Office Management and Control

THE ACTIONS OF
ADMINISTRATIVE MANAGEMENT

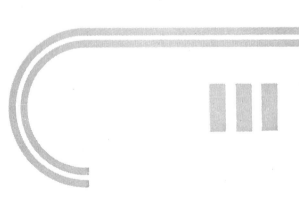

FOURTH EDITION
1962
RICHARD D. IRWIN, INC.
HOMEWOOD, ILLINOIS

OFFICE
MANAGEMENT

AND CONTROL

The Actions of Administrative Management

By GEORGE R. TERRY, Ph.D

SCHOOL OF BUSINESS
NORTHWESTERN UNIVERSITY, AND
MANAGEMENT CONSULTANT, CHICAGO

FOURTH EDITION

First Printing, May, 1962

Library of Congress Catalogue Card No. 62–16523

PRINTED IN THE UNITED STATES OF AMERICA

To My Mother

PREFACE

Office Management and Control is now appearing in its fourth edition. In it are included the very latest developments in this highly dynamic and increasingly important field of management study. Modern operations of today's enterprises, be they in business, government, education, or military, necessitate an understanding and a utilization of the work of the office. The trend in management is definitely toward more and better facts, quicker and more accurate data, more comprehensive planning, more effective controlling—all of which rely to a significant degree upon the contributions of office management. Keeping in mind the dynamics of the office and being guided by the recommendations and experience of many educators and students using the previous editions of the book, it is believed that this new fourth edition offers a thoroughly modern, balanced, practical, and helpful book which meets completely the current requirements of both the teacher and the student.

So great have been the recent changes in office management that some feel this name itself is inadequate. A number of alternatives have been suggested with the intent that a title more descriptive of the true meaning of this managerial area be adopted. The term *administrative management* appears to be winning significant favor. It conveys well the breadth, importance, and modern use of managerial actions dealing with paper work and related services. Hence, in this edition, the subtitle *The Actions of Administrative Management* has been added. By this addition, it is believed that the subject area is better identified, communication about it is clarified, and recognition of its status is signified.

A room called "the office" never has housed all the activities of office management. Down through the years, office work has had a greater and greater influence upon every member of management. Primarily this is because office work deals fundamentally with information, a necessary ingredient basic to all management. Data must be assembled, processed, retained, and distributed so that management members can do their work effectively. The current dynamics of data and information handling represent an accelerated continuation of efforts to improve our techniques, understanding, and contributions in this vital area of management.

The computer and other electronic operating machines have sharpened the focus upon information handling. Now more than ever before the emphasis is upon having adequate information in the most usable form at the proper time and place. Development of new office machines, new planning techniques, new means of decision making, improved methods of employee motivation, and recent improvements in work measurement, all reflect this intense modern effort which is the core of progressive office management.

Yet with all the changes of the current office evolution, the basic objective of this book can be described by the same sentence stated in the first edition, some years ago, namely, to present fundamental principles and successful practices used in getting office work accomplished. With time, new practices proven superior have come into use and the interpretation given the meaning of office work has been modified, but the principles are enduring. Getting the necessary office work done in the best way remains the chief stabilizer of office management study.

The managerial viewpoint is stressed. Encompassed in this approach is the ability to recognize a situation requiring managerial action, determining the alternate actions that might be taken, deciding upon the particular action to follow, and putting the decision into effect. To augment this approach and for clarity of presentation, the material of this book is presented around the concept of office management being a distinct activity which can be segregated into fundamental functions making up what can be termed a management process. Under each fundamental function is included the various types of managerial work pertaining to that function. This arrangement provides a logical and readily comprehended theme as well as supplying continuity and revealing the vital interrelatedness among the fundamental functions.

A total of nine new chapters feature this edition. Appearing in print for the first time is an entire section of five chapters devoted to "Office Automation," an area increasing daily in importance and destined to occupy greater prominence in office management. The entire book has been updated, all chapters have been reworked, and nonessential material has been deleted. Thus, a concise yet comprehensive book in office management is provided.

Over forty new case problems are included in this fourth edition. Some of the former cases are retained, the selection being based on the issues raised by the case, interest of class members, and suggestions from experienced instructors using the former edition. In addition, many new questions have been included at the end of each chapter. They include questions which can be classified as emphasizing thought provocation, review, or a small project activity by the student. Ample material is therefore supplied to make the office management course interesting and to permit purposeful participation by the class members.

I am indebted to many sources for help in preparing this edition. The exchange of ideas, discussion of office management problems, and the sharing of information and viewpoints rank high in the activities with others and have contributed immensely to this present edition. The list of names and companies is too long for inclusion here, but their help, interest, and co-operation are sincerely appreciated. Special acknowledgment is extended Professor Betty M. Weaver of Ohio University who offered detailed comments and suggestions which proved especially helpful. All the many practicing office managers, executives, teachers, and students who helped to shape this book did so in order to provide a means for advancing our modern office management knowledge and its application, and also to attract qualified people to this vital area of activity. Writing this fourth edition under this strong influence has been uncommonly challenging and deeply motivating.

GEORGE R. TERRY

May, 1962

TABLE OF CONTENTS

PART 7. ACTUATING IN OFFICE MANAGEMENT

INDEX

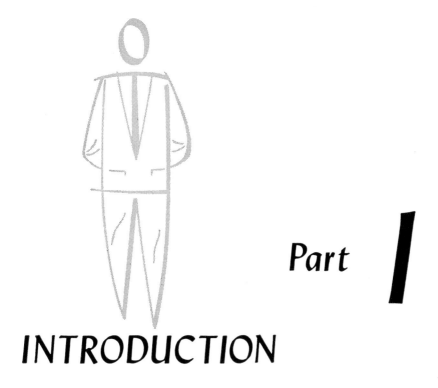

Part *1*

INTRODUCTION

The study of office management begins with the concept of management applied to office work. The basic managerial functions and their use in the office, the adequate supplying of business information, the fundamental activity elements necessary to process data, and the characteristics of office work comprise the subject matter of the first two chapters.

Chapter 1

THE ROLE OF OFFICE MANAGEMENT

Knowledge comes by taking things apart: analysis.
But wisdom comes by putting things together.
—JAMES A. MORRISON

WE ARE in the midst of a revolution in office work. Only a few decades ago, the office was generally viewed as a secondary activity in most enterprises. Typically, it was symbolized by green eye shades, chief clerks, and papers heaped upon desks located in congested, dark, and ugly surroundings. But this has all changed or is currently being subjected to sweeping stages of evolutionary advancement.

THE OFFICE OF TODAY

The office of today has grown up. It constitutes a major, vital, and expanding activity of every enterprise. It is a giant force in all work accomplishment. It is gaining status, exercising greater influence, attracting high-caliber executives, and contributing more and more. It has its fingers in practically every activity that takes place. What has brought about this change in the office and continues to cause upheavals in office work performance? Fundamentally, two developments: (1) the need today for more and better factual information to manage an enterprise, and (2) the technological improvements for processing this required factual information.

More and more, the modern manager is basing his work upon facts in place of guess and intuition. This trend toward management by factual information is taking place from the top to the lowest managerial level, in all types of enterprises, and for all types of situations and circumstances. Today's mode of operation simply does not permit the successful manager to carry in his head all the information needed to carry out his work effectively. Helpful information on costs, sales, production, personnel, plans, accomplishments, inventories, machines, customers, prices, markets, and taxes, for example, represents masses of data which

3

must be collected and put into an easily accessible form in order to have maximum value and benefit.

Since the advent of the first commercially successful typewriter, or about 1872, there has been a continuous parade of new office machines designed to accomplish office work more efficiently. During the last twenty-five years or so, the pace has quickened. Perhaps the expression "The pace is full speed ahead" more adequately describes events of the past decade or so, with the availability of computers capable of processing enormous quantities of paper work at fantastic speed. The adoption of computers and other electronic machines has already made deep modifications in office work methodology, but they are destined to cause even greater changes in the future.

IMPACT UPON OFFICE MANAGEMENT

As a result of this current status of affairs, office work is undergoing many significant changes; and in turn, the impact of these changes upon office management is profound. The recognized need for information, the cost of obtaining such information, and the advent of new tools and techniques for getting this information have placed office management in the limelight. And office management enjoys a rather unique niche because most activities are preceded, started, stopped, or permitted to continue as a result of information on a piece of paper supplied by the right personnel, in the right manner, and at the right time, place, and cost. As we shall see, this constitutes the essentials of office management. Competent management of office work is therefore highly desirable, if not actually imperative. The required information must be processed satisfactorily and efficiently.

CONSIDERATIONS OF MANAGEMENT

Office management is one—and a most important one—of the various specialized areas of management. Among the other areas are manufacturing management, sales management, personnel management, finance management, farm management, city management, traffic management, and credit management. Although the areas of application differ, the concept of management is the same regardless of its area of application. That is, management is a universal concept. Furthermore, it is made up of definite functions or activities. Hence, the statement can be made that management is a universal activity. Its definite functions are applied to different areas; but the application varies with regard to type of function, amount, quality, and timing, depending upon the circumstances as the manager sees them and what he is trying to accomplish.

OBJECTIVES

To clarify the meaning of office management, it is helpful to begin with consideration of the predetermined objective or objectives. Office management concerns the achievement of certain desired goals or results; and basically, the efforts of the office manager center around ways and means to accomplish these goals. There is a mission to perform, a project to initiate, a service to supply.

The predetermined objectives may be specific or general, written or unwritten, long or short term, temporary or permanent, or applicable to certain segments of the office only. Whatever their form or content, these predetermined objectives are set and accepted, for without them the meaning of management becomes nebulous and there is no satisfactory basis for determining the effectiveness of management.

To provide examples of predetermined objectives of office management, the following are presented:

1. To furnish all necessary and complete information to whom, when, and where it is required for the efficient operation of the enterprise.

2. To provide adequate records and reports at lowest possible cost.

3. To assist the enterprise in keeping competitive.

4. To supply accurate paper work and assist in rendering service to the customer.

5. To make better and better written records at lower and lower costs.

Such statements may sound purely academic, but they serve a practical purpose in that they point out the sought-for goal. They define the target. Other objectives, subordinate but related to the over-all goal, can be used to designate the aims for specific office groups or individuals.

In the office, predetermined objectives can be conveniently classified as pertaining primarily to (1) service, (2) social responsibilities, or (3) profit. Service is of foremost importance in the objectives of office management because office work is done to assist others in doing their work more effectively. Also of significance is the objective dealing with social responsibilities which stresses the attainment of the goal in accordance with certain moral and ethical codes as set forth by the industry and society in which the enterprise operates. Lastly, predetermined objectives emphasizing profit or gain to the owners can be assisted tremendously by office management. Performing the office work more effectively can mean more profit inasmuch as less expenditures for clerical work are made. Greater emphasis of the importance of the office to management and profit is in order. Acceptance of this obligation by office management members strengthens their status and identifies their role.[1]

---

[1] The concept of profit as the objective of any enterprise or segment of an enterprise is actually quite limited. Profit, as such, can be the indirect or the direct aim, depending upon the thinking of the particular company involved. Profit is residual in nature, a by-product resulting from other direct goals.

OFFICE MANAGERIAL FUNCTIONS

Objectives can be achieved only through action. The determining, initiating, and carrying-out of definite and purposeful actions to achieve a predetermined objective is the content of management. This content is made up of a process—called the management process—consisting of fundamental functions or activities.

These fundamental functions of management include:

1. *Planning*—to lay out a means or a course of action giving consideration to the factors influencing the particular situation.

2. *Controlling*—to determine what is accomplished, evaluate it, and apply corrective measures, if needed, to insure results in keeping with the plan.

3. *Organizing*—to distribute the planned work to be done among the members of the work group, establish proper work relationships among them, and supply the proper work environment.

4. *Actuating*—to stimulate and maintain the desire of the members of the work group to execute their respective work enthusiastically in order to achieve the predetermined objective in accordance with the plan.

These four fundamental functions are the distinguishing characteristics of management. They apply universally to management, be it production management, sales management, finance management, or office management. Specifically, they are the means used by an office manager to perform office management. They identify the office manager from the nonoffice manager. The student of office management will do well to fix these functions in mind for they provide an all-inclusive viewpoint of office management activities and assist greatly in the understanding of office management.

OFFICE MANAGEMENT PLANNING

The fundamental function of planning in office management includes the methodic technique of looking ahead and selecting a course from among alternative actions in order to accomplish a predetermined aim. It is a foreseeing action—related facts and assumptions are considered and established for the purpose of determining what must be done, when, by whom, where, and how. Planning requires visualization of future action. It includes determination of proposed actions and knowing what steps will produce the desired results and in what sequence they should be taken.

Effective planning necessitates creative, reflective, and imaginative thinking. Such vision marks the progressive office manager; and in today's office, planning is rapidly becoming ever more and more important. It is the core of much modern managerial thinking. Perhaps more than ever before, office management planning contains a dynamic element due to the pace at which technology and innovations are being made available to the office and introduced into our economy. In these changes, office managers should contribute, not simply adjust, to the plans, thus adding to the progress and advancing the status of the office management field. Good planning emphasizes prevention rather than correction of delays. It anticipates and defines future possible difficulties and makes provision to care for them.

Consider the illustration of a company which, wishing to mechanize its weekly payroll procedures, purchased, without proper planning, a specialized machine costing $15,000. The machine performed all the payroll work very satisfactorily and required only 1½ days a week to do it. About six months later, the manager decided to mechanize accounts payable and accounts receivable, and hence purchased a general-purpose accounting machine costing $7,500. Within a short period, the capacity of this machine proved too small, so an additional and identical machine was purchased at the same price. The total capacity of the second general-purpose accounting machine was not required, so efforts were undertaken to find work to utilize it full time. It was discovered that the entire weekly payroll work could be done on it. This eliminated the need for the original specialized payroll machine. Its cost, or $15,000, could have been avoided by proper planning. But is having all the work done on two $7,500 general-purpose accounting machines the best plan? Could one $10,000 general-purpose accounting machine accomplish the total work? Adequate planning would have taken into account all the alternative possibilities and determined the one best course of action for the company to follow.

OFFICE MANAGEMENT CONTROLLING

A long-standing practice of a manager is to check results in order to see if the work is progressing satisfactorily and in keeping with what is expected, that is, in accordance with the planning. "Follow-up" is an essential part of management and is included under the term "controlling." The best plan may not bring about the desired results. Variances, misunderstandings, and unexpected events may occur. Such contingencies must be quickly ascertained so that corrective action can be taken.

In order to apply controlling to any activity, measurable performance factors must be established. These include such things as quantity, quality, cost, or time bases. The actual performance is compared with the expected or pre-established standard. For example, the number of payroll cards processed per hour is compared to the number expected for acceptable performance, and deviations from the established base are subject to analysis and evaluation.

Much of the office manager's contribution to the entire enterprise is in the area of controlling. Records and information help provide answers to the question: "How well is the work being done?" However, controlling within the office area is the chief consideration of this book, since it is an essential part of office management. Controlling must be exercised by the office manager to carry out his office management activity successfully. In instances where the office manager is in charge of all office work, some of which is done by people other than those in the office, the function of office management controlling takes on added importance. Also, when people in organizational units throughout the enterprise decide certain matters involving paper work, the problem of proper control in office management and how to maintain it becomes one of major significance.

OFFICE MANAGEMENT ORGANIZING

Organizing means literally to make organic—i.e., serviceable or helpful—by means of establishing a structure or a definite operating relationship among various components of the entire entity. An office manager organizes the work for which he is responsible by apportioning it in an orderly fashion among the various structural units for achieving the task. The personnel for each structural unit are selected, delegated appropriate authority, and held responsible for the satisfactory completion of their respective work. If, within the company, no group exists from which personnel can be selected, the manager must recruit and hire the needed personnel from outside the company. In addition, the personnel are provided proper workplaces, that is, the appropriate equipment, machines, lighting, and area. In brief, organizing deals with the establishing of proper relationships among the components of the work to be done, designating the people who are going to do it, and providing the work environment in which the tasks will be done.

Knowledge and skill in organizing are vital in office management. Organizing makes it possible for the office manager to spread his influence and to get goals accomplished effectively through a group. Organizing is a key to group efficiency. It helps the group serve as a unit with all its efforts blended together toward a specific objective.

OFFICE MANAGEMENT ACTUATING

The fundamental function of actuating includes the creating and continuing of the desire by each member of the work group to achieve the objective in accordance with plans. The work of planning, controlling, and organizing does not accomplish the predetermined goal. The plan must be put into effect by people working willingly at prescribed tasks and at given times and places. To accomplish this, people must be properly motivated to work along these guided lines. This activity constitutes managerial actuating.

The type of person, the component activity to be performed, the facilities provided, and the manager's judgment determine the measures utilized to execute this actuating function. Leadership, human-relations practices, training programs, and proper compensation are among the more common means.

Actuating concerns intangible subject areas, but success in these areas brings high rewards. When members of the work group are inspired to use their highest attainable skills and capacities, when they are genuinely interested in their work, when they are enthusiastic about accomplishing their assigned task, and when they believe in and understand the plan and how the objective is to be accomplished, the burden of management is lightened, and the accomplishments attained frequently are startling even to the experienced manager proficient in actuating efforts.

Figure 1–1 recapitulates the concept of the basic office management

Basic Office Management Functions	Performed by People, but Concerned Primarily with. . . .
PLANNING AND CONTROLLING Determining the future courses of action and seeing that they are accomplished within reasonable limits.	. . . things and materials. What procedure? Equipment? Machines? Cost? Accuracy? Time limits?
ORGANIZING AND ACTUATING Dividing the work, maintaining proper work relationships among members of the group, and getting them to want to accomplish what the manager wants them to do.	. . . employees and their work. Who does what? Who reports to whom? What motivates whom? How acquire dedication to work?

FIG. 1–1. The basic office management functions.

functions in a concise tabular form. It serves to fix in mind the process of management as a distinct activity consisting of planning, controlling, organizing, and actuating.

INTERDEPENDENCE OF FUNDAMENTAL FUNCTIONS

The four fundamental functions of office management are interdependent—they should never be thought of as being mutually exclusive. Each depends upon the others. Actually, there is no sharp delineation designating the terminating of one function and the starting of another in the process. For instance, planning constitutes a part of determining the work-to-be-done components, an activity included under organizing. And controlling influences the establishing of proper relationships among the organizational units normally included under organizing.

Nor is there a definite sequence of the functions which the office manager must follow. In presenting the fundamental functions, the sequence of planning, controlling, organizing, and actuating was followed. But a manager performs only the function or functions required by the situation and in the order deemed advisable. Thus, actuating efforts may be employed, followed by planning and subsequently by controlling.

OFFICE MANAGEMENT IS A DISTINCT ACTIVITY

From what has been stated, it follows that office management is a distinct entity; it can be studied, and proficiency in it can be attained. Management is not a person or a group of people. One who performs the activity of management is a manager. Hence, those who perform this activity of management in the office work area are office managers.

The concept of management as an activity, and of those performing this activity as managers, helps to clarify thinking on this subject. Unfortunately, many common expressions used to describe the work of the office manager are not very helpful. For example, identifying an office manager as the one who "runs" an office or the person who sees that office work is accomplished does not provide much assistance. Also, the condition that a person has subordinates reporting to him does not make that person a manager in the true meaning of management. Having a group of faithful followers is not a guarantee that management exists.

To reiterate, an office manager, to qualify as an office manager, performs four fundamental functions making up the management process. The use of this management process marks the essential difference between a clerk and an office manager, or between an accountant and the manager of the accounting department. Knowing how to write letters, for example, is not sufficient to manage the correspondence department. Office management is a distinct entity, it is an activity in itself, and it requires the use of certain knowledge, skills, and practices.

OFFICE MANAGEMENT AND THE BASIC ELEMENTS

A manager has six basic elements to which he can apply his activity of management. These basic elements, commonly referred to as the "six M's," include Men, Materials, Machines, Methods, Money, and Markets. In other words, a manager, by the application of the management functions, i.e., planning, controlling, organizing, and actuating determines what is done with these basic elements.

Figure 1–2 shows this concept in graphic form. To manage effectively requires a knowledge of the objectives, i.e., knowing what is to be accomplished is a prime requisite. In most cases, planning helps to set forth the objectives. With the stated goals as a background, an office manager utilizes the "six M's" in achieving the objectives. These basic

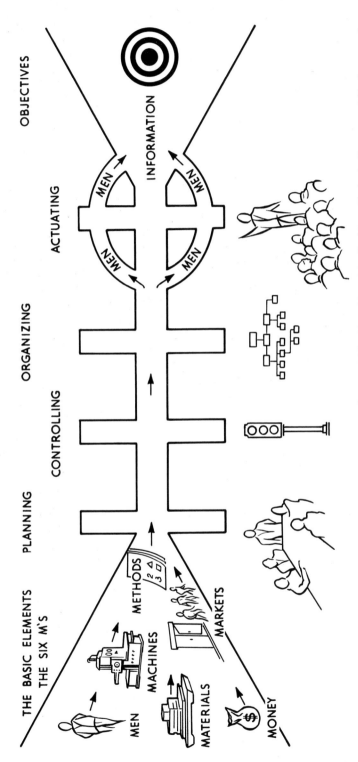

FIG. 1–2. The objectives of the office are obtained by subjecting the "six M's"—Men, Materials, Machines, Methods, Money, and Markets—to the application of the managerial functions of planning, controlling, and organizing, and, in addition, subjecting the basic element of Men to the activity of actuating.

"M's" are intertwined, as shown at the left of the figure. They are subjected to planning, controlling, and organizing. The men, or members of the work group, are actuated to want to achieve the objectives and help insure that the end results will be the stated objectives.

DEFINITION OF OFFICE MANAGEMENT

Office management can be defined as *the planning, controlling, and organizing of office work, and actuating those performing it so as to achieve the predetermined objectives.* The predetermined objectives include such things as getting the office work accomplished within reasonable limits of time, effort, and cost expenditures; supplying adequate information (both written and verbal) to manage effectively; and implementing the performance of other major functions of the enterprise by providing the required service and facilitating activity of written and verbal information.

Several observations should be noted concerning the definition given above. First, office management is considered in the broad, inclusive sense. It includes managerial efforts over office work anywhere in an enterprise. It is not confined to efforts of the person called "the office manager" or some similar title, nor to the work performed in "the office" only.

Second, office management is not a purely mechanistic activity. The effective application of the fundamental functions of office management is fraught with great difficulties. No fixed formula can be followed in all cases. There is an art of management as well as a science or body of knowledge of management.[2] The art of management deals with skill or the application of knowledge. This is of special importance in management. One may have all the facts and pertinent relationships but fail to use them effectively.

Office management necessitates the ability to make decisions. Each of the fundamental functions of management requires decision making in its execution. Determining the course of actions to follow (planning) or appraising a situation (controlling) involves decision making. Decisions should be based on adequate facts, and these facts are often difficult to obtain. The successful manager carefully distinguishes between facts and opinions and utilizes only those data which are definitely related and pertinent to the problem at hand. Frequently, all the facts cannot be secured, in which case the best decision based on the known facts should be made, with the realization that future adjustments may be necessary. Normally, decisions should be based on a logical or reasoned approach, with due regard given to the intent of the enterprise.

Lastly, office management members must be able to exercise ingenuity. To a considerable extent, all managerial progress is dependent

---

[2] Science and scientific management are discussed in the immediately following pages.

upon the creation and the development of successful ideas. Most improvements start as ideas—for example, a better way of performing an office task, a simplified means of securing applicants, and the rearrangement of data on the paper form to make calculating easier. Such ideas stem from observation and thinking.

COMMON APPROACHES IN APPLYING THE MANAGEMENT PROCESS

In applying the management process, an office manager can follow one of several general approaches. Among these are (1) the scientific approach, (2) the artistic approach, (3) the conventional approach, (4) the observational approach, and (5) the systematic approach. All are utilized, all are valid. However, the scientific approach employing the "scientific method" has probably contributed more to the fundamental knowledge of office management than has any other approach. Office managers who use the scientific approach are commonly termed scientific office managers.

SCIENTIFIC OFFICE MANAGEMENT

"Science" is a body of knowledge discovered by means of the scientific method, which knowledge has been accumulated and accepted in reference to the discovery or understanding of truth. The facts which make up this body of knowledge are expressed by statements or data generally believed to be representative of the phenomena and supposedly free from bias and prejudice. Science is entirely objective; there is no place in it for personal influence, likes, and dislikes.

The scientific method consists of well-defined steps taken either to confirm or to disprove a stated proposition under consideration. The method tests the proposition under carefully prescribed and controlled conditions. These steps are shown in Figure 1–3. In essence, a tentative solution to a stated problem is tried out under specific and known conditions. In a sense, it can be viewed as controlled experimentation.

Frederick W. Taylor is generally credited with the beginning of the application of the scientfiic method to management. He conducted many studies or tests under controlled conditions, i.e., employed the scientific method, and obtained vast new funds of knowledge. Among his important conclusions were that high wages were compatible with low unit costs; that standards were needed to control production; that employees, materials, and procedures should be scientifically selected; and that cooperation between management and nonmanagement members was required for highest productivity.[3]

---

[3] These fundamentals are expounded in F. W. Taylor, *Scientific Management*, which comprises the previously published works *Shop Management*, *The Principles of Scientific Management*, and *Testimony before the Special House Committee* (New York: Harper & Bros., 1947), pp. 1–47 and 130–31.

BASIC ACTION	STEPS	
CREATE	1. RECOGNIZE THE PROBLEM	
	2. MAKE PRELIMINARY OBSERVATIONS AND ANALYSIS	
	3. DRAW UP A HYPOTHESIS OR TENTATIVE SOLUTION TO THE PROBLEM	
PROVE	4. MAKE A THOROUGH AND DETAILED ANALYSIS	
	5. COLLECT ADEQUATE DATA	
	6. CLASSIFY THE DATA COLLECTED	
	7. MAKE A TENTATIVE ANSWER TO THE PROBLEM	
CONCLUDE	8. TEST THIS SOLUTION OR ANSWER	
	9. ADJUST IN LIGHT OF RESULTS UNDER STEP 8.	
	10. STATE THE ANSWER TO THE PROBLEM	

FIG. 1–3. The scientific method consists of well-defined steps.

ARTISTIC OFFICE MANAGEMENT

By artistic office management is meant the approach emphasizing the art of management. Art stresses the skill in bringing about a desired result. The art of management enhances the science of management because the former determines the adroitness and best manner of applying the fund of management knowledge. Skill in perceiving where and when to take certain actions or to refrain from any action is essential to managerial success.

Judgment, experience, understanding, and feeling appear to be important in developing an art of management. Management really becomes personalized and a part of the manager when the art of management is developed and employed. Science lays the groundwork, but it is the art of management that causes managerial achievements to soar to heights consistent with highest professional levels.

CONVENTIONAL OFFICE MANAGEMENT

The adherence to custom characterizes conventional office management. It follows the manner and method which have been handed down from the past; emphasis is placed on doing a managerial task in a manner similar to that which one's predecessor used. The fundamental theme is expressed by the statement: "What was good enough for my father is good enough for me." The follower of conventional management seldom asks why or questions the purpose of a particular managerial activity. He is little concerned with efforts to discover new managerial techniques.

OBSERVATIONAL OFFICE MANAGEMENT

This type is characterized by the use of observations as the basic media for managing an operation. The observational manager observes how other managers achieve their goal and uses this information in determining his own course of action. He copies and attempts to select what he believes to be the best of his fellow managers' techniques and then applies them to his own particular problems. The observational manager's attitude is: "Find out how the other fellow performs a managerial task similar to one which you have—then solve your managerial problem by using the same approach and method."

Observational management helps to distribute managerial ideas and techniques among managers. Furthermore, it requires little effort. Most managers like to discuss their activities, especially those in which they are successful. Also, observational management offers dynamic sources of information for the changing managerial problems, but does not necessarily contribute to the improvement of managerial techniques. An office practice which works well for one office might produce poor results for the firm which copies it, as a result of differences in objectives, in the size of the office, or in the personnel of the two firms. Nevertheless, observational management is used by many managers of small offices where the facilities and time may make other approaches difficult to follow.

SYSTEMATIC OFFICE MANAGEMENT

A systematic manager strives to manage mainly by means of systems. These automatically encompass the plans, policies, relationships, and controls used by the managers and provide the required written managerial records. Systematic management differs from both conventional management and observational management more in degree than in kind, for there is usually some systematic management in every type of management. Actually, it is a necessary supplement to each of the other managerial types.

For the most part, systematic management is static because it tends to fix or to stabilize a given procedure and attitude. It tends to keep things as they are and to develop definite and rigid habits for handling the work. When this approach is the over-all guide, serious limitations in a manager's operation and breadth of vision may result.

OFFICE MANAGEMENT ACTIVITIES

Office work should always be appraised by the results it accomplishes; to consider it in and of itself leads only to confusion. To reiterate, office work is the means to a desired end; it is not the end in itself. There is little value in records and communication as such. They are made to expedite the work of producing or selling the product or of giving better service.

The activities included in office management are quite numerous; among them are the following:

1. Deciding the extent of office automation to be used.
    a) Selecting and utilizing office electronic machines.
    b) Handling the training and transferring of employees in keeping with mechanization plans.
    c) Establishing integrated data processing (IDP).
2. Maintaining adequate office services and communication facilities.
    a) See that correspondence work—stenographic and typing—is performed.
    b) File records and reports.
    c) Handle incoming and outgoing mail.
    d) Supply reception and messenger services.
3. Determining the complete course of action to accomplish the office work.
    a) Keep informed of latest developments in performing office work.
    b) Select office methods and procedures.
    c) Co-ordinate the work of the office with that of the nonoffice.
    d) Maintain proper balance among the various office activities.
    e) Specify and purchase office furniture, machines, and supplies.
    f) Arrange the office layout—location of office furniture and machines.
    g) Determine effective work environment—adequate lighting, elimination of noise, and proper ventilation.
    h) Select the office location.

4. Measuring and evaluating quantity and quality of office work.
    a) Establish standards for office work.
    b) Apply work simplification to office work.
    c) Schedule and dispatch office work.
    d) Time-study office operations.
    e) Maintain quality of office work.
    f) Keep office costs within acceptable limits.
    g) Prepare office budget.
    h) Write office manuals.
5. Providing an effective office organization.
    a) Apportion the work among the organizational units.
    b) Identify the organizational units.
    c) Establish definite and known relationships among organizational units.
    d) Know the individual jobs in the office.
    e) Assign proper personnel to organizational units.
    f) Delegate authority.
    g) Fix responsibility among personnel.
    h) Provide for proper work facilities.
6. Inspiring the office personnel to do the best of which they are capable.
    a) Motivate office employees.
    b) Give adequate supervision.
    c) Analyze and evaluate office jobs.
    d) Give office training programs.
    e) Provide adequate communication among office employees and between office and nonoffice units.
    f) Administer office salary plan.
    g) Promote office safety.

THE TITLE "OFFICE MANAGER"

Since office work is present in every phase and level of management, it follows that most executives have something to do with office work, although this is not their primary responsibility. Any department head or other executive can improve the management of the office work under his direct supervision by applying the managerial practices developed in this book. He need not necessarily have a large clerical staff. However, when the scope and extent of activities are limited, the degree of specialization may be somewhat reduced.

The scope of the office manager's job is quite flexible. Strictly speaking, the one in charge of managing office work is the office manager. As already stated, in some enterprises the office manager has charge of the work done by all the departments of the office; in other enterprises, he is the general manager not only of the office work in the office but of all office work, whether it is done in or out of the office.

THE ADMINISTRATIVE MANAGER

In actual practice, the one in charge of managing office work is not always titled "office manager." He may have the title of "controller," "auditor," "head accountant," "chief clerk," "systems analyst," or "manager, office services"; or he may have no title at all.

Since about 1960, the title "administrative manager" has gained considerable favor. Many believe that this title is more descriptive of the managing of information and better denotes the company-wide range of activities centered in the office. This can be viewed as another change in the current evolution of the office. The increasing importance of information and the availability of elaborate data-processing equipment have given increased status to those managing paper work, and have made the office the communication transfer point for a company's entire activities. As one speaker so aptly described it: "The office has become the nerve center of the enterprise."

With this change, the person in charge of office work, whatever his title, has been given greater authority and responsibility, and more company-wide activities have been transferred to the office area. Recognition of this significant growth and trend is encompassed by the title "administrative manager."

In a study based on the response from two hundred managers of paper work, it was found that the title "administrative manager" was held by over one third of them. "Office manager" identified but one eighth of them, while "vice president" or "treasurer" was the title for only one tenth of them.[4] From the same study, it was discovered that more than two thirds of the respondents report to top management. The two top categories were "vice president" (19.7 per cent) and "controller" (18.8 per cent).

The title "administrative manager" is winning favor, and the trend seems destined to continue. In many cases, the duties and title of the office manager have changed. He is proving himself to be an indispensable adjunct to the top management of the company and is occupying an increasingly important role in the over-all management of the enterprise.

QUESTIONS

1. What are the important reasons for the major changes taking place in the office during the past several decades? Discuss fully.
2. Do you agree with the following statement? "To achieve objectives requires action. This being true, planning can be considered nonproductive because nothing is achieved simply by planning." Elaborate on your answer.

---

[4] John Allan Rhea, "What's Happened to the Office Manager?" *Administrative Management*, July, 1961, p. 12.

3. Describe the meaning of Figure 1–2 in your own words.

4. Relate an experience in some phase of business, preferably dealing with office work, which illustrates poor planning.

5. Visit an office with which you are familiar and find out its major objectives. What do you deduce from the information obtained?

6. Office management is defined by some as the accomplishment of office work by others. Does acceptance of this definition mean that actuating office employees represents and is the same as office management? Discuss.

7. Is there any difference between what might be termed "experimental management" and "scientific management"? Explain.

8. In your opinion, is there any relationship between:
   a) Planning and organizing?
   b) Planning and controlling?
   c) Organizing and actuating?

9. Briefly relate your reaction to this statement: "The key to being an expert office manager is to know how to practice effective controlling. It is the results that count, and managerial controlling gets the results."

10. Discuss the concept and activities of administrative managers in modern business enterprises.

11. What steps of the scientific method do you feel are probably most difficult to apply to office management problems? Discuss.

12. How successful do you believe an office manager can be by following the approach of observational management in his work? Discuss.

CASE PROBLEM

Case 1–1.   The Sullivan-Culbert Company

This company, a manufacturer of kitchen utensils, has enjoyed a considerable increase in sales during the past twelve months. Many new items have been added to the company's line of products, and distribution has been expanded to a national basis, resulting in the selling of a large number of accounts by the company. Sales are made direct to dealers. The officers of the company include Mr. Daniel Sullivan, president; Mr. Neal Culbert, vice president; and Mr. Theodore Buffington, secretary-treasurer.

Mr. Culbert, in charge of sales, has received many dealer complaints during the past several months. Delays in billing, incorrect invoices, and mistakes in pricing and discounts are mentioned most frequently.

Mr. Culbert has spoken several times about these complaints to Mr. Buffington, who is in charge of the office. Mr. Buffington states that there is a sufficient number of employees in the office to get the work out promptly and correctly. The difficulty is that they just do not work. He has repeatedly cautioned them about the quality of their work, but it does no good. Office help is difficult to find, so he cannot be too severe. Probably the whole condition is a part of growing pains which the company is now experiencing.

The office force totals 12 men and 42 women. Most of the men have been with the company four years or longer, while nearly 80 per cent of the women have been with the company less than one year—some 40 per cent having been hired within the last four months.

Mr. Culbert also spoke with Mr. Sullivan about the complaints and the general condition of the office. Subsequently, Mr. Sullivan had a talk with Mr. Buffington, at which time it was decided that Mr. Buffington should proceed to correct the office situation, using all reasonable and necessary means.

Mr. Buffington took the following measures:

1. Hired an additional six male clerks and eight female typists.

2. Announced by means of a personal note to each office employee that the quality of the office work must be improved and pointed out that far too many errors were being made.

3. Stated that all office supervisors would become working supervisors in order to locate sources of mistakes in papers being prepared. Any employee caught preparing an incorrect billing or invoice would be given five demerits by his supervisor. A total of fifteen demerits means automatic employment termination.

4. Appointed Mr. Herbert Welsh as his assistant to whom all office supervisors would report. However, carefully stated that decisions involving major issues remain his (Mr. Buffington's) prerogative.

5. Indicated a greater activity on his (Mr. Buffington's) part in work of credit extensions, collecting accounts, and trying to keep sufficient cash and funds on hand to meet the needs of the expanding business.

6. Made it clear that if the quality of the office work did not improve, changes in personnel would be made.

7. Informed both Mr. Sullivan and Mr. Culbert that adequate means have been taken to improve the management of the office work.

Problems:

1. What is the main issue in this case?

2. What is your opinion regarding the measures taken by Mr. Buffington?

3. After talking with Mr. Buffington, do you believe Mr. Culbert did the correct thing in seeing Mr. Sullivan? Why?

4. What is your recommendation to Mr. Sullivan? Discuss.

Chapter 2

APPLICATION OF MANAGEMENT TO INFORMATION HANDLING

More erroneous conclusions are due to lack of information than to errors of judgment.

—LOUIS BRANDEIS

THE OFFICE is the fountainhead of business information. And in turn, information is the lifeblood of a modern enterprise. To be useful, proper, and adequate, information must go to the right person at the right time and in the right form.

WHAT IS INFORMATION?

Information is meaningful data that conveys usable knowledge. What is usable depends upon the following:

1. *Objective of the recipient.* If information is to help, it must assist the recipient in what he is trying to do.
2. *Accuracy of the data transmission and processing.* The real essence and significance of the information must be retained regardless of how it is handled and manipulated.
3. *Time.* Is the information current?
4. *Space or place.* Is the information available at the right place?
5. *Form.* Can the information be used effectively? Does it show needed relationships, trends, and areas requiring managerial attention; and does it emphasize pertinent situations?
6. *Semantics.* Is the relationship between the words and their intended meaning absolutely clear? Is there any likelihood of misunderstanding? The word "duck," for example, may mean a type of cloth, a type of fowl, or to move quickly.

It is well to point out that as defined above, not all data are information. There are today many useless records being handled in the office. In contrast, there are gaps of information that need to be bridged by useful

21

data. Generally, it is the responsibility of the office manager, administrative manager, or whatever his title, to supply needed information in order that the entire enterprise can be managed efficiently.

SUPPLYING INFORMATION

To supply needed information requires fundamentally four activities. These include data (1) collecting, (2) processing, (3) retaining, and (4) distributing. Figure 2–1 shows this concept graphically. First of all,

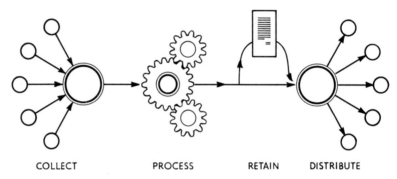

COLLECT PROCESS RETAIN DISTRIBUTE

FIG. 2–1. Data must be collected, processed, retained, and distributed to provide needed information to manage an enterprise effectively.

the data must be collected; and, as discussed in the following paragraphs, there exist major sources of data in most enterprises. Next, the collected data must be processed. In brief, the descriptive information must be arranged according to a predetermined pattern, numerical values calculated, and helpful relationships shown. Typically, some information either is retained by the office for additional data, when available, to be added to what has been processed, or is retained simply for future reference purposes. Lastly, the processed data are distributed to those requiring the information and include all types of communication. More will now be discussed for each of these four activities.

THE COLLECTING OF DATA

Practically every operation in a modern enterprise gives rise to data. While the terms may differ from enterprise to enterprise, depending upon the type of enterprise, the following operations or activities can be considered basic sources of data.

Operation or Activity	Give Rise to and Need for:
Purchasing:	Vendors' list, prices, quotations, delivery dates
Receiving:	Receipt of material, inspection, quantity
Stockkeeping:	On hand, coming in, location, allocation
Production:	Process times, orders, waiting times
Selling:	Customers' orders, sales analysis, price

Delivery:	Date, carrier information, bills of lading
Billing:	Customer's name, merchandise, price
Collecting:	Credit, invoice, discounts
Disbursing:	Payroll, materials purchased, taxes

Actually, all this type of information is obtained from data expressed as words, numbers, and symbols. The challenge is to put the proper data together and make them available to the proper party at the proper time. For instance, under purchasing, for a vendors' list to be useful, it should contain (1) names, preferably alphabetically, by type of commodity or by location; (2) terms of sale; (3) past experience with vendor (4) name of representative with vendor; and (5) telephone number. Likewise, certain data must be put together meaningfully for (say) billing, collecting, and disbursing.

THE PROCESSING OF DATA

Data processing is a series of planned operations upon information in order to achieve a desired objective or result. Usually, a formula or pattern is followed to arrive at a result that shows the data in some standard and useful form. Bookkeeping, inventory record keeping, payroll, accounting, and the solving of mathematical equations are all included under the heading of processing of data.

The performance of the operations in predetermined sequence and the device or machines employed to perform these operations constitute a data-processing system. There are many types of devices that can be employed and hence many types of data-processing systems. For example:

1. The device may be simply pen and paper.
2. The device may be an adding machine and an accounting machine.
3. The device may be a computer.

Likewise, the sequence of operations may differ from one system to another, depending largely upon the devices to be utilized. However, regardless of the data-processing system, *the plan of processing is always of human origin.* Furthermore, the system is or should be performed essentially to serve human beings. Data are processed to put them into a form that has greatest utilization.

BASIC ELEMENTS OF DATA PROCESSING

Specifically, what are some basic elements of data processing? In answering this question, many will mention "writing" and "calculating," and a few will include "storing." But study of the processing effort reveals that there are not three, but eight basic elements of processing. These are shown in Figure 2–2. For each element, the reason why it is performed and the result obtained from applying each element to the data

Basic Element of Data Processing	Why Performed	Results in:
1. Reading	To interpret data by going over characters, words, and symbols	Awareness of data existence
2. Writing, typing, card punching, or paper-tape perforating (frequently called *input*)	To facilitate processing by putting data on or in medium, i.e., alphabetical or numerical marks on paper, holes in paper, magnetic areas on tape, and magnetic ink on paper	Start of data processing
3. Recording or printing (frequently called *output*)	To obtain results of processing, the data—in medium form for processing purposes—are converted to form easily read by a human being, if not already in that form	End of data processing
4. Sorting	To classify the data	Data being related to one or more bases
5. Transmitting	To disseminate the data	Data availability for specific purpose and place
6. Calculating	To manipulate the data mathematically	Numerical data being added, subtracted, multiplied, or divided
7. Comparing	To check data for accuracy and completeness	Quantitative and qualitative inspection of data
8. Storing	To retain or keep the data	Data being available when needed

Note: The meaning of each of the following terms, frequently used in office management, is included in the above listing:

a) "Interpreting" (usually associated with No. 2 or No. 3) is imprinting the meaning of the punched holes in a punched card on that card.

b) "Reproducing" (usually associated with No. 2) is duplicating an exact copy of a punched card.

c) "Collating" (usually associated with No. 4) is merging sets of related data into a single set.

d) "Segregating" (usually associated with No. 4) is separating sets of related data into several sets

FIG. 2–2. The basic elements of data processing.

are also included in the figure. To illustrate, sorting (No. 4) is performed to classify the data and results in the data being related to one or more bases.

It would be difficult to overstate the importance of these basic elements of data processing. They serve as the nucleus around which all paper work revolves. Various combinations of these elements, in kind as well as in degree, are required to supply the needed information which the office is expected to furnish.

PROCESSING AND PRODUCTION UNIT EMPLOYED

The development and use of the modern electronic computer has brought emphasis and recognition to the basic elements of data proc-

essing. Terminology such as "input," "output," "transmitting," and "recording" is commonplace with computer installations. However, these
terms are actually not exclusive with computer usage. These elements of
processing are basic and universal. They exist in all data processing,
whether noncomputer processing or computer processing.

To highlight this important fact, Figure 2–3 is included. In this

OFFICE PRODUCTION UNIT EMPLOYED	READING, TYPING ECT. (1)	WRITING, TYPING, PRINTING (2)	RECORDING, PRINTING (3)	SORTING (4)	TRANSMITTING (5)	CALCULATING (6)	COMPARING (7)	STORING (8)
ACCOUTING MACHINE		V	V	V		V	V	
ADDING AND CALCULATING MACHINES		V	V			V		
ADDRESSING MACHINE			V	V				
COMPUTER WITHOUT SPECIAL ATTACHMENTS			V	V	V	V	V	V
COPYING MACHINE			V					
ELECTRONIC READER	V	V						
HUMAN BEING	V	V	V	V	V	V	V	V
MICROFILM UNITS			V					V
PNEUMATIC TUBE					V			
PUNCHING MACHINE			V					
SORTER				V				
TABULATOR			V			V	V	V
TELAUTOGRAPH		V	V		V			
TELEGRAPH		V	V		V			
TELETYPEWRITER		V	V		V			
TYPEWRITER		V	V					

BASIC ELEMENT OF DATA PROCESSING

FIG. 2–3. Each office production unit performs specific
basic elements of data processing.

figure, the basic elements of data processing are shown across the top,
while the common office productive units are listed vertically in the left
column. The basic elements of processing performed by each production unit are indicated by the check marks. For example, an accounting
machine performs the basic elements of writing, recording, sorting, calculating, and comparing. In contrast, a copying machine performs just

one basic element of processing—recording. A human being performs all the basic elements of data processing.

This figure helps to identify the make-up of office work. It assists in grasping the important over-all picture of office work and in understanding better the role and operation of various office production units. It also demonstrates that what has been done with papers for years is still being done, whether essentially by hand, by ordinary office machine, or by computer.

THE RETAINING OF DATA

The very nature and reason-to-be of much paper work requires that data be retained. The more obvious reason is to keep it for future reference requirements. The work of what to retain, for how long a period, and under what arrangement is a vital part of providing needed information. However, equally important is the retaining of data either mentally, manually, or mechanically so that subsequent data can be appended to the already existing fund and thus keep the information current.

The retaining of data for subsequent processing and bringing them up to date has been emphasized by the use of the computer—the function of its so-called "memory unit." But data retention is also basic in office work performed by hand, or where records are kept solely in the owner's head.

THE DISTRIBUTING OF DATA

Collecting, processing, and, when necessary, retaining data are insufficient for information to be utilized by employees and customers. The information must also be distributed to those who have need for it. This task includes the proper placing and timing of the information. It includes all the means of communication such as mail, telephone, telegraph, intercommunication systems, and electronic communication devices.

An employee's effectiveness depends upon the accuracy, timeliness, and precision with which his contribution is geared to the over-all plan. When this thesis is followed, reports are distributed only to employees who are in a position to take direct action; only information which, directly or indirectly, helps get the job done is provided. Violations in the distributing of data are common sources of inefficiency in office management.

CHARACTERISTICS OF OFFICE WORK

To point out the important distinguishing features about office work and its performance serves to supply a better concept of what is being managed. Accordingly, the major characteristics of office work will now be briefly discussed.

1. *A facilitating function.* Office work is a facilitating function; it is the essential medium through which the various activities of an enterprise are fused together. In a sense, office work can be called the "catalytic agent" of modern management.[1]

The work of the office assists in efforts to increase output, lower costs, stimulate employees, pay wages, purchase materials, ship orders, and communicate with others. The individual work of practically every department in an enterprise is implemented by office work. For example, a credit department cannot operate successfully without current records of creditors, amounts and dates due, lists of delinquent accounts, credit histories of customers, and a quantity of correspondence.

2. *A service work.* Another distinguishing feature of office work is that it is a service work. In and of itself, office work serves little purpose; it is performed to help others do their work more effectively. For example, office work is a service to the top executive officers, to the production department, to the sales department, and to the finance department. It helps supply top executives with data which are necessary in order to manage the enterprise. By means of records, the production department is helped to improve its service and to lower costs, the sales department is aided in its work of selling the product, and the finance department is assisted in maintaining written evidence of the financial status of the enterprise.[2]

Service is also the primary objective of the office manager. Consideration for office costs, as well as for the utility, quality, and quantity of the office services, is also important; but these should be recognized as secondary objectives. An eagerness to slash all costs or a decision to compile only records which the office believes are useful might result in failure to provide the necessary office services to the other departments. Thus, losses occur in these departments that probably far exceed the savings in operation. However, the service should be evaluated in terms of cost; elaborate and excessive service usually means waste, while, on the other hand, inadequate service represents false economy.

3. *Volume determined by outside.* Unlike many major business activities, the volume of office work is determined by factors outside the

---

[1] "Catalytic agent" is a term used in chemistry and means an element the presence of which is necessary to bring about a desired reaction between other elements but which does not itself enter into the reaction. In a similar manner, office work brings about a desired reaction of business elements but does not enter into the reaction itself.

[2] See Policyholders' Service Bureau, Metropolitan Life Insurance Company, *Functions of the Office Manager* (New York, undated), pp. 5–6.

office. These factors include the number of shipments, the amount of collections, the number of open accounts, the quantity of sales letters, the number of factory employees, and the number of items manufactured or sold—all factors outside the control of the office.

4. *An indirect contributor to profit.* No profit is realized directly from office work, since it acts through the operative departments, such as the production, sales, and finance departments.[3] In this sense, office work contributes indirectly, not directly, to the profit-making ability of the enterprise. However, some feel that office work produces profit. This belief stems primarily from considering the office as a complete unit within itself.

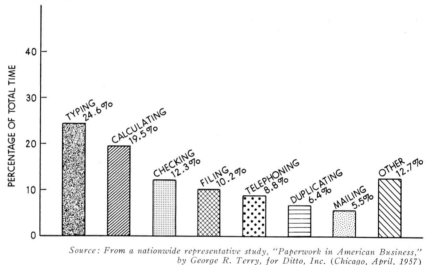

Source: From a nationwide representative study, "Paperwork in American Business," by George R. Terry, for Ditto, Inc. (Chicago, April, 1957)

FIG. 2–4. Major activities making up office time.

5. *Contents.* The make-up of office work is predominantly typing and calculating, which together account for approximately 44 per cent of all office time.[4] This percentage is increased to 90 per cent when the seven major activities of the office are included. The data are shown in Figure 2–4. Part III of this book, consisting of Chapters 8–13, inclusive, deals with these major office activities. A complete discussion is presented of correspondence and reports, of calculating and checking, of filing, and so forth.

6. *Dispersion.* Office work is not performed exclusively in any one department; some of it is performed in every department of a company.

---

[3] "Profit," as used here, is the residual income accruing to the owner of an enterprise after he has paid all the economic aids of production—that is, rent on all land used, interest on all capital used, and wages to all labor used.

[4] From the study *Paperwork in American Business*, by George R. Terry, for Ditto, Inc. (Chicago, April, 1957).

The swing to mechanization and especially computers has resulted in much office work being handled within a single location; but there is still considerable paper work in other areas, for example, in the purchasing, engineering, or inspection department. Furthermore, a milling machine operator in a factory usually performs some clerical work in the normal course of his daily duty. Where financial incentives and production control are used, the operator may be responsible for a considerable amount of clerical work, yet he is not classified as an office worker. Likewise, most salesmen are accountable for sizable amounts of paper work; and the same is true of many employees of a personnel department, who are quick to point out the voluminous paper work used in the execution of their tasks.

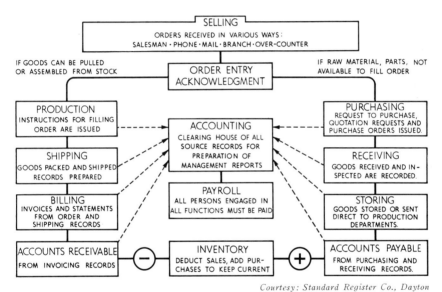

Courtesy: Standard Register Co., Dayton

FIG. 2–5. Records permeate an entire enterprise. Information is required by every department.

Figure 2–5 indicates the dispersion of paper work and the basic functions of business. Selling gives rise to the order entry acknowledgment, and the subsequent paper work flow affects many departments, whether the goods are shipped or assembled from stock, or needed raw materials are obtained to take care of the customer's order.

7. *Personnel performing.* One of the interesting developments among office employees is the increasing proportion of women in this category. In the year 1870, for example, only 2 per cent of office personnel were women; by 1930, the percentage was nearly 50; by 1950, the number of women office employees reached 60 per cent of the total; and in 1960, women held nearly 75 per cent of all office jobs.

There is, however, a tendency for certain office jobs to be occupied by men. These include accountant, collection clerk, credit clerk, and correspondent. Other office jobs are commonly held by women. In this group are the jobs of file clerk, machine operator, receptionist, typist, stenographer, and telephone operator. Still other jobs are held by either men or women and include those of bookkeeper, cashier, mail clerk, and private secretary.

Also, the proportion of office workers to total workers varies considerably with different industries. For example, nearly one half of the workers in finance, insurance, and real estate are office workers. In contrast, the proportion is about 11 per cent in manufacturing and only 0.3 per cent in agriculture, forestry, and fisheries.

GROWTH OF OFFICE WORK

The amount of office work has grown tremendously in our economy during the past several decades. This growth can be verified in a number of ways, but the increase in the number of office employees is probably most conclusive, especially when one observes the productive capacity of present-day office equipment and machines to enable a large work

Year	Total Population of the United States	Total Working Force	Clerical Workers	Percentage— Clerical to Total Working Force
1960	181,057,000	66,681,537	9,783,632	14.6
1950	151,230,000	55,835,340	6,866,374	12.3
1940	131,950,000	45,166,083	4,612,356	10.2
1930	123,080,000	48,829,920	4,025,324	8.2
1920	106,970,000	41,614,248	3,111,836	7.5
1910	92,410,000	38,167,336	1,718,458	4.5
1900	76,090,000	29,073,233	1,068,993	3.7
1890	63,056,438	22,735,661	801,505	3.5
1880	50,262,382	17,392,099	518,439	3.0
1870	39,904,593	12,505,923	305,502	2.4

Source: U.S. Department of Commerce, Bureau of the Census, "Statistical Abstract, 1960" (Washington, D.C.: U.S. Government Printing Office, 1961), pp. 7, 23–27.

U.S. Department of Commerce, Bureau of the Census, "1955 Annual Report on the Labor Force" (Washington, D.C., March, 1956), pp. 3–5.

U.S. Department of Commerce, Bureau of the Census, "1950 Census of Population," Vol. I: "Population" (Washington, D.C.: U.S. Government Printing Office, 1953), pp. 110–12.

U.S. Department of Commerce, Bureau of the Census, "Sixteenth Census of the United States, 1940," Vol. III: "Population" (Washington, D.C.: U.S. Government Printing Office, 1943), p. 76.

U.S. Department of Commerce, Bureau of the Census, "Fifteenth Census of the United States, 1930," Vol. V: "Population" (Washington, D.C.: U.S. Government Printing Office, 1933), pp. 10–22.

U.S. Department of Commerce, Bureau of the Census, "Twelfth Census of the United States, 1900," Special Reports: "Occupations" (Washington, D.C.: U.S. Government Printing Office, 1904), pp. 1 and li.

FIG. 2–6.   Total population of the United States, total working force, number of clerical workers, and percentage of clerical workers to total working force for the years 1870–1960.

volume per employee. The rate of growth in the number of office employees has been much greater than in that of either our total working force or our total population. For example, in the United States, during the period 1870–1940, the total working force increased less than four times, while the number of clerical workers increased fifteen times. From 1940 to 1960, the total population increased 38 per cent, the total working force expanded 47 per cent, and the number engaged in clerical occupations increased approximately 121 per cent.

The basic information concerning the growth in total population of the United States, in the total working force, and in clerical and kindred workers is set forth in Figure 2–6. The ratio of clerical to total working force has been calculated for each year, and these values are shown in the last column to the right. For example, in 1870, the ratio of clerical to total working force was 2.4 per cent; whereas in 1960, this ratio had increased to 14.6 per cent. Each decade since 1870 has shown a greater percentage of the total working force performing clerical work. Stated differently, in 1870, about one worker in forty was an office worker; in 1960, about one in seven was an office worker.

REASONS FOR GROWTH

This increase in office work and in office personnel is attributable to many forces. The industrial growth of the United States is a major cause. With it has developed the concentration and specialization of efforts, with the resultant more intricate relationships between major segments or occupations making up the working force, which circumstance pointed to the need and use for more paper work. For example, during the period 1900–1960, the number engaged in manufacturing occupations increased from 6 million to 16.4 million, and the number engaged in "service industries" spurted from 4 million to nearly 14 million. These growths emphasize the necessity and the use of more paper work. In addition, the employment of more factual information by managers has influenced the growth of the office. Demands for statistics, accurate information, and carefully prepared statements can be cited as examples. Then, too, as more information of a general but applicable nature has become available, the tendency is to get this information into the hands of interested persons, thereby increasing the office work of recording and communicating this information.

Another contributory cause is the influence of a tremendous expansion in legislation, especially that pertaining to business. On the part of private enterprises, this increased government-business activity has made for more office work and employees in order to fulfill the requirements of the numerous statutes and governmental regulatory bodies. And from government's side, both the amount of governmental clerical work and the number of governmental office employees have been stimulated. There were nearly 4 million office workers in public administration work in 1960.[5]

Finally, some portion of the growth in office work is undoubtedly due to inadequate efforts to control it. The preparation of essential paper work only, the extended use of efficient office machines, the adequate motivation of office employees, and the development of proper procedures and methods are examples of efforts which assist in reducing the amount of paper work.

WILL GROWTH CONTINUE?

Opinions differ regarding the future growth of office work. Some believe it will continue to grow at a rate exceeding that of all other types of work. They view it as basically a self-perpetuating situation—more people, more paper; more paper, more people. They point out that we have become attuned to the use of the products of the office.

In contrast, many believe that the upward trend in office work cannot continue. They insist we are drowning in a sea of paper and that some office work has become a ritual performance for its own sake. They observe that the past increase in office work has resulted in an overwhelming increase in overhead costs, and this process cannot continue indefinitely.

THE FUTURE OF THE OFFICE

A number of available studies point out that there exists considerable waste office work. The exact amount is unknown, but the gains to be won by eliminating just a portion of this unnecessary processed information staggers the imagination. It seems that a simple approach could be followed: (1) Eliminate the unnecessary paper work being done, and (2) perform the necessary paper work more efficiently. The first criterion is to determine what office work serves effectively a definite and essential need, that is, provides essential information. Opinions, of course, will differ in this evaluation. The second criterion stresses such things as simplification of the office processes, training of office employees, and more office mechanization.

There are some who believe the office of the future will become so mechanized that paper itself as an instrument will be supplanted to a great extent by drums, tapes, and wires. Payroll checks might be replaced with information fed by wire from the employer's machine directly into the bank's machine for credit to the individual employee's account. Collectors will receive payment by drawing on their customers'

---

[5] U.S. Department of Commerce, Bureau of the Census, *Statistical Abstract, 1960* (Washington, D.C.: U.S. Government Printing Office, 1961), p. 713.

checking accounts. Whether these things come about is conjectural, but the trend toward greater mechanization is taking place.

As office mechanization increases, it would seem that clerical personnel will become more technically proficient, require more training, and become more productive. Real wages are likely to increase;[6] but the many problems stemming from the relationship of the employee to a machine, specialization of work, and employee work satisfaction are likely to be multiplied.

Increased emphasis will probably be placed upon analysis and interpretation of information made available by the office. As more facts are needed and can be made available within a reasonable period, the task of determining what data are necessary, and why, will take on new and increasing meaning. But the facilitating and service elements of office work will remain of prime importance. Determining and providing essential information effectively, and thus contributing to the success of the entire enterprise, will continue to be the vital task of office management.

THE CHALLENGE OF OFFICE MANAGEMENT

Opportunities are abundant in the field of office management. The rapid growth in the amount of work and in the number doing it have emphasized the need for managers trained in this field. As the importance and contributions of the office are gaining greater recognition, the status of the qualified office manager is increasing.

Challenges are indeed numerous for the executive specializing in the managing of information handling. The following list is representative rather than exhaustive. Among the significant challenges are:

1. Preparation for the "automated office."
2. Unwarranted application of office mechanization in certain areas.
3. Upgrading the status of office management.
4. Increasing the number of office executives with the management viewpoint.
5. Application of greater creativity to office management.
6. Reduction in the amount of unnecessary paper work performed.
7. Improvement in office procedures and methods.
8. Establishment of more and better office work standards.
9. Simplification of office practices and operations.
10. Careful analysis and evolvement of remedial actions for coping with mounting office costs.
11. Attracting and acquiring the better graduates from schools for office jobs.
12. Extent of specialization in individual office jobs.

---

[6] Real wages are the goods and services that money wages will buy at any given time.

13. Greater delegation of authority by the office manager to his subordinates.

14. Development of better means of motivating office employees.

There exist in companies almost everywhere vast possibilities for qualified executives. This is especially true for office managers. The future is brilliant for the qualified office manager who recognizes the real importance of information handling, can manage it effectively, and can contribute to the successful operation of the entire enterprise.

QUESTIONS

1. Select three common types of paper work found in an office with which you are familiar; and for each type, name the basic elements of data processing required to prepare the paper work.
2. Discuss the distributing of data in office management.
3. What is the meaning of information from the viewpoint of the modern office manager?
4. In the typical business enterprise, enumerate five activities giving rise to data; and for each activity, give the type of common data which are created.
5. Can office work do a service job without being facilitating? Can it be facilitating without doing a service job? Explain.
6. Explain the meaning of Figure 2–3 in your own words.
7. Would you say that office work is an end in itself? Why?
8. What is a data-processing system, and why is it important in office management?
9. Discuss the major deductions you believe should be made from Figure 2–4.
10. Name five current challenges of office management, and discuss the one you feel is most important.
11. Do you feel that the future possibilities and opportunities of office management, compared with those in other fields of management, are (a) greater, (b) about the same, or (c) fewer? Give reasons for your answer.
12. What is your opinion regarding the future growth of office work?

CASE PROBLEM

Case 2–1.   The Driscoll Company

The Driscoll Company was founded in 1920 by Mr. Harold Driscoll. The chief product of the company is injection sprays. The enterprise started in a small one-story flat; and through the persistent efforts of Mr. Driscoll, the company grew in size and scope of operations, until today it employs 450 men and nets about $5 million a year. Currently, in addition to sprays, the company manufactures decontaminators and spreaders.

Two years ago, Harold Driscoll retired as president of the company and took the inoperative position of chairman of the board of directors. Clarence Driscoll, the eldest son, took over the position of president at that time. About twelve months ago, members of the sales department of the company bitterly complained of having to spend too much time in adjusting accounts and handling customer grievances. An increasingly large amount of the equipment delivered by the company either was defective or would not meet the specifications supplied by the customer. At about this same time, profits started to dwindle, and turnover of employees increased.

Clarence Driscoll, the president, called a meeting of the eight department heads to discuss the problems which were confronting the company. The following points were brought out during the discussion: (1) The haphazard method of spot checking for quality was undoubtedly the cause of much of the trouble; (2) the plant manager explained that the sales department was not giving him enough time to fulfill orders, a rush order always coming through when the production facilities were taxed to capacity; (3) processing of a cancellation of an order by a customer took an excessively long time to reach the factory and the office billing department; (4) items were purchased that were not in immediate requirement, while purchase of other items of an emergency nature was delayed; (5) it required four working days to answer the typical letter of inquiry from a prospective customer; and (6) the sales department claimed that many credit records of the company did not reflect current data. The discussion ended without any final conclusions drawn to meet the situation. Clarence Driscoll stated that now that all knew what the problems were, the department heads could work harder to meet them, and this was all that was needed.

During the following months and up to the present, matters have grown worse. Labor turnover is higher than ever; and as of the end of last month, a $300,000 credit is owed to customers due to rejections.

Problems:

1. From the viewpoint of office work, what is the major problem here?
2. What actions do you recommend the company take? Why?
3. Outline how you would try to gain acceptance for your recommended actions.

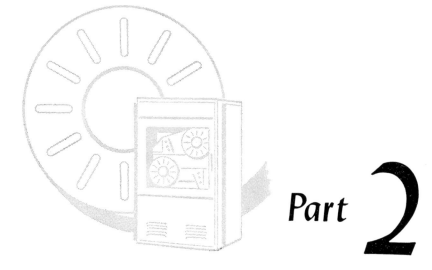

Part 2

OFFICE AUTOMATION

Automation is becoming commonplace in the office of today. Slowly but surely, it is working into a key position in the performing of office work. The reasons for adopting these new ways of doing office work, their effect upon office management, important aspects concerning their technical operation, and vital considerations in their use as a basic processor of data are discussed in the following five chapters.

This discussion of office automation includes the latest developments in this interesting, fast-moving, challenging, and somewhat disturbing subject area. The various chapter headings include (1) the new office technology, (2) electronic computers—managerial considerations, (3) electronic computers—technical considerations, (4) applications of computers, and (5) integrated data processing.

Chapter 3

THE NEW OFFICE TECHNOLOGY

*How poor are they that have not patience! What
wound did ever heal but by degrees!*

—WILLIAM SHAKESPEARE

MACHINES and their application to office work
are bringing about startling evolutionary changes and a new era in the
management of office work. Current achievements stagger the imagination, yet predictions are of even greater things to come. Work is being
accomplished at fantastic speeds; monotonous and routine jobs are being
eliminated; and the entire make-up of office work, as it has been known,
is undergoing significant changes.

ILLUSTRATIONS OF THE NEW OFFICE TECHNOLOGY

Scientific break-throughs are speeding the accomplishment of the new
office technology. A reading machine scans written material at a rate of
nearly 2,000 words a minute—the equivalent of one page in this book in
about twelve seconds—and converts the words to holes punched in a tape.
In turn, the tape operates automatically a machine for long-distance
transmission of messages. Machines sort bank checks, debit and credit
depositors' accounts, and make out monthly statements. Machines record
inventory items sold, items to be replaced, volume of inventory, and
quantities on hand of each item.

The new office technology is actually a part of the great technologic
advances being applied to every branch of industry, and the trend is toward new and better machines. These applications in the factory, in
sales, in research, in medicine, in the military, and in transportation
are giving greater impetus to the importance of paper work and to its
processing in keeping with developments in these other areas. For example, in the machine-tool industry, while an operator makes a machine
part by hand, his motions and their sequence are recorded on magnetic
tape. Subsequently, this tape can be run through the machine any number of times, duplicating exactly the original part. An oil refinery, com-

39

pletely automated, requires only three men to operate the control buttons. And a steel-pipe plant employing automatic machines produces four times as much pipe with one third the number of employees formerly used. Machines can multiply two thirteen-digit figures in 31 millionths of a second, that is, at the rate of 32,000 such multiplications in *one* second. In one day, this unit can perform not millions but hundreds of millions of operations without a single error—an amount of work equivalent to that accomplished using the entire work life of one thousand people. Thus, analysis of much data required for modern research is performed by means of machines.

Airplanes can be guided in "blind" take-offs and landings, movements of trains can be controlled, and the course of storms can be charted and weather maps quickly sent to stations across the nation. All these applications, which might be classified as "nonoffice," actually enhance both the importance and the scope of paper work and give increasing recognition to its dominance and the necessity for its proper management in the emerging technical age.

NEW HORIZONS OF OFFICE MANAGEMENT

Greater effectiveness of office operations is being encouraged by the new tools and techniques being made available by the new office technology. At the same time, all management members are making bigger demands of the office because of the need for specific information. The effect is to give the manager in charge of information a much larger scope of operation, much more opportunity, and much greater responsibility.

The trend of developments appears to be toward the swiftest possible reaction by an *entire* enterprise to any given stimulus. The enterprise is being viewed more and more as a responsive body instead of a cluster of individual and, to some extent, isolated departments. Rather than letting each other know eventually what is taking place, the demand is for almost instantaneous, pertinent, and complete information to all departments. In fulfilling this need and in playing this role, the office is attaining major status and serves to direct and co-ordinate the activities of all the various components making up the enterprise.

DEFINITION OF OFFICE AUTOMATION

The word "automation" first appeared in print about 1948. Since that time, this word has stimulated much discussion and controversy; it has been accorded many different meanings. Some consider automation as a synonym for technological change, while others believe it denotes mechanization. Commonly, the word is used solely in connection with the processing of products in a factory; but, while popular, this concept is obviously incomplete, since data processing and the compilation of information have been subjected to technological improvements.

In performing work of any kind, automation means the arrangement whereby one or more machines are operated without human participation except to press the starter button. It is the regulation of processing by which high-speed, self-correcting instruments or machines control the operations of other machines. In a very real sense, automation is the extension of mechanization. If an office machine can be operated and controlled by other machines or devices, office automation can be said to exist. The situation, however, is primarily one of degree and terminology.

Actually, automatic devices are not new. Nineteen hundred years ago, the Romans used a hydraulic float valve to regulate the water level in their reservoirs and tanks. However, today the simultaneous introduction of many electronic devices to control the kind and flow of office work and their outstanding accomplishments are of significant value.

Office automation relieves mankind of menial work. Most office work requires some human cerebration; but when the work is repetitive in nature or subject to exact formulation, it can be effectively handled by machine. By such means, man is free to employ his mind for work which the human brain *alone* can encompass.

THE EXPANDING OFFICE TECHNOLOGY

The uses of new techniques and machines to supply needed information multiply daily, and so do the users. The trend is unquestionably upward, whether measured by casual observation, surveys, statements of managers, or the number of office machines in use. Computer manufacturers, for example, now do an annual business of over $1 billion.

Each week, noteworthy applications of data-processing machines are announced, and news is given of many more in various stages of development. To illustrate, for large construction projects, a computer is now being used to indicate what portions of the total work should be expedited for any given time reduction for completing the project and to keep the additional cost accruing from such changes at a minimum. In another application, the trend, production run, and standard quality control systems are classified and processed so that quality control can be maintained with the help of three instead of twenty-seven clerical employees. Managers of retail stores can find which items are selling satisfactorily, which poorly, which items to discontinue, which to promote, which to purchase, and where to display (shelf and location in store), all by means of a point-of-purchase analysis rapidly calculated by an electronic office machine. In addition, there is now available an automatic engineering drawing system. It employs an aperture card which is a combination microfilm and tabulating card. An original penciled drawing is microfilmed. The film is mounted on the card, and all copies or prints are obtained from this combination microfilm and tabulating card. A design retrieval program using these cards can easily be established, thus helping to eliminate duplicate engineering design work.

WHY AUTOMATE?

Managers of present-day enterprises need considerable data to help them make effective decisions. As the managerial need for information becomes more and more pressing, the means for supplying this information quickly and completely have been stimulated. This is reason No. 1 why companies automate their data-processing work. In the quick tempo of today, events affecting enterprises seem to happen with increasing rapidity, and many decisions must take into account at least part of these events. Under such conditions, the gathering, processing, and distributing of data must be done as quickly as possible. In certain areas, the tremendous amounts of paper work required can be handled within a reasonable period only by machine. In the case of supplying scientific and research data calculated from mathematical formulas, a machine accomplishes in several hours what would require years of manual calculation.

A second major reason for office automation is to reduce office costs. In some instances, this goal is achieved; but in others, cost reduction is more fancy than fact. One is inclined to believe that in any installation, because of the speed and versatility of office machines used in automation, paper work costs are reduced. Unfortunately, it is difficult to make accurate comparisons of a "before and after" office automation. Usually, many innovations are effected by automation. The report requirements may change, due mainly to these innovations; and the volume of work may increase, since the processing time is stepped up and "we have the necessary machines." Also, some of the departmental operations may undergo transitions of one type or another. If all factors remained on a *status quo* basis before and after automation, and there is an adequate volume of work, the costs under automation will be reduced. But a very likely condition that develops is more data processing with approximately the same dollar expenditure.

This does not mean that office automation is not an attractive investment. Quite the contrary, it usually is a good investment; otherwise, managers would not utilize it. A well-planned, -installed, and -managed installation will return a saving of approximately 30–40 per cent on the total investment each year. To achieve this return, it is necessary in many cases to operate the equipment five days a week, sixteen hours a day. In each case, individual circumstances govern and must be taken into account for the particular conditions present.

In a study of the Chicago area, it was found that the average estimated cost of automated equipment per company was about $110,000, whereas the average estimated clerical saving was about $50,000. This means a "pay-out" period of a little over two years—an attractive inducement.

Frequently overlooked, but an important reason for office automation, is reduction of errors. Machines seldom commit mistakes; and when they do, it usually is the fault of the person operating them. Office automation tends to integrate data processing and thus minimizes the number of times the data are handled; hence, it reduces the possibilities of committing errors. Higher-quality office work can be viewed as a by-product, even though it is an important contribution of office automation.

As pointed out in Chapter 2, the office work force represents one of the fastest growing groups in our economy. The search for competent office help is continuous. Ways of getting out the necessary work with a limited number of people have been eagerly sought, or an arrangement requiring employment of only the more competent office employees has won favor. Both these conditions are met by automating office work. In many cases, the capacity of the automated system is greater than current needs; and as the clerical work load increases, it will not be necessary to add people, but rather depend upon the system to take on most of the additional load. This assures adequate clerical help for perhaps the next decade.

The last reason to be discussed is the desire to have an internal status symbol. Automating office work signifies progress; and in some instances, it appears that equipment was ordered and installed simply because certain executives insisted upon having it. Whether the type and amount of equipment were adequate and proper for their needs was hastily reviewed, and full utilization of the equipment has never been made. Instances of this nature are relatively minor, yet they demonstrate that the basis of some automation is impulsive and personal, not rational and logical.

THE FEASIBILITY OF AUTOMATION

Automating the paper work of an enterprise can be a detailed and complicated task. For best results, it is imperative that the entire cycle of the work to be automated be taken into account, that the real objectives be carefully defined and used as guides in designing the system, and that the proper equipment be selected and employed for the intended use. Actually, two aspects of data processing are involved: (1) the make-up of the paper work itself and (2) the processing of the data as such. Under the former are included the design of the entire cycle, what data are included, in what form, to what form, and how utilized. Under the second point are the actual uses of the equipment typically operating on a continuing basis. These two aspects of data processing are interrelated, and the experts in each area should work together as a team, with each aware of the other's problems.

In some "feasibility" studies, the erroneous assumption is made that office automation is desirable regardless of the procedures and methods currently being used. The result is that inefficiencies in paper work are automated or some data are permitted to remain in a form which is incompatible with best automation practices. As a result, both the good and the bad features of the present system are preserved. Experience clearly demonstrates that it is extremely difficult to remove unnecessary data or to change basic procedures once they are incorporated in the office automation arrangement. The proper approach is to conduct a thorough and sound procedure and method study *prior* to the decision to use any form of automation. Only in this way is a solid and reliable foundation established for all the subsequent phases of improvement, simplification, and mechanization.

Also, too much emphasis may be placed on the practicality or desirability of utilizing particular types of machines and equipment. Attention is focused on speeds, peak loads, scheduling, and other technical considerations. While these are important, it must also be remembered that the data are being processed for utilization, to help somebody do his job better because of the processed data provided to him. Furthermore, concentrating on the processing of the data *per se* may permit inadequate consideration for such things as acquiring the source data, converting the data into suitable form for machine processing, supplying the processed information in the best format, and getting it to the right personnel at the right time.

A sincere effort to improve the total management information system necessitates a knowledge of, and adequate consideration for, a number of factors. These include the objectives of the enterprise and the contributions expected of each functional area or organizational unit to the achievement of these objectives. The decision-making activity vested in each management member should be clearly identified so that the information needs of each member can be determined. Familiarity with the organization structure assists in answering who decides what, who is expected to inform whom, and what information is needed. Generally, it is also helpful to know the relative importance of the various basic functions of the enterprise—manufacturing, marketing, financing, engineering, and personnel—in order to obtain some impression of the probable characteristics of the data to be handled. Also, any future increased work loads and contemplated changes should be taken into account, as well as the existing management information systems, no matter how primitive, because such facts can have an important bearing upon the information system that is recommended.

INFORMATION IMPROVEMENT

As implied in the statements above, office automation provides an opportunity to improve existent information by streamlining procedures and processing essential information in a format that stimulates effective usage of the information. To this end, the office manager should capture the initiative and suggest what types and arrangements of information might be of greatest assistance to the recipient. Too frequently, it is assumed that identical information and reports should continue after automation as existed before automation. The common practice of asking the recipient what information he wants usually results in a continuation of the existent information because the recipient does not know what other types he might have or how what he is receiving might be bettered. In short, he is not an expert in designing the information needs and report structure of his company. Perhaps no one man is— or for that matter, no one group; but certainly, efforts of reasonably skilled people in this area will assist in achieving better information.

Two illustrations will demonstrate the challenge of information improvement in the typical enterprise, which improvement can usually be won during the time of office automation installation. In a well-known company headquartered in Boston, the vice president of finance is provided on a monthly basis with information on (1) items having a nonrecurring profit impact, (2) items having a continuing profit impact, and (3) financial managerial subjects requiring policy determination or modification. Such information differs from the rigid and common standardized financial data, yet it provides valuable assistance in vital decision making concerning financial matters.

In another company, information was limited to traditional accounting statistics. For example, the manager was informed that his company enjoyed a 13 per cent sales increase over last year, now held a 40 per cent share of the market, employed 90 employees, and was awarded 53 patents during the past twelve months. This information sounds favorable, and the facts are not deliberately overstated. But are they complete, and do they supply enough information upon which to base important decisions? For this company, the answer appears to be "No," because further information, carefully selected, revealed that while the company's sales were increasing 13 per cent, sales of the highly specialized industry of which this company is a member increased 37 per cent. The 90 engineers constitute two thirds of all engineers employed in the industry; hence, in engineering skill, the company is missing the mark by more than 50 per cent, since only 40 per cent of the market is being sold and a total of 103 patents pertaining to this industry were awarded last year.

OFFICE AUTOMATION AND PLANNING

The office management process affects and, in turn, is affected by office automation. An exhaustive treatment of this interesting transition in management is beyond the scope of this book; hence, the discussion here will be limited to the high points of the more basic considerations involved. The first to be discussed is planning.

As already stated, an office automation study should commence with planning efforts directed at improving procedures and methods, combining reports, records, and office forms wherever possible, and point the entire effort toward handling only information that is truly essential. Much of this work can be done by company personnel; but in many cases, the services of a consultant experienced in this area can save much time and direct the work to a satisfactory conclusion. However, excessive reliance upon outside assistance, particularly from manufacturers of automated office equipment, may prove unwise. The manufacturer's representative frequently is not familiar with the specific and detailed needs of the company. In many instances, he is not aware of the human problems confronting company personnel should the decision to automate be made. He can and does render valuable assistance in helping the prospect become more aware of what the equipment can do and the possible aids it can provide for the prospect.

There should be no restricted areas or restrictions in the initial development stages of automation. Compromises can always be made later, but beginning with circumscribed areas inevitably means ending with restricted areas. The usual pattern in the application of automation is to a smaller range of activities than was initially considered. Seldom can the best results of automation be achieved by confining it to predetermined limits of activities or to certain organizational limits. Automation commonly cuts across conventional lines originally established for non-automated purposes.

The use of an automation committee can assist in attaining a unified program of preparation and installation. Important groups such as the methods department, the personnel department, and the departments in which changes will occur can be represented on such a committee. Planning pertaining to the feasibility of automation; the how, when, and where of the changes to be made; and the means for handling these changes, especially with reference to personnel, can be handled quite successfully by a committee.

Adequate planning will avoid the establishment of unrealistic deadlines for the change-over to automation. Frequently, it requires more time to get into office automation than is at first realized. The usual pattern is pressure for early installation after long delay in trying to decide whether to automate. Planning helps establish practical schedules and ties together the various required activities for automation into a coordinated program.

OFFICE AUTOMATION AND CONTROLLING

When an automation committee is used, this body can perform periodic follow-up of the installation to smooth out operating difficulties. There usually are a number of such difficulties. The follow-up should also include the comparison of achievements under automation with what was anticipated prior to the change-over. In this way, the original objectives of the automation can be promoted, in that areas requiring managerial attention are identified and remedial action is applied to them.

Office automation is commonly of a multiproject nature, and this fact emphasizes the importance of establishing effective progress-reporting techniques and carefully monitoring them in order to maintain proper control over each project. Effective reporting techniques are simple, comprehensive, and easy for either the technical or the nontechnical employee to understand. To maintain the support of top management members, it is a good practice to provide them with clear, concise, and up-to-date reports which reveal how each project is progressing and to what extent established goals are being attained.

Job completion dates must be realistic and adhered to; otherwise, control efforts become dissipated. Failure to provide sufficient lead time and allowances for unexpected contingencies is a common cause of establishing completion dates that cannot be fulfilled. The delay of one project aggravates the entire program because work scheduling under automation closely interrelates all projects within the system. As a result, certain projects may be subjected to completion on a "crash basis," which usually means higher costs and extra follow-up efforts.

OFFICE AUTOMATION AND ORGANIZING

For office automation to achieve real success, its various activities must be integrated with the operational activities of the company. It should not be regarded as a new, mysterious entity separated from the main body of the company or as an interesting, captive consulting facility. To achieve the needed integration between information and action functions, it is essential that those in the automated activities have a clear understanding of their working relationships with those in other units of the company and that the authority of the personnel in automation be clearly defined. This brings up questions of organization.

In many cases, the area of office automation was initially placed in the controller's office. Reasons for this vary, but many top managers feel that for office automation this is a logical organizational location and provides an ideal spot for it to prove itself a valuable asset. In other instances, office automation is made a part of the treasurer's office, or at least some similar top post in the finance segment of the company. This arrangement is justified because the finance department is generally responsible for the development of records and reports, has jurisdiction over control of costs, is charged with protecting the company's assets, and deals with matters which affect all phases of the enterprise. This latter consideration is of great importance because office automation should be so placed organizationally that it can serve all functions of the enterprise. If this is not done, the full potential of office automation is never realized.

There are many today who believe that office automation should occupy a separate organizational unit and that the manager in charge should report to the president. This arrangement not only accords great importance to office automation, but it also permits a broad scope of operation and a cutting-across traditional organizational boundaries, considerations which probably are necessary for a truly integrated information-processing system to exist.

Organization and office automation give rise to the question: "Should centralization or decentralization be followed?"[1] The situation is primarily whether to have (1) a single large installation to serve the office needs of the various operating units of a big enterprise or (2) a number of smaller facilities, each designed and located to serve the needs of one or several of the company's various operating units. The decision depends upon many factors. The physical size of the enterprise and of each operating unit probably ranks high on the priority list. The total volume of work must be sufficiently large to make possible its division among various units; otherwise, a decentralized arrangement is impractical. The degree of uniformity in office work and reporting practices of the company presently existing or hoped for are also influential. In addition, of prime concern is the capacity of the proposed automated equipment to meet schedule demands made on it. Finally, the investment required must be given adequate attention. For many types of office automated equipment, the larger the size of the equipment used, the lower the job cost. This is due to the speed and capacity of the larger machines relative to those of the smaller machines. This suggests a centralized arrangement. On the other hand, save for information processed for use of corporate officers, the need for adequate communication equipment to handle information to the various operating organizational units may prove costly. Generally speaking, under decentraliza-

---

[1] Centralization and decentralization are thoroughly discussed in Part VI, Chapter 28.

tion there is less of a communication problem on consolidating results from each of several processing centers for use by corporate officers than in the case of a centralized unit, where there is the problem of communicating information to all operating units.

From the organizational viewpoint, there is also the task of determining clearly the authority and responsibility assigned to those in charge of the automated equipment. Likewise, each subgroup within the unit handling automation must understand how it is to work with other groups and the particular duties that it is expected to carry out. In too many companies, office automation has been established in the organization mainly on an empirical basis, without proper definition of the authority and the responsibility of those in charge of this specialized work.

OFFICE AUTOMATION AND ACTUATING

With all the glamour now being associated with the new office technology, it is easy to forget that people are still vital to office management and will continue to be so. It requires people to operate and maintain machines, and it requires people to interpret and utilize the information made available to them. The manager's task of actuating may well increase in importance as further advances are made in office technology.

Successful office automation requires effective managerial actuating. The office employee confronted with change in his work methods becomes very concerned about his economic security and mode of work life. He may assume an attitude of apathy, indifference, surprise, or even hostility. Despite the great amount of literature that has been written about implementing satisfactory solutions to the "human problems of automation," it appears that the solutions are not always effective or managers are remiss in applying them properly. Some obvious needs are not fulfilled, and good intentions apparently are not translated into realities.

The introduction of automated equipment poses the problem of manpower displacement. In turn, this frequently necessitates the establishment of certain policies in order to cope with the human considerations involved. Among the policies of greatest significance are the following:

1. To tell the office automation story as it is developed, so that all employees will know what is going on.
2. To terminate the employment of no employee because of the new machines and equipment.
3. To reduce the salary of no employee because of automation.
4. To change job content with reassignment, retraining being provided.

Briefly, the approach is to keep employees informed, let normal attrition of office help take up the excess number of office employees, maintain salaries because productivity per employee will increase under automation, and adjust the work force to new methods by required transfers and training.

Employees to be affected by the change should be encouraged to participate in designing the change. Normally, this practice brings favorable results. Not only are excellent suggestions offered, but by this practice a needed sense of belonging and importance are enjoyed by the employee. High employee participation usually means high employee cooperation. However, it is a mistake to by-pass employees in the planning stages and initially invite them to be a part of the program at the time of installation.

A positive attitude by supervisors helps to dispel gloom among the employees. Favorable expressions about the proposed changes, logical explanations giving frank answers to "How does this affect me?", a willingness to find answers to questions to which he does not know the answers, and following through on questions to a mutually agreeable conclusion—these are the types of actuating work that appear not only helpful but actually mandatory in most instances.

It must be remembered that with the passage of time, people tend to become more ready to accept change. The attitude toward office changes almost always becomes more favorable several months after completion of the planning and installing periods than it had been during these periods. People tend to adjust to their surroundings. Experience with new work methods usually demonstrates that many of the fears and unpleasantnesses believed associated with the change actually do not exist or are of much less importance than originally conceived.

OFFICE AUTOMATION AND MANAGERIAL DECISION MAKING

Among the greatest influences of the new office technology is its effect upon managerial decision making. There are three major efforts to consider:

1. *Aid in establishing a more sound basis for managerial decision making.* Modern office technology makes it economically feasible to compile data on a current basis. A manager can now know where he is rather than where he has been. To make decisions, reliance need not be placed on facts conditioned by the old traditional lags in information. Furthermore, it is possible to relate different units of measurement regarding company activities. No longer need production reports be expressed as units stamped per day, or shift, and inventory in some other measurement unit. The entire fund of information can be in a measuring unit common and meaningful to all concerned departments. Also, all the interrelated data can be of a comparable time period. For example, the

period and frequencies for production reports can be precisely identical to those of inventory, or of sales reports. Thus, valid correlation of the information can be calculated.

2. *Making feasible the use of new analytical techniques in managerial decision making.* Mathematics has long been applied to engineering and production problems, but it is now being utilized in management decision-making problems. The significant relationships of the important factors are determined and related mathematically. Then, different values for the variable factors are substituted in the equation and tentative answers calculated. In this way, the best combination of factors for the most desirable answer is determined. In the past, the physical inability of clerical staffs to process all relevant information according to the limits prescribed by the mathematical equation made it impractical to determine many alternative decisions under different sets or conditions or factors. The techniques employed depend upon the problem and conditions under which the factors must operate. Among the more common techniques are linear programming, queuing theory, games theory, and optimization formulas.

3. *Making possible the pretesting of decisions by means of simulation.* Office automation makes it physically possible to solve tomorrow's problem today, before a real crisis develops. Simulation includes the building of a model of a company that behaves exactly like the real thing; in other words, this model reflects actual operating conditions. Different tentative decisions are followed through to their respective different answers—what would happen as a result of each solution. The best answer can then be selected from various alternatives, and what decision to make for this desired answer is identified.

Simulation provides the answers to "what if" questions. It is made practical through office automation, which can solve problems that are too complex and have too many variables to solve through human effort alone. However, the use of a model to acquire knowledge is nothing new. Engineers have used this technique for years. Models of new designs are constructed and subsequently subjected to varying conditions of operation in order to determine the design providing optimum favorable results. In like manner, the manager using simulation does the same thing.

EFFECT UPON MANAGEMENT STRUCTURE

One of the most important effects of the new office technology upon the management structure is the increased emphasis given to taking a broader viewpoint or perspective of the entirety, rather than of one single component. In the future, the work of the office manager will be carried out in more sweeping, yet integrated lines. The management of information should be viewed as an activity affecting all parts of an enterprise and areas outside the enterprise as well. The trend of managerial thinking is definitely toward this broader concept of achieving a fully integrated information system. However, as of the early 1960's, actually only a few companies have achieved much *intra*functional information, and a very limited number have achieved *inter*functional information.

The objectives of office management must be and are becoming more clearly defined. Abundant factual information is available, for example, to establish goals. In addition, the data the office can supply makes for improved aims of the entire enterprise. More thought is being given to the subject of information handling and to its proper management.

Another effect upon the management structure is the emergence of a management information group or department. Such a group will probably become more and more common and will occupy a relatively high organizational level. As office automation increases and experience in obtaining full utilization of office technology is acquired, fuller integration of information will be accomplished. This, in turn, will mean less paper work and reports by personnel of the operating departments. Supervisors, for example, will not be required to spend two to three hours daily on paper work. This shift will enable employees to devote more of their time to their primary function. Also, it is quite likely that a reduction in the size of the clerical staff groups of the operating departments could result. To illustrate, sales analysis of sales and labor costs of production might well be transferred to the information center.

For a given office, automation usually increases relatively the machine cost and decreases the labor cost. In turn, the greater machine expenditure spotlights attention upon questions of depreciation; scheduling and maintaining even work flows, and keeping the mechanized units in top working condition; utilization of records; and format of reports. Automation in the office stresses managerial problems; in the factory, the problems are primarily technical.

Office technology influences the management structure not only of the large company, but also of the small one. The present and relatively limited routine processing performed by a service bureau for small companies will probably expand to cover complete integrated information systems.[2] Equipment considerations alone will not bring this about, but the scarcity of competent and experienced analytical talent will make the service bureau arrangement the logical choice of the small enterprise.

DANGER OF OVER- AND UNDERMECHANIZATION

Like all innovations concerning methods, the contributions of the new office technology give rise to formidable problems. Of particular im-

---

[2] Service bureaus are discussed in Chapter 22, page 426.

portance is the achieving of the best correlation between the demands made on the information system and the physical equipment itself. This involves the danger of overmechanization or of undermechanization in the office. From this problem of optimum fit stem many automation difficulties. For example, the equipment may turn out to be too elaborate for the specific company's needs, thus making the equipment investment excessive. Or frequent and expensive breakdowns may occur primarily because too much work or too many different types of work are being attempted with the particular machines. In other cases, the installation cost may greatly exceed estimates—a condition commonly arising from inadequate analysis of all the demands of the information system.

A prime cause of office overmechanization is failure to determine specifically what work is and what work is not to be done by the machines. Some work is best done by a willing hand and a pencil, especially when the cost of operating the machine is taken into account. Likewise, a policy of charging each department for the machine time of a centralized unit can have the effect of loading too much work on the machine. This comes about quite innocently, in that a department head charged with a machine cost customarily sees to it that he gets something in return. Net result: Some work which should not be handled by the center is sent there for processing. The remedy lies in educating every management member to the economic considerations and limitations of each piece of office equipment and to the idea of total information integration.

In contrast, office under mechanization commonly arises from indifference, fear, or lack of direction. The attitude of "Let us alone; we've been doing it this way since 1930" is one of the chief contributors toward undermechanization. Seldom do office employees demand mechanization or hover around the machine, praising it, after installation. Their normal reactions are not to make any changes. Also, the lack of well-defined directions by top managers can lead to undermechanization. Failure to perceive the broad implications of office automation and personal preference for other areas may be cited as the major reasons for this lack of needed direction.

SOCIAL ASPECTS OF OFFICE AUTOMATION

Social change stimulated by office automation emphasizes employment modifications, which can be viewed as offering either (1) greater opportunities or (2) fewer opportunities, even to the point of mass unemployment. The former is indicative of the attitude under which office automation will come to maturity. It stresses: "What will automation help us do better, or assist us to achieve that has never been achieved?" There is a problem, however, in adapting to this greater opportunity. In this connection, much human effort will shift from manual to mental work and from menial to more challenging tasks. In the second view-point, the dominant force is fear. Employees are quite naturally con-cerned whether the higher rates of office work performance will result in unemployment or in raising living standards. Past experience seems to indicate that technological advancements have increased the over-all level of employment. New demands have developed, the machines themselves creating a large labor force required for their construction and maintenance. However, many people are *displaced*, not *replaced* to other areas of duty. For example, a large installation of electronic office machines in a Chicago office required the shifting of several hundred employees to other jobs. Not a one lost his job; each was trained and placed in new work. This called for real management ability and, of course, necessitated an adjustment on the part of each employee.

Many times in the office, the normal rate of attrition will bring about the smaller work force required. But older employees with seniority and relatively little flexibility pose difficulties. In a large insurance com-pany, the personnel whose jobs were eliminated in the advance to more office automation were divided into three classes:

> The largest class includes relatively unskilled junior personnel in clerical jobs of a repetitive nature—filing, sorting, recording, and performing other tasks where only a bare minimum of insurance knowledge is required. The second class consisted of personnel with more experience, and many years of seniority, who are in relatively routine jobs which require slightly more knowl-edge of insurance. Jobs of this class do not require original thinking, nor judg-ment beyond that necessary to identify an exception to usual routine which must be passed along to higher authority for action. The third class is com-posed of more highly skilled people engaged in supervisory and senior staff work. Their duties are primarily in the judgment area, and they require a more advanced knowledge of insurance.[3]

The writer of this quotation goes on to say that relocation of the un-skilled junior personnel and of the skilled senior people create relatively few problems. It is the experienced employee performing routine jobs not in the judgment area who presents troublesome personnel disloca-tion difficulties because there are few job openings for a person with these qualifications and usually such an employee is relatively inflexible.

Many are of the opinion that skill requirements will increase for most office jobs as a result of automation. From the over-all viewpoint, this might be, but it is well to observe that many jobs of relatively low skill will remain. The automated office is not a 100 per cent mechanized robot. The best current estimates are that some 30 per cent of the

---

[3] E. W. Martin, Jr., "Practical Problems of Introducing a Computer," *Business Horizons*, Fall, 1960, p. 8 (published by the Indiana University School of Business, Bloomington, Indiana).

total office work is performed by electronic systems in a typical present-day "automated office," but it can well go higher.

Undoubtedly, the number of irksome, monotonous tasks is reduced by automation. Much laborious and time-consuming office work is done by the machine. This is desirable from the social point of view and is a benefit to mankind. Many feel that we are at the beginning of what might be described as a second Industrial Revolution, which will substitute machines for human beings in performing mental drudgery, just as the first Industrial Revolution substituted machines for carrying out most backbreaking physical drudgery.

ANTICIPATED PROGRESS OF OFFICE

It is a natural human instinct to anticipate what future progress can be expected in office management and what events of the future might change the office as we know it today. Experience of the present, although limited, suggests possible changes to be expected due to office technology. It appears fairly certain that many of the present processes and procedures will fall by the wayside. Much of the required writing and calculating will be done automatically by machine which will operate from sound. Communicative devices will probably revolutionize the distribution of information, and it could be that most conferences will be handled on closed TV circuits or some adaptation thereof. Future reproducing processes are almost certain to establish an entirely new concept of filing and storing records. Many of these changes may not come about until many years ahead, while others may take place within the present decade.

It is reasonable to predict that decision making will be improved. The qualification of data, made possible by office improvements, will improve the amount and the quality of facts. The availability of a wider range of alternatives evaluated factually could reduce decision making based either on intuition or on historical data projection. Also, decision making will be carried out on a broader base. Company goals, not departmental goals, will be stressed; and the interaction of decisions pertaining to departments will be emphasized.

The handling of information will be carefully planned and engineered. The haphazard, "just let it grow as needs develop" attitude will decline to a minor position. And office work will become more closely related to managerial planning and controlling, and will be used to the full. The products of the office will increase in value and importance.

With all these changes, it is logical to state that an office manager's work will take on greater importance. With larger amounts of accurate and timely factual information available, the operational consequences of a decision will be measured more precisely, but the decision cannot be an automatic response to the impact of information. Judgment, consideration for nonmeasurable but influential factors, and responsibility for consequences are not transferred to the office automation equipment. They remain, at least in the foreseeable future, with the manager.

QUESTIONS

1. For any given enterprise, should identical information continue after automation as existed before automation? Why?
2. Briefly describe your concept of the meaning of "office automation."
3. Justify the viewpoint that both office automation and office technology are expanding.
4. Do you agree with the following statement? "Although there is much glamour and sophistication about automation in the office, the real reason for its development is the reduction in office costs that it brings about." Why?
5. Discuss the subject area of "Office Automation and Controlling."
6. What is meant by the statement that office automation permits a manager to reach better decisions by means of simulation?
7. Discuss several general but important factors to be considered in determining the feasibility of office automation for an enterprise.
8. In your opinion, have some companies installed computers in their office in part for reasons of their prestige and reputation? Discuss.
9. Are the social aspects of office automation of major concern to the office manager? Elaborate on your answer.
10. Do you believe that in the enterprise of the future there will be a management information department? Why?
11. As you see it, will office managerial actuating become less important as office automation increases? Justify your viewpoint.
12. What are the major considerations that help decide for a given enterprise whether to have a single large installation of office automated equipment or a number of smaller facilities, each designed to meet the needs of a component of the entire enterprise?

CASE PROBLEMS

Case 3–1.   Bates Products Corporation

Accounts receivable have been processed manually for the past forty years. New markets developed as a result of new products offered by the company caused the volume of work to increase to a level such that the decision was reached to convert the manual tasks to a punched-card installation. Accordingly, a representative from an office machine manufacturing company was called in and requested to analyze the work and devise the new system to be followed. The representative was introduced to the supervisor of the accounts receivable department and her two assistants. It was requested that they give the representative complete co-operation because he was developing the new machine process that would be followed in the future. At the same time, to each of the twenty-seven nonmanagement members of the accounts receivable department, a brief letter was given:

This is to advise you that as soon as possible the handling of accounts receivable manually will be discontinued and a system using punched cards will be installed. This move will necessitate some transferring of employees, but rest assured that this will be worked out to the mutual advantage of all concerned.

(Signed) HENRY L. WOOD
Office Manager

The accounts receivable supervisor was unfavorable toward the change. She believed it would necessitate many adjustments, would make the work monotonous, and reduce her importance within the company. She spoke with a company methods analyst, who also was negative about the contemplated change. He favored use of late-model accounting machines which, in his opinion, were ideally suited for the accounts receivable work. "Henry claims punched cards are the best and is determined to see them used, so who am I to oppose him?" commented the analyst. He thought he would be called in to design the punched-card arrangement, but later was told that this was all being done for the company by the machine manufacturer.

Everything went along as usual for the next five months. Then, one morning, various pieces of punched-card equipment arrived and were located within the accounts receivable area. At the same time, the office manager held a meeting in his office with two representatives of the punched-card equipment company, the accounts receivable supervisor, and her two assistants. During this meeting, the representatives carefully explained each step of the new process to be followed. Many questions were asked, and the representatives answered each one of them. The meeting took all morning. After lunch, the office manager introduced the representatives to the employees of the accounts receivable department, informed them of the meeting held during the morning, and requested that any questions they might have should be directed to their immediate supervisor, who would either answer the question directly or find out the answer and give it to them. The change-over date was set for ten days hence; and the names of six employees, with the respective departments to which they were being transferred, were announced. During the next several days, there were few questions, since the general feeling among the employees was that the best way to learn the new process was by actually working with the machines and on the new system.

Two weeks after the change-over date, the president of the company visited the accounts receivable department, as he was quite interested in the new system. To him, the employees of the unit appeared confused. He spoke with the supervisor, who said: "Well, it is a mess right now. My desk is piled high with work. We're working overtime but not making much headway. Getting the information on the cards is the big task right now. That will take time. We have a manual that appears to give all the details about the operation. It reads O.K., and I must admit that the representatives are very willing to help in every way possible. But we are still just processing accounts receivable; and for the life of me, I can't see how this new setup is an improvement over the old method that we all know so well."

Speaking with several employees of the department, the president received these reactions: "There are plenty of headaches. I'll stay with it for another week or so; but as of right now, I certainly don't like it." Another employee stated: "We have no precedent to go by. I don't know how to operate this thing. They told me to read the manual, but I don't understand what I'm reading." Another said: "I don't mind the overtime—in fact, I can use the extra money. Other companies use punched cards, and I guess we can, too.

I think this gives us a chance to learn more about punched cards. This might give me a chance to get ahead."

One of the assistant supervisors said: "These people know the finished paper work that is wanted, but little about the machines or their operations. Sure, there are problems. I'd say we are trying to work with something we don't know much about."

Problems:

1. Do you feel that, given a reasonable amount of time, the present difficulties in the accounts receivable department will take care of themselves? Why?

2. What action, if any, do you suggest the president take? The office manager? Substantiate your viewpoint.

Case 3–2.   Twenty-first Century Office

Professor Dean Sager is extremely interested in the development of the new office technology. He conducted several personal interviews with practicing office managers, and the following are the highlights of the responses he received.

"The office in the year 2065? Almost all the work will be done by machine. It will be a push-button age. Information will be kept right in the machine and will be delivered to you automatically upon request. In many respects, the information won't be on paper at all, but will be on some mechanical medium, like wire or tape, and will be available to us when we want it."

"In the office of the future, we'll find the executive sitting at a small table; his mail will consist of a tiny packet of plastic transparencies similar to microfilm. These transparencies will be enlarged on a visual screen. If he wishes, he can dictate directly into a machine that will simultaneously either type the letter or paper, or put it on an electronic medium by which it can be quickly transmitted to its recipient. Direct wires connecting the two offices will be unnecessary. The transmission will be wireless, similar to present-day TV."

"The importance of human relations as we know it today will be a thing of the past. Automation will have taken over, and this means a minimum number of people will be required. Minimum people mean minimum trouble. If you have no people, you have no human relations. It's as simple as that."

"Office conferences will be virtually eliminated. Low-cost closed TV circuits connecting executives located in widely separated cities will be commonplace. And this same screen will serve to view wanted materials from a file. In the future, filed material will be housed in narrow wall compartments. By means of a push button, material from a designated file will be brought to view on the executive's screen within a few seconds."

"The term 'office' will be seldom used. Within the next hundred years, 'administrative information center' or something like this will be the common term designating what we currently refer to as the office. But we'll never have a fully satisfactory name for the office because it means so many different things to so many different people in so many different activities."

Problems:

1. What is your reaction to the comments secured by Professor Sager?
2. In your opinion, what might the office of 2065 be like?

Chapter 4

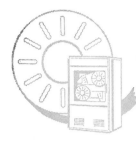

ELECTRONIC COMPUTERS— MANAGERIAL CONSIDERATIONS

Unless a capacity for thinking be accompanied by a capacity for action, a superior mind exists in torture.
—BENEDATTO CROCK

PROBABLY the best-known and -publicized machine of the new office technology is the electronic computer. The year 1944 brought the completion of the first machine which could handle successfully a sequence of arithmetic operations specified in advance. This so-called "sequential control" accomplishment paved the big breakthrough for the computer. Several years later, a machine entirely electronic in internal operation was offered on the market; and soon to follow was the "stored program" idea of placing instructions in memory, the storage of digited information on magnetic tape, and magnetic cores and memory drums for retention of information. Developments followed in rapid order, and the rate of technological advance in computers continues at an astonishing pace. The electronic computer is becoming the hub of business information in the modern office.

EXAMPLES OF COMPUTER INSTALLATIONS

Airplane reservations are now handled with the help of a computer. Information about all seats on over one thousand separate flights is contained in the unit. At each reservation desk is a small push-button machine, a "reservor," connected to the centralized computer. Upon a call for a reservation, a metal card is inserted into the reservor, and a proper key is struck. As a result, some lights either do or do not flash, which indicates to the agent whether seat space is available. As reservations are accepted, the computer subtracts from the total number for that flight; and likewise, for a cancellation, an addition is made to the number available. The entire operation requires but a few seconds, and waiting time by the customer is minimized. Formerly, the agent was required to do a great deal of telephoning; and behind the scenes, much tallying and sorting were necessary.

In another computer installation for a federal government agency, the calculating, writing, and proofing of 4,600,000 bank checks a month are accomplished. In addition, the computer is capable of keeping up to date revised addresses, amounts due, and changes occurring from time to time, so that the information and check writing are current and correct for each month. Any corrections or changes can be recomputed by day, month, or year. The computer is practically error-proof.

An example of pretesting the results of alternative decisions is provided by computers used by advertising agencies. The computer takes the risk out of media buying by trying hundreds of media combinations electronically in order to determine the best combination for a particular advertising campaign. To duplicate manually the information of many combinations would be extremely costly and time-consuming. In one such experiment, it required a four-man crew three months to duplicate what the computer provided in six minutes.

MANAGEMENT AND THE POTENTIAL OF COMPUTERS

The real potential and future of computers for business data processing is up to the members of management. Significant improvements in management are possible by use of the computer, but managers must be truly objective and honest with themselves if they are to gain the marvels which the computer can bring about. It is erroneous to think that depositing a modern computer in the midst of inept management policies, outmoded practices, and an archaic organizational structure will somehow or other cause corrective miracles to take place.

The awe-inspiring electronic computers, with their fantastic accomplishments, have led some to refer to them as machines that think. This is not true. The machines do not think. They operate only as instructed and must be told what to do in the minutest detail. Decision making is not their prerogative except what decision making is given them. They must follow a predetermined pattern of action. This means that managers must still think; they cannot turn this vital requirement over to the computer. However, it must be noted that computers are capable of making simple decisions; they can modify their own instructions as dictated by progressive stages of their data processing. Erroneously, the simplification and improvement in computer operation have given rise to some calling a computer a thinking mechanical human being. It is mechanical, all right; but it is not thinking, and it is not a human being.

What computers actually do is enhance the power and the influence of the human mind, not minimize its importance. They provide help never before believed possible or even conceived. Instead of being overburdened with the processing of data, the human mind can be relieved of such mental drudgery and concentrate its efforts and attention to create, to plan, to ponder and reflect about information, to decide what should be done and whom to inspire. Guesses, hunches, and risks in decision making can be minimized; and decision making on facts and adequate, usable information can be maximized.

Computers increase the responsibility of managers. And managers, by their thinking or lack of it, regulate the real potential of the computer. With the assistance given by computers, the human mind can soar to new heights of accomplishment and acquire knowledge and judgment not yet imagined. The computer can show the way to great progress in the way we employ our talents, and help us keep the values that make the human being so distinct and his life so worth while.

Since computers do exactly what they are instructed to do, it is obvious that the accomplishment of hoped-for outputs and gains of a computer are regulated by the person issuing the instructions or figuring out how the computer can be utilized to do what he wants it to do. The potential lies with the manager, not with the moronic metal monster. In essence, computers are tools to be exploited by managers. The challenge is not to be satisfied with the processing of data as such, but to initiate revolutionary and new applications and concepts which are made possible by the use of computers.

MAJOR CATEGORIES OF COMPUTER APPLICATION

Many difficult tasks are being accomplished by computers for all types of enterprises. For convenience, these tasks can be segregated into four major categories: (1) control, (2) simulation, (3) design, and (4) specific processing of data. All computer applications can be classified under one or more of these categories.

As pointed out in Chapter 1, controlling means "to determine what is accomplished, evaluate it, and apply corrective measures, if needed." When a computer is used for controlling purposes, the facts about what has taken place are put into the machine, in order to obtain specific performance measurements; these values are compared to information showing what is desired; and the respective differences reveal the areas in which corrective action is to be taken. Information on cost, inventory, production runs, and quality of raw materials is illustrative of control material.

Simulation, as pointed out in the previous chapter, is the testing of numerous operating plans to determine the most productive plan. Frequently, but not always, the plans are expressed in mathematical form. However, in all instances, the data must be of a measurable type. In aircraft research, for example, computers are used to simulate different flights for jets. Such factors as allowable pay load, fuel consumption, and speed can be determined accurately without even putting the plane in the air. The example given above of advertising agencies deciding the best combination of various media to employ is illustrative of simulation.

A third category of computer application is design. By this is meant the confirmation or rejection of an intelligent guess or hypothesis by the results obtained from carefully directed experimentation. The characteristics of each guess are calculated and checked against specifications. The computer performs these calculations very rapidly. A wide range of possibilities can be considered by the designer; and as a result, the best possible design is identified and used.

Computers are also employed for what may best be termed specific processing of data. This includes the preparation of bank checks, bills, inventory records, and reports of various types. To justify a computer for this work, there usually must be a relatively large volume of work requiring considerable calculating, sorting, or comparing. Otherwise, available machines designed especially to perform the particular work will provide entirely satisfactory results at lower costs.

SHOULD A COMPUTER BE USED?

Executives of many firms have asked themselves: "Should my company use a computer?" Upon what bases should this decision be made; and if favorable, which computer should be selected? The choice is wide; different features are stressed on different units. Some are desk-size models with monthly rentals of around $300, while others are a series of several machines costing $60,000 a month rent.

Decisions regarding computers can be guided by adequate study given to certain subjects; but before listing and discussing these factors, it is well to make certain observations. First of all, the computer industry is still in its infancy. The future holds improvements and opportunities for computer applications far above any present usage envisioned. The potential is vast. Companies have ordered and installed computers even though studies indicated an operating loss from them for a number of years. But these decisions were reached because it was recognized that some pioneering with a tool as powerful as a computer is probably necessary, that usage begets further usage with the discovery of new applications, and that first-hand experience gained in the use of computers helps to reap the benefits of computerization. However, it is possible to "go overboard" in deciding such issues and wind up in a precarious managerial position.

Returning to the factors that merit study by a company in deciding basic questions regarding computer usage, the following will be discussed:

1. The objectives of the company.
2. Status of present information system.

3. The selection of the type of computer.
4. Personnel considerations.
5. Adjustment of policies.
6. Physical requirements and tasks of conversion.

THE OBJECTIVES OF THE COMPANY

The fundamental goals of any enterprise set the stage for evaluating possible changes in the use of resources and means for achieving these goals. However, this evaluation frequently takes the form of understanding possible advantages claimed for a new machine, material, or method and then judging whether these advantages are feasible and desirable for the particular company.

Among the important objectives sought by most companies from the use of a computer are savings in clerical cost; capacity to handle increasing work volume; greater accuracy and uniformity in data processing; the securing of better information in less time; better information upon which to base decisions, including the means to enable the technique of either simulation or design to be employed; and improved service to customers. These objectives are not mutually exclusive, but the selection and weight given to each helps formulate a "blue-sky" concept of the ideal computer installation from the viewpoint of the particular company.

STATUS OF PRESENT INFORMATION SYSTEM

Many office executives feel that an important step in deciding whether to use a computer is to analyze the present office procedures and methods in order to spot any weaknesses and to determine any foreseeable inability of the present system to cope with probable future needs. In addition, the possibilities for improving the present information system should be investigated. In many cases, study brings to light hidden potentials within the existing setup. Taking advantage of these opportunities and improving the present system may adequately fulfill the requirements. A chemical manufacturer found that certain revisions and additions in his current conventional way of processing papers would result in substantial savings, and that the use of a computer was possible but would necessitate a high overhead burden and relatively expensive operating payments.

The volume of transactions is commonly a deciding factor. Computers handle tremendous work volumes within extremely short periods. When a company is faced with an increasing volume of accounts to be processed, the signal for computer utilization may be at hand. Especially is this true when the current noncomputer equipment has limited capacity and prohibits procedural refinement and expansion to more mechanization.

Speed of processing is another worthy consideration. Reference is commonly made to speed as an outstanding gain in the use of computers. It may be vital, but more often than is frequently the case, speed of processing should be considered in relation to service required. To know that with a computer, information for a report can be completed in two hours, in contrast to four days under the present setup, is convincing, provided the report will be used in two hours and will not be ignored or filed away for four days before any use is made of it. The challenge here is to get management members to improve their usage of the material made available. Perhaps this starts with more rapid processing to make information available more quickly and hence more up to the minute.

In addition, speed of processing may directly influence the company's standard of service in comparison with that of its competitors. When an advantage in service is keenly sought, the computer should be evaluated to determine how much its contribution in speed and service will mean in sales and in customer relations.

THE SELECTION OF THE TYPE OF COMPUTER

As is the case in most office automation, and as related in Chapter 3, the selection of the equipment usually involves the establishment of a committee. The computer is no exception. The ideal committee consists of experienced managers, preferably from the upper organizational levels. This group can be supplemented by another group representative of the major areas to be affected by the installation of the computer. In some instances, a committee has been used to carry out the previous step, namely, studying the status of the present information system; and when this practice is followed, the same committee continues to serve in the selection of the type of computer.

Knowledge about various computers must be acquired by the committee members; and this is best done by attending schools offered by the computer manufacturers, reading available literature on the subject, and conferring with executives of companies having computers in operation. After a period of several months, an effort is made to determine what types of work should be done by a computer and what type of computer appears best for the company's present and reasonable future needs.

Competent consultants can be employed to give assistance in drawing up the recommendations pertaining to the company's work to be done on a computer, the type of machine, steps in application, and pitfalls to be avoided in these efforts. The consultant's wide and varied experience can save much time and tend to spark the action to move ahead. But participation by the company personnel is essential, for it provides them with practical insight as to what is going on and why. Furthermore, familiarity with the proposed processing is gained, and the background needed for successful installation and operation is obtained.

A number of criteria can be used in the task of selecting a particular computer. Among the more common are (1) completion of operations within a fixed time, (2) cost, (3) the most versatile computer within a given maximum expenditure, (4) specific computer features, (5) proven performance, and (6) the manufacturer. Under this latter consideration, the manufacturer, such bases as experience in computer manufacturing, installation and training service, and caliber of maintenance service usually rank high.

It may be that the best decision is to utilize a computer owned and operated by a computing service center which does work for a number of offices in its general vicinity. Work which is either of a relatively small volume or of a highly specialized nature generally is most suited for computer center work. Several computer manufacturers maintain such service centers. The National Cash Register Company, for example, has a nationwide network of centers to provide inexpensive sales analyses and payroll reports for any company using a cash register or office machine equipped with a punched-tape recorder to serve as a communication medium.[1] Processed information can be supplied within several hours on customer trends in style, color, prices, and model.

PERSONNEL CONSIDERATIONS

A delivery date of one year from receipt of order is a common practice for computer manufacturers. This waiting period can be viewed pessimistically; but on the other hand, it permits time to make adequate preparation for the computer's use. This includes, first of all, the selecting and training of analysts, operators, and programmers—new skills required for computer operation. A standard practice is to select from among present employees, but a few from outside the company may be added. Various tests are available to assist in the selection work. Experience shows that these tests give reliable results. Training is normally supplied by the school of the equipment manufacturer, but only basic principles and a working knowledge are supplied. Supplemental reading, study, and experience in operating the computer are needed to acquire acceptable proficiency.

In going to a computer system, additional major personnel effects usually must be considered. These consist of transfers, reduction in work force, and morale. They were discussed in Chapter 3. However, additional comments about these important considerations seem warranted and are included here. The transfer of certain employees to other clerical jobs and the reduction in the number of new employees hired stem from a common practice followed in many offices. This practice is not to terminate employment because of a computer installation. The approach is basically to take care of displaced employees, but the displaced are not replaced.

---

[1] Communication media in connection with computers are discussed in Chapter 5; see pages 76–87, inclusive.

The effect of these changes upon morale can be very great. Announcement of the use of a computer at a future date is likely to give rise to fear among clerical workers concerning their job security. The necessity of changing work habits to which they have grown accustomed sometimes causes resentment. But the problems can be solved satisfactorily. Employee dislocations can be handled in the manner described above. Morale can be maintained by proper, timely, and effective communication and action to all the office employees. Asking for their ideas, pointing out what the problems are, giving reasons for decisions, and keeping them fully informed on developments as they take place are among the management activities that should be followed.

Properly handled, the computer system becomes a means of office work that is easier and more practical than any former way. Generally, employees will like the computer way; success or failure depends in large measure upon the quality of personnel relations performed. The installation should be employee-oriented, not computer-oriented. In the final analysis, the new method is dependent upon the good will, understanding, and cooperation of the employees. To ignore the personnel considerations is certain to invite disaster.

ADJUSTMENT OF POLICIES

The installation of a computer can open the door to great savings and service opportunities, but it is only the initial step. To gain maximum utilization, it is necessary and desirable to adjust policies so that the advantages of these opportunities can be won. Also, as previously mentioned, as experience is gained in computer use, additional and special applications tend to appear.

Included in the types of popular changes made are (1) elimination of many special files; (2) greater degree of centralized filing; (3) use of "centless accounting"; (4) uniform "days in period" for comparable reports; (5) more data retained on previous functions, such as sales, costs, and collections, to provide helpful trends or comparisons with current data; and (6) greater availability of pertinent data to lower levels of management. In addition, periodic reviews of current computer applications help to uncover other uses and take advantage of available computer time. This state of affairs seems to exist no matter how carefully and thoroughly the initial feasibility study was conducted. It is difficult to envision all the applications and the best arrangement for each at the time of the initial investigation. The "universe" of possible computer applications tends to be limited, despite all the talk and encouragement to think in terms of a truly integrated, company-wide information system. One large public utility, for example, installed a computer to handle many of its accounting applications. Subsequent experience with the computer, modifications in records processed, and improved management resulted in 42 per cent of the computer's available time not being used. Further study showed that the computer would be most helpful in engineering and in special applications. Figure 4–1 shows some of these additional

1. Meter test statistics.	5. Industrial relations trend problems.
2. Power plant efficiencies.	6. Accumulation of meters by route.
3. Material price comparisons.	7. Material usage report.
4. Rate conversion tables.	8. Pension survey.

FIG. 4–1. Additional applications for computer developed by one large public utility company.

applications. As a result, the company modified its policies to take advantage of its idle computer time and thus secured greater help than was initially believed possible.

PHYSICAL REQUIREMENTS AND TASKS OF CONVERSION

Usually, it is necessary to provide nonvarying, disturbance-free electrical power and also office space that is regulated as to temperature, dust, and humidity. The layout of the office may have to be changed to place the heavy machine where ample structural support is provided and the flow of office work can most efficiently be handled. Channels under the floor in which to run electrical cables connecting the various units sometimes pose a technical problem, especially when a controlling factor is the maximum lengths of cable specified by the computer manufacturer.

Converting large amounts of written material into language required by the computer can represent a herculean task and too often is brushed off as a minor consideration in a computer installation. Conversion difficulties include inaccuracy and lack of uniformity in existing records, missing papers, unexpected deviations of records from a supposed format, errors in reading or in putting information on tape, the maintenance of an adequate work force to accomplish the conversion work, and the accomplishment of the work within reasonable budget limitations.

The conversion process must also take into account what is known as "application in parallel." This means the practice of continuing the processing of information in the normal way and also through the computer, then comparing the results in order to check the accuracy of the computer program. Normally, the work is run in parallel for several complete cycles, or until the new process is completely "debugged." This can be a very frustrating period. Consistent results are obtained; and then, without warning, inconsistencies prevail. Finding and correcting the sources of errors frequently pose major tasks. In some installations, conversion problems are minimized by beginning with areas that are already using punched cards or have been subjected to a certain amount of office mechanization, but there is no guarantee that this approach will eliminate conversion difficulties.

NUMBER AND COMPARISON OF COMPUTERS

Since 1951, when the U.S. Bureau of the Census installed the first large electronic data-processing system for business data, approximately 3,000 systems have been put into operation. This estimate is for general-purpose systems; it does not reflect specialized installations, as in banks, except in the case of the larger banks where large general-purpose systems are in use. Included in this estimate are the small or desk-size computers, which have opened up a number of users with relatively limited amounts of data processing to be handled.

A study related by *Fortune* magazine in 1959 estimates 2,000 computers in use by American business and government. The units included in this study are those costing $1,000 or more monthly rental. This excludes many of the desk-size models. In addition, the *Fortune* study estimated that 400, or 20 per cent of the total, are large-scale machines costing $12,000 or more monthly rental. Governmental sources reveal that the number of computers in federal government use was about 550 as of June, 1960.

These statistics clearly indicate the importance of computers in the information handling of business today. The increase in office automation has grown steadily, and it is reasonable to predict that this trend will continue. Improvements in computers and greater knowledge in their application appear to assure development of such events in the future.

Figure 4–2 shows a comparison of computers and highlights certain important differences among them. Although the computers were se-

NAME	SIZE CLASSIFICATION	AVERAGE PRICE (IN THOUSANDS)	AVERAGE MONTHLY RENTAL	MEDIA		YEAR FIRST OFFERED
				Input	Output	
IBM 705.........	Large	$2,000	$40,000	C–MT	C–MT–PR	1955
NCR 304.........	Large	900	17,500	C–PT–MT	C–PT–MT–PR	1960
RCA 501.........	Large	800	16,000	K–C–PT–MT	C–PT–MT–PR	1959
Univac 1101......	Large	1,600	32,000	C–PT–MT	C–PT–MT–PR	1950
Burroughs 205....	Medium	250	5,000	K–C–PT–MT	C–PT–MT–PR	1954
IBM 650.........	Medium	200	4,000	C–PT–MT	C–MT–PR	1955
RCA 301.........	Medium	290	6,500	K–C–PT–MT	C–PT–MT–PR	1961
Burroughs E101...	Small	26	1,000	K–C–PT	PT–PR	1955
IBM 632.........	Small	6	200	K	C–PR	1958
Royal Precision L6P–30........	Small	50	1,200	K–C–PT	PT–PR	1956

Code: K = Keyboard   PT = Perforated tape   PR = Printer
         C = Punched card MT = Magnetic tape

FIG. 4–2. A comparison of computers.

lected arbitrarily, they do represent many, but not all, of those in common use. Most computers are equipped with some special components in order to meet the operating conditions specified and desired by the user.

MODULAR IDEA OF COMPUTER

As already implied, it pays to plan for a complete data-processing system at first. Subsequently, purchases for a single-unit application that fits into the total plan can be made. Thus, the old units will be compatible with the new units.

Developments in computer design have made it possible to install machines which will not become obsolete as the processing needs expand in volume or in diversity. New devices can be added in building-block fashion. This makes it possible to avoid large expenditures necessitated by processing the data in a new manner or sequence as different volume levels or types of processing are added.

WILL IT PAY TO WAIT?

With a field as dynamic and fast-growing as computers, the question arises: "Will it pay to wait in order to obtain a better buy to fulfill our data-processing needs?" Computers, like any other machine, wear out; but experience to date shows that most electronic equipment functions perfectly even after 10 years of use, and engineering estimates are that a usable life of 20–25 years is reasonable. The usefulness of a computer can be reduced by failure of the unit to meet changed requirements. However, proper planning, taking into account probable future needs for five to 10 years, can minimize most of this loss so that it should not become serious. Furthermore, the utilization of computers employing modular-type design that "grow with the user" helps to meet the problem.

Delay in acquiring data-processing equipment might be thought the best decision when consideration is given to the amazing advances made possible by engineering improvements. In the relatively brief history of computers, improvements have been more in the nature of speed, convenience, and capacity rather than a radically different basic design. Likewise, computers to serve the special needs of a particular industry or type of application have been developed and employed. In many respects, efforts have concentrated on perfecting components which are made available, but certainly not mandatory, to existing systems. Seldom do these components make the rest of the system obsolete. In the case of rental units, the newest components, as they become available, are commonly incorporated into the system. This is a major advantage in renting versus buying the equipment.

The subject of costs and the pay-out period arouse some interesting considerations in deciding the question of whether to wait or to proceed with a computer installation now. The total period in a projected installation must be considered. It is unrealistic and incomplete analysis to begin with some future date and ignore the interim period from the present to the start of that future period. Savings, if any, should be considered from using what is available today. Displacements of this system by future changes can be taken into account.

The data of Figure 4–3, while hypothetical, serve to illustrate a common situation regarding timing and pay-out period for data-processing systems. Under process system No. 1, a net saving appears in the fifth year, with total savings at the end of ten years being $540,000. Process system No. 2 illustrates waiting until a new machine is on the market and installing it in the third year. Under this arrangement, total savings at the end of the tenth year are $375,000, not as favorable as under process

Year	Process System No. 1		Process System No. 2		Process System No. 1 and No. 2	
	Yearly	Cumulative	Yearly	Cumulative	Yearly	Cumulative
1..........	− 50	− 50			− 50	− 50
2..........	− 65	−115			− 65	−115
3..........	− 70	−185	− 50	− 50	−120	−235
4..........	+105	− 80	− 70	−120	+ 15	−220
5..........	+ 90	+ 10	− 75	−195	+ 75	−145
6..........	+100	+110	+100	− 95	+150	+ 5
7..........	+100	+210	+100	+ 5	+160	+165
8..........	+110	+320	+110	+115	+175	+340
9..........	+110	+430	+120	+235	+175	+515
10..........	+110	+540	+140	+375	+175	+690

FIG. 4–3. Loss or savings for each of three different installations of data-processing systems for a ten-year period (in hundreds of thousands of dollars).

system No. 1, but toward the end of the period increasing yearly at a faster rate than those of system No. 1. However, if system No. 1 is started in the first year and converted to the improved machine, and system No. 2 in the third year, the cumulative savings amount to $690,000, a sizable increase over either those of system No. 1 or those of No. 2 used singly.

In addition, it should be pointed out that the initial conversion to a computer system involves a great deal of work and time. But it is highly probable that the second conversion necessitated by adopting process systems No. 1 and No. 2 will be relatively far less difficult due to previous experience, and that the second conversion will stress "debugging" the new system rather than the physical work involved in converting to the new system.

SUGGESTIONS FOR COMPUTER USERS

Many of the problems of computers must be solved in managers' offices rather than in the laboratories of the designing engineers. Experts in the area of computer installation quickly point out that each installation has its unique difficulties, but certain general practices usually aid in achieving complete satisfaction within a minimum of time. Among the suggestions covering these practices are the following:

1. View the computer as a data-processing system, not as a single machine. See it as a means for supplying information to an enterprise, not as a replacement for a single or particular office machine.

2. Learn as much as possible about the various uses of computers. This knowledge will broaden your viewpoint and assist in maximizing utilization of the computer.

3. Have top managers or a top group decide what work should be done with a computer. Do not permit one involved department head to make this decision.

4. Never consider a computer the cure-all for all current paper work ills. A computer assists in attaining improvements, but employees must improve the system. The computer does what it is told to do.

5. In planning a data-processing system, take into consideration the probable needs for the future five to ten years.

6. Always relate computer capability to the specific requirements of the installation being considered. Capacities and special types of work performed which are not needed by the system at hand are superfluous.

7. With sufficient training, use present personnel for computer operation, as they usually can operate a data-processing system very satisfactorily.

8. Work closely with the computer manufacturer, who is anxious to assist in attaining a completely satisfactory installation.

QUESTIONS

1. Should an office manager look to a computer as the cure-all for his current paper work ills? Substantiate your answer.

2. Name the four categories of computer application, and give an example of each.

3. In your opinion, do computers increase or decrease the status and importance of the office manager? Why?

4. Discuss the importance of the present status of the information system of an enterprise in deciding whether that enterprise should use a computer.

5. Do you agree with the following quotation? "It is true that most of our customers must wait from 12 to 15 months for delivery of their computer ordered from us. However, this is a distinct advantage to them, not a disadvantage." Give reasons for your answer.

6. In your own words, describe what is meant by the modular idea of computer.

7. Upon what basis and by whom should the selection of the type of computer be made? Elaborate on your answer.

8. As an office manager, would you install a computer even though careful

study indicated an operating loss would probably result from it for at least several years? Defend your stand.

9. Does experience tend to show that for a given enterprise it is usually possible, by means of competent managerial planning, to prescribe accurately the uses for a computer prior to its installation? Discuss.

10. Does not the fact that computers are being improved month after month suggest that the astute manager should wait, if he possibly can, until computers are more perfected, desirable features are available as standard equipment, and the entire unit is less likely to become obsolete? Why?

11. Discuss the various important aspects in the task of converting to computer operation in a typical business enterprise.

12. What is your reaction to the following? "The over-all effect of the computer in the office is voluminous records of all sorts processed quickly and accurately. But to management members, too many records confuse rather than help, and herein lies the problem of computer usage for office work. It is also the significant difference between the desirability of factory automation and that of office automation as we know it today." Elaborate on your answer.

CASE PROBLEM

Case 4–1.   Gordon-Grunow Company

Chairman of the Board Benjamin Coleman commented: "It's about time we took action. Our chief competitor has a solid-state Datiac 999. Our rising labor costs, especially in the white-collar class, are hurting us. In billing, sales analysis, and research and development, we employ 47 clerks and four supervisors. Think of it—53 people for this type of work. We must move ahead, men."

Immediately after this board meeting, President Ronald Hall instructed his secretary: "Call the local Datiac office and set up an appointment with its representative." Ronald Hall felt uneasy and insecure in his job. He had come up through the ranks in the sales department; but since his appointment to the presidency three years ago, profits had dwindled, important mergers of competitors had been consummated to the disadvantage of Gordon-Grunow, and the board members were beginning to question Hall's leadership. He was within twenty months of retirement and had a strong desire to end his presidency in a blaze of glory with a significant contribution to the company. He believed the acquisition and use of a computer by the company might be a step in this direction, but interviews with key people during the past six weeks had left him undecided. Now, with the board "breathing down his neck," he believed the computer should be ordered. Problems which were certain to arise could be worked out after they had the computer. And, he reasoned, it would certainly provide faster and more complete information than was now available to company officials.

Generally known throughout the company's office management members, numbering thirty-eight, was the fact that Donald Fromberg, the controller, believed he was passed over when Ronald Hall was made president. Approximately the same age as Hall, Donald Fromberg had known him for some thirty years and believed he always had been, was now, and probably always would be a plugging, well-liked, not too intelligent salesman. Fromberg still nurtured some thought of being president of the company some day; but as the months rolled on, he realized in his more practical moments that such a possibility was getting more and more remote.

Mr. Fromberg repeatedly expressed the opinion in conversations with Mr. Hall that the installation of a computer would open the door to opportunities for savings, but current operations in the office would have to be reviewed to take full advantage of the computer system. Comparing the company's paper work with that of other companies, Gordon-Grunow was, in Mr. Fromberg's opinion, in a favorable position. Actually, to take full advantage of a computer, the entire accounting system would have to be revamped and rebuilt from the ground up, and this would cause confusion and involve more cost during a period when cost reduction was a prime need of the company. In reply to Mr. Hall's observation that other companies having computers must have faced the same problems of adapting their accounting system to the computer, Mr. Fromberg agreed that they probably did; but he pointed out that their needs were different from the viewpoint of volume of work, the initial system of record keeping followed, and the cost needs of the company.

Allan Wright, aggressive chief of the company's research and development section, was all for the company getting a computer. As head of twenty-six engineers and researchers, Wright figured the computer would accelerate the work of his unit and would make possible a reduction of five engineers from the payroll, leaving his section still able to perform the same amount of research work as was currently being done. These savings in salary alone, contended Mr. Wright, would enable the company to get the computer for practically no new outlay of funds. He strongly urged that the computer be obtained and placed in his unit under his jurisdiction. "We'll make it hum—day and night," he added. "We could start right here in my unit and gradually spread out into the other units of the company. Improved sales analysis, for example, is an area where we could certainly use some help. If the company needs anything, it is sales—a lot more sales."

Problems:

1. What is the problem as you see it?
2. What is your general impression of Mr. Fromberg? Of Mr. Wright?
3. What do you believe Mr. Ronald Hall should do? Why?

Chapter 5

ELECTRONIC COMPUTERS— TECHNICAL CONSIDERATIONS

Be wiser than other people if you can, but do not tell them so.

—Lord Chesterfield

A COMPUTER is actually a group of mechanical and electronic devices connected into a unit or system to process data. Accurate terminology would designate a computer as an electronic data-processing system. This is actually the outgrowth of a continued advancement in office mechanization. Here is a unit that can take a bundle of facts, process the necessary string of operations, including any or all eight of the basic elements of data processing discussed in Chapter 2, turn out the answers with fabulous rapidity, without error, and proceed automatically to the next bundle of data and process them.

THE ANATOMY OF A COMPUTER

The top portion of Figure 5–1 diagrams the essential make-up of an electronic computer; the bottom portion, the general appearance of actual units. Different models will vary somewhat in detail and specific purposes, but the fundamentals outlined here are common to all computers.

Data in a suitable form such as punched cards, perforated paper tape, or magnetic tape are fed into the input units, where the data are converted into so-called "computer language" or, more accurately, electric pulses. Input units usually are either card readers, tape units, or magnetic drums, depending upon the particular design of the equipment. These data, now in computer language, are stored or retained in a memory unit, which commonly consists of magnetic cores, magnetic drums, and pulse emitters. They hold standard or current facts and sometimes instructions. When needed, the data are released to the process or computer section. Figure 5–2 gives illustrations of these memory types of equipment.

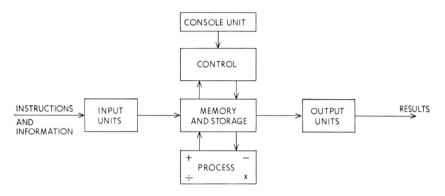

FIG. 5–1. Basic components of an electronic computer.

Directing the entire operation is the control section, which issues a program, or chain of instructions, to the process unit for each new group of data. It can send stored data required by the program, examine any step to select the following one, and start the processing of the next group of data. Frequently, a console unit, illustrated by Figure 5–3, permits a human operator to enter data if necessary, determine the status of the operations, and exercise complete supervision of the processing work. By means of the output units, completed processed data are converted from the "computer language" to a usable form such as printed records, punched cards, magnetic tape, or perforated paper tape. Figure 5–4 shows a printing unit having a capacity of six hundred lines per minute —each line approximately twenty words.

A   B
SIMULTANEOUS CURRENT
THROUGH WIRES A AND B
WILL REVERSE MAGNETIC
CHARGE OF ONLY THE CORE
AT THEIR INTERSECTION.

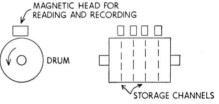

MAGNETIC HEAD FOR
READING AND RECORDING

DRUM

STORAGE CHANNELS

FIG. 5–2. *Left:* Magnetic core provides access to data faster but is presently more expensive than the magnetic drum. Each core holds one binary digit. About 75,000 can be stored per cubic foot of core and are available at the rate of about 50,000 per second. *Right:* Magnetic drum is mounted on its axis and rotates at from 2,000 to 8,000 r.p.m. Information is stored on channels around the drum by means of magnetic spots. The desired information is brought to a magnetic head and read. More than 1,000 digits can be stored per square inch of surface and are available at a rate of about 25,000 per second.

Courtesy: Remington Rand Inc., New York

FIG. 5–3. Panel of a supervisory control console unit of an electronic computer. This is the "nerve center" of the electronic system, giving the operator a continual picture of the internal operation.

CODING THE WORK FOR A COMPUTER

Information is conveyed by symbols. In the English language, there are familiar letters of the alphabet, numbers, and punctuation marks. For everyday correspondence, these symbols are recorded on paper according to a prescribed sequence and grouping. When transported to another person reading and writing English, these symbols convey a particular message.

In the same manner, to com-

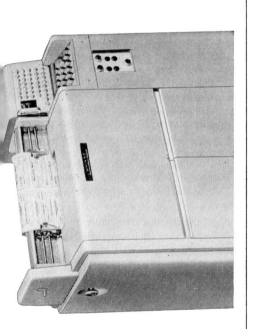

THE UNIVAC HIGH-SPEED PRINTER PRINTS ON PAPER UP TO 78,000 CHARACTERS IN A SINGLE MINUTE - EQUIVALENT TO PRINTING THE CONTENTS OF THIS PARAGRAPH 60 TIMES A MINUTE. NOW, FOR THE FIRST TIME, IT IS POSSIBLE TO GET UNIVAC RESULTS PRINTED AT SPEEDS TO KEEP PACE WITH THIS FAMOUS COMPUTING SYSTEM. 7,500 PAYCHECKS CAN BE PRINTED, FOR EXAMPLE, IN LESS THAN ONE HOUR. OPERATING ON UNIVAC OUTPUT TAPE, THE HIGH-SPEED PRINTER OFFERS A SELECTION OF 51 CHARACTERS - LETTERS, NUMBERS, AND PUNCTUATION MARKS - ON A LINE 130 CHARACTERS WIDE. ITS EXTREME VERSATILITY PERMITS PRINTING, IN ANY FORMAT DESIRED, ON SPROCKET-FED PAPER - EITHER BLANK OR PREPRINTED - FROM 4 INCHES TO 27 INCHES WIDE, AND UP TO CARD STOCK IN WEIGHT. INTERCHANGEABLE PLUGBOARDS PROVIDE COMPLETELY FLEXIBLE CONTROL OVER THE PRINTED OUTPUT. ACCURACY IS ENSURED IN HIGH-SPEED PRINTER OPERATION, AS THROUGHOUT THE ENTIRE UNIVAC SYSTEM, BY EXCLUSIVE SELF-CHECKING FEATURES. THIS PHENOMENAL NEW UNIVAC AUXILIARY IS ALREADY AT WORK IN LEADING COMPANIES, PRINTING THE PAYCHECKS AND THE OTHER BUSINESS FORMS NEEDED IN COMMERCIAL DATA-PROCESSING. NOW, AT LAST, ELECTRONIC COMPUTING IS PRACTICAL FOR OFFICE ROUTINES.

FIG. 5-4. A high-speed printer complete with control panel. In just one second, the entire paragraph illustrated was printed with this unit. A total of 7,500 pay checks can be printed in less than one hour.

municate with a computer system necessitates that the information be expressed in symbols and in a form that can be read and interpreted by data-processing devices. In the case of the computer, this language has been called "computerese." It is language the machine can understand and act upon, in keeping with the desired processing. Man invented "computerese" to utilize the machines. It represents symbols making up a mutual language to provide communication between people and machines. In other words, every detail which the machine is to follow must be put into language that the machine can handle. This includes the use of special codes and numbers which, put on or into the data-transmitting medium, will cause the machine to perform the operation desired.

There are a number of different media that can be used. For input data, the following are included: (1) punched card, (2) perforated paper tape (3) magnetic tape, (4) magnetic tape ledger record, (5) magnetic ink characters, and (6) imprints of specially formed characters or fonts that are read by machine. The processing of output data, being basically the reverse of that for input data, means that the same media can be used for output data as for input data. However, since output data are either for human use or for subsequent machine use of a relatively limited sort, not all the communication input media are used for output. For the latter purpose, the communication media include (1) punched card (2) perforated paper tape, (3) magnetic tape, (4) magnetic tape ledger record, and (5) ordinary print on paper. The concept of input data, output data, and data processing by a computer is shown by Figure 5–5.

BINARY MODE

Before discussing each of the data-transmitting media, some fundamentals in their representation of the data should be pointed out. The flow and storage of data are accomplished by the use of codes appropriate to the medium. These codes are made up on the basis of what is known as a binary mode, which means the use of only two possible conditions. For example, holes in a punched card or in a paper tape are either present or absent. Likewise, magnetic spots are either present or absent, electric current is in one direction or in an opposite direction, switches are closed or open, and electric current is on or off. In other words, the base is of two, just as decimals refer to a base of ten. The two number symbols are zero and one, represented, for example, by "off" and "on" conditions in the electrical circuits of the machine.

The binary notation of zero and one are called "bits." "No bit" means zero and "a bit" means one. This arrangement, plus a columnar pattern, enables information to be translated into "machine language." A columnar pattern is shown in Figure 5–6, in which the lights have been assigned arbitrary positions or location values of 8, 4, 2, and 1.

The coding system can be a seven-bit alphameric, six-bit numerical, a

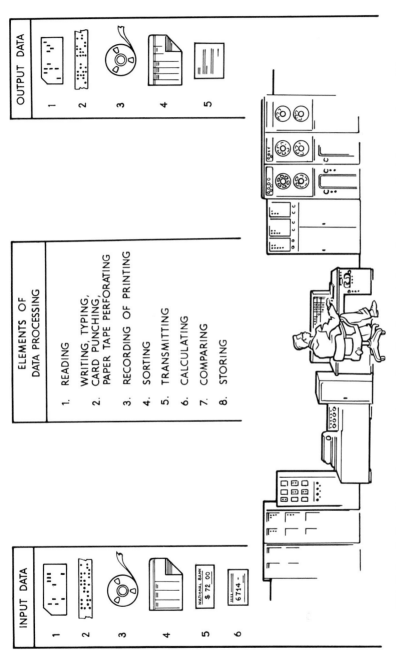

FIG. 5-5. Media of input data, processing, and media of output data of an electronic data-processing system.

INPUT DATA

1
2
3
4
5 NATIONAL BANK $72 00
6 6714-

ELEMENTS OF
DATA PROCESSING

1. READING

2. WRITING, TYPING,
   CARD PUNCHING,
   PAPER TAPE PERFORATING

3. RECORDING OF PRINTING

4. SORTING

5. TRANSMITTING

6. CALCULATING

7. COMPARING

8. STORING

OUTPUT DATA

1
2
3
4
5

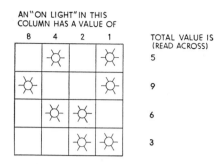

AN "ON LIGHT" IN THIS COLUMN HAS A VALUE OF

8	4	2	1	TOTAL VALUE IS (READ ACROSS)

FIG. 5–6. Illustrating the binary arithmetic employed to put data into machine language in order to machine-process them.

two-out-of-five, a biquinary, or a binary. Coding requires a thorough knowledge of how the machine operates and what can and cannot be done by it. This knowledge is specialized and is offered by the manufacturers of the machines. A concentrated course of several weeks' duration is usually required. Assistance is also made available by the manufacturers after installation of the machine.

PUNCHED CARD

The typical punched card is about 7⅜ inches long by 3¼ inches high. In the IBM type, the card is divided into 80 vertical columns, each one containing 12 units which, read from the top down, are: 12, 11, 0, 1, 2, 3, 4, 5, 6, 7, 8, 9. The 12 and the 11 zones are frequently called R and X, respectively. Data from original records are put on the cards by means of punched holes; that is, when certain holes are punched in the card, these holes represent definite information. High-speed machines are used for this purpose. The letters of the alphabet number 26, and there are 10 digits (0–9), making a total of 36 characters, each of which must be assigned a coded representation by a positioned hole in the card. Since there are 12 units in a vertical column on the card, it requires three different vertical arrangements totaling 36 (3 × 12) characters to represent all possibilities. This is clearly illustrated by Figure 5–7.

Information represented or coded by means of the presence or absence of holes in specific and exact locations is read as the card travels through a card-reading mechanism. The reading is automatically converted to an electronic language utilized by the computer in its data processing.

One method of recording binary information on cards is row binary, in which the data are arranged serially across each row beginning at the lower left, moving across from left to right for each horizontal row, and progressively upward on the card. A punched hole in the card represents 1, no punch indicates 0. It is also possible to arrange the binary information in parallel columns, with each column of the card containing twelve information bits. For certain computers, where the basic unit of information is a word consisting of a maximum of thirty-six consecutive bits, a total of three adjacent card columns is used.

PERFORATED PAPER TAPE

Another common medium for the transmission of data into a computer system is perforated paper tape. It is a continuous recording medium and

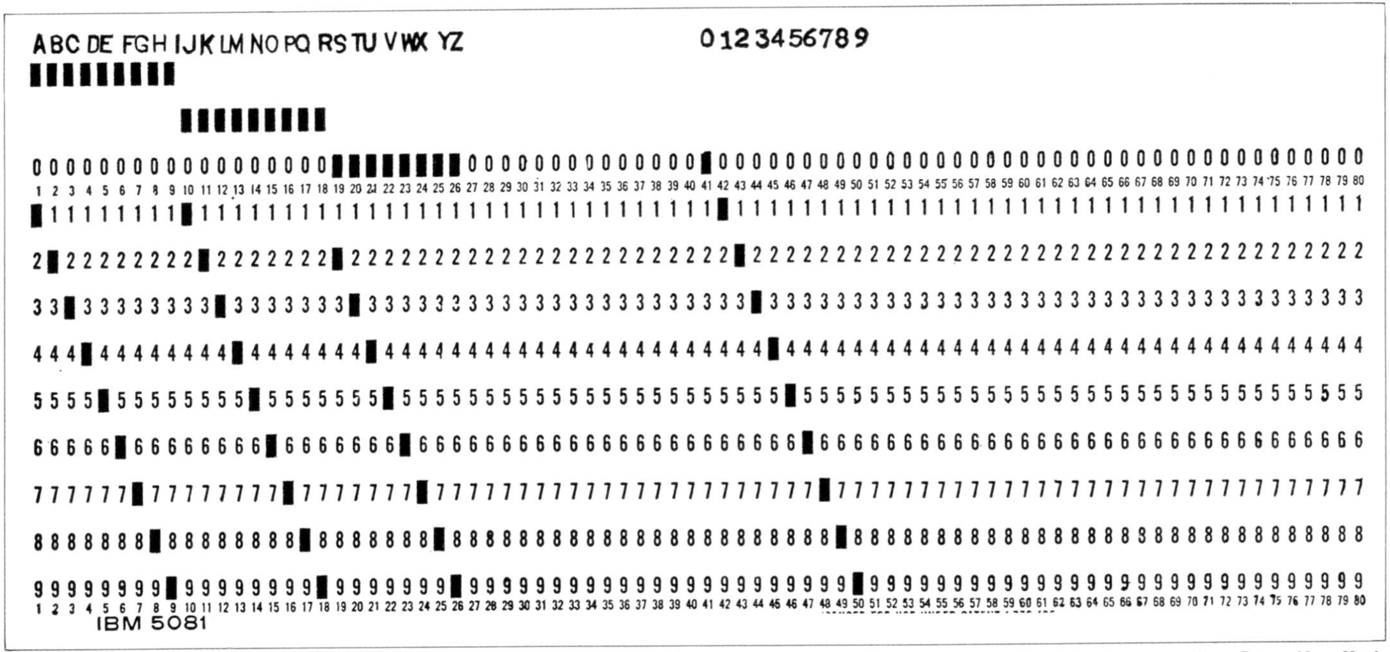

FIG. 5–7. A code used for punched holes which represent letter and figure data.

Courtesy: International Business Machines Corp., New York

can be used to record long runs of data, being limited only by the capacity of the storage medium into which the data are being placed.

Most perforated paper tape is either of an eight-channel code or of a five-channel code. A channel runs the length of the tape. In any column across the width of the tape, the number of possible punching positions is equivalent to the number of channels of the tape. That is, in the eight-channel tape, there are eight possible punching positions; and in the five-channel tape, there are five positions.

Figure 5–8 shows the code of an eight-channel paper tape. Observe that the lower five channels, identified as channels 1, 2, 4, and 8, and "check," are used to record numeric characters. The sum of the position values indicates the value of the character. For example, 3 is expressed by holes in positions 1, 2, and "check," while 7 consists of holes in 1, 2, and 4. For alphabetic characters, two additional channels at the top, X and O, are used with the 1, 2, 4, 8, and "check" channels. The arrangement is

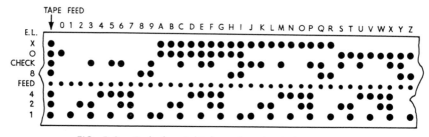

FIG. 5–8.   Code for eight-channel perforated paper tape.

similar to that of the 12, 11, or R and X zones of the punched card being used in conjunction with the 0–9 or digit punches of the punched card. To illustrate, the letter A is represented by holes in the following channels: X, O, and 1; K by holes in channels X, "check," and 2.

The channel identified as "check" is used for verification purposes. Each column is punched with an odd number of holes. If the sum of the holes punched in channels X, O, 8, 4, 2, and 1 is an even number, a hole in the "check" channel must be present. This explains why the column for the letter Y shows holes in channels O, "check," and 8. The "end of line" or "El" channel at the top of the tape is used to indicate the end of a record or the tape.

MAGNETIC TAPE

The principal input medium for computer systems is magnetic tape. It is one-half inch wide, made of plastic, and coated on one side with a metallic oxide. Information recorded on magnetic tape is permanent, but previous recordings are destroyed as new information is put on the tape.

It is possible to utilize the same tape many times, thus saving in recording costs. Magnetic tape is supplied on plastic reels containing approximately 2,400 feet of tape.

The data are recorded on the tape in the form of magnetic dots or spots. The code employed is illustrated by Figure 5–9. Starting at the top, the first channel is C, for checking, followed in order by B and A, commonly called zone tracks, and 8, 4, 2, and 1, the numerical tracks or channels. In similar manner to that described under perforated tape, numbers are coded, using the numerical channels. The number 5 is coded as 4 and 1; and 7 is 4, 2, and 1. The zone tracks are used in combination with the numerical tracks to indicate letters. In this code, for every column, the total spots add to an even number. If for a column the total of the spots in the zone and numerical tracks is an odd number, a spot is added at track C.

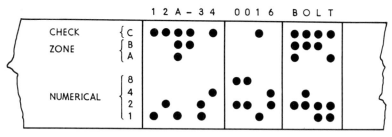

FIG. 5–9. Coding of magnetic spots on tape to transmit information. This is the seven-bit alphameric code. Translation of the spots is shown at top of sketch.

It is appropriate to state at this point that an electronic system is not infallible. Therefore, it checks itself to find any error. The impulses on channel C, or "check," of the tape are used for this purpose. For example, every transfer of information from the memory units might be tested on an odd-even basis. If the sum of the group of digits is an even number when it is supposed to be odd, the machine indicates the error and stops. This is all done automatically by the machine.

MAGNETIC TAPE LEDGER RECORD

This medium consists of magnetic strips imbedded on the back side of a ledger record. It serves as a dual-purpose record that is readable by machine and by people. Ordinary typing of information on the front side is translated into computer language on the magnetic strips of the same ledger record. The strips are capable of storing a large variety of information. Normally, one of the strips is for positioning purposes prior to an entry being made on the ledger record; the remaining strips contain data, some in what is called a positive coding, some in just the opposite or negative code. The positive and negative codes are used for verification purposes and to insure accuracy. An illustration of the magnetic tape ledger record is shown in Figure 5–10.

The advantages of this medium are unique. They include unlimited access to external memory and to familiar, hard-copy accounting data. Also, simultaneous access to both electronic and human language is provided, thus eliminating separate searching operations. Instructions to the machine can be stored on the magnetic tape ledger records along with human language instructions on the front side, thus expediting the handling and processing work. Changes in instructions are easy to make. In

Courtesy: Burroughs Corp., Detroit

FIG. 5–10. A magnetic tape ledger record.

addition, the stored information on the magnetic tape is introduced into the machine as needed, or on a random access basis, thus permitting greater processing flexibility and more utility of the internal memory of the computer for processing.

MAGNETIC INK CHARACTERS

Information can be printed with magnetic ink on ordinary paper. This serves as a medium that can be read by either man or machine. As of mid-1962, this medium is popular for bank checks and deposit slips, but has not as yet been extensively adopted for other types of paper work. Study is being given to the extension of magnetic ink to business documents other than checks and deposit slips. Best prospects seem to be documents used in mortgage loan accounting and payment coupons.

Numerals and characters of the same style and size are used on all checks. The information conveyed by these imprints is utilized in processing the check in its journey back to its maker, with the proper bank and individual account being debited or credited. The printing is done with an ink containing iron oxides which are electronically charged and read by magnetic ink character-reading equipment. A special type of design is used in order that the characters can be read visually and maximum machine readability is provided. The printing type employed is of a style called "Font E–13B" and is illustrated by Figure 5–11. The characters are located on the bank documents in specific areas, such as definite

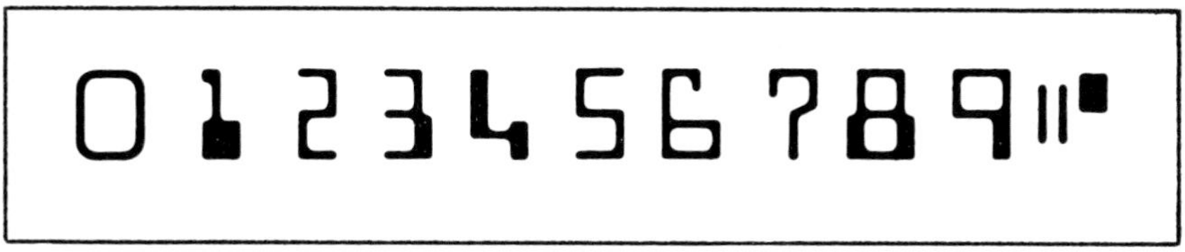

Courtesy: Moore Business Forms, Inc., Niagara, N.Y.

FIG. 5–11. Type font selected for magnetic ink characters. It can be read visually and also provides optimum machine readability.

distances from the bottom and right edge, in order that the machines may perform automatically and not have to search for the data.

SPECIAL IMPRINTS FOR MACHINE READERS

There are machines that can do what you are doing right now—reading. A machine reader can read letters and numbers without the use of special ink. Research has demonstrated that to the machine, ordinary printing may be difficult to read because of the variations in normal printing quality. Hence, certain printing type faces resembling conventional type facings have been developed to counter typical printing shortcomings and to meet better the needs of the machine reader. However, the machine can read most printed type, but special imprints are preferred because they give better results. As of 1962, most commercially feasible machines are required to read within a relatively small area of the document. It may be an account number, an amount to be paid, or a name and address. In the near future, machines to read a page of typed material probably will be available and, beyond that, perhaps a machine to read handwritten material.

The machine reader actually does two operations: (1) It reads, and (2) it translates what it reads into computer language. In short, the machine performs human reading and the time-consuming and laborious manual punching required by some of the other media for input data. Manufacturers of the reader state that when three or more operators are continuously employed in reading and punching, the machine reader is to be preferred.

Being very versatile, the machine reader can be used for the input of data in many different applications. Credit invoices, checks, order cards, and bill stubs of public utility companies are among the more common uses. Its main areas of application can be classified under two groups: (1) where the input information consists of a long number of separate units recorded in a great number of places and must be processed quickly

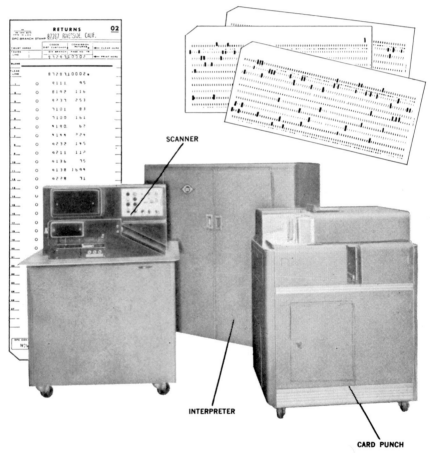

SCANNER

INTERPRETER

CARD PUNCH

Courtesy: Farrington Electronics, Inc.,
Needham Heights, Mass.

FIG. 5–12. A machine that reads. The unit on the left is the scanner or reader; the center unit, an interpreter; the unit on the right, a card punch machine.

and economically, and (2) where the output data of today becomes the input data of tomorrow. To illustrate, if a statement with a stub is sent to a customer who subsequently returns payment and the stub, it is feasible to put critical portions of the printed matter of the stub in a form that the machine reader can easily handle when the stub is returned and becomes input data. Figure 5–12 shows a machine reader. This particular machine reads a varying number of lines from a printed listing and translates these data into punched cards which are fed into the computer.

PROGRAMMING

The anatomy of the computer and the coding of work for computer processing are two essentials in the technical discussion of electronic data-processing systems. There remains another essential to be discussed in order to complete a basic presentation of the operating aspect of computers. This third essential is programming.

A data-processing system is designed to handle a specific number and type of operations. When included in the system, a computer is directed to perform each basic element of processing by specific instructions, which normally include the identification of the data, the basic elements to be performed, the sequence, and what to do with the results. This complete package of instructions is commonly known as a program. It is developed by "programming," which can be considered as the breaking-down in most complete detail of the work to be electronically processed.

Assume, for illustrative purposes, that the processing requires multiplication. In this case, the computer must be informed or directed to perform multiplication as well as (1) the operation that precedes the multiplying, (2) the operation that follows the multiplying, (3) the identity and location of the multiplicand, and (4) likewise that of the multiplier. In addition, after the multiplication is completed, the result must be transferred to storage at a specific location in the storage device, from whence it can be discharged, if desired, by the output device or retained in storage for future processing, as the individual case might be.[1]

In other words, an operation usually involves a chain of operations such as reading, locating information in storage, transferring to the processing device, processing, returning the result to storage, perhaps also returning the initial information to storage, sending out the result from storage to the output device, and finally discharging the result in the prescribed medium from the output device. Thus, the simplest portion of a procedure requires a number of carefully planned steps that must be designated in detail to the computer.

---

[1] When magnetic tape ledger records are used as the input medium, part of the stored data are on the tape or strips of the ledgers. In the case of magnetic ink characters being used as the input medium, little of the data is stored in a storage unit of the computer.

The preparation by computer of customers' invoices, for example, may require 1,500 or more steps. A computer program usually is designed and evolved in the form of a flow chart listing the precise step-by-step action to be taken. Subsequently, these actions, in proper sequence, are coded as an instruction in a form the computer can follow and are placed in the storage device. As such, these instructions are commonly termed a *stored program.*

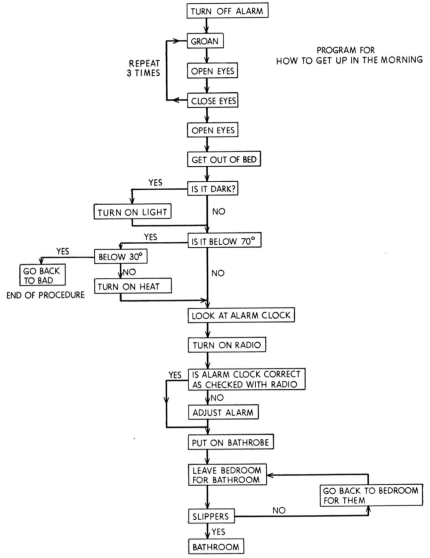

FIG. 5–13. This diagram illustrates how programmers have to instruct the electronic system to work.

Intimate knowledge of existing procedures, methods, and routines is extremely helpful in performing programming work. The broad, over-all picture should be taken, for one large programming job may encompass many small jobs, thus eliminating duplication and needless waste. A background in office procedural analysis and a complete understanding of the purposes for which the finished data are used appear paramount in this work. A humorous, but helpful, illustration explaining how a programmer instructs a machine to work is shown by Figure 5–13.

One computer can be supplied with a number of different procedures by simply putting in, or *loading*, the proper programs into storage. The stored programs are accessible to the computer, providing it with the ability to alter its own program in response to conditions revealed as the processing takes place. Hence, it can be said that the computer exercises some judgment within the limits established by the programmed operations to be performed. In this sense, it can be stated that computers are capable of making simple decisions.

It should be added that not all programs are stored in and accessible to the computer. By means of the console unit, programs can be entered directly into the computer step by step as the processing work progresses. This permits tracing a procedure one step at a time and affords high human-operator or external control. In some instances, limited data can be entered directly by control keys on the console. In addition, limited output information may be obtained, thus enabling the console operator to supervise the operation of the computer.

BUSINESS AND DATA-PROCESSING PROGRAMMING

Progress in programming has been significant to those wishing to use computers for the processing of normal business data. Typically, this type of work requires many programs providing for relatively small amounts of processing to large quantities of data. Comparatively simple additions, multiplications, and recordings are required. Programming is especially important in adopting computers for business purposes.

In contrast, the use of the computer for research and much scientific work entails a small amount of data being processed many, many times. Frequently, the task of processing is to substitute various values in mathematical formulas and determine whether a critical value, such as the stress in a structure or the amount of chemical produced, is within a safe, allowable technical limit. Processing data for scientific work frequently involves complex mathematics such as extracting square roots, raising numbers to decimal powers as exponents, and handling repetitive processing using different numerical values. Programming for the computer to handle this type of work is fairly simple. The procedure is determined and repeated over and over again with different mathematical values.

It is interesting to note that computers were first used for scientific work, in so far as large-scale commerical usage is concerned. This was probably due to the restricting influence of programming in connection with the computer use. We simply had not figured out how to tell the computer economically the manner of handling much data with little processing. However, during the past decade or so, the rapid strides in the advancement of programming and the knowledge being built up about it are probably the most outstanding factors contributing to computer progress for the processing of ordinary business data.

COMMON BUSINESS ORIENTED LANGUAGE (COBOL)

To operate a computer, it is necessary to have a network of preprogrammed packages which range from simple service routines to highly complex compilers. A compiler accepts a special code or a natural language, interprets it for the computer, selects the proper routine from a library retained by the computer, supervises the coding, allocates data, assembles a complete program, and gives a report on this program. The first compilers were all algebraic or mathematical, because the language of mathematics is concise and definite. With time, however, attempts were made to orientate the input language of a compiler to the natural language of the user. Subsequently "Math-Matic," "Fortran," and "Unicode" were developed.

With the great interest developing in computers for processing business data, efforts were directed and stimulated toward developing new system languages more suitable for this type of processing. As a result, "Flow-Matic" was pioneered, followed shortly by "AIMACO" and "FACT." The situation seemed to be that each computer manufacturer was developing his own language, a condition not only costly and unnecessary, but extremely difficult for users of several different types of computers. Accordingly, in January, 1960, the Conference on Data Systems Languages, or CODASYL, accepted and approved a plan for perfecting and advancing a common and simplified English language for business system programming. This simplified language is called COBOL and stands for Common Business Oriented Language. Figure 5–14 illustrates COBOL.

This advance in having a common computer language suitable for all computers, regardless of their manufacture, is the most significant advance in programming. Once a program is written in COBOL, it need not be rewritten if switching from one data-processing system to another takes place. Exchange of business programs is therefore expedited. Costly and time-consuming rewriting from one machine language to another is eliminated, and the burden of programming is eased by the use of COBOL. As an indirect result of the COBOL influence, many business-oriented "canned" or subroutine programs have been created for each type of computer. Also, automatic compilers and translators have

---

This language is COBOL:

SUBTRACT QUANTITY-SOLD FROM BALANCE-ON-HAND. IF BALANCE-ON-HAND IS NOT LESS THAN REORDER-LEVEL THEN GO TO BALANCE-OK ELSE COMPUTE QUANTITY-TO-BUY. . . .

COBOL eliminates the use of detailed and difficult computer language instructions such as:

06011	′	12040	12047
06028	C	12048	
06074	?	12046	12014
06145	S	12012	12010

FIG. 5–14. COBOL permits instructions to computers with simple English words of everyday business language.

appeared on the market. Thus, another hurdle has been removed, so that the progress of computer processing of business data can continue upward to even greater heights.

QUESTIONS

1. For an electronic computer, name the basic components and the function of each component.
2. What is the meaning of binary mode, and how is it used by a computer?
3. Explain Figure 5–5 in your own words.
4. Identify clearly each of the following:
   a) Stored program.
   b) Magnetic drum.
   c) COBOL.
   d) Magnetic tape.
5. Discuss the code used for an eight-channel perforated paper tape.
6. As you see it, is there any substantial difference between the use of magnetic ink characters and the standard magnetic tape as media for data communication? Discuss.
7. What are the present major considerations in the application of the machine that reads?
8. Discuss the subject area of "Magnetic Tape Ledger Record" as a medium for data transmission.
9. Do you feel that the machine reader will eventually replace man as the reader of office records? Elaborate on your answer.
10. Discuss programming as a requirement in the use of an office electronic system.
11. Relate briefly the history, present use, and significance of the common business-oriented language as employed for computer operation.
12. What are the important differences between programming for processing business data and programming for processing scientific data? Elaborate on your answer.

CASE PROBLEMS

Case 5–1.   Gibbons Sales Service

It is desired to resolve a specific problem for a stored-program, general-purpose computer. The problem deals with the calculation of sales commissions. Under the present compensation plan, salesmen are paid 5 per cent of their sales on the first $100 of sales each day and 10 per cent on sales in excess of $100 for the same day. To encourage salesmen to sell the higher-priced units, the company is contemplating revising the plan so that the higher commission will apply before the $100 daily sales level is attained. To this end, it has been suggested that the amount by which the average price of units sold by the salesman exceeds $10 be subtracted from the $100 sales level to determine the amount on which the 5 per cent commission will apply. Commissions on sales in excess of this new level would be 10 per cent.

To illustrate, salesman James Hendrick sells $150 worth of merchandise, the average price of which is $15. As the plan now is, salesman Hendrick will receive $10, calculated as follows:

$$
\begin{array}{lr}
\text{5 per cent of } \$100 \dots\dots\dots & \$\ 5.00 \\
\text{10 per cent of } \$\ 50 \dots\dots\dots & 5.00 \\
\hline
\text{Total} \dots\dots\dots\dots\dots\dots & \$10.00
\end{array}
$$

Under the contemplated revised plan, salesman Hendrick will receive $10.25, calculated as follows:

$$
\begin{array}{lr}
\text{5 per cent of } (\$100 - [\$15 - \$10]) \dots\dots\dots\dots & \$\ 4.75 \\
\text{10 per cent of } (\$150 - [\$150 - \$100 + \$5]) \dots\dots & 5.50 \\
\hline
\text{Total} \dots\dots\dots\dots\dots\dots\dots\dots\dots\dots\dots\dots\dots & \$10.25
\end{array}
$$

It is not possible, of course, simply to tell the computer, as described above, how to compute the commissions. The various operations to be performed by the computer must be determined. The computer cannot guess what is intended for it to do. The logical steps, in proper sequence, must be determined as the beginning of the necessary programming.

Problems:

1. Draw the computer diagram for salesmen's commissions, using the present plan of compensation. Refer to Figure 5–13 and use it as a guide
2. Draw the computer diagram for salesmen's commissions, using the contemplated plan of compensation.
3. Briefly discuss the observations you have made in preparing these diagrams, especially from the viewpoint of programming.

Case 5–2.   Madison Manufacturing Company

A check and stub unit is to be written by a high-speed printer which is a component of the data-processing center at Madison Manufacturing Company. The printer is made up of a cylinder of print wheels, arranged side by side, which rotate. Raised characters for imprint are located in bands around the rim of the cylinder. Usually, there are some 50 characters in each band. Each character provides one printing position. Opposite each band is a little hammer that presses the paper against the desired character at the proper time while the paper is stopped at each print line. The printer of this company has a printing speed of 700 lines per minute. The maximum number of characters on any one line is 20, and there are six lines to an inch. The printer can skip one or two lines at printing speed; but for three or more lines, it has a speed of 2,000 lines per minute. For estimating purposes, the time required to print a line of less that 20 characters with a distance or length of six inches is the same as that for 20 characters.

The check and stub unit to be printed is 3½ inches by 5¾ inches, the latter being the horizontal distance. Flow of units through the printer is vertical. The check position is to the left, and on it will be printed three lines of 10 characters each on the top three lines, plus five lines of six characters each on the bottom five lines. On the stub, the following will be printed:

From top of stub:
Line 1.....................8 characters
Line 2.....................6 characters
Line 3.....................6 characters

From bottom of stub:
Line 1.....................12 characters
Line 2.....................12 characters
Line 3.....................10 characters

For mechanical reasons, a top and a bottom border of one quarter of an inch each must be maintained. No printing can be placed in these borders. In other words, the bottom of line 1 is five twelfths of an inch (one quarter plus one sixth) from the top edge. In addition, one quarter of an inch must be allowed between successive units to compensate for the slight differences in sizes of the units and for a spacing interval for feeding the paper stock through the printer.

Problems:

1. Draw a layout of the check and stub unit.
2. Compute the printing time for one thousand check and stub units.

Chapter 6

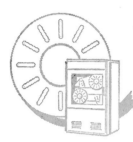

APPLICATIONS
OF COMPUTERS

*Courage is rightly esteemed the first of human quali-
ties, because . . . it is the quality which guarantees
all others.*

— WINSTON CHURCHILL

ALMOST every week, one hears or reads of a new
application of a computer in some activity of our economy. The growing
list seems almost endless, but it is reasonable to expect that any machine
like a computer, with its versatility, flexibility, speed, and performance
of essential work, will be applied to a multitude of uses. In this chapter,
some idea of the various and interesting types of applications will be
briefly discussed. The discussion is certainly not inclusive, but some
indication of the part the computer is playing and is destined to play in
our future is revealed.

Included in the selected applications are (1) insurance premium billing, (2) inventory control data processing, (3) visible record–MICR
automation system, (4) processing of public utility customer accounts,
(5) information retrieval—automatically, and (6) computer process
control (CPC).

INSURANCE PREMIUM BILLING

Paper work is a vital element to insurance operations. A leader among
insurance companies began its computer program by forming a management committee to investigate the computer field and to study the feasibility of computers for processing information in its business. Company
history revealed that for the past 60 years, the company's volume of
paper work had doubled about every 10 years, and this in the face of a
shrinking supply of competent office help. It was believed that a comprehensive office automation program was the answer. The committee's
task was to determine if this was true and, if so, to set up such a program in action.

Current office procedures and methods of processing the work were carefully analyzed; and from these data, a test pattern was developed against which to study specific computers offered on the market. Over a period of fifteen months, committee members attended programming courses offered by leading manufacturers of computers. In addition, meetings were arranged with representatives of these manufacturers at which time the feasibility, application, comparative costs, times required for processing, conversion techniques, and the like were discussed.

Work to Be Done. The initial work to be placed on the computer was the writing of premium notices to policyholders. Volume consisted of 400,000 premium notices a month, based on the current 2,000,000 insurance policies. It soon became apparent to the committee that the work of premium billing would require only a part of the computer's total capacity. Inclusion of other essential work for the computer was therefore added. This work included payroll preparation of approximately five thousand home office employees; the accounting of premium payments; the calculation, payment, and record keeping of commission payments to agents; and the determining of actuarial data including for each policy the anniversary cash value, cash value monthly changes, policy dividends, loan interest due, interest payable, accumulated dividends, and cash values of paid-up additions.

Based on the information secured, judgment, computer experience of others both in and out of the insurance field, and recommendations of the several computer manufacturers' representatives, the committee chose a particular computer of one of the manufacturers and decided to start the switchover to computer processing with the premium billing and follow in turn with the other areas of application. It was estimated that the computer would be delivered, installed, and ready to handle the premium billings at the end of 16 months. For the remaining applications, an additional period of approximately 28 months was estimated.

Accomplishment of Objectives. The computer was delivered approximately 11 months after order. Four months later, it processed the first batch of premium notices for policyholders. Under the former system, ten weeks of lead time were required, that is, monthly billings to be sent out June 1 would be started through their processing not later than March 15. Even then, the work involved considerable overtime, especially making last-minute changes in amounts and addresses of policyholders. With the computer system, lead time is twenty-one days, and the need for overtime is practically nil.

Some interesting details of the present computer system are as follows. Pertinent data from the policy are put into a punched card which serves as a ready reference to the policyholder and a basic source of data for the system. Key filing unit is the policy number. Information required for premium billing includes the amount of the premium, the period of time for which the premium is due, the date due, the name and address of the policyholder, and, of course, the policy number. Utilizing a card-to-tape converted, the data are put into the computer by means of the tape medium. Likewise, information on additional policies, as well as on changes in old policies, is fed into the computer by means of tape. The data are retained in the computer's memory units and, upon specific instructions, are taken from the memory unit, processed if required, needed information sent to the output unit, and basic information returned to the memory units. A high-speed printer puts the information on a continuous form which is separated along perforations for insertion in envelopes and mailing to policyholders.

The second major application, that of payroll preparation for some five thousand home employees, was completed eight months after the computer installation. Dramatic accomplishments include starting the payroll work two days before the payday, whereas previously it had to be started five days before the payday. The writing of the pay checks necessitates less than one hour of the high-speed printer. Also, required payroll reports for the government and for the company's cost accounting are prepared by the computer, and with greater accuracy than ever before achieved.

INVENTORY CONTROL DATA PROCESSING

Like many applications, the work of inventory control, as it is normally thought of, must be modified so that it is in a form that meets the physical operational requirements of computer handling. In this respect, a common arrangement for inventory control by computer is the cumulative or "cum" system, in which all activity is directed toward the new cum or total quantity. Information can be thought of as being gathered by degrees, and quantities increase in number until the entire records are started again from a new base. In essence, if cum is available, inventory is available at the proper time and in the proper quantity. There is no need for balance-of-stores records common in noncomputer inventory control systems.

An understanding of the basic operations performed is essential for comprehending the working of the inventory control data processing. Hence, before discussing what the computer does, a brief description of the basic operations will be given. The initial step is the sales forecast, which is reviewed monthly and adjusted in light of market conditions. A "release for production" is made against the sales forecast, which release authorizes procurement of materials, production schedules, and final assembly. Comparison is made between the cumulative requirements and the amount available. If the latter exceeds the former, no order for parts is entered. On the other hand, if the amount available is less than the cumulative requirements, the deficit is filled by ordering the parts.

MODEL	To Date Release	To Date Cum Shipped	February Releas	February Cum Shipped	March Release	March Cum Shipped
124	5,000	2,400	1,000	3,400	1,500	4,900

FEBRUARY

	Week A		Week B		Week C		Week D	
	R*	CS*	R	CS	R	CS	R	CS
	250	2,650	250	2,900	250	3,150	250	3,400

MARCH

	Week A		Week B		Week C		Week D	
	R	CS	R	CS	R	CS	R	CS
	375	3,775	375	4,150	375	4,525	375	4,900

COMPONENT NO. 1 FOR ALL MODELS

FEBRUARY

Week A		Week B		Week C		Week D	
R	CS	R	CS	R	CS	R	CS
1,500		1,500		1,500		1,500	

MARCH

Week A		Week B		Week C		Week D	
R	CS	R	CS	R	CS	R	CS
1,625		1,625		1,625		1,625	

* R = Release; CS = Cum Shipped.

FIG. 6–1. Data utilized in "cum" method of inventory control.

The Data Utilized. In Figure 6–1 (page 97), the top illustration shows that for Model 124, the amount released is 5,000; shipped, 2,400; February scheduled shipment, 1,000; March scheduled shipment, 1,500. Thus, the cum for February is 3,400 and for March, 4,900. The data are converted to weekly amounts, as indicated by the middle illustration of Figure 6–1. So far, our data are by model, and each model may require a number of components. Quite probably, some of these components will be common to several models. Our need is to determine the total number of each component that will be required for the scheduled product mix represented by the various models. Assume the monthly data illustrated by the bottom illustration of Figure 6–1 represent these values. The amounts required will be determined primarily on the sales forecasts of each model, with important modifications for in-plant lead time. This is to say that some components are required for subassemblies, others for the final assembly; those for subassemblies must be available in the plant for consumption before the components intended for final assembly. In many instances, the same type of component will be used for the subassembly and again in the final assembly.

For each component, comparisons are now made between the cum and the availability. Based on this comparison, the decision to "order schedule" is determined. Referring to Figure 6–2, the cum requirements

COMPONENT NO. 1 FOR ALL MODELS

	USED TO DATE	FEBRUARY			
		Week A	Week B	Week C	Week D
Cum requirements....	13,400	14,900	16,400	17,900	19,400
Available............	22,000	22,000	22,000	22,000	22,000
Order schedule.......		0	0	0	0

FIG. 6–2.

for component 1 are 13,400 for the "used to date." As indicated in Figure 6–1, the requirements for the first week of February are 1,500, making the cum 14,900; for the second week, 1,500, making the cum 16,-400; and so forth. The availability of component 1 is 22,000, which, compared to the cum of February week A, shows ample supply; hence, no order schedule would be made, and the value of 0 is entered under week A. In like manner, it can be seen that no order schedule for component 1 would be issued during any of the weeks of February. Even the last week shows the cum will be 19,400, with 22,000 available. Production planning is quite unlikely to match exactly sales forecasts because of the varying need for finished goods inventory, variations in estimated lead times, rates of production, and capacity to produce exactly to requirements. But the system provides reasonable checks between weekly needs and availability, so that deviations are kept within practical limits; thus, satisfactory inventory control is achieved.

Automating the Process. This system is suited to automation. It utilizes a computer designed to approach in-line accounting on a mechanized basis. Such a computer is equipped with a random access storage device which permits the storage of and rapid access to any of many millions of characters comprising the records. In other words, any of the records in the computer can be reached quickly without scanning the intervening records. The various accounts may be posted in random order. For example, interrelated transactions might involve (1) secure raw materials, for which the transaction is posting receipts to raw material record; (2) make up subassemblies, for which the transactions are posting production of subassemblies to subassembly account and deducting

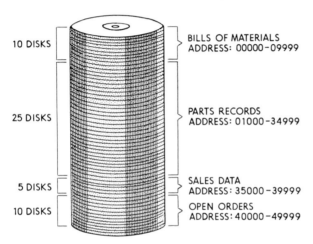

FIG. 6–3. Each of the fifty thousand records has an address or specific location on a disk of the storage unit of the computer.

components used in subassemblies from components accounts; or (3) ship finished goods, which requires for the record a deduction from the finished goods account by the amount of finished goods shipped.

In this application, the equivalent of 62,500 eighty-column punched cards, or 5,000,000 characters, is stored in the storage device of the computer. A total of 50,000 different records of 100 characters each constitutes the master information and previous balances. These 50,000 are prorated among the types of basic information and constitute addresses or identities by which specific records can be located by the computer. This is shown graphically by Figure 6–3.

The Processing by Computer. For programming the cum system, each part contained in the bill of materials for each model has a parts record stored in a separate section in the computer. For example, the parts record for a purchased part contains the part number; the percentage allowance for loss, waste, or spoilage; the origin; the cum receipts; and the balance due on open purchase orders.

For the given period of thirteen weeks, a master schedule or sales forecast by week by models is punched on a tape which is fed into the computer. This schedule is first processed by the bill-of-material section, or portion showing the materials needed. The computer calculates requirements by periods, namely, by multiplying usage by schedule by shrinkage factor. Next, the schedule period is adjusted for lead time on each piece part. These data are carried forward to the parts record, where they are stored awaiting information from other models. As this information from other models becomes available, it is combined with other like information so that the cum requirements by periods are accumulated on the parts record for each component. When and how much to purchase or make is determined by comparison of the accounts scheduled with the amounts available for each component, as discussed above.

What was previously long, tedious labor required for inventory control is now accomplished in several hours by means of the computer. In addition, it is now a simple matter radically to revise the production program. Information can be quickly obtained regarding the position materialwise if a new production plan is attempted. Shortages and excesses of materials are pointed out, and the status of all components is revealed.

VISIBLE RECORD–MICR AUTOMATION SYSTEM

A prominent and long-established bank in the Midwest is now enjoying the fastest check handling at the lowest cost per item and highest accuracy in banking history. How is it doing this? By means of a visible record computer using MICR (magnetic ink character recognition) source documents. This office automation system is specifically designed for financial accounting. Flexible MICR and punched-card inputs are utilized; electronic processing and retention of accounting records in ordinary visual form (printing on paper) are features of this process. The accounting records are maintained on magnetic tape ledger cards which, as pointed out in Chapter 5, are regular-appearing ledger cards with magnetic tape imbedded on the back side of the card. Information typed on the front side is translated into computer language on the magnetic strips of the same card.

The system is made up of four essential units. These are illustrated in Figure 6–4 and include, viewing from left to right, (1) the sorter-reader, (2) the record processor and console, (3) the card reader, and (4) the data processor. The latter is the nerve center of the entire system. It performs all calculations, gives instructions, and directs the operations of the other three units.

Courtesy: Burroughs, Inc., Detroit

FIG. 6–4.   The essential units of the visible record—MICR automation system.

Encoded MICR items—for example, bank checks in the case of our bank illustration—are read and sorted automatically by the sorter-reader unit to provide on-line and buffered data input for the record processor unit. In other words, the check is read regarding such information as the account number, process control number, and amount from the magnetic ink markings on the check and sorted to a batch of checks, which expedites the posting of the transactions to the check writer's account or statement. The sorter-reader processes mixed items of varying sizes and thicknesses at rates of over 1,500 per minute.

The information read by the sorter-reader is transmitted to the record processor and console, which automatically selects from its file of records the desired record by account number, reads the data stored in the magnetic tapes or strips on the back of the account ledger record, updates both the printed side and the magnetic storage area of each currently active record amount, and returns the ledger record to the file. The recording of data is accomplished by means of a printer capable of over two hundred lines per minute, each line consisting of 156 characters. The accounting records are filed by batches in the processor, and the record needed for posting is brought to the front part of the unit for posting operations. Those records requiring special attention are segregated by means of an auxiliary unit called a stacker. Three input stations for forms provide operating versatility. The console supplies the means of communicating between the supervisor and the system.

One of the important functions of the card reader is to supply on-line data input to the system from punched cards. It does this at a rate of two hundred cards per minute. In addition, this unit puts programs into the core memory of the data processor, input data for selected data-processing applications, and the processing of exceptional items.

The entire system supplies up-to-the-minute information of current status and previous activity for each account. Simultaneous daily printing of the ledger, statement, and journal avoids the end-of-period statement-printing peaks. In addition, vital analysis of the records can be conducted quickly, the records are balanced step by step to insure complete accuracy, and lower operating costs provide better operational control.

PROCESSING PUBLIC UTILITY CUSTOMER ACCOUNTS

The preparation of bills for more than 500,000 electric and gas meters is another interesting application of an electronic data-processing system. Readings from the meter readers' reports are typed on a special report using a machine which simultaneously makes a perforated tape of the information. This tape is fed into the computer, which reads the information at high speed. Being given the customer's number and present meter reading, the computer locates the information it has on the particular customer number; subtracts the previous from the present meter reading; computes the cost and discount, if any; and along with the customer's name and address, sends the processed information to the output unit, where the customer's bill is printed. Subsequently, the bills are sorted automatically by cities and mail zone numbers for putting in the mail.

The monthly bill has the customer's account number preprinted in magnetic ink. This number identifies the account. When bill stubs are returned for crediting customer payments, they are sorted by customer number and read by a sorter-reader unit similar to that described above. From this unit, the information is fed into the computer, which posts the payment to customer ledger cards in the form of magnetic tape ledger cards. Approximately twelve thousand customer bills are prepared in one hour. It required about one year to complete the switchover to the new system, but this conversion was accomplished without any inconvenience to the customers of the public utility.

New meter installations and changes of address and number of meter are handled in the same manner as the input of monthly billing data. The new meter is assigned a customer's number; or if the case requires, the new address is added, and the old address is removed from the data in the computer's memory units. These additions and changes create extra work. However, initial estimates placed this work at not more than 2,200 per month, whereas the actual requirements have never exceeded 1,720 in any one month. The system does provide needed flexibility as well as great accuracy and speed.

In addition to processing customer accounts, the company intends to use the computer for the handling of engineering computations and studies. This will facilitate design and planning work so essential to the improvement of new electric and gas facilities necessary to meet future requirements. Other areas for future exploration include payroll, accounts payable, property and plant records, and inventory.

INFORMATION RETRIEVAL—AUTOMATICALLY

Much of the money spent for research and development will be spent more effectively or not at all when available literature on the subject can be searched thoroughly beforehand. There are thousands of technical journals carrying literally millions of articles on a vast array of scientific subjects. Screening and retrieving what is pertinent to a particular study represents a herculean task for the searcher. In many cases, research is started on a project already completed or in process elsewhere, or not all the available knowledge has been reviewed before launching the new study.

This gives rise to another facet of office technology, called automatic information retrieval. Succinctly stated, this can be called mechanization of the intellectual effort of information input to provide quick screening of voluminous available information on any of a multitude of subjects. It is a terrific time consumer, if indeed physically possible, to follow through all the reports and journals to keep pace with developments in a given field of study. The need is for a fast way to have access to information on specific subjects. This, in turn, requires some means by which masses of data are assimilated, classified, and compressed into complete and understandable indexes; and if desired, the complete information itself can be retrieved quickly.

It is estimated that some $1.5 billion are spent each year for research and development, and a goodly portion of this amount goes for "information services" or searching the literature. Much of this can be handled by the use of computers, but it should be pointed out that other mechanical means are possible and in use. For example, a large pharmaceutical house maintains a punched-card index file on fifteen thousand drug-journal articles that goes back five years. Cost for this arrangement is only $550 a month. Other systems use a combination punched card and microfilm, with the latter located within the center portion of the card. The card is used to locate the title and subject, the microfilm for showing a portion or all of a copy of the original article. The microfilm can be projected on a special screen for reading convenience.

Different but closely associated with information retrieval is the belief by many that the computer will help bring about the common world language so long sought. The belief is that as man learns to communicate with machines, this communication will spread to man-to-man communication. Thus, "computerese" may end language barriers.

On the other hand, it seems that to eradicate any language of long standing will certainly not be an overnight accomplishment. But communication between men of different languages is an accomplished fact of the computer. It can translate information from one language into another. Such units are feasible, but this application to date has been relatively minor compared to the host of other uses to which computers have been applied.

COMPUTER PROCESS CONTROL (CPC)

One more category of computer applications will be discussed. This application is computer process control (CPC), whereby the computer starts actions and acts upon the results of such actions, thus, in essence, allowing complete automation of the production line. Under this arrange-

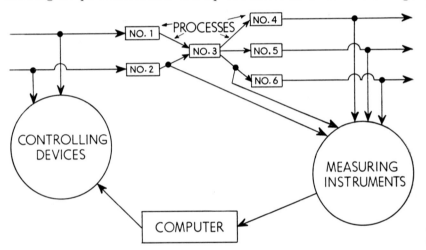

FIG. 6–5.   The general arrangement for computer process control (CPC).

ment, the computer makes a running analysis of the process and compensates for changes as they occur. The general arrangement followed is graphically represented by Figure 6–5.

The computer is connected to many and various instruments which provide pertinent readings on variables critical to the process. These readings are analyzed, related, and processed at fantastic speeds, thus recording if the process is progressing satisfactorily or what, if any, part of the production process needs remedial action. If the latter is the case, the computer dispatches back through the communicative network a series of actions that cause individual controls on various pieces of production equipment to make necessary adjustments.

Different processes put different demands upon CPC. Chemical industries typically require a large number of calculations; other industries may necessitate relatively few checks, but they must be made with great rapidity. Complete CPC may cost upwards of $1 million, depending upon the complexity of the process. But CPC can be achieved by stages.

This normally begins with the use of a computer "off line," that is, the computer is not an integral of the process, but is used to assist human operators who have complete control of the manufacturing process. It is also possible to put the computer "on line," but not in control. This is accomplished by the programming and the work which the computer is permitted to do, commonly monitoring and results of analysis to serve as guides for the human operators.

Illustrative of CPC is the adaption of blast furnace operations in steel mills to computer control. This arrangement is an off-line application and enables the blast furnace operators to know the ideal and exact conditions for the most efficient operations for producing the best-quality finished product. Indications of difficulties and mechanical failures are detected in advance. A typical blast furnace consumes daily 4,800 tons of raw materials, mainly iron ore, limestone, and coke, and turns out 1,700 tons of iron. The grade of ore, quality of limestone, amount of heat, iron composition and purity desired, and a host of other variables are representative of the type of information which must be properly co-ordinated to operate the furnace in keeping with predetermined goals.

COMPUTERS AND THE FUTURE

Change is always taking place; the direction and degree of this change in the way paper work is accomplished is, and will inevitably be, modified by the computer. Everywhere, the tempo of technological advance has quickened. The need for more and more information is being accelerated. Discoveries not yet imagined will be made. In such an era, the computer will occupy an increasing role of importance in the hopeful advances of human progress. Properly understood and applied, the computer will assist man to employ his talent, his time, and his ideas most effectively in the pursuit of values which make man so distinctive and his accomplishments so significant.

QUESTIONS

1. Do you feel that the major areas of computer applications can be considered fairly well explored as of the present? Substantiate your answer.
2. With reference to the six illustrations discussed in this chapter, what common attributes do you observe in each system? What major differences? Briefly discuss.
3. Discuss the approach taken by the insurance company in the premium-billing illustration, pointing out wherein you feel the approach was good or bad.
4. Identify each of the following:
   a) A sorter-reader unit.
   b) Cum system of inventory control.
   c) Computer process control (CPC).
   d) Random access computer.

5. Outline the major steps as you envision them for preparing payroll with the computer by the company using the computer for premium billing.

6. With reference to the processing of customer accounts by the public utility, determine:

   a) The time required to process the acounts each month.

   b) The percentage of accounts changed each month due to additions and corrections.

   c) Several alternatives to the system curently used for getting the input and for putting it into the computer.

7. Could the cum method of inventory control be used for noncomputer data processing in this managerial area? Why?

8. Explain Figure 6–3 in your own words.

9. Using the material included in this chapter as a background, if you could choose one feature of a computer to be improved at no additional cost to you, what feature would you choose? Why?

10. Outside of bank checks and bill stubs, what other types of documents do you feel might be processed advantageously by the use of MICR? Discuss.

11. Consult several business periodicals and read a report on a CPC installation. Relate the interesting aspects of this installation and what would seem to be the limiting factors of additional installations of this particular type.

12. Discuss the meaning, operation, and potential of automatic information retrieval.

CASE PROBLEM

Case 6–1. The Burton Company

One of the largest department stores in the entire United States, the Burton Company, operates six stores located within a large city and suburban shopping areas adjacent to the city. Studies conducted by the controller, Mr. Lief Huff, show that the paper work performed by the company in connection with the conduct of its business with its customers has been growing, with the costs for this work exceeding the rate of the volume growth. Both the processing and the cost of papers dealing with company purchases and inventory are considered satisfactory by Mr. Huff.

At a top executive meeting yesterday, the controller was authorized to proceed with the necessary work relative to reducing costs and improving the handling of papers created by store customer relations, including such work as the preparing of billings or statements for customers and the processing of customer accounts receivable. Currently, for this work the company uses accounting machines purchased some seven years ago.

A customer extended open credit by the company produces her "charge plate" at the time of making a purchase. This plate is inserted into a small unit on the counter by the store clerk. The plate imprints the customer's number, name, and address upon the purchase order made out by the clerk in longhand. At the same time, the customer's number is relayed to the central credit department, where a check is made to determine if the credit is in good standing. If so, approval is relayed to the originating small unit used by the store clerk who, being thus informed, proceeds with consummation of the sale. On the other hand, if credit is refused, the customer is politely informed of the condition by the clerk, who terminates the sale unless cash payment is made on the account or for the current merchandise being purchased. In some instances, it requires five to ten minutes to get the check on credit. Mr. Huff feels the present arrangement can be improved. Copies of the order written by the clerks are sent to the accounting department, where monthly statements to customers are prepared. As stated above, accounting machines are currently used for this work.

The company has approximately 300,000 customers sold on open account. Of the total number of sales transacted, some 22 per cent are cash sales. Peak loads occur during the Easter period, late summer before school starts, and the Christmas period. Accounts are divided by stores, with the statements sent out for each store on approximately the same day of each month. For example, billings for store No. 1 are put in the mail on the second day of each month, and those for store No. 2 on the ninth day of each month. It is estimated that during the past five years, the number of accounts has increased an average of 3 per cent per year. It is believed that this growth will continue and may even rise to 5 per cent per year.

Problems:

1. What approach do you recommend that Mr. Huff follow? Why?

2. In your opinion, what are some major considerations that will help determine the feasibility of the use of a computer by the company? Discuss.

3. Assuming a computer is being considered, describe in general the type of computer and the step-by-step procedure of the computer processing that might be adopted by the company.

Chapter 7

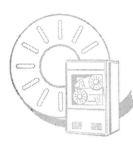

INTEGRATED DATA PROCESSING

We cannot advance without new experiments in living, but no wise man tries every day what he has proved wrong the day before.

—JAMES TRUSLOW ADAMS

ANOTHER important and major aspect of office automation is integrated data processing, commonly referred to as IDP. Actually, this is an identification for purposes of convenience and discussion. The last several chapters have dealt with data processing by means of computers; and as indicated, computers integrate the processing of data. However, the identification of IDP is given to data processing that primarily, but not exclusively, ties together various types of office machines by common media and integrates their respective operations so as to form a whole from the various machines utilized. Computers can be and frequently are a part of a data-processing arrangement which includes geographically dispersed input and output centers, each connected with a centralized computer center. This can be thought of simply as an extension of a computer or data-processing system, or it can be considered a type of IDP. It is the latter view that has been adopted in this chapter. The concept of IDP will be developed fully in the following pages.

THE EVOLUTION OF IDP

In 1954, executives of the U.S. Steel Corporation introduced the concept of IDP by using the media of punched cards and perforated tapes. This concept included the mechanization of the original data and the use of systems for processing these data with various office machines that instruct one another. The original data serve all subsequent purposes, the processing is integrated, and those work portions which are different each time are performed manually.

This new idea was quickly exploited by many companies for various portions of their paper work operations. Some concentrated on reaping benefits from systems and utilizing office machines other than computers, while others viewed the new concept as a means to a more effective way to use their computers. But each sought a common goal: to simplify data processing and improve the usage of information provided.

MEANING OF IDP

In the processing of business data, it is customary to find certain data copied and repeated over and over again, rearranged according to many different formats, and originated in or sent to different locations; that is, spatial differences are present. In addition, business data are interrelated. For example, data showing price figures alone mean little. Required, in addition to price, are vendor's name, address, and terms of sale. Likewise, a single figure showing the quantity of an item on hand is insufficient. The units of measurement, location, cost, and source may also be necessary.

Consider the paper work required to handle a customer's order. Raw materials must be purchased or, if stocked, the inventory records consulted, release orders to manufacture issued, production-scheduled shipping tickets and bills of lading prepared, and invoices made out to the customer. Much of the information used in preparing these various documents is similar, and the data are written many times. Distribution of the information may be made to a considerable number of locations, some of which are miles apart, as, for example, a branch factory and the central office building.

It is logical to attempt simplifying and integrating the writing of these various office forms. The elimination of duplicate writings can be accomplished by using carbon copies, an accounting machine extends and totals, and information punched in code on cards can be used repeatedly to reproduce all documents required. But in general, these deal with a single process and are not interchangeable among various processes. However, in some instances, as in duplicating copies containing essential information for specific purposes, such as purchasing or production control, the copies serve in several processes, and all the writing is integrated by use of the one master.

In addition, attention can be directed to mechanizing the writing and the handling of customers' orders to cover all related and subsequent needs. Since IDP includes nearly all types of office machines, it means that a variety of machines can be considered in seeking improvements via the mechanization route. Successful achievement of simplifying the necessary writing, integrating it, and mechanizing the entire work will provide faster processing, improved accuracy, and better customer service.

DISTINGUISHING FEATURES OF IDP

From the viewpoint of semantics, integrated data processing means the formation of an entirety of processing derived from all the constituent parts in accordance with their proper interaction to each other and utilizing the best means for handling the data. Strictly speaking, an advanced means, such as an electronic machine, need not necessarily be used. The processing can be integrated using manual methods, and high levels of efficiency can result from such efforts. Based on the individual conditions, the manual means may be recommended.

All IDP studies should first be systems-oriented and then machines-oriented. The former concept is one of long standing in office management, but the mechanization of data processing from original entry to finished result is relatively new. This latter concept extends by means of mechanization the systems' only approach to greater economies, if the individual circumstances justify it. Experience shows that it can bring about exceptional effectiveness.

IDP, as discussed here, can be described briefly as automation of source data. The writing for an office operation is put into such a form that subsequent operations requiring this writing can be processed automatically. IDP therefore tends to tie office work together, to integrate it, or to form a whole from the various parts. Mechanization is used. The term IMDP, integrated mechanical data processing, would be more precise; but the modern and common term is IDP and hence will be used here.

The distinguishing feature of IDP is the preservation of source data, determined by thorough system analysis to be necessary, in a mechanical and reasonable form at the time of origination, so that all subsequent processing of the data can be performed and preserved in this reusable form. This concept applies to all office processing and is distinguished from conventional approaches by the original and necessary data being (1) recorded at the point of origin in a mechanical form, (2) processed exclusively in a mechanical form, and (3) utilized in all subsequent operations, where needed, resulting in the integration of the processing work.

To implement this approach, all conventional office machines must be adapted to speak the same language; that is, a basic and direct compatibility, so to speak, between different types of machines, and between machines of different manufacturers, must be achieved. In this manner, data originating on one type of machine can be used later on other types, without human reading, interpreting, and writing.

THE COMMON LANGUAGE LINK

The common language medium joining all machines utilized is the key to the mechanization aspect of integrated data processing. The medium is acceptable to all the machines, permits each to perform its particular task, passes the result on to the next machine, which utilizes this information and passes on the accumulated data. In essence, the group of conventional machines is connected into a single harmonious system. The various machines can be widely dispersed geographically. The necessary communication is achieved by use of appropriate media, usually perforated tape and electrical impulses. This idea of the common language link in IDP is shown graphically by Figure 7–1.

There are three common language media in use today: (1) perforated tape, (2) punched card, and (3) edge-punched card. Whatever the medium, it is prepared simultaneously with the initial writing of the data. To reiterate, when a sales order is initially typed, a mechanism at-

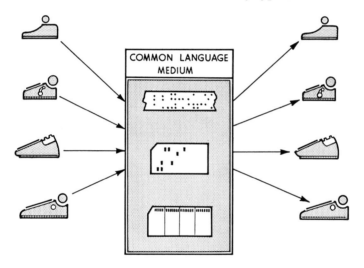

FIG. 7–1.   The key to IDP is the common language medium.

tached to the typewriter automatically prepares the medium. As stated above, this medium is then used to operate all subsequent machines required. Normally, each machine is equipped either to prepare the medium or to "read" it, or both. Figure 7–2 illustrates a nondescriptive accounting machine connected to a tape perforator. In this application, the following is performed in one operation: A voucher is posted, the voucher check is computed and printed, and a voucher register is prepared. Integrated with this operation, a perforated tape is made for subsequent preparation of punched cards used in the processing and the analyzing of the data.

The most widely used perforated tape has five rows or channels of perforations; and for technical reasons, this five-channel tape can be considered standard. Various combinations of holes in these five chan-

Courtesy: Burroughs Corp., Detroit

FIG. 7–2. Installation of an accounting machine connected to tape perforator providing perforated tape for subsequent integrated data processing.

nels give a total of thirty-two symbols, including the twenty-six-letter alphabet, letters, figures, space, carriage return, line feed, and blank. A shift symbol provides for numerals. Figure 7–3 shows the five-channel code for perforated tape.

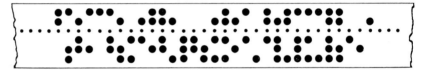

	A	B	C	D	E	F	G	H	I	J	K	L	M	N	O	P	Q	R	S	T	U	V	W	X	Y	Z	LETTERS	FIGURES	SPACE	CHR. RETURN	LINE FEED
FIGURES					3				8						9	0	1	4		5	7		2		6						
	1	1		1	1	1				1	1						1		1		1		1	1	1	1	1	1			
CODE	2		2				2		2	2	2	2				2	2	2			2	2	2				2	2			2
CHART	o	o	o	o	o	o	o	o	o	o	o	o	o	o	o	o	o	o	o	o	o	o	o	o	o	o	o	o	o	o	o
			3			3		3	3		3		3	3		3	3		3		3	3		3	3		3		3		
		4	4	4		4	4			4	4		4	4	4			4				4		4			4	4		4	
		5					5	5				5	5		5	5	5			5		5	5	5	5	5	5	5			

FIG. 7–3. *Top:* Five-channel tape. *Bottom:* Five-channel code.

It must not be concluded that perforated tape is limited to five channels. Actually, up to eight channels can be used; this permits more characters, check, and control symbols. A seven-channel tape, for example, would require all equipment using this tape to be so equipped for it. As long as the operations are within an enterprise, no particular difficulty would be present; but in dealing with outside firms, difficulty would be encountered because, as stated above, the five-channel tape is standard and by far the type most widely used.

Punched cards are also a medium for conveying data in an IDP arrangement. The data are put into punched cards which serve to operate all subsequent machines in the process.

Courtesy: Commercial Controls Corp., Rochester, N.Y.

FIG. 7–4. The Flexowriter Programatic prepares documents from unit edge-punched cards automatically. The machine reads, reproduces, or punches card or tape.

The edge-punched card is, as the name suggests, punched along the edge of the card. The code used is that of the five-channel perforated tape. Cards are easy to handle and file; however, the information on one card is limited by its length, generally about seven inches. This is sufficient, however, for many purposes. Figure 7–4 shows a typewriter equipped to utilize edge-punched cards.

ACHIEVING IDP

The applications of IDP are practically limitless. Every major procedure either by itself or along with other procedures, offers possibilities. The gains to be realized are usually substantial. For best results, a definite program should be followed, patterned along these steps:

1. *Review areas and departments for study.* This can be started by preparing check lists revealing pertinent facts about present paper work activities in the manufacturing, procuring, and distributing departments. Information on the present methods of preparing papers, and their route or travel in the normal operation of the business, is the type to be obtained. By studying and evaluating this information, specific goals will emerge, such as improving production control communication, reducing processing time for purchase orders, providing quick shipping information, sending out invoices promptly, and eliminating copying errors.

2. *Secure top management approval.* Being integrated, IDP will cross departmental lines, involve many employees from different organizational units, and affect what they do. Hence, authorization of and support for the IDP effort must be given by top management; otherwise, the program will be seriously hampered, and little, if anything, will come of it.

3. *Appoint director to head all IDP activity.* Along with its blessing, top management should appoint an individual to manage the activity, giving him the necessary authority and help to direct the study to a successful installation. Designated groups, carefully selected, should be appointed to assist the director in finding and evaluating all the necessary facts. These groups will include members from the departments affected by proposed changes, personnel from the systems and procedures and the methods departments, and possibly specialists from a management consultant firm.

4. *Establish target dates.* IDP programs have a tendency to bog down or to extend over long periods unless they are controlled and adherence to a definite schedule is maintained. Target dates for completion of work should be established for each major element in the program. Activities such as finding the facts, charting present procedures, analyzing current procedures, and determining recommendations seem to go on and on unless specific dates for their completion are established and enforced.

5. *Gather and analyze pertinent information.* Many details are required, and suitable forms should be used for securing them in order to expedite identification, comparison, and evaluation.[1] To all participating members must be supplied proper instruction, so that they observe and understand what information to obtain and how to record it. The analysis should seek to disclose the major advantages and the disadvantages of the present manner of performing the work.

6. *Make recommendation and install.* As study and analysis proceed, possibilities for improvement are disclosed and verified. Substantiation of all gains should be made. Decisions must be made regarding what office machines are to be used and what arrangement of the information on the

---

[1] Discussion of such forms is included under Chapters 23 and 24.

paper forms will be followed. Finally, the proposal of what to do and why is presented to all interested management members, followed by a discussion to modify the proposal if necessary, but primarily to secure full agreement and approval. As soon as practical thereafter, the installation of the program should commence.

In applying the above steps, certain guides are helpful. These include the following: (1) Permit no restricted areas; instead, make the program comprehensive and truly integrated; (2) code first-hand material as much as possible in order to reduce future looking-up time; (3) use an adequate number of control totals between transmissions of data to insure accuracy; and (4) relate data from various sources and for various purposes to the greatest possible extent.

ILLUSTRATIONS OF IDP

Large department stores have the problem of inventory control so that the proper quantity and quality of each item are on hand in order to maximize sales and gross margins. To help solve this problem economically, IDP is being used. At the time a customer transaction is originally entered into a National Cash Register, a perforated tape recording is made. The recording shows whether cash or credit sale; salesperson's number; customer's number; description of merchandise, including material, size, style, and retail price; and the vendor's number. A prepunched price ticket—actually a small card about 2½ inches wide and 1 inch long— inserted in a unit called a Media Reader automatically starts the tape recorder and produces a detailed record of the item sold. Complete information on inventory control, by units, is thus accurately and economically provided. Figure 7–5 illustrates the machine, tape, and price ticket used for this purpose.

Another example that is simple but very effective in processing work is the use of a multi-entry, flexible-unit combination called Cardatype for

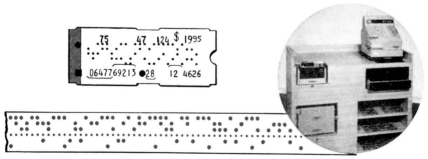

Courtesy: National Cash Register Co., Dayton

FIG. 7–5. Machine, perforated tape, and price ticket used for effective unit inventory control by large retail outlets.

Courtesy: International Business Machines Corp., New York

FIG. 7–6. Basic machine units for a Cardatype installation.

many applications of recording and accounting. The basic machine units include a typewriter, an auxiliary keyboard unit, and a card-feeding and -reading control console. These are illustrated in Figure 7–6.

Consider a manufacturer with a large number of customers. A punched card is prepared in advance for each customer, showing name and address. Also, a separate card is prepared for each item sold, providing information such as the item's description, weight, and price. These are kept in a reservoir file convenient to the operator. Upon receipt of a purchase order, the customer's name card and the cards for each of the items ordered are pulled from the file and fed into the feeding and reading control console, which actuates the typewriter, causing information on the cards to be typed on the paper forms. Semipermanent information, such as preliminary digits of a serial number or the date, is handled by means of the auxiliary keyboard unit, while variable or individualized information is manually typed on the paper forms by means of the typewriter. If it is desired, simultaneously with the writing of the forms, a punched card or a perforated tape can be produced for subsequent processing of the information in a different format for different purposes. Figure 7–7 shows examples of billing performed by this system. Note that the invoice, invoice register, stock selection tickets, and shipping tags are produced. Only the information encircled was inserted by manual key strokes; the rest, or over 95 per cent of the work, is automatic—obtained by automating the source data. Several typewriters can be used, if necessary. The console unit performs all computations, such

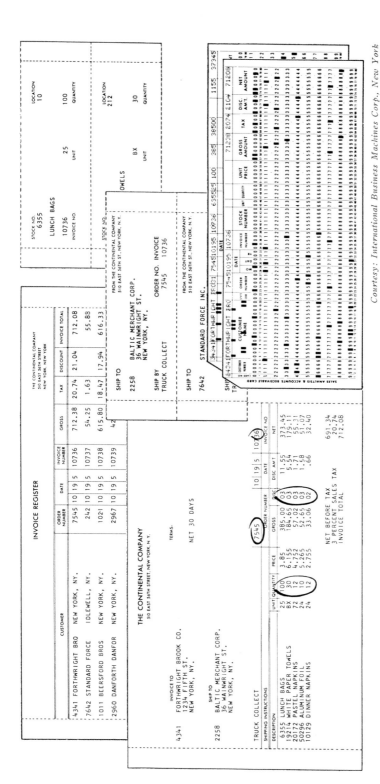

FIG. 7-7. Different papers pertaining to billing filled out simultaneously by Cardatype installation. Only the encircled portions were written by manually operating the typewriter.

Courtesy: International Business Machines Corp., New York

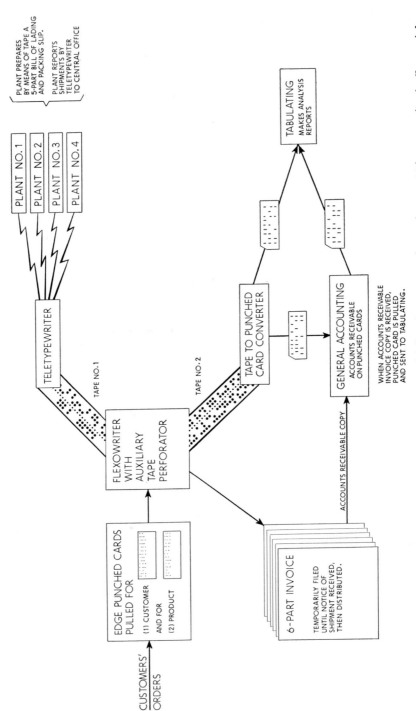

FIG. 7–8. Integrated data processing of order entry, shipping, and billing by a national manufacturer with a centralized office and four widely separated plants.

as tax, discount, and net amount. While the unit is handling one invoice, the operator refiles the cards from the previous invoice, so that they are ready for reuse as needed.

Figure 7–8 illustrates an interesting application of IDP for a national manufacturer having four widely separated plants. All production scheduling, stock control, receiving and billing of customers' orders, releases to manufacture, and routing of shipments are made from the centralized office located in a large city, different from that of any of the plants. All customers' orders sent direct to one of the plants by customers are immediately forwarded to the central office. Referring to Figure 7–8, and beginning at the left, the sequence is as follows. Customers' orders are received; edge-punched cards are pulled for customer name and for products ordered, and are sent to the Flexowriter with auxiliary tape perforator. Insertion of the edge-punched cards into the Flexowriter reader causes a six-part invoice to be typed automatically and two perforated tapes of the transaction. Tape No. 1 is sent to a teletypewriter, which using the tape, transmits the order, by means of electrical energy, to the proper plant. The tape made at the receiving unit of the plant is used to write a five-part bill of lading and packing slip. Tape No. 2 from the Flexowriter is used in a tape-to-punched card converter. Two sets of punched cards are prepared, one set being used by general accounting accounts receivable, the other set for statistical analysis purposes and tabulated open orders file. Plant shipments are teletyped daily to the central office. Upon notice of shipment, the invoice copies are distributed, the accounts receivable copy being sent to general accounting, upon receipt of which the punched card of the transaction in their possession is pulled and sent to tabulating, where costs and other reports are prepared.

THE COMPUTER AND IDP

As stated in the beginning of this chapter, a computer or data-processing system integrates the processing of data, but the identification of IDP is not normally applied to a computer installation. In many instances, the computer makes up the entire data processing within itself. However, this circumstance is being modified by developments in the transmission of data over considerable distances, whereby widely dispersed machine units are connected or tied with a computer in a central location. When any of the dispersed machines mechanizes the source data which are utilized by the computer serving as the central processing unit, or vice versa, the element of joining machines together for integrating the data processing can be viewed as qualifying more as an IDP installation than a computer installation. The difference, however, is more of degree than of kind.

A centralized accounting operation necessitates that information be consolidated from source data received from widespread locations. This

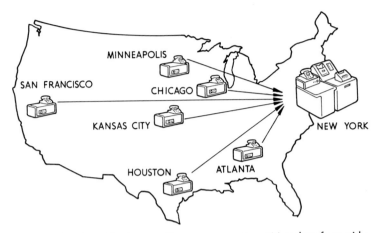

FIG. 7–9. Centralized accounting arrangement requiring data from wide-spread locations.

arrangement is shown by Figure 7–9. Data can be sent to the computer headquarters by mail, messenger service, telegraph, or telephone. For any of these communication means, the data can be sent in computer language, but telegraph or telephone provides much faster service. Tele-

Courtesy: Illinois Bell Telephone Co., Chicago

FIG. 7–10. The units to the left constitute Data-Phone. To the right, punched cards are being prepared.

graph has been used extensively, but developments now tie the ordinary telephone to a computer and provide multiple and direct access to it. The development making this possible is called Data-Phone; the machine utilized is illustrated by Figure 7–10.

Regular telephone lines comprising a nationwide network are used, and there are no intermediate steps. To utilize the Data-Phone, a customer picks up the telephone and dials the service number. A dial tone signals connection, after which he inserts an identification card into the device attached to the telephone, which identification is required by the computer and confirms the customer's right to order. Then, the data, in the language of the computer—punched cards, perforated tape, or magnetic tape—are fed into the device; and these data are transmitted at speeds up to 1,600 words a minute directly into the computer. Machines talk to one another, cross-town or cross-country. Payment for each Data-Phone call is made just like a telephone call and at the same rate. Its potential is believed to be so great that in the not too distant future, conversations between machines over regular telephone lines may equal the volume of voice communications.

CONCLUSIONS ON OFFICE AUTOMATION

At the risk of some repetition, several fundamentals of office automation from the managerial viewpoint will be cited in concluding this section of the book. Whether it is the use of an electronic system, integrated data processing, or any combination of the two, it is essential to keep in mind what is to be accomplished—what the real need of the enterprise is. This is fundamental. The better approach might be to analyze and know the needs thoroughly, then get the machines that will best do the required work. On the other hand, knowing the machines and what can be done with them can prove a satisfactory approach. With machine knowledge as a background, it might be possible to adjust the procedures, and the form and type of records determined as essential, to fit what the machine can perform most economically. However, in either event, the real need of the enterprise in terms of its paper work requirements should receive top priority.

Office automation stimulates thinking of office work as a whole, not just a component of it. All the papers and records should be considered, not simply the payroll records, or the inventory statistics, or the order-handling procedure. Automation is geared to volume. There should be a sufficient quantity of work—frequently, this means grouping the components and performing the work for all. Elimination of waste and duplication is more easily attained when the entire office work picture is taken. Furthermore, office automation cuts across divisional lines—divisional in the sense of organizational structure, problems, and vested interests.

The benefits of office automation are numerous; yet problems are entailed, and greater emphasis is placed on sound, competent office management. To adopt successful office automation requires comprehension, much thought, and study. Difficult decisions must be made. Deeply intrenched habits and beliefs may have to be dispelled. The design of office papers may require revision, the retraining of office personnel may be needed, and an extensive educational job conducted with nonoffice personnel and customers. A committee with a member of each participating function represented can prove helpful as an educational means, for the collection of facts and exchange of ideas, and in the eventual steps of installing the new and better way of doing office work. But efforts of people working on problems of automation must be properly co-ordinated. Many will participate on an advisory basis only, but others will be expected to make decisions and put them into action. Specific authority and responsibility for determining the extent and kind of office automation should be carefully spelled out. In each case, there should be an executive who is the active and recognized head of automation efforts. This helps provide leadership, co-ordination, and an enthusiastic, purposeful managerial effort. Office automation is an area in which a manager *must* manage.

QUESTIONS

1. What is your definition of integrated data processing; and in general, what purpose does it serve in office management?
2. As you see it, what is the distinguishing feature of IDP, and how does this differ from so-called "conventional" approaches in the processing of data?
3. Identify clearly each of the following:
   a) Common language link.
   b) Cardatype.
   c) Edge-punched card.
   d) Flexowriter.
4. Are machines, special or conventional, required for IDP to exist in the normal and widely accepted usage of integrated data processing? Defend your answer.
5. Name and discuss each of the common language media used in integrated data processing.
6. Discuss the subject area of "The Computer and IDP," from the viewpoint of office management.
7. In your own words, describe the meaning of Figure 7–5.
8. Discuss the importance of providing target dates in the establishing of integrated data processing by an enterprise.
9. What is Data-Phone, and how is it used in connection with IDP?
10. Discuss the possibilities and a manner of using IDP for any series of office tasks with which you are familiar, such as (*a*) processing the purchase orders by a bookstore and its sales to students; (*b*) maintaining students' records in a large university; (*c*) handling the requisitions, purchases, and inventory records of a manufacturer; or (*d*) any selection of office work you care to make. Indicate the process now followed and also the

suggested IDP way, and why you feel IDP would prove beneficial in the particular application.

11. Describe an IDP application for the work of billing in which application of the use of punched cards is employed to advantage. Make your answer specific and complete.

12. What significance do you attach to the statement that office automation stimulates thinking of office work as a whole, not in terms of components or segments of the entire job of processing and distributing data?

CASE PROBLEMS

Case 7–1.   Dixon Boat Company

A new distribution center is to be constructed in Atlanta, Georgia, to provide a large centralized stock of all parts for Dixon boats and engines within easy access of customers throughout the United States. Service to customers is to be given high priority; in fact, top managers of the company indicate that this is the controlling requirement. In total, there are 57 company-owned sales offices scattered around the country, and shipment of an order to any customer should be made within twenty-four hours of the receipt of the order at a sales office.

The distribution center will serve as a warehousing point for all parts presently distributed from the 57 sales offices. Because of its size, the center will carry in inventory a far greater number of items than any of these offices could afford to stock. Parts will be shipped to the center from three Dixon factories. All customer orders from the sales offices will be handled by the center; no customer orders will be handled directly by any of the three factories.

Study shows that there are approximately 40,000 different items; and of this number, about 12,000 are sold in relatively large volume. About 90 per cent of the total items will be carried in inventory, and it is believed that back ordering will not be a problem. Shipments will be made to between 15,000 and 18,000 customers. Remittances will be sent to the center. In co-operation with the center, each sales office will establish an account or identifying number for each of its customers to assist the center in its paper-handling work. Invoices will be sent out from the center.

It is believed improved control over inventory can also be accomplished by the operation of the center. The immediate invoicing should provide better control for the company and possibly encourage prompt payments by customers.

Problems:

1. Outline the means you recommend for handling the order entry–billing work by the company's new distribution center.
2. Draw a graphic representation of your proposed arrangement.
3. Discuss the strong points of your proposal.

Case 7–2.   Public Utility Suppliers, Inc.

This corporation, in business for over fifty years, manufactures and handles many different types of equipment and maintenance parts used primarily by public utility companies. About 40 per cent of the business is from products manufactured by the company; the remaining 60 per cent is jobbed and warehoused by the company for some eighteen small manufacturers. General offices are in New York City, but all shipments to customers are made from the corporation's seven warehouses dispersed throughout the United States. Quite a few of the products have a high dollar value and are expensive to handle and ship. Service is important, since usually the ordered items represent materials needed for emergency work.

The records of all sales transactions must be quite detailed. This requirement is brought about not only because the corporation wants to have complete information on its business but also because vendors to the corporation wish complete information concerning sales of their products. Also, the customers need complete data on their purchases to comply with government regulations concerning public utilities.

Currently, upon receipt of an order, it is typed on a five-page multiple copy form. Copy No. 1 is retained by the general office; copies No. 2, 3, and 4 are air-mailed to the warehouse nearest the customer's designated place of delivery; and copy No. 5 is mailed to the customer to acknowledge the order. The warehouse, upon shipment of the order, encloses copy No. 4 with the merchandise. Copy No. 2 is returned to the general office, and copy No. 3 is retained by the warehouse for its records. Upon receipt of copy No. 2 by the general office, it is matched with its copy No. 1, which is then completed regarding date of shipment, pricing, etc., and mailed to the customer. Copy No. 2 is retained by the general office for its records.

There is considerable writing required to designate the name of the customer to be billed and the items of each order. The work, as now performed, requires a skilled and experienced order writer who receives a weekly pay of $104. Present rate is seven orders written an hour. The average quantity is 382 orders a day. Study shows it takes about four days, on the average, from the time the order is received until it is shipped. There have been cases where copies No. 2, 3, and 4 were delayed in transit to the warehouse or were not sent to the nearest and proper warehouse.

The president of the company wants to mechanize the entire order-handling paper work and asks you for recommendations.

Problems:

1. What are your recommendations for this corporation?

2. Enumerate the important assumptions made in answering question No. 1.

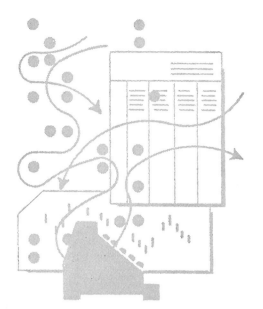

Part *3*

WORK OF INFORMATION HANDLING

The basic office tasks of writing, duplicating, calculating, comparing, mailing, telephoning, and filing are commonly referred to as office services. They deal with information handling, exist in every office, and are normally included in the work supervised by the office manager.

In each of the following six chapters, the application of the management process—planning, controlling, organizing, and actuating—is included, so that a practical conceptual pattern of management operation in these major areas is provided.

The order of the chapters is (1) correspondence and reports, (2) duplicating, (3) calculating and comparing, (4) mail and office communicative services, (5) storage—effective filing, and (6) storage—records retention.

Chapter 8

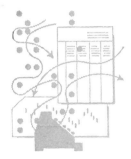

CORRESPONDENCE AND REPORTS

On the clarity of your ideas depends the scope of your success in any endeavor.

—JAMES ROBERTSON

IN EVERY enterprise, much of the writing work deals with correspondence and reports. The work of writing is a basic element of data processing; but in addition to putting the words and data on paper or some other medium, we are concerned here with what to put on the paper. A creative or thinking process is involved. Writing a letter or report begins with what should we tell the reader, how we should express our thoughts, and when the writing should take place.

THE CHALLENGE OF WRITING

One of the most powerful factors in the world is helpful ideas in the minds of energetic men of good will, presented to others in writing so that they can understand and use them. Clear thinking is a requisite of clear written communication. Most newly created thoughts and ideas are fuzzy and must be put in writing which is edited and rewritten before clarity is obtained. Skill in writing can be developed. It is not an ability with which some are blessed and which others can never hope to achieve. A strong will to do plus the application of basic practices underlying all forms of effective written communications are fundamental in getting messages across clearly, concisely, and simply.

Writing can be stimulating, and it is a powerful tool. It is the means of transferring information on paper; it can help win men's hearts to a stated cause; and it can implement effective action, both mental and physical, that otherwise would not take place. A person you have never seen will change his course of action, send an inquiry, or start a new program—as a result of a report or a letter. This should inject a pride of accomplishment in writing really good letters and reports, and inspire one to be satisfied with only the best.

But too often, the challenge is not even recognized, let alone mastered.

Much business writing fails to follow Shakespeare's "Speak plain and to the purpose." Consider this exchange of letters between a state highway department and another office.

Will you please forward two more certified copies? We can't send copies to the auditor's office so we must have at least two carbon copies which are certified. We have one carbon now, so we still need two certified copies, one of which must be a carbon. Also, if you send a copy, please send a certified copy rather than a copy of a certified copy. Thank you.

The reply:

I cannot send you two certified copies since it seems the only carbon copy was sent to you previously. Unless I have a carbon copy, I can't obtain a certified carbon copy and without a certified carbon copy, I cannot obtain a copy of a certified carbon copy; therefore, I will have to send two certified copies of carbon copies or have your carbon copy certified and get a copy of your certified carbon copy certified. Please return carbon copy.

This may be an extreme example, but various studies show that much of the written matter of American business is not understood by the recipient. The ideas are jumbled, statements are ambiguous, the sentence structure is poor, and the intended meaning is camouflaged. As a result, the value of the communication rendered to others is diminished, and the criteria of how well the job has been done are obscured.

IMPORTANCE OF LETTERS AND REPORTS

Most executives spend at least two hours a day reading and writing letters and reports. In some cases, they spend twice or three times that amount of time. Many are aware that they probably spend too much time and money in this activity, yet there seems to be a reluctance to let go of the old weighty methods holding them down.

Letters are one of the main carriers of the corporate image. Public relations can be developed tremendously by the use of effective letters. The good will of many companies is due directly or indirectly to their effective correspondence work. Many stories attest to the fact that a friendly, well-written letter paved the way for a million-dollar sale with a previously unknown party. Or what might have been a devasting blow to a company was avoided because the proper letter was sent to a certain party at a particular time. Obviously, such letters are important—worth every ounce of thought and imagination the writer can pour into them. But what about the other letters—the ordinary or supposedly unimportant ones? Individually, they may seem trivial, but their cumulative effect is great. Each one is an opportunity to make friends and influence others favorably toward your company. This gives them enormous potential.

Not only are letters powerful tools of managers, but reports are very important in managerial activity. The work of carrying out the functions of planning, controlling, organizing, and actuating is greatly aided by reports. For example, the work of planning requires information on what must be accomplished, and within what time periods. Reports help to supply this needed information or to suggest possible avenues of approach which might reveal potent information.

As an enterprise grows, various levels of management develop, and many management members find they cannot keep in personal touch with all phases of the enterprise. As a result, reports are used to keep executives informed, to develop favorable interdepartmental relationships, and to help get the work accomplished through the work force.

CLASSIFICATION OF LETTERS AND REPORTS

Efforts to classify letters and reports into major types help to identify them and to designate the main purpose of each communication. Such information can be helpful in managing this area of office services.

A study of the correspondence in any enterprise will reveal that most letters can be classified into those dealing with complaints, employment, purchasing, sales, or credit. In turn, letters in each of these major groups can be classified further according to individual type. To illustrate, under:

Complaints—replies are usually of four types:

1. Acknowledgment of complaint and promise to investigate and report later.
2. Adjustment of complaint, giving date and amount, and thanking addressee.
3. Refusal to adjust complaint, with reasons explaining why.
4. Request that the goods be returned for inspection and advice that further consideration will be given.

Employment—three types of replies are generally given:

1. Acknowledgment of application, stating that there is no opening at present.
2. Acknowledgment of application and request to report for work.
3. Welcome to newly hired worker of the company and explanation of company policies.

Purchasing—three kinds of letters are common:

1. Request for prices and delivery dates.
2. Request to trace shipment.
3. Inquiry about disposition of order.

Reports can be classified into many different types, including private, public, company, departmental, restricted, nonrestricted, technical, and nontechnical. However, for purposes of office usage, the three groups of executive, periodic, and special are quite satisfactory. Under each of these classifications are the following:

Executive reports—include:

1. Balance sheet.
2. Statement of cost of goods sold.
3. Statement of profit and loss.
4. Budgetary statement.
5. Annual departmental report.
6. Report to stockholders.

Executive reports stress broad concepts and results rather than details, usually covering a three-, six-, or twelve-month time period. For the most part, they are prepared for members of top and intermediate management levels.

Periodic reports—deal mainly with departmental activities, including:

1. Monthly reports on operation.
2. Departmental records of performance.
3. Monthly credit reports.
4. Purchasing reports.
5. Material-handling reports.
6. Salesmen's reports.
7. Advertising and sales promotion reports.
8. Personnel management reports.

Periodic reports typically cover weekly, monthly, or quarterly periods. Usually, they contain some detailed information which is pertinent to the operation of the particular department. A printed form is commonly used to assist in obtaining the needed data for a periodic report.

Special reports—concern subjects of:

1. Product development.
2. Marketing research.
3. Plant location.
4. Company insurance and pension revisions.
5. Various projects of a nonrecurring nature.

Activities covered by special reports are those activities not covered by other reports. Special reports are published at infrequent intervals. A portion of a special report dealing with the findings of a market research study is shown by Figure 8–1.

35–E   X Research Company   N 58

SUMMARY OF FINDINGS

OBJECTIVE:

To obtain a measure of consumer acceptance of Product Y.

RESULTS:

1. Product Y is not as well liked as Product No. 17.
2. The market potential of Product Y is somewhat between 50% and 80% of the market for Product No. 17. These are the limits indicated by consumers' stated preferences and test-package consumption.
3. The preference for Product No. 17 over Product Y prevails in all geographical areas and among all types of consumers. The greatest liking for Product Y was found among women.
4. Product No. 17 is preferred chiefly because it is crisp, easy to eat, and has a sweet, mild flavor.
5. Product Y is preferred by those who like a harder and heavier cereal than Product No. 17. Most cold cereal users, however, thought Product Y too hard to chew.
6. While food value is not a dominant factor in consumers' preferences between cereals, Product Y was the choice of consumers who emphasize this point.

CONCLUSION:

There is a limited market for an expanded cereal that is harder and heavier than Product No. 17. The potential volume of one such cereal— Product Y—is between 50% and 80% of the Product No. 17 market.

FIG. 8–1. A portion of a special report.

SUGGESTED WRITING PRACTICES FOR BUSINESS

A long list of suggested writing practices could be reviewed here; but in view of the purpose of this book, only the more important points will be discussed. These include the following:

1. *Make the writing serve a known and definite purpose.* In the case of letters, for example, know exactly what is to be accomplished by the letter. Do not confuse the issue; settle on one main point and concentrate on it. Letters pertaining to a single subject are easy to understand, and they expedite filing.

Every business report should be tied to and used as a reference point, a specific portion of the company's plans. Reports are written to help keep the recipient informed and, in many instances, to help determine what action to take. For the former purpose, there are far too many reports that simply give "a recital of past activities." As such, they possess relatively little value as managerial reports. If actions are proceeding according to plan, this is all the recipient needs to know in order to be informed. If they are not proceeding according to plan, he needs to know where and when, so that he can take the proper remedial action. But much effort is wasted in writing reports that relate, in minute detail, quantities of material that in the end boils down to "progress to date is satisfactory, in keeping with our plans." And it is essential that the aim of the letter or the report be known to the person preparing it because this knowledge guides the writer and helps him point the communication toward its intended uses.

2. *Keep the recipient in mind.*   The aim of a letter or of a report stands a much better chance of accomplishment if its text is understood. To expedite this understanding, the needs, wants, and interests of the recipient should be given prime consideration. The reader is put in the center of what is written. Look at the subject from his viewpoint; visualize the reader while writing, and tailor the material and expressions to him.

In letter writing, for example, the technique of the "you viewpoint" can be followed. To illustrate:

Write:

"You may have quick service if you'll just telephone ORchard 1–7777."

Do not write:

"We wish to call attention to the fact that we are in the dry-cleaning business and have a fifteen-year record of excellent service."

Or write:

"Thanks for your letter of May 14. Your order will be shipped today by parcel post."

Do not write:

"We have received order dated the tenth and in reply we wish to state delivery is being made today under separate cover."

It is helpful to bring associated considerations to the receiver's mind, so that he can compare what is in the letter or report with what he knows. This, in turn, greatly increases his interest in and comprehension of the material. For the most part, a reader acquires from a written business communication only such knowledge as he brings to it. That is, a person who has broad training and an extensive background in a particular subject will acquire more from a report in that subject than the individual who does not possess such training and background.

3. *Be factual and unbiased.*   Accuracy is essential to good writing regardless of the scope, subject, medium, or level for which it is in-

tended. The facts should be relevant to the subject; opinions should be identified as such. Irrelevant details should be excluded. What is basic to the stated purpose should be included. Information which is incomplete and not essential to the purpose should be avoided.

The motive and the ideas should be presented without bias. The objective viewpoint should be stressed. Fundamentally, the writing is being done to inform the reader of the situation or subject as it is. A letter or a report can be colorful, yet not filled with emotional statements. Remember that the content and the words should be tools of straight thinking, not stumbling blocks.

4. *Use simple words and short sentences.* Word choice is vital; simple words are bold and clear, and usually convey the intended meaning. Some writers never use a simple word if they know a big one of similar meaning, and such practice weakens a letter or a report. Employing words in common usage is a good rule to follow. Benjamin Franklin said: "Never use big words when little words will do." This is well illustrated by a story. When still a lad, Benjamin Franklin told his mother: "I have imbibed an acephalous mollusk." His mother, believing young Franklin had swallowed something poisonous, forced him to take a large dosage of medicine to induce vomiting. When he got over the effects of the medicine, he explained to his mother: "I have eaten nothing but an oyster." Whereupon his mother thrashed him for deceiving her. Franklin vowed never again to use big words when little words would do.

Clear sentences are one of the most helpful ingredients of clear reports. Although variety in sentence length is desirable, short sentences are normally preferred. Some say that no sentence should be longer than twenty-five words. However, it should be long enough to convey the thought. A practical suggestion is to fit the sentence to the reader's span of attention. Omit involved phrases, and weed out the extra words. Tabulate lists for greater clarity. Unity, coherence, and correct sentence structure are more readily achieved in short than in long, complex sentences. Correct punctuation also helps.

5. *Establish an acceptable mood.* All business writing should be in a tone that wins co-operation or puts the reader in a mood to read the communication and give adequate thought and consideration to it. Positive expressions help to accomplish this goal. Greater acceptance and motivation are gained by writing in an optimistic tone. For example, in a letter, write: "We can send you tickets for the November 27 performance," instead of "We cannot send tickets for any performance prior to that of November 27."

Being friendly is also helpful in establishing an acceptable mood. Let your writing reflect your own natural self. Letters and reports are written to human beings, not merely to names. Write naturally and humanly. Stilted, highly formalized statements are taboo. Avoid the use of so-called "whisker" expressions and dead diction. Examples of whisker expressions in letter writing, along with suggested improvements, are:

Do not use	*Use*
I am not in a position	I cannot
My attention has been called	I notice
Enclosed please find	We enclose
Has come to hand	Referred to me
Acquaint me with the facts	Tell me
Under separate cover	Separately
Contents duly noted	I have read
At this time	At present
We have reviewed our records	We find
It is our opinion	I believe
At all times	Always
Take pleasure	Are pleased
We have yours of the 10th	Your letter of November 10
Your esteemed favor of the 6th and its enclosures	The papers you sent

The top of Figure 8–2 illustrates a letter written in a stilted manner and using whisker expressions; an improvement is shown in the bottom portion of this figure.

6. *Make the writing clear.* This requires knowing what must be included and in what sequence it should be presented. The writer should express each thought so clearly that the reader is certain to understand it. Normally, the transcriber helps in acquiring clarity by straightening out improper sentence structure and switching words. It is well to have a competent person edit a report to insure that the meaning is clear.

Have your writing say exactly what you intend it to say, and mean what the writing says. These eight words form the basis of all great writing: "Write so that you cannot possibly be misunderstood."

7. *Interpret findings adequately.* Care must be exercised to avoid exaggeration or the inclusion of unqualified interpretations which cannot be reasonably derived from the available information. It is usually best to understate rather than to overstate conclusions. Also, recommendations must be practical and sound.

8. *Summarize briefly.* Normally, it is best to state the results in a summary statement. Convey the essentials to the reader easily; under no circumstances should the receiver be required to dig through quantities of words and figures to find out what the writing discloses or is all about.

9. *Make the writing conclusive.* Be certain to include what action, if any, is desired of the reader, what the writer will do, or what the writer wants done. Be decisive; let the reader know exactly the recommended course or disposition. Presumably, the writer is or has become thoroughly familiar with the information he has worked with, and his

recommendations have value. This does not mean necessarily that the recommendations will be followed, but they provide a springboard for action.

March 15, 19--

Dear Sir:

    Your letter addressed to our Chicago plant has been referred to the undersigned for reply. We wish to advise that it is our long standing policy to limit our sales promotion efforts to ideas originating with our advertising agencies. Therefore, we cannot accept your suggestion.

    Enclosed herewith is your letter and under separate cover your display unit is being returned.

    Needless to say, we want to extend our thanks to you for your interest in our products and their sales.

Very truly yours,

March 15, 19--

Dear Mr. Hayes:

    Thanks for your suggestion concerning the display unit for our products.

    Our executive committee has decided not to change the current means of display. This was decided in view of our present sales and the costs for changing our sales program at this time. There are also some legal difficulties to which the use of this display unit might expose both you and ourselves. We would want to clarify these legal points before considering your suggestion for future action.

    We will keep you informed of developments.

Very truly yours,

FIG. 8–2. *Top:* A letter written in a stilted manner. *Bottom:* An improvement over the letter above.

In presenting a single proposed action, do not hedge. Avoid double meanings. Long, qualified explanations usually offer little help. Strive to set forth the recommendations so clearly and cleanly that they will be followed.

PROCEDURE FOR HANDLING WRITING WORK

A definite procedure is required to handle the work of writing effectively; it cannot be left to chance. Relying upon haphazard methods or hoping that the work will be accomplished promptly is wishful thinking. A way of getting the writing accomplished effectively and economically must be established and followed. The following is suggested:

1. *In the case of correspondence, get letters to those who answer them.* Letters on ordinary and routine subjects can be quickly routed to the proper party for reply. In contrast, letters dealing with out-of-the-ordinary subjects frequently offer some difficulty. The eternal question in such cases is: "Who handles matters of this sort?" Frequently, these letters are addressed to the wrong person within the enterprise and must be rerouted. The task of getting letters to the proper persons for answering is usually the responsibility of the head of the mailing department or the office manager.

For reports, the subject area to be covered, time for completion of report, and designation of the writer are basic decisions to be made. In many cases, established policies regarding report writing guide the initial planning steps of report preparation.

2. *Get facts to the correspondent.* In order to write meaningfully, it is necessary for the writer to have all the facts. To write a sales letter, for example, one must have information on what the product will do, its good points, its price, and the like. Likewise, to compose a report requires access to pertinent information and some knowledge of the facts in the particular subject area.

When filed material is required in order to write a letter, it is secured by the writer in one of several ways. The incoming letter may be (1) routed by the mail room to the filing department, which attaches the filed material to the letter and then forwards both to the writer; or (2) sent directly to the writer, who decides if he needs the file covering previous correspondence and, if so, requests it from the filing department. In some cases, both the writer and the file are located in the same area, so that the writer can himself secure any filed material he needs.

3. *Permit correspondent to analyze facts and to organize the writing.* To a considerable degree, every written business communication is an effort to have the recipient believe and act toward a subject as the writer does. Hence, the writer should try to visualize the type of reader to whom he is writing and select an approach that will invoke the reader's response to action. Sometimes, this necessitates guessing or taking a chance. The opening statement in letters, for example, should be designed to get the reader's attention. Following this, the reader's interest should be developed. Then, lead this interest into a desire and finally culminate the en-

tire letter with action—to order the service, to accept the adjustment, to pay the bill, or whatever the case might be. For reports, a simple statement of what the report is about, what it shows, and how the information should be used are of major interest.[1]

4. *Provide correspondent with a stenographer or a dictating machine when ready to dictate.* The assignment of stenographic help to a writer is done by the stenographic supervisor or by the office manager. When the writing is correspondence, the stenographer should report to the correspondent at stated times throughout the day; this permits better organization and execution of work on the part of both the stenographer and the correspondent. In actual practice, however, the task of regulating stenographic work is not so simple. Most offices have a certain amount of irregular correspondence which is best handled by adapting it to a schedule setting definite hours when emergency dictation can be handled. This helps accomplish all the work with a minimum of confusion. On the other hand, emergency work can be sandwiched in with the regular work. However, when this is done, allowance must be made in the regular schedules.

Many report writers prefer to write out the material in longhand before having it typed. Others put most of their material directly on the machine. The type of material, difficulty of composing, and the amount of statistical tables help determine which procedure to follow.

5. *Get material typed.* The final step is the actual physical work of typing the material, and this is by no means a small job. When completed, the material is sent to the correspondent, who reads, checks, and, in the case of correspondence, signs the letters. Subsequently, the material is prepared for mailing or distributing.

TYPEWRITERS

Machine selection is a part of planning. In the work of correspondence and report writing, the typewriter is the basic office machine, is widely used, and speeds the handling of all written work. A convenient classification of office typewriters is (1) standard and (2) electric.

The standard typewriter is actuated by hand or human energy, i.e., by the depression of a key. While typing, the carriage is moved to the left by action of a spring. In contrast, the electric typewriter is motivated mainly by electricity. Manual energy is still used to touch the keys, but the energy input is about one fifth of that required for manual machines. Work done on an electric typewriter is of uniform type impression, and a greater number of copies can be obtained without any increase in manual energy.

Most typewriters on the market today are excellent machines and have

---

[1] The designing of letters and reports is discussed in Chapter 15.

many common features which are recognized as standard equipment. Most are equipped with the "set" and "clear" tabulators, either of a single- or decimal-key type. Tabulators are very helpful for the rapid movement and alignment of the carriage which is required in reports and other written work that have frequent indentations. Typewriter platens are available in different degrees of hardness. A soft platen should be used where the number of copies are few and quietness is desired. Conversely, a hard platen is recommended when a large number of copies is required. It causes more noise, however, than does the soft platen.

Various type styles are also available. Whatever the job, there is a type face designed to handle it. The styles vary somewhat among manufacturers. Most typewriters are equipped with a standard keyboard. Special keyboards or parts of keyboards, such as engineering, mathematical, chemical, or foreign language signs and marks, are available at an additional cost.

AUTOMATIC TYPING MACHINES

The automatic typing machine has won wide adoption for the typing of similar letters when they are in (1) large quantities and (2) similar format having slight changes only, such as name and address and dates. It consists of a regular typewriter to which a special mechanism has been attached. The paper is inserted in the machine in the same manner as in a regular typewriter; and the date, name, and address are typed in by hand. At the touch of a button, the machine takes over and automatically types the letter, stopping at the first place where a special fill-in is required. This is typed in by hand, and then, after another touch of the button, the machine continues typing the letter to the next stop. Figure 8–3 shows a letter typed in this manner. All paragraphing, spacing, and the like are handled by the machine. If possible, the location of each fill-in should be at the end of a line or paragraph, to provide the required elasticity in space. Words or numbers of varying lengths can be inserted without difficulty. The entire letter has been typed automatically by machine, with the exception of the individualized parts as noted on the illustration.

As many as 200 short letters a day can be typed with this machine. Multiple combinations of machines requiring one operator can produce approximately 500 short letters a day. Such a battery is a mass producer, flexible and efficient. For most applications, an operator can employ a battery of four automatic typing machines.

Form letters or paragraphs are originally cut on either (1) a record roll or (2) a tape.[2] This perforating work is done in the individual office or at the local service office. The record roll, resembling that used on a

---

[2] Form letters and paragraphs are discussed in Chapter 15.

player piano, is mounted in the machine and, when released, passes over a trucker bar in which a vacuum is maintained. Any opening in the roll causes a change in pressure, which actuates the type, thus causing the machine to write. The capacities and details of operation vary with the machine and the manufacturer.

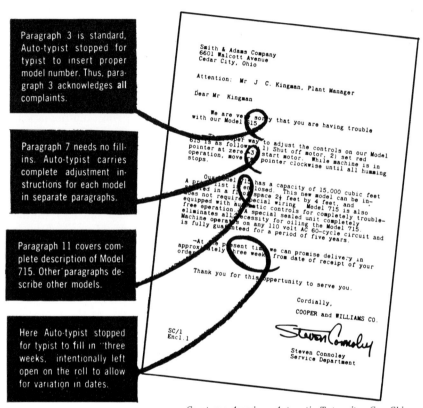

Courtesy: American Automatic Typewriter Co., Chicago

FIG. 8–3. A letter typed by an automatic typewriter. Paragraph selection and individual fill-in material are easily handled as described in the illustration.

About twenty different letters or an equivalent of form paragraphs can be placed on one record roll. The operator selects the material to be machine-typed by means of simple controls. In one method, a series of push buttons is used to make the operation entirely automatic. See Figure 8–4. In another, the operator inserts a coded and punched card indicating the desired material into a selecting device and presses the "start" button. The desired material, in the proper sequence, is typed automatically. It is possible to switch from one letter to another or from one paragraph to another simply by turning a dial to the identifying number of the material to be typed.

Courtesy: American Automatic Typewriter Co., Chicago

FIG. 8–4. An automatic typewriter featuring push-button controls.

Courtesy: Commercial Controls Corp., Rochester, N.Y.

FIG. 8–5. An automatic writing machine that is actuated by a punched tape.

When a perforated tape is used, the operation of the automatic typewriter is quite similar to that described above. Such a typewriter unit is illustrated in Figure 8–5. The holes in the tape cause the mechanism to operate specific typewriter keys which result in the desired letter. Perforated tape is being used more and more to operate office machines automatically. Its growth has been stimulated by the application of integrated data processing (IDP), which was discussed in Chapter 7.

PRODUCING LETTERS BY DUPLICATION PROCESS

To produce a substantial quantity of written material exactly alike, any one of several duplicating means described in Chapter 9 is satisfactory. Duplicating is fast and economical. It is used for both letters and reports. When used for letters, the name and address are omitted, and simply "Dear Sir" is put on each letterhead, with the name and address on the envelope only. As an alternative, the name and address can be typed carefully on the letter, but it will not match precisely the dupli-

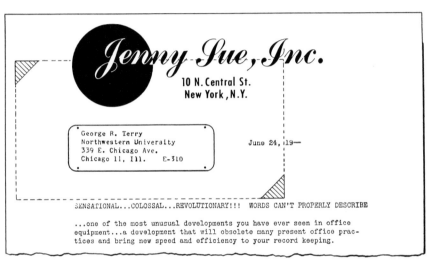

Jenny Sue, Inc.

10 N. Central St.
New York, N.Y.

George R. Terry
Northwestern University   June 24, 19—
339 E. Chicago Ave.
Chicago 11, Ill.   E-310

SENSATIONAL...COLOSSAL...REVOLUTIONARY!!! WORDS CAN'T PROPERLY DESCRIBE

...one of the most unusual developments you have ever seen in office equipment...a development that will obsolete many present office practices and bring new speed and efficiency to your record keeping.

FIG. 8–6. A "window letter" which features the use of a preaddressed card to individualize a form letter. The card, also used as a business reply card, is held in place either by a pocket in the back or by slots into which opposite card corners are inserted (as illustrated). The name and address appear through a window opening in the letter. The mailing can also utilize window envelopes.

cated part of the letter. However, with typing skill and experience, satisfactory results are possible.

Another possibility for volume mailings is to use a "window letter." A preaddressed card is attached to the back and top of the duplicated letter, so that the name and address appear at the normal location and can be read through a window opening in the letterhead. The card also serves as a business reply card with necessary postage and name and address of the sender on the reverse side. This arrangement is illustrated in Figure 8–6.

For correspondence, a machine is available that will write a complete letter from blank paper in one run—individual name and address, salutation, letterhead in color, date, text, and facsimile ink signature—all with one operator. Since the same basic process is used at the same time, the name and address are perfectly matched with the text of the letter. In addition, the machine will print and personally identify a reply card. Sheets of paper are fed automatically to the machine, which progressively prints name, address, salutation, letterhead, date, body of letter, closing, and signature. The machine speed is one hundred complete letters per minute.

PERSONAL OR MACHINE BASIS

Dictating machines are also used in letter and report writing; but before discussing them, it should be pointed out that either a personal or a machine basis can be followed, and it is only when the machine basis is followed that dictating machines are used. Under the personal basis, the dictator talks to a stenographer, who manually takes down the statements in shorthand. Later, these notes are transcribed. When a machine is used, the dictation is recorded and subsequently played back to the transcriber, who types the letter.

The choice between the personal and the machine bases rests upon the relative evaluation of the advantages of each in each particular case. No standarized formula can be applied, and the comparison cannot be made wholly on factual data—certain indeterminate subjective factors enter into most decisions covering this subject.

Advocates of the personal basis are quick to point out that a feeling of close co-operation, better understanding of the type of letter to be written, and consideration for the important human element are induced when letters are dictated to a stenographer. Second, the personal basis permits the transcriber to work from written notes, which are usually easier to comprehend than audible data. Third, shorthand is not difficult to learn, and satisfactory speeds suitable for most office work are attainable by most employees. Fourth, dictation is possible anywhere. A special machine need not be available. Fifth, the cost of a machine is avoided, as well as the costs of operation, special supplies, and maintenance.

It is possible for the transcriber to use a machine for recording dictation. The notes are printed in letters on a tape in accordance with a special code. The machine looks like a small typewriter and requires special training for proficient operation.

The important advantages of the machine basis include the following: First, dictation is expedited—material can be dictated when it is on the dictator's mind. His thoughts can be recorded as they occur to him. Second, the distribution of work among transcribers can be balanced. Steady and even work throughout the day frequently minimizes the number of transcribers needed. Third, the transcriber's time is saved, since her presence is not required while the dictation is being recorded. Fourth, convenience is provided. The dictator can work independently;

he can dictate at his convenience; he need not wait for his stenographer. Fifth, the dictator is alone; thus, concentration and clearer and better thinking are encouraged.

DICTATING MACHINES

When the machine basis is used, a selection is offered from modern machines employing electronics to provide clear, high-fidelity recording of the human voice. A recorder unit is used by the dictator, and a transcriber unit is used by the typist to play back the recorded dictation; or a combination unit featuring both recording and transcribing can be used. The latter is practical when the dictator and transcriber can plan their day for separate periods of dictation and transcription.

The recorder is equipped with either (1) hand microphone, recommended for ordinary dictating practices or when the surroundings are somewhat noisy; or (2) desk microphone, for recording over-the-desk conference discussions or important telephone conversations, assuming the consent of both parties has been obtained. Furthermore, when the recorder is equipped with a foot-control device, the desk microphone permits free use of both hands during correspondence dictation. It is possible to start and stop the recorder as desired and to listen to what has been dictated. A signaling device is also provided whereby the amount of dictation and places of correction can be indicated.

Transcribers are equipped with special features which assist the typist, including special headphones; foot or hand controls for starting and stopping the machine; backspacer for repeating dictation; voice-control adjustments to regulate speed, volume, and tone; and a signaling device to inform the transcriber of length of dictation and places of correction.

Dictating machines can be classified according to the type of medium used, including (1) plastic belt, (2) plastic disk, and (3) wax cylinder.

PLASTIC BELT

In this type, the recording medium is an endless belt of thin, tough plastic, 3½ inches wide and 12 inches in circumference. This belt withstands rough handling, provides constant recording qualities, and permits uniform backspacing for convenient and accurate corrections. Every recorded groove on the belt is the same length and of the same recording quality. One belt will accommodate about 15 minutes of dictation and serves as a permanent, one-time recording medium. As many as five belts, nested one within the other, will fit into a small business envelope and can be mailed for about 4 cents.

The machine is a recorder-transcriber, sturdy and compact; it weighs only 20 pounds and covers a desk area slightly larger than a standard business letterhead. The units may be used in the office or, in the case of

Courtesy: Dictaphone Corp., New York

FIG. 8–7.   Close-up of the recorder-transcriber "Time-Master," which records on a small, flexible plastic belt.

the portable model, are especially convenient for traveling representatives who send communications to the home office. A close-up view of the machine, with the plastic belt partially removed, is shown in Figure 8–7.

PLASTIC DISK

As the name implies, the plastic disk method of voice recording employs a thin disk of plastic material. The disk can be used once, then thrown away or filed for future reference. One hundred disks are approximately 1 inch in thickness; and three sizes are available—3, 5, and 7 inches in diameter, respectively—for 4, 15, and 30 minutes of recording. The disks are light, tough, and unbreakable, which makes it possible to send them conveniently through the mail. They can thus be used to improve the communication between salesmen and the office, executives and their associates, and the main office and its branches.

WAX CYLINDER

This is one of the oldest means of recording and transcribing used in the office. The equipment consists of a recorder and a transcriber with various features such as hand or desk microphone, foot control device, and special headphones, described above, plus a shaver. This latter unit is used to shave or cut off the engraved surface of the used cylinder so that it can be used again for dictation. The shaver works on the same principle as a lathe. Each wax cylinder will record about eight one-page letters and can be shaved about sixty-five times.

CONTROLLING LETTER AND REPORT WRITING

Unnecessary letters and reports are a tremendous waste of time, money, and energy. The office manager should see to it that only necessary materials are prepared and that they fulfill a vital need.

In modern business, there is little doubt that there are too many letters. When the sender keeps a copy of the original and the receiver's reply, and the receiver the original and a copy of his reply, there is a total of four letters in company files. In certain cases, a reply to the sender is not necessary. In other cases, the reply is not clearly stated, necessitating a follow-up letter, with more letters to be written subsequently.

The habit of writing reports frequently tends to remain long after the original need for the report has ceased. It is well to check periodically and to re-evaluate the importance of and necessity for all reports. This practice will not only weed out the reports no longer necessary but will also help to bring about improvements in the reports which are deemed necessary. Progress requires that a critical attitude be taken toward current report writing.

Also, distribution of reports should receive close attention by the office manager. Too often, distribution is made to a long list which includes names of persons who neither need nor read the report. Many practices reputed to be truthful are cited in office management circles regarding efforts to screen the distribution of reports. One such practice is to review the distribution list and remove the names of certain individuals believed nonessential as report receivers. No notice is given those whose names are removed. Subsequently, in most instances, the absence of the report is not noticed by the new nonreceiver; seldom is a complaint or an inquiry made about the report.

COST OF LETTERS AND REPORTS

Office letters and reports cost more than most people realize. For example, each business letter that is individually composed and typed costs its sender about $1.00, perhaps more. The time of the dictator and stenographer, the office overhead, and the mailing and filing costs make up the bulk of this total. A rough estimate, based on an allowance of 10 minutes for dictation and 15 minutes for transcription, gives a labor cost of around 75 cents, to which must be added the cost of paper, envelope, and postage, plus office overhead costs. The cost varies, of course, depending on the length, difficulty of material, method of transcription, and nonproductive time.

For large quantities of almost identical letters, the cost can be reduced considerably by using the automatic typewriter. One operator with four machines will produce approximately 500 short letters a day. For this arrangement, the cost data are as follows:

DAILY COST

Depreciation on four machines (five-year basis)...............	$ 6.25
Overhead expenses (floor space, heat, interest on investment).......	0.70
Electricity...	0.20
Maintenance..	0.30
Supplies..	1.05
Labor..	12.00
Total...	$20.50

Twenty dollars and fifty cents divided by 500 letters equals 4.1 cents a letter.

Likewise, the cost for identical letters produced by a duplicating process is less than for those individually typed, the exact figure depending mainly upon the process used and the quantity involved. Of course, a comparison of costs for a letter individually typed to that for a duplicated letter is not strictly comparable, since it is unlikely that quantities of identical letters would be individually typed.

The cost of a report depends upon many factors. The time of the writer is the key cost; and frequently, this is most difficult to control. Studies show that what appears to be a simple twenty-five-page report may cost upwards of $1,500 to prepare. Most executives underestimate what a report costs.

Expenditures for writing should be compatible with those for achieving the objectives and plans for the work of business writing. Usually, the manager has two alternatives: (1) to strive to gain the same goals but at less cost, or (2) to improve the present quality and effectiveness at the same or, if possible, at lower cost.

SUGGESTED CONTROL TECHNIQUES

In any particular case, an office manager may determine the importance of letter-writing costs by the following simple program: Determine the payroll for one month for employees engaged in letter-writing activity in the office. Add to this the monthly investment in machines, space, and supplies. This total will give some idea of the importance of letter writing in the office. If compared with the total office expenses, this figure becomes even more meaningful; in most cases, it represents quite a sizable percentage.

An effective technique with respect to reports is first to determine the total cost of preparing a report; then to attach to each copy delivered a statement similar to that shown in Figure 8–8. Or another approach is to advise the recipient of the cost of preparation and to indicate that in the future, his unit or department will be charged for this work, with records being maintained in the company's internal bookkeeping accounts. If the costs do not justify the use made of the reports, the recipient will request his name to be withdrawn from the distribution list. Discretion and judgment must be exercised in this approach, but it is effective.

It may be argued that the additional cost of running off extra copies of a report is relatively small; that is, to make 24 copies costs little more than to make 14 copies. But while the cost of labor, paper, and machine time for the differential 10 copies may be relatively small, the fact still remains that 10 more people receive the report. They take time to look it over, become interested in functions or problems which may not be their concern, waste some of their time on these "foreign" activities, and

Dept._____   Report _____
                                                 Date_____

                        PLEASE NOTE

Dear_____:

    The cost of preparing this report for you is $_____. Is it worth this much to you?
    We wish to eliminate, simplify, or combine reports which "cost more than they are worth."
    Will you let us have your comments on the following lines?

    _____
    _____
    _____
    _____
    _____
    _____
    _____
    _____
    _____
    _____

Return to *Neal Graham*   Sign your name here_____
              Office Manager   Your title_____
                                                Department_____

FIG. 8–8. Suggested form to be attached to all reports to make receiver cost-conscious and to eliminate unnecessary report work.

require additional filing space and help to retain the reports for some doubtful future reference.

In order to reduce expenses incurred in preparing letters and reports, the following questions might be asked:

1. What is the purpose or aim of this business writing?

2. Is the best duplicating process being employed in making the copies?

3. To whom are copies sent? Should they be sent?

4. Should the material be continued in its present form? If not, what is your recommendation?

5. Can the readability be increased by illustrative material and better grammar and English?

6. Is the cost justifiable?

7. Are there instances where one copy can serve several present recipients, thus reducing the number of copies needed?

8. Are parts of the report duplicated elsewhere? If so, can this be eliminated?

When given sufficient thought and properly applied, the answers to these questions will assist in writing better—not bigger—letters and reports. And office managers will have achieved a noteworthy accomplishment.

Some measurement of quality and output should be determined, for only by such means will a manager be able to determine the success of efforts toward improving the work of writing. Consideration for such factors as accuracy, clearness, conciseness, completeness, and naturalness can be used to rate the quality of the work. Output might best be determined by sorting letters according to type and counting the number of each type written during the period of a week or two weeks. For reports, number of pages, by type, usually gives satisfactory results.

An accounting of such things as what machine is assigned to each correspondent, the amount of work turned out by each machine, the extent of machine idleness, and the amount and frequency of repairs can also be employed. These data, plus proper follow-up, will help to improve the work output. Desirable in certain instances is the drawing of a daily record or chart for each stenographer or typist, showing the amount of work completed, the amount currently being handled, and the amount scheduled to be done. This information can be used to distribute the work evenly among all employees and to check accomplishment with task.

The use of an office manual is another effective means of controlling. Manuals provide the employee with standard practices and instructions in a form that is convenient and easy to use. They help the employee to help himself and assist in eliminating many needless errors.

ORGANIZING AND BUSINESS WRITING

Like most writing in the office, letter writing is done by different employees located in many different departments. Many top executives prefer to handle their correspondence work in their own unit, i.e., by their secretaries and themselves. However, the bulk of correspondence work is usually performed by personnel designated as correspondents who either have transcribers permanently located in the various departments performing letter writing or have transcribers in a centralized transcribing department or "pool."

Whatever the organization arrangement, the producing of letters consists of dictation and transcription. Each affects the other, for the dictator must correct or redictate if the transcriber's work is in error, and the transcriber cannot be efficient if the dictator does his work poorly. The organizational relationship should encourage the needed co-ordination among those engaged in letter-writing work.

In a typical enterprise, many employees have the task of report writing. In some cases, the total job content is report writing; while in others, a report is required but once a week or month. Report writing can be found in almost any organizational unit—it is not confined to "the office." For example, the assistant sales manager may have the responsibility of writing the monthly sales report; the technician, a research report; and the personnel manager, a report on the company's industrial relations.

It is the belief of many managers that reports should be written by the employee having the needed technical familiarity with the subject. This means report writing is dispersed or operated on a decentralized organizational basis.[3] These managers further claim that decentralization reduces communicative problems in giving needed explanations, and insures privacy of confidential material.

ACTUATING—CORRESPONDENCE AND REPORTS

A program which acquaints all correspondence personnel with effective letter-writing fundamentals, enumerates specific practices preferred by the enterprise, and supplies the best writing tools will help tremendously in attaining effective letter writing. Many actions can be taken. For example, Mutual of New York undertook a comprehensive correspondence simplification program and, among other things, drafted a series of "guide letters" for its correspondents. Figure 8–9 shows an example. These letters were meticulously prepared to give customers the answers they wanted in understandable terms and in a friendly, helpful manner.

It frequently is helpful to appoint a correspondence counselor. He or she may be selected from among present employees, or the services of a consultant may be used. The duties of the counselor include those of an adviser, a teacher, and a salesman for effective writing within the enterprise. He is the nominal head of the program for correspondence improvement.

Also, weekly or semimonthly meetings at which correspondents will discuss the principles of good letter writing should be established. The counselor acts as the group leader, and letters written by the employees can be criticized. It is also possible to hold conferences with individual employees. Frequently, this method is more effective than the group

---

[3] Decentralization is discussed in Chapter 28.

Example of The "Long" and "Short" of It

DEATH CLAIM - EXPLAINING AGE ADJUSTMENT

Original

We are enclosing a letter addressed to the payee under
the above numbered policy, explaining the adjustment
which we made because of a difference in the Insured's
age.

Will you see that we are furnished with the best
evidence available as to the correct date of birth? A
copy made by a notary of a family or public record,
made at or near the time of birth, of the date of birth
together with a statement by the notary as to the date
of publication of the book from which the record is
obtained, and by whom the record was made and when, is
the most satisfactory evidence. Form 3593 covers such
information. If no such record is obtainable, an
affidavit to that effect should be furnished together
with the best information available with a full
statement as to its source and why it is believed to
be correct.

Please forward the above information to us at your
earliest convenience.

Yours very truly,

Revised
To Manager

DCA-14   We will gladly make adjustments on this claim, if
necessary, when correct birthdate is established. If
(name) is unable to complete Form 3593, please get an
affidavit stating why the date is believed correct and
return with the best evidence available.

Also, kindly give the enclosed letter* of explanation.

Thank you.

* Key No. DCA-15

Original 160 Words: Revised 53 Words: Saving 67 Per cent

Note: The Original is a splendid example of a letter
that goes to great unnecessary length in stating
the obvious. Notice that the Revised states all
that a manager need be told to know how to proceed.

Courtesy: Mutual of New York

FIG. 8–9. A guide letter furnished company correspondents to assist them in writing more effectively.

meetings, for samples of the employee's work can be inspected and personalized help given.

Each correspondence employee should be kept busy at the level of skill for which he or she is hired. Stenographers should not be tied down to typists' jobs. Correspondents should not spend a great deal of their time filing. High-salaried executives should not dictate letters in those cases where a correspondent will do an equally effective job. Full utilization of all correspondence facilities is the goal. In addition, the machines must be kept in good repair to insure high volume and quality of work.

The same motivating techniques can be used for writers of reports. But in this area, it is extremely helpful to establish the importance of report writing. This will add prestige to the writer as a doer of work that is needed and is beneficial to all members of the enterprise. More specifically, it should be pointed out to the writer how report writing will help him, that reports can be a means to desirable ends—to get certain actions started and others curtailed. The reading of good reports is also helpful. A study of expressions, choice of words, and organization of material can be especially beneficial. In addition, contests stimulating competitive efforts to write effective reports can be used. Regular meetings to encourage the exchange of ideas helpful to writers are another effective medium. Also, writers should be told to draft their material currently—while it is on their minds. Make a brief written note when you think of an idea which you can use in your writing. Ideas come when least expected and are easily forgotten unless noted.

As stated in the beginning of this chapter, the ability to write good reports is seldom a natural gift; it must be developed, and this is best accomplished by means of specific training. Reluctance by managers to do something about improving report writing exists for several reasons. Some managers do not bring up the subject for fear that the responsibility of developing such a program will be added to their already full schedules. Others have never thought about improving report-writing efforts, while still others are reluctant to start an activity which might subject them to criticism of their own handling of written words.

BETTER DICTATING PRACTICES

Dictation can be made effective by motivating the dictator to follow a few simple suggestions that reflect, for the most part, ordinary common sense. In brief, the dictator should:

1. Have complete information at hand and organize his thoughts before dictating.
2. Refrain from unnecessary interruptions.
3. Speak clearly, pronounce each word correctly, and avoid the "ah" and "oh" when thinking about the next sentence.
4. Be concise—avoid unnecessary details and repetition. During World War II, Sir Winston Churchill, in asking for a report on a very important subject, ended with the request: "Pray, put it on one page."
5. Give complete information regarding work requirements—number of copies, general make-up of material, and whether rough draft or final copy is desired.

BETTER TYPING PRACTICES

Typing proficiency can be developed most quickly by proper instruction, adequate supervision, and regular practice. There are no substitutes for these essentials. The office manager should do everything possible to promote these factors. In addition, he can provide a good working area, including adequate space, good light, a posture chair, a desk or stand which insures that the base of the typewriter is about thirteen inches above the chair seat, and supplies within easy reach. The office manager should also give encouragement to and co-operate completely with typing efforts designed to develop fast finger strokes, rhythm, and proper touch.

QUESTIONS

1. Are letters and reports important in modern business operations? Substantiate your viewpoint.
2. Under what specific conditions would you recommend the use of the personal basis—stenographer and shorthand—to accomplish correspondence work? Of the machine basis—a recording and transcribing machine?
3. In general, how can dictating practices be improved? Typing practices?
4. What is an automatic typing machine, and when and how should it be used, from the viewpoint of effective office management?
5. Discuss the meaning of the writing practice, "Establish an Acceptable Mood," in preparing business correspondence.
6. Discuss the cost of letters.
7. In your opinion, what is the best way to get report writers to want to improve their writing?
8. Would you say that a report based on opinions is of little or no value to an office manager? Why?
9. Do you agree with the following? "Admittedly, some reports cost a lot of money to prepare, but the cost is usually minor when the report is viewed in the light of its importance. Reducing the funds allocated for report writing is foolish economy. Greater and more tangible savings can usually be acquired elsewhere in an enterprise." Elaborate on your answer.
10. Identify clearly each of the following:
    a) "Window letter."
    b) "Guide letters" for correspondents.
    c) "Whisker" expressions.
    d) Special reports.
11. Discuss several effective techniques for controlling business-writing activity in an office.
12. Secure a report written for an executive. Study its contents, and determine the main purpose it is intended to serve. Assuming that the purpose is a valid one, explain in what specific ways you feel this report can be improved.
    Sources for reports are friends in business, government reports, and various articles in newspapers and magazines available in the library.

CASE PROBLEMS

Case 8–1.   Hill and Dooley

Arnold Hill and Patrick Dooley are partners in a law firm. Mr. Hill is physically handicapped and is unable to attend any court proceedings or to perform any field work. Cases are assigned to Mr. Dooley and the two associates of the firm, Mr. Roger Brun and Mr. Edgar Eden. Full-time secretaries are assigned to Mr. Dooley and Mr. Brun. Two part-time court-reporting students from a nearby school handle the dictation of Mr. Hill. These students rank high in their class and work from 1:30 P.M. to 4:30 P.M. each workday. Mr. Eden reports to Mr. Hill by means of memorandums dictated to the part-time students. However, the amount of this work is small and is usually done after 4:00 P.M., when Mr. Hill leaves the office for the day.

Upon arrival in the afternoon, the two part-time students alternate in taking dictation from Mr. Hill. He insists on using these court-reporting students and wants them to become fully acquainted with legal work before they go out and do court-reporting work. Based on past experience, the part-time girls remain with the law firm of Hill and Dooley for about eighteen months.

Mr. Hill demands exacting and perfect work in every detail. He has the work first "rough-typed"; then, after he has made all necessary corrections, the work is typed in final form. An afternoon of a part-time student is spent in taking dictation, checking the rough draft with Mr. Hill, and waiting while the other part-time student is taking dictation. Statistics show that the full-time secretaries are able to perform over three times the transcription accomplished by either of the part-time court-reporting students.

Mr. Brun believes the employment of the part-time students reflects poor management. Mr. Dooley feels it is a question to be decided solely by Mr. Hill.

Problems:

1. As you see it, what is the problem to be solved in this case?
2. Justify both the expressed and what you feel are the implied viewpoints of Mr. Hill; of Mr. Brun.
3. Outline a plan for improving the correspondence work of the Hill and Dooley law firm. Justify the actions you propose.

Case 8–2.   Whitehurst Vending, Inc.

Arnold Pierson, president of this corporation, has jotted down the following notes covering items to be included in his report to shareholders for the year just ended.

1. Sales are down—$40,272,396 this year compared to $49,335,840 last year. But sales of the general products line are up 20 per cent. The general products line is the growth area of our business. Included in the general products line are vendors for milk, coffee, candy, cigarettes, and hot and cold foods.
2. Earnings this year—61 cents per share; last year—$1.07 per share.
3. Paid four quarterly dividends of 12½ cents a share; total for year, 50 cents.
4. Federal income tax $1,825,000 this year.

5. Believe new dollar-bill and coin change units will result in substantial sales by the company.

6. Inventory may be high, but we are in a position to capitalize on rapidly expanding automatic retailing sales on cards, and toiletries look good. Especially suited semi-attended locations are motel lobbies, service stations, and drugstores. Refreshments (carbonated drinks) continue to be our big market.

7. Experimenting with all-automatic grocery. Running tests here. Will permit grocers to expand with displays in places such as apartment houses, parking lots, and service stations. Market is tremendous here.

8. A new hospitalization and group insurance program was started. Higher benefits to employees are provided by the modified plan.

9. Company outlook is favorable. With business adjustments back of us, we can reasonably look forward to a greatly improved sales and profit picture this forthcoming year.

Problems:

1. Prepare the report to shareholders that you feel appropriate for Mr. Pierson to have distributed.

2. What are the major features of your report? Elaborate.

Chapter 9

DUPLICATING

It's the little things that annoy us. We can sit on a mountain but not on a tack.

—HELEN WATERMAN

DUPLICATING is a basic office operation and is increasing in importance as the work of the office is being modernized. Single copies of papers rarely suffice in the modern office; duplicated copies are needed—in some instances several copies, in other cases thousands. The task is commonly to make or "run off" copies of a report, form letter, bulletin, price lists, charts, drawings, or financial statements.

DUPLICATING AND OFFICE PROCEDURES

Duplicating is not limited to making copies that provide convenience. Duplicating is also important in many procedures constituting an essential component of the procedure. In some applications, basic information is put on a master and subsequently duplicated as needed onto paper forms designed to direct and control a particular business activity. For example, in purchasing, master sheets for duplicating can be prepared. When an item is to be purchased, its master is withdrawn from the file, and the needed information duplicated on all the purchasing forms. These forms are then processed, and the master is returned to the file for future use. The result is accurate, fast work and much saving in writing time.

An interesting variation of this procedure is used when several of the requisitions to purchase can be assembled for the preparation of one purchase order for one supplier. The requisitions are sent to the purchasing department, where the buyer groups them respectively under the names of the vendors whom he selects. The card for each selected vendor is removed from the vendor file and assembled with the requisitions which will make up the purchase order to that vendor. These are placed in a shingled or overlapping position and held in place by a large clip. In addition, a variable information form is added, so that the composition of the purchase order can be completed. Figure 9–1 shows the purchasing requisitions, giving complete specifications, assembled on

155

Courtesy: Eastman Kodak Co., Rochester, N.Y.

FIG. 9–1. Preparation of purchase orders from component parts is expedited by the use of a duplicating machine.

the left, with the variable information such as purchase order number, date, and quantities being written in on the right. When entries are completed, the entire assembly is placed over a purchasing order master giving heading and shipping instructions—common to all purchase orders —and duplicated. Thus, a complete purchase order is prepared with a minimum of manual writing. Different-colored papers can be used for convenient color coding. After the purchasing order copies are completed, both the vendor and the item or specification cards are returned to their respective files for future use.

Another example illustrating duplicating as an essential part of a procedure is the use of a short reply written at the bottom of a letter to lessen correspondence work. The answer or comment is written in the margin or at the bottom of an incoming letter. A copy is then made and sent to the interested party, the original being retained for the files. While this procedure is not suited for all correspondence, it does save considerable typing and filing space when it is followed.

PLANNING IN DUPLICATING WORK

Two areas are usually the main concern in the planning of duplicating: (1) determining the sequence of the duplicating work to be done and (2) deciding what duplicating process to use. Regarding the first, consideration must be given to the urgency of the material; but in general, a first-come, first-serve basis is satisfactory. Grouping the work and establishing its sequence for each duplicating machine gives orderliness to the duplicating efforts. Effective is the use of a requisition form showing the duplicating process preferred, the number of copies, size of paper, date needed, destination, and general comments.

Deciding what duplicating process to use is relatively simple when the question is the selecting of one of the existing duplicators within the company. To decide what new duplicating machine, if any, should be added brings up the question of what basic types are available, what are the trends in duplicating equipment, and what choice will best meet the particular requirements.

DUPLICATING PROCESSES

There are numerous reproducing processes available to the office. Aside from the carbon copy method, by which means from one up to about 12 copies can be made on a standard typewriter and about 20 on an electric, the more common reproducing processes are (1) stencil, (2) direct or liquid process, (3) indirect or gelatin process, (4) multigraph, (5) photocopy, (6) contact, (7) whiteprint, (8) dry electrical, (9) offset, and (10) noncarbon.

Individual considerations should determine the reproducing process to use, and this requires knowledge of what means of duplicating are available along with their respective major characteristics. For this purpose, Figure 9–2 has been included, thus giving pertinent information on a comparative basis for each of the ten duplicating processes. The stencil method, for example, provides a low cost per duplicated sheet, en-

Process	Relative Cost of Duplicated Sheet	Usage	Usually Economical for Number of Copies Up to:	Main Type of Material for Which Suited*	Speed in Sheets per Minute
1. Stencil	Low	Wide	5,000	L–N	200
2. Direct	Medium	Average	300	L–N	150
3. Indirect	Medium	Limited	300	L–N	200
4. Multigraph	Low	Average	10,000	L–N	150
5. Photocopy	High	Limited	5	L–N–I–P	5
6. Contact	High	Average	10	L–N–I–P	4
7. Whiteprint	High	Limited	500	L–N–I	8
8. Dry electrical	High	Limited	10	L–N–I–P	5
9. Offset	Low	Average	10,000	L–N–I–P	150
10. Noncarbon	High	Limited	4	L–N	5

Code: L = Letters   I = Illustrations
N = Numbers   P = Pictures

FIG. 9–2. Comparison of various duplicating processes.

joys wide usage, is usually economical for up to 5,000 copies, is best suited for material made up of letters and numbers, and is produced at a rate of 200 sheets per minute. The information in this figure is approximate and is intended to serve as a general guide only. For a specific installation, additional factors meriting evaluation would include the cost of the equipment and the supplies to run it, the quality of copy desired, time and place considerations, and employees' preference.

DESCRIPTION OF DUPLICATING PROCESSES

To assist in providing a basic knowledge of duplicating, helpful in office management, a discussion of each process will be given. The order followed is the same as that given above.

1. *Stencil.* This is a common method and consists of "typing a stencil," either by typewriter with ribbon removed or nonoperative, by special hand tools (styli), or by a die-impressed operation performed by the manufacturer. The openings thus made in the stencil, i.e., openings caused by the stencil coating being pushed aside and exposing the base fiber, permit ink to pass through so that paper held against the surface receives the image. Even, sharp, and clear strokes on the stencil give the best results. Corrections can be made on the stencil by using a special fluid to reseal the surface and then retyping. It is also possible to block out and remove an area and replace it by attaching a new portion of stencil. For the stencil process, the paper should be slightly absorbent, so that the ink does not smudge or blur. A 16-pound bond, when one side is used, and a 20-pound bond, when both sides are used, generally give satisfactory results. A quick-drying ink is available, and its use minimizes the possibility of the ink blurring. The image or printing is usually in a jet-black color, although several other colors are also available. It is possible to store the stencil for use at a later time; about 5,000 copies can be made from one stencil. Machines are available which provide such features as accurate registration for fill-in material, a capacity of 200 copies per minute, and the use of several colors at the same time. Such a machine is shown in Figure 9–3.

2. *Direct or liquid process.* In this process, the material to be reproduced is put on a master sheet which has behind it a special carbon sheet. The carbon places the image in reverse on the back of the master sheet. Different carbons are used for different colors. The master is placed in a machine, and copies are made directly from it in this manner: The copy sheet is slightly moistened with a special fluid before contacting the back side of the master; and as the copy sheet presses against the master, a very small layer of the carbon is removed and impressed on the copy sheet. Four colors can be reproduced in a single machine operation, and about 300 copies can be made from one master. Production rates of

about 150 sheets a minute are possible with a fully automatic machine. Master sheets can be stored for reruns. Figure 9–4 shows a liquid duplicator.

3. *Indirect or gelatin process.* From a technical viewpoint, this process is similar to the one above, with the exception that an intermediate agent, gelatin, is used. The material to be reproduced is put on a master sheet made of special paper; the master sheet is pressed against the gelatin, thus depositing the image on it. Copies are then made by pressing the sheets against the image in the gelatin. The ink remains concen-

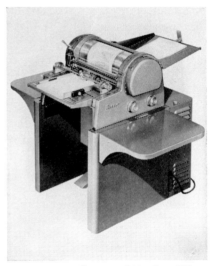

Courtesy: A. B. Dick Co., Chicago

FIG. 9–3. A duplicating machine using the stencil process.

Courtesy: Ditto, Inc., Chicago

FIG. 9–4. A direct or liquid-process duplicating machine.

trated long enough to permit the duplicating of several hundred copies, but it is gradually absorbed and dispersed by the gelatin. This makes it possible to use the gelatin over and over again. However, new impressions on the gelatin are required for reruns. The form of the gelatin is that of either a continuous roll or separate flat sections, depending upon the design of the machine. Since the middle 1950's, the manufacture of gelatin-process duplicators has been reduced. Today, it represents a smaller proportion of the duplicator business than that of former years.

4. *Multigraph.* Machines using this process of reproduction are either of an imprinting or a ribbon process. In the imprinting method, it is possible to use type, rubber strips, or electrotypes. Ink is applied to the type by an inking attachment which controls and furnishes the exact amount of ink needed. The paper, coming in contact with the wet type, forms the copy.

In the ribbon process, the duplicating is done through a ribbon similar to that used in standard typing. Type is composed directly onto a blanket or railed segment. Approximately 65 to 70 lines of type are held by one blanket. The ribbon goes between the blanket and the paper, so that when the paper is pressed against the type it receives the impression and the copy is made. Work made by this process closely resembles original typing; and when such appearance is considered important, this method is commonly used. Direct-mail and multiple letters can be cited as examples.

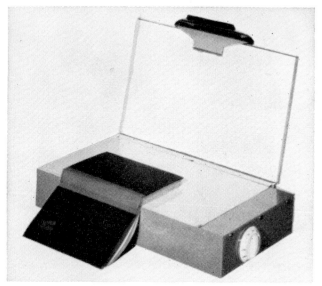

Courtesy: American Photocopy Co., Evanston, Ill.

FIG. 9–5. A portable machine for duplicating a page from a book.

Signature attachments are also available, changes or corrections can easily be made in the type, and the process is speedy, as up to 9,000 copies can be run in one hour.

5. *Photocopy.* Photocopy machines are so constructed that readable negative paper prints are obtained by directly photographing the original material. By a photocopy of the negative, it is possible to make a positive paper print (black lines with white background). Photocopy prints can be made in the same size as, or larger or smaller than, the original. The use of this process is normally confined to one or at most perhaps a half-dozen copies of an existing original.

6. *Contact.* This method is rapidly growing in popularity and consists basically of placing a sensitized paper in contact with the material to be reproduced and inserting it into the machine, which exposes, de-

velops, and fixes the copy sheet. The process is technically known as thermography and means literally a "burning" process. Dark areas, such as typewritten words, absorb more heat than the blank areas. Exposure to infrared light causes the words of the original to burn an image onto the heat-sensitive copy paper. For purposes here, three types of contact reproduction will be included: (*a*) Apeco, (*b*) Verifax, and (*c*) Thermo-Fax.

a) Apeco. This method gives a finished and exact copy of any office record, regardless of type or color; for example, a black-on-white copy

Courtesy: Eastman Kodak Co., Rochester, N.Y.

FIG. 9–6. A Verifax Signet Copier is an effective and economical machine for copying papers.

just like the original is produced in a matter of seconds. The advantages in using the Apeco method of contact reproduction include the following: The method is simple and clean, and no chemicals are required; it is fully automatic, and the machines require no special installation. Figure 9–5 shows a unit specially designed to copy a page from a book.

b) Verifax. Figure 9–6 shows a secretary operating a Verifax Signet Copier. A unit such as this can prove a very valuable tool in industry. Experience indicates that increased efficiency and tangible savings pay for such a unit in about a month or two. Exact copies of letters, including original letter head and signature, can be obtained; other material of interest to more than one member of a company can also be copied.

To operate, place the material to be reproduced in contact with a sheet of sensitized paper, expose to light for a few seconds—controlled by light switch of the machine—place exposed sensitized paper with developing paper, insert in developing and fixing bath, remove and permit copy to dry. It is possible to secure several usable copies from the same negative.

c) Thermo-Fax. Thermo-Fax Copying Machines make direct copies in a matter of seconds. Figure 9–7 shows such a unit. The machine is turned on with the flick of a switch, exposure timing is set on a dial, the original and sensitized papers are placed together and inserted into

Courtesy: Minnesota Mining and Manufacturing Co., St. Paul

FIG. 9–7. This Thermo-Fax "Fourteen" Copying Machine copies originals up to 14 inches wide—important in accounting and legal departments—and features speed, economy, and convenience.

the machine, the material is quickly processed and rolls out of the machine. There is no special training required to operate it. Ready for instant use, it gives dry, ready-to-use copies and emits no detectable odor of any sort. The process is effective wherever carbon is present in the writing, as with pencil or typewriter.

7. *Whiteprint.* In this process, positive prints are produced directly from translucent originals. This process features the feasibility of making additions or corrections on a master. For example, its use in certain types of cumulative reports is illustrated by copies of a payroll sheet containing constant data such as name, social security number, and department being made from a master. Subsequently, for each payroll period, a copy is used to which has been added the variable information, such as gross earnings, deductions, and net earnings for each employee. Likewise, customers' statements can be typed on a translucent paper

and retained as permanent copies by the company. At the end of each month, a whiteprint is made of the entire statement and is sent to the customer. Important advantages include the following: No copying work is required; errors are held to a minimum; and each time, the customer receives the full story on his account.

Additional advantages of the whiteprint process include speed; flexibility; low cost of operation; capacity for large sizes—42 inches and almost any length; color coding—a choice of white and five colors of tinted paper, in addition to four colors for lines; and convenience of blocking out—any unwanted lines may be blocked out by covering them with opaque material during exposure.

Whiteprint machines employ either of two development processes. In one process, the copy is given a light coating of a special solution which permanently develops the copy. In the other, the copy is developed by exposure to controlled aqua ammonia vapors. The machines are made in a variety of sizes. Figure 9–8 illustrates a whiteprint machine.

8. *Dry electrical process.* This is sometimes referred to as the electrostatic process. The reproducing units include a fuser, a copier, and a special camera; each about the size of a typewriter.

"Xerography" (pronounced zē-rog'ra-fē) is a combination electri-

Courtesy: Charles Bruning Co., Inc., New York

FIG. 9–8. The Bruning Copyflex Model 14, illustrated above, makes direct, positive, errorproof copies of practically any original comprised of the opaque markings from typing, printing, writing or drawing on paper or on cloth.

cal and mechanical process using powder but no ink or sensitized paper. A specially coated plate is charged with positive electricity and is subsequently exposed to the material to be reproduced, *A*, by means of a camera. As a result, the reflection of *A* on the plate is retained and remains charged positively. The remaining area of the plate loses its charge because of light exposure permitted by the camera. Then, a negatively charged powder is adhered to the positively charged *A*. A sheet of paper is placed over the plate and given a positive electric charge. The positively charged paper draws the powder from the plate, forming a direct copy which is heated in a few seconds to fuse the powder into a permanent print.

Copies of pages for reports and other written work are made quickly and accurately by this process. The copy is permanent, and the same plate can be used hundreds of times. Although not yet commercially available, the xerography principle applied to commercial printing is being studied.

9. *Offset.* The offset process is subject to many variations. Basically, the principle involved is that the material to be reproduced is (1) prepared on a plate, which is (2) transferred to an intermediate agent, which is (3) printed on the paper. Frequently, the intermediate agent is made of rubber.

One important offset process is photo-offset. The material to be reproduced is photographed, and the negative is transferred to a sensitized plate. This plate is then used in a photo-offset printing unit. Slight variations in this method are commonly termed "planographing" and "offset lithography." Frequently, the dry electrical process is used for making offset master paper plates.

A well-known process known as "multilith" is based on this offset principle. Either a metal or a paperlike master can be used. The latter is more widely used, since it can be handled like a piece of paper. That is, a regular typewriter plus pencil, pen, ink, brush, or crayon furnished by the supplier are used in preparing the master. Erasures and corrections are handled as with ordinary paper, and the paperlike masters can be filed in the office like paper sheets. The process is recommended for quantities of from 500 to 10,000 copies.

10. *Noncarbon.* While not a common means of duplicating material, as such, nevertheless this method is applicable and convenient for making copies of initial writing—same as carbon paper. Noncarbon designates the carbonless "NCR paper" of the National Cash Register Company. Colorless chemicals on the paper itself eliminate the necessity for carbon paper. The bottom side of the first sheet is coated with one chemical and the top side of the second sheet with another chemical. Writing on the first sheet reproduces instantly on the second sheet, and similar reaction takes place between the remaining sheets of the pack. "NCR paper" is available in quantities for processing into various records. Among the advantages cited for its use are that very clear copies are obtained, smears and smudges are eliminated, and hands and clothing are not soiled.

FUTURE TRENDS

Improvements and advances in duplicating processes have made this area one of the most dynamic of the entire office. Changes have been rapid and revolutionary; growth has been strong and steady. Further advances and improvements upon the performance of office work by efforts in duplicating are certain to take place.

Recent developments in the design of duplicating machines are pointing to units capable of duplicating by any of several of the methods described above. Actually, they are multiduplicators. Figure 9–9 shows a unit that (1) makes masters for either the direct process or the offset process of duplicating within fifteen seconds, without typing or chang-

Courtesy: Ditto, Inc., Chicago

FIG. 9–9. Duplicating machine employing several duplicating processes.

ing the original, and (2) produces low-cost facsimiles from the original, which remains unchanged by the process.

CONTROLLING THE DUPLICATING WORK

The controlling efforts over duplicating work should be thorough and understood by all affected by them. Scheduling of work and duplicating material in economic lot sizes are important in managing the work of duplicating. The necessary follow-ups to insure delivery of work when promised are likewise essential. Quality, too, must be watched, for unless proper attention is directed to it, the work tends to get marginal and below satisfactory standards.

Material and handling costs are probably the two big items to watch in controlling duplicating work. Rigid controls over the issuance of paper are usually in order. Likewise, an accurate accounting of how much time is spent on each duplicating job lot is normally needed to exercise really effective control. Frequently, records such as those shown in Figure 9–10 assist in these efforts. Reasonable levels of performance should be established and made known to each duplicating employee, so that he knows what is expected of him. Making the duplicating employee cost-conscious about his work is a strong, positive force toward achieving adequate control. However, when corrective action is required, it should be taken immediately.

DUPLICATING REPORT

HOURS AND ACTIVITY REPORT   WEEK ENDING

Regular jobs: Total paid hours:
Special jobs: Time available:
Machine down time:

STD. HRS. OPERATION	UNIT	ACTIVITY	STD. HRS.			
			Std.	All.	Taken	Diff.
Stencils	Stencil		.040			
Run copies	Copy		.00008			
Gather and staple	Copy		.00004			
Plastic binding	Fin. unit		.025			
Material						
20# stock	Ream					

FIG. 9–10. Comparative data are helpful in controlling the work of duplicating.

ORGANIZING IN DUPLICATING WORK

Duplicating lends itself to a centralized organizational unit. Such an arrangement makes for better utilization of the necessary equipment and machines, encourages adequate supervision, fixes responsibility, and expedites the development and the retaining of efficient operators in duplicating work. Depending upon the individual circumstances, however, duplicating is found as a part of the correspondence organizational section, or whatever unit utilizes duplicating most. Also, in recent years, with the availability of low-cost, easy-to-operate machines, such as those using the contact process giving several copies of letters, billings, or notices that are needed in a hurry, the trend is to disperse these machines throughout the office, placing them at locations where they are used frequently and are convenient to the person needing the copies.

ACTUATING IN DUPLICATING WORK

Much duplicating work is of a routine, repetitive nature, and managerial efforts usually must be made to maintain the employee's interest and desire to turn out good-quality duplicating work within reasonable time periods. At least a modicum of training in the proper use of the duplicating equipment is necessary. Instruction should be provided and required. It is erroneous and wasteful to place an employee in duplicating work and assume that he knows how to operate the duplicating machines. Many of the manufacturers of such machines supply voluminous material on the proper operation of their respective units, and quite a number will provide training help free of charge through their sales representatives.

Employees in duplicating work need definite work goals. The nature of the work seems to require that a sense of accomplishment be emphasized by management. Also, the employee's desire to have the manager know what is being achieved in duplicating must be satisfied. The practice of establishing work objectives helps to fulfill these basic desires.

Full utilization of the employee's time should be stressed. Either not enough or too much duplicating work can result in a dissatisfied employee. Or expecting the work to be accomplished within practically no time at all can dull the duplicating employee's enthusiasm. Members of a duplicating department must work as a team, with the various members performing several different jobs throughout the day. It is therefore especially important to maintain a congenial group.

COLLATING AND BINDING

Affiliated with duplicating work are collating and binding of the duplicated material. Collating is the assembling of several different sheets of paper to form a report or booklet. This work can be done manually or by a hand or electrically operated machine. Figure 9–11 shows collating machines.

In many cases, the material is held together by a binding, of which there are many different types. First, there is side wire stitching, i.e., on the side. Also, there is saddle wire stitching, i.e., through the fold at the back of the booklet. Usually, the latter is preferred, since it enables the sheets to remain flat and open once they are placed in that position.

Courtesy: Collamatic, Wayne, N.J.   *Courtesy: Thomas Collators, Inc., New York*

FIG. 9–11. The collating machine on the left is electrically operated. A feed roller at each bin ejects one sheet of paper; the operator grasps the sheets, gathers them, and staples each pack with the electric stapler. The unit on the right is an effective hand-operated collator; as many as thirty-two sheets can be gathered in one continuous operation.

Mechanical fasteners are used extensively, including ring or loose-leaf binders, prong fasteners, or screw-post fasteners.

The use of wire and of plastic bindings has won widespread favor. Wire binding is spun or coiled onto the packet of punched paper; plastic binding is fastened onto the paper via punched holes by means of a clasping action. Plastic bindings are available in diameters ranging from ⅛ to 1¼ inches and in a variety of colors. Binding equipment, consisting of a punching machine and a binding machine, each about the size and weight of a portable typewriter, is commonly used where it is preferred to bind various manuals and booklets in the office. This practice offers definite advantages, including the following: (1) A variety of stock, such as stiff divider pages, metal foils, samples, photographs, and maps, can be bound together; (2) various page sizes can be securely bound in one manual; (3) revisions and renewals in the manual can be made conveniently and quickly right in the office; (4) the cost is reasonable—the two units of equipment and the binding are popularly priced —and one girl can bind approximately one hundred manuals in an hour; and (5) the binding is sturdy and durable.

COMPOSITION FOR DUPLICATING WORK

So-called "cold-type" composition required to prepare the master copy is made from (1) pictures or sketches which provide the illustrative material and (2) typed material produced by the use of office typing machines. In several of the processes, the complete composition is photographed as a part of the preparation of the master.

Frequently, among the office typing machines are typewriters with various styles of type, but office composing machines are widely used. These machines provide different sizes and styles of type, bold headings, and straight left and right margins. In brief, the versatility of a well-equipped printing shop is brought to the office by use of these machines. They have found wide use in the preparation of all types of reports, bulletins, booklets, catalogues, price lists, and house organs, where variety in composition is desired.

Figure 9–12 shows an office composing machine. It resembles a typewriter in both appearance and operation. Each type face is on a removable disk which can be quickly inserted into or removed from the machine. Each disk is complete with capital and lower-case letters, numerals, and symbols. Over six hundred different sizes and styles of type, ranging from 5½-point newspaper style to 14-point Heavy Gothic type, and including boldface headings and italics, are available. The machine has different impression adjustments to provide the proper intensity of typing. Various vertical spacing choices permit the desired space between lines. In addition, all kinds of rule work—single, double, and vertical lines as well as dots and dashes—can be produced by the machine.

Courtesy: Addressograph-Multigraph Corp., Cleveland

FIG. 9–12. Changes from one type to another are accomplished quickly by means of small type fonts weighing less than one fifth of an ounce. Two such fonts fit into the machine at one time, and changes are made in less time than it takes to refill a mechanical lead pencil.

Even margins on both the left and the right, similar to those of regular type-set composition, are obtained by typing each line twice. To illustrate: line 1 of the copy is typed in the regular manner on the left half of the piece of paper. Then, it is retyped on the right. The machine spaces the second typing so that both margins are even. The procedure is repeated for each line. When completed, the typed material on the right half of the paper constitutes the finished or master copy.

QUESTIONS

1. Discuss duplicating as an essential component of an office procedure.
2. Explain Figure 9–1 in your own words.
3. Point out the major differences between the concepts in each pair of the following:
   a) Multigraph and multilith duplicating processes.
   b) "Cold-type" composition and whiteprint.
   c) "NCR paper" and a "multiduplicator."
   d) Side wire stitching and saddle wire stitching.
4. Discuss the managerial work of actuating as applied to duplicating.

5. As you see it, in the management of duplicating work, which is most important: planning, controlling, organizing, or actuating?

6. Describe concisely five common duplicating processes found in offices today.

7. What are office composing machines, and for what purposes are they used?

8. What are the major topics of information regarding collating and binding with which an office manager should be familiar?

9. What duplicating equipment would you recommend for each of the following?

   a) Eight copies of a chart 8½ × 11 inches.

   b) Copy of a letter.

   c) A company president's speech of fifteen pages, copy to be made for each of eight thousand employees.

   d) Copy of photograph.

   e) One hundred copies of a one-page announcement.

   f) A copy of a map 8½ × 15 inches.

10. What are the main considerations in the planning of duplicating work?

11. Do you favor having duplicating work on a centralized or on a decentralized organizational arrangement? Why?

12. Visit a medium-sized or large office and inquire regarding the duplicating processes utilized, along with the respective reasons given for the adoption of each process. What deductions do you make from your investigation? Elaborate.

CASE PROBLEM

Case 9–1.   Butler Products Company

Stencil-duplicated material has been processed and used in the office of the Butler Products Company for a number of years. Last year, for example, there were duplicated 1,645 memorandums of one page each, 276 reports of six pages each, and 183 reports of eight pages each. For each memorandum, an average of nine copies was made; for the six-page reports, eight copies; and for the eight-page reports, six copies.

The suggestion has been made by an employee in the duplicating unit that a duplicating machine using the contact method be installed to replace the present stencil machine, which is worn and must be replaced within the near future. The employee states that since a large part of the work is single-page memorandums, the contact method would be faster and less costly.

Current costs of the company are 25 cents each for a stencil; ink, about $20 a year; labor for typing or operating the duplicator, $2.00 per hour; paper, $1.50 for 500 sheets when purchased in quantity. It requires approximately one minute per line to prepare stencils. The memorandums average 15 lines and therefore require 15 minutes to prepare. The reports are made up of 20 lines to a page. It takes about 12 minutes to put the stencil on the machine, adjust it, and later remove and file it. Speed of the machine is 75 sheets a minute. For hand collating and stapling of reports, a flat rate of 10 cents per report can be used.

The office manager investigates the possibility of adopting a contact duplicating machine from the viewpoint of cost. He finds that the sheets of sensitized paper, one of which is needed for each page duplicated, will cost the company 4½ cents each; depreciation on the contact machine will be $57.50 per year, compared to $80.45 for a new stencil machine. Material costs, in addition to sensitized paper sheets, will approximate $30 per year for the contact machine. The office manager believes that the same employees can be used regardless of the process selected. With the contact method, he estimates two hundred copies an hour can be duplicated, which includes the work of loading the machine. The operations of adjusting the stencil and removing it from machine are, of course, not required under the contact process.

Problems:

1. Based on cost, should the office manager decide to adopt the contact process of duplicating? Substantiate your answer.

2. In addition to cost, what other important factors should be considered by the office manager in arriving at a decision?

3. What should be the decision of the office manager? Why?

Chapter 10

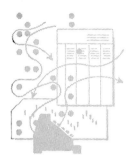

CALCULATING AND COMPARING

The only way to get rid of responsibilities is to discharge them.

—WALTER S. ROBERTSON

OFFICE WORK involving calculating and comparing is present in every enterprise. Figuring of some kind is necessary during the course of normal operations. Costs must be estimated, sales must be added, discounts computed, and interest rates figured. In addition, the data must be compared to insure that the invoices are correct, the calculated quantities balance with each other, and the written copy is accurate. Material requisitions, sales analysis, prorating, percentages, labor distribution, and inventories all require calculating and comparing work.

TYPES OF CALCULATING

In the typical office, adding, subtracting, and multiplying make up the common types of calculating. Studies show that dividing, extracting square root, and solving mathematical formulas constitute a relatively small amount of the total calculating work performed in offices; estimates are that it is some 5 per cent of the total calculating work. The tasks involving calculating are many; calculating is required in the preparation of many different types of records.

The preparation of an invoice, for example, requires calculating. As shown in Figure 10–1, to determine the amount for each item, multiplication or extension work is performed; as indicated, in line 1 of the illustration, three items at $0.62 each equals a total of $1.86 (3 × $0.62). The sum of these extensions is determined by means of addition. This is illustrated by the amount of $210.74 in the figure. Applying the discount entails subtraction in order to determine the total net amount due. This simple illustration is typical of the need for calculating in order to prepare many common forms of paper work.

172

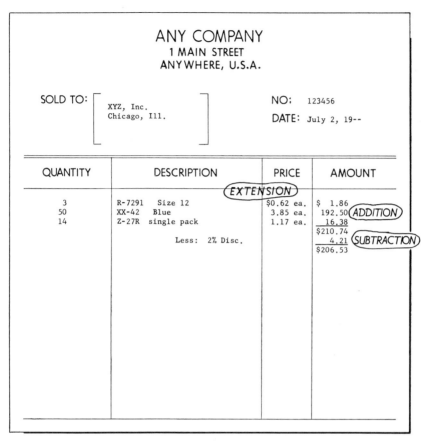

FIG. 10–1. Typical calculating work includes extension or multiplication, addition, and subtraction.

METHOD TO USE

In the modern office, much calculating work is done by machine, but other methods are also employed. These include performing the work mentally, working it out in longhand with pencil and paper, utilizing tables and charts of various kinds, and using a slide rule. For convenience, the discussion here will be viewed from two bases, including use of (1) the mental or personal basis and (2) the machine basis.

CALCULATING BY MENTAL OR PERSONAL BASIS

The personal basis is commonly used for short and relatively simple calculating work. Different methods can be followed; some represent much less work than others. A few effective short cuts will be included here. *In adding a column of figures, it helps to combine pairs or groups of successive numbers that add up to 10.* The addition can proceed from the top down or from the bottom up. For example, to add:

$$5$$
$$3$$
$$7$$
$$6$$
$$3$$
$$1$$
$$4$$

say to yourself (working from top down): 5, 15, 25, 29. The 3 and 7, and the 6, 3, and 1, are grouped as units of 10.

Left-to-right addition is speedy and accurate. This is accomplished by adding the tens of one number to the tens of the next number, then adding the units, and following this pattern successively to the last number. To add:

$$78$$
$$81$$
$$33$$
$$45$$

say 78, 158 (78 + 80), 159 (158 + 1), 189 (159 + 30), 192 (189 + 3), 232 (192 + 40), 237 (232 + 5).

Horizontal addition is helpful in adding numbers not arrayed in column form. Assume the total is wanted from a number of billings, including $42.50, $1.11, $34.77, $9.81, $7.83, $25.40, and $17.08. It is not necessary to arrange the numbers in the form of columns. Simply add the units, then the tens, then the hundreds, and so forth, and write the sums of the successive additions in the form shown below, then add.

Sum of:

Units..................	20	(0 + 1 + 7 + 1 + 3 + 0 + 8)
Tens..................	33	(5 + 1 + 7 + 8 + 8 + 4 + 0)
Hundreds.............	35	(2 + 1 + 4 + 9 + 7 + 5 + 7)
Thousands............	10	(4 + 3 + 2 + 1)
Total...............	$138.50	

Multiplication by near number is simple, yet it is not commonly practiced. By this procedure multiplying quickly by numbers near 10, 100, or 1,000 is possible. For example, 368 multiplied by $0.98 consists of

$$368 \text{ times } \$1.00 = \$368.00$$
$$\text{less } 368 \text{ times } 0.02 = \underline{7.36}$$
$$\$360.64$$

In other words, multiplying by 100 is accomplished by simply adding two zeros to the end of the number being multiplied, then adjusting this figure for the amount the multiplier deviates from 100. In like man-

ner, if the multiplier had been $0.12, the multiplier used would be 10
and the calculation would be

$$
\begin{array}{rl}
368 \text{ times } \$0.10 = & \$36.80 \\
\text{plus } 368 \text{ times } 0.02 = & \underline{7.36} \\
& \$44.16
\end{array}
$$

The breakdown method of multiplication is a timesaver when the
personal method of calculating is followed. Actually, this is similar to
multiplication by near number and differs in degree, not in type. To
multiply by 50, for example, multiply by 100, which is easily done,
and take one half, since 50 is one half of 100. Likewise, to multiply
by 25, take one fourth of that found by multiplying by 100. To illustrate, $1.95 times 25 equals one fourth of $195.00, or $48.75. In mul-
tiplying $1.95 times 26, an additional amount for one unit, or $1.95,
would be added to $48.75, giving $50.70.

The use of reciprocals represents another short cut. A reciprocal of
a number is one divided by that number. The reciprocal of 4, for example, is ¼. Figure 10–2 shows the reciprocals for numbers 1–20, in-

Number	Reciprocal	Number	Reciprocal
1........	1.000000	11.......	0.090909
2........	0.500000	12.......	0.083333
3........	0.333333	13.......	0.076923
4........	0.250000	14.......	0.071428
5........	0.200000	15.......	0.066666
6........	0.166666	16.......	0.062500
7........	0.142857	17.......	0.058823
8........	0.125000	18.......	0.055555
9........	0.111111	19.......	0.052631
10.......	0.100000	20.......	0.050000

FIG. 10–2. Numbers from 1–20, inclusive, and their
reciprocals.

clusive. Calculating work involving percentages and prorating can be
expedited by the use of reciprocals. For example, one day of a 31-day
month is the reciprocal of 31, that is, $\frac{1}{31}$, or 0.03226: one day of a
365-day year is equivalent to the reciprocal 0.00274; one ounce of a
pound, to 0.0625. Assume, from the following data, the percentage
figures are to be calculated:

Department	Sales	Percentage Total
A................	$ 3,905.40	
B................	7,041.62	
C................	2,052.98	
Total........	$13,000.00	100.00%

The reciprocal of 13,000.00 is 0.000076923. Multiplying the sales for each department by this reciprocal gives the respective percentages of 30.04, 54.17, and 15.79. In many cases, even though machines are employed, the use of reciprocals for this type of calculating is followed.

To divide by any number is to multiply by that number's reciprocal. The problem, 159.5 divided by 5, can be solved by looking up the reciprocal of 5. Figure 10–2 shows this is 0.2, and multiplying 159.5 by 0.2 which gives 31.90. When this method is followed, tables of reciprocals are usually made readily available. The method is quite effective when the divisor is not an uneven or uncommon figure, such as 156.18. Also, the method is used for division work by means of machines that multiply only, or where it is deemed desirable to have the operator stay with multiplying work only, that is, not mix the work of multiplying with that of dividing.

Calculating of discounts is another area where short cuts can be used. Discounts are an important feature in the transaction of exchange of goods or services. Among the important discounts and the reason for granting them are:

Discount	Reason
Quantity:	Less expensive to handle large orders
Trade:	Different types of buyers perform different marketing functions
Cash:	Inducement for prompt payment

Customarily, a full or list price is used as the base from which the discount or discounts are applied. When two or more discounts are in effect, each is applied to the net amount remaining after the previous discount has been taken. For example, with a list price of $25.00 and discounts of 30 per cent and 10 per cent, denoted as 30 and 10, the net price is $15.75, calculated as follows:

List price	$25.00
Less 30% (first discount)	7.50
Balance	$17.50
Less 10% (second discount)	1.75
Net price	$15.75

This method is too cumbersome. A simple method follows. A 30 per cent discount means 70 per cent ($100 - 30$) remains; hence, the amount can be determined by multiplying the list price by 70 per cent. Likewise, a 10 per cent discount means 90 per cent applies. In the above example, the calculation is therefore

$$\$25.00 \times 0.70 \times 0.90 = \$15.75.$$

Another simple method is to determine the single rate equal to the two discounts. To do this, add the discounts and subtract the sum obtained by multiplying the discounts:

$$0.30 + 0.10 = 0.40$$
$$\text{less } 0.30 \times 0.10 = \underline{0.03}$$
$$\text{Equivalent discount} = \overline{0.37}$$

or $(1.00 - 0.37)$ remains, applying to $25.00 equals:

$$0.63 \times \$25.00, \text{ or } \$15.75.$$

Where the calculating work includes various discounts, it is common practice to make up a table showing the equivalent single discount and the net that is applicable. Such a table is illustrated by Figure 10–3.

CALCULATING BY MACHINE BASIS

Modern office machines have reduced calculating work to very simple tasks. Lengthy columns of figures can be added in a matter of seconds; and if wanted, a written record is available for checking the accuracy or for future reference. Errors due to handwriting figures incorrectly, carelessly, or out of column are eliminated by the machine basis. In this chap-

Discount per Cent	Equivalent	Net
10	0.10	0.90
10 & 5	0.145	0.855
10, 5, & 5	0.1878	0.8122
20	0.20	0.80
20 & 10	0.28	0.72
20, 10, & 5	0.316	0.684
40	0.40	0.60
40 & 5	0.43	0.57
40, 5, & 10	0.487	0.513
40, 10, & 5	0.487	0.513
50	0.50	0.50
50, 10, & 10	0.595	0.405

FIG. 10–3. Discounts, their equivalents, and net amounts.

ter, adding machines and calculating machines will be discussed. Other types of machines, such as a billing or an accounting machine, perform calculating work; these will be discussed in Chapter 17.

ADDING MACHINES

Basically, these machines are of two types: key-driven and crank-driven. In the former case, the machine mechanism is actuated by depressing a key; in the latter case, the number is "put in the machine" by depressing the key, and the mechanism is actuated by pulling a lever or pressing a motor bar.

These two basic types are subject to important possible variations, which include the following:

Listing or Nonlisting. This simply means that the former type lists or provides a written record of the figures on a tape. This can serve as a machine record, for visual comparison, or as proof of work. Where a long column of numbers, over five hundred, for example, is involved, a listing is usually desired. However, when a nonlisting machine is used and proof of work is required, the work can be checked by going through the addition twice and comparing answers. In some instances, this method is as quick as checking a tape record. The nonlisting type is excellent for short batches of numbers, and for totaling columns and running cross-column checks.

Full Keyboard or Ten-Key Keyboard. A full-keyboard machine provides a column of keys from 1 to 9 for each digit position. Thus, a five-row machine can handle a number like 628.47. The full keyboard permits high speeds where numbers of four or less digits are involved, such as 4.67, 3.26, 9.00, or 12.95, because the keys can be depressed simultaneously. For best results, a skilled operator is necessary. There are many short cuts available in the over-all use of this type of machine. The latter or "10-key" type has, as the name suggests, 10 keys from 0 to 9. Within the machine capacity, all numbers are recorded by means of

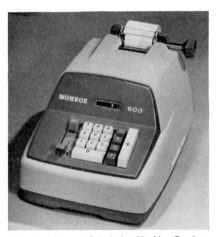

Courtesy: Monroe Calculating Machine Co., Inc., Orange, N.J.   *Courtesy: Burroughs Corp., Detroit*

FIG. 10–4. Adding machines. *Left:* Listing ten-key model. *Right:* Listing full-keyboard, ten-column-capacity machine.

these 10 keys. The number 629.43 would be handled by first pressing the key 6, then 2, and then 9, and so on until the number is completed. The 10-key machine is usually very satisfactory for large numbers. The hand travel is small, since it is confined to 10 keys. Numbers with five or more digits are quickly handled on this machine.

Manual or Electric. In a manual machine, the mechanism is actuated by hand; in the electric machine, by electricity. In both cases, the keys are depressed by hand. Comparing these two machines, the manual usually has lower maintenance cost, is lighter, and no electric cords are necessary; the machine can be operated anywhere. In contrast, the electric machine is faster and saves the operator's energy; however, its initial cost is usually greater. Most adding machines can also be used for subtracting, and a number are adaptable for work involving multiplying and dividing. Illustrations of several different types of adding machines are shown by Figure 10–4.

CALCULATING MACHINES

These machines are specially built for multiplication and division work, which is really repetitive addition and subtraction, respectively; that is, 3 times 3 is the same as 3 plus 3 plus 3, and 9 divided by 3 is equal to the number of times 3 can be subtracted from 9, i.e., 9 less 3,

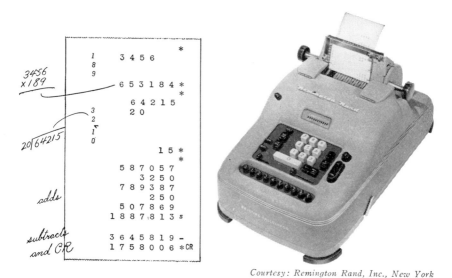

Courtesy: Remington Rand, Inc., New York

FIG. 10–5. A fully automatic printing calculator, with an example of its work.

less 3, less 3. The same considerations apply to calculators as discussed above under adding machines.

A fully automatic calculator that prints a record of the work done is shown by Figure 10–5. In multiplying, there is no repetition of figures on the tape—just the problem and the answer, as shown in the upper right of the figure. The same is true for division—the answer is read directly from the tape. Likewise, calculating work of addition and subtraction is simplified, as illustrated by the lower right portion of the figure. The machine is available with capacity up to $1 trillion.

There is also available a listing calculator featuring a wide range of application, high speed, and interoperation transfers, making it possible to perform sequences of combined operations such as storing data in the machine and recalling for use in subsequent operations. An illustration

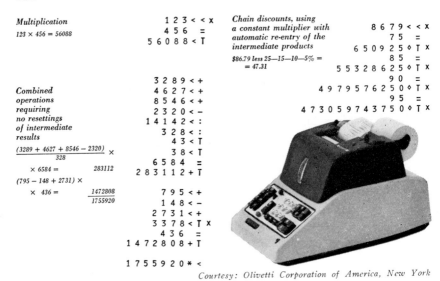

Courtesy: *Olivetti Corporation of America, New York*

FIG. 10–6. A listing automatic calculator with a wide range of applications. Illustrations of the printed tape supplied by the machine are shown.

of this machine and several examples of the calculating work it can perform are shown by Figure 10–6.

LOCATION OF CALCULATING GROUP

When the volume of calculating work warrants, it is usually economical and satisfactory to have a centralized computing group with all the proper machines operated by skilled employees. If established, the centralized unit should be the department having the largest quantity of calculating work—probably the bookkeeping section, which utilizes calculating machines of various types and is staffed by employees competent in calculating work. In most offices, however, it is not feasible to have *all* the calculating work done by a centralized group. Having some of the calculating work handled by employees throughout the organization has merit. Such employees are familiar with the particular material, and the calculating work represents a relatively small portion of the total.

COMPARING WRITTEN MATERIAL

Reading handwritten or typed copy and columns of numbers for accuracy accounts for a sizable portion of office workers' time. Progress in reducing these comparing efforts for checking purposes has been made, as evidenced by proofing devices on office machines, short-cut means for checking calculations by the personal method, and proofing masters only of duplicated material. For the most part, material to be checked falls into two categories: (1) material that requires exact comparison with the original and (2) material that necessitates general checking for correctness of intended meaning and satisfactory appearance.

When exact comparison is required, it is common for one employee to read from the original while another employee checks the material. A word-for-word comparison is made. The employee reading indicates headings, quotations, and punctuation marks, and spells difficult words. Care must be exercised by the employee checking to catch omissions, misspelled words, and incorrect syllabifications. Along with this, an examination is made to see that the general format, margins, and appearance are correct.

Material requiring general checking is carefully read, but a word-for-word comparison is not made. Frequently, general checking work is done by one employee—commonly the one who wrote the material. The meaning of the material must be clear and the general appearance satisfactory. Special attention should be given dates and amounts. In this respect, comparison with the original is recommended.

The checking of numbers is best performed by reading the columns vertically. Placing the original list side by side to the written list, so that the numbers are matched on the same line, helps to eliminate possible error. Also, the doubling of figures and using the comma division should be practiced whenever possible. For numbers that repeat, use the expression "two times," "three times," and so forth. To illustrate:

When the number is:	*Say:*				
157	One	fifty-seven			
2157	Twenty-one	fifty-seven			
2,157	Two	one	fifty-seven		
3,845,157	Three	eight	forty-five	one	fifty-seven
341 ⎫ 341 ⎬ 341 ⎭	Three	forty-one		—three times	

UNIT ANALYSIS COMPARATIVE REPORTS

Most data, to have maximum value for an operating manager, must be timely and provided in a format that expedites usage. The summarizing of much data in a neat and concise form emphasizing comparisons describes the unit analysis comparative report which is illustrated by Figure 10–7. The data are written on specially designed forms held in place by binder rings through holes at the top of each form. At the close of each period, such as a month, the data for the current month are posted in the left-hand column of a strip and the year to date figures in the right-hand column; the center of the strip is used for identifying information. By properly positioning the newly completed monthly strip in the binder, comparisons between figures for the current month and

PERIOD JANUARY THIS YEAR	PERIOD FEBRUARY THIS YEAR	PERIOD MARCH THIS YEAR	PERIOD APRIL LAST YEAR	PERIOD APRIL THIS YEAR	OPERATING REPORT	% OF SALES	TO DATE APRIL THIS YR
					SALES		
60,125	62,411	63,147	51,875	57,355	PRODUCT A	55.2	243,038
51,312	61,387	62,298	44,375	55,467	PRODUCT B	44.8	230,464
111,437	123,798	125,445	96,050	112,822	TOTAL	100.0	473,502
					COST OF SALES		
42,066	42,439	43,571	35,643	41,295	PRODUCT A	69.9	169,371
35,462	43,279	43,921	30,234	38,272	PRODUCT B	70.0	160,934
77,528	85,718	87,492	65,877	79,567	TOTAL	70.0	330,305
					GROSS PROFIT		
18,059	19,972	19,576	16,032	18,060	PRODUCT A	30.1	73,667
15,850	18,108	18,377	14,141	17,195	PRODUCT B	30.0	69,530
33,909	38,080	37,953	30,173	33,255	TOTAL	30.0	143,197
					COST OF SALES ADJUSTMENTS		
1,211	857	752	418	456	INVENTORY ADJUSTMENTS		3,076
2,075	1,947	1,846	1,157	1,411	OVER OR UNDER ABSORBED BURDEN		7,279
3,286	2,604	2,598	1,575	1,867	TOTAL	1.9	10,355
30,623	35,476	35,355	28,598	31,388	GROSS PROFIT AFTER ADJ.	28.1	132,842
					GENERAL EXPENSES		
6,317	7,185	7,321	5,732	6,930	ADMINISTRATIVE – SCHEDULE A		27,753
8,245	9,345	8,580	7,048	6,742	SELLING – SCHEDULE B		32,892
3,612	4,762	5,121	3,848	4,637	SHIPPING – SCHEDULE C		18,132
2,098	2,417	2,860	2,461	2,420	BRANCH – SCHEDULE D		9,795
20,272	23,709	23,882	19,089	20,729	TOTAL EXPENSES	18.7	88,572
10,351	11,767	11,493	9,509	10,659	NET PROFIT FROM OPERATIONS	9.4	44,270
					OTHER INCOME		
251	187	252	142	210	INTEREST EARNED		900
516	518	675	567	572	DISCOUNT ON PURCHASES		2,281
122	158	145		112	DIVIDENDS RECEIVED		537
			250		PROFIT ON SALE OF ASSETS		250
218					PROFIT ON SALE OF INVESTMENTS		218
1,107	863	1,322	709	894	TOTAL OTHER INCOME	.9	4,186
					OTHER DEDUCTIONS		
376	112	87	123	75	INTEREST PAID		650
678	458	567	482	420	DISCOUNT ON SALES		2,123
	100				LOSS ON SALE OF ASSETS		100
					LOSS ON SALE OF INVESTMENTS		
1,054	670	654	605	495	TOTAL OTHER DEDUCTIONS	.6	2,873
53	193	668	104	399	NET	.3	1,313
10,404	11,960	12,161	9,613	11,058	NET PROFIT BEFORE TAXES	9.7	45,583
					TAXES		
55	55	55	45	55	CAPITAL STOCK		220
145	152	159	127	121	STATE INCOME		577
3,675	3,742	3,815	2,655	3,420	FEDERAL INCOME		14,652
3,875	3,949	4,029	2,827	3,596	TOTAL TAXES	3.1	15,449
6,529	8,011	8,132	6,786	7,	NET PROFIT FROM ALL SOURCES	6.6	30,134

JUST LIFT UP

Courtesy: Royal-McBee Co., New York

FIG. 10–7. Comparative and accumulative operating and financial information is presented in an effective arrangement.

TO DATE APRIL LAST YEAR	TO DATE MAY LAST YEAR	TO DATE JUNE LAST YEAR	TO DATE JULY LAST YEAR	TO DATE AUGUST LAST YEAR	TO DATE SEPT. LAST YEAR	TO DATE OCTOBER LAST YEAR	TO DATE NOVEMBER LAST YEAR	TO DATE DECEMBER LAST YEAR
212,966	265,648	322,377	380,739	441,106	506,089	576,913	651,284	716,671
195,033	238,744	286,557	334,678	387,159	442,183	501,494	559,179	615,890
407,999	504,392	608,934	715,417	828,265	948,272	1078,407	1210,463	1332,561
150,092	188,548	228,527	271,129	313,991	358,719	407,341	458,628	503,750
136,676	168,147	202,572	236,256	272,467	310,328	351,012	390,713	429,433
286,768	356,695	431,099	507,385	586,458	669,147	758,353	849,341	933,183
62,874	77,100	93,850	109,610	127,115	147,370	169,572	192,656	212,921
58,357	70,597	83,985	98,422	114,692	131,855	150,482	168,466	186,457
121,231	147,697	177,835	208,032	241,807	279,225	320,054	361,122	399,378
1,723	2,234	2,711	3,161	3,886	4,268	4,822	5,643	6,264
4,318	5,578	6,735	7,615	9,199	10,360	11,676	12,894	13,881
6,041	7,812	9,446	10,976	13,085	14,628	16,498	18,537	20,145
115,190	139,885	168,389	197,056	228,722	264,597	303,556	342,585	379,233
21,908	27,338	32,972	38,783	44,604	50,539	56,786	63,284	69,205
27,909	34,726	41,868	48,805	55,740	62,860	70,244	77,826	84,741
15,607	19,327	22,846	26,691	30,515	34,283	38,450	42,837	46,757
10,361	12,933	15,249	17,767	20,734	24,878	29,328	34,483	39,569
75,783	94,324	112,935	132,046	151,593	172,580	194,808	218,430	240,272
39,407	45,561	55,454	65,010	77,129	92,037	108,748	124,155	138,961
541	707	853	1,035	1,228	1,400	1,581	1,737	1,864
2,081	2,773	3,288	3,900	4,525	5,337	6,102	6,724	7,439
110	110	110	110	325	465	595	595	595
163	163	163	163	287	287	287	487	487
251	251	251	251	251	251	251	251	251
3,146	4,004	4,665	5,459	6,616	7,740	8,816	9,794	10,636
505	615	702	817	911	1,021	1,206	1,378	1,535
1,660	2,055	2,483	3,045	3,583	4,085	4,647	5,372	5,993
215	215	215	215	361	361	361	361	361
2,380	2,885	3,400	4,077	4,855	5,447	6,214	7,111	7,889
766	1,119	1,265	1,382	1,761	2,293	2,602	2,683	2,747
40,173	46,680	56,719	66,392	78,890	94,330	111,350	126,838	141,708
180	225	270	315	375	430	498	570	637
479	601	725	850	1,002	1,183	1,377	1,587	1,774
11,107	13,687	16,504	18,685	22,103	25,791	29,813	34,093	37,958
11,766	14,513	17,499	19,850	23,480	27,404	31,688	36,250	40,369
28,407	32,167	39,220	46,542	55,410	66,926	79,662	90,588	101,339

those of previous periods are supplied. In the illustration, for example, comparisons are expedited between (1) April this year and previous months of this year, (2) April this year and April last year, and (3) the year to date this year with the same period last year. The unit analysis method assists in determining trends, measuring the efficiency of the operations, and highlighting the status of different components making up the entire activity. It assists in presenting calculated data in a convenient and usable pattern.

PEGBOARD AND PAPER STRIPS

Pegboard accounting, also known as shingle-strip and summary-strip accounting, is another type of strip arrangement for accumulating or summarizing a large number of items with minimum time, maximum accuracy, and convenience. The equipment consists of a special board and ready-made paper strips, about 2 to 3 inches wide and 16 inches long, fastened to the board. Original data are written on the strips. These strips are held in alignment by means of holes across the top which fit into a peg strip at the top of the board. The arrangement of the paper strips is offset so that a vertical margin of each strip is exposed, thus disclosing a column of figures. Quick summaries and "recaps" can be run off. A movable horizontal bar is used to guide the eye to the proper line across the forms.

Pegboard accounting is particularly effective in making distribution analyses of various kinds, including cost, payroll, stock control, and sales, and it can be designed to serve almost every type of business. The boards are made in various sizes, ranging from approximately 20 × 18 inches to 36 × 18 inches. The advantages of the use of peg strips include the following: Copying of the data is eliminated—the original forms are used to obtain final results; accurate information can be provided; flexibility is permitted, since variations in the number and kind of distributions are possible; and the cost is economical—there is a minimum of handling, and the equipment required is simple.

EMPLOYEE TRAINING FOR CALCULATING AND COMPARING WORK

Basic training is paramount to acquire proficiency in calculating and comparing work. Many people have the background for acquiring acceptable competency, but this ability remains dormant until properly developed through training. To develop skill in calculating necessitates the acquiring of a *number sense*, that is, an ability to recognize relations that exist between numbers and to think of numbers in their broad relations. Basic training in the use of calculating machines is also important. While not difficult to operate, the use of a machine is limited by the knowledge of the operator. The machine calculates only what the operator puts into it. Instructional material is helpful; but to provide maximum benefits, it should be prepared in a step-by-step, easy-to-follow plan, and amply illustrated. Work of comparing requires reading skill, patience, and a strong desire for work accuracy. It takes practice and a sincere determination to perform either calculating or comparing work speedily and competently. The techniques must be understood, but skill in applying them is essential.

QUESTIONS

1. Using the horizontal addition method, what is the sum of the following invoices? $19.77, $8.03, $22.98, $12.55, and $16.46.

2. With the advent of the computer in the office, do you feel that calculating and checking will become less important in the future? Why?

3. Give a brief description identifying each of the following:
   a) Shingle-strip accounting.
   b) Horizontal addition.
   c) A number sense that a person should acquire.
   d) The reciprocal of a number.

4. By the near-number or breakdown basis, multiply each of the following:
   a) 427 by 13.
   b) 728 by 25.
   c) 956 by 9.
   d) 6,131 by 50.

5. Discuss the subject of "Comparing Written Material" as it applies in office management.

6. Calculate manually the net price to a buyer extended a chain discount of 25, 10, 10, and 5 per cent from a selling price of $60. Extended a discount of 50 per cent from a selling price of $60. Extended a chain discount of 25, 10, 10, and 5 per cent from a selling price of $30. What basic observations do you make from your answers?

7. In general, would you say that centralization probably works out better for corresponding work than for calculating work? Why?

8. In your opinion, could all checking work in the office be considered controlling work? Explain.

9. Explain the calculations illustrated by Figure 10–6.

10. Calculate the total of the following numbers, using left-to-right addition. (State the intermediate numbers as you proceed.)
    15
    82
    36
    93
    47

11. Explain the following terminology used in connection with adding machines:
    a) Listing and nonlisting.
    b) Key-driven and crank-driven.
    c) Full keyboard and ten-key keyboard.
    d) Manual and electric.

12. In your own words, explain the purpose and use of a unit analysis comparative report as illustrated in Figure 10–7.

CASE PROBLEM

Case 10–1.   The Vitek Company

Upon receipt of a customer's order, it is entered in two ledgers; one is by item, the other by salesman. This is done in order to determine total weekly sales for each item and for each salesman.

Wendell Adams, office manager of the company's New York sales branch, believes this method of tabulating sales data involves excessive entry work and increases the chances for committing errors in copying and adding the figures. He suggests that printed strip tickets be used to simplify the work and at the same time increase the accuracy. According to his idea, the tickets could be shingled several different ways as desired, and only one entry of each order received would be necessary.

The Vitek Company manufactures and distributes nationally toilet preparations, including a well-known soap, hair shampoo, a men's hair-grooming preparation, nail polish, tooth paste, tooth powder, mouthwash, and a liquid deodorant. Most of the items are offered in several different sizes. The total number of products, including the various sizes of each, is thirty-eight. The company has a sales force of fifty-four salesmen operating out of four branches. The main office is located in Detroit. Weekly reports by each branch are sent to the main office, where they are analyzed and made up into a final company report.

Data on the quantity and dollar sales of each item and the items sold, and dollar sales by each salesman and to what customers, are required. Many of the items are sold in lots of a dozen, in which case the quantity entered is 12. To illustrate the present work, suppose an order for six hair shampoo size No. 2 and two dozen tooth paste giant size is received from the Baker Drug Store, located in the territory of John Doe, a Vitek Company salesman. Entered in the hair shampoo size No. 2 ledger are date, saleman's name, quantity, and the amount of sales dollars. In the tooth paste giant-size item ledger are entered date, salesman's name, quantity, and sales dollars. Also in the John Doe salesman ledger are entered date, code number of the Baker Drug Store, quantity, item, and sales dollars.

Problems:

1. Do you agree with the viewpoints expressed by Wendell Adams? Discuss.

2. Write the proposed means for handling this work according to Wendell Adams, giving sufficient details to convey complete understanding of the proposed plan. Include the design of the printed strip ticket, and explain how it would be used.

Chapter **11**

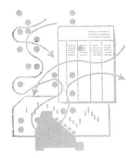

MAIL AND OFFICE COMMUNICATIVE SERVICES

The eyes believe themselves; the ears believe other people.

—Greek Proverb

Success of any enterprise depends in great measure upon the ability to use communicating devices effectively. Man's ability to convey his ideas and thoughts accurately to another person adds immeasurably to managerial accomplishment. The various communicative services in an enterprise, such as the mail-handling, telephone, and messenger services, must be operated in an efficient manner for sustained high office productivity to exist. There are no substitutes for these office services. They must be provided if the office work is to be accomplished effectively.

AVAILABILITY AND SELECTION OF COMMUNICATIVE MEANS

Typically, a business enterprise has a variety of communicative means available to it. These include such means as mail, telephone, intercommunication systems, messenger service (either personal or mechanical), teletypewriter, television, and a host of others, which will be discussed in this chapter. Before the proper means can be selected, however, it is necessary to know what the real communicative needs of the company are. Various considerations enter into the picture. Figure 11–1 lists some major questions to be asked to determine the communicative means. Answers to these types of questions serve as helpful guides in the selection. Unless careful analysis is made of the genuine needs, there is likely to develop a hodgepodge, overlapping, and nonco-ordinated communicative system that is not tailored to serve best the requirements of the company.

THE COMMUNICATION OF MAIL

It is doubtful that a modern enterprise could exist without mail; it is imperative that some written means of offering the services of the enterprise and of issuing answers to inquiries, statements, and invoices be available. Promptness and accuracy are the major requisites of the mail service.

Proper arrangement of the equipment in the mail room will help keep the mail moving in and out of the office without interruption or confusion. The work of the mail room can be greatly simplified and performed quickly and smoothly by using the proper number of units, correctly arranged.

1. What quantity and type of communications are or should be provided? This information, segregated for supervisors, salesmen, customers, vendors, and the general public, will provide helpful, factual, and basic information.
2. Is cost a prime consideration? An approximate cost range from the minimum to the maximum, and related to the service provided, is helpful.
3. Is speed of major importance? Certain devices transmit messages in a matter of seconds, but cost is relatively high. Adequate planning reduces much of the need for speed in communicative devices.
4. Should written or oral communications be utilized? The former tend to be more specific, provide evidence, and help to lessen misunderstandings. In contrast, oral communications are quicker, cost less, and are superior when the exchange of ideas to reach a mutual agreement is desired.
5. How long is the average communication? Certain devices are ideal for lengthly communications, while others are designed for short, terse messages.
6. Are there peak periods of communicative activity? If so, the capacity of the selected communicative means must satisfy this load.

FIG. 11–1. Questions to assist in determining the communicative needs of an enterprise.

Figure 11–2 suggests a layout for a modern mail room. The equipment has been arranged in a room with dimensions of 12 × 16 feet. Beginning at the lower right of the figure, the route of incoming mail is first to the table where the mail is opened and the time stamped, then to the adjacent tables and sorting racks, where it is sorted. It is then delivered to the proper stations throughout the office.

Outgoing mail is first taken to the outgoing-mail sorting racks and tables, shown at the upper left of the figure, where it is grouped with other mail having the same destination. When necessary, each piece is weighed and proper postage determined; then, it is put through the metered-mail machine and finally into the mailbag located at the upper right portion of the figure. Mail is delivered to the post office in these bags.

Weight is also an important consideration in determining proper post-

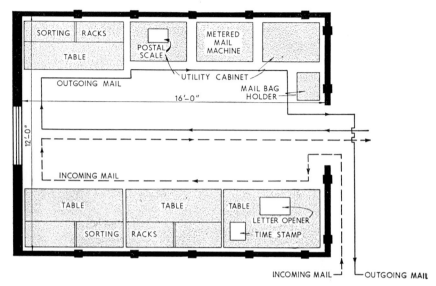

FIG. 11–2.   Arrangement of mail-room equipment.

age. A mail room should be equipped with an accurate postal scale. Many different models are offered on the market.

PROCEDURES FOR MAIL ROOM

Additional comments regarding the procedures followed in mail handling are in order, for they may suggest areas for managerial improvement. The procedure for handling *incoming* mail is fairly uniform. The major areas are as follows:

1. *Receiving and opening the mail.* Mail is delivered to the office by the postman or a company representative who calls for it at the post office. The latter is preferred by many large enterprises, especially in the case of the first morning mail, because when called for at an early hour, it can be distributed by the time the office formally opens. In this event, it is well to have the employees handling incoming mail report for work about one-half hour before the regular opening office hour.

Mail is opened either by hand or by machine, depending upon the volume of mail. An efficient mail-opening clerk can open by hand about 15 pieces per minute. Machines of various models and capacities are also available for opening the mail; some will open as many as 500 letters per minute. Mail marked "Personal" or addressed to specific individuals is not company mail and may or may not be opened, whichever is the policy of the company. The common practice is not to open it. In some instances, mail so addressed is forwarded immediately to the employee's home address.

2. *Sorting and time stamping.* The next step is to remove the contents of the envelopes and, at the same time, sort the mail according to who handles the particular type of mail under question; this might be a department, a division, or an individual. Usually, the name of the person or of the department to whom the letter is addressed determines where it is to be delivered. When this is not given, a quick glance or scanning of the paper is necessary to determine its proper destination. In exceptional cases, the entire contents must be read.

Courtesy: First National Bank in Dallas

FIG. 11–3. Handling the incoming mail in a large bank.

Figure 11–3 shows a portion of a large mail room. The man in the foreground is opening letters by means of a machine. The man in the background is sorting to the proper compartments in the sorting racks. The general pattern of the various compartments in the rack is similar to that of the mail stations in the office, for in this way the sorted mail can be kept in a logical order for ultimate distribution.

In the case of mail containing money or checks, a listing showing the senders' name and address and the amount enclosed is made out by the mailing department. The cash and checks, along with the listing, are later sent to the cashier department. In other instances, the check is attached to the letter; or in the case of cash, the money is placed in a small envelope and attached to the letter, with appropriate notation. The checks and cash are then delivered to the cashier department.

A letter referring to previous correspondence can either be delivered to the department concerned, which, if necessary, requests the file from the filing department; or it can be sent to the filing department, where the needed file is attached and forwarded to the proper correspondent. The method used depends chiefly upon the number of such letters received and the system of filing used.

At the time the mail is read and sorted, it is customary to stamp the hour and date received on each piece of correspondence. This provides a timed receipt that can be used as evidence in controversial matters regarding the correspondence. It can also be used for checking the efficiency of mail distribution in the office. Either a hand stamp or a machine can be used for the stamping.

3. *Distributing the mail.* This is the final step in the handling of incoming mail and is usually done by messengers, although other means, such as conveyor belts and pneumatic tubes, may be utilized.

For *outgoing* mail, the major areas of mail handling are as follows. Normally, the same employees handle both incoming and outgoing mail.

1. *Collecting and grouping by destinations.* To help in collecting, outgoing mail is usually placed in special desk trays specified as mail stations. Upon receipt at the mail room, the mail is first grouped according to geographical area, then by city, and then by name of addressee. Sorting racks are commonly used for this purpose. All mail of a similar class, and addressed to the same wholesaler, branch, or company, is put together so that it can be mailed as a single piece. Frequently, large Manila envelopes with the address printed or stenciled thereon are used for these large firm mailings. In some instances, each of the outgoing sorting racks contains an addressed envelope which is handy for instant use. Replenishments are made either the first thing in the morning or at regular intervals throughout the day.

2. *Inserting, sealing, and stamping.* If necessary, the material is folded and inserted by the mail department. When ordinary envelopes are used, the name and address on the material must be checked with that on the envelope. Sealing and stamping can be done either by hand or by machine; the volume of mail should determine the method used. It is possible to seal and stamp around 350 letters an hour by hand. It is advisable to appoint one mail-room employee as sole custodian of the stamps. He should control their use either by affixing the postage to the letters or packages personally or by seeing the letters or packages it is going on before issuing postage to someone else.

When manual operations are used, the stamps are usually kept in an "out in the open" manner, and this may result in stamp losses owing to carelessness in handling and borrowing. To minimize these losses, an accounting should be maintained to show the number of letters mailed in comparison with the amount of stamps purchased. Special care must be exercised in the case of packages.

Many companies now use a meter-mail machine that imprints the postage seal either directly on a letter or, in the case of a package, on an adhesive paper tape which is affixed to the package. At the same time the postage seal is imprinted, a "meter ad," postmark, and date are also imprinted. This is illustrated by Figure 11–4. The machines are offered in an array of capacities and designs; many seal as well as stamp the envelope.

An important part of this machine is the meter, which is a detachable, portable unit containing the printing die for the postage and a recording mechanism. In buying postage, the meter is taken to the post office and set for a lump sum which is paid in advance. The set meter is then returned to the place of business and inserted into the machine, from

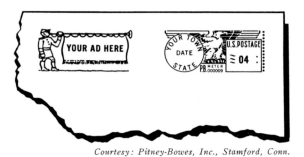

Courtesy: Pitney-Bowes, Inc., Stamford, Conn.

FIG. 11–4. Illustrative of metered-mail imprints, showing "meter ad," postmark, date, and amount of postage.

which metered stamps can be printed as and when needed. In essence, *a postage-meter machine is a government-licensed device for affixing postage.* Figure 11–5 illustrates a postage-meter machine. Meter mail has many advantages, including the following: (1) Time and effort are saved; (2) stamp losses are stopped; (3) accurate accounting of postal expenditures is provided; (4) date of mailing is shown; (5) quicker handling is provided by the originating post office, since no canceling is required; (6) the prestige of the user is increased; and (7) postmark, slogan, and advertising are added.

3. *Mailing the material.* It is advisable to post mail at regular intervals throughout the day. This practice smooths out the work load, minimizes the usual late afternoon peak, and helps the post office to deliver mail promptly. On distant mail, this practice might save a day. Also, knowledge of train and plane schedules is helpful in expediting mail. It is necessary to deliver certain classes of mail to the post office.

PERSONNEL OF MAIL ROOM

Competent help must be employed if the activities of the mail room are to be performed satisfactorily. Manual dexterity, dependability, and an ability to read rapidly are among the important attributes desirable in mail-room employees. Training designed to inform about postal regulations, company policies affecting mail handling, and the company's organizational units and the specific types of work done by each is strongly suggested and will usually pay big dividends. Some managers hold periodic meetings with the mail-room personnel, briefing them on regulations, postal data, and the importance of accuracy, neatness, and care in handling all mail. After investigating and establishing effective

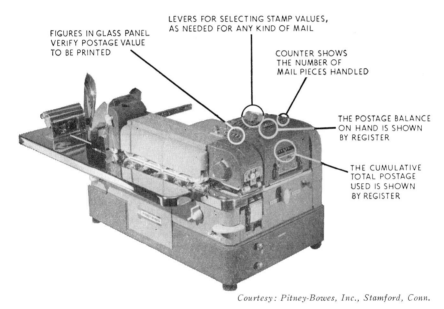

FIGURES IN GLASS PANEL VERIFY POSTAGE VALUE TO BE PRINTED

LEVERS FOR SELECTING STAMP VALUES, AS NEEDED FOR ANY KIND OF MAIL

COUNTER SHOWS THE NUMBER OF MAIL PIECES HANDLED

THE POSTAGE BALANCE ON HAND IS SHOWN BY REGISTER

THE CUMULATIVE TOTAL POSTAGE USED IS SHOWN BY REGISTER

Courtesy: Pitney-Bowes, Inc., Stamford, Conn.

FIG. 11–5. A postage-meter machine, with the important operations of the meter illustrated.

mail-room practices and procedures, the work of handling the mail will normally undergo relatively few changes. They will be more of degree than of kind. Hence, a manual carefully outlining the directions and instructions to be followed will prove highly beneficial.

CONTROL OF MAIL-ROOM OPERATIONS

Most control efforts affecting mail-room operations deal with either cost or conformity with postal standards and requirements. Hence, the head of the mailing department and key personnel must know the postal requirements, so that the proper amounts of postage—no more and no less—are affixed. Knowledge of the various classes of mail is basic. In general, first-class mail includes correspondence, securities, and documents; second-class mail, newspapers, magazines, and other periodicals; third-class mail, unsealed printed matter and form letters; fourth-class mail, packages and parcels. Special services, such as registered mail, certified mail, special delivery, and special handling, are available but should be used only under the right circumstances.

The following suggestions should be adopted:

1. *Include zone number in the address.*   This speeds delivery. The post office will indicate zone numbers on mailing lists free of charge. To receive this service, segregate the addresses by cities that have zone numbers and then turn these lists in to the local postmaster. He will zone the local addresses and forward the others to the respective proper cities, where they will be zoned and returned at no charge.

2. *Use standard-size envelopes.*   Standard-size envelopes are best suited for most purposes. The No. 9 or No. 10 envelope for correspond-

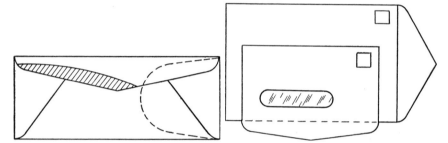

A postage-saver envelope requiring only third-class rate can be top-sealed like a first-class envelope. One end of flap remains unsealed to permit postal inspection.

With the two-in-one combination envelope, first-class mail in one compartment and third-class or fourth-class mail in the other can be mailed as a unit.

FIG. 11–6.   A postage-saver envelope and a two-in-one combination envelope.

ence is preferable, since only two horizontal folds in the enclosed material are necessary.

The postage-saver envelope permits third-class rates, yet gives the appearance of first-class mail. Also, the two-in-one combination envelope is recommended where a folder or booklet is sent with a letter. With this type of envelope, the letter or other first-class mail is in one compartment, while the folder or other third-class mail is in another compartment. Illustrations of the postage-saver and the two-in-one envelope are shown in Figure 11–6.

3. *Use window envelopes when feasible to do so.*   The risk of getting a letter in the wrong envelope and the necessity of sending individually addressed envelopes to the mail room are eliminated by the use of window envelopes. There is also a saving in cost. With regular envelopes, the labor costs for addressing are about $8.25 per thousand (assuming a rate of three a minute and wages at $1.50 per hour). Window en-

velopes cost about $2.00 per thousand more than regular envelopes, so the net saving realized by using window envelopes is $6.25 ($8.25 less $2.00) per thousand, or 75.7 per cent.

However, some people believe that window envelopes are less attractive and dignified than regular envelopes. Certain types of correspondence are probably best handled by regular envelopes. The final decision in this matter rests with the manager.

4. *Employ enclosed business reply envelopes to increase returns and lower costs.* A permit, for which no fee is paid, must be obtained to use these envelopes. The postage for such envelopes is of a collect-on-delivery type for which the initial sender pays 6 cents for each reply, based on a 4-cent regular charge plus 2 cents for the return privilege. If the return is less than 67 per cent of the original mailing, the use of business reply envelopes results in savings. When regular stamped envelopes are enclosed, the postage for 100 replies is $4.00; postage on 67 business reply envelopes is $4.02.

5. *Have posters, books, and guides available to mail personnel so that they can find out and apply the proper mail procedures.* The *United States Postal Guide* (which can be obtained from the Superintendent of Documents, Washington 25, D.C.) is especially recommended. The office manager should cultivate close co-operation with authorities of his local post office. They are always very helpful and can greatly assist in solving mailing problems.

TELEPHONE

Good telephone practices aid in building the good will of any enterprise, save time and energy, and help get work accomplished. The telephone has come into wide usage because it provides an inexpensive, convenient, and rapid means of communication. Being verbal in characteristic, the telephone is not well suited to convey information concerning drawings, sketches, or dimensions of parts. Conversing over the telephone places the participants in a peculiar relationship. The persons talking can hear but cannot see each other. The impression must rely entirely on the voice—its tone, clearness, and pleasantness; the selection of words; and the manner of speaking. All of these factors, properly blended, constitute the art of telephoning, which can be acquired.

Telephone systems can be classified into two types: (1) the outside telephone with extensions handled through a company switchboard (PBX) and (2) the private internal telephone (PAX). The former provides service for external calls coming into or going out of the office and for internal calls between telephones within the office. However, by using the new Dial PBX, outbound calls are dialed directly from every desk, so the telephone attendant can handle incoming calls and perform other work. Figure 11–7 shows a Dial PBX. In contrast, with the

Courtesy: Illinois Bell Telephone Co., Chicago

FIG. 11–7. The new Dial PBX provides an easy, part-time job for the attendant.

private internal telephone, "inside" calls do not go through the switchboard. Since, in the typical company, more than one half of the telephoning is internal—between telephones within the company—use of the private internal exchange relieves the regular telephone lines. This clears the way for better service on "outside" calls—those from customers and other important callers.

TELEPHONING BY THE PRIVATE SWITCHBOARD OPERATOR

Certain characteristics distinguish the seasoned and efficient telephone switchboard operator. For convenience, these characteristics may be divided into technical aspects and speech aspects. Under technical aspects are included the best way to handle the levers, the manipulation of the cords, the dialing of numbers, and the writing of messages, each of which constitutes an important segment of switchboard telephone efficiency. The best way of performing these tasks can be found by consulting the telephone company's special representative.

Speech aspects include the proper use of the voice over the telephone, the manner of speaking, and the standardization of certain phrases and words in conversation. They help to obtain faster service, better co-operation, and company good will. It may be well to secure the help of a trained consultant in this field. The following expressions are effective:

1. Identify the company immediately. To illustrate, say:

"Good morning. American Manufacturing Company," or
"American Manufacturing."

2. If the party must be delayed, the operator should say:

"The line is busy right now. Will you wait?"

3. When the caller agrees to wait, the operator should report about every thirty seconds, saying:

"The line is still busy."

When able to complete the call, the operator should say:

"I'll connect you now. Thanks for waiting," or "Here's the line now. Thanks for waiting."

When the caller cannot wait, his name and number should be obtained and the call returned.

TELEPHONING BY THE INDIVIDUAL

The good work of a private switchboard operator must be supplemented by proper telephone techniques on the part of the individual using the telephone. Again, these considerations can be viewed from the technical and also from the speech aspects.

Under technical aspects are the following:

1. To be heard clearly, speak directly into the transmitter, with the lips about 1 to 2 inches from the mouthpiece.

2. To hear better in a noisy office, place your hand over the mouthpiece, not over your ear.

3. To attract the operator's attention, move the receiver hook up and down slowly and evenly.

4. After finishing a conversation, replace the receiver gently on the hook, making certain the receiver is all the way down. Unless the receiver is all the way down, the line is either "out of order" or "busy" to anyone calling.

Speech aspects emphasize the following suggestions in order to gain the most satisfactory results:

1. Answer the telephone immediately and identify the department and yourself. For example, say:

"Cost Department, Mr. Allen."

If answering for someone else, give his name and then yours. Say:

"Mr. Brown's office. Miss Kenny speaking."

2. Handle, if possible, but transfer the call when it requires handling by someone else in the organization. To do this, advise the calling party he is being transferred to another phone. Say:

"I will transfer you to our accounting division. One moment, please."

Then flash and tell the switchboard operator:

"This call to Mr. Kohl."

3. When using the telephone, do not leave the line unless it is necessary. If this is the case, tell why and for how long. Say:

"Will you excuse me for a moment? I must look at our file on this."

4. On outgoing calls, introduce yourself promptly. Say:

"Hello, Mr. Briggs. This is Spencer of National Sales."

The office manager should maintain periodic checkups on the use of the telephone by company personnel. All calls should be handled in the prescribed manner. Data can be obtained on the time required to handle calls and on the manner of speech and use of words. Important activities upon which to focus control efforts include promptness in answering the telephone, helpfulness on all calls, and a pleasing telephone personality. Employees should be informed that periodic checkups are made. When necessary, remedial action should be taken without delay.

AUXILIARY TELEPHONE SERVICE

It is possible for several executives in different parts of the country to hold a conference by means of a simultaneous telephone hookup known as *conference call service*. The savings in time and trouble from this type of service are obvious. In some instances, the connections are monitored or recorded for possible future reference. When this is done, approval by the parties is necessary. The signal that the call is being recorded is a "beep" tone every fifteen seconds.

A perpetual telephone receptionist is afforded by the *automatic answering device*. This unit, about four times the size of a telephone, is linked to the telephone. Incoming calls are answered by a recorded message something like this:

"This is the Avenue Realty Company. Your call is being answered by an automatic answering device. Will you leave your name, telephone number, and message after you hear the 'beep' tone? You may leave a half-minute message for me, and I'll call you when I return. Thank you."

After returning to the office, all messages recorded by the unit are audited and the return calls made. The device is especially convenient not only for small, one-man offices and for medical doctors, but also for large offices during the nonworking hours, thus providing around-the-clock service. The cost is $30 per month after an installation fee of $15.

Radio-telephone service provides communication between moving units and any Bell System telephone. It is particularly adaptable for use by trucking, taxicab, and public service companies, and by police and fire departments.

To call a mobile unit, the regular desk phone is used. A request is made for the mobile service operator who, by means of radio, signals the driver of the mobile unit. This is done over an approved radio channel. The driver answers the call on his dashboard telephone, and the conversation takes place. In a similar manner, the driver can call his office from his mobile unit. Control over the radio frequencies used is under the jurisdiction of the Federal Communications Commission.

The above description covers the so-called "two-way" voice communication using a telephone instrument. There is also a one-way signaling service which signals only to the mobile unit. By means of a code, the driver translates the message, such as "Go to Warehouse R immediately," or "Drive to Third and Foster Streets at once."

WATS, or wide-area telephone service, provides unlimited interstate telephoning within specific areas for a flat monthly rate. It is designed for the customer who makes frequent calls to widely scattered and distant points.

INTERCOMMUNICATIONS SYSTEMS

Quick verbal communication is provided by means of intercommunication systems. The various individuals or stations are each equipped with a speaking-talking unit. By turning a switch or depressing a key, instant right of way is obtained with anyone in the circuit, and conversations can be conducted with great clarity of tone. When privacy is desired, the microphone in the unit can be turned off and a hand set substituted.

Many different capacities and features in units are available; usually, it is advisable to consult with the manufacturer or sales representative for specific data regarding individual requirements. The units can be connected in various circuit arrangements, depending upon the needs of the particular enterprise. Figure 11–8 shows various models of intercommunication units.

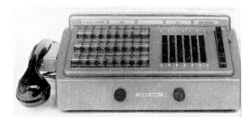

Courtesy: Executone, Inc., New York   *Courtesy: Du Kane Corp., St. Charles, Ill.*

FIG. 11–8. Intercommunication units enable the user to converse with any other master station or any staff station in the system. The hand set is optional; it provides complete privacy of conversation.

PAGING SYSTEMS

Important in most companies is the means of locating people through the use of flashing lights, tone bells, and buzzers. These paging devices are usually run by the telephone switchboard operator, or they may be a part of a private internal telephone system. The light or noise outlets are located throughout the office and plant, so that key personnel are free to leave their desks without fear of missing any calls. By means of a code, such as two long and two short rings for the president, one long and one short ring for the controller, and so on, these men are notified of calls. By telephoning the switchboard operator, the message is obtained. The system is quite effective, for it is convenient and is a time-saver to all concerned.

DELIVERY SERVICE

In the normal course of office work, many papers are handled successively by several employees, and this entails getting the papers from one employee to another. Notices and memorandums must be distributed, and reports must be sent to the executives. All these activities necessitate adequate delivery services.

Either a personal or a mechanical method can be employed. Selection depends upon the specific objectives of the delivery service. Usually, the following factors are of prime concern:

1. The total number of messages.
2. The frequency of the messages.
3. The number of delivery points.
4. The number of messages at each delivery point.
5. The distance between delivery points.
6. The maximum allowable time between delivery points.
7. The expense, including investment and operating costs.
8. The flexibility of the service to meet changing office conditions.

PERSONAL METHOD FOR CARRYING MESSAGES

The personal method is the oldest and the most common method of handling messages. To be of greatest benefit, the service must be regular and frequent. Schedules should call for deliveries about every half hour throughout the office. This time interval can be varied, depending upon the needs of the office. In some cases, calls every fifteen minutes might be required; in others, calls every hour might suffice. Very often, calls are made with greater frequency in the early morning and late afternoon business hours, in order to take care of the peak loads.

Deliveries can be made either on a desk-to-desk or on a departmental basis. The former is preferable and should be used whenever possible.

Desk-to-desk calls insure that the person intended to receive the material actually gets it, that messengers do all the messenger work, and that the distribution and collection are accomplished with a minimum of effort and confusion. In contrast, deliveries by departments require further distribution within each department and often result in costly delays.

The personal method for carrying messages provides excellent training for new, inexperienced employees. They can quickly learn the names of key employees, location of their work stations, layout of the office and plant, and the work of each organizational unit. Some large companies start all young office help as messengers before transferring them to their initially selected jobs.

Adequate control of the messenger service requires close supervision and adherence to practices and procedures, including the following:

1. The complete route must be established to include all desks designated as stations. The course to be followed must be defined, and the allowable time for one trip must be known. Adequate rest periods between trips are desirable and usually amount to about 20 per cent of the total travel time.

2. All desks designated as stations must be visited on each trip. Even though there is nothing to deliver, there might be something to pick up.

3. Messengers should confine their efforts to the delivery and pickup of written materials along the prescribed routes. The running of miscellaneous errands for members of the office should be forbidden.

4. Each member should be instructed to sort the papers as they are collected, so that on each trip, deliveries can be made to stations not yet called upon. Papers designated for stations already called upon are delivered on the next trip. This eliminates backtracking.

5. A designated area or receptacle for "incoming" and another for "outgoing" messages should be used at each station desk.

6. Each messenger should be provided with an accordion file with one section for each station or some similar arrangement. The file should be equipped with a shoulder strap for carrying, or mounted on wheels for pushing, from station to station.

7. A card-control system provides a check upon the activities of messengers. Several plans are possible.

a) The messengers can be required to check in, that is, to sign or punch a card at several well-selected stations along the route. These cards can be collected daily and inspected, and any irregularity of service can be investigated and corrected immediately.

b) The messengers can pick up a card and replace it with another at each station on the route. Different cards, identified by number or color, can be used for each trip; and by noting the card in the basket, spot checks can be made to find out if schedules are being maintained.

8. To inform employees politely of the last trip for the day, the messenger can either say, "Good night," or leave a card printed "Last collection has been made" in the basket.

MECHANICAL METHODS FOR CONVEYING MESSAGES

Mechanical conveyors are well suited to convey messages and papers when the work volume is large and fairly constant, and where stations remain fixed. Belt conveyors are probably the most common type used in an office. Brush-off stops can be provided at each station in order to permit the delivery of papers at specific points.

In the office of a mail-order wholesaler, order and form units coming down the belt conveyor are removed, information is checked and posted, and the units are returned to the conveyor in a series of various combinations of successive stations along the conveyor. The line of stations permits effective and rapid processing of stock record information. The conveyor moves at the rate of twelve feet a minute.

Pneumatic tubes are effective, easy to use, and do not require special skill to operate, Material is carried quickly and accurately to its destination. The initial cost of the tubes is rather high, but the maintenance cost is low. The use of pneumatic tubes is most economical where the volume of work is large. Different-sized tubes and tube carriers are offered. For example, a "4-inch tube carrier" is a popular size and has maximum inside length of 14 inches. Rectangular-shaped carriers are also available for handling bulky items.

In the case of a large aircraft manufacturer, the installation of pneumatic tubes linking seven buildings into one unit resulted in annual payroll savings of over $100,000. The manager of a medium-sized metal-processing company reduced messenger service costs by $4,200 a year by means of pneumatic tubes.

MECHANICAL METHODS FOR TRANSMITTING WRITTEN MESSAGES

This group constitutes those methods whereby the message is converted to energy impulses, transmitted by means of electrical or electronic circuits, and translated to a written or printed form at the receiving end. The original copy of the message remains in the hands of the sender, but the contents of the communication are transmitted to the recipient. Included in this classification are (1) teletypewriter, (2) telegraph, (3) telautograph, and (4) television.

TELETYPEWRITER

The teletypewriter, or TWX service of the telephone company, is a machine resembling a large typewriter that transmits messages between stations using telephone lines. The operation is based on the principle of combining the telephone and the typewriter. The machine has basically the same keyboard as a standard typewriter. When the keys are depressed, electric impulses reproduce the message in typed form on one machine or on many similar machines, the number being determined by the number of connections desired. Figure 11–9 shows a teletypewriter.

The machine is used very much like a telephone. To send a message, the TWX subscribers' directory is consulted, the call is placed by number, and the connection is made. Some 15,000 subscribers are listed in the TWX directory. Any two teletypewriters can be connected for communication in the same way as two telephones. Transmission is at the

Courtesy: Illinois Bell Telephone Co., Chicago

FIG. 11–9. A teletypewriter.

rate of seventy-five words per minute. The communication is two-way; a written conversation can be carried out. The service is especially effective over long distances. Charges are made on the basis of time and distance, similar to the long-distance telephone. Rates are approximately one third to one half less than those of the telephone.

TELEGRAPH

Another means of handling communications over relatively long distances is the telegraph. Telegrams secure attention, provide terse businesslike messages, and impel immediate action. They are used for practically all subjects or phases of business activities.

Telegraphic communications can be sent by any of four main ways: (1) over the counter—giving it to the operator at any branch office; (2) by messenger; (3) by telephone—similar to an ordinary telephone call, charges being made to the telephone account or paid by coins dropped into a public pay telephone; and (4) by mechanical tie lines, such as direct telephone connection, and the teleprinter. The direct telephone connection is simply a direct wire between the sender's office and the local telegraph office, and the teleprinter is a device similar to a typewriter which transmits the typed message electrically to the telegraph office. The message is recorded on paper tape both in the sending office and in the telegraph office. The former serves as the sender's reference copy; the latter is used to transmit the message to a circuit for its destination.

The cost of telegraphic communications varies with length of message, distance, and speed of delivery. Domestic messages are classified into the following main types: full-rate telegram—most expedient service; base rate applies to 15 words; (2) day letter—deferred slightly in handling; base rate applies to 50 words or less and is roughly 40 per cent more than that for a full-rate, 15-word telegram; (3) serial—a deferred message sent in sections to the same addressee during the day; cost is about 20 per cent more than for a day letter containing the same number of words; and (4) night letter—an inexpensive overnight service; base rate applies to 50 words or less and is about 75 per cent of that of a full-rate, 15-word telegram.

Cablegrams or services to foreign countries are classified as (1) ordinary—the standard full-rate service, (2) urgent—priority over all other messages except government messages, (3) deferred—no priority over other types, and (4) night letter—messages permitting overnight delivery.

Code words are sometimes used for telegraphic communications in order to reduce costs or to insure secrecy. For example, the code word "ROEUZ" might mean: "What action shall I take?" Commercial codes are available, or a special code can be created.

Anything printed or drawn, such as layouts, drawings, or charts, can now be transmitted instantly and accurately by WIREFAX, a special service using telegraph equipment. Actually, WIREFAX is a public facsimile system that transmits in units up to 7½ by 9½ inches. Cost depends upon amount and distance. Charges for the initial unit between Chicago and New York are $4.60, and each additional unit is 55 cents.

TELAUTOGRAPH

Another mechanical means for transmitting messages is the telautograph. As the name suggests, it transmits a handwritten message. The writing is electrically reproduced over comparatively short distances, such as between main office and receiving room, department and department, and warehouse and main office. In order to send a message, a switch is turned on, and the message is written with a metal stylus on a

metal platen. In order to
see what is being written,
the sender watches the pen
of the instrument writing
on a roll of paper. Figure
11–10 illustrates a telautograph. As the message
is written, it is reproduced
almost simultaneously at
one or a number of con-
nected receiving points.

A telautograph pro-
vides economical and high-
speed transmitting and
receiving of messages.
Handwritten records are
furnished and can be at-

Courtesy: TelAutograph Corp., Los Angeles

FIG. 11–10. A TelAutographic transceiver,
which transmits and receives electronic handwritten
messages, including special symbols and sketches.

tached to such things as inquiries, notices, and shipping instructions. It
is possible to carry on a written conversation—messages can be sent and
received.

TELEVISION

One of the newer methods for transmitting written messages is television. Although its current application in business is limited, television
holds much promise for the future. By means of closed circuits, it is
possible to transmit and have instantaneous receipt at many points. Television presents the message visually and in motion—a series of events.
However, it does not provide a written message to the recipient.

A television-telephone, enabling the caller to see as well as hear the
party at the other end of the line, is available. When the caller lifts the
television-telephone, his image appears simultaneously on one half of
his screen and upon one half of that of the party being called. When the
party answers, his image appears on the remaining halves of the two
screens. The unit is about the size of a conventional television table model
set. Maximum effective distance is about one mile. Television-telephone
applications include those in large industrial plants to compare drawings
and materials, in banks to check signatures, and in penal institutions to
serve as an electronic guard.

RECEPTION SERVICE

To many visitors, the first impression of a company is frequently
gained from the receptionist. Courteous and prompt treatment should be
extended visitors in order to build and develop company public relations
and good will. The receptionist's basic job is to (1) find out with which

person, if any, the visitor should talk; and (2) arrange for the visitor to see the proper person quickly.

A pleasant manner of speech and a winning personality are highly important; but in addition, certain standardized procedures have been found most effective. For example, in securing information from callers, the receptionist should ask: "What company do you represent?" or "May I help you?" Should the visitor say he is calling about a personal matter, or words to that effect, it is well for the receptionist to inquire: "Does Mr. —— know you?" If an evasive or a negative reply is given, the receptionist should ask if someone has sent the caller. If no one has, a recommended procedure is to say: "I'll let you talk with Mr. ——'s secretary, who will try to help you."

When the person called on is too busy to see the caller, the receptionist should address the visitor with: "I'm sorry, Mr. —— is busy and will not be able to see you. Can you come back or phone first for an appointment?" In situations where the person is absolutely not interested in talking with the caller, the receptionist must be tactful and courteous. Refusals to grant short interviews with callers should be held at an absolute minimum; but when necessary, the receptionist might say: "I am sorry, but Mr. —— is not interested in what you have to offer." Under no circumstance should the receptionist suggest that the visitor call later if the person being called upon has no intention of seeing him. Honesty is the best policy.

The receptionist must be fully familiar with what matters are handled by each employee who has callers. Normally, a guide or booklet is available for reference. Customarily, the receptionist keeps a report of callers, including the date, the name of each caller, the name of his company, and the person called on. When individual conditions permit, the receptionist might also perform office work of sorting, stuffing envelopes, typing, or operating the telephone switchboard. However, if there is too much extra work, the regular duties of the receptionist might be neglected. The office manager should watch this carefully.

TAPE AND WIRE RECORDERS

These devices are being used for a large number of applications, including the recording of inventory counts, personnel interviews, laboratory tests, and sales talks. In the case of inventory counts, the person taking the count is equipped with a microphone attached to the recorder in the office. As the inventory count is obtained, it is spoken and thus recorded. A typist then plays the recording and types the inventory lists. Intermediate paper work, tally sheets, and the like are eliminated. Likewise, interviews with prospective employees or, in the case of lawyers, talks with clients can be recorded and studied for complete information —a more effective practice than the use of handwritten notes, which often inhibit the speaker. However, when conversations are recorded, approval by both parties is necessary.

Tape or wire is used in the operation of the machine. The tape is a narrow, thin, flexible, paper-like material coated on one side with magnetic oxide of iron; when wire is used, it is of a special type. The sound is recorded by a magnetic principle. A recorder is slightly larger and heavier than a portable typewriter. Figure 11–11 shows a popular tape recorder.

Courtesy: Webster-Chicago Corp., Chicago

FIG. 11–11. A high-fidelity recording and playback tape recorder.

QUESTIONS

1. State concisely the difference between each of the following:
   a) A window envelope and a business reply envelope.
   b) Mail and interdepartmental memorandums.
   c) Metered mail and nonmetered mail.
   d) Postage-saver envelope and regular standard envelope.

2. What is a postage meter? Explain in nontechnical language what must be done in connection with its use in an office.

3. Discuss a satisfactory approach to the determining of a company's communicative needs.

4. What practical suggestions would you give to a newly hired head of the mail room of an office in order to help him succeed on the job?

5. Briefly describe each of the following, pointing out for what type of communication and under what circumstances it is best suited:
   a) WIREFAX service.
   b) TWX service.
   c) WATS telephone service.
   d) Television.

6. What are the major considerations you feel necessary for acquiring adequate control of a personal messenger service in an office?

7. In your opinion, which three of the following attributes would you emphasize in managing the mail room?
   a) Speed.
   b) Cost.
   c) Economy.
   d) Dependability.
   e) Training area for other office jobs.
   f) Accuracy.
   Justify your selection.

8. Under what general circumstances would you suggest that an enterprise use (*a*) the telegraph, (*b*) the long-distance telephone, (*c*) an air-mail

letter, (d) the teletypewriter, and (e) the telautograph. Give reasons for your answers.

9. Mr. Burns comes to you for advice concerning the management of the reception service of his company. What specific suggestions would you give him?

10. Enumerate and discuss briefly the minimum activities you feel necessary to insure adequate control of outgoing mail in a large office.

11. Relate how you would apply managerial actuating work to a messenger boy.

12. Do you believe that the management of mail and office communicative services should be under the jurisdiction of the office manager? Justify your viewpoint.

CASE PROBLEMS

Case 11–1. Hoosier Pharmaceuticals, Inc.

This company sells a variety of pharmaceuticals to a large number of customers, including hospitals, drugstores, and physicians' supply stores. Distribution is nationwide, and the company is well known and established. About 75 per cent of the company's shipments are in small packages—not over 8 × 8 × 6 inches.

Many of the packages are sent by (1) air mail, (2) special delivery, or (3) special handling, because the customer usually wants the pharmaceuticals as soon as possible. Mailing the packages in this manner incurs additional fees charged by the post office. Special delivery provides immediate delivery at the post office of the addressee; special handling applies to fourth-class mail only and insures prompt and expeditious handling by the post office. Starting at 3:00 P.M., several truckloads of packages are taken to the post office. The last load leaves the company building at 4:30 P.M.

A careful investigation by Mr. Charles Meyers, the office manager, showed that a great majority of the packages could be sent by regular mail, provided the packages were ready to go at stated times throughout the day, and would reach their determination as quickly as by the use of special mailing services. Mr. Meyers estimates the savings from planned scheduled mailing and the use of regular mailing service at about $65 a day.

He feels that some loss is suffered due to stamp pilferage. Currently, stamps are kept in a desk drawer of the packing room and distributed by Mr. James Lange, the foreman. However, this distribution is loosely handled, in the opinion of Mr. Meyers. The foreman contends that he cannot sit at the desk all day long to issue the proper amount of stamps, nor can he check each package mailed for correct postage. He has suggested that the company get a postage-meter machine; but Mr. Meyers has not taken this suggestion seriously, as quite frequently emergency letters or packages must be sent out during nonregular working hours, that is, at night or during Saturdays and Sundays. Mr. Meyers contends that under such conditions, a key to the postage-meter machine would have to be given to each of several people; consequently, control over its use would be diluted.

It is also believed that orders to the same customer on the same day could be grouped and packed in the same box, thus reducing handling expense, as well as being more convenient for the customer. Mr. James Lange disagrees with this suggestion, pointing out that the postage will be about the same and the time spent in grouping orders to the same customer will slow the work of his men.

Problems:

1. Do you agree with the viewpoints advanced by Mr. James Lange? Why?
2. What action do you recommend be taken? Justify your viewpoint.
3. How should Mr. Meyers proceed in this situation?

Case 11–2. Eggert Chemical Company

On a tract of thirty-one acres of land, this company operates three plants in which asphalt products, roofing materials, and naphthalene are respectively manufactured. In addition, a fourth building, housing a control laboratory, is located near the north side of the tract. This laboratory building is about half a city block from the asphalt products unit, a city block from the roofing materials unit, and a city block and one half from the naphthalene unit.

Under the present arrangement, operators from each of the three operating plants bring samples to the control laboratory for testing. Later, they return for the results. The work of the laboratory is vital, for the products must meet specific chemical specifications.

Since the samples are brought into the laboratory from different sources, there is no control of the flow of the receipt of this work. At times, peak loads occur, and samples cannot be run immediately.

Frequently, the operators make several trips to the laboratory to get the results on the samples brought in. If the tests are not completed, the operators may linger in the laboratory waiting for their completion. On some occasions, a great deal of unnecessary conversation with the technicians and other operators takes place, thus interfering with both manufacturing and laboratory efficiency.

Problems:

1. Enumerate the more important possible actions which the manager of the Eggert Chemical Company might take to improve the communicative services within the company.
2. Which action do you recommend be followed? Why?
3. Explain how you would proceed to justify your recommendation.

Chapter 12

STORAGE—EFFECTIVE FILING

Fool me once, shame on you; fool me twice, shame on me.

—CHINESE PROVERB

FILING CONSTITUTES a major segment of office work. Pertinent written information concerning decisions, thoughts, contracts, obligations, drawings, and transactions must be available when needed, in order that the office may provide its needed service.

Filing is the placing of papers in acceptable containers according to some predetermined arrangement so that any paper, when required, can be located quickly and conveniently. Emphasis is upon the "finding," not the "storing," aspect. The written information is retained for future possible use. Placing it in safekeeping is important; being able to find it promptly, when wanted, is vital. One needed paper lost or mislaid can delay a dozen employees in their work.

THE FILING PROBLEM

Filing is becoming more important and more complex. Each year, greater quantities of papers must be filed; and the problems of how best to handle them for quick reference, what arrangement to follow, what policies to adopt, and what equipment to utilize require competent office managerial action. The current condition is the result of many influences, but leading factors include the extensive use of credit buying, dispersion of operations, increase in products and services offered, governmental requirements, and the capacity to create more records, especially as a result of office automation.

Our ability to utilize effectively and to control records has apparently not kept pace with our ability to produce them. For the increase in records has not resulted directly in increased office efficiency. Failure to realize that every record created and processed must have proper disposition, and lack of control over the interrelated functions which produce nonessential and excessive records, are an important part of the filing problem. It cannot be viewed as a separate entity; it is an integral part of paper work processing.

ARRANGEMENT OF PAPERS IN FILE

Consideration for the type of material handled, the nature and size of the enterprise, and the peculiarities of the particular business influence the selection of the filing arrangement. There are numerous ready-made filing arrangements from which to choose. Different manufacturers stress different features. The arrangement adopted should provide for distinct classifications or divisions of the material, allow for possible expansion, and be inclusive of all the material to be handled. Fundamentally, the arrangement should stress this condition: When searching for information, there should be as few places to look as possible, preferably one.

Material can be filed according to four basic arrangements: alphabetical, numerical, geographical, and chronological. Various combinations of these are possible and, in fact, are commonly used. For example, an alphabetical-numerical plan is often employed; and in many alphabetical files, the material in each subdivision is arranged chronologically, i.e., the latest paper always on top. Likewise, the usual filing practice under the geographical plan is to arrange subdivisions alphabetically.

ALPHABETICAL

The alphabetical arrangement is the most widely used form of filing. It stresses the name or topic as the important item; and it can be considered the foundation of practically all filing, since in most instances, when other forms are used, the arrangement of the smaller units is usually alphabetical.

Under the alphabetical arrangement, all material is filed in dictionary order. If the first letter is not sufficient for determining the proper place of the material, the second and, if necessary, the third and fourth succeeding letters are used. See Figure 12–1. For any given total of names, the probable number which will occur in each subdivision of the alphabet is known. For example, names beginning with the letters S, B, M, and H, respectively, are most common; those beginning with X, Q, and U occur least frequently. For a given quantity of names, there are usually about three times as many names under B as under A, twenty times as many under H as under I, and ten times as many under T as under U. Information of this sort is utilized scientifically in determining filing guide subdivisions, which can be purchased as standard equipment. Sets ranging from 24 to some 2,600 subdivisions are available.

To provide for expansion, sets are available that permit the inserting of additional subdivisions to the original set. For example, a set of 300 subdivisions is converted into one of 400 subdivisions simply by adding

FIG. 12–1. Alphabetical filing.

an expansion package of 100 subdivisions. None of the original sub-divisions are discarded; there is no waste.

The advantages of alphabetical filing are that direct reference is provided, a quick check is offered on misfiled material, and common names are grouped. It is sometimes considered "the natural way to file." Figure 12–2 illustrates a modern alphabetical filing arrangement for correspondence. From this illustration, the following can be observed:

1. The primary guides, or partitions segregating the material, give the chief breakdowns of the alphabet and are identified by green tabs occupying the first three positions which are shown along the top left portion of the guide.[1] These tabs are marked with letters and numbers, i.e., $A = 1$, $Abr = 2$, $Ad = 3$, $Ag = 4$, etc. The number expedites the filing work. When considering the letter d, it is a little difficult to recall that d is between c and e. In contrast, no thought is required to remember that the number 3 is between 2 and 4.

2. Individual folders containing regular correspondence are filed behind their proper primary guide and tabbed in the fifth or extreme right position: "1. Aaron, Carl"; "1. Abbott, A. M."; etc.

3. Miscellaneous folders, used for occasional and miscellaneous correspondence, are marked with red tabs in the first three positions. These folders correspond in identification and number with the primary guides and are placed in the back of each primary-guide spacing. When regular

---

[1] Tabs are located by position along the width of the guide. At the left is the first position, and moving to the right are the second, third, fourth, and fifth positions; the fifth position is at the extreme right.

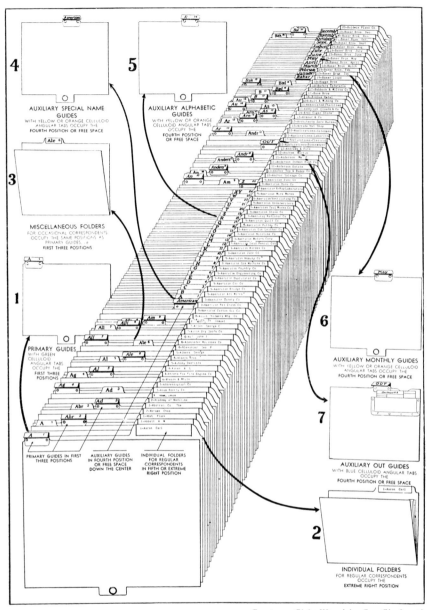

Courtesy: Globe-Wernicke Co., Cincinnati

FIG. 12–2. Filing arrangement under a modern alphabetical correspondence-filing plan.

material is moved to the transfer file, the miscellaneous folders are moved also and serve as primary guides in this file.[2]

4. Auxiliary guides, tabbed in the fourth or right-center position, are used to simplify and to speed the filing by dividing primary-guide spacings according to individual needs. Auxiliary guides may include (*a*) common titles and names, such as "American," "Brown," "Smith," and "United States"; (*b*) alphabetical listings which segregate the material under the common title or name—"American Art Works" or "American Bridge Co.," for example; and (*c*) monthly listings which separate the material under the common title or name by months— "Baker Bros.—Jan.," "Baker Bros.—Feb.," and "Baker Bros.—March."

5. Out guides are tabbed with blue in the fourth position and are inserted in the file when any folder is taken out. Each out guide is equipped with a holder device for a charge-out card. Entries on this card show when a folder is removed, by whom, and when returned. Out guides are also available in folder form, in which case spaces are ruled on the side in order to record data on removals.[3]

SUBJECT FILING

A modification of the alphabetical arrangement is subject filing, in which the arrangement of material is according to subject or descriptive feature instead of name. For example, all material pertaining to insurance is put in one main division and all material on taxes in another division. If necessary, subdivisions of each subject are made. For Insurance, the subdivisions might be Accident, Fire, and Group; and the material is usually filed alphabetically under each classification. The choice of subject heading should be inclusive and descriptive of the contents.

Subject filing is helpful in indicating the main classifications for separate files in an office. To illustrate, a separate file may be used for each main subject, such as costs, orders, personnel, purchases, and taxes. Subheadings are included under each main subject, for example, under Orders are Adjustments, Collections, Complaints, Correspondence, and Shipments. In addition, subject filing places all material of a common descriptive feature together, so that it can be used conveniently. Common examples of subject filing include executive files, files of material going between home office and branches, interdepartmental written material, research data, clippings, and notes.

NUMERICAL FILING

In this filing arrangement, each item filed has a number, and location of the material is by numerical sequence. Numerical files are used for such material as bank checks, invoices, engine numbers, and papers pertaining to freight cars. However, the numerical arrangement is not con-

---

[2] The transfer of filed material is discussed in Chapter 13.

[3] The subject of charging material out is discussed on page 221.

fined to prenumbered material. Items such as letters, memorandums, and notices are also filed according to this plan; and in such cases, an auxiliary alphabetical card file is employed to learn the proper filing number. The system of numbers can be basically one of two types: (1) serial—to provide unlimited expansion, or (2) coded—to indicate specific types of items. An illustration of the latter type is given below:

Divisions

100. *General Sales*	200. *Production*	300. *Research*
110. Recap of orders booked	210. Purchasing	310. Consumer studies
120. Recap of sales shipped	220. Payroll	320. Radio ratings
130. Expenditures	230. Budget	330. Television surveys
140. Budget	240. Recap of items completed	340. Readership records
		350. Product testing

The numerical plan offers simple provisions for expansion, some degree of secrecy, ease and speed of operation, and an effective means of identification. Numbers are easy to work with; in fact, most alphabetical filing systems use numbers on the file guides, in addition to the letters, in order to expedite finding. Figure 12–3 shows the arrangement of a numerical file.

Terminal-Digit Filing. Although ordinary numerical filing is a conventional way to file numbered records, it has certain serious disadvantages. Among these are the following: (1) "Misfiles" increase, as the filing personnel must read numbers of six or more digits; and (2) the newest records, usually those referred to most frequently, are placed at

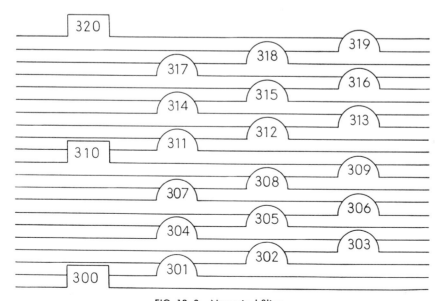

FIG. 12–3. Numerical filing.

one end of the file, thus causing filing activity to be concentrated and congested in the newer sections.

Terminal-digit filing eliminates these difficulties, yet retains the benefits of the numerical file. In terminal-digit filing, numbers are used, but they are read from right to left instead of the conventional left to right. Hence, records are filed according to the last digit or, more commonly, the last two digits, then the next two or subdivision thereof. To illustrate:

		In Terminal-Digit File Last-Two Number Breakdown with Sub-divisions Thereof
In Numerical File	*In Terminal-Digit File Last-Two Number Breakdown*	
160 79	3 25 41	5 17 41
174 63	5 17 41	3 25 41
325 41	1 74 63	1 74 63
517 41	1 60 79	1 60 79

GEOGRAPHICAL FILING

The main filing divisions in the geographical arrangement include states, counties, cities, branch-office territories, and salesmen's areas.

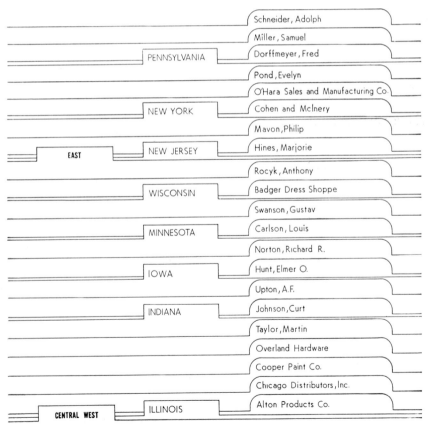

FIG. 12–4. Geographical filing.

Usually, the subdivisions are arranged alphabetically; for example, a sales area by cities in alphabetic order, and each city by customers' names in alphabetic order.

The geographical arrangement, sometimes called location arrangement, is easy to understand, simple and direct, and can cover the over-all work division, particularly that of sales. The files are generally less unwieldy than is frequently the case with the other basic arrangements. Also, several people can work at the files simultaneously—for instance, one in the Philadelphia file for "Cupper Manufacturing Company" and the other in the Los Angeles file for "Cizzla Sales Corporation." In addition, the geographical arrangement makes it comparatively simple to compile mailing lists by states or cities; and the segregation of material for tax, political, or mailing reasons is readily provided.[4] Figure 12–4 shows a geographical plan of filing.

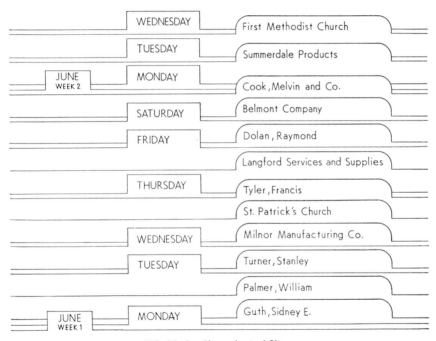

FIG. 12–5. Chronological filing.

CHRONOLOGICAL FILING

The chronological filing arrangement simply arranges material according to its time sequence. The main divisions are either months or weeks, with the subdivisions being days. Some correspondence, bills,

---

[4] For a thorough discussion of geographic methods of filing, see B. M. Weeks, *How to File and Index* (3d. ed.; New York: Ronald Press Co., 1956), chap. vi. This book presents the principles and practical aspects of office filing in a concise and understandable manner.

and pending accounts payable can be handled on a chronological plan.

The advantages of this plan are simplicity, ease of filing, and a convenient signal or reminder of unfinished work, which is shown by the material in the file with reference to a specific date. Figure 12–5 (page 217) illustrates chronological filing.

Tickler File. The "tickler file" is an adaptation of chronological filing. Future matters requiring attention within fairly well-defined time limits are filed under due dates or the time when action should be taken. A glance at the file shows for any given time what matters are to be followed up, what ones are behind schedule, and what ones must be handled in the near future.

FILE INDEXING

The file index furnishes the key to how the materials are arranged. For any given set of material, a choice is made from several possible indexes. In some cases, the subject is the best index; in others, the name of the customer or the point of destination might be most useful. To illustrate, the following material could be indexed in any one of the several different ways indicated:

Material	*File according to:*
Catalogues:	Date, name of company, or name of product
Correspondence:	Date, subject, name of company, name of customer, name of seller, point of destination, or point of origin
Invoices:	Date, name of customer, or number
Personnel application forms:	Name of applicant, or type of work (subject)
Purchase orders:	Date, name of vendor, name of product, or number
Tax reports:	Date, subject, or name of taxing body

Cross Indexing. Cross indexing is used when more than one subject is covered by the material or when several indicators are helpful in finding it. A report dealing with the subjects of market expansion and finances could be filed under the subject of markets, sales, future sales, finances, or costs. Cross indexes provide information as to where to place and to find the report; however, numerous cross references should be avoided in order to simplify the work as much as possible. It is best to have these indexes on reference cards which can be maintained in a separate file. To find material on wages, the index card might read:

Wages	*See also* Compensation
	Fringe Benefits
	Job Evaluation
	Salary

This means that material on Wages may be found under all five terms.

Phonetic Indexing. In a great many instances, a name can be spelled in different ways, thus causing a filing problem when extensive lists of names are included. For example, the name "Barnett" can also be spelled "Barnet," "Bornet," "Bornett," and so forth. Under which spelling is such a name filed or found? Poor handwriting and errors in transcribing might add further to the filing perplexity. To meet this problem, a system of file indexing based on the pronunciation or sound of the name has been developed.

Under this system, all names are coded by use of the "Soundex Code," which is:

Code Numbers	Key Letter Equivalents
1	b, f, p, v
2	c, g, j, k, q, s, x, z
3	d, t
4	l
5	m, n
6	r

The letters *a, e, i, o, u* and *w, h, y* are not coded. In addition, the following practices apply:

1. The initial letter is not coded but is used as a prefix to code a number which always has three digits.

2. The zero is used where there is no key letter equivalent.

3. Doubled key letters are coded as one, that is, *rr* as *r*.

4. A key letter and its equivalent are likewise coded as one, that is, *ck* as *c*.

To illustrate, the name "Barnett" would be coded B–653; "Barnet," B–653; and "Bornet," B–653. Thus, all names which sound alike, although spelled differently, have identical index numbers. This means that they are in the same classification or grouping in the file and hence are quickly located. A phonetic filing system can therefore be considered a special type of alphabetic-numeric arrangement. Among the important advantages of phonetic indexing are the following: Ninety per cent of all family names are grouped automatically, duplications are detected, unlimited expansion and flexibility are provided, the effect of transcribing errors is minimized, and a uniform and precise indexing method is provided.

FILING PROCEDURE

One of the means for accomplishing an effective filing system is to follow a definite, well-planned filing procedure. The chief steps in such a procedure include the following:

1. *Checking release for filing.* Before any material is prepared for filing, it must first be checked to be sure it is released for filing. Material

which is still being processed or referred to, or which, because of policy, is not retained by the company, should, of course, not be placed in the files.

2. *Reading and marking for filing*. Reading is done to determine the proper filing classification. Care must be exercised in the reading; otherwise, a "misfile" or "lost record" will result. Immediately after reading, the material is marked to identify its filing classification. This marking can be done by underscoring or circling a word or two on the paper or

Courtesy: Erie Railroad, Cleveland

FIG. 12–6. Sorting waybills in a large office. Approximately three million waybills per year are sorted in this office.

by stamping or writing the proper file data in the upper right-hand corner. A colored pencil usually works very satisfactorily, as the contrast aids future reference. If the filing is by subject or there is a possibility of filing under several headings, a cross-reference card should be made out and placed in the separate cross-reference file.

3. *Sorting*. When properly handled, sorting speeds up the operation of filing. Sorting can be performed entirely manually or with the use of a sorting device. In the former, the material is divided into neat piles on a table or desk, each pile being of a different classification. When this method is followed, it is best to sort all material according to major divisions, then each major division by subdivisions, and finally each subdivi-

sion as required. Figure 12–6 shows sorting devices being used in a large office. The device consists of dividers properly indexed and hinged, at intervals of about ¼ inch up to 1 inch, to a common base section. Thus, a series of pockets is formed, and each item of the material to be sorted is dropped into the proper pocket. Different sizes are available, ranging from around 30 up to as many as 2,000 divisions or pockets.

4. *Filing material.* Each piece is filed under the proper classification, with the newest addition always on top or at the front of the contents in its respective folder. This actually amounts to dropping the material into the file at the right place.

5. *Charging material out.* This last step deals with the removal of papers from the file. A definite manner for handling this work is necessary in order to know where items are, in the event that several people want the papers at the same time, and also to minimize indiscriminate removals from the files with the resultant high loss of material. Records of charged-out materials can be handled in any one of four ways: by substitution card, out folders, out guides, or multiple charge-out forms. Figure 12–7 illustrates these different media.

When the removed material is a single card or piece of paper, its place in the file can be occupied by a substitution card showing the name of the person to whom the material is issued, along with the date and the initials of the file clerk issuing the material. Upon return of the material, the entries on the substitution card are lined out, and the card is reused.

The "out folders" are ordinary file folders with one side printed for the recording of data concerning removals. The out folder serves as a substitute for the regular folder and permits the removal of only single papers.

When an entire folder is removed, either the out folder or the out guides can be used. The "out guide" is a pressboard guide with tab printed "Out" and a pocket or device to hold a charge-out slip. The out guide replaces the material taken from the file and serves both as a record and as a marker for the borrowed material.

Multiple charge-out forms are used to keep a record of the transfer of charged-out material from one user to another. The date, identification, and route of material are written on the card. Depending on the system used, one copy of the form is attached to the substitution card, placed in the out folder, or inserted in the pocket of the out guide. A second copy is filed in a tickler file for follow-up. Other copies are attached to the material so that, as each individual or department using the material finishes with it, a line is drawn through the name or department on the route list; the top copy is returned to the filing department; and the remaining copies and material are forwarded to the next name on the route list. The returned copy received by the filing department is attached to the tickler file copy; thus, there is a record of who has the material, with-

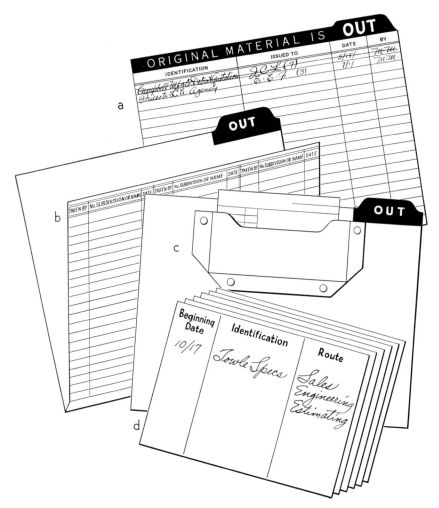

FIG. 12–7. Media used in controlling charge-outs from filed material: (a) substitution card, (b) out folder, (c) out guide, and (d) multiple charge-out form.

out clearance of the filed material each time through the filing department.

FILING PRACTICES

Certain filing practices have been found helpful, and adherence to them will probably bring best results. However, in certain individual cases, slight deviations might work out advantageously, depending upon the circumstances. A complete list of these filing practices is beyond the scope of this book, but the more important ones include the following:

1. Use a sufficient number of guides to help place and find the material quickly. This usually means a guide for each inch of filing.

2. File material *behind* the guides.

3. Use colored tabs and labels to increase identification and to prevent misfiling.

4. Provide, with reference to correspondence files, individual folders when five or more papers have accumulated. Crowded miscellaneous folders frequently indicate that more breakdowns of the alphabet are needed.

5. Arrange material in folders chronologically, the latest at the front.

6. Leave 3–4 inches of working space in the file drawer to avoid jamming the files and wasting time in obtaining materials.

7. File each name according to (*a*) surname, (*b*) given name or initial, (*c*) middle name or initial, and (*d*) title, if important to retain.

> Alexander, Charles D. (Dr.)

8. File "nothing before something."

> Carter
> Carter, George
> Carter, George L.

9. File alphabetical material in exact sequence of letters, *A* through *Z*, to the last letter of the last word.

> M & A Stores, Inc.
> Maag, Robert C.
> MacArthur, Thomas P.
> Mack, Henry
> MacTavish, Sam W.
> Maleski, Franck C.
> McGuire, William F.
> Mead-Carters Co.

10. Treat compound words as one word.

> Cohen, Julius I.
> Co-operative Sales
> Co-Workers Order of Bart
> Cutter, Frederick J.

11. Spell out abbreviated names.

> Safety Tool and Tire Company
> Saint Louis Poultry and Egg Company
> Saint Paul Club
> Salk, Meyer L.
> Street, Theodore P.

12. Spell out numerals and abbreviations.

> First National Bank
> Three Thirty-Three Lake Building
> Young Women's Christian Association

13. When names are identical, file by city; then state; and if necessary, by street address in city.

> Carson, John M.
>   Bangor, Maine
> Carson, John M.
>   Springfield, Mass.
> Carson, John M.
>   3719 Lyndale Road
>   Springfield, Ohio
> Carson, John M.
>   5127 Western Street
>   Springfield, Ohio

14. Sort material alphabetically by first segregating into four groups,
such as *A–F*, *G–L*, *M–R*, and *S–Z;* then, sort each group according to
the first letter. Likewise, with numeric material, first sort 0–2, 3–5, and
6–9; then, sort each group by the first digit. This procedure usually
saves a great deal of time.

15. Use top drawers for current filing, bottom drawers for most recent transfer. This expedites quick reference.[5]

16. Transfer material to inactive file regularly and at stated intervals.

FILING CABINETS

Filing cabinets are available in many different sizes and types designed to fulfill every filing need. They are made to accommodate many
different sizes of material, but those for cards— 3 × 5-inch or 5 × 8-
inch—letter, and legal-size papers are most popular. The equipment is
available in sizes from one to six drawers. The one- and two-drawer
models are used on a desk or table; the three-drawer is desk height and
is usually used beside a desk, providing ready accessibility to papers
frequently used. Four-drawer models are used for counter purposes. The
five- and six-drawer files provide extra large filing capacities for the
floor space occupied. A standard file drawer holds about 5,000 sheets of
paper, 300 file folders, and 26 file guides.

The mechanical details of files differ with the manufacturers. Most
files feature a ball-bearing, full progressive side-arm suspension which
provides smooth rolling action of the drawer and permits easy opening
and closing. A sliding, adjustable device known as a "follower" holds
the papers upright in the drawer. It can be pulled up tight and snapped
or locked in position; a slight force releases the device and permits it to
be moved to another position. In some files, when the drawer is opened,
the front of the drawer tilts forward and, at the same time, the back of
the drawer tilts backward, thus opening the filed material like pages of a

---

[5] Transfer of filed material is discussed in the following chapter on records
retention.

book. This permits easy and rapid access to the filed materials. Steel cabinets have won general acceptance and favor. The equipment is available with or without locks, insulated for fire protection, and in several colors and finishes to harmonize with the color scheme of the office.

MOTORIZED CARD FILES

When the work requires access to a large number of filed cards, a motorized card file may be useful. It is electrically operated and brings in a few seconds any desired tray of cards in the unit at convenient writing height to a seated operator. The cards are filed vertically, and the trays are removable. Units are available in various card sizes and capacities. Savings in time and effort result from the use of motorized card files. Demanding specifications in respect to space limitations, floor layout, and operational problems can be met. A motorized card file unit is shown in Figure 12–8.

Courtesy: Remington Rand Inc., New York

FIG. 12–8. A motorized card file providing an ideal work station with availability to a large number of cards.

SIDE-FILING CABINETS

Filing cabinets are also available in which the compartments swing open sideways, thus exposing the entire contents on an open-faced shelf providing increased visibility and accessibility. These files are available in letter and legal size, and in two-, three-, and four-compartment units. Advantages claimed for filing equipment of this design include the following: (1) It permits full and easy accessibility to all materials; (2) it conserves energy, since the folders can be slid instead of lifted out; and (3) it saves floor space—the file depth is approximately 12 inches and the projection of an open compartment is 7 inches, much less than in the case of the ordinary filing cabinet. Side-filing cabinets have won extensive favor in executive offices. The two-compartment model can form a part of an executive L-shaped desk unit and works in well with the executive decor.

ROTARY FILES

In this equipment, the material is held to the periphery of a wheel which, when revolved, affords ready and quick means for locating any record at writing height. Posting is convenient without removal of the card. The unit provides speedy handling, enormous saving of motion— up to 75 per cent has been estimated—and compactness.

Many different models are available. The range of sizes is from small units about the size of a telephone to large units approximately 36 inches high. The capacity varies, of course, with the size of the wheel;

Courtesy: Wheeldex and Simpla Products, Inc., White Plains, N.Y.

FIG. 12–9. A multi-wheel unit of rotary filing equipment.

for example, a unit having a 21-inch-diameter wheel, handling 5 × 8-inch cards, has a capacity of 6,000 cards. Both single- and multi-wheel units are offered, as well as a special mechanism for stabilizing the rotation. A four-unit model is illustrated by Figure 12–9.

In the majority of cases, the cards have a slot-punched opening at the bottom in order to provide a gripping effect of the card to a retaining rod. For large cards, double openings and two rods are used. However, revolving file units are also available in which plain cards, i.e., not slotted or punched, can be used. Since no mechanical fastening is employed, it is possible to file the same type of material as that used in a vertical file, including such items as file folders, sketches, photographs, and folded drawings.

RECIPROCATING FILES

The employee can either go to the work, or the work can be brought to the employee. This latter situation is stressed in reciprocating file equipment. Figure 12–10 shows an installation of this type of equip-

Courtesy: Rol-Dex Division, Watson Mfg. Co., Jamestown, N.Y.

FIG. 12–10. Reciprocating filing equipment in which the file can be moved back and forth in the long, troughlike container. This is known as the "lateral-type file," since the work is to the side of the operator. A "left-right" arrangement, in which the file moves across the front of the operator, is also possible.

ment. The employee remains comfortably seated, and the file can be moved forward and backward as required. Use of this type of file (1) reduces employee fatigue, (2) eliminates travel time, (3) minimizes waiting time at files, and (4) allows full supervision, since all equipment is at desk-level height and under full view of the supervisor.

VISIBLE FILES

The name "visible file" reveals its outstanding feature, namely, providing to the user, at a glance, visible information in the files. Visible files are a very important means of filing. For convenience, the types of visible files can be divided into three groups: (1) filed strips, (2) cards filed horizontally, and (3) cards filed vertically.

FILED STRIPS

This type of visible file is used when quick reference to records containing a small quantity of data is needed. It is useful for maintaining lists which undergo changes, such as names and addresses of customers, prices, rates, bin locations, directories, reservations, hospital indexes, telephone and switchboard data, and routings.

Either of two methods can be followed. The first consists of (1) typing or otherwise writing the data on scored and special sheet material, which is made of resilient veneer covered on both sides with paper; (2) separating the sections by breaking along the scored line; and (3) placing the strips in a frame by bending them slightly and snapping the ends under the side channels of the frame. The second method consists of writing the data on small die-cut cards which snap or button on

Courtesy: Remington Rand, Inc., New York

FIG. 12–11. Two types of visible reference record equipment used where the amount of data is small and where fast, frequent reference is required.

a receiving device or runway in the frame. This places the cards in an offset arrangement with the upper margin of the card exposed or plainly visible. With either method, the frames can be suspended on desk stands, wall brackets, and rotaries. Figure 12–11 shows illustrations of this equipment.

To indicate special conditions applying to a particular name or account in a list, signaling devices can be used. These signals are either opaque or transparent and are available in several contrasting colors. They are either slid over, or attached to, a record and thus serve as a warning or indication of a special consideration applicable to that account. Different-colored strips and cards are also available and can be used for signaling purposes, if desired.

CARDS FILED HORIZONTALLY

In the second type of visible files, cards are filed horizontally in a shallow slide or tray in such a manner that the bottom margin of each card is exposed, providing for quick visibility. In this margin are pertinent data concerning the information on the major area of the card. Varying widths of margin exposure may be used; standard equipment provides $\frac{3}{16}$-inch to $\frac{5}{16}$-inch margin visibility. Card capacity per tray depends upon the card size and the margin exposure used, but eighty cards per tray is a good average figure. Each card is fastened in such a way that it can be raised and flipped by pivoting about the top edge. Thus, the complete information on any card can be viewed in full, or additional data can be written on the card with the tray used as an armrest. Units are available with different numbers of trays.

Electrical visible file units (cards filed horizontally) are also available. Stooping, reaching, pulling out trays, writing at inconvenient levels, and pushing trays back are eliminated by this electric unit. It excludes many causes of operator fatigue, raises productivity, and saves floor space. One popular unit holds sixty trays, counterbalanced in two equal banks which travel up and down when the unit is actuated. Figure 12–12 shows illustrations of the visible file operated manually and also the unit operated electrically.

Fastening of Cards. Several arrangements are available for fastening the card into the tray. In some equipment, the top edge of the card is fastened directly onto the tray; while in other equipment, "pockets" made of strong kraft paper are fastened directly onto the tray. In the latter case, a card is held in place by inserting the bottom edge into a flap made by a U-shaped plastic strip at the bottom of the pocket. The top of the card is held by inserting the corners into slots precut in the pocket. Each arrangement offers benefits. Fastening the card directly into the tray is advantageous in that markings can be made directly on the exposed visible margin of the card; the tray is utilized solely for

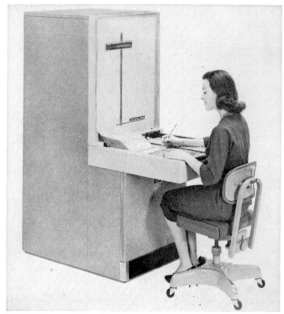

Courtesy: Remington Rand, Inc., New York

FIG. 12–12. Visible file equipment where cards are filed horizontally. On the left is the manually operated unit with tray withdrawn and ready for posting. On the right is the electrically operated unit. The operator presses one of several bars in front of her, causing the desired tray to come out of the unit at writing height in a matter of seconds.

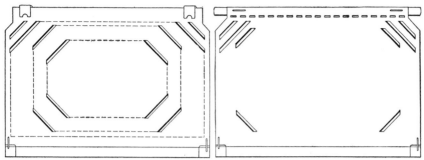

Courtesy: Acme Visible Records, Inc., Chicago

FIG. 12–13. Pockets are slotted to take care of various-sized cards. *Left:* The use of the hinge and hanger-pocket method. *Right:* The use of the bar-pocket method.

cards. In contrast, the use of pockets with the plastic material at the margins affords protection for the visible margin of the card, prevents cards from getting dog-eared, and affords a uniform space for signal devices. Figure 12–13 illustrates pockets used in visible record equipment.

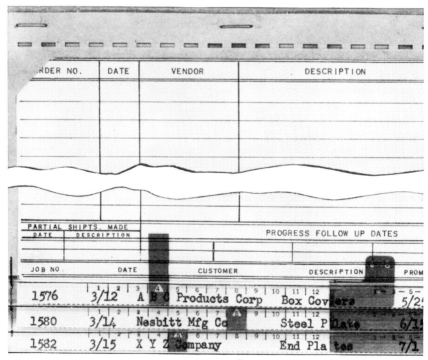

Courtesy: Remington Rand, Inc., New York

FIG. 12–14. An effective follow-up signaling system. On the top card, the signal over the 4 indicates April, the month in which follow-up should be made. The signal at the right of the card at the 3 indicates the day of the month on which the follow-up is due.

Signals on Card. Effective signaling to denote certain information on the card is one of the outstanding features of visible filing equipment using cards filed horizontally. By sliding different-colored plastic markers along the visible margins, definite dates or quantities, which are signals for specific actions, are brought out in bold relief. By such signals, a whole tray of cards can be scanned and the items requiring immediate attention quickly spotted. Figure 12–14, page 231, illustrates a signaling system for accurate follow-up.

Book Form. It is also possible to secure visible equipment which is suitable for keeping all card information in book form. Approximately two thousand cards can be kept in one binder. The book form affords portability and a posting surface always at desk height. Binders are made to lie perfectly flat when open, to lock against any possible accidental shifting of record sequence, and to lift and guide sheets into proper position when the binder is closed.

CARDS FILED VERTICALLY

The third type of visible files to be discussed is that designed for use where cards are filed vertically in an open-tub type of file. The cards

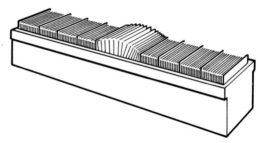

FIG. 12–15. Side view of magnetic-card visible file. A batch of cards can be fanned out to permit visibility and ease of finding card information.

vary in size from about 4 to 20 inches in width and 6 to 12 inches in height. They are similar in appearance to the printed forms for machine- and hand-posting work. Two types will be discussed here: (1) the magnetic card and (2) the shingled, clipped-corner card.

In the magnetic-card visible file, the records are instantly visible and accessible. They are not fastened in any way to the tray, making rearrangement, removal, or addition of cards to the file a very simple task. Very thin metal strips are included in the cards during manufacture. The unit is powered by magnetic force and operates on the basis of the repellent force of magnets separating one card from the next at any point of reference. A batch of 15 to 20 cards can be fanned out quickly with just a touch of the fingertips, and information on these cards can be read very easily. Figure 12–15 illustrates a side view of the magnetic-card file.

In the shingled clipped-corner-card file, one or both of the upper corners of the card are cut away in order to provide diagonal indexing margins; in addition, the horizontal and one of the vertical margins of the card are used for indexing. Cards are placed in the file in an offset arrangement, so that the top, diagonal, and side margins of the card are exposed or visible. The card is held in position by means of a notched

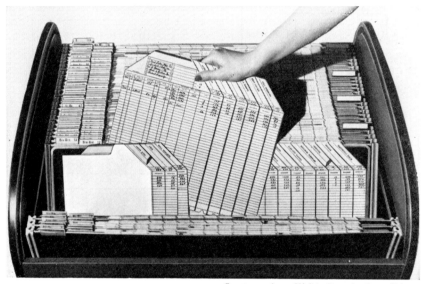

Courtesy: Acme Visible Records, Inc., Chicago

FIG. 12–16. The arrangement of cards in a file. Groups of cards can be removed and replaced just as easily as one card.

arrangement at the bottom of the card which fits into a receiving device at the bottom of the file, and the design is such that cards can easily be inserted or removed. Both sides of the card can be used, and signaling devices similar to those already discussed can be employed. Figure 12–16 shows the arrangement of cards in the file. With this equipment, the finding time is minimized, thumbing through cards is eliminated, and exceedingly quick scanning over large numbers of cards is possible— for example, nearly seven thousand cards, 10 × 5 inches in size, can be accommodated in one file unit.

FILING SUPPLIES

Guides, tabs, file folders, plastic signals, labels, and printed cards are among the items designated as filing supplies. For each item, as-

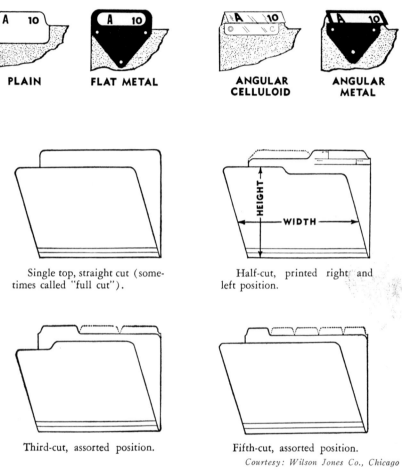

PLAIN   FLAT METAL   ANGULAR   ANGULAR
                                   CELLULOID   METAL

Single top, straight cut (some-   Half-cut, printed right and
times called "full cut").   left position.

Third-cut, assorted position.   Fifth-cut, assorted position.

Courtesy: Wilson Jones Co., Chicago

FIG. 12–17. *Top:* Styles of tabs for file guides. *Bottom:* Offset cuts at top of file folders.

sorted sizes and forms are available. Figure 12–17 shows several popular styles in tabs for file guides and the choice of offset cuts at the top of file folders.

STANDARDS AND FILING

If possible, production standards for filing operations should be developed. With these as a guide, the manager can determine whether the proper amount of filing work is being obtained. Standards will vary among different companies due to the type of records and the conditions surrounding the work. However, to give an idea of what can be done, expectancies are shown, based on data from a number of companies:

Task	Units per Hour
Sorting letters and filing alphabetically	180
Filing 5 × 8-inch cards in an alphabetical vertical file	315
Locating and pulling letters from an alphabetical file	110
Filing vouchers numerically	700
Marking one-page letters for filing	220

AUDITS AND FILING

Spot checks for neatness and accuracy of a company's files are advisable in order to administer adequate control over filing. Also, periodic inspection can be made to determine if misuses of filing equipment exist or if new or different equipment is needed. This work can be done by the person in charge of filing, but a better practice is to use a committee or council. With the latter arrangement, more interest in filing is generated, prestige is added, the thinking of a number of people is utilized, and awareness of needed improvements is enhanced.

COST OF FILING

It is difficult to generalize on the cost of filing. Where such data have been calculated, the amounts depend greatly upon the circumstances of the individual office. Studies show a cost of about 1 cent for each paper filed in an ordinary four-drawer correspondence file. Stated differently, the cost of filing using a four-drawer correspondence file is about $200 per year. Thus, a company with twenty-five files has an annual filing expense of $5,000. The substantiating data for one file cabinet per year follow:

Rent for 5½ sq. ft. per cabinet and aisle at $2.00 per sq. ft.	$ 11.00
Depreciation on cabinet	6.00
Transfer cases	8.00
Labor	140.00
File guides and folders	8.40
Overhead and supervision	15.00
Miscellaneous	3.00
Total	$203.40

Cost data such as illustrated by the above can be helpful in controlling filing. From cost information, an approximate basis for satisfactory filing can be established and subsequent filing operation costs compared to this base in order to determine if, for the most part, filing operations are satisfactory.

CENTRALIZATION AND DECENTRALIZATION OF FILES

One of the major issues in the area of filing and the fundamental function of managerial organizing is the question of whether to have centralized or decentralized filing. Convincing arguments can be stated for either side of the question. The trend, however, appears to be toward centralization from the viewpoint of management operation and decentralization regarding the physical files. This combination stems from the fact that with centralized managerial activity, the best of filing knowledge and practices from the over-all company viewpoint can be put into use. At the same time, decentralized physical records provide accessibility for those needing the files, flexibility in arrangement, and a satisfactory cost of operation.

However, the decision to centralize or not depends upon the requirements of the particular enterprise. Filing needs differ. Adequate thought must be directed to the type of material, the work habits of the people using the records, and the normal manner in which they are used, i.e., the flow of work, frequency of records use, and information required.

FILING AND PERSONNEL

Better placement of personnel for filing work is needed. In too many instances, the attitude prevails that the untrained office employee who cannot be fitted in elsewhere because of lack of some office skill should

---

1. Eliminate useless originals and copies of material being put in the file.
2. Adopt a suitable filing system with adequate indexing to fit the needs of the enterprise.
3. Supply proper filing equipment to facilitate the particular filing system followed.
4. Hire and develop personnel suited for filing work, and delegate required authority to them.

FIG. 12–18. Four cardinal points in acquiring highly efficient filing work.

be given filing work. Entirely overlooked is the fundamental truth that filing personnel should possess certain attributes, including a sense of orderliness, accuracy, manual dexterity, quick reading comprehension, and a liking for detail.

A realistic approach consisting of four facets appears in order. First, appoint one person to be in charge of all filing. This will help promote needed study and improvements in filing. Second, establish what can reasonably be expected from the filing personnel. For example, are all requests clear and complete? Frequently, the file clerk is expected to have an ability to find a piece of paper even though she has never seen it and does not know what it was about, who it was from, or when it was written. Third, make sincere efforts to upgrade filing. All key and office personnel should be made aware of the importance of filing and of the helpful contributions of those performing this work. Fourth, adjust wages of the filing personnel. Of the total cost for filing, most is for labor, and filing can never be more efficient than the people doing the filing.

To enable personnel to perform filing work efficiently, the four cardinal points shown in Figure 12–18 are suggested. Success in each of these activities will insure a large degree of success in acquiring effective filing.

QUESTIONS

1. Discuss the subject of indexing as an important part of filing.
2. For each of the following filing troubles, suggest a feasible solution:
   a) Correspondence papers piled up in miscellaneous folders.
   b) Necessity of fingering many folders before finding the right one.
   c) Search through many papers in a folder to find the one wanted of a certain date.
   d) St. Louis correspondence may be found under "St. Louis," "Saint Louis," or "Missouri."
   e) File drawers jammed tight with material.
   f) Too many files in which a needed paper might be found.
3. As you understand it, what is "the filing problem" in business today?
4. Explain several means for the charging-out of filed material, i.e., for controlling the removal of papers from the files.
5. Name four different types of files; and of this group, discuss the one that interests you the most.
6. Identify each of the following, and explain how it is used:
   a) Tickler file.
   b) Terminal-digit file.
   c) Primary file guide.
   d) Individual file folder.
   e) Magnetic-card visible file.
7. Explain Figure 12–2 in your own words.
8. It is desired to use a convenient signaling system in connection with a visible file (cards horizontal) for items in an inventory. For each item, a minimum and a maximum quantity has been calculated. An ordering point has also been established; it is the quantity on hand at which additional units should be ordered, so that the quantity on hand will always remain between the minimum and maximum levels determined. Using Figure 12–14 as a guide, sketch a signaling system to show the minimum, maximum, and ordering points. Also, include an indicator for the present quantity on hand. This will vary between the maximum and the minimum as units of the item are withdrawn from inventory. When the stock-on-hand indicator coincides with the ordering point, a requisition to purchase is made. Explain the operation of your suggested signaling system.
9. Discuss eight filing practices that you feel are of major significance.
10. Draw a tabular chart showing the file indexing used in connection with various types of material handled in your school office or in some other office with which you are familiar.
11. Discuss the cost of filing. Do you feel that cost is an adequate means of controlling filing work? Why?

12. Office manager Arvid Svenson is reasonably certain that present difficulties in his filing department are personnel in their make-up. In general, what actions do you feel Mr. Svenson should take to help remedy the present situation?

CASE PROBLEMS

Case 12–1.   Hennings Construction Company

Custom-built houses in the $27,500–$30,000 price range are constructed by the Hennings Construction Company, which maintains a main office, an on-the-site sales office, and two construction offices located about 35 miles apart. The main office is approximately 20 miles from the sales office or either of the construction offices.

The sales office and the construction offices require immediate information on costs, delivery of materials, and dates subcontractors performed work on the houses, and telephone the main office for this type of information. Unfortunately, the desired data are not always available, primarily because the bookkeepers in the main office are two to four months behind in their work, and each bookkeeper keeps all the pertinent information in her desk drawer until she has posted the cash receipts and the payments to the subtrades, or put the sales through the books. There are a total of three bookkeepers who do general ledger and accounts payable work.

When a call is received from the sales department or from the construction department, the bookkeepers usually cannot get the information requested until the following day—or in some cases, not for several days. This is because, to find the data requested, it is frequently necessary to search through many papers in the desk drawer and six broken wooden filing cabinets along the wall of the office. Completed records are placed in these filing cabinets. All information pertaining to purchases, for example, is filed alphabetically, year after year, without any division or subdivision as to chronological order. Material for a house built in 1952, for example, might be next to that for a house built in 1961, or 1959.

Under the present state of affairs, canceled checks and monthly bank statements are not reconciled for periods of two to three months. This work is handled by the chief bookkeeper, Betty Dougherty, who guards the canceled check work and will permit no one else to perform work in connection therewith. Some difficulty is experienced in getting the checks written out for accounts payable. None of the bookkeepers want to do this check writing because it takes time from their bookkeeping work.

The situation became so bad that Carl Hennings, president of the company, called in Professor Franklin Swope, from a nearby University, to review the situation and make recommendations regarding what corrective action to take. Professor Swope studied the entire operations and at the end of two days discovered that:

1. The company managers do not believe in overtime work.
2. Office morale is low.
3. Carl Hennings is thinking of firing the entire office force.
4. Carl Hennings has no objections to the company having two checking accounts—one for general payables, the other for payroll.
5. One key area for improvement is to get the processed papers into the files in accordance with an arrangement that will expedite usage of the filed material.

Problems:

1. What pertinent recommendations do you feel Professor Swope should make to Mr. Hennings? Be specific.

2. What contributions do you believe improved filing management practices and procedures can contribute to this company? Why?

3. What difficulties do you anticipate in implementing the recommendations you feel Professor Swope should make? How would you overcome these difficulties?

Case 12–2. Charleston Veneer Company

Manufacturer of tropical and domestic wood veneers, with general offices located in Chicago, the Charleston Veneer Company is considered one of the largest in the industry, producing over one hundred million feet of veneer annually. Three manufacturing plants are located in Suffolk, Virginia; Kansas City, Missouri; and Sisters, Oregon. Warehouses and sales offices are located throughout the United States. The company employs thirty-four salesmen operating out of Chicago and six district sales offices.

To maintain records of veneer is a task of considerable magnitude and must be done accurately. Each log, when cut, is identified by a number. The log is cut into segments, called flitches, and designated alphabetically. To illustrate, a customer may buy flitch K from log 8932. The company manufactures about 60 species of wood veneers.

As the veneer is manufactured, samples are drawn from stocks, graded, priced, and sent to the various sales offices. The salesmen, in turn, sell from these samples. When the veneer is cut, sample sheets are sent to the Chicago office, and the footage and price for each flitch are entered on inventory cards. There is one card for each log. These cards are filed numerically by log number. So-called "slicer reports," showing the amount and type of veneer cut, are sent daily to the Chicago office by the manufacturing mills. When a sale is made, the flitch is canceled on the inventory card. This information is taken from sales orders at the beginning of their processing in the Chicago office. A cancellation notice is sent by the Chicago office to all sales offices, notifying them of the depletion of the particular veneer.

However, too often a flitch is resold before the cancellation notice of its depletion reaches the various sales offices. In addition, the Chicago office keeps no record of total footage on hand of each species of wood. In the event of a large order, the customer usually wants the same type of wood, although the veneer pattern will vary due to the make-up of the log itself. To take care of this sales contingency, it would be well to know how much veneer of a certain type, or at least how many flitches from the same log, are on hand at any given time. Furthermore, there are no adequate records of salesmen's sales. Who is selling what is not known accurately, and it is believed such information would be helpful in guiding sales efforts.

Problems:

1. Recommend specific improvements for recording and filing information concerning sales and inventory records which the company needs.

2. What are the major disadvantages to your recommendations, and how would you try to minimize them?

Chapter 13

STORAGE—RECORDS RETENTION

Beaten paths are for beaten men.

—ERIC JOHNSTON

RECORDS retention is another important office service. It is closely akin to filing in that, like filing, it provides for the basic data-processing element of storing. Most enterprises find themselves inundated by the mass of records of all kinds. The problem is how to decide which records to keep and which to discard. Typically, too many papers are filed or stored because some day somebody may ask for them. The result is row upon row of filing cabinets, many useless papers retained, and needless office expense.

The National Records Management Council, Inc., a nonprofit organization, estimates that corporate records occupy office and storage space valued at $350 million a year. This is the space equivalent of about two-hundred buildings the size of the Chrysler Building in New York City. Furthermore, according to the Council, 95 per cent of the corporate records over a year old are never used, and 95 per cent of the references made deal with records less than five years old. The problem is clear: Keep worthless materials out of files, and periodically review filed materials to eliminate what is no longer necessary. In many instances, one half of the filed papers can be destroyed, and half of the rest can be transferred from the office to storage space.

MEANING OF RECORDS RETENTION

Records retention deals with the disposition of records and concerns filing those that must be retained and destroying those that are or become worthless. The time to effect a records-retention program is before the materials are filed. Permit only carefully defined "useful materials" to be filed. Keeping worthless materials out of the files is easier and more realistic than getting worthless materials removed once they are filed. In addition, periodic checks should be made in order to remove and dispose of filed materials that have become worthless.

Records retention is an essential part of records management, including the entire life span—the birth and death—of a record. The work of records retention must be co-ordinated with that of other office management activities, so that the necessary paper work is done at lowest cost and yet provides the necessary information quickly and accurately.

CONTENT OF RECORDS-RETENTION PROGRAM

Included in the activities of a sound records-retention program are provisions to—

1. Establish a tight schedule of retention periods for every type of record and all its copies.
2. Remove from files all material that has become useless, employing well-timed and orderly procedures for this work.
3. Establish and maintain a convenient, low-cost, and safe area for records storage.
4. Index the exact location of each type of record, showing where it is stored, and in what type of container.
5. Take charge of all microfilming of records to insure that only necessary copies are made.
6. Show facts on volume of records, how much is in office, how much is in storage area, and how much is discarded.
7. Revise schedules of records-retention periods based upon facts derived from analysis of the use made of the records, by major types.
8. Participate in purchasing decisions for new filing equipment and supplies.

ADVANTAGES OF RECORDS-RETENTION PROGRAM

Such a program can be quite extensive. It requires good management, foresight, judgment, and especially a steadfastness of purpose. The rewards, however, are high. Better filing efficiency is gained since inactive material is removed, thus reducing finding time. Space savings are also achieved—throwing out records that have become useless means less space is needed. Also, storing useful but inactive records in an inexpensive storage area means dollar savings. Furthermore, the retained records are better protected and safeguarded. Equipment designed especially for storage can be utilized, and the records are not subject to possible mutilation as a result of frequent handling.

Figure 13–1 shows the results from several selected cases. For example, a large insurance company located in the New England area found that 58 per cent of all filed material could be eliminated, 14 per cent could be placed in a storage room to be consulted when required, and the remaining 28 per cent remained in the office area as material needed for reference from time to time in order to operate the business. As a re-

| TYPE OF ENTERPRISE | LOCATION | FILED MATERIAL | | REMAINING IN OFFICE AREA | FILING AND STORAGE SPACE SAVED |
		Eliminated	Placed in Storage Area		
Large insurance company......	New England area	58%	14%	28%	44%
Large bank.................	New York City	62	17	21	55
Manufacturer...............	Chicago	71	15	14	62
Air-line company............	East Coast area	55	19	26	43

FIG. 13–1. A records-retention program usually reduces the amount of useless papers stored.

sult of these changes, 44 per cent of the filing and storage space was saved and made available for other purposes. Comparable results for other types of enterprises are shown in the figure.

Think of it. In each case, from one half to two thirds of the carefully filed and retained records could be discarded as waste paper. Only about one paper in four remained in the office files. Imagine the savings in finding time and space. The general effect upon the disposition of records by a records-retention program is shown graphically by Figure 13–2.

In the case of the federal government, record-cleaning efforts were directed at the government's nearly 20 million cubic feet of files. Within several years, federal agencies were destroying over 2½ million cubic feet of records annually—the equivalent of over 1½ million file drawers.

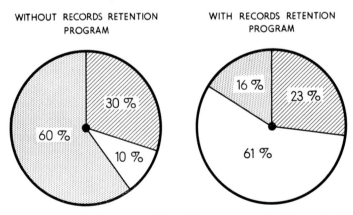

WITHOUT RECORDS RETENTION PROGRAM   WITH RECORDS RETENTION PROGRAM

30 per cent retained in active files   23 per cent retained in active files
60 per cent retained in inactive files   16 per cent retained in inactive files
10 per cent destroyed   61 per cent destroyed

FIG. 13–2. Typical disposition of records by companies without and those with records-retention programs.

In addition, nearly 1 million cubic feet of paper was being transferred from active to storage areas at centers.

TRANSFER OF MATERIALS TO INACTIVE FILES

A systematic transfer of materials to inactive files is desirable in order to prevent current files from growing unmanageable. Material cannot remain in files indefinitely—the physical space becomes exhausted.

In a four-drawer filing cabinet, the top two drawers can be used for current material and the bottom two for inactive material. This arrangement affords convenient reference to inactive material, necessary from

1 INACTIVE	3 INACTIVE	6 INACTIVE	8 INACTIVE
1	4	6	9
2	5	7	10
3	4 INACTIVE	8	9 INACTIVE
2 INACTIVE	5 INACTIVE	7 INACTIVE	10 INACTIVE

FIG. 13–3. Arrangement for active and inactive material in five-drawer files.

time to time in every office. When the five-drawer file is used, a common arrangement to follow is illustrated by Figure 13–3.

The transferring of material can be done in one of two main ways: (1) the entire unit, or periodically; and (2) the individual, or perpetually.

The entire-unit method requires that all material be transferred at a scheduled time. Usually, this is done on an annual basis and at the beginning of the calendar year, fiscal year, or busy season. The material remains in the original folders and is moved bodily. New folders are used for the new material in the current file.

The individual or perpetual method places time limits on individual papers by appropriate marks on the folders. Then, periodically, at intervals of about two or three months—or perpetually, at irregular intervals—the files are screened, and papers found to have been in the file past the allowable limit are transferred to the inactive file. In cases where the transaction is terminated, i.e., a settlement granted or a sale closed, the material is transferred immediately, regardless of date.

WHAT KIND OF COMPANY RECORDS TO RETAIN

Most offices are confronted with the problem of how long to retain active and inactive file material. The answer lies in knowing what to save and how to store it. This, in turn, depends primarily upon the usefulness of the material to managers, and the legal requirements. The period of retention differs among companies, but there is a tendency toward the development of standard practices.

Group decision making is advisable to establish needed policies affecting the determination of what papers to retain and for how long a period. Usually, the controller, the legal counsel, the tax counsel, and the manager of records retention should be included in this group; they can decide basic issues essential to the program. For the most part, this group sets forth policy instructions on which operating decisions can be based by the manager of records retention.

Papers that are essential to the company's security should be kept. Proof of assets and liabilities is important. Papers giving proof of ownership, property, inventories, machinery, and buildings are included in this category. Insurance is recovered on proof, not guesswork. Records dealing with transactions should be saved. These include receipt of money, proof of payment, proof of expenses or purchases, and payroll. Also, documents providing proof of usage should be retained, for they are vital in matters dealing with research, engineering, and patents. If the company becomes involved in infringement or other patent-suit claims, certain drawings, properly coded, numbered, and preserved, form the basis for prosecution or defense. Historical data of various types often prove valuable in that they provide trends and statistical analysis helpful in the company's planning efforts. Such data should be retained if there is a reasonable possibility that they will be used in the future or will be referred to for improving decision making by relating the reasons given *why* certain decisions were made in the past with the outcome of such decisions.

APPROACH TO RECORDS RETENTION

Each company should strive to develop its own records retention based on an analysis of the actual use made of its own records. To copy what another company has decided frequently results in serious shortcomings. The analysis might begin with a cursory review of the entire enterprise to obtain background and understanding of the current work and to spot what records are used and what ones are filed for satisfactory operation. Following this, a survey is in order to determine (1) what is filed; (2) how much is filed—its size and quantity; (3) where it is filed—including the copies, if any; (4) how often it was used during specific preceding periods; (5) when, if ever, it is permanently removed from file; and (6) what is done with permanently removed material. In some instances, this survey work is expedited by classifying the material by type or by department. Information applicable to several departments can be studied as a group, thus relating the types of information common to several units.

From the survey data, the value of each record is weighed. Questions decided are: Should this record be filed at all? How long should this record remain in the file? Is it advisable to retain this record in storage? Particular attention is paid to records presently having long-term retention. Experience shows that many retention times can be cut measurably below the periods formerly believed necessary.

DETERMINING CLASSES FOR RETAINED MATERIALS

Results from this survey will show the records of varying importance from the viewpoint of retention. For convenience, they can be grouped into four classes: (1) nonessential, (2) helpful, (3) important, and (4) vital.

Records classified as nonessential should never be filed. They may have value for a relatively short period—perhaps as little as a few seconds—but retaining them is wasteful. Included in this category are penciled notations, routine inquiries, announcements, and acknowledgments.

Helpful records are those that can assist, but only for a very limited time, perhaps four to five weeks. After this period, their usefulness is completed. If filed, they should be placed in a separate drawer or cabinet and destroyed as their helpfulness ceases. In this group is general correspondence, most of which has a useful life of not over four weeks.

Important records include those containing information of value for relatively long periods—up to five or six years. They should first be filed in the office for handy reference; but ultimately, as they lose their current usefulness, they should be transferred to storage. How long they remain in the office depends upon the type of record and the policy established. Many firms keep records such as invoices, accounts receivable, sales records, quotations, and financial statements in active files for one to two years, then transfer to storage. With sufficient time, important records lose their essentiality and should be discarded. As stated above, this may take place at the end of five or six years. However, in this connection, the statute of limitations must also be taken into account. It specifies the length of time a record is alive according to law. This period varies for various documents and among states, as shown by Figure 13–4.

STATE	OPEN ACCOUNTS	CONTRACTS IN WRITING	
		Under Seal	Not under Seal
Alabama	3	10	6
Alaska	5	6	6
Arizona	3	6	6
Arkansas	3	5	5
California	varies	4	4
Colorado	6	6	6
Connecticut	6	17	6
Delaware	3	20	3
District of Columbia	3	12	3
Florida	3	20	5
Hawaii	varies	4	4
Georgia	4	20	6
Idaho	4	5	5
Illinois	5	10	varies
Indiana	6	20	10
Iowa	5	10	10
Kansas	3	5	5
Kentucky	5	15	15
Louisiana	varies	varies	varies
Maine	6	20	6
Maryland	3	12	3
Massachusetts	6	20	6
Michigan	6	6	6
Minnesota	6	6	6
Mississippi	3	6	6
Missouri	5	10	10
Montana	5	8	8
Nebraska	4	5	5
Nevada	4	6	6
New Hampshire	6	20	6
New Jersey	6	16	6
New Mexico	4	6	6
New York	6	6	6
North Carolina	3	10	3
North Dakota	6	6	6
Ohio	6	15	15
Oklahoma	3	5	5
Oregon	6	10	6
Pennsylvania	6	20	6
Rhode Island	6	20	6
South Carolina	6	20	6
South Dakota	6	20	6
Tennessee	6	6	6
Texas	2	4	4
Utah	4	8	6
Vermont	6	varies	6
Virginia	3	10	5
Washington	3	6	6
West Virginia	5	10	10
Wisconsin	6	varies	6
Wyoming	8	10	10

FIG. 13–4. Statutes of limitations, in years, for specified documents.

Vital records, as the name implies, are paramount. They are retained permanently. They may be transferred to the storage area after a given period of time, but they are never destroyed. Vital records include legal papers of incorporation, titles to ownership, deeds, reports to stockholders, and insurance policies.

If records are placed in storage, many records managers suggest marking the destruction date on the material at the time of its transfer to storage. This may be a date stamped on the material or a notice to destroy in "one year," "two years," or "retain permanently." In any event, all transferred material should be classified, properly labeled, and indexed so that it can be found if needed.

A RECORDS-RETENTION PROGRAM

Figure 13–5 shows a sound program of records retention. As previously stated, material classified as nonessential should never be filed, but should be destroyed immediately. "Helpful" material is filed in a separate file for the limited period, then destroyed. Material considered important or vital is filed (step No. 1) and subsequently transferred to the inactive file as a normal procedure (step No. 2). Periodically, all material is removed from the inactive files and sorted (step No. 3). It is either important or vital material. The former is handled in three different ways: microfilmed, records destroyed, films placed in storage, and ultimately destroyed (step 4A); records placed in storage and eventually destroyed (step 4B); or records destroyed, having outlived their span of importance (step 4C).[1] If the material is classified as vital, step 4D, consisting of microfiling, destroying records, and placing films in storage, can be followed; or step 4E, placing the material in storage, can be adopted.

This program may vary somewhat in individual applications. For example, microfilm may not be used at all, or it may be found more practical to eliminate step No. 3 (sorting), microfilm all records, and use the microfilms for reference in all cases.

For records in storage, a system of indexing should be adopted, so that all such material can be located quickly. The information can be kept on small index cards or on sheets in a loose-leaf notebook. It should include subject classification, shelf number, box number or name, and scheduled date for ultimate destruction. It is important that each container be labeled plainly.

At least once a year, a list should be prepared showing what stored original records should be destroyed. It can be compiled readily from data on the index cards. The list is then submitted to the office manager or designated executive for approval and authority to proceed. When

---

[1] Microfilming is discussed immediately below.

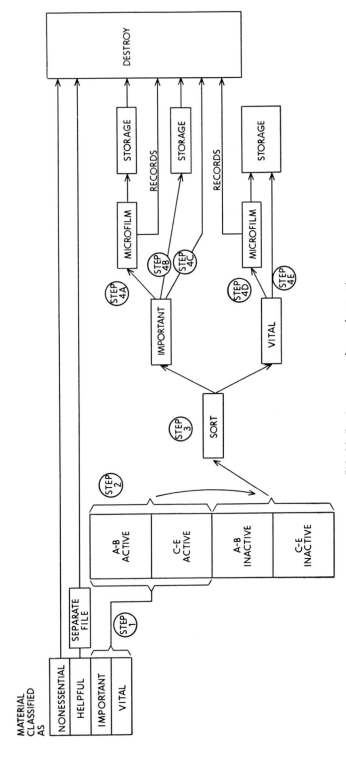

FIG. 13–5. A program of records retention.

this has been granted, the material is destroyed and the list filed permanently for future reference.

MICROFILMING

"Microfilming" is a photographic means of retaining the information given in office papers. The materials are first photographed on film at reduced sizes; then, the film is developed, to serve as the permanent record. Figure 13–6 shows several popular arrangements in microfilming material and a modern microfilming machine.

One of the first commercial applications of microfilming was in banks, where it was used in connection with checks. The list of applications grew steadily, and microfilming is now associated with many types of paper materials. It is an accepted part of many records-retention programs. The records classified as important or vital which are needed for continuance of an enterprise can be microfilmed and stored in a safe or in a remote area, in order to avoid loss in case of disaster.

Microfilming is available to the small as well as to the large enterprise. Outside concerns specializing in microfilming work will microfilm records either in the office of the company or in their own plant. The cost for this service, including film and developing, varies from $4.00 to $6.00 for each one thousand pieces, depending upon the size and quantity of the material, whether hand or automatic feed can be used, and whether one or two sides are to be microfilmed.

Advantages. The use of microfilming effects a great savings of storage space. About 98–99 per cent of storage space can be saved, since one to two file cabinets of film hold the equivalent of a hundred cabinets of original records. In addition, the chances of losing a document are minimized. The photographs on the film are in sequence like links of a chain; once a paper is photographed, there is no danger of the photograph being lost unless the whole roll of microfilm is lost. Furthermore, with microfilm, the retained materials are clean and easily handled; and they reduce the fire hazard, because the film is of the acetate, noncombustible type.

Disadvantages. On the other hand, microfilming has its drawbacks. The courts usually prefer original documents, but will accept microfilmed material when failure to produce the original is adequately explained. Usually, microfilming must be established as a regular procedure and one not motivated by any suspicion of fraud. Microfilming may perpetuate the habit of keeping old records. It is easier to microfilm all records and file the films than it is to decide what should be saved, sort the material, and retain only what has future use. Also, the use of microfilming requires special equipment; a viewer is the minimum requirement. Furthermore, employees must be trained for the specialized techniques required, and these skills are somewhat different from those required for most office work.

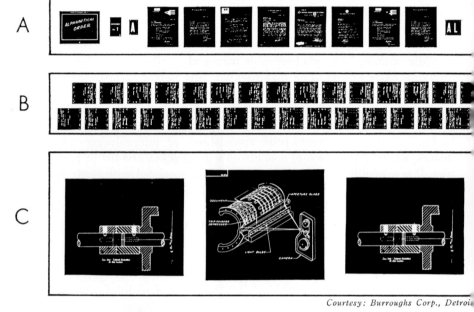

Courtesy: Burroughs Corp., Detroit

FIG. 13–6. *Top, A:* For standard size letters, 16-mm. film and 17-to-1 reduction are popular. *Top, B:* For infrequent reference, a double line—one for front, the other for back of the document, 23-to-1 reduction, is recommended. *Top, C:* For engineering drawings and ledger sheets, a 17-to-1 reduction and 25-mm. film are used. *Bottom:* One compact machine handles all microfilming needs, including high-fidelity filming to high-clarity reading.

THE PHYSICAL WORK ENVIRONMENT

A clean, dry area should be designated for records retention. Proper conditions of temperature, circulation of air, and humidity should be provided. Traditionally, storage rooms have been the attics of business;

they should be regarded as attractive work areas. The floor area must withstand a relatively high weight per square foot. For example, about 200 pounds per square foot may be required. This is based on a full drawer holding 75 pounds of records, drawers stacked eight high, occupying a floor area of about 3 square feet.

Various types of equipment can be used for storing records. The following are of special interest: (1) open-shelf file units, (2) storage boxes on shelving, and (3) specially designed fiberboard drawer files.

An open-shelf file unit is illustrated by Figure 13–7. Such a unit provides instant accessibility to records at low cost. It is available in various sizes, is completely prefabricated, and is easy to assemble without tools. Follower blocks keep records upright for convenient reference. Another common storage means is storage boxes on shelving. These boxes are built of high-test corrugated fiberboard especially designed to withstand rough usage and to prevent mildew and damage from dirt or moisture. A variety of sizes is supplied so that the stored material fits snugly in the box. The shelving is assembled quickly without tools and can be extended by adding extensional units. The shelving can be dismantled and reassembled in a new location in a matter of minutes. In the third and last method, specially designed fiberboard drawer files combine the drawer, shelving, and base all in one unit. A steel framework carries the entire weight

Courtesy: Bankers Box Co., Franklin Park, Ill.

FIG. 13–7. A ready-reference open-shelf file unit.

load. The drawer files are interlocking, as illustrated by the insert in Figure 13–8. It will be noted that a single drawer is within a steel shell. The drawers are locked together solidly, each locking to the others around it. The unit "builds its own steel framework as you stack it." As many as twenty drawers can be stacked in one tier. There is no buckling, sagging, or warping. In this method, space is entirely devoted to drawer units. Also, different available drawer sizes and separators for inside the drawers mean practically no waste space. The result is a compact, efficient use of space. With space utilization expressed as a ratio of cubic feet of records to square feet of space, the specially designed

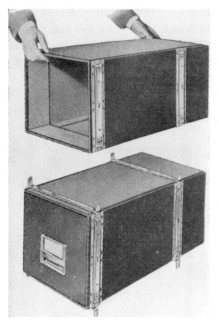

Courtesy: Bankers Box Co., Franklin Park, Ill.

FIG. 13–8.   Interlocking fiberboard drawer files form a compact and substantial storage file.

drawer files method can easily reach a ratio of 8 to 1. Many storage areas do not attain a ratio of 5 to 1. From actual measurement, one New York bank, after installing fiberboard drawer files for storage, reported a 30 per cent saving in valuable floor space.

CONTROLLING AND RECORDS RETENTION

An effective means of control is to limit the quantity of records per employee. The amount permitted will depend upon the type of business operation. In public utilities, for example, an amount of 5 cubic feet of records per employee on payroll is considered satisfactory. For an assembly plant, a comparable figure may be only 1 cubic foot of records; whereas in a purchasing department, the amount may be as great as 12 cubic feet, yet still qualify as an effective records-retention practice.

Cost is used by many companies to keep records-retention work within reasonable limits. Cost for labor and space will vary depending upon the particular location, but cost for equipment is relatively much more uniform. For this latter, an average cost figure is $2.00 per cubic foot of records stored. If the cost of records-retention equipment is higher than this amount, remedial attention is probably in order.

Additional cost information that adds to the need to control the amount of records retained is revealed by the fact that it costs about

$1,200 to create the contents for one file drawer of correspondence. As- suming five thousand papers in one file drawer, one fifth of the papers being letters produced at a cost of $1.00 each, the remaining papers carbon copies at a cost of 4 cents each, the calculations are:

$$1,000 \times \$1.00 = \$1,000$$
$$4,000 \times 0.04 = \underline{\quad 160}$$
$$\text{Total} = \$1,160$$

Helpful ratios can also be derived. To illustrate, a "usage" ratio re- veals the extent to which the materials stored are being used. The formula is:

$$\text{Usage ratio (in \%)} = \frac{\text{Requests} \times 100}{\text{References filed}}$$

For example, if last month, 200 requests were made from 20,000 items stored, the usage ratio in percentage would be 200×100 di- vided by 20,000, or 1 per cent. This ratio for stored materials will sel- dom exceed 5 per cent. For active materials in the office files, it should run about 15–20 per cent. Further analysis of usage ratios can be made, taking into account the rate of reference by type of record versus the age of the record. Such studies assist in better controlling of records- retention efforts.

Another ratio is the "accuracy" ratio, which is calculated by this formula:

$$\text{Accuracy ratio (in \%)} = \frac{\text{Number of items not found} \times 100}{\text{Number of items found}}$$

For 10 items not found and 10,000 found, the ratio is 0.1 per cent. For a rating of excellent, the accuracy ratio should not be greater than 0.5 per cent. A value of 3 per cent or more signifies that remedial action is required. The accuracy ratio can be used for either active only, inactive only, or all stored records.

HEAD OF RECORDS-RETENTION PROGRAM

In most cases, it is best to have one person in charge of a records- retention program. The person should have adequate authority to di- rect and maintain the program. To a great extent, the success of the program is throttled by the caliber of person heading the unit and the relationship of the records-retention unit to the other office units. Pref- erably, this head should report to an executive in a high enough organi- zational level to get top management support and opinions.

Committees should be used to assist the designated head of the records-retention work. As stated earlier in this chapter, a committee to establish policies and decide retention periods for each type of paper is effective, but putting into action and managing the program is better vested in a competent individual. Consultation with department heads is in order because they usually are well qualified to suggest which of their own records probably should be retained and for how long a period.

INSTILL CONFIDENCE IN RECORDS RETENTION

The manager of records retention must instill a feeling of confidence in the records-retention activities and results. All office personnel, as well as key management people, must believe in the accuracy, completeness, and usefulness of the filed material. Unless they do, they are quite likely to keep important records in their own desks or special files than to trust them with records retention.

A manual supplying information on the procedures and practices of the records-retention group is also helpful. Data on the type of material stored, the indexing system, retention schedule, and specific duties of records-retention personnel should be clearly written and made available to anyone whose work is affected by records retention. Such a manual is extremely beneficial for obtaining better understanding and for training new employees in records-retention work.

QUESTIONS

1. Do you favor the entire-unit or the individual method in the transferring of filed material? Why?
2. For how long a period do you suggest each item in the following list of filed material be retained:
   a) Sales prospect lists?
   b) Invoices from suppliers of raw materials?
   c) Real estate deeds?
   d) Payrolls and pay rates?
   e) Application forms from prospective employees?
   f) Quotations to customers?
3. What activities are included in a complete records-retention program?
4. Interpret the data given in Figure 13–2.
5. Discuss the physical requirements for a records-retention area.
6. Write a two-sentence identifying description of each of the following:
   a) Fiberboard storage box.
   b) Fiberboard drawer file.
   c) Microfilming.
   d) Statute of limitations.
7. Do you agree with the following? "The availability of reliable microfilming machines and supplies solves the retention-of-records problem for most offices. This is substantiated by the fact that accurate copies at a cost of a fraction of a cent each and a saving of over 95 per cent storage space are obtained through microfilming."
8. Can you see anything wrong with using old vertical filing cabinets for the storing of records? Discuss.
9. Investigation shows the following facts about the records-retention depart-

ment of the Greenwood Manufacturing Company. Accuracy ratio = 0.35 per cent; total employees on payroll, 183; usage ratio = 6.17 per cent; current cost of records-retention equipment, $723.45; weekly gross payroll for records retention, $109.70; cubic feet of records in records retention, 214. Evaluate the records-retention work of the Greenwood Manufacturing Company. Substantiate your viewpoint.

10. Do you favor the use of a well-selected committee to handle a records-retention program? Why?

11. When and where should microfilming be used, and what are its advantages?

12. An office which has never had a records-retention program is now interested in establishing one. Suggest an approach which can be followed to meet this purpose.

CASE PROBLEM

Case 13–1. Martin-Durkee Manufacturing Company

RALPH HESS: Come in, please. You're Mr. Fred Ford, the management consultant?

FRED FORD: Yes. Thank you very much.

HESS: I'll be glad to assist you in every way. I suppose you'd like me to start by discussing what we do here?

FORD: Yes, if you will.

HESS: The engineering design division is divided into three sections: design, administration, and design drafting. I am in charge of the latter. We are responsible for all mechanical drafting work in the designing of new products, improvements in the design of existing products, production drawings relative to the building of prototype products, and products to be built under contract to customers.

FORD: You handle improvements in existing design?

HESS: Yes, sir.

FORD: What does the design section handle?

HESS: They handle the design of new products only. Now, to be able to use the latest commercially offered items as components of design—and this is true for new product design as well, that is, for the design section—it is necessary to have readily available a file of catalogues and design manuals offered by various manufacturers. All these cabinets you see in the room out there are filled with such material. In addition, we have correspondence, blueprints, original drawings, and even samples of various items. Some of these, both papers and samples, are odd sizes and shapes, and are difficult to store; and my guess is that part of what we have out there could be discarded.

FORD: Do the files out there represent all the stored reference material?

HESS: No. There are stacks of stuff in a basement room. The material is stacked up in neat little piles on the floor; each stack is tagged, but it's a mess to find anything down there.

FORD: Do you have need to go to this basement room from time to time?

HESS: Yes, every once in a while. The men resent being sent there to look for something—all except Harvey Pair, who doesn't seem to mind. In fact, I guess you could say he even enjoys it. Gets lost down there for half a day at a time.

FORD:　About how frequently do you refer to the files out here in this next room?

HESS:　That's hard to say. Sometimes, quite often; at other times, maybe just once or twice a day.

FORD:　How is the material arranged in these files?

HESS:　It's supposed to be alphabetical by manufacturer's name, that is, for the design manuals. General literature from vendors is kept in a separate tier of cabinets, by vendor's name. Several times a week, a young lady from the main office brings current material and files it. But my designers and draftsmen are constantly coming to me and complaining they can't find the material they want, and they insist it was in the files. Sometimes, we find it misfiled; sometimes, the young lady tells us we never did have the material; sometimes, it is lost but turns up later.

FORD:　What do you think should be done?

HESS:　Well, now. . . . I understand you're the expert, so what I say may not make any sense. But for whatever it is worth, I think there is too much junk in the files—stuff we'll never use. And some way to find what we want would be a big help, too. Why, we've requested new copies of booklets and catalogues from a supplier only to discover before we receive them that we have the same booklets or catalogues in our file. Just could not find them when we wanted them.

Problems:

1. What further information do you feel Mr. Ford should obtain from Mr. Hess?

2. As Mr. Ford, would you hold any other interviews or make any observations within the company? Why?

3. What recommendations would you make to the company's managers? Discuss.

Part *4*

PLANNING IN OFFICE MANAGEMENT

A more thorough study of the management process— planning, controlling, organizing, and actuating—and its application to the office work of information handling is now in order. This portion of the book, Part IV, is devoted to planning.

First, development of the general concept of planning as it applies to the office is discussed. Following this, a chapter is devoted to each major area of office planning. They include office papers, office equipment, machines, layout, physical environment factors, and location. These seven chapters provide a co-ordinated and concise presentation of office management planning and include all concepts believed to be of major significance.

Chapter 14

PLANNING THE WORK OF THE OFFICE

We can't cross a bridge until we come to it; but I always like to lay down a pontoon ahead of time.
—BERNARD BARUCH

IF AN OFFICE manager finds that certain office work never seems to get done, deadlines are missed, peak loads are ever present, working overtime is common, office machines and equipment are poorly selected, and office space is inadequate—that office manager needs planning. Dominant under these conditions are foggy notions of what the office is supposed to accomplish and how it is to be done. There is a dearth of prescribed patterns of action and who is assigned to do each one. No sequence of work order is followed. Little work foresight is employed, and few preparations are made for tomorrow's work. Such an office reflects a confused, hodgepodge hindrance to successful operation of the enterprise.

PLANNING AND OFFICE MANAGEMENT

Planning helps establish orderliness and efficiency in getting office work accomplished. It keeps the office moving along smoothly, stressing simplicity, maintaining a work balance, and eliminating nonessentials. Planning assists in producing superior office work in record time with a minimum of effort.

As pointed out in Chapter 1, planning is the basic ingredient of the management process—planning, controlling, organizing and actuating. From planning result plans, and it is in order to make actions conform with these plans that controlling, organizing, and actuating are undertaken. If an office manager's plans are weak or incomplete, his controlling can never attain extraordinary accomplishments, simply because the controlling is being applied to plans that are mediocre. And the same applies to organizing and actuating being applied in conjunction with weak plans.

Office management planning includes prescribing the use of each basic resource available to the office manager. This takes into account, for example, the paper forms to be used, be they plain or printed sheets, or cards, or tape. What, if any, machines should be employed and which of several methods should be followed are typical questions answered by managerial planning. Furthermore, ample consideration for cost, time, and space requirements must be included. In addition, the planning effort must give considerable attention to the people who will be doing the work. Gaining their acceptance, training them, and maintaining their interest and co-operation are vital to the success of any plan. Later in this chapter, more will be stated about these components making up the scope of planning. This permeating of planning into every facet of proposed activity should be kept in mind in order to gain the full meaning and significance of planning.

PLANNING DEFINED

Stated formally, *planning is the visualization and formulation of proposed activities designed to achieve certain results.* It deals with future or hoped-for actions and is of a predetermining nature.

Thorough planning requires reflective thinking, imagination, and foresight. It is mental work. It is preparatory and should precede the physical effort. For this reason, planning is sometimes referred to as a "pre-executive" function, in that it constitutes work done prior to physical efforts by a manager. The preparatory efforts determine the goal, select the various activities, set their respective scope, integrate them, and identify them to interested parties.

PLANNING AND OBJECTIVES

Objectives result from planning; and in turn, planning is affected by objectives. This sounds paradoxical, but it simply signifies the importance of planning as both a determinant of goals and a medium for showing how these goals can be achieved.

For the office manager, the basic objectives are generally set forth by others—members of the board of directors, or top managers. Through planning, these men have determined what goals the enterprise should strive to attain. However, with the basic objectives known, the office manager frequently has to determine certain objectives for his organizational unit and its respective subordinate units. This necessitates planning. The immediate objective of each organizational unit must fit into and be part of the basic objective of the entire enterprise so that integrated objectives from top to bottom are actually stated and known.[1]

Most of the everyday planning of the office manager is determining the type and timing of work in order to achieve given goals. In other

---

[1] For specific examples of office management objectives, see Chapter 1, page 5.

words, it involves what sequence of what office work operations should take place in order to accomplish the stated objectives. In this planning, the goals affect the course of action to be followed.

Objectives are vital, not only to planning but to all management work. The whole justification for management existence is to achieve desired objectives. They set the targets for the entire management process because, as previously stated, the fundamental functions of management—controlling, organizing, and actuating—are essentially activities to implement the plan, which in turn is designed to achieve certain objectives. The obvious is frequently soon forgotten, and this is far too often the story with objectives. No one disagrees with the statement that a common goal must be established in order that a group may work together effectively and management may operate efficiently. But in quite a number of cases, the objectives are not known, are forgotten, or are ignored. This hampers effective management. Periodically, an office manager should state his objectives and then check his activities to see if he is managing toward the achievement of those objectives.

It should be noted that most offices have several objectives. They must of course be compatible, integrated, and to some extent interrelated. Seldom is it wise to try and state the real purpose of an office in one single, inclusive objective. Usually, such a statement is inadequate for managerial purposes. Objectives must be meaningful to every office employee, in terms he can understand, and of a type for which he can strive enthusiastically.

As time and conditions change, objectives are shifted, adjusted, added, or eliminated. There is, however, a stability about many objectives—they do not change perceivably over long periods. Many changes, if made, are slowly evolved, although some take place relatively quickly as a result of emergencies or major events such as legislative acts, world developments, or economic emergencies. But even in these instances, there are frequently forewarnings or indications that a change is likely to occur.

Some executives state that one mark of an effective work group is its ability to adjust quickly to new conditions, to maintain flexibility, to shape to new demands. This is another way of recognizing that all objectives of an enterprise do not remain constant; adjustment to change is a basic requirement.

STEPS IN PLANNING

Planning is highly individualized and is greatly influenced by such things as the subject area, the type of plan being created, the people who will carry out the plan, the person or persons doing the planning, the wishes of top managers, and the type of work included. However, there are fundamental components common to all planning work. Although not always followed by all planners, close adherence to them assists in evolving effective plans. These components are made up of the answers to these questions:

1. *What work has to be done?*   This includes the nature of the work, the amount, time allowed to accomplish it, and when it should start and when it should be finished.

2. *What manner or process will be followed?*   For example, will the work be done manually or by machine? If the latter, what kind, etc?

3. *What is the sequence of the work?*   How does the work progress from beginning to end? What is the work flow? What organizational unit or units are concerned with the work?

4. *What skill or type of employee is included?*   This answers the question: "Who is going to do the work?" The plan spells out this information in detail. For the operative level, instructions to the individual employees should be provided.

These questions sound simple enough, but application of them to a specific project raises many considerations. Further query is necessary. To illustrate, how long a period should the planning cover—a few days, a week, several months, or years? Can the planning be based entirely on factual data, or must certain calculated guesses as well as straight hunches about the future be made? Is there more than one way to accomplish the work to be done; and if so, how is the favored alternative to be chosen? Finally, but of great importance, what provisions or arrangements should be included in the plan to gain acceptance of it and to win the hearty co-operation of those selected to implement it? Each of these important and qualifying considerations will now be discussed.

LR AND SR PLANNING

Long range (LR) and short range (SR) are two basic types of planning. LR plans usually are for periods of five years or more. Among the objectives of such plans are utilization of improved office machines and equipment, better utilization of office space, and improved physical working conditions such as better light, ventilation, and sound control. The plan for achieving these goals is carefully devised, with the various necessary activities scheduled and integrated to take place according to a predetermined blueprint of action. LR planning provides perspective to office management; it helps achieve a needed balance of activities. Also, significant savings are made possible by LR planning. In the office of one manufacturer, for example, a 22 per cent reduction in space per office employee was achieved and, at the same time, a 36 per cent increase in output.

SR planning commonly identifies planning for the immediate future, that is, for the next several months, or possibly a year ahead. It is especially effective in the office for establishing timetables for billing, duplicating work, and other similar activities. Many office training programs are of a short-run type. Likewise, efforts to institute an office machine maintenance program, to improve correspondence, and to raise the efficiency of filing and records retention are suited to SR planning.

PLANNING—FACTS AND PREMISES

Facts are a basic ingredient of practical and effective planning. The facts should be obtained, carefully evaluated, and possible relationships uncovered before attempting to formulate a plan. Sometimes, when the facts are difficult to ascertain or are unpleasant, there is a tendency to discount them or to ignore them in the planning. Such action should be avoided. A planner must face the facts and take into account the actions that the facts dictate. Planning founded upon hopes or opinions may represent wishful thinking and prove impractical in efforts to apply it. Most successful planners stick to the facts. However, this certainly does not imply that visualization of hoped-for achievements cannot be made. Actually achievements are visualized, but the planning to achieve them should be based on facts, on the realities of the things and conditions upon and with which the hoped-for goal is to be attained.

But planning deals with the future, and facts about the future are unknown. Hence, facts alone are insufficient for the foundation of planning; probable events of the future must also be assumed and included in the planning. Such events are termed premises or assumptions, and they facilitate planning. That is to say, premises form the background against which the planner believes future events affecting his plan will take place.

As future events unfold, planning premises change, in turn causing changes in plans. To illustrate, on the premise that sales would increase 20 per cent during the coming year, an office manager planned his operations to take care of the additional office work resulting from this anticipated increase in sales. The increase in sales materialized and soon exceeded the 20 per cent gain forecast. Concurrently, the office manager had to adjust his plans in keeping with the facts and the new premise established—in this case, an additional 10 per cent sales increase.

Typical of planning premises are business forecasts, governmental actions, price structures, population projections, business cycles, quantity of work, quality of work, process used, and market demand studies. These are assumptions about the future upon which the planning efforts are based. Planning premises within any given enterprise should be harmonious; otherwise, integration of the various planning efforts throughout the enterprise will not be achieved. However, different premises can and should be used. This leads to alternative plans, discussed in the following paragraphs.

PLANNING—CHOICE OF ALTERNATIVES

From the viewpoint of management, embracing all planning are alternate goals and courses of action. If there is only one goal, attempts to evolve a possible array of related goals from planning are superfluous. Likewise, if there is only one means of achieving a goal, planning becomes a rigid, mechanical activity. The concept of planning in management implies determining a choice from several possibilities. There are a number of worthy goals. Which ones should a manager select? There are a number of means to accomplish a given goal. What means should be given preference by the manager? These questions are answered by planning.

Since the future is uncertain and conditions are dynamic, most managers agree that planning should provide alternatives, so that changes in plans, when needed, can be applied. As stated above, this can be the outcome when different premises are used. A plan based on premises A, B, and C may be dissolved when events show premises B, D, and E are in effect, and another plan substituted, based on these premises B, D, and E. Planning for a range of plans, not just a plan, provides a needed practical aspect and flexibility to plans, so that a manager can perform his work better.

PLANNING—WINNING ACCEPTANCE

Although planning is a fundamental function of management and all managers require planning in their work, it is common for a manager to perform planning efforts with others. Consultation with others to gain suggestions, facts, basic information, and advice is a fairly common practice in modern management. This approach is more democratic, helps to gain hearty acceptance and co-operation of those affected by the plan, and probably gives a better plan than if it were conceived by one person. Joint participation gives recognition to the fact, mentioned above, that no matter what is planned, it must be carried out by people and the success of any plan depends in some degree upon people's knowledge, comprehension, and desire to make the plan work.

In some cases, participation by nonmanagers in planning work is on a highly informal basis; in other cases, it is quite formalized. Committees are used by many enterprises for planning. Customarily, they are advisory, with the final approval on their recommended plans residing with the manager in charge. Committees provide an excellent means for making employees more aware of the importance of planning and of the difficulties in its formulation.

The success of any plan depends in great measure upon the manner in which employees perform their respective jobs. It is easy to think of planning as concerning primarily papers, machines, and methods—void of the influence of the human element. But the most effective planners give due consideration to the abilities and skills of the people involved and realize that a workable plan includes preparing the information for use and determining the steps for action by various individuals.

STRATEGIES IN PLANNING

A vital consideration in all office planning is the manner in which the plan is applied and the subsequent reaction of people affected by it. The approach should be well thought out, with the timing and details given special attention. The term "strategy" has been used in this connection, meaning the manner in which the plan is introduced or applied in order to help insure its success. There are many strategies employed by planners. Among the more common are the following:

1. *Strike while the iron is hot.* This stresses proper timing. When a situation appears favorable for adoption of a plan, it should be proposed without delay. Thus, unexpected opposition or difficulties possibly arising in the future are avoided.

2. *Time is a great healer.* This strategy points out that through patience and enforced delay, time is spent; and with it, acceptance of the proposed plan can be won. In other words, with time, events will happen which will make the plan acceptable and, in some instances, requested.

3. *Camel's head in the tent.* The infiltration approach is followed by offering a small portion of the plan and winning acceptance for it; subsequently, successive portions are offered, and accepted, until the entire original plan is in operation.

4. *Mass-concentrated offensive.* Here, the aim is to perform a major surgical operation—cut out the old, install the new—and handle the entire change in the shortest practical time. The rapidity and the "get it over with" aspects feature this strategy.

5. *Sewing seed on fertile ground.* The best place to gain acceptance for a plan is from those who favor it. Under this strategy, favorable members of a group are indoctrinated with the merits of the proposed action. In turn, they explain the plan to other group members, thus enlarging the number favorable to the plan. When sufficient members have been "won to the cause," the plan is formally offered and usually accepted.

The above strategies have been included for illustrative purposes only. The list is not all-inclusive; there are many, many different strategies. It should also be observed that some strategies are the direct opposite of others. This follows because the situations to which they apply, especially the human element make-up of the group, may be directly opposite. Considerable skill is required to apply strategy successfully in office planning.

TYPES OF PLANS

Generally speaking, repetitive work is best suited for planning. However, much nonrepetitive work has in its make-up portions of repetitive work; and by analysis, it will be found that more repetitiveness and hence more planning are possible than might at first have been believed. Also, work that is nonrepetitive but is performed frequently can usually be planned successfully.

In office work, most concern is usually given these types of plans: (1) objectives, (2) policies, (3) procedures, and (4) methods. Objectives and planning were discussed several pages back. Policies are formu-

---

POLICIES

1. Billing and Receivables
   1.1 Cash discount allowances
   1.2 Error allowances
   1.3 "Spin-offs" for handling large and small orders
   1.4 Customer satisfaction and relationship
   1.5 Compliance with industry practices
2. Cash and Payables
   2.1 Number of banks
   2.2 Periods of payment
   2.3 Dual signatures
   2.4 Advance notice periods for check requests
   2.5 Advances on standard expense account

FIG. 14–1. Areas covered by two office policies common in many enterprises.

lated by planning and assist in deciding what work must be performed. *A policy is a basic guide to action.* It sets forth over-all boundaries within which activities are to take place. Policies result from managerial planning; and they, in turn, affect planning. They tell the intentions of the managers in respect to various activities. For example, a company may have a policy of purchasing each year a quantity of office machines based on an amount determined by a percentage of net sales. This establishes that certain activities are to take place and puts limits upon them. However, it does not set forth what machines are to be purchased. That is, a policy permits planning and decision making within the prescribed limits of the policy.

Figure 14–1 shows, in topical outline form, two policies common in most offices, with the probable make-up of contents under each policy. For example, the policy covering cash and payables includes the number of banks used by the enterprise, periods of payment, the use of dual signatures, and so forth. These are areas covered by policies; and as stated above, they do not specify preciseness, but rather the broad boundaries within which exacting decisions are to be made. The policy content pertaining to the number of banks might place the limit at two, but the policy does not specify which two banks. Likewise, the periods of payment, not the exact dates, are set forth by the policy.

Procedures are of special interest in the management of office work. An "office procedure" can be defined as *a series of related clerical steps, usually performed by more than one person, which constitute an established and accepted way of carrying on an entire major phase of office activity*. Procedures are obtained by preplanning the various steps believed necessary to accomplish the work. Procedures are applied to the handling of such things as incoming orders, accounts payable, purchase orders, making up payrolls, sending out statements, and handling mail. An office procedure is broad in scope and frequently extends throughout a large portion of the entire office.

The term "method" designates *the manner of work performance of a task consisting of one or more clerical acts by an individual employee*. Thus, a series of methods which are cumulative and integrated make up a procedure.[2]

In planning, it is more logical to determine first the procedure and then the methods making up this procedure. In this way, the broad activities are established, co-ordination is enhanced, and the end result of the total effort is more clearly visualized. Actually, consideration is usually given to the methods while in the stage of planning the procedure. It is possible, however, to start with the methods and tie them together for the procedure.

PROCEDURES AND OFFICE MANAGEMENT

For purposes of discussing office planning, the remainder of this chapter will be confined to office procedures. Procedures are basic in getting office work accomplished. They are, indeed, the basis for a completely harmonious and orderly operation of office work. More than this, the success or failure of any enterprise depends in great measure on how orderly the office procedures are developed and how well they are controlled in expediting the intended functions and flow of information into and out of the enterprise.

An office procedure handles cycles of business activity, that is, it identifies and establishes the sequence of specific operations for achieving a definite type of office work. Some of the more common office proce-

---

[2] Some believe it is helpful to think of procedures as answering questions regarding the *what, when,* and *where* of office work; and of methods as answering *how* office work is to be done. To a degree, this is true; actually, however, *what, when, where,* and *how* can be applied to either a procedure or a method.

dures are those pertaining to sales, inventory, production, production control, payroll, cost, and purchasing. An office procedure for sales might include this series of specific operations: (1) Write the order, (2) deliver to warehouse, (3) fill the order, (4) reduce inventory on hand, (5) ship the order, (6) invoice customer, (7) collect payment, and (8) record receipt of payment. If well planned, this sales procedure will tie in with an inventory procedure, a purchasing procedure, and a production control procedure, plus other small and minor procedures operating at the same time, supposedly aiding the major ones to function more smoothly and efficiently.

A challenge of planning is to determine what combination of office procedures is best for a given enterprise. The complexity of modern information handling negates the approach of considering each office procedure as a separate and independent entity. The office manager cannot plan piecemeal and add parts together, taking a paper here, a machine there, a tape from somewhere else, and an intercommunication system from still another area and hope they all will fit together, work right, and give agreeable results. Today, he must start with the objective and work backwards, by asking how best this goal can be reached by the use of those facilities available to him or those that can be made available to him.

This kind of planning for office procedures can be termed the "total-concept" approach. It necessitates a thorough understanding of the total information requirements before trying to design and utilize various

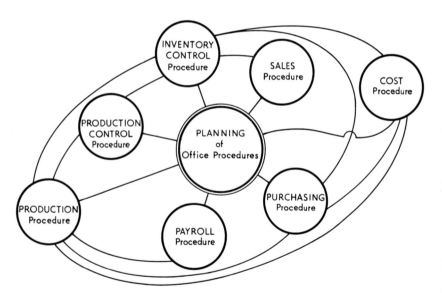

FIG. 14–2. In office management, a complex of interrelated procedures is involved in the handling of selected basic information processing.

office procedures. A mass of interrelated variables must be correlated, and the best means should be used to provide accurate, quick answers to information needs.

Figure 14–2 shows in graphic form the interrelation of various office procedures involved in planning office procedures. Many procedures are interdependent and have common areas of paper work contact or similarity. The figure does not attempt to show the relative importance of these procedures. If it did, the sales, production, and cost procedures might well assume larger proportions.

ESTABLISHING A PROCEDURE

The total-concept approach in procedures planning may, from the viewpoint of planning any one procedure, establish certain limits; but still, there usually exists a choice of alternative procedures. A certain type and amount of office work can normally be performed in several different ways. In determining the procedure to establish, adequate consideration should be given several important factors, including the following:

1. *Study the entire office process.* This includes the total concept or the assuming of an over-all picture of the total paper work procedures. With this as a background, find out the type of paper work to be handled by the particular procedure under investigation. Determine its volume, any characteristic peaks and valleys in its normal flow, and the importance of the time limit for getting the paper work finished. Consider also the present office layout and how the current arrangement will tie in with the procedural requirements. Keep in mind that procedures are far-reaching—they frequently affect the work of several departments.

2. *Establish the best sequence of the necessary steps.* Use the minimum number of steps required to do the work adequately. Each step should make a definite contribution toward the completion of the office work, i.e., each step should be entirely justifiable. There should be no delay, no duplication, and no backtracking.

3. *Hold the writing to a minimum.* As far as possible, the work of copying should be eliminated. Original source data should be used to eliminate posting to or recopying of records. The operations of checking and comparing should be the smallest feasible amounts. Likewise, the number of copies should be limited to a quantity necessary only for carefully selected persons or departments—those really concerned in the operation. There is no merit in making copies and in distributing them simply for the sake of doing so or because they are available.

4. *Wherever possible, source data should be put in a form suitable for reuse in subsequent operations.* Actually, this is the basic idea of

IDP (integrated data processing), discussed in Chapter 7. Commonly, the processing of data requires the repeating of identical information on different documents; hence, having such data in a form that expedites duplicating in whole or in part saves time and energy.

5. *Adopt a procedure best suited to the individual need.* The best procedure is tailored to accomplish a specific and particular goal—no more and no less. Frequently, this necessitates modification of a procedure used by another enterprise under similar conditions. Use by others is no valid justification for adopting a certain procedure, unless it can be shown, by thorough study, that the procedure will accomplish the objective better than any other procedure that could be devised within reasonable time and cost limitations.

6. *Wherever possible, perform multiple operations by machine.* Research studies are now ample to show that multiple office operations are more efficiently performed by machine than by hand. Automatic features of many modern machines, the time required for loading and unloading the machine, and the complexity of much data processing have made mechanization of multiple operations the preferred means.

7. *Give consideration to the personal preference of the employees who will do the work.* Consulting with the employees, getting their ideas as to what the make-up of the procedure should be, and incorporating these ideas whenever possible usually results in obtaining better work. The practice of employee consultation helps to raise morale, gives consideration to the small but important details of the work, and pro-

---

1. Is it a definite fact that the information produced is not available more simply or economically from another source?
2. Is every part of the information on the record really necessary?
3. Is it possible to eliminate or shorten any proposed step of the procedure, or combine them with other steps?
4. Is any step in the procedure being accepted on the basis that "it has always been done this way"?
5. Can the sequence of the necessary steps of the procedure be changed to expedite the work or make the work less fatiguing?
6. Are the employees designated to do the work specially trained and qualified to do their individual tasks?
7. Are the batches of work large enough to promote efficiency and, on the other hand, small enough for ease in balancing and handling?
8. Are codes being used, and are they simple and short?
9. Are all the workplaces well arranged for performing the work?
10. Are files that are used extensively readily accessible?
11. Does the office layout assist in getting the work to flow smoothly?
12. Are physical conditions such as light, noise abatement, and office temperature the best for proper office work execution?

FIG. 14–3. Helpful questions to ask in efforts to design the best possible procedure.

vides due regard for custom and tradition in establishing the procedure.

8. *Perform one type of office work with one procedure.* Attempts to secure a general over-all procedure for all types of work result in ineffectiveness. For example, special work processed through a regular work procedure usually results in delaying the former and slowing down the latter. But as indicated above, all procedures within a given enterprise are interrelated to some degree and have certain common areas of contact.

A helpful summary check list is shown by Figure 14–3. Answers to these questions provide a penetrating review of the procedure to be followed and help achieve a superior means of getting the office work performed.

EXAMPLE OF OFFICE PROCEDURE

To illustrate a definite office procedure, a brief discussion of a procedure for handling invoices and sales orders will be related. Enterprises where merchandise is delivered or services are performed in return for compensation have the task of invoicing their customers for this merchandise or service. In many instances, the same information is required on both the invoice office forms and the order office forms. This suggests the use of a combination invoice-order form which requires only one writing, reduces the possibility of errors, minimizes the possibility of shipping merchandise without issuing an invoice, and bills each customer immediately after shipment of merchandise.

Figure 14–4 shows graphically a procedure for using the combination invoice-order form. Starting at the top of the illustration, the order is received from any of a number of sources. The first step is to edit the order, i.e., check for correctness of model, part number, description, price, and credit. The order is then written on a stub-type unit-arrangement office form, omitting date shipped, quantities shipped, how shipped, total price, and usually the invoice number and invoice date. These omitted items can usually be determined only after the shipment is made. The form is then separated into (1) an invoice section and (2) an order section. The latter is sent to the factory or shipping room. When shipment is ready, the quantity shipped is written on the order section, the packing copy is inserted in the package, and the order copy is sent to the office, where it is matched, by order number, with the invoice section. Prices are filled in on the order copy, and the writing on the invoice section is completed. The invoice copy is then mailed to the customer, and the posting copy is sent to the bookkeeper.

This procedure is simple, effective, and practical. It will give very satisfactory results for most invoice and sales-order handling. However, in some instances, because of the particular details of the opera-

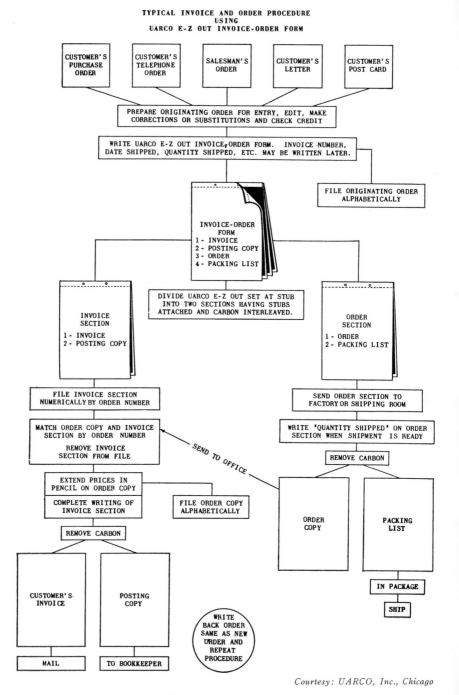

Courtesy: *UARCO, Inc., Chicago*

FIG. 14–4. Procedure using a combination invoice-order form.

tion, the procedure may prove deficient. Among the more common of such cases are (1) when the description of the merchandise or service frequently changes from the original writing, (2) when descriptions or specifications of service needed on the order copy differ considerably from those on the invoice copy, (3) when the number of items is large and many back orders are required, and (4) when a large single order is received for frequent-release shipments over a long period of time.

AVAILABLE PROCEDURES

There are a number of ready-made procedures which are available to the office manager. Quite a few companies offer preplanned procedures and engage in the business of selling "office systems." Some can be adopted in total with little or no alteration, while others require a great deal of modification in order to answer the specific needs of a given case.

No one type of procedure can be universally recommended. When a ready-made procedure is to be used, the selection depends chiefly upon such things as (1) the volume and regularity of the flow of the paper work; (2) the kind and amount of data; (3) the relative costs, including both installation and maintenance; (4) the policies of the company; and (5) the attitude of top management members, including the influence of key personnel.

The office manager should keep informed as to what procedures are available, carefully evaluate them, and study them to determine how they can be modified, if necessary, to improve the operations of his office. For the most part, he should neither adopt all ready-made procedures nor reject all of them consistently. Satisfactory results are usually obtained by taking an open-minded attitude and having a will to progress. He should never forgo his planning work entirely to others.

ADVANTAGES OF OFFICE PROCEDURES

Procedures bring order and a mode of operation to office work. They reduce everyday work to a routine, thus simplifying the execution of the work and minimizing the task of decision making in the handling of that work.

Executives are relieved of many details of execution, making it possible for them to devote most of their time to other work. The carrying-out of the usual and frequent tasks is taken care of by the procedure. Thus, only the out-of-the-ordinary or exceptional matters are referred to the executive, who decides what is to be done in these cases. This practice is referred to as the "exception principle" in management literature.

Uniformity of action is obtained through use of office procedures. Common clerical tasks are handled in an identical manner each time they occur. Work can be easily located, and quick checks on progress can be made. Well-designed paper forms, work habits, and controls can be utilized.

Procedures usually result in savings in costs of office operations. The work is kept moving, delay is minimized, employees are guided in their respective tasks, and unnecessary steps are eliminated.

In addition, the work of training personnel is simplified. The duties and operations of each job are clearly defined. Information is determined regarding what the employee must be capable of doing to perform the work satisfactorily. Selective training programs can be focused on the particular requirements needed by the employee.

Procedures formalize the successive clerical steps, and an omission of any one of them is unusual. Thus, the chances of error are reduced. Furthermore, the possibility of any inaccuracy in the work at any one point is minimized, since an employee becomes particularly efficient and adept at his operation because of specialization and repetition.

Lastly, procedures improve the service of the office. It is by means of procedures that the modern office is able to meet the large demands placed upon it. Getting the work out on time and in an acceptable form is possible through the help of office procedures. They make it possible to render the type of office service desired.

QUESTIONS

1. What do you understand by the term "premises of planning," and of what importance are they in managerial planning?
2. Do you believe that long-range planning is of major significance in office management? Why?
3. Summarize the chief points under the subject of "Office Management Planning and Objectives."
4. Should all office management planning include a strategy? Why?
5. In planning, is there always a choice of alternatives? Explain.
6. What is meant by each of the following terms?
    a) Policy.
    b) "Camel's head in the tent."
    c) Total-concept approach in procedures planning.
    d) Method.
7. Explain the meaning of Figure 14–2 in your own words.
8. Name and discuss five advantages in using office procedures.
9. Give an acceptable definition of office management policy, and relate several examples of policies with which you have had experience.
10. Select an office procedure with which you are familiar, and write a short report about it, explaining its major features so that a chart of it, similar to that of Figure 14–4, could be constructed from your report.
11. Discuss the use of ready-made procedures by an office manager.
12. In establishing an office procedure, is it important to study the entire office process? Why?

CASE PROBLEMS

Case 14–1. Overton Trust Company

The transfer agent of stock of the Frey Manufacturing Corporation, an Illinois corporation, is the recently appointed Overton Trust Company. Included among the duties of a transfer agent are maintaining an up-to-date list of the corporation's shareholders' names and addresses, disbursing dividends to these owners, and transferring title of any stock certificate of the corporation presented for recording of ownership change.

Upon being presented with a certificate for transfer of ownership, it is the practice of the agent to cancel the old certificate, properly endorsed and assigned, and issue a new certificate for a like number of shares in the name of the assignee, or new owner. The recording of the transfer details, including the adjusting of the transfer records to reflect the change of ownership, requires at least twenty-four hours. In addition, under Illinois law, it is necessary for the new certificates created by the transfer to be forwarded for countersignature by a registrar, who acts as a check against the overissuance of authorized shares. This registrar must by law be separate from and independent of the transfer agent.

The managers of the Overton Trust Company desire to keep adequate records of transactions, handle the receipt of certificates, cancel them, issue new certificates, forward them to the registrar for countersignature, and subsequently deliver new certificates as quickly as possible to the new owners. The source of certificates presented for transfer can be classified into two types: (1) over-the-counter items, that is, those presented in person to the transfer agent by a broker or an individual; and (2) mail items, that is, those sent to the transfer agent through the mail.

With this in mind, Clark Gates, a member of the office staff at the Overton Trust Company, suggested that a three-section receipt form be used. This form would provide appropriate space for pertinent information, including the name of the stock seller, the number of shares to be transferred, and the old and the new certificate number. The following is a sketch of the proposed three-section receipt.

Receipt No. _____	Receipt No. _____	Receipt No. _____
Received for transfer of _____ shares of Frey Manufacturing Co.	Received for transfer of _____ shares of Frey Manufacturing Co.	Received for transfer of _____ shares of Frey Manufacturing Co.
Old Certificate No. _____	Old Certificate No. _____	Old Certificate No. _____
New Certificate No. _____	New Certificate No. _____	New Certificate No. _____
Section 1	Section 2	Section 3

For over-the-counter items, the receipt is filled out; and section 3 is given the customer, with the information that the new certificate will be available the following day from the office of the registrar. Transfer of the old certificate will be completed, a new certificate issued, and both, accompanied by section 2 of the receipt form, forwarded by messenger to the registrar. Section 1 will be retained by the Overton Trust Company as a record of the transaction. After the registrar has noted his records and added his signature, he delivers the new certificate to the party presenting section 3 of the receipt form. At this time, the recipient is asked to acknowledge delivery of the new certificate by signing a "statement of receipt" appearing on the reverse side of the receipt.

In the case of mail items, the work is handled in similar manner. The three-section receipt form is filled out; the mechanics of transferring are carried out; and the new certificates, together with section 2 of the receipt, are delivered to the registrar. The following day, the messenger of the Overton Trust Company, using section 1, picks up the new certificate from the registrar and returns it to the transfer agent. Meanwhile, section 3 has been retained with the correspondence for identification. As soon as the new certificate is returned to the transfer agent, it is mailed to the transferee with a letter of transmittal, in duplicate, describing the enclosure and asking for acknowledgment of the contents on the duplicate copy. Upon its return, the receipted duplicate copy is filed in the central filing section.

Problems:

1. Draw a graphic representation of how the three sections of the receipt form will be used for (*a*) over-the-counter items and (*b*) mail items. Use any form of graphic representation that you feel helps visualize the paper work followed.

2. Evaluate the plan suggested by Clark Gates.

3. Suggest other practical means for handling the transfer agent's work as described in this case. Which alternative do you prefer? Why?

Case 14–2.   Northwestern Typewriter Company

In order to stimulate sales, the Northwestern Typewriter Company encourages its dealers to send in names of prospects, who are then written a letter by the company, offering to send free of charge a booklet entitled *How to Reduce Your Typing Costs*. Likewise, the company sends out letters (offering the free booklet) to names on various mailing lists which it purchases.

If the prospect replies that he would like to receive a copy of the booklet, he is sent one by the company. Subsequently, the company wishes one of the salesmen of the dealer in the particular area to call on the prospect who replied and either (*a*) sell him a Northwestern typewriter or (*b*) get him to use a Northwestern typewriter on a free trial basis. The company has found that a high percentage of trials result in sales.

Ordinarily, the salesman's call should occur within 30 days after the booklet is mailed. Frequently, two calls are necessary—one 30 days after booklet mailing, another 60 days after mailing. Where trials are obtained, a third call 90 days after the salesman's initial call is generally necessary. In some instances, a sale is made on the initial call by the salesman.

The sales manager of the Northwestern Typewriter Company wishes to have a paper work procedure installed whereby the handling of the necessary paper work would be reduced to a system, and which would indicate the status of every prospect to whom a letter was sent.

Problems:

1. Define the company's policy regarding its sales efforts.
2. Discuss the strategy in the planning of this company.
3. What procedure do you recommend for the Northwestern Typewriter Company?

Case 14–3. Warner Company

Some eighteen thousand accounts are handled monthly by the Warner Company of Detroit, Michigan, a distributor of a morning newspaper. The average amount for each account is about $1.75 per month.

Currently, the procedure for handling collections is as follows: A file card is made out for each subscriber, showing name, address, period of subscription, monthly due date, and the amounts of credit, debit, and balance. These cards are filed alphabetically according to the subscriber's surname.

Each collection day, the office clerk goes through the file and makes out a list stipulating the name, address, and amount of accounts due. The collection sheets are given the collectors. Upon collection, the customer is given a receipt, and the amount paid is written by the collector opposite the proper name on the collection list. From these sheets, the office clerk posts the collection date and amount on the proper file cards.

Mr. Henry Madison, the office manager of the Warner Company, feels that the present procedure does not permit sufficient flexibility—for example, when only partial payments or advance payments are made. Furthermore, he believes that the procedure can be simplified and that constant combing through the file and drawing up lists can be minimized or possibly eliminated. At the same time, Mr. Madison realizes that the number of accounts is large but that the amount per account is small. He believes that any proposed change must of necessity require little or no new equipment.

Problems:

1. Do you agree with Mr. Madison, the office manager? Why?
2. Indicate the procedure you recommend for the Warner Company.

Chapter 15

PLANNING OFFICE PAPERS

The future that we study and plan for begins today.
—CHESTER O. FISCHER

MUCH INFORMATION supplied by the office is written on paper. This medium, whether it be letterheads, cards, printed forms, or just plain pieces of paper, can be considered the raw material of the office. While not inclusive of all office work, the processing and distributing of information involves, sooner or later, the use of various papers. This is basic to most office work. To list all the various types of paper media would be cumbersome and unnecessary. For convenience and to serve adequately the purpose here, the types included in this chapter are letters, reports, and office paper forms of various kinds and sizes.

OFFICE PAPERS AND PLANNING

Planning involves the design and the specification of characteristics and features of office papers. But the office paper requirements are only a part of the total requirements. As already stated, office managerial planning involves consideration for the entirety of the work accomplishment—the use of the papers, the office machine, the method, and the office employee. Planning of office papers emphasizes considerations for the papers themselves, but adequate consideration must also be given to the basic work elements intimately associated with them. Questions such as what information is needed, in what format it should be provided, how many copies are required, what arrangement best fits the machine or manual process to be followed, the preference of the employees working with the information, and which arrangement of information will be most pleasing to customers are typical of those encompassed in the work of planning office papers.

ARRANGEMENT OF LETTER

A business letter should make a favorable first impression. To do this, it should be well placed on the page, have margins as even as possible, have a uniformity of typing or print, and give a clean and neat appearance.

There is probably no one best form for a business letter. Usually, a general pattern is in common usage; but slight variations are the rule, depending upon the particular needs and wishes of the writer. Most readers are accustomed to the general pattern and look for certain information in certain locations. Figure 15–1 shows the forms of several different types, including (1) block paragraphs, (2) indented paragraphs, and (3) simplified letter. The difference between indented paragraphs and block paragraphs is that in the latter, the paragraphs are started at the left margin. In the simplified letter, all material starts at the left margin, the salutation is omitted—in its place the subject of the letter is written—and the complimentary close is omitted. Slight variations from

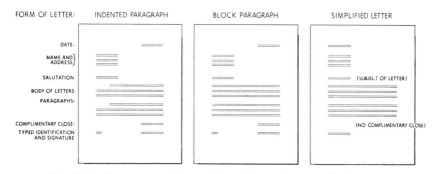

FIG. 15–1. The respective forms of three different letters used in business.

these three forms of letters are employed. One large national distributor, for example, uses the block paragraph form with open punctuation, that is, commas and periods are omitted at end of date, address, and close.

SPEED LETTER

In order to simplify the work of correspondence, the so-called "speed letter" is used by many business writers. The speed letter is a preprinted form designating certain spaces for filling in desired information. Commonly, two carbon copies of the letter are provided, making a pack of several sheets. A simple arrangement provides spaces for "From" and "To" at the top of the sheet; and a line for the "Subject" to be written in, below which is a space for the "Message" and below it, the "Reply." In the three-copy arrangement, the original is retained by the sender; copies No. 2 and 3 are sent to the receiver, who writes in his reply, returns copy No. 2, and retains copy No. 3.

In other styles, space is provided for a listing of recipients making up a mailing route, and preprinted information is included so that the appropriate information can be indicated by a simple check mark. Addi-

DEMPSTER CORP. CHICAGO, ILL. SPEED LETTER			DATE		
TO: 1		LOCATION		INITIALS	DATE
2					
3					
4					
5					

APPROVAL		NOTE AND FORWARD
AS REQUESTED		NOTE AND RETURN
COMMENT		NOTE ENDORS'T OF ACTION TAKEN
FOR YOUR INFORMATION		PER CONVERSATION
INITIAL FOR CLEARANCE		PREPARE REPLY
NECESSARY ACTION		SIGNATURE

MESSAGE

SIGNATURE	TITLE

FIG. 15–2. A well-planned printed form to expedite written communication.

tional space is provided for such individual information as may be required. Figure 15–2 shows a speed letter of this design. The letter can accompany other written material or convey a message in and of itself. Either single- or multicopy design is available.

FORM LETTERS

As pointed out in Chapter 8, most letters can be classified into a relatively small number of types. This fact suggests and has led to letter standardization, or the use of form letters. A form letter is *a standardized letter which is used by an enterprise to answer all correspondence of a similar and recurring subject, or which is used to give the same infor-*

mation to many addressees. A form letter may be sent to accounts past due. Such a letter, keyed "Delinquent Collection Letter No. 1," is sent to all accounts in arrears, with the appropriate name and address added at the top. After a certain amount of time, a "Delinquent Collection Letter No. 2" may be sent to those accounts which remain unpaid.

Benefits in Use of Form Letters. The chief advantages in the use of form letters are that they (1) afford a uniform operation, (2) conserve both the dictator's and the typist's time, and (3) help reduce letter costs. On the other hand, there are disadvantages in the use of form letters, including these: (1) They are not keyed to the requirements of individual cases, (2) they may be a little stilted, and (3) they are very often discounted by the receiver because of the lack of a personal touch.

Generally speaking, form letters serve a very useful purpose. They are tailored to fit certain conditions and are usually worked over by several correspondents to create the best possible results. They need not be impersonal, and it is not necessary to send the same letter again and again to the same customer. When properly handled, there should be no objection to form letters.

FORM PARAGRAPHS

Form paragraphs are similar in idea to form letters but apply to standardized paragraphs only. Under this practice, letters are composed of form paragraphs plus individual ones. Experts are frequently engaged to develop the form paragraphs.

It is customary for the dictator to use several variants of a form paragraph. This permits some diversity. The approved form paragraphs are listed, keyed, and indexed, and are made available to all correspondents.

DEVELOPING FORM LETTERS AND PARAGRAPHS

Form letters and form paragraphs can be "armchaired" from handy references, or they can be determined by using a factual approach. The latter is recommended. To do this, simply take these steps:

1. For a period of four weeks, make an extra copy of every letter written.

2. At the end of this period, sort the copies by major subject and further by types under each major heading.

3. Determine the types of letters most frequently written and also, under each type, the most frequently used paragraphs.

4. Select the best reply to each frequently asked question and also the best expression of the necessary information.

5. Standardize these forms, and incorporate them as form paragraphs and form letters.

6. Repeat this entire procedure every twelve months; then, adjust and improve form paragraphs and letters as suggested by findings.

For this work, the office manager should enlist the services of all letter-writing people in his office. Participation will not only help win acceptance of the program of improving correspondence but will also utilize the best personnel for this work, raise morale, and increase efficiency.

FORMAT FOR REPORTS

There is no one best way to arrange the information of a report. In some instances, a standardized format is well established and accepted; but in many cases, the writer is free to choose the make-up. Material should be presented logically. Aids which will help in the reading should be provided—for example, simple statements, sectional headings, summaries at the beginning, and a table of contents. A reader often glances through a report, noting the various headings and reading a sentence here and there. For this reason, it is advisable to make it possible to obtain a "quickie" on what the report is all about and what it includes. This approach will maintain the reader's interest and lead him to correct conclusions and proper actions.

Every report should follow a carefully developed general outline. The first step in preparing such an outline is to select the information to be included in the report. This is ordinarily dictated by the purpose of the report, what information is available, or what can be uncovered. Next, the items of information should be classified under headings which normally are grouped as major and minor, or as many groups as judgment suggests.

There are a number of general outlines for reports; the following is preferred by many:

1. Summary of findings.
   a) Objectives.
   b) Results.
   c) Conclusion.
2. Methodology.
   a) Techniques.
   b) Sample.
3. Detailed results.
4. Appendix.

Another outline which is effective and adaptable for many subjects, especially those of a technical nature, includes:

1. Summary.
2. Objective and scope.

3. Equipment used.
4. Methodology.
5. Data obtained.
6. Conclusions.
7. Recommendations.

The following has also won considerable favor:

1. Introduction and definition of problem.
2. Conclusions and recommendations.
3. Discussion of procedure and results obtained.
4. Summary.

It should be observed that in each of these outlines, either the summary, conclusion, or recommendation is included near the beginning of

---

April 25, 19—

To: T. E. Miller
SUBJECT: Storing purchased parts in our stores.
OBJECTIVE: To reduce damage to parts while in transit
                        or in stores.
SCOPE OF PROJECT: Try to attain:
                        1. Better package design and material.
                        2. Improved physical inventory taking.
                        3. Better utilization of stores space.
                        4. Efficient housekeeping in stores.
TIME REQUIRED: Approximately six weeks.
SUBMITTED BY: J. D. Black

FIG. 15–3. Example of an effective short memorandum.

the report. This may seem illogical; but actually, it is not. The sequence of items need not be chronologic; however, there should be *some order* in presenting the material. The great majority of report readers want the gist of the findings or the conclusions right away, so it is effective to put this information at the beginning.

In many instances, a short, well-written memorandum is very effective. Figure 15–3 illustrates such a memorandum. Short headings simplify the job of writing because they unify short, simple sentences into a condensed and informative message.

Charts, drawings, pictures, and maps help to convey the meaning to the reader, but they must be carefully selected and employed in "reasonable" amounts for maximum assistance to be derived. The accuracy and completeness of the illustrative material must be carefully checked. In many cases, the chart or drawing must be explained and significant developments and relations pointed out to the reader, because the exact meaning may not be gained simply by looking at the illustrative material. Pictures are especially helpful in dealing with technical subjects.

OFFICE FORMS

Among the most important and most widely used papers in an office are office forms. Succinctly stated, *an office form is a printed piece of paper which provides space for entering records, information, or instructions which are to be conveyed to other individuals, departments, or enterprises.* Office forms are used in various sizes, designs, types of paper, and number of copies. Common examples include cost tickets, expense accounts, factory orders, requisitions, sales data, purchase orders, invoices, and credit memorandums.

Office forms are used because they meet the demands of modern office activity. More specifically, the use of office forms:

1. *Reduces copying.* Office forms are particularly helpful where several copies are necessary. The monotonous work of copying, as well as the chance of committing errors in copying, is eliminated. Items common to many transactions are printed on the form.

2. *Insures uniformity.* Forms give standard appearance to the format of records. Identification and recognition of data are made easier; filing and sorting are simplified.

3. *Serves as work guides.* An office form guides the office employee in his work. He knows where to begin and what he is doing, and understands what he is expected to do. His job is made easier.

4. *Gives official sanction.* An office form gives a mark of approval to written work which is viewed as authentic when appearing on a printed office form.

5. *Implements mechanical operations.* For office mechanization, the paper on which data are recorded must meet certain machine requirements, such as a definite size, a certain arrangement of information, uniformity of spacing, and provisions for punching and notching. Forms meet these requirements and thus facilitate the use of office machines.

PLANNING OF OFFICE FORMS

In the planning of an office form, it is usually wise to enlist the help of forms-design engineers. These men are trained and experienced in this type of work and are usually able to suggest improvements in a form. Most companies manufacturing office forms are very willing to be of help and offer services of design engineers. In addition, the employee who will use the form can frequently offer helpful suggestions as well as evaluate a proposed form. A check list such as that shown by Figure 15–4 assists in forms-improvement efforts. In this list, twenty-six perti-

HAMMERMILL FORM ORDER SHEET • PART 1

a *5 minute* FORM CHECK LIST

[A quick and easy method of checking the efficiency and economy of any form—new or old—before placing your printing order. Read the text at the bottom of this sheet.]

Necessity

	OK	?
1 Has the entire system been checked and would a written procedure for the use of this form help put it into more efficient operation?		
2 Are all copies of the form or report necessary?		
3 Have the actual users of this form been consulted for suggested improvements, additional requirements and possible eliminations?		
4 Can the data furnished by this form be combined with some other form or can some other form be eliminated or consolidated with it?		
5 Has everyone responsible for the form or the form system approved it?		

Purpose

	OK	?
6 If form is to be sent from one person to another, are proper spaces for "to" and "from" provided?		
7 Will routing or handling instructions printed on each copy be helpful?		
8 Should this form be consecutively numbered, or have a place for inserting a number?		
9 If this is an Outside Contact Form, should it be designed to mail in a window envelope?		
10 If this form is to take information from, or pass information to, another form, do both have the same sequence of items?		
11 Have we taken into consideration the number of forms which will be used in a given time (4 to 12 months)—the possibility of changes, and how long the form will remain in use?		

Size and Arrangement

	OK	?
12 Is the size right for filing, attention value, ample room for information and to cut without waste?		
13 Is all recurring information being printed, so that only variable items need be filled in?		
14 Has space been provided for a signature?		
15 Is spacing correct for handwriting or typewriting? (The Hammermill Form Layout Sheet will help check this.)		
16 Are the most important items, which should be seen first, prominently placed? (Near the top, if practicable.)		

Wording

	OK	?
17 Does the form, by title and arrangement, clearly indicate its purpose?		
18 Is there a proper space for the date?		
19 Is the form identified by company name and firm name or code number to aid reordering?		
20 If this is a revised form, can it be distinguished from the previous form?		

Paper and Printing (SPECIFICATIONS)

	OK	?
21 Should the form be on colored paper to speed up writing, distribution, sorting and filing; to designate departments or branch offices; to indicate days, months or years; to distinguish manifold copies; to identify rush orders?		
22 Have we specified paper which will be thoroughly satisfactory, economical enough for form use, consistent in performance and surely available for later reorders?		
23 Is proper weight of paper used for original and each carbon copy? (Bond Substances 9, 13, 16 and 20. Ledger Substances 24, 28 and 32. Mimeo-Bond Substances 16 and 20. Spirit and Gelatin Duplicator Substances 16 and 20.)		
24 Are detailed specifications complete? (Paper, type, ink, rules, punch, perforate, score, fold, gather, pad, carbon sheet, stitch, etc.)		
25 Can other forms, printed on the same paper as this one, be ordered now to reduce production costs?		
26 Have requirements been estimated correctly and is the quantity to be ordered most economical? (Consider probability of revision and rate of use.)		

Remarks ON POINTS QUESTIONED (?)

Pt. #

DATE _____ 19_____ SIGNED_____

HOW TO USE THIS FORM Run through this list and appraise a new or revamped form point by point with an initial (rather than a check mark) either in the column headed "OK" or "?." This will help in working out the most efficient form size and specifications and the best working arrangement of items and copy. Points marked (?) for further study can then be appraised systematically and discussed with those who will regularly use the form. Findings and further details can be elaborated upon in the column for "Remarks" at bottom of the second column.

To pin down responsibility, the person or persons giving the final OK should place their initials opposite the remarks. The whole Check List should be filed with a copy of the form for future reference.

FIG. 15–4. A form check list which aids in improving office forms.

nent questions are classified under five main headings: the necessity, purpose, size and arrangement, wording, and paper and printing of the form. Use of this list helps reveal information which is basic in designing the form. A separate sheet is recommended for each form analysis.

The planning of office forms can be conveniently considered in terms of functional considerations and physical considerations. The former deal with factors such as the way the form is used, its purpose, the information supplied on it, and the number of copies required. Physical considerations include the ink, print type, paper, and size.

An excellent illustration showing the improvements possible by proper arrangement of necessary information and the use of space is shown by the "before and after" comparisons in Figures 15–5 and 15–6. The old form was 11 × 8½ inches and contained numerous opportunities for improvement, as noted on the illustration. In contrast, the new form is smaller, 8½ × 8½ inches, yet is far more effective.

FUNCTIONAL CONSIDERATIONS

There are seven factors that merit discussion here, including:

1. *Purpose of the form.* The foremost consideration is to determine the job for which the form is to be used. An office form is actually a

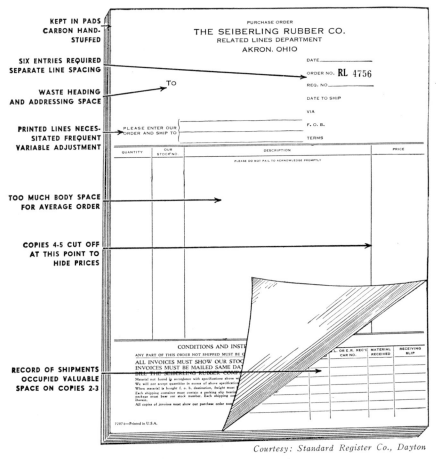

Courtesy: Standard Register Co., Dayton

FIG. 15–5. Original form before redesign.

road map of a job: It shows the flow and sequence of the work. A form should start where the job starts, stop where the job stops, and include the necessary intermediary steps according to the most efficient logical

sequence of operations. The form directs employees from the beginning
to the end of the job.

2. *What information to include.* Knowing the purpose of the form,
the next step is to decide what information the form should include.
Help along this line can be secured by answering questions such as:

    a) What information is needed to accomplish the stated purpose?
    b) Is the information really vital?
    c) How is it to be used?
    d) Who uses it, and in what manner?

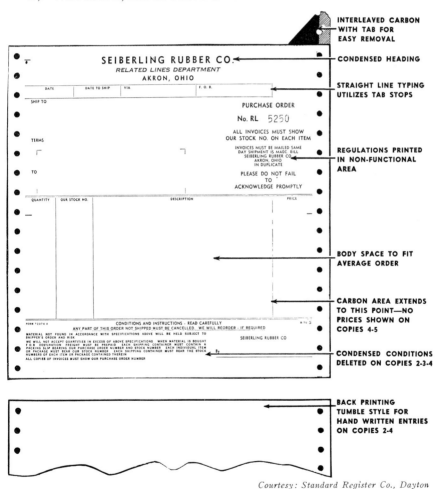

Courtesy: Standard Register Co., Dayton

FIG. 15–6. Form after redesign.

A complete list of the items to be included is prepared. Then, a careful
review of this list should be made in order to eliminate duplications and
information not absolutely necessary.

3. *Sequence of items.* The order should be mainly that of the normal flow of the work, and related items should be grouped. When items are transcribed from one form to another, the items should be arranged in the same sequence on both forms. If instructions are necessary, they should be located just above the portion of the form to which they have reference. This helps to have them read at the proper time, which is just before filling in the form. All instructions should be brief and to the point.

4. *General pattern of the form.* The method of completion is important. If the work is to be done manually, ample writing space is necessary, and horizontal lines on the form are desirable. Spacing should be three or four lines to the inch.

If the work is to be done by machine, the form should be spaced in accordance with the demands of the machine. The data should be arranged to utilize a tabular alignment, and horizontal lines on the form should be omitted. The following illustrates correct and incorrect arrangement when a machine is used:

Correct	*Incorrect*
Name:	Name _____
Address:	Address _____
S.S. Number:	S.S. Number _____
Age:	Age _____

The use of "boxed" style should be employed whenever appropriate. This style saves filling-in time, conserves space, and improves legibility. It is helpful to provide a reference number for each space to be filled in. By this means, tabulation, comparison, and interpretation of data are expedited. Where long sentences are necessary, it is desirable to have them printed in columnar form instead of across the full width of the sheet, as this expedites reading and makes for better appearance. However, when the information to be filled in is lengthy, the boxed style is usually inappropriate; the regular or "open" style is better. An illustration of a form featuring the boxed style for answers and numbers to expedite machine tabulation is shown in Figure 15–7.

5. *Adequate identification.* The form name should suggest its purpose. For example, the title "Sales Records" is not complete; "Weekly Sales Records by Territories" is more descriptive. Usually, the center or the upper left corner is preferable for the location of the name of the company and the upper right area for reference data in filing. Numbering all forms helps identify them and serves as a quick reference. The identification number should be in a convenient location, preferably near the title. In the case of multiple forms, it is usually advisable to number each copy for handy reference. Quick identification can also be gained by using different colors of papers.

6. *Number of copies.* Whether a single or multiple copy form should be used depends mainly upon two considerations: (1) who requires a copy and (2) when the copy is needed. Multiple forms afford a quick means of supplying many copies. However, it is best to keep the number of copies at a minimum. Only the required number of copies

INVESTIGATOR START HERE:

Is this a personal interview with____________________?

IF NOT: Be sure to obtain answers for questions 1, 2, 3 and 4 for this person from an adult member of the family.

5
Yes [1]
No [2]

Key No. [ ]

1. Have you, yourself, tried both of the tubes of tooth paste we left you? 6

If "No," skip rest of questionnaire and interview other family members.

Yes [1]
No [2]
Don't Know [3]
[4]

2. Which sample tooth paste do you like best? 7

No. 53 [1]
No. 59 [2]
No Difference [3]
Don't like either [4]
[5]

3. What is there about the one you prefer that makes you like it?

EDITOR ONLY
8: [1] [2] [3] [4] [5] [6]
8: [7] [8] [9] [0] [X] [R]

AGE GROUPINGS:

10		10		10	
0-4	1	20-24	5	40-49	9
5-9	2	25-29	6	50-59	0
10-14	3	30-34	7	60-69	X
15-19	4	35-39	8	70	R

PASTE BRAND:

11	11	11
1	5	9
2	6	0
3	7	X
4	8	R

SEX: 12
Male [1]
Female [2]

PRINCIPAL FAMILY PURCHASER: 13
Yes [1]
No [2]

FIG. 15–7. A printed form using the boxed style for recording answers, numbers to expedite machine tabulation, and columnar arrangement of material. This form saves time in writing, conserves space, and expedites reading.

should be made; and extreme prudence and care in this respect is recommended, as excess papers tend to clutter up an office and contribute to inefficiency.

7. *Type of form.* There are in general five different types or arrangements of office forms: single, stub type, continuous stub type, fan or Z arrangement, and continuous semistrip arrangement. The single type is used where the original copy only is required, as, for example, in the case of an employment application form. When necessary, copies can be obtained simply by using carbon sheets and as many form sheets as required. Many single-unit forms are used in an office.

The other four arrangements mentioned above are multiple forms. Illustrations and features of each are shown in Figure 15–8.

Multiple forms require only one writing, minimize mistakes, help attain uniformity, improve departmental co-ordination, and save time. The equipment used for multiple forms is either ordinary office equipment or the same type of equipment with simple attachments, for example, a spe-

Can be made with stub at top, bottom, either side, or top and bottom. The latter is used when set must be separated into two sections after initial writing for subsequent fill-ins. Carbon is fastened to stub, is used once, and can be of same or different widths and lengths to permit selective copying.

STUB TYPE UNIT ARRANGEMENT

This is the same as the stub-type unit arrangement except that the bottom sheet of each set is attached to the following set by perforations.

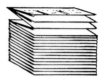

CONTINUOUS STUB TYPE UNIT ARRANGEMENT

These are provided in continuous strips with perforated accordion folds at left and right edges. The arrangement is available in either packs or rolls. Being joined at alternate sides, the forms can be separated from the strip but still retained in sets. The fan arrangement is available with or without interleaved carbon.

FAN OR Z ARRANGEMENT

This arrangement is similar to the continuous stub type except for the absence of stubs. The forms are perforated at fold. Depending upon method and equipment used, these may be utilized either with or without carbon interleaving.

CONTINUOUS SEMI-STRIP ARRANGEMENT

FIG. 15–8. The main types or arrangements of multiple office forms.

cial roller on the typewriter platen, or a holder. Figure 15–9 illustrates units of this sort.

PHYSICAL CONSIDERATIONS

Improvements in office forms can also be made along the lines of ink, print type, paper, and means of carbonizing copies. Although technical in nature, the office manager should possess some knowledge of them.

1. *Ink.* The ink selected should provide proper contrast to the paper and should give a clear, uniform, and smooth imprint. Certain printing processes require a certain type of ink. Use of more than one color of ink adds to the cost of the form.

This attachment, called a "dual feed," makes it possible to produce two records in one operation. Common information is typed on two forms of different size, with independent spacing as the work requires.

This device provides vertical tab spacing. The lever at the left is pulled down, causing the next form to be drawn to exact positioning for typing.

Courtesy: Standard Register Co., Dayton

A pack holding refold tray used for continuous multiple form.

FIG. 15–9

As discussed in Chapters 5 and 6, one of the latest "inks" is a magnetic type containing iron oxides. Typing or printing with this type of ink makes impressions on the paper which can be read by electronic means used to put various counting and sorting mechanisms into action.

2. *Print type.* The print type should be selected primarily on the basis of readability, with some thought given to making the printed page distinctive. For any one form, it is best to keep the type sizes and type styles to a minimum. Items of equal importance should be printed in the same type throughout the entire form. Normally, italic and boldface type should be used for emphasis, but it should be confined to those items or words where special stress is required.

3. *Paper.* Acquaintance with the more salient facts about paper used in forms is desirable. The five important properties of paper are weight, grade, grain, color, and size.

a) Weight. Paper is usually sold by weight. Normally, the mill supplies paper in standard sizes according to the different grades and the intended purposes for which the paper is to be used. To illustrate, the purposes and corresponding sizes are shown in this table:

Use of Paper	*Size*
Bonds, ledgers, general writing	17″ × 22″
Book papers and offset pages	25″ × 38″
Cover stock	20″ × 26″
Newsprint	24″ × 36″
Bristol board	22½″ × 28½″

A ream is the common measurement for quantity of paper and is approximately 500 sheets. For example, bond paper listed as 17″ × 22″ —20 means that 20 pounds of this grade and size of paper includes approximately 500 sheets. Likewise, bond paper 17″ × 22″—13 means that 13 pounds of this grade and size of paper contain approximately 500 sheets. Comparing these two, the latter sheets would be thinner, since, based on the same size and approximate quantity, their weight is less (13 pounds) compared to the former (20 pounds).

The lightest paper which will give satisfactory results should be used. Among the factors which determine the proper weight of paper are number of copies, amount of handling, purpose of the form, how filed—on edge or side, length of time retained, and whether printed on one or two sides. The following weights are usually recommended:

Application	*Weight of Paper Recommended*
Legal documents	28 pound
Ledgers	24 pound
Letterheads	20 pound
When 1–4 copies are made	16 pound
When 5–8 copies are made	13 pound
When over 9 copies are made	Tissue

b) Grade. The grade of paper means the quality and is chiefly based on the kinds of materials used in the manufacturing process. Paper is made from rags, mechanical wood pulp, sulphite wood pulp, soda wood pulp, and sulphate wood pulp, which are used in varying amounts, depending upon the kind of paper.

The grade of paper selected for a form depends upon such things as the life of the form, the amount of handling, and the appearance. The following table can be used as a guide:

Life of Form	Grade of Paper
1–5 years	100 per cent sulphite
6–12 years	50 per cent sulphite and 50 per cent rag
Over 12 years	100 per cent rag

c) Grain. Like wood, paper has a grain characteristic. The direction of the grain is determined by the alignment of the fibers making up the paper. The expression "with the grain" signifies the longitudinal direction of most fibers. Grain direction is the result of the manufacturing process.

The grain of paper is important because it determines the rigidity of paper. Some processes require that the grain of the paper run with the length of the printing roll. The grain should be parallel to the type-writer platen, because the paper then rolls around the platen better and there is less tendency for the sheets to slip. Paper folds more easily and quickly when it is parallel with the grain. Furthermore, when the graining runs vertically on forms posted by machine or filed on edge, there is less tendency for the forms to buckle and curl.

d) Color. The possibility of using colored paper for office forms should be considered. This frequently affords an effective medium for securing a strong appeal, a unique identification, and a simple means of facilitating the handling of forms. However, colored paper usually costs more than white.

e) Size. The size of the paper form is determined by such things as the amount of information, the economical paper size, the size and types of office equipment and machines, and the mechanical requirements. The limitations of the printing process must, of course, be considered in determining the physical dimensions of a form.

For purposes of economy and to eliminate waste, forms in the process of development should be made to be cut from stock sizes of paper. It is advisable to discuss the subject of economical stock sizes with the prospective supplier.

4. *Means of carbonizing copies.* The providing of carbon paper for use with the forms can be achieved in several ways: (*a*) inserting carbon by hand, (*b*) one-use carbon interleaved into the form, (*c*) carbon in the machine—using a simple "floating carbon" device, and (*d*) spots of wax

carbon applied to the back of the form during the manufacturing process.

As indicated in Figure 15–8, some multiple forms provide one-use carbon paper interleaved into position. When the fan and continuous semi-strip arrangements are used without carbon interleaving, the "floating carbon" device can be used. In this case, the forms slip over the carbon sheets which remain in the machine, and these sheets are used many times over until the impressions indicate the need for a carbon change. The fourth method, application of spots of wax carbon, makes it possible to apply the carbon to certain parts of a form, thus permitting only certain portions of the original writing to appear on the copies. Frequently, price information or specification data do not appear on all copies, since this information has little value for the purpose of some copies. A similar result can be achieved in the other carbon methods by cutting off certain carbon sheets or blacking out, with a solid mass of dots or other marks, that portion of the form which is not to receive an impression. The carbon mark is not visible on the blackened area.

As indicated in Chapter 9, carbonless "NCR paper," manufactured by the National Cash Register Company, can also be used for making copies simultaneously with the original writing. All that is required is to use NCR paper for the sheets of the form.

QUESTIONS

1. Give circumstances under which a form letter can generally be used to advantage.

2. Relate four important reasons why office forms are utilized.

3. Do you approve of the use of speed letters? Why?

4. Which form of letter—(*a*) block, (*b*) indented, or (*c*) simplified—do you favor? Why?

5. Discuss the general subject area of "Managerial Planning and Office Papers."

6. Discuss the property of weight in the identification and utilization of paper for office forms.

7. Do you agree with the following? "Reports are expensive in the typical enterprise because a standardized format or arrangement of presenting the information is not followed. If a standard pattern were followed, both the cost and the effort to prepare would be greatly reduced."

8. Referring to Figures 15–5 and 15–6, point out and discuss four improvements that you deem of special importance in designing a more effective office form.

9. What is meant by each of the following?
   a) "Floating carbon" device.
   b) Grain of paper.
   c) Stub-type unit arrangement.
   d) Boxed style for printed office forms.

10. In the writing of a report, do you favor presenting the material chronologically if it is at all possible? Why?

11. Explain how the information secured from a check list, as shown in Figure 15–4, can be used to improve office forms.

12. Discuss the various means of carbonizing copies of office forms.

CASE PROBLEMS

Case 15–1. Metric Products Corporation

J. Gregory MacLeish, sales representative of the Metric Products Corporation, believes that his company's invoice form can be improved. He would like the invoice to provide a better corporate image and impress customers more favorably than does the form presently being used. Accordingly, he discusses the subject with Pierre du Vall, the corporation's advertising manager, and asks him to design an invoice form that will be noticed and considered outstanding. Mr. du Vall agrees and after several days submits the design shown by the accompanying sketch.

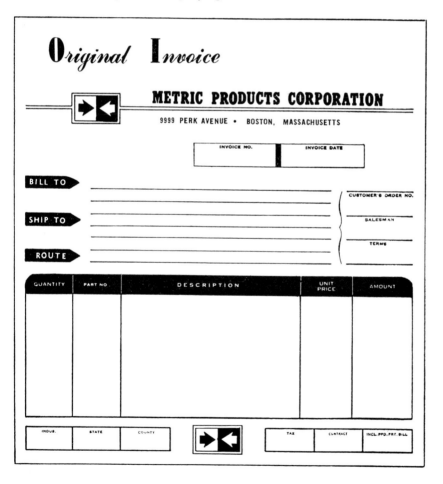

Mr. MacLeish then telephones Kenneth R. Perkins, the office manager, explains he would like to show him an impressive design for the company's invoices, and arrange a conference.

Problems:

1. As Mr. Perkins, what would you say to Mr. MacLeish after he shows you the proposed new invoice form?

2. Using this form as a guide to information that the form should provide, what improvements do you believe should be considered in the form design? Justify your views.

Case 15–2.   Hughes, Thomas, and Weaver, Inc.

The assistant office manager has designed a new customer order and invoice form. He asks you what you think of it. You observe that the size is 7 inches by 10½ inches; an original and five copies will make up one unit; different colors of paper will be used for each copy; five type styles are used in the composition of the form; and all printing is in black ink except the company's name, which is in light blue. The shipping route is in red, so that it will stand out. The spacing of lines on the form is five to the inch. In answer to your specific questions, the assistant office manager tells you that he intends to get reactions to the form from the company's various sales executives, both in the home office and in district sales offices; a good price from the printer can be secured in quantities of sixty thousand, which is about a two-year supply; a standard typewriter billing machine, pica type, is used for writing invoices; and in about 40 per cent of the invoices written, two extra copies are needed (seven copies total), and these will be inserted in the five-copy pack as required.

Problems:

1. Outline your reply to the assistant office manager.

2. Discuss the specific recommendations you would make to the assistant office manager.

3. Explain the probable reasons for the weaknesses of the proposed form.

Chapter 16

PLANNING FOR OFFICE EQUIPMENT

It's amazing what ordinary people can do if they set out without preconceived notions.

—CHARLES F. KETTERING

OFFICE PLANNING usually necessitates decisions regarding certain types of equipment and machines to implement the proposed manner, sequence, and skill required to accomplish the work. Knowledge of office equipment and machines is therefore essential for office planning. The office manager cannot reasonably expect maximum potential output unless the best physical means are provided. Analysis and study of various types of office equipment and machines are usually in order. From these data, along with the consideration for the work to be done and the people to do it, the office equipment and machines are selected and utilized.

This chapter deals with office equipment, the following chapter with office machines. However, before proceeding with office equipment, attention will be directed to important managerial considerations especially helpful in planning, and applying to both office equipment and machines.

EQUIPMENT, MACHINES, AND OFFICE MANAGEMENT

The use of equipment and machines is one of the most interesting aspects of modern office work. Suitable facilities have contributed tremendously to the increased efficiency of the office. Office mechanization, with its fabulous developments, is contributing greatly to the advance and status of office management. Office automation, which can be viewed as the ultimate of office mechanization, is having such a tremendous effect on office management that an entire section of this book, Part II, was devoted to it. There is little doubt that the proper use of office equipment and machines will become increasingly important in office management. It is one of the popular and powerful forces of office management today.

However, the expanding use of office equipment and machines places an increased burden and responsibility upon the office manager. He must marshal all available facts about possible facilities and help decide for each task the best manner of performance consistent with his particular requirements. Adequate consideration must be given to such important factors as the types of equipment available, the characteristics of each, the cost per unit of output, the initial outlay, the maintenance cost, the accessories to be provided, and the suppliers of equipment and accessories.

SELECTION OF OFFICE EQUIPMENT AND MACHINES

Careful evaluation of several aspects is usually necessary in order to select wisely a particular unit of equipment or machinery. The decision should never be made hastily or impulsively.

The sales representatives of most office equipment manufacturers are excellent sources of helpful information about their particular products. They are very willing to be of service and will cheerfully give or try to find out the information requested. The office manager will do well to work with them, for they can keep him informed of latest developments and advise him of any special applications in other offices. This may prove an important source of ideas for improvements. Furthermore, these representatives can help in working out special applications and uses. The representative should be considered as one who is trying to help. His aggressiveness adds to his merit, as this characteristic is desirable in sales representatives.

On the other hand, the office manager, or whoever selects office equipment or machines, has definite obligations to fulfill. Good management dictates that these objectives cannot be ignored, passed over lightly, or left entirely to the sales representative.

EQUIPMENT AND MACHINE SELECTION FACTORS

In performing the work of office planning, the following twelve factors should be carefully considered:

1. *The work and the manner of accomplishing it.* The purpose of the work should be clearly defined and critically examined, to assure that it is essential and that all unnecessary detail has been eliminated. Knowledge of what is probably the best way of doing the work, along with alternative effective ways, should be determined.[1] Sometimes, work of a similar nature, currently performed in the office, can be used as a guide. A careful analysis of the work prior to the purchase or rental of office equipment is always in order. If this is omitted, there is danger that unsatisfactory equipment may be acquired. For example, a desk may have

---

[1] Office methods are discussed fully in Chapter 24.

been purchased when a table would have been better, or a different model of machine from the one purchased might have answered the specific requirements of the office more completely.

2. *The individual requirements.* The decision to utilize a particular piece of office equipment or machine should be based upon the *individual* requirements of the particular office. Use by others is not sufficient grounds for adoption. The questions of whether to use a certain unit and, if so, what size and type to use are extremely important. They necessitate careful weighing of all the facts to determine the proper plan with a logical and unbiased attitude.

This individual requirement approach is especially important in regard to the use of office machines. The efficient office manager does not mechanize an office operation whenever it is possible to do so. Instead, he considers the available machines in the light of the way each one will assist in getting the work accomplished in his particular office. Basing his decision upon these factual data, he decides what, if any, machine to utilize and include in his final plan.

However, as implied in the chapters on office automation, there is emerging a universality of data processing and distributing adaptable for all enterprises to meet their information requirements. Adequate consideration of these universal concepts of what is necessary and what is not, from the viewpoint of effective information handling via automation, may prove them sufficient for the individual enterprise's requirements. It could well be that in certain cases, individual requirements are stressed too much, necessitating special and high-cost operations being added.

3. *Amount and value of total time saved.* A new office machine might foster greater speeds of accomplishment, but the important consideration is not comparison of speeds but savings in total time, both in amount and value. The amount will depend a great deal upon the volume of work. Economies are usually not realized unless the unit is operating a good portion of the time. Volume is affected mainly by the possibility of combining work, the flexibility of the unit for handling various types of work, and its capacity for expansion and contraction in order to handle varying amounts.

In addition to the amount of time, the utilization of time saved must be evaluated. To be advantageous, time saved should be used for other productive office work. If the time saved is simply dissipated and spread over other tasks, there are no economic benefits.

4. *Flexibility of use.* The economies gained from the use of office equipment or machines are influenced by the extent to which the units can be used for various types of work in the office. Generally speaking, if a unit being considered can be effectively employed for many types of work in the office, justification for use of that unit is usually indicated.

Likewise, the feature of expansion and contraction in order to accommodate varying amounts of paper work is normally advantageous.

5. *Price and investment.* The question of price is always an important managerial consideration. However, price should be considered along with the services provided and made available by the unit. In other words, due consideration must be given to what is received as well as what is paid out. In many instances, purchases of equipment are made on the basis that expected savings will recoup the initial investment within about one fourth the life of the unit.

However, the factors which determine how quickly an office unit should pay for itself vary somewhat with the policies of the individual purchasing company and with the importance attached to each factor.

Salary per Year (1)	Approximate Salary per Minute (2)	Cost per Day for $10,000 Accounting Machine (3)	Personnel Time Required to Save (in Minutes) (4)
$ 5,000..................	5.0¢	$4.00	80.0
7,500..................	7.5	4.00	53.4
10,000..................	10.0	4.00	40.0
12,500..................	12.5	4.00	32.0
15,000..................	15.0	4.00	26.6

Column 2 is based on 250 working days a year, eight-hour day, and 83 per cent efficiency.
Column 3 is based on 250 working days a year, ten-year life span.
Column 4 is Column 3 divided by Column 2.

FIG. 16–1. A quick and convenient means of determining whether an office machine will pay for itself within a reasonable period. The approach is based on determining the time required to be saved by the employee who will use the machine.

In any given case, however, the decision is usually based on an evaluation of such things as (*a*) the current complete price, including installation and delivery; (*b*) if a replacement, the make, model, type, and condition of the replaced unit and its probable current market value; (*c*) the percentage of working time the unit will be used; and (*d*) the investment percentage return to the company (the effect of income taxes and overhead expenses in reducing the gross earnings should be included in this calculation).[2]

Figure 16–1 shows a quick rule-of-thumb approach to decide whether to purchase a particular piece of office equipment or machine. It is based on timesaving by personnel, as illustrated by a ratio of personnel to equipment or machine. For example, the salary cost per minute for an employee receiving $5,000 a year is approximately 5 cents. The number of thousands of dollars per year is approximately the equivalent

---

[2] Depreciation and the influence of trade-ins are discussed later in this chapter.

number of cents per minute. For a $10,000 accounting machine, the cost per working day is $4.00. Hence, $4.00 divided by 5 cents per minute gives eighty minutes as the time required to be saved by a $5,-000 employee to pay for the accounting machine.

6. *Capacity of unit.* It is imperative that the unit be of sufficient size to permit efficient operations. Nothing is gained by getting a smaller desk or accounting machine than the reasonable expectancy of work volume indicates is necessary. In the case of many machines, the expected output can be judged from experience of actual users of the machine, data from the manufacturer, and actual test runs in the office. When feasible, this latter source is recommended; in fact, it is always advisable to obtain a demonstration of an office machine. Free trials, however, should be carefully qualified as to purpose, use, and extent of time; for unless this is done, a machine originally brought in for trial tends to remain, and eventual purchase may be required, regardless of selection efforts.

7. *Aesthetic values.* The appearance of the office—a desire to impress by having the latest or the finest in office equipment and machines —is an important, although sometimes subdued or concealed, consideration. Aesthetic values are highly subjective and are controlled primarily by one's preferences, not by any factual data. Justification for certain selections is based on personal likes. In some instances, benefits resulting from aesthetic values are advanced as considerations; for example, it may be claimed that an attractive office has a favorable effect upon office morale and makes it less difficult to hire new employees.

Actually, office equipment and machines should be looked upon not only as *physical* means of assisting employees to accomplish their work but also as *mental* stimuli, because supplying the proper equipment makes for a positive and co-operative attitude and helps place the employee in the right frame of mind to work efficiently.

8. *Employee preference.* This consideration is of great significance because the human element is vital in determining whether the equipment is properly utilized or operated. A strong bias against a particular unit prevents maximum benefits from being realized, regardless of the suitability of the unit to the work. The highly successful office manager will not force the use of a particular unit against a prejudice which the employee may have concerning that unit. Most office employees will turn out consistently the maximum work of acceptable quality when they are supplied with the equipment and machines *they feel* are the best available.

9. *Effect upon personnel requirements.* In many cases, the installation of office equipment or machines changes the requirements regarding both the number of employees and the level of their skill; and the problems of transferring, reducing, and training the work force must be con-

sidered. For example, in the case of machines, trained operators or the availability of those who are trainable as operators are foremost considerations. Furthermore, when machines are adopted to perform monotonous work, the effect upon personnel is also important, because usually a happier and more satisfied work force is the result.

10. *Forecast of work load.* As in all planning, not only must the current volume and type of work be considered, but also the probable future requirements and the adequacy of the unit to fulfill these future needs. Future requirements should be estimated for about five years, and such forecasts are sometimes quite difficult. Good management requires, however, that the unit neither become inadequate to handle the work volume several months after its installation nor stand idle a large portion of the time because of a decline in work volume which could have been predetermined.

11. *Quality of paper work.* The effect of the unit upon the accuracy and appearance of the papers should also be considered. When a machine is to replace a manual operation, increased accuracy usually will result, for machines tend to make fewer errors than human beings. Also, forms executed by machine generally have a better appearance; they are neater, more legible, and more uniform than papers which are handwritten.

12. *Need for copies and statistical data.* This consideration applies mainly to office machines selection. A contemplated machine may provide more copies of a record, and it may furnish a great deal of data of a sort and in a form not currently available. However, the important consideration is whether these available copies and data are necessary and whether they serve useful purposes which significantly aid management efforts. Unless these conditions are fulfilled, the availability of additional records and papers may lead to inefficient instead of efficient management practices.

DEPRECIATION

There is no one set of answers to the questions of how to figure costs of machine operation, rates of depreciation to use, and when it is economically sound to purchase a machine or to make a trade-in. The planner must refer to the accounting practices followed. Most companies consider office equipment and machines as assets; and over a period, they write them off because of depreciation. The rate will depend upon the kind of product. For example, the following are common:

Desks	20 years
Files	15 "
Accounting machines	10 "
Rugs and carpets	10 "
Typewriters	5 "

Some companies follow the practice of charging to expense any equipment purchase of less than a stated amount, for example, $100; and any equipment purchase over this amount is put into an assets account. Other practices are also followed, but they must be reasonable and within the meaning and intent of income tax laws.

INFLUENCE OF TRADE-IN

The question of trade-ins further complicates the work of office planning. Some general over-all guiding policy should be followed, tempered with certain adjustments based upon the individual circumstances. A trade-in depends mainly upon three factors:

1. The availability of the cash and capital resources of the enterprise. This is always present in any trade-in discussion.
2. The expected cash savings to be derived from the new unit's use. If these savings will pay for the net outlay within twenty-four months, a trade-in is usually in order.
3. The difference between the accrued net depreciation and the expense necessary to keep the unit operating; that is, if the net (present book value minus trade-in) is less than the cost of repair, a trade-in is probably best.

BUY OR RENT

At one time, only certain types of office equipment and machines could be obtained on a rental basis. Now, the practice of rental has spread to practically every type of office facility. Details of rental agreements vary widely. For example, some grant a right to purchase, after rental for a period of time, commonly three to five years, by crediting a portion of the rental payments toward the purchase price.

Advocates of the rental basis claim better maintenance is provided and the renter is free from the expense and worry of keeping all units in top operating condition. In addition, renting permits capital to be utilized in other more productive facilities. A large portion of the renter's funds are not tied up in long-term equipment and machine needs. Furthermore, renting permits the payments to be considered as expenses from the tax viewpoint, not as assets, as is the case with purchase. To some companies, this can be a distinct advantage. In contrast, many managers always buy equipment and machines if it is possible to do so. They state that in the long run, purchasing is less costly than renting, they are free to move the facility as they like, and they can arrive independently at decisions affecting equipment or machines. Also, it should be noted that if funds are available, investment in equipment and machines in one's own business can be attractive.

MAINTENANCE

All office equipment and machines require attention periodically in order to keep them in satisfactory condition. Ordinary use results in wear and tear, making cleaning, oiling, adjusting, and installing new parts the rule rather than the exception.

Preventive maintenance, rather than remedial maintenance, should be stressed. The former seeks to catch trouble before it happens; this is accomplished by scheduling inspections at carefully determined intervals. The latter, or remedial maintenance, deals with trouble after it occurs. Preventive maintenance provides greater employee satisfaction and efficient product performance.

A program of orderly maintenance will eliminate most of the unexpected breakdowns and costly repairs. Uninterrupted service at the lowest cost should be the chief objective. If the facility is rented, the landlord or owner usually provides for the maintenance. In contrast, if purchased, the owner can handle the maintenance in any of three ways: maintenance contracts, individual service calls, and company-operated service.

Maintenance Contracts. Many manufacturers, or their sales distributors, prefer to service their products in order to insure complete satisfaction; and to this end, they offer maintenance contracts which call for regular inspection, cleaning, adjusting, and oiling. Charges are made on a predetermined basis, and the rates and conditions for special service calls are usually stated. Advocates of this type of maintenance service claim that the regularity of service, the use of genuine parts, the employment of skilled, factory-trained mechanics, and the over-all, long-range low cost warrant its use. Research indicates this method is probably the most popular for offices of all sizes, but it represents the highest maintenance expenditures.[3]

Individual Service Calls. Individual service calls can be thought of as a "when required" type of service. This is sometimes called "no service contract" maintenance. It is of a remedial nature. The age and number of units are the chief factors which influence the choice of this policy. If most of the units are new, it is reasonable to expect that they will not require repair service; likewise, when a large number are in use, it is logical that not all will require maintenance service. However, a service call on an individual basis usually costs more than one under a maintenance contract. Also, the regular cleaning and oiling of most equipment and machines are usually advisable, and these must be provided on an individual service basis when this plan of maintenance is used.

Company-Operated Service. The third alternative is a company-operated service. Companies which follow this policy do so primarily

---

[3] National Office Management Association, *Value of Maintenance Contracts on Office Machines: A Quarterly Survey* (Willow Grove, Pa., September, 1958).

because of considerations of cost, control, or availability of service. Maintenance costs may be lower under this plan, provided there are a sufficient number of machines and amount of work to warrant the full-time services of maintenance employees. With a company-operated service, it is possible to exercise close control over the progress of the work, the expenses, and the regularity of inspections. Finally, in some instances, available outside services are inconvenient, owing to the remoteness of the office—for example, an office located with a factory in an out-of-the-way small town. In such cases, it may be desirable to adopt the company-operated service plan.

OFFICE EQUIPMENT

The remainder of this chapter will be devoted to office equipment. As previously mentioned, knowledge of equipment must be obtained before effective planning involving its use can be created. Information on electronic computers and machines used in integrated data processing was included in the chapters of Part II. Those facilities commonly associated with "office services" were discussed in Part III. In the following pages, material on additional and important units is given.

OFFICE CHAIRS

The office chair is probably the most important physical facility in an office. It is personal to the employee and vitally affects the ease and comfort with which the work is done. Most office work is of a sedentary nature, a fact which further stresses the importance of the office chair. Some believe that the progress of office modernization can be judged by the kind of chairs furnished clerical employees. Although extremely important, the effective use of posture chairs appears to be a blind spot of many office managers, both for themselves and for their fellow employees.

CHAIR TYPES AND FEATURES

There are many types of office chairs, including the familiar straight-back chair, the swivel chair, chairs that tilt, the posture chair, plain or upholstered chairs, wood or metal chairs, and chairs with or without armrests. Certain features about chairs require careful consideration by the office manager. Upholstering generally adds to appearance and comfort; but it requires periodic cleaning and, in the case of leather, "dressing" in order to preserve the material. The materials used in the seat construction and base and the chair balance are further considerations. Caster wheels made from relatively hard material are usually best for use on carpeting, while casters of softer material should be used on composition tile and wood flooring. The self-lubricating type of caster helps reduce maintenance.

In the office, posture chairs are especially important. Figure 16–2 illustrates an executive posture chair. According to the dictionary, posture means the "relative arrangement of the parts of anything, especially the body." A posture chair helps the user to attain the proper relative arrangement of the body parts in the correct position. Support is provided so that the body weight is properly distributed and correct body balance is maintained. The chair has three adjustments, thereby making it possible to "tailor-fit" it to the occupant. These adjustments include:

Courtesy: Harter Corp., Sturgis, Mich.

FIG. 16–2. An executive posture chair.

1. The seat height—so that the feet are comfortably placed on the floor and no undue pressure is present on the underside of the leg just above the knee.

2. The back-rest height—so that support is provided the small or lumbar region of the back. The swivel joint of the back rest should be approximately one inch higher than the top of the hip bone.

3. The back-rest horizontal position—so that the muscles covering the two pelvic bones, i.e., the glutei muscles, overhang slightly the rear edge of the seat, thus placing the body weight forward on the underside of the leg muscles.

The proper use of posture chairs can improve the appearance of office employees, reduce fatigue, improve morale, and aid in the functioning of important body actions, including breathing, circulation, and elimination. An adequate supply of oxygen for the lungs, a free flow of blood throughout the body, and proper positioning of the vital abdominal organs are seriously retarded by a slumped position maintained for long periods of time.

The major consideration about a posture chair is that it be used properly. Simply supplying a posture chair seldom assures that the benefits of good-posture seating are being enjoyed. The occupant must know how to sit in the chair and must sit that way. Adjustability of the chair is a key so that the occupant can sit high enough for leg comfort, with the spine erect and supported in its natural curve, well back in the chair, and the body relaxed for freedom of movement. Figure 16–3 illustrates examples of common incorrect seating with posture chairs.

Chair Too High
Seat pressures nerves and stops circulation just above the knee.

Chair Too Low
Steady pressure on spine causes great fatigue.

Chair Back Too High
No needed support to spine, causing slumping and a strain on back and shoulder muscles.

Chair Tilts Back Too Far
Occupant easily gets off balance, with excessive back strain.

FIG. 16–3. Examples of common incorrect seating.

OFFICE DESKS

The office desk is the workplace of many office employees. Its purpose is to provide a work surface, a temporary storage for materials being processed, and a convenient area for selected tools and machines required in accomplishing the work. However, a desk is more than just a place where work is done; actually, it is a basic working tool, and this should be kept in mind when planning. Viewing a desk as a working tool emphasizes the meaning of desk efficiency, which is influenced by (1) the design features of the desk and (2) the person using the desk.

The first factor—the design features of the desk—stresses the old adage: "A place for everything, and everything in its place." The desk and its interior are planned to give maximum service to the user. Tailor-made desk-drawer arrangements are available to aid work production. As new requirements arise, the drawers can be interchanged and rearranged as desired. Figure 16–4 suggests efficient arrangement of materials in desk drawers to meet specific requirements. Consideration for these facts assists in achieving better office planning.

The second factor—the person using the desk—emphasizes the influence of the desk user's work habits and attitudes upon desk efficiency. The personnel element is vital and necessitates adequate instructions, training, and supervising. To assist in achieving desk efficiency, the following guides are listed:

1. Work on one task at a time and finish it before starting another. Abstain from trying to do several tasks at the same time.

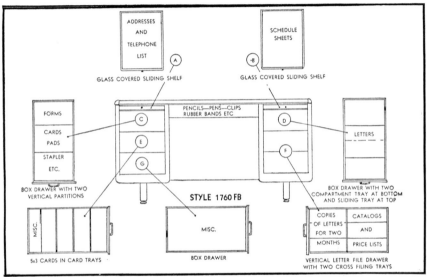

Courtesy: Art Metal Construction Co., Jamestown, N.Y.

FIG. 16–4. Suggested desk-drawer layout to meet individual requirements for order department manager.

2. Keep the desk free from excess papers and supplies. Have only those items on the desk that are needed. The desk top is a work surface and should facilitate immediate action.

3. Shelve material that is not urgent. For example, insert slips in magazines to articles to be read and then put them to one side for reading in off moments.

4. Strive to keep the work moving over the desk. Take action on each paper coming to the desk as quickly as possible.

5. Act on important paper work first. Have a daily schedule, and make use of a desk calendar to guide the sequence of work.

6. Dispose of all mail before going home. Do not permit a stack of mixed-up papers to remain overnight and cause a poor start the next day.

7. Adopt a convenient standardized arrangement for papers and supplies in the desk drawers.

DESK APPEARANCE AND DIMENSIONS

The trend in desk appearance is toward smooth, streamlined surfaces. Edges are rounded; offsets are not being used to any noticeable degree; the supports touching the floor are recessed in order to conceal them from view, to permit ample toe room when standing near the desk, and to facilitate cleaning the floor. Steel desks are equipped with linoleum, plastic, or composition tops; and lighter colors and finishes seem to be preferred. Many wood desks are finished with light stain and bleached colors; for steel desks, a light gray finish is being used extensively. Hardware and exposed metal parts are of dull finish to avoid annoying highlights.

Generally speaking, there is no standard size of desk top, as the dimensions vary with the type of desk, the material used, and the manufacturer. Executive desks are usually the largest, sizes ranging from 76 × 36 inches to 60 × 32 inches being the most common. For general office work, sizes from 60 × 34 inches to 42 × 30 inches are popular. There is an increasing use of smaller executive desks, especially of general office desks which are 50 to 55 inches wide instead of 60 inches, and 30 inches deep instead of 34 inches. In some companies, however, certain sizes are specified for certain uses. For example, in one company, the following applies:

Employee	*Desk-Top Size*
Department head	78 × 38 inches, triple overhang
Supervisor	60 × 36 inches, front overhang
Staff	60 × 30 inches or special-purpose desk
Clerical	60 × 30 inches

Desks are made of various heights. At one time, the popular height was 30½ inches; but the trend is toward a lower desk, 28½ or 29 inches high. Small adjustments are provided mainly to level the desk due to variations in the floor level. Certain industrial engineers claim that, for the physical characteristics of the average employee, the lower desk working level is a better height, since it maximizes the employee's comfort.

A specially built desk for the board of directors' room of a well-known midwest distributor is shown by Figure 16–5. The decor of this office is a rich blending of modern functional office equipment, creating an attractive atmosphere.

DESK DESIGNS

Desks are available in single- and double-pedestal styles. The pedestal is the support or foundation of the desk, and it contains the drawers or a fold-away platform which houses a typewriter or some special machine. The single-pedestal desk is used in cases where a single tier of desk drawers and a smaller-size top are sufficient.

FIG. 16–5. A well-designed board of directors' room.

Desks are designed to serve particular needs. Among the most popular are those for executives, junior executives, stenographers, typists, adding and calculating machine operators, and billing clerks. Figure 16–6 illustrates several different types of desks designed to serve particular requirements.

The term "conference desk" is usually applied to a desk having an oversized top that overhangs the pedestals at one or both ends and at the back. At meetings, it is possible for five or six people to sit comfortably around a conference desk, since ample work space and leg room are provided. The conference desk has become quite popular. It is impressive and adds prestige to an executive's office.

Especially where an electric typewriter is used, a great many com-

Courtesy: Art Metal Construction Co., Jamestown, N.Y.

FIG. 16–6. This office features desks designed to meet specific work requirements. Observe in the foreground the fixed-bed typewriter desk; in the left background, the general-purpose desk; and in the right background, the desk with an overhang top.

panies have adopted the machine platform arrangement in conjunction with the ordinary desk. Figure 16–7 shows such an arrangement. The platform can be attached to either side of the desk. Economy and effi-

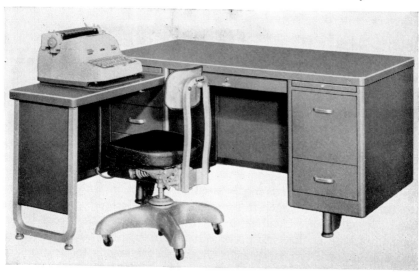

Courtesy: Art Metal Construction Co., Jamestown, N.Y.

FIG. 16–7. A machine platform attached to a steel office desk.

ciency are gained. Provided is a firmer base than the disappearing platform, more knee space, and desk drawers for supplies.

MODULAR OFFICE FURNITURE

This type of furniture consists of easily and quickly assembled modular components which, when assembled, comprise an effective functional and modern arrangement. Basic units include such "building blocks" as desk tops, desk pedestals, auxiliary tops, end supports, and shelving units. In a number of installations, modular components have been put together to form a U-shaped desk and platform arrangement as illustrated by Figure 16–8. Partition panels for privacy can be

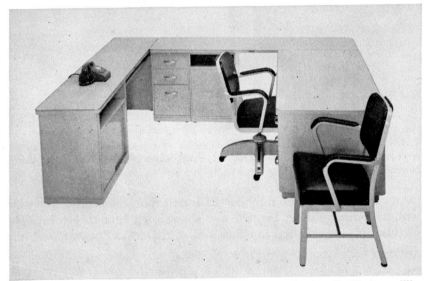

Courtesy: Invincible Metal Furniture Co., Manitowoc, Wisc.

FIG. 16–8. Modular office components assembled to provide an efficient U-shaped unit.

added to meet individual requirements. Components are standard and interchangeable, thus supplying flexibility and many various combinations.

POSTING-TRAY UNIT

This equipment is commonly used in connection with machine installations and is designed to provide convenient reference to sheets or cards. Rapid removal and return of the material, quick access to accounts, locking in sheets to prevent unauthorized removal, clear vision, and a clean, orderly arrangement of records are among the features of this posting unit. The tray can be purchased separately, or the equip-

Courtesy: LeFebure Corp., Cedar Rapids, Iowa

FIG. 16–9. Posting-tray equipment adjustable in height from 31¼ inches for standing position to 22 inches for seated position. The specially designed trays keep the work convenient to the operator and at a distance providing comfortable vision.

ment can be secured as a unit consisting of tray and stand which in some models houses a file drawer. To meet individual requirements, a variety of types, sizes, and capacities are available. Illustrations are shown in Figure 16–9.

MISCELLANEOUS DEVICES

Copyholders are especially helpful for stenographers doing copy work, for, as the name implies, they hold papers in place at a convenient reading level. A horizontal bar guides the eye to the proper line. Correct posture is aided, because the material is held in a proper reading position. Since the copy is held directly in front of the operator at a constant distance, eyestrain, head twisting, and fatiguing refocusing of the eyes are eliminated.

Numbering devices are used to place numbers chronologically on incoming orders, memorandums, and other papers in order to plan and process the papers more effectively. They are offered in a variety of sizes, capacities, and prices. They are well designed and will give satisfactory service for many years.

Check protectors are employed to make out checks in perforated print so that the chances for altering the words or figures are eliminated. Different styles and types of print are available. Most check protectors are manually operated. Also offered are units that sign checks with official names, thus eliminating much laborious and repetitious work for some executives.

QUESTIONS

1. Would a scientific office manager ever purchase a particular piece of office equipment primarily because of the aesthetic values it offered? Explain.

2. Comment on the following quotation: "Trying out the office equipment or machine under actual conditions can go a long way toward determining its adequacy and desirability in a particular office. However, a trial has a tendency to obligate the user and may result in a purchase when such is not in order."

3. Assume an office manager is considering the purchase of a calculating machine costing $750 for use by an employee receiving $4,800 a year. Explain how Figure 16–1 might assist the office manager to reach a decision regarding the purchase of the calculating machine.

4. Discuss the advantages of renting office equipment and machines rather than purchasing them. Do you favor renting or buying? Why?

5. Carefully distinguish between each in the following pairs:
   a) A secretarial desk and a conference desk.
   b) Posting-tray unit and modular office furniture.
   c) Office chairs and posture office chairs.
   d) Copyholder and check protector.

6. List five guides helpful in achieving desk efficiency, and discuss one of these guides thoroughly.

7. Rank the following factors—flexibility of use, price and investment, amount of time saved—used in the selection of office equipment and machines in the order of their importance as you see it. Justify your answer.

8. Do you think it wise for an office manager to purchase (a) only what he currently needs in the way of office equipment and machines, (b) a little less than is needed—to encourage better production rates and full machine utilization, or (c) more than is needed—to provide for future expansion and possible breakdowns? Why?

9. Does the supplying of a posture chair insure that the office employee who occupies it will have good posture while seated? Why?

10. Evaluate the following information sources for an office manager who is considering the purchase of an office machine which has a list price of approximately $2,000:
    a) Sales representatives of manufacturers.
    b) Present users of the type of machine considered.
    c) Local branches of professional management groups.
    d) Advertisements of manufacturers.
    Give reasons for your answers.

11. What arrangement to provide for the proper maintenance of a new accounting machine do you favor for a small office employing nine people? Justify your answer.

12. You are contemplating the purchase of seven electric typewriters for a centralized stenographic department. Three different manufacturers'

makes are being considered. Basing your decision on the following data, which make of machine would you purchase?

	ELECTRIC TYPEWRITER		
	A	B	C
Unit cost.............................	$425.00	$382.50	$439.00
Done business with manufacturer in past...............................	Yes	No	No
Employees' preference................	Third	Second	First
Quality of work done by machine......	Satisfactory	Satisfactory	Satisfactory
Aggressiveness and competency of sales representative................	Very satisfactory	Average	Average

Justify your decision.

CASE PROBLEMS

Case 16–1.   Zenith Finance Company

Employing a total of fifty-two persons, the Zenith Finance Company handles all types of commercial financing, but an important part of its business is financing by means of discounting accounts receivable of clients. This work is performed by an accounts receivable supervisor, Miss Arlene Brinker, and six clerks. The average weekly salary of the clerks is $105. Miss Brinker has been told by Edward O'Day, the office manager, that her unit is consistently behind in its work, although it is within the budget allowances. He does not know whether the unit is understaffed, the method of processing is wrong, the employees are not as efficient as they should be, or what the trouble is. Miss Brinker indicated that in her opinion the girls in her unit were above-average employees and were working at a very satisfactory pace. "That might be," replied Mr. O'Day, "but something is wrong, and we must find out what it is and correct it."

Subsequently, Mr. O'Day talked with several suppliers of office equipment and machines. He thought some type of mechanization might be the answer, but the type of work apparently did not lend itself to any readily available means. No vendor appeared to have an available machine adaptable for this type of work.

Basically, the work consists of the following. Clients send in their invoices for discount by listing them on a schedule form and attaching a copy of each invoice plus a copy of its corresponding bill of lading. The clerk checks to see that all the standards have been met and, if so, issues a check for the prescribed percentage of advance to be made to the client. Then, the invoices are posted to client account cards and filed.

When a client receives his customer's check, he lists it on a remittance form stating the invoice paid and the amount of the attached check. When the remittance form is received by the clerk of the Zenith Finance Company, she goes to the file, finds the client's account card, returns to her desk with the proper card, and marks remittances that are being paid. Accuracy of the client's work is checked at this time. Sometimes, the remittance form list is eight to ten pages long. After processing remittances, the card is returned to the file, from whence the next client card needed is removed and the work process is repeated.

In order that accounting can prepare the daily bank deposit, remittances are processed before noon of each workday. Also, since the company does local banking for some of its clients, some invoice schedules are processed during the morning.

About two weeks after her interview with Mr. O'Day, Miss Brinker went to Mr. O'Day's office and showed him the results of a study she had conducted of the "pattern of time spent" by her employees. The data are as follows:

EMPLOYEE	Two Weeks—Time Spent on:				
	Scheduling Invoices	Posting Remittances	Walking to and from File	Idle	Total
A.....	16.4 hrs.	47.3 hrs.	11.8 hrs.	4.5 hrs.	80.0 hrs.
B.....	5.8	54.5	13.5	6.2	80.0
C.....	19.1	39.7	17.1	5.1	80.0
D.....	18.7	41.0	15.4	4.9	80.0
E.....	11.7	48.3	14.6	4.4	80.0
F.....	9.8	52.8	12.2	5.2	80.0

Mr. O'Day's reaction, among other things, was that an excessive amount of time was spent in walking to and from the file. He asked Miss Brinker if a clerk could take several cards with her per trip to and from the file, and thus reduce the walking time. Miss Brinker replied that the practice of taking only one card maintained maximum availability of cards in the file for others who might need a certain card to process the work. Furthermore, she pointed out that the present practice reduced the possibility of having lost cards.

Further thinking about the situation led Mr. O'Day to believe that placing cards nearer the clerk certainly would be an improvement. Inquiry from local equipment suppliers revealed that a specially equipped desk, costing $433.50, could be used for each accounts receivable clerk. Special small card files, available for $82.00 each, are also suitable, and could be located near the clerk; but according to Mr. O'Day's calculations, eight such files would be needed to hold all the cards, and there is not sufficient floor space near the desks to accommodate this additional equipment.

Problems:

1. What are the alternatives available to Mr. O'Day?
2. What is your general impression of Miss Brinker?
3. What interpretation do you give the "pattern of time spent" data submitted by Miss Brinker?
4. What actions do you believe Mr. O'Day should take? Why?

Case 16–2.   Security Insurance of Saint Louis

For the past several months, discussions dealing with modernization of office facilities have been held by executives of Security Insurance of Saint Louis. At the last meeting, approval to proceed was passed, and a committee was authorized to formulate a complete plan and submit it to the president of the company within sixty days. Approval of the committee's recommendations would be a routine matter. The prime purpose of the committee was to determine what office equipment to purchase, and to keep expenditures within the authorized limits. The committee consisted of the office manager, the controller, and the personnel manager.

Since the prescribed expenditures were somewhat limited, the committee decided to purchase what was probably most important—desks and chairs. It was believed this would be a good start in the company's office modernization program. Suppliers of this type of equipment were called in and requested to submit bids. It soon became apparent that the company's tentative appropriation for this purpose was insufficient to purchase as many desks and chairs as the committee had in mind.

The controller suggested that a survey of the present equipment be made and purchases be limited to what was most in need of replacement. Several suppliers agreed to make this survey free of charge and to take the used equipment as partial payment on the new equipment. The personnel manager, however, objected to this plan, explaining that an office employee with a new desk and chair working alongside an employee with an old desk and chair might cause difficulty and some misunderstanding among employees.

The idea was also advanced that either new desks only or new chairs only be purchased. But disagreement over which should be purchased existed among the committee members. One committee member strongly advocated new desks, since these provide the working areas, are in full view, and contribute a great deal toward improving the general appearance of an office. In contrast, it was pointed out that a new comfortable chair probably would mean more to an employee and would result in more favorable comments by the employees.

The office manager rejected the idea that the project be held in abeyance pending the availability of more money to purchase both desks and chairs and perhaps other modernization work. He believes a beginning must be made now and eventually the entire office probably will be improved. In his opinion, to delay will bury the office modernization program indefinitely.

Problems:

1. Evaluate the viewpoints of the controller; of the office manager.
2. What alternatives are available to the company?
3. What action should be taken? Why?

Chapter 17

PLANNING FOR OFFICE MACHINES

True opinions can prevail only if the facts to which they refer are known; if they are not known, false ideas are just as effective as true ones, if not a little more effective.

—WALTER LIPPMANN

THE NUMBER and type of office machines are very extensive. For simplicity, the discussion here will concentrate on the most important units so that fundamental and helpful information is supplied for the planning that is necessary to get office work performed effectively. Mention of certain machines and their use was made in previous chapters dealing with office automation (Part II) and the work of information handling (Part III). The machines included in this chapter are in addition to those previously discussed.

OFFICE MACHINES AND PLANNING

Office management planning includes the *what, where,* and *when* of office machines in formulating the work to be done. In planning, it is decided what machine is well suited for a particular task set forth by the procedures and methods planning work, in keeping with company policy, and the personnel requirements. For effective planning, it is of course necessary to know what machines are available and what can be done with them. In many respects, office planning is a back-and-forth type of analysis and decision making for determining future actions. That is, the procedures and methods influence the machine to be used; and likewise, the machine influences the procedure and method to be followed. And consideration for the people doing the work affects both machines and methods that are followed.

After a company has a machine, there are planning efforts to use it for new work as such work arises, assuming machine time is available. Also, the work originally intended for the machine may be modified, necessitating new and additional planning to perform this modified work with the same existent machine. Planning is a continuous activity, and this is especially true in the planning of office machines.

ACCOUNTING MACHINES

There are many different kinds of accounting machines. In some discussions, the classifications of billing machines, posting machines, bookkeeping machines, and accounting machines are used. However, a clear definition of each type is difficult to state and serves no real practical purpose. In this discussion, the one inclusive identity of accounting machines is used.

These machines do not perform accounting work in the same sense that an accountant does accounting work. They are basically mechanical aids which simplify and expedite the paper work. They are not wholly automatic, since such things as the form to use, what numbers to put in the machine, and how the data obtained are used from the accounting point of view remain the task of the human brain and hand.

Although accounting machines are used for a great many different purposes, nevertheless they perform fundamentally writing and calculating. The extent, manner, and combination of these functions found in any one machine type are determined by the main purpose and use intended for that machine. Some billing machines, for example, are designed to write in the name, address, and descriptions, to multiply and to extend, to figure discounts, and to add for the net total. For each entry, the proper keys are depressed, but the movement of the machine is automatic. In others, the machine is equipped with a calculating mechanism for multiplying and adding. The operator picks up the number from the reading on the mechanism and types it in the appropriate column.

To minimize errors, a checking or proofing device is featured on many accounting machines. These accuracy devices are of several types. In some instances, they consist of showing a number which is compared with an original, such as "old balance," or with an entry number, for proof of accuracy; in other cases, the machine locks and will not print if old entries have been picked up incorrectly. Figure 17–1 illustrates a

John Doe 2124 Dayton Drive				Account No. 342			
Old Balance	Date	Debit	Date	Credit	New Balance	Proof Line
37.85	Nov. 7	8.12			45.97	37.85
45.97	Nov. 30	10.60		20.00	36.57	45.97

FIG. 17–1. Ledger sheet used in machine, showing comparison between old balance and proof line for proof of accuracy.

ledger sheet showing old balance, date, debit, credit, new balance, and proof line. For each horizontal line of figures, the proof-line figure must be equal to that of the old balance; otherwise, an error is in that horizontal line. Different machines handle this so-called "direct-proof" feature in slightly different ways.

Many accounting machines are equipped with "heads" or "bars" or accumulating registers which make it possible to summarize and to dis-

Basis of Classification	Types	
Keyboard....	*Descriptive Machine.* Equipped with both typewriter and numerical keyboards.	*Nondescriptive Machine.* Has numerical keyboard only.
Bed.........	*Flat Bed Machine.* The printing surface and the papers are placed horizontally onto this flat bed. Advocates claim it simplifies insertion of papers.	*Platen or Carriage Machine.* The papers are inserted in the carriage, and platen is turned similar to that of a typewriter.
Print........	*Single-Print Machine.* Prints two or more copies simultaneously. Papers are inserted into machine as a pack with carbon interleaved.	*Multiprint Machine.* Papers are placed side by side into the machine, which prints one paper and then moves over and prints the same data or portions of it on the other paper.
Style........	*Window Machine.* Papers are placed in an opening or window; machine entries are printed while papers are held in this position. Easily handles entries in booklets, as in a bank, and expedites visual checking by operator and customers.	*Nonwindow Machine.* Papers are placed in the carriage or on the flat bed—there is no window opening of the machine.

FIG. 17–2.   Common classifications of accounting machines.

tribute accounts. This feature is very valuable in most accounting work, particularly with records dealing with cost, sales, and payroll.

Accounting machines can be classified in a number of ways. One common distribution is whether the machine is nondescriptive or descriptive. In the former, the machine is equipped with a numerical keyboard only; if letter material is required with this machine, it is usually accomplished by means of either an addressing or a stamping machine. In the latter, the machine has both typewriter and numerical keyboards, permitting the entry of letter as well as figure data. Figure 17–2 shows some common bases for classifying machines, along with comments on each type of machine.

DESCRIPTIVE ACCOUNTING MACHINE

To illustrate further the types of accounting machines and the kind of work done with them, several brief descriptions will be included. The first is the descriptive accounting machine, for which the work of accounts payable can be used. The exact requirements will vary from industry to industry as well as from company to company. For illustrative purposes, the work of a purchase journal, remittance advice, and distribution expense ledger are used. These are shown by Figure 17–3. These data are printed simultaneously by the descriptive accounting machine. Requiring the machine's typewriter keyboard is the descriptive material giving the vendors' names on the purchase journal. For example, referring to Figure 17–3, the purchases from Smith Supply Company are posted January 9, for $16.00 and $8.50, making the balance due $170.00. For inventory or expense purposes, the items are distributed directly to the proper column, shown in the upper right of the figure. The first item from Smith Supply Company for $16.00 is charged to Miscellaneous account 84; and likewise, the second item of $8.50 is charged to Miscellaneous account 92. These data are printed on the respective distribution ledgers, as shown by the illustration. Distribution totals are accumulated automatically. The same machine can be used if a voucher check is used instead of a remittance advice. When due, the remittance advice is paid, less any discount allowed. Illustration of this work is not included here; but for this payment work, a check and a

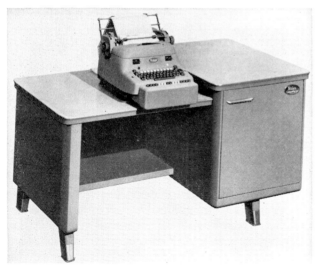

Courtesy: Friden, Inc., San Leandro, Calif.

FIG. 17–4. A machine unit that performs descriptive accounting work extremely effectively.

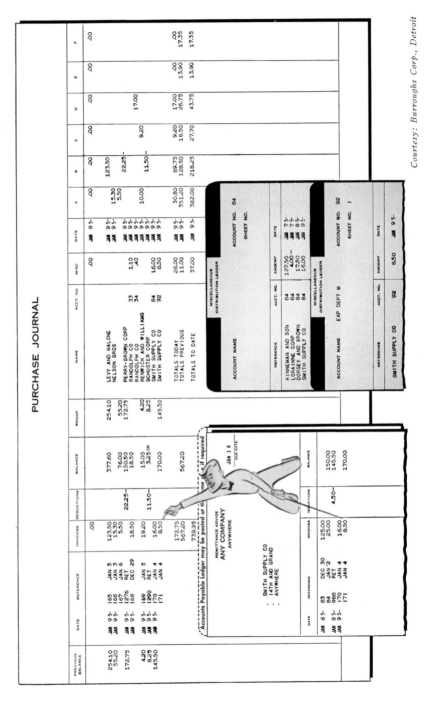

FIG. 17-3. Remittance advice, purchase journal with distribution, and distribution ledger prepared simultaneously with a descriptive accounting machine.

Courtesy: Burroughs Corp., Detroit

check register are prepared simultaneously by the same machine. A carbon copy of the check is made on the office copy of the remittance notice. Partial payments are handled by posting to suppliers' accounts during the check-writing operation. Checks written that do not affect accounts payable, such as those to replenish the petty cash fund or for transportation charges, are written and distributed directly to the columns affected.

Different features are stressed by different descriptive accounting machines. Most are adaptable for many different types of work and are useful for any one or all types, including general ledger, accounts payable, accounts receivable, and payroll. Figure 17–4 shows a popular model. This machine features a single keyboard, program keys on the typewriter, and a processing unit housed in the pedestal of the desk-like unit. For the work of billing, the operator has only to enter figures and descriptions, and the machine automatically does the rest, including extensions, additions, deductions, percentages, discounts, subtractions, and totals.

NONDESCRIPTIVE ACCOUNTING MACHINE

Figure 17–5 shows a nondescriptive accounting machine. In discussing the work of this type of accounting machine, sometimes referred to as a numerical keyboard accounting machine, consider accounts receivable work in which the ledger, statement, and proof-tape journal are

Courtesy: Burroughs Corp., Detroit

FIG. 17–5. A modern nondescriptive accounting machine.

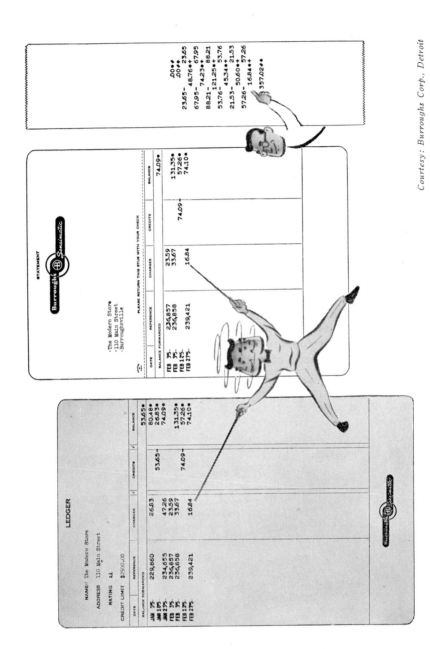

Courtesy: Burroughs Corp., Detroit

FIG. 17–6. Accounts receivable work consisting of original ledger, statement, and proof-tape journal. The entries are made by the machine shown in Figure 17–5.

prepared. Figure 17–6 shows these records. To illustrate, for the last entry, the operator inserted the forms into the machine; entered the old balance, the reference numbers, and the charge by depressing the proper keys; then actuated the machine by the motor bar. The machine automatically prints all the needed information, including date, reference number, charges, and the new balance, on the three forms. To reset the machine for other accounting forms, such as accounts payable, a quick adjustment is provided by turning a knob at either side of the machine. The letter material at the top of the ledger and the statement can be written by means of a typewriter or an addressing machine. The ledger copy is permanent and retained; a statement is mailed monthly to the customer.

WINDOW-POSTING ACCOUNTING MACHINE

The window-posting cash register type of bookkeeping machine is different in operation and appearance from the majority of others and is especially adapted to use by retail stores, banks, and hotels. With this type of machine, the payment of a bill or a deposit in a bank is handled by inserting the customer's ledger card and statement or book into the machine. The proper keys are depressed; and when the machine is actuated, the entries are printed on the inserted forms and also on a machine audit sheet or roll which shows the total transactions. The necessary calculations are then made automatically by the machine, and the new balances are printed on the forms. A window-posting cash register accounting machine is illustrated by Figure 17–7.

Courtesy: National Cash Register Co., Dayton

FIG. 17–7. A window-posting cash register type of accounting machine. The work illustrated is an instalment registration of accounts receivable for a piece of furniture.

ADDRESSING AND LISTING MACHINES

Affixing addresses or other information in applications where the same information is used periodically typifies one of the popular uses for addressing and listing machines. Their widest application is probably addressing envelopes or advertising literature. The use of these machines is beneficial wherever a small quantity of identical information must be written repeatedly. In addition to mailing lists, the following are typical applications: names of employees along with standardized payroll information, i.e., check number and social security number; addresses on shipping labels and tags; headings on invoices and ledger cards; listing of customers; items ordered; items of storekeeping; lists of tools; tax roll; names and addresses of stockholders; and the list of dividend recipients.

There are two types of addressing and listing machines: those using metal-embossed plates and those using fiber or tissue stencils. Metal plates are made in a machine especially designed for that purpose. The plate is stamped, thus forcing the required impressions in the metal. Metal plates give very long service; they practically never wear out. The fiber stencils can be prepared on a typewriter equipped with a special platen, last a long time, but should be handled carefully. It is also possible to type or cut a punched tape which, when fed through an automatic machine for making plates, will produce them at a high rate of speed.

In operating, addressing and listing machines position a plate over the material and impress the data on the plate onto the material. A ribbon is between the plate and the material. One plate is used for each item, or name and address. Machines are available which handle over 100 items or plates per minute, each item consisting of up to 360 typewriter characters. For listing purposes, the spacing between impressions can be adjusted from ⅙ inch to 4 inches. This makes it possible to line up the impression on a ruled form.

Attachments Used. The great majority of the machines using metal plates permit attachments which add considerably to their value for specific operations. Among the more common attachments are:

1. A cutoff device which permits only part of the plate to print at one time. This is especially useful where a portion of the information on the plate is printed in the first column of a spread sheet, another part in the second column, a third part in a third column, and so on.

2. A selector which permits certain plates to pass through the machine without writing. This feature is desirable, for example, when certain plates are wanted for a particular mailing. The sequence of the plates remains unchanged.

3. A repeater for printing duplicate impressions from each plate be-

fore advancing to the next plate. To illustrate, the name and address might be required on the check stub and on the check, or on the statement and on the envelope. Settings for triplicate impressions are also available.

4. A dating device for entering the date simultaneously with the printing of other data. This is used a great deal in connection with statements and letters.

SPECIAL APPLICATIONS OF ADDRESSING AND LISTING MACHINES

It is also possible to use this type of machine not only for writing but also for distribution and addition of figure information simultaneously. This is accomplished by means of carefully located punched holes in each plate. Figure 17–8 shows the code used for punched holes and illustrates several types of plates. A sensing mechanism translates the information coded by punched holes into figures which are printed on a suitable form. Various capacities for coded figure data are available, including the writing and listing of annuity checks in insurance companies, the listing of

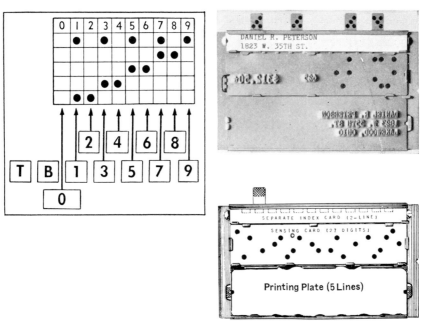

Courtesy: Addressograph-Multigraph Corp., Cleveland

FIG. 17–8. *Left:* Code for hole punching and keyboard of key punch used in addressing-accounting type of machine. *Right:* Two different types of plates used in addressing-accounting machines. The plates shown provide index-card and sensing and printing areas; the tabbing sockets at the top provide the primary selective classifications. Many styles of addressing plates are available.

various statistical data, the processing of billing records, and the preparing of payrolls.

PUNCHED-CARD MACHINES

Among the most important and versatile of all office machines are punched-card machines. They are used to punch holes in cards, tabulate desired information by means of these punched cards, and write data based on the information revealed by the holes in the cards. Sometimes, these machines are called "Hollerith machines" (International Business Machines Corporation punched-card machines) and "Powers machines" (Remington Rand punched-card machines).

Punched-card machines put data and information in such a form that it can be easily handled for any of a number of subsequent operations. These machines provide flexibility, accuracy, and rapidity. They are employed for many different uses, including the analyzing and summarizing of statistical data, the writing of invoices, payrolls, inventory control, labor distribution, market research, sales reports, and accounts payable. In fact, punched-card machines can be used for nearly all parts of the accounting function. Furthermore, it is possible to obtain correlated data very easily by using this type of machine. In market research studies, for example, the number of respondents who answered "Yes" to a given question, broken down according to age, income, and occupation, can be quickly obtained. Likewise, sales analyses by units, dollars, territories, and months, or manufacturing costs by various types of labor operations, can be easily determined.

ARRANGEMENT OF DATA ON CARD

The "punched card" is the fundamental and key physical unit about which the whole process revolves. A vertical column or columns of the card are allocated to different items, depending upon the nature of the data and what information it is desired to include. Information on months may be given two columns so that the 1 in the first column and the 0 in the second can be punched to indicate 10, or the month of October. Figure 17–9 shows the allocation of space on a punched card covering accounts receivable. In this illustration, the number 1 punched out in each of the first two columns indicates the eleventh month, or November. The code followed for punched holes was given in Chapter 5.

Laying out the punched card or deciding what information to punch in the card warrants careful thought. This emphasizes the planning function. Only information which is valuable to management, which will reveal pertinent major relationships, and which will provide the basis for meaningful subanalyses should be included.

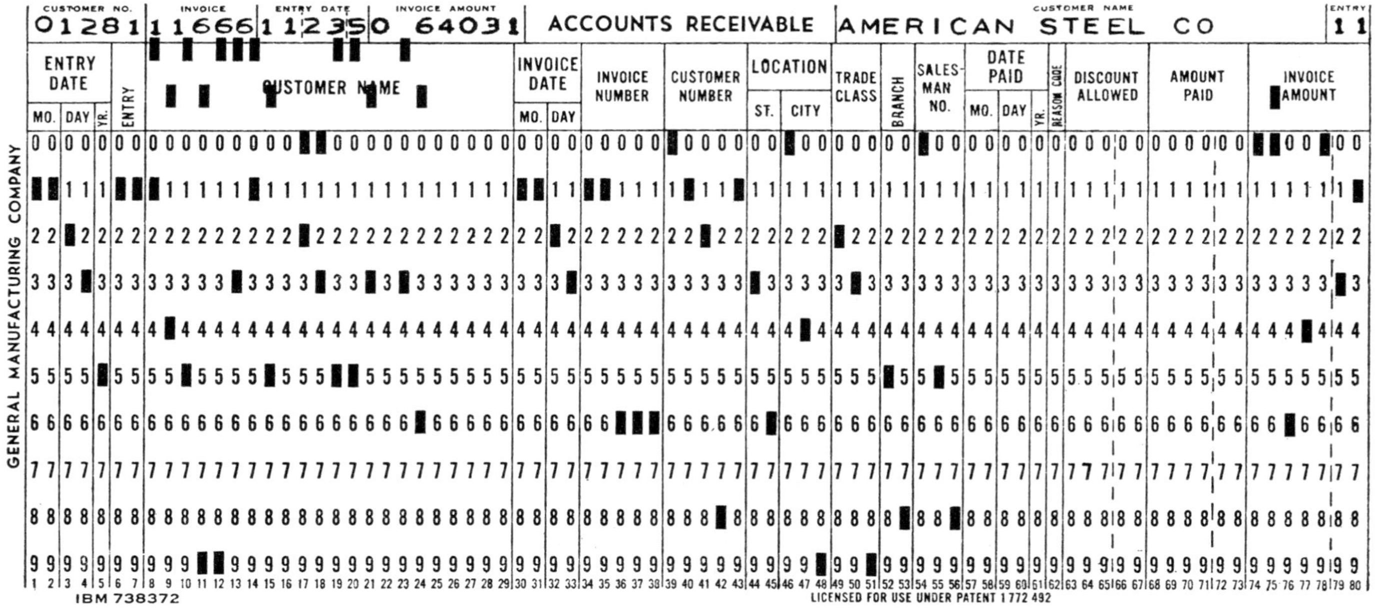

Courtesy: International Business Machines Corp., New York

FIG. 17–9. The space on the punched card is allocated according to the needs of the particular study.

BASIC PUNCHED-CARD MACHINES

There are three basic machines for a punched-card arrangement. They include a punching machine, a sorter, and a tabulator. A punching machine punches small holes in the card, representing the numerical and alphabetical information desired. The machines have many automatic features, depending upon the model and the manufacture. Figure 17–10 shows a card-punching machine.

The sorter arranges the cards according to any desired classification and in alphabetical or numerical sequence. The sorting is really a box sort. Cards are passed through the machine; and the punched hole causes a mechanism to operate, resulting in the card being directed into a specific box or pocket of the machine. Sorting at any one time is done according to one vertical column, i.e., a unit number or a letter. For example, consider the numbers in the left column of Figure 17–11 as the data to be placed in proper numerical sequence. The first sort arranges the data in sequence according to the unit column. Then, the second sort rearranges this sequence according to the 10's column. In like manner, the third sort rearranges the 100's column, thus placing the cards in proper numerical sequence. Sorting machines are capable of handling 1,000 cards per minute, or 60,000 per hour.

Courtesy: International Business Machines Corp., New York

FIG. 17–10.   A card-punching machine which features an automatic card control of skipping and duplicating, a fast method of duplication when desired, and a design which permits efficient and rapid operation.

The tabulator prepares printed reports from the data contained on the punched and sorted cards. These machines can print individually or in summary; a great variety of reports is possible. The number of reports that can be printed is almost limitless but depends mainly upon the information to be "read" by the machine, the forms on which the reports are prepared, and the arrangement and rearrangement of the cards. A tabulator—or as it is sometimes called, a punched-card accounting machine—is illustrated in Figure 17–12.

Unsorted Data	Arrangement after First Sort	Arrangement after Second Sort	Arrangement after Third Sort
	↓	↓	↓
828	750	904	107
107	460	107	191
542	191	212	212
904	542	828	375
212	212	542	388
375	904	750	460
191	375	460	542
750	107	375	750
388	828	388	828
460	388	191	904

FIG. 17–11.

Courtesy: *International Business Machines Corp., New York*

FIG. 17–12. A punched card accounting machine that provides an economic and rapid method of printing and punching card documents during a single pass of the file.

SPECIAL PUNCHED-CARD MACHINES

Special machines for specific operations are also available. A complete listing of these is beyond the scope of this discussion, but the more common ones should be included. A machine called an "interpreter" prints at the top of the card the data represented by the punched holes. This information is sometimes desired for quick identification and reference. However, many experienced and skilled operators can read the punched cards as easily as the average person reads normal print. A "verifier" can be used to check the accuracy of the holes punched in the cards. Another machine, called a "gang punch," is designed to punch standardized information on cards. For example, data such as date and location of customer, which are repetitive for a batch of cards, can be punched at one time and not performed individually for each card. There is also a "multiplying punch" which senses, for example, two factors prepunched in the card, computes the product, punches it into the card, and records the factors and the product on a paper.

Variable information such as meter readings, job data, and stores requisitions can be pencil-marked in appropriate spaces on a punched-card area. Then, by means of a machine called an "optical scanning punch," the variable information is read and automatically punched into the card, thus making it ready for processing.

With the developments in office automation and especially integrated data processing, many punched cards are now produced simultaneously with the typing of the information on a typewriter equipped with special attachments or units "connected with" the typewriter. Such machines were discussed in Chapter 7.

USAGE OF PUNCHED CARDS

Punched-card machines are employed most commonly for (1) correlating, analyzing, and summarizing data, such as sales by customer, and net revenue by salesman, as illustrated by Figure 17–13; (2) preparing bills or invoices—the data on cards can be easily grouped and totaled; (3) handling accounts payable—each payment to a creditor is processed via a punched card; (4) keeping inventory records—purchases and usages by items are simple operations with punched cards; (5) preparing payrolls and distributing labor costs—checks are prepared from information on the card for each employee, and tabular lists can be quickly run as well as labor cost allocated to predetermined groups; and (6) production control—for each production operation, pertinent data and its relationship to other operations are put on separate punched cards, from which production routing and dispatching information are easily prepared.

Competent help and assistance should be secured in the selection, adoption, and use of punched-card machines. The proper and full use of the equipment requires adequate knowledge, ingenuity, and a fundamental understanding of the work and of the objectives to be achieved. The expert in this field can be of great and genuine assistance.

Key considerations in the usage of punched cards include the cost and time of getting the raw data punched into the cards, the extent to which correlated or listed information will be helpful, and the value of addi-

SALES AND GROSS PROFIT BY CUSTOMER

CUSTOMER		COMMODITY		QUANTITY	UNIT	COST OF GOODS SOLD	SALES AMOUNT
BR.	NO.	CODE	DESCRIPTION				
1 3	6 7		ACE DRUG CO				
1 3	6 7	0 3 0 1	BEAUTY SOAP REGULAR	1 2	D Z	1 9 8 0	2 4 0 0
1 3	6 7	0 3 0 2	BEAUTY SOAP GUEST	1 2	D Z	2 0 4 0	2 5 2 0
1 3	6 7	0 3 0 3	BEAUTY SOAP BATH	1 2	D Z	2 1 6 0	2 7 0 0
1 3	6 7	1 3 1 4	SHAVE SOAP LARGE	2 4	D Z	4 8 0 0	6 9 6 0
1 3	6 7	1 3 5 2	BRUSHLESS CREAM LRG	2 4	D Z	3 1 2 0	4 3 2 0
			(FOR THE PURPOSE OF THIS EXHIBIT, ONLY) (A FEW COMMODITIES ARE ILLUSTRATED)			2 7 5 0 0 ✻	3 7 5 0 0
1 3	1 0 5		ADAMS DRYGOODS CO				
1 3	1 0 5	0 3 0 1	BEAUTY SOAP REGULAR	2 4	D Z	3 9 6 0	4 8 0 0

NET REVENUE ANALYSIS BY SALESMAN

BRANCH	SALESMAN		GROSS SALES	RETURNS AND ALLOWANCES	NET SALES	COST SALES	TRAVEL AND EXPENSE	COM
	NO.	NAME						
1 3	2 9	A ANDREWS	5 4 0 3 0 0	3 7 5 0 0	5 0 2 8 0 0	2 9 6 0 0 0	2 5 7 0	
1 3	3 2	G DRISCOLL	6 1 1 9 0 0	4 3 5 0 0	5 6 8 4 0 0	3 8 2 5 0 0	2 6 4 0	
1 3	4 5	R M EDWARDS	3 9 0 5 0 0	3 4 0 0 0	3 5 6 5 0 0	2 2 4 0 0 0	2 9 0 0	
1 3	4 7	A H FRANKLIN	7 5 1 3 0 0	4 5 0 0 0	7 0 6 3 0 0	5 1 3 5 0 0	2 8 0 0	
1 3	5 1	J A HOLLAND	6 2 5 7 0 0	4 4 1 0 0	5 8 1 6 0 0	3 8 5 5 0 0	2 6 2 5	
1 3	5 5	L B LAWSON	6 1 2 0 0 0	4 2 9 0 0	5 6 9 1 0 0	3 8 5 0 0 0	2 5 7 5	

Courtesy: International Business Machines Corp., New York

FIG. 17–13. Samples of the work prepared by a tabulator of punched cards.

tional facts gained from being able to interpret the data in a more feasible form.

The use of punched cards is not confined to large companies. The following quotation illustrates the extent to which punched-card accounting is used in enterprises employing several hundred people:

One company employing less than two hundred people furnishes a fair example of what may, in the future, become more common. . . . Investigation showed that 95 per cent of items ordered were for six different quantities (in cases). This permitted even the punching to be preponderantly automatic. Two files of prepunched cards were set up, one for each popular quantity of each commodity and the other containing master cards for each customer. Orders originate in branches and are forwarded to headquarters. An operator pulls a master code card for the customer and a commodity card for each time ordered. No key punching is necessary except when the quantity ordered is unusual (5 per cent of the items). From then on the order analysis, sales accounting including costs, inventory control (factory and five warehouses), accounts receivable, production planning, production explosion (the breakdown of the effect of orders upon raw materials and packages) becomes completely automatic. Of course, cards other than those for orders come into the picture. As a matter of fact, all records of production, including inventories, costs, and payroll, are handled on one set of machines.[1]

And in another case, the following:

Another company employing less than three hundred men, in this case a small subsidiary of a national organization, manufactures wire which is distributed through the branch offices of the parent company. Here all payroll, production, sales, and inventory records are handled on one set of machines. The inventory records include control of wire stocks not only at the factory but also at more than fifty branches.[2]

MARGINAL NOTCHED-CARD MACHINES

These machines are used to notch precoded holes *along the edge* of a card so that sorting of the data by key classifications can be accom-

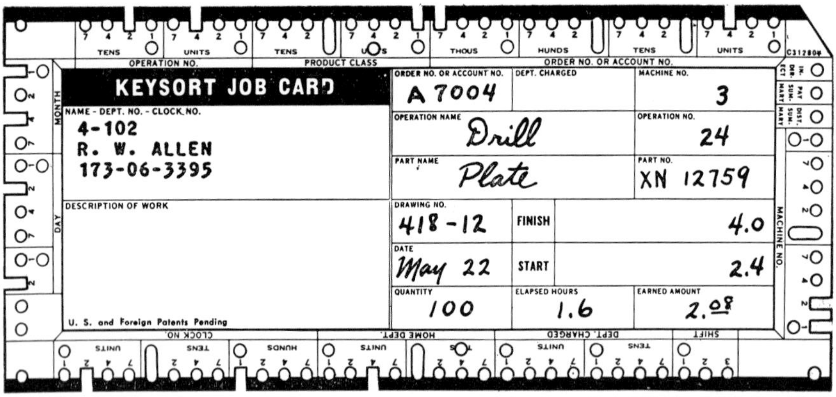

Courtesy: Royal-McBee Corp., New York

FIG. 17–14. Card punched with holes and notches to indicate definite information.

plished quickly and accurately. After sorting, data referring to a similar attribute, such as sales, inventories, or indirect labor costs, can be totaled and used in management reports. The process is versatile; it is applicable to many transactions, including sales orders, stock requisitions, purchase and expense vouchers, and payroll records.

The cards are available in varying sizes; for example, there are 2 × 3½-inch and 7½ × 8½-inch cards. As on most record cards, pertinent information is written in the center position of the card. Holes located adjacent to one or more margins are assigned definite values or meanings, depending upon their location. Identification with a particular classification is made by notching away the portion of the card between the hole and the edge. For example, in Figure 17–14, the operation number

---

[1] Leon E. Vannais, "Punched Card Accounting from the Audit Viewpoint," *Journal of Accountancy* (New York: American Institute Publishing Co., Inc.), September, 1940, p. 17.

[2] *Ibid.*, pp. 20–21.

24 can be identified by the notches in the upper left margin of the card where the 2 under the 10's and the 4 under the units have been notched. Likewise, the date, May 22, is coded in the left margin, indicating that the month is 5 and the day is 22. Observe that for any one segment, the holes of values 7, 4, 2, and 1 make possible any value from 1 through 9. Zero is indicated by no notches.

The cards can be notched by means of either a hand punch or a machine especially designed for that purpose. To sort the cards, it is common to use a single or a multiprong fork. The prong is positioned so that it slides through a designated hole in a stack of cards. Then, by the shaking of the pack, the cards with notched holes at the prong location fall clear of the other cards. Thus, a fast, accurate sort is provided. When large amounts of notched cards are to be sorted, a machine can be used. It utilizes the same principle as that of hand sorting described above, but handles much larger volumes very quickly.

MISCELLANEOUS MACHINES

Labeling machines prepare addressed labels in long, continuous-length strips. The back of the labels is mucilaged. The strips are cut automatically and individually for each label just prior to its being affixed to an envelope, package, or periodical. The labels are available in a variety of sizes. The speed of the machine is relatively high.

Electric staplers, used for attaching sheets of paper together, are employed for large volumes of this work. The stapling of booklets or reports, for example, is illustrative. Savings of much effort and time are gained by using an electric stapler.

Counters provide quick measurement of units and the speed of certain office work. Bank checks, cards, and labels, for example, can be quickly counted by use of these machines. Some are operated manually, while others are attached to common office machines to indicate such information as the number of strokes of typing on a typewriter or the revolutions of the cylindrical drum of a duplicating machine.

QUESTIONS

1. Would you say that the installation of accounting machines frequently necessitates changes in office procedures and methods? Why?
2. Discuss four of the more common uses for which punched cards are used, that is, the general types of reports or information obtained from them.
3. Discuss the use of the nondescriptive accounting machine in the office.
4. Discuss the "before and after" planning necessitated by the use of office machines.
5. In your own words, describe the work being done as illustrated by Figure 17–3.
6. For what type of work are addressing and listing machines usually well adapted?

7. Relate the important considerations to be taken into account in laying out the punched card for the processing of data.

8. Briefly discuss the considerations for office machines that should be included in office management planning.

9. What are the three fundamental machines in a punched-card setup, and what does each machine do?

10. Do you agree with the following? "Marginal notched cards and punched cards are used for practically the same purposes in an office, the selection depending upon the size of the office and the volume of work handled." Explain.

11. Distinguish carefully between the concepts in each of the following pairs:
    a) Nondescriptive and nonwindow accounting machines.
    b) Gang punch and "optical scanning" punch.
    c) Fiber stencil and window-posting accounting machine.
    d) Electric stapler and punched-card sorter.

12. What are the major differences between an accounting machine and a punched-card tabulator?

CASE PROBLEMS

Case 17–1. The Underhill Company

A current problem in the office of the Underhill Company is keeping notes receivable accounts up to date. The majority of these notes are monthly, although some are weekly. Currently, a general ledger and a supplementary ledger in the form of a visible card index are used. When a payment is received, a receipt, in duplicate, is made out; the original is sent to the customer, and the copy is retained by the company for its records. From this copy, payments are posted to the customer or account card, all of which make up the visible card file. When posting, the balances due, discounts earned, and total paid to date are calculated and entered upon the card. Because of the volume and urgency of other work, the posting to the cards is performed about every sixth day and to the general ledger about every three weeks.

Under the present arrangement, it is difficult to be aware of all delinquent accounts immediately. Also, from time to time, serious errors have occurred in the posting of the information to the cards and to the general ledger. Finding such mistakes is a problem in itself, but more serious is rectifying the error with the customer. In addition, during the past three years, there has been a constant growth in the number of accounts, and there is good reason to believe that this growth will continue.

The office manager has considered several actions that might be taken. He is of the opinion that an office machine should be used for this work.

Problems:

1. What are the major actions that the office manager should take?

2. Assuming that you agree with the office manager that a machine should be used, what type of office machine would you recommend? Why?

3. Describe in necessary detail how the work would be handled, utilizing the machine recommended in the answer to question No. 2, above.

Case 17–2.   Robertson and Davis, Inc.

The following letter was received by a professor of office management in a large midwestern university:

Robertson and Davis, Inc.
6140 Plum Street
Cincinnati

February 3, 196–

Dear Professor:

About six years ago, I was a member of several of your most helpful classes and since graduation have realized more and more what you did for me while I was on campus. Probably you will recall that it was through your help that I got a job with Robertson and Davis, Inc. As you can see from this letter, I am still with them and like my work very much.

Since a year ago last November, I have been supervisor of our IBM tabulating department. About two weeks ago, the controller of our division, the midwest one here in Cincinnati, requested that I devise a way of handling accounts payable and the general ledger for our division. At present, we are using a manual operation consisting of hand-posting entries and subsequently typing voucher checks. Although I have no data on the time it takes to handle an account payable under our current system, it appears that a great deal of time is consumed in processing the invoices and in compiling information necessary for the trial balance at the end of each accounting period.

My thoughts are along the following lines, and I would appreciate your comments regarding them and any suggestions you care to offer. In this respect, my company will gladly compensate you for your time and services.

I propose to lay out the tab card so as to include space for all pertinent information, including invoice date, number, due date, vendor number, and so forth. Also, suitable paper forms will be designed for an invoice register, cash disbursements register, and an account distribution for running trial balance.

Invoices will be sent to my department after checking and approval by the purchasing department and accounting department. We will code vendor lists, each vendor being assigned a number. Upon receipt of invoices, they will be coded and stamped with a number for reference purposes. This information will be punched into cards, one for entry on invoice register and payment, and another for account distribution for the general ledger file. After punching and balancing, this information will be listed on the invoice register from payable cards and then put into a due date file for future payment. The account distribution cards will be filed into the current month's general ledger file.

When payment is due, cards will be pulled from this due date file and machine-tabulated on the cash disbursements register. The cards will then be collated by vendor name and the payments or checks run off by the machine.

For each accounting period, journal entries will be prepared and punched for entry into the general ledger file. A trial balance will be run after all entries are made. This trial balance will show account number and entries, giving totals by major accounts.

Sincerely yours,

JAH:r   (Signed) John A. Hemminger

Manager, Tabulating Department

Problems:

1. In your own words, describe the proposed means for handling the work under discussion.

2. Evaluate the proposed use of the IBM equipment by Mr. Hemminger.

3. Draft the reply you feel the professor should write.

Chapter 18

OFFICE SPACE PLANNING—LAYOUT

When nothing seems to help I go and look at a stone-cutter hammering away at his rock perhaps one hundred times without as much as a crack showing in it. Yet at the hundred and first blow it will split in two, and I know it was not that blow that did it, but all that had gone before.

—JACOB RITS

THE USAGE of office space is another important area of office management planning. Like any segment of the office productive process, the office should be tooled for production. Poor office space arrangement wastes the employee's time and energy by failure to provide the means for effective work habits. If there is no place to put needed papers and books, the telephone is on the wrong side of the desk, recessed light fixtures provide an inadequate amount of light, employees must sit beneath a ceiling vent or face a window, the carpet shows dirt easily, and the flow of work is uneven—the result is obviously less production.

OFFICE SPACE PLANNING DEFINED

As the term suggests, office space planning is the determining of the arrangement of all physical components of work considered necessary for the office work performance and the co-ordinating of these components into an efficient and attractive unity. Some people consider an office to be a room with office equipment and machines in it. But it is far more than that; it is a work area for handling information. Every physical component in the area or space is a tool to help do the work. The equipment and machines have a purpose; and their arrangement should help, as a co-ordinated unit, in the accomplishing of the office work. But this broader viewpoint is not confined to equipment and machines. It includes all areas of office planning, i.e., the work to be done; the process adopted; the equipment and machines used; the spaces provided; the physical surroundings—light, color, ventilation; and the personnel doing

338

the work. Some refer to this as "integrated space planning," meaning that all components utilized for performing the given work should be tied together as a unit.

INTEGRATED SPACE PLANNING

Under integrated space planning, the separate contributions of all factors utilized are co-ordinated into a unified program for desired work performance. These are harmonious and integrated efforts toward a common goal. For example, a particular type of desk is provided at a designated area because this location helps most in accomplishing the required work. The chair, the color and treatment of the walls, the location of the office area, and the machines utilized are all co-ordinated toward a common ultimate purpose. Both beauty and effectiveness are attained. An office can serve practical needs, yet possess distinctiveness and impressive appearance. Helpful, workable surroundings make up good design and are never out of style. If an office is workably correct, it can be aesthetically pleasing.

Integrated space planning stresses functional analysis as its basis. This is essentially a data-gathering, question-asking approach so that effective space utilization can be evolved into a plan. It includes the type of information to be gathered and digested before calling in the architect or construction engineer. Figure 18–1 shows an interesting example of functional analysis being applied to a private office. The "before" pictures illustrate the drab, nonfunctional office. The old desk without overhang top did not lend itself to the formal conferences required daily, and the old sofa kept visitors at a distance for informal conferences. The "after" views show the functionalization, comfort, and warmth supplied. The L-shaped desk placed along one wall provides ample work, storage, and conference areas. Informal conversational groupings can be held away from the desk and in pleasant surroundings. Proper lighting, draperies, and carpeting were added to complete the dignified yet functional office.

OFFICE LAYOUT AND WORK FLOW

The movement of office work through and between departments is a fundamental consideration in determining the arrangement of the physical units. If the basic circulation patterns are clogged, the effects multiply outward and hinder the entire enterprise. Flow is either (1) by papers or (2) by people. Usually, it is better to bring the papers to the person than the person to the papers, although both are and must be used. Careful planning is required to provide a minimum amount of travel from one department to another, from machine to machine, and from desk to desk. Ideally, the work is directed along the shortest distance between two points, which sounds simple, but commonly is difficult to apply.

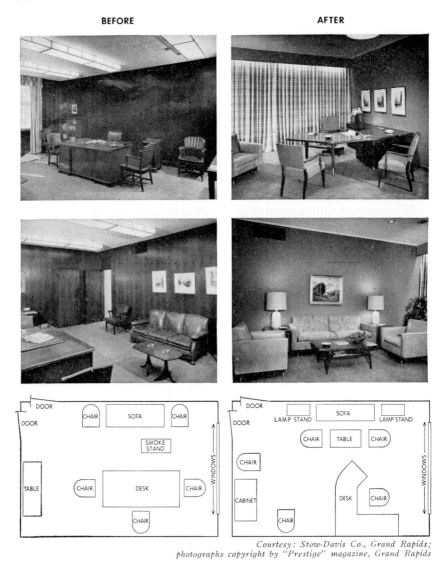

BEFORE   AFTER

Courtesy: Stow-Davis Co., Grand Rapids;
photographs copyright by "Prestige" magazine, Grand Rapids

FIG. 18–1. The "before and after" views of a private office, showing the improvements and better design brought about by space planning guided by functional analysis.

In most large offices, there is a key paper or set of papers about which the various office operations revolve. For example, in the office of a wholesaler or a sales department, the key paper is the customer's order. The key paper forms the core of nearly all the work that takes place in the particular office area. Tracing the movement of this document, or that required by employees working on it, supplies the clue as to what physical units should be related and in what sequence. Work activities other than those of the key paper exist, but they will be related and subordinated to the key paper.

Since the flow of work in the large office is usually of a constant pattern, i.e., the sequence of steps, the work volume at the various stations, and the particular type of work performed at each station remain fairly constant, the layout can be designed to accommodate these fairly uniform conditions. In contrast, when the office is small, many different flows must be handled with the same layout. In these cases, the layout should be made to handle best the flows representing the largest volumes of work, usually those of orders, accounts payable, invoices, and purchases. The relatively minor flows can be fitted to the layout as best possible.

The flow, when plotted on the floor plan, should conform to a straight line, circle, or some regular shape. This helps insure that wasteful backtracking or deviation is avoided. In addition, a minimum of time and cost should be required in going from beginning to end of the flow.

FUNDAMENTAL CONSIDERATIONS

Everyone seems to have ideas about office layout. Some of these ideas are excellent, while others are so impractical or incomplete that they are useless. In most instances, the help of an office layout specialist is recommended, for this assures that a reasonably efficient office layout will be obtained. This approach, however, does not prohibit the office manager or any executive from talking with the layout specialist and contributing to the task of evolving the best office space plans. General knowledge in this subject area by laymen assists in these efforts. The person responsible for office layout work is a key man in office planning and therefore should be selected carefully.

Office layout has a number of objectives. Among the more common are to facilitate an efficient flow of office work; to assist good supervision; to use space effectively; to locate equipment, machines, and aisles conveniently; to add to the employee's comfort; to impress favorably customers and visitors; and to provide for future expansion, contraction, or move, as the case may be. All are important, and all are provided in an excellent layout.

From the viewpoint of layout, most large offices are made up of four separate types of areas, including (1) private offices, (2) general office area, (3) service areas, and (4) storage areas. It commonly helps to keep these in mind when preparing office layouts so that the over-all viewpoint is maintained and the essentials for each type of area are included.

In order of their increasing difficulty, office layouts are for either new, remodeled, or currently used areas. New areas normally permit the most effective space utilization; completely co-ordinated space planning is possible. The next group—remodeled areas—sometimes poses difficult-to-solve problems, in that the building facilities are inadequate or the space modernization is incomplete. Finally, the planning of existing areas for space improvement can be both fascinating and frustrating, in that considerable improvement in space utilization can usually be brought about, but certain rigidities prevent a desired level of space efficiency being attained.

Space planning is similar to other types of planning, in that it is continuous or nearly so. Specifically, when is space planning in order? First, when the work flow is changed by a new or modified work procedure. This may be when a piece of equipment or a machine is replaced or sold. The signal for performing space planning is also given when additional work space is needed. This could be due to an increase in work volume or personnel. Likewise, a change in organization frequently suggests consideration for layout modifications. Especially is this true if functions are either added or taken from an organizational unit. Also, complaints from employees about their work areas suggest space-planning efforts to eliminate the poor areas that infest the office layout.

The presence or the absence of certain building facilities may be the vital issue in deciding upon a layout. In too many cases, the ideal arrangement does not fit in with the physical working conditions of the space or building. Adjustments that weaken the layout must be made. In some buildings and spaces, a number of shortcomings must be taken into account.

IMPORTANCE OF OFFICE LAYOUT

Good layout assists in accomplishing the work efficiently, while a poor arrangement can seriously retard the work output. Adequate space must be provided and must be properly utilized, for too much or too little office space can make for inefficiencies. In the former case, needless energy is wasted in such things as messenger service and the flow of work through the office; likewise, excessive costs of heating, ventilating, and lighting frequently result. When too little space is provided, it usually results in crowded conditions which not only interfere with the work output but also encourage employee complaints, which are reflected in low morale.

Ineffective use of office space is a continuous liability. It contributes to office inefficiency daily, and it will continue to do so until an improved layout is planned and put into effect. Frequently, the individual daily loss is small; but when consideration is given the cumulative amount—for a month or a year, for example—the importance of proper layout is brought into bolder relief.

In addition, it must be remembered that occupancy of office space represents a definite cost. While, in most cases, office space does not represent the largest portion of office expenditure, it usually does represent a sizable outlay, and it must be kept within reasonable limits. Adequate consideration to the office layout helps insure proper space provision as well as space utilization.

BASIC LAYOUT GUIDES

Over a period of time, there have been developed a number of layout guides which should be followed in order to provide an effective office arrangement. Not all of these can be followed in any one layout; but in general, the more that are included, the better the layout. A list includes the following:

1. Utilize one large area in preference to an equivalent area of small parcels. The single large area permits better lighting, ventilating, supervising, and communicating.

2. Use uniform-size desks in any one area. This gives better appearance and promotes the feeling of equality among employees.

3. Keep filing cabinets and other cabinets at uniform height in any one area to improve general appearance.

4. Use straight symmetry in layout. Avoid offsets, jogs, and angle arrangements.

5. Provide for work to flow in straight lines as nearly as possible. Avoid backtracking, crisscrossing, and unnecessary movement of papers. Give major preference to the dominant flows of work.

6. Provide for maximum work loads.

7. Have the work come to the employee, not the employee go to the work. Keep employee flow to a minimum.

8. Reduce walking and waiting time by installing pencil sharpeners and duplicating machines in each area of need.

9. Place related departments adjacent, and keep jobs of a similar nature in close relationship.

10. Anticipate and provide for future changes. Keep the layout flexible.

11. Locate supervisors at the rear of their work groups, so that they can easily observe what goes on in the work area.

12. Place all employees so that they face in the same direction. Do not have employees facing one another.

13. Arrange desks so that ample natural light comes over the left shoulder.

14. Avoid private office locations which cut off natural light to the adjacent general office area.

15. Do not have the employee facing a window, too near heat sources, or in line of drafts.

16. Use movable partitions for walls, as they are easy to install and can be quickly rearranged at will. Part-way partitions with plain or opaque glass permit good light and ventilation.

17. Provide sufficient floor electrical outlets for office equipment and machines.

18. Place units requiring noisy equipment and machines in an area with soundproofing to avoid disturbance to others.

19. Locate departments which normally have many visitors from the outside near the entrance; or if this is not feasible, make provisions so that this traffic will not disturb other departments.

20. Locate vending machines, fountains, and bulletin boards where they will cause least distraction and congestion.

21. Put files and frequently used equipment near the employees who use them. Abstain from putting all files at dead-wall space.

22. Place filing cabinets back to back.

23. If a corner is required, consider the possibility of providing it with filing cabinets.

24. If possible, provide lounging areas where employees can relax during rest periods, talk informally, and eat lunch.

25. Provide convenient and adequate rest-room facilities.

26. Allocate the generally prescribed number of square feet per employee for his particular work station. These space quantities are discussed in the following paragraphs.

SPACE STANDARDS

The amount of space to be allocated for any given work station or department is subject to a great many considerations. The type of office work, the physical units, the shape of the area, the general effect desired, and the location of service facilities are examples of factors to be taken into account. Of prime importance are the individual circumstances of each case. Certain guiding data are available, but judgment and experience must be used in determining the correct amount of space.

Desk Space Standards. Fairly uniform space standards have been evolved for common office units, such as desks, chairs, and files. For example, when 60 × 34-inch desks are arranged as single units with aisles adjacent, or when they are arranged in pairs, end for end, with aisles adjacent to each desk, the minimum space standard from back to back of desks is about 72 inches. See Figure 18–2 (top illustration). These arrangements provide about a 3-foot strip for the chair and for getting to and from the desk. However, when three desks are used end for end, with aisles adjacent to outer desks only, the minimum standard for space from back to back of desks must be increased to about 84 inches, thus providing a chair space of around 4 feet. This extra distance is necessary so that the employee at the middle desk can get in and out without unnecessary disturbance to the occupants at the outer desks. The bottom illustration of Figure 18–2 shows this case.

Generally speaking, the arrangement of two desks end for end, as illustrated by plan No. 2, necessitates the smallest area per clerk of any conventional desk arrangement. In contrast, the arrangement of desks in single units, as shown in plan No. 1, requires the greatest amount of space per clerk.

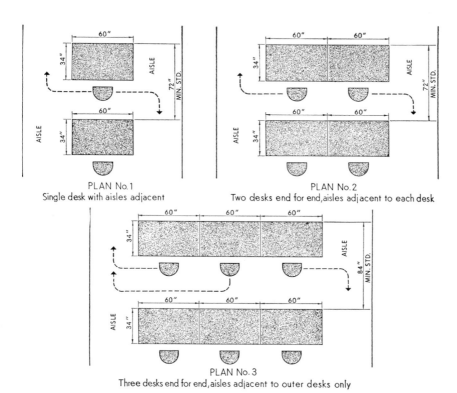

PLAN No.1
Single desk with aisles adjacent

PLAN No.2
Two desks end for end, aisles adjacent to each desk

PLAN No. 3
Three desks end for end, aisles adjacent to outer desks only

FIG. 18–2. Minimum standards for back-to-back arrangement of desks under different floor plan layouts.

Office Corridor Standards. Main corridors should be from 5 to 8 feet wide, depending upon the amount of traffic to be handled. A 5-foot aisle can normally accommodate around 850 people in five minutes. Main aisles in an office area should be from 4 to 5 feet wide, and the range of secondary aisles should be from 3 to 4 feet wide. Cross aisles should be provided about every 50 feet.

Filing Cabinet Space Standards. The spacing of ordinary filing equipment depends upon frequency of use and function of the material filed. For *active material* and files facing the same direction, the aisle space should be equal to the drawer depth plus 24 inches, or two drawer depths plus 36 inches if files are arranged back to back. These concepts are illustrated by Figure 18–3. In contrast, if the material is storage or inactive, the aisle between filing tiers should be equal to the depth of the drawer, or about 28 inches.

To save space, file cabinets should always be arranged back to back. This arrangement, for four files, results in a *distance* saving of 24 inches for active and two-drawer lengths, or about 56 inches, for inactive material.

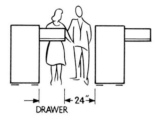 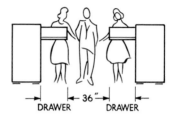

Files facing same direction   Files back each other

FIG. 18–3.   Recommended aisle spaces for active files according to their arrangement.

OVER-ALL SPACE ESTIMATES

Studies show that a value of 60 square feet of space for each *ordinary clerical employee* is a desirable standard; and when an office layout calls for this amount, the space utilization may be considered highly satisfactory.

The value of 60 square feet per ordinary clerical employee is arrived at in this manner:

$$
\begin{aligned}
\text{54-inch desk and chair, } 54'' \times 72'' &= 27.00 \text{ sq. ft.} \\
\text{Aisle per desk, } 18'' \times 72'' &= 9.00 \text{ sq. ft.} \\
\text{Miscellaneous (files, aisles, etc.)} &= 24.00 \text{ sq. ft.} \\
\text{Total} &= 60.00 \text{ sq. ft.}
\end{aligned}
$$

In actual practice, however, this value is frequently very difficult to achieve. An average of around 70 is probably better, and this applies to people in a large clerical area. For a small department, the average will run about 80 square feet per employee. Space estimates for other personnel include:

$$
\begin{aligned}
\text{Top executive} &\dots \dots \dots \dots \dots \dots \dots 400\text{–}450 \text{ sq. ft.} \\
\text{Intermediate executive} &\dots \dots \dots \dots \dots 275\text{–}300 \text{ sq. ft.} \\
\text{Supervisory executive} &\dots \dots \dots \dots \dots 110\text{–}125 \text{ sq. ft.}
\end{aligned}
$$

However, there is no fast rule for the standard number of square feet per office employee. The data above can be used for comparison or reference purposes. The space that can or should be used is influenced by the nature of the work, the available total area, the extent of service areas, the need for privacy, the number and type of equipment and machines, and the shape, exposure, and obstructions within the total space itself.

SURPLUS AREA

As far as possible, efforts should be made to determine what amount of space appears to be appropriate, and this amount should be allocated —no more and no less. In cases where the total space available is greater than that deemed necessary, the surplus should be either immediately utilized for other purposes, screened off and held in readiness for future use, or rented to other interests. Following a "do nothing" attitude and permitting the space to remain open and idle usually results in current adjacent activities spilling over into these areas; and after this happens, it is difficult to get them back into the area where they belong. Also, any semblance of space control is lessened, and an orderly, planned expansion program is ignored.

STEPS IN PLANNING AN OFFICE LAYOUT

For general expediency and satisfactory results, the following twelve steps are recommended for determining an office layout.

1. *Secure a drawing or blueprint of the available area.* In obtaining the drawing or blueprint, care should be exercised to insure that the information shown is accurate and complete. In the event that no print is available, the space should be measured and the dimensions indicated on a neatly drawn hand sketch. A convenient scale is $\frac{1}{4}'' = 1'$, which means that $\frac{1}{4}$ inch on the drawing is equal to 1 foot of actual floor dimension. The exact location and size of radiators, windows, building offsets, and door swings, and the location of columns, pipes, electric light outlets and wiring, ducts for telephone wiring, running water facilities, and entrances and exits are important. Frequently, the ability to adapt a suggested layout depends upon the completeness and accuracy of these data. A building offset incorrectly spotted, or the omission of a radiator, can necessitate changes and alterations in a proposed layout and cause an otherwise acceptable layout to be rejected.

2. *Determine the areas of main traffic movement.* These areas will depend upon such things as the size and shape of the space available and the general type of office. The location of building facilities such as entrances and exits, stairways, elevators, rest rooms, and the like will suggest areas of greatest travel. From this information, the location of the main corridors, storage rooms, reception rooms, and wardrobe rooms in the layout will be suggested. These represent space required for other than personnel occupancy.

3. *Gain a complete over-all picture of the work to be done in the area.* Gaining an over-all picture is not easy; yet at the same time, it is not especially difficult. The organization of the office will assist in determining what unit does what work and, in turn, what employee performs what work.[1] Study of this information will be helpful. In addition, this over-all picture might suggest to the office planner the reassignment of certain duties among the groups in order to gain a better layout. Subsequently, the suggestions can be evaluated and decided.

Study of the flow of work must be made. There is always a basic circulation plan around which the office layout is constructed. An analysis of the various procedures used, the specific work involved in preparing the number and type of reports, and the various services rendered are

---

[1] Organizing is discussed in Part VI of this book.

among the important considerations to be included. The usual sequence of operations in performing the work should be listed so that the space relationship of desks or machines will be in a convenient, logical order, according to the progressive steps of the work.

4. *Determine the quantity, size, and type of physical units to be included.* There are several ways in which this can be done. For example, they can be calculated by dividing the estimated quantity of work by the accepted standard of performance. To illustrate, for 750 orders daily and a standard of 250 orders per day per unit, the requirements are $750 \div 250 = 3$, which means that provision for three units must be made in the layout to take care of these orders.

Another way is to use a list showing the various types and sizes of the units to be included. Such a list usually is a copy of what has been used in the past or is based on estimates of what probably should be included. There is usually little, if any, scientific determination of the items on such a list; and for the most part, it represents an opinion of what should be used. This approach is satisfactory as a temporary expedient, but efforts should be made as soon as possible to determine with some accuracy what physical units are really needed. This may require close co-operation with the procedures planning and the methods of performing the work.

Data should also be available regarding any type of work, machine, or equipment which is exceptionally noisy or otherwise objectionable. Such physical elements should be noted and, as stated previously, consideration given to the possibility of locating them in areas isolated from the office proper.

5. *Identify the basic groups making up the office.* These data can be obtained from the organizational structure.[2] Normally, they include the top management and various departmental and divisional groups; however, sometimes units smaller than a division can be used, depending upon the individual requirements. Among the more typical groupings are top management, sales, purchasing, accounting, billing, cost, stenographic, and estimating; and these form the nucleus around which the layout will be made. They serve as small segments for convenience in handling the entire layout.

6. *Consult briefly with the head of each basic group.* This is primarily to gain some idea of what each group leader has in mind regarding his particular unit, and it affords the leaders an opportunity to speak up and to have some voice in the layout work. Frequently, very valuable suggestions are received. In some instances, conflicts, such as several groups wanting the same space, are encountered; but these can usually be worked out as the entire layout work proceeds. The impor-

---

[2] See Part VI in this book on subject of organizing.

tant point is that by consulting with the group leaders at this step, an opportunity is given for an expression of their space needs and how these needs can be provided for.

7. *Formulate tentative answers regarding the use of reception room, conference rooms, and private offices.* A complete discussion on the use of these areas is made in the following sections of this chapter. For purposes of illustration, assume that, for the time being, the tentative answer is to use a reception room, two conference rooms, and six private offices in the top management group and one in each of the five departmental groups. These data are then added to the physical units information discussed previously under point 4.

8. *Make templates to scale of all physical units (or use models), and identify clearly.* A template is a scaled pattern, made of cardboard or paper, which is used to represent the floor area occupied by a physical unit. The scale of the templates must be the same as that of the drawing showing the available area; as already pointed out, a scale of $\frac{1}{4}'' = 1'$ is convenient. Frequently, the shape of the templates is confined to that of a square or a rectangle; and in most cases, this is satisfactory; but there are instances where the details of cut-off corners, rounded corners, and the like should be included in the templates, as the final arrangement may hinge upon these considerations.

A separate template should be made for each physical unit considered in the layout. For purposes of identification, the name of the unit and of the basic group by which the unit is to be used should be stamped or printed on each template. It is also possible to use different colors representing different physical units to help visualize the work. Where a conference room and private offices are considered, templates covering the over-all floor dimensions should be made and clearly identified. Details of the arrangement within these areas can be postponed temporarily until it is determined if the entire space will be available for use.

Instead of templates, small-scale, three-dimensional models of the physical units can be used. These office models are dimensionally accurate and show at a glance the arrangement of the office. Many people can visualize the layout more clearly from scale models than from a technical drawing with which they may be unfamiliar. Complete kits, consisting of several hundred pieces including desks, chairs, files, machines, coat racks, and building columns, are available.

Also available are magnetic templates and magnetic models that can be used along with a steel-covered piece of plywood serving as a base. The magnetic templates or models hold fast to the steel-plywood base, yet they can be moved to show different layouts. The base can be attached to a wall, thus providing convenient viewing adequate for a group of people. In addition, some companies have found sandpaper-backed templates on flannel boards to be highly effective. They are inexpensive, permit vertical display of office layouts, and are well suited for meetings.

9. *Arrange templates or models for each basic group within its respective tentative area in accordance with basic effective office layout guides.* The suggested layout is determined by moving and shifting the templates or models to various positions so as to arrive at an effective arrangement. This phase of layout is a tentative trial-and-error process. It requires considerable time and cannot be rushed. If magnetic templates or models are used, they can be moved about as desired; yet, when released, they hold a fixed position. When the contemplated layout is completed, a picture of it can be taken and white paper copies made so that convenient reference sheets are provided.

10. *Check entire tentative layout, and make minor adjustments as required.* After the units in each group have been arranged in the best manner, the next step is to review the entire layout in order to see that it is a well-knit arrangement which will meet the particular needs. Provision for the smooth flow of all work through the entire office is checked, the extent of complementary units along common division lines is noted, and the general appearance of the entire layout is reviewed. Usually, minor adjustments are made to achieve the over-all effect desired.

11. *Indicate by appropriate markings the major flows of work and the telephone and electric wiring; also, include the name of the employee to be located at each unit.* This information is necessary in order to gain a complete understanding of the layout. The location of electric wiring outlets is especially important where groups of electrically driven machines are used. In many cases, some wiring arrangements must be provided for getting current to each desk.[3] The name of the employee at each work unit is helpful to the office executive in visualizing the arrangement.

12. *Recheck related layout with each respective basic group and, after securing respective sanctions, submit the over-all plan to the top managers for final approval.* The first basic group to consult, of course, is the top managers. Point out where the executives will be located, what facilities are provided, and the chief considerations determining the recommended layout. Generally, minor changes will be suggested, and they can usually be incorporated. The same approach is followed with each group head. If the plan follows closely the suggested ideas of the group head, as disclosed in step 6 above, it is well to point out this fact. If not, an explanation of the recommended layout should be made, with the reasons carefully pointed out in a simple, logical way. After all groups have O.K.'d their respective layouts, the entire plan is submitted to the top managers with the statement that this layout has the

---

[3] See pages 385–87 of Chapter 20.

approval of each group head. Acceptance by the top managers is then usually little more than a formality.

RECEPTION ROOM

Careful attention should be given to the reception room. It creates the initial impression of the enterprise upon the visitor, and it is true that initial impressions are often lasting ones. The reception room can, therefore, help create favorable reactions and assist in building public good will.

The reception room should have an attractive, inviting appearance. Many managers have found that displays of the company's products or illustrations of its services are very effective. Keeping the room clean also helps. Chairs should be kept in a straight line, with newspapers and magazines arranged neatly on a table, and ash trays kept clean.

To add to the caller's comfort, it is well to include some sort of cloakroom facilities to the reception room. A convenient place to leave one's hat and coat is appreciated by many callers, particularly in inclement weather and when the call is of fairly long duration. The providing of a telephone and a washroom are additional conveniences, but the decision on these should be based on the requirements and the cost of providing and maintaining them.

Whenever possible, the reception room should not handle ordinary and necessary traffic between different areas in the office. Employees walking across the reception room create a disturbing influence and distract from the dignity of the entire office. To prevent this condition, it is best to provide a passage for regular office traffic which by-passes or goes around the reception room.

The possibilities for the arrangement of the reception room are almost endless. The illustration at the top of Figure 18–4 gives a satisfactory layout for a small room. Sometimes, the work of receptionist and switchboard operator can be combined when the amount of work can be conveniently handled by one person. However, very often this is not the case.

CONFERENCE ROOM

For meetings in privacy, a conference room is highly recommended. Most private offices are not suited for the handling of meetings. With a conference room, the participants can be arranged more satisfactorily, a greater number can usually be accommodated, and each one can have a convenient place to write or to take notes. Furthermore, the meeting is placed on a businesslike basis, with a minimum of interference and distractions. The conference room should be located conveniently where traffic in and out of the room will be least disturbing to the other office employees. The bottom illustration of Figure 18–4 shows an effective layout for a conference room.

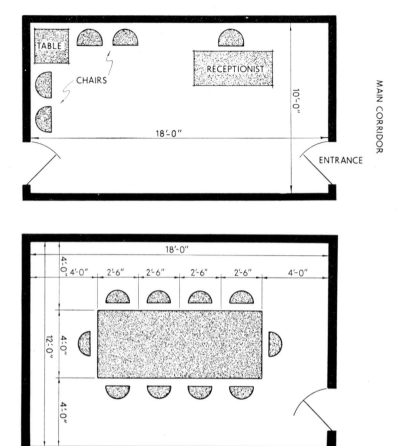

FIG. 18–4.   *Top:* Suggested layout for small reception rooms. *Bottom:* Suggested layout of conference room for ten people. The table size is 4 × 10 feet. For each two additional people to be accommodated, add 2 feet 6 inches to table length and to room length.

THE PRIVATE OFFICE

Decisions regarding the use of a private office should be made only after ample consideration has been given to the individual circumstances. A private office should be employed when its use is dictated by facts and unbiased judgment. It should never be provided simply because it has always been provided for a particular job or because requests and sometimes pressure have been brought to bear.

Justifications for Private Office. A proponent for a private office will usually seek to justify his views upon three considerations: (1) prestige, (2) suitable space for work requiring high concentration, and (3) proper accommodations for confidential work. Because of prestige considerations, most top management members are supplied with private offices.

This helps add weight, influence, and respect to this group in the eyes of other employees and of visitors to the office. Aside from top managers, there are other members of the office who, for reasons of prestige, probably merit separate private offices. They include department heads and professional people. In many cases, however, the department head can perform the most effective supervision when located in the general area of his unit with additional individual space.

The second major consideration, to provide suitable space for work requiring high concentration, can usually be determined objectively. Creative work, such as writing advertising copy and preparing difficult reports, usually justifies a private office. Likewise, employees doing intricate analysis, original planning, close mental work, and work requiring exclusive attention with a minimum of distraction merit a private office.

The third important reason, proper accommodations for confidential work, is significant in work involving research, planning, control, and consolidating recapitulations of important statistics. Likewise, the conversations during personnel selection interviews are of a confidential sort, and it is best to conduct them in a private office. However, the importance of confidential work can be overemphasized by employees, and extreme care should be exercised in determining whether this consideration actually warrants a private office.

Objections to Private Offices. The relatively high cost is a paramount objection to private offices because, with them, space utilization is about 35–50 per cent that of the open-area arrangement. In addition, the buying, erecting, maintaining, and, in case of alteration, moving of partitions entail expenditures which cumulatively amount to quite sizable figures.

Another objection often made is that the use of private offices may tend to slow up the work by interfering with supervisory effectiveness. The closeness of the supervisor to the employees, his familiarity with problems as they arise, and his being at the heart of all happenings in his unit are the types of things that are usually lost when the supervisor is segregated by a private office. In order to see that an order is carried out properly, it is frequently best to be close at hand to give instructions, check performance, and provide encouragement.

Furthermore, private offices complicate the heating, ventilating, and lighting of these areas as well as of adjoining areas. Individual segments of space, set off from the large area, require special arrangements to supply these services, all of which mean additional materials and labor.

Moreover, the use of private offices may prevent other arrangements which work out equally well or better. Such arrangements include the use of dwarf partitions, railings, and modular furniture with partitions. These are discussed in the following paragraphs.

MOVABLE PARTITIONS

For segregating the private offices needed and dividing the office space as the approved layout requires, the use of movable partitions is winning increasing favor. Movable partitions are made from metal or wood and are easily erected, dismantled, and relocated. They are prefabricated and factory-finished. Wiring and outlets are laid in the baseboards and joints. A variety of styles, colors, and finishes are offered. Panels with recesses for bookcases, alcoves for drinking fountains, provisions for door openings, and with or without glass (crystal or obscure) in the top areas are among the many available kinds offered to fit requirements for every type of working space. Various heights, ranging from the railing to the ceiling, are available. Door units can be selected from either single or double models; they may be hinged, double-acting, or sliding. The partitions are soundproof, with insulating material in the center or core.

Partitions from about 36 inches to 84 inches in height are very popular. They afford privacy, yet do not interfere with ventilating and lighting as much as partitions extending from the floor to the ceiling. In many cases, a 36-inch partition is used to surround the work area of one person, thus affording many advantages of a private office at much less expense and trouble. However, movable partitions creating the effect of private offices have, in some instances in their initial usage, resulted in employees behind the partitions becoming loud and boisterous. In such cases, an educational job on how to use "partitioned offices" has corrected the situation.

For partitions higher than 36 inches, the use of clear or crystal glass for the upper portion of the partition is highly satisfactory. This design permits the occupant to look out and see what is going on—an important consideration for a supervisor's office; it also minimizes the obstruction to light, and the cost is reasonable. Sometimes, a frosted or obscure glass is preferred. Figure 18–5 shows an installation of movable office partitions.

Movable partitions afford great flexibility in office layout; they make it economically possible to fit the available space to new layouts whenever the need occurs. The panels can be used over and over again. Not only space flexibility but also space control and high material salvage are thus realized. Changes in layout can be made overnight or during a week end. In many instances, the cost of erecting movable partitions is only 15 per cent of that of immovable tile and plaster walls. Furthermore, the use of movable partitions eliminates objectionable inconveniences such as noise, commotion, debris, dirt, waiting for plaster and paint to dry, and, after partition installation, the cleaning of rugs, draperies, and furniture.

Railings are used, especially in banks, with outstanding success. The

Courtesy: General Fireproofing Co., Youngstown, Ohio

FIG. 18–5. Effective use of movable office partitions.

old layout idea of having executives in private offices concealed in the rear of the bank has given way to the modern plan, whereby executives are in the front, open portion of the bank area, with offices divided by low railings. This arrangement is of relatively low cost, minimizes the need for special lighting and heating facilities, makes a pleasing appearance, and is convenient for both the officers and the customers.

MODULAR EQUIPMENT

Modular equipment and its availability with partition panels was pointed out in Chapter 16.[4] Such units give a private office effect and satisfactorily meet many privacy and prestige requirements. Popular arrangements can be assembled from interlocking, interchangeable component units.

Modular-type arrangements save floor space and increase efficiency. Figure 18–6 illustrates a comparison between conventional desk units and modular units, with a saving of 22.4 per cent of floor area resulting from the use of the modular units. At the same time, the smaller space is more convenient and provides an adequate work area.

WARDROBE FACILITIES

Wardrobe facilities can be provided either by having separate rooms —locker or cloakrooms—or by placing wardrobe racks in the office areas. If the former plan is used, provision should include separate rooms for men and women. When racks are used, they can be located throughout the office areas. Units are available which provide storage for coats, hats,

---

[4] See Chapter 16, page 312.

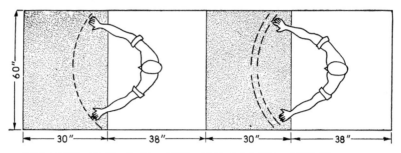

DESK AREAS = 3,600 SQ. IN.   TOTAL AREA OCCUPIED = 8,160 SQ. IN.

CONVENTIONAL DESK UNITS

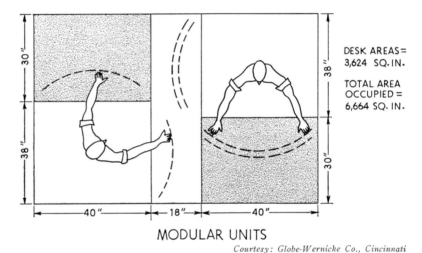

DESK AREAS =
3,624 SQ. IN.

TOTAL AREA
OCCUPIED =
6,664 SQ. IN.

MODULAR UNITS

Courtesy: Globe-Wernicke Co., Cincinnati

FIG. 18–6. A comparison of conventional desk units with modular units shows that, for the same number of employees and approximately the same desk areas, the modular units save nearly 23 per cent of floor space (8,160 square inches compared with 6,664 square inches).

overshoes, umbrellas, and the like for as many as three persons per square foot of floor area.

REVIEW OF CREATED LAYOUT

After finishing the office layout, it is helpful to review the work and make certain that proper provisions for specific key considerations are being supplied in the recommended layout. Asking these questions helps to confirm the thoroughness and completeness of the space planning.

1. Will the work travel mainly in a straight line, without backtracking, congestion, or "backups"?

2. Are aisles adequate and properly located?

3. Will the employees receive the work with minimum effort at proper times and in adequate amounts?

4. Is space used to maximum efficiency?
5. Are the proper equipment and machines at the proper places?
6. Are management members satisfied with the layout?
7. Will nonmanagement members be comfortable, and are they provided sufficient space?
8. Are there proper provisions for future space addition? Reduction?

In some cases, a real difficulty is the lack of a co-ordinator for office space planning. Some companies have such a co-ordinator, and it is his duty to gain the desired uniformity, interrelationships, and equitable space distribution. Viewing office layout solely as a part-time, intermittent task can give rise to serious problems. Another difficulty is a tendency of top management members to stay with an old, inefficient layout, thereby retarding progress and making needed layout changes very difficult. Alertness to new ideas, comparison of costs, and strong desires to improve space utilization must be stimulated in order to overcome this "keep the layout as it is" attitude. Also, in some instances, the mistake is made of not being alert to indicators of employee discomfort caused by physical facilities and evidenced by complaints, drop in work output, and increase in errors. Quite often, the solution is revising the layout, getting the physical units in proper repair, or updating the layout in keeping with current demands.

QUESTIONS

1. What meaning do you give the term "integrated space planning"? Of what importance is it in office layout? Justify your answer.
2. Discuss the relationships between office layout and work flow.
3. Name eight layout guides that you feel are of major importance.
4. What are some office space standards that you would use in making an office layout?
5. What are your ideas concerning the use of private offices in a modern office layout? Substantiate your viewpoint.
6. In your opinion, should an office supervisor be located at the front, rear, or center of his or her work group? Should he or she be facing in the same direction as, or in an opposite direction from, the work group? Give reasons for your answers.
7. Comment on the following statement: "Money spent in redecorating and refurnishing a reception room can be better spent in fixing up the office proper. The reception room has little, if any, relationship to the efficiency with which the paper work of an office is accomplished."
8. In your opinion, should office space planning be considered a continuous activity? Why?
9. Explain Figure 18–6 in your own words.
10. Describe the layout of an office with which you are familiar, and point out several ways in which you feel it might be improved. Give reasons for your suggested changes.
11. Approximately how much office space would you allot to each of the following?

    a) Two desks end for end (60 × 34-inch desk), aisle adjacent, chair for each desk.

    b) Private office for top executive.

    c) General office space for eight clerks.

    d) A conference room for ten persons.

12. Select a local business concern which employs about 20 to 30 office workers. Visit this office and make a rough sketch of the present office layout, indicating the approximate dimensions and location of equipment and furniture. Be sure to note the location of such things as electric light outlets, windows, radiators, running water, and doors (also whether they swing in or out, or both).

    Take these data home and make a scale drawing, using a scale of $\frac{1}{2}'' = 1'$. Clearly identify all parts of the drawing.

    Carefully study this layout; and using the principles of office layout as a guide, note the places where you believe the present layout can be improved. Give reasons for your opinions.

    Now, prepare a revised layout and support it with a brief discussion, pointing out the effective features incorporated in your improved layout.

CASE PROBLEMS

Case 18–1. Hanover Company

To provide needed warehouse space and locate the production control department near the center of its major operations, it has been decided to make certain layout changes. Production control has a manager, an assistant manager, and eight clerks. Currently, they share an office area with the traffic department, which employs thirty-two persons, including four managers. The present arrangement is illustrated by the drawing on page 359.

Production control is located in the area shown by the upper part of the drawing. Two of the available private offices are vacant. All production control will be moved to another floor of the building. The traffic department, now located within the lower three fourths of the illustrated area, will be moved and consolidated within the upper portion of the illustrated area, specifically the top 80 feet, making an over-all area of 50 feet wide and 80 feet long. The traffic department is growing; and if possible, adequate space for four managers and forty clerks should be provided. The remaining or lower space, namely, 50 feet wide by 30 feet long, will be taken over for needed warehousing purposes.

Problems:

1. Prepare your recommended office layout for the traffic department. A scale of one-quarter inch equals one foot is very satisfactory.

2. Point out the desirable features of your proposed layout.

3. Do you believe that your proposed layout will be better for the traffic department than that which they are now using? Substantiate your answer.

Case 18–2. Universal Cork Company

Representatives of this company just signed a ten-year lease for office building space as shown in the drawing on page 360. The area will be used as the district sales office. To meet the company's requirement, an effective arrangement for the following minimum equipment within this space is needed:

Three salesmen's desks, 60" x 32", and chairs
Two stenographers' desks, 60" x 32", and chairs

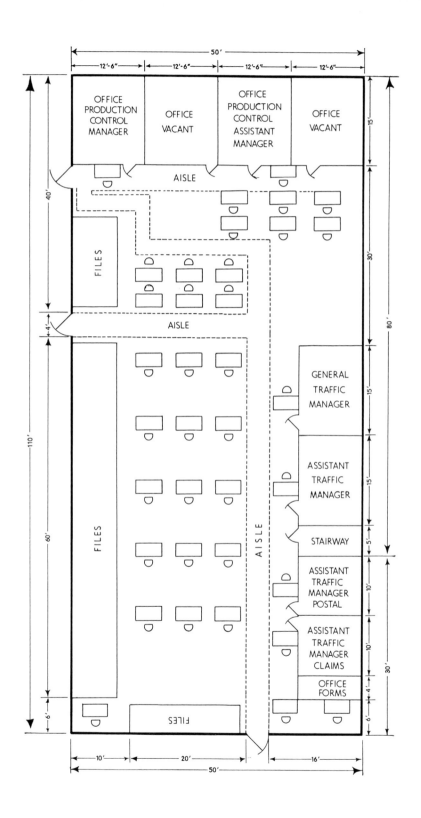

Two bookkeepers' desks, 60″ x 32″, and chairs
One 60″ x 32″ table
One 72″ x 38″ drafting table and stool
One 44″ x 23″ blueprint rack
One 36″ x 18″ telephone switchboard and chair, to be located as shown on drawing
Three five-drawer filing cabinets
One private office for district manager
One reception room or area

Problems:

1. Draw your recommended office layout for the company.
2. Justify your recommendations.

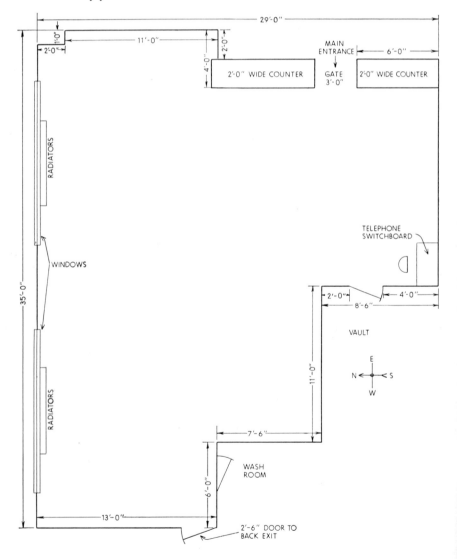

Chapter 19

PLANNING FOR OFFICE PHYSICAL ENVIRONMENT

He who would distinguish the true from the false must have an adequate idea of what is true and false.
—BENEDICT SPINOZA

THE OFFICE equipment and machines used and the layout followed affect the general office physical environment, but of even greater influence are the physical working conditions under which the work must be done. These working conditions should be pleasant, comfortable, and conducive to good work habits. Providing them properly requires planning.

Among the major factors of physical working conditions in most offices are (1) light, (2) color, (3) music, (4) air, and (5) sound. As previously stated, planning for physical environment cannot be considered independently of the other major areas of office planning. They must all be carefully co-ordinated. For example, office layout should be tied in with lighting, and the use of machines with noise control. Furthermore, light is dependent somewhat upon the color scheme employed in the area, and sound conditioning of an office influences the effectiveness of music. The benefits of proper air conditioning may be reduced considerably by lack of sufficient light in the area.

THE SEEING SYSTEM IN THE OFFICE

Adequate light is perhaps the most important consideration in office physical facilities. Many office tasks are of an exacting and close nature. Small print, carbon copies of typed material, and poorly handwritten notes are among the regular hard-to-see materials that must be handled. The successful execution of this paper work requires good light.

A balanced integration of lighting and surroundings in an office creates a visual climate which assists employees to see rapidly, easily, and comfortably. Figure 19–1 shows the advantages of proper lighting-seeing conditions.

Without light, there can be no sight; and for light itself to be seen,

361

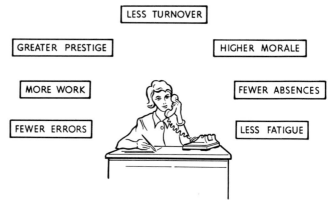

FIG. 19–1.　A well-balanced co-ordination of lighting and surroundings provides many advantages.

it must be *associated with surfaces*. Light and surfaces are closely linked. This means that the entire working environment must be taken into account when considering lighting questions because the surfaces affect the light which, in turn, regulates the ability to see. For an object to be seen, it must stand out from all other things around it. That is, contrast is necessary. The subject of contrast and light is discussed under "Quality of Light" later in this chapter.

It is universally agreed that the smaller the object, the more difficult it is to see. Visual perception of size depends not only upon the dimensions of the object but also upon the distance of the object from the eyes. Hence, the ability to see can be improved by increasing the size of the object, for example, by enlarging the type size of printed material and by adjusting the distance of the eye from the object. Adjustments, from the practical office viewpoint, can only be made within a limited range.

A great deal of physical and nervous energy is required to see. Certain eye muscles can relax only when viewing distances of about 10 feet and over. To read material under normal working conditions of an office requires the eyes to converge and to focus for the near distance. The eyes must also adjust for the brightness of the light; this is accomplished by the contraction and expansion of the pupils of the eyes. With age, the pupil of the eye becomes smaller, necessitating a greater amount of light. On the average, an employee 55 years old requires nearly twice as much light as an employee 25 years old to attain the same visibility.

QUANTITY OF LIGHT

In order to determine the proper amount of light for any given case and to make reasonable comparisons, a measurement of light is necessary. One such measurement is a *foot-candle*, which technically *is the amount of direct light one foot distant from a standard candle*. A rule of thumb for rough estimating is that, for small rooms, one watt per square foot of area provides 15 foot-candles. Thus, a 100-watt bulb in a room 10 feet × 10 feet will provide approximately 15 foot-candles of

RECOMMENDED VALUES OF ILLUMINATION FOR OFFICE WORK

	Foot-Candles Recommended at Working Height
DIFFICULT SEEING TASKS..75	

Involving:
    a) Discrimination of fine detail, such as 6–8-point type
    b) Poor contrast
    c) Long periods of time
Such as:
    Auditing and accounting
    Business machine operation
    Transcribing and tabulation
    Bookkeeping
    Drafting
    Designing

ORDINARY SEEING TASKS..45

Involving:
    a) Discrimination of moderately fine detail, such as 8–12-point type
    b) Better-than-average contrast
    c) Intermittent periods of time
Such as:
    General office work (except for work coming under "Difficult Seeing
       Tasks," above)
    Private office work
    General correspondence
    Conference rooms
    Active file rooms
    Mail rooms

CASUAL SEEING TASKS..30
Such as:
    Inactive file rooms
    Reception rooms
    Stairways
    Washrooms and other service areas

SIMPLE SEEING TASKS..10
Such as:
    Hallways and corridors
    Passageways

Source: Illuminating Engineering Society, "Recommended Practices of Office Lighting" (New York, March, 1960), p. 11.

FIG. 19–2.

light. The amount of light also depends upon the distribution of the light sources; for example, that provided by a single 100-watt bulb will differ from that supplied by four 25-watt bulbs, because of the difference in the light dispersion over the area.[1]

Figure 19–2 shows the recommended values of illumination for

---

[1] The subject of light dispersion is discussed on pages 365–66.

office work. To illustrate, for ordinary seeing tasks, a quantity of 30 foot-candles is recommended. These values are guides; some variation from them is possible according to individual conditions.

QUALITY OF LIGHT

Quality of light is as important as quantity of light in a proper seeing system. Under quality of light are such considerations as brightness, diffusion, and glare. These qualities are related; they are not independent of each other. Brightness is a quality determined by the amount of light reflected from an object. The effective light for seeing is the reflected light, not the light from the source. If the object to be seen reflects very little of the light cast upon it, the object is relatively difficult

FIG. 19–3.   Light concentrated on a small work area is an enemy of good seeing.

to see and in this case possesses a low reflectance value. The ratio of the light a surface reflects, divided by the amount of light it receives, is the reflectance value of that surface. For example, a smooth finish in white has a reflectance value of about 0.90, or 90 per cent; in medium yellow, 0.65; and in dark green, 0.07.

Brightness is also important because of its contrast, which affects seeing. The human eye sees best when all areas within the field of vision, such as a desk and its immediate surroundings, are approximately of the same brightness. An undesirable situation is that in which the area is much brighter than the desk. Consider the condition illustrated in Figure 19–3. The light is concentrated on the desk area, and the surroundings are dark. Under these conditions, the pupils of the eyes are continually expanding or contracting in their adjustment to the bright and dark areas. This makes for eye fatigue and difficulty in concentrating on the work.

For the visual area, which is generally described as about 30 degrees in all directions from the eye, there are certain current guides for brightness contrast. One such guide is that the ratio of the brightness of the light source itself to its background should also not exceed 3 to 1. The design of the fixture and its arrangement influence this ratio. From a practical viewpoint, too great a brightness contrast can cause glare, which comes either from the source of light or from smooth, highly polished surfaces. This means that a lighting plan should include not only the proper type of fixtures but also the light-reflecting characteris-

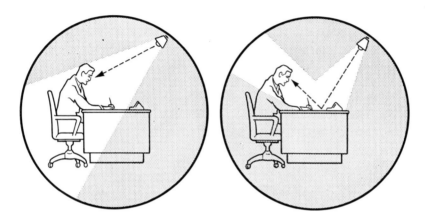

FIG. 19–4. Glare prevents office employees from working effectively.

tics of all surfaces within the office area. In some instances, the correct amount of brightness contrast is obtained by having several sources of light, not just one. See Figure 19–4.

Greatest visibility is usually reached when there is a maximum color contrast between writing and its background. It is difficult to read when there is little contrast between the paper and the printing, for example, white on white, white on cream, or black on black. On the other hand, white chalk marks on a blackboard or black print on white paper affords a high contrast and helps the seeing process.

Because of color contrast, it is usually recommended that the ceiling of an office be of a very light color with a reflectance value of around 0.80. Walls should be of a material and color having about 0.50 as a reflectance value. The floor should have a reflectance value of at least 0.25, since it is the background against which much work is seen.

Diffusion of light is also important, in order that an object in any spatial position may be seen clearly and easily. The quality of light should not be absolutely uniform. Some shadow effect is normal to the eye; but harsh, strong, contrasting shadows are annoying and should be avoided. Well-diffused light is sometimes referred to as a "soft" light. Proper diffusion of light is obtained by having light in different amounts come from an adequate number of sources and directions.

SOURCES OF LIGHT

Sources of office lighting include natural, fluorescent, and filament bulb. Natural light is probably the best source, but it varies throughout the day and from day to day. Usually, other sources of light must be used to maintain the required amount of light. Natural light has certain beneficial psychological effects. An employee usually feels better and has a sense of less confinement when he can look out occasionally and see daylight, observe the weather, and the like. It is advisable to have natural light visible even in cases where it is a very minor light source.

Fluorescent light enjoys wide acceptance in offices. Practically all new offices and most of those remodeled are using this type of light source. Fluorescent light is closer than any other artificial light to the color of natural light, and it provides large amounts of illumination at relatively low operating costs. To illustrate, the light output of a 40-watt fluorescent tube is nearly twice that of a 40-watt filament bulb. Also, the surface area of a 48-inch-long fluorescent tube is roughly ten times that of the filament type; this characteristic helps to distribute the light more uniformly.

Filament-bulb light is still an important source of artificial lighting. Improvements in filament-bulb shape, type of glass, and length of life have been achieved. However, the filament bulb has certain objectionable characteristics, including the yellowish color of its light that looks different from the color of natural light, the large number of bulbs that are necessary to supply a sufficient amount of light under today's office-lighting requirements, and the heat generated from these masses of bulbs.

Sources of light can also be classified as either (1) general lighting or (2) supplementary lighting. In the former, the entire area is lighted to a prescribed level of illumination. The source is usually a number of fixtures in or suspended from the ceiling. The second, or supplementary lighting, consists of illuminating a relatively small area, like a desk top or a portion of an office machine. Supplementary lighting can be used advantageously not only to provide the desired *décor*, as in private offices, or from lamps on tables and desks, pulldown lamps, and lighting effects in reception rooms and hallways, but also for increasing the illumination when the office work is in a fixed position or where the area involved is relatively small.

The central working areas of desks and most office machines meet these conditions. The light intensity on a desk top from a one-tube fluorescent desk light is 35-foot-candles at a distance of 24 inches from the lamp—the area in which difficult seeing tasks are performed. Such a lamp supplies an effective auxiliary lighting source when used in conjunction with a suitable lighting system to illuminate the surrounding area in order to supply the proper quality of light, as discussed above. Normally, local lighting should never exceed five times the light intensity of the general surrounding illumination.

BASIC DESIGNS OF LIGHTING SYSTEMS

Whether the fluorescent or filament-bulb type of lighting is used, the four basic designs of lighting systems include (1) direct, (2) semidirect, (3) indirect, and (4) semi-indirect. Under direct, light from the luminaire is permitted to travel directly to the working surface. This gives a "hard" type of light, and diffusion is not too good. Glare may be high, shadows are sharp, and the ceiling is usually dark. Generally, it is the least preferred type.

The design of semidirect lighting allows some of the light from the luminaire to travel upward to the ceiling, whence it is reflected downward to the working area. Most of the light, however, travels downward directly to the working area. A semidirect system illuminates the ceiling and lessens the effect of deep shadows.

In the case of indirect lighting, the light travels upward to the ceiling, where it is reflected downward to the working area. This provides a light which is "soft" and relatively free of sharp shadows. Actually, the ceiling is the source of light to the work area; therefore, it should have a high reflection value. But since the employee cannot completely ignore the ceiling, the possibilities of glare and too intense ceiling brightness must be taken into account.

With semi-indirect lighting, most of the light travels upward to the ceiling and then down to the work area, but some of the light is allowed to travel directly downward. As with indirect lighting, the ceiling is, in effect, the main source of light. The direct light helps increase the amount of light on the work area, but consideration must be given to its possible contribution of objectionable shadows and glare.

ARRANGEMENT OF FIXTURES

Generally speaking, with fluorescent lighting, it is more comfortable to view the fixtures *crosswise*, not lengthwise. Especially is this true in a large office. In a small office, this consideration is relatively unimportant. However, there is one important exception—the use of luminous-sided fixtures with glass or plastic sides. These units should be viewed lengthwise for greatest comfort, regardless of the area size.

Some uniformity or symmetry of the lighting fixtures is usually desirable for better general appearance. The arrangement should bring out the architectural and decorative features that assist in producing a cheerful working environment. Long rows of fixtures may be interrupted or designed with an occasional break, but the foremost considerations are proper lighting without serious glare; the impression of co-ordinated lighting—not a group of individual lights; and cost of installing and of maintaining. Fixtures can be suspended from the ceiling or recessed in it. The design of having the ceiling completely luminous is gaining favor. For this purpose, "floating-panel luminaires" can be used. They

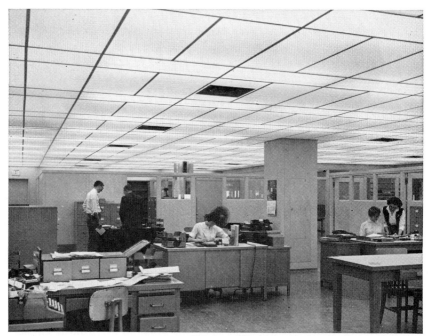

Courtesy: Illuminating Engineering Society, New York

FIG. 19–5. An office with ceiling completely luminous can supply excellent light.

are economical, easy to install, and create a pleasant atmosphere. Pre-assembled by the manufacturer in a variety of convenient sizes, an excellent quantity and quality of light are provided. Since the panel floats free of the wall, no cutting or fitting of materials to the room perimeter is required. Figure 19–5 shows a seeing system of this design.

OFFICE LIGHTING AS AN INVESTMENT

Expenditures for improved lighting represent a sound investment. A well co-ordinated seeing system represents about 2 per cent of total operating costs of a large office, compared with 0.5 per cent normally spent for obsolete, inadequate lighting. This increase of 1½ per cent is minute when related to all the comfort, greater accuracy, and psychological advantages of proper office lighting. And it is even more so when compared with office productivity. Many studies show 15 per cent increases in productivity from providing an adequate quantity and quality of light. The gain varies with the individual situations. In a two-year test made in the office of the Bureau of Internal Revenue in Washington, D.C., it was found that supplying adequate light and introducing light-colored finishes for balanced brightness resulted in an increased productivity of 5.5 per cent. The work consisted of card punching. The increase in productivity amounted to about $12,000 annually, whereas only $6,500 had been spent in improving working conditions. The dollar investment paid for itself in about six months, not to mention the returns in better employee morale, reduction in absenteeism, and more accurate work.

SELECTION OF SEEING SYSTEM

To assist in determining the best seeing system for a given office, the following provocative questions can be used.

1. Are adequate quantities of light being supplied?
2. Are the quality characteristics of the light suitable—brightness and contrast satisfactory, no glare, and absence of dark shadows?
3. Does the lighting enhance the equipment, machines, walls, and floor, contributing to an uplifting work environment?
4. Is the appearance of the seeing system pleasing both lighted and unlighted?
5. Is the construction of the luminaires sturdy and of good wearing qualities?
6. Can the lighting facilities be cleaned conveniently and inexpensively?
7. Is the usable illumination provided per light unit efficient?
8. Is the seeing system flexible in that the quantity of light can be increased if office changes so require, or can wall partitions be relocated without costly relocation of luminaires?

To elaborate on one point, maintenance has a significant influence upon the adequacy of office lighting. Needed are periodic cleaning of the luminaires, proper wattage of bulbs, and correct voltage. In one study involving eight locations, the foot-candle output was raised from an average of 11.8 to 46.2 foot-candles, or an increase of over 350 per cent, by cleaning the dirty fixtures, using color of high reflecting value for the walls and keeping them clean, replacing aging bulbs, and supplying the correct voltage.

COLOR CONDITIONING IN THE OFFICE

Color not only beautifies an office but also improves conditions under which office work is performed. The gains from proper use of color are, therefore, not only aesthetic and psychological, but economic as well. Color cannot be used indiscriminately. This is especially true in the office, where the aim is a dignified yet cheerful and comfortable atmosphere. The intelligent use of color requires constant attention and an understanding of color harmony and compensation.

PSYCHOLOGICAL EFFECT OF COLOR

A full comprehension of the psychological effect of color on human beings must await the more complete assessment of color science and color philosophy. There are unknowns in the use of color, but it is well established that color affects the human emotions, senses, and thought processes. For example, color usually has an important influence upon one's blood pressure and disposition to relax. A certain color will impress the minds of some individuals with a particularly favorable feeling or thought; another color will have the opposite effect. Some colors give a lift; others impart a depressed feeling. Some tend to hasten mental action, others to retard it.

Colors in the range of yellow, orange, and red are regarded as "warm" colors; they usually have the psychological effect of encouraging warmth and cheer. In contrast, cool colors, including blue, violet, and dark green, generally produce a subduing effect of restraint and calmness. Tints such as buff, beige, and ivory are moderately stimulating, while pale violets and blues are depressing.

SELECTION OF COLORS

Colors should be selected very carefully for an office. Warm colors should be used to counteract the effect of a drab, cheerless area. Color seems to change the temperature, in that a room with blue walls, for example, feels cooler; this is actually the result of a mental process stimulated by the blue color, which appears to reduce the sensitivity to heat.[2]

For example, during August, the walls of a New England office were painted blue. The following winter, the employees complained of the office being cold, even though the normal temperature of 70 degrees was maintained. Then, the temperature was raised to 75 degrees, but complaints still continued. The blue walls were then redecorated to warm yellow and green. The temperature continued at 75 degrees.

---

[2] Robert C. Daly, "The Power of Color," *Buildings* (Cedar Rapids, Iowa: Stamats Publishing Co.), November, 1951, p. 28.

Now, the employees protested that the office was too warm. A return to the temperature of 70 degrees resulted in the ceasing of the complaints.

The general color scheme of an office can follow one of many arrangements, depending upon individual preferences. An office of all one color sameness should be avoided. If the one color is a light color, it will create an area which is too somber, tending to induce relaxation. Under such conditions, a person is not mentally alert. On the other hand, if all the color or too much of an area is of a strong or brilliant color, the result is excessive stimulation and discomfort—likewise nonconducive to sustained office work output. A proper color balance is needed. Usually, this means the use of a few colors correctly, not a variety haphazardly.

The current trend is toward the monochromatic, which describes the

When Desk Is—	Use Carpet of—	Use Walls of—	Use Draperies of—	Use Chair, also Pictures, Desk Accessories, and Lamps of—
Gray	Gray	White	Gray	Red
Gray	Rust brown	Light gray	Rust	Yellow
Walnut or mahogany	Green	Beige	Chartreuse	Dark yellow
Walnut or mahogany	Beige	Light blue	Light blue	Dark yellow
Bleached or blond finish	Light brown	Beige	Beige	Orange
Bleached or blond finish	Charcoal	Gray	Yellow	Coral

FIG. 19–6. Suggested color guide for an integrated color pattern.

use of various shades of one color for floors, walls, and draperies, together with one bright accent color. As a beginning point, the desk is selected in a particular color. With this basic color determined, the floor covering is selected to harmonize correctly with the desk. Then, lighter shades of the floor covering can be used for walls and draperies. The accent color can be in the chair or accessories such as pictures, desk pieces, and lamps. Figure 19–6 shows a suggested color guide to obtain a co-ordinated color pattern in an office.

The use of the monochromatic does not mean that insipid, spiritless colors are employed. Quite the contrary is true. A stimulating office environment can be created by a variation of warm and cool colors, but in totality of a proper blend. Unless unusual features characterize certain office areas or the manager has strong preferences concerning color, it is usually best to follow basic recommendations regarding colors in the office. These are presented in outline form in Figure 19–7.

Area	*Colors Suggested*
General office	Ceiling in white, walls faced by employees in soft, cool colors—one or more of the other walls may be in a warm color like light yellow. Wall colors should harmonize.
Conference room	Light and neutral colors are preferable, but some carefully utilized strong colors are usually necessary to stimulate occupants.
Reception room	Neutral colors are usually best. Avoid sharp contrasts. Limited and careful use of vivid colors is in order.
Corridors	Light colors are usually needed because of lack of daylight.

FIG. 19–7.

PRIMARY, SECONDARY, AND COMPLEMENTARY COLORS

The primary colors are red, yellow, and blue; and they can be located on a color wheel at equally spaced distances. Secondary colors are obtained by mixing adjacent colors on the wheel. For example, red and yellow give orange. (See Figure 19–8.)

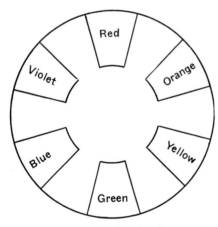

FIG. 19–8. Sketch of color wheel, showing relationship of primary colors— red, yellow, and blue. Secondary colors are made by mixing adjacent colors named on the wheel. A combination of all the colors shown produces a neutral gray.

Complementary colors are those directly opposite each other on the wheel. Green, for example, is the complement of red; blue, of orange. When used with discretion, complementary colors tend to enrich each other and afford contrast without a color clash.

Color experts usually employ considerable quantities of the grayer shades, i.e., colors toward the center of the color wheel. These are subdued, and their use minimizes the possibility of color violence. The brilliant colors are used here and there to give accent and distinction.

Pleasant and harmonious color effects are obtained by securing a balance among the colors used. Three ways in which this can be done are as follows:

Harmonious Color Effects	*Description (Refer to Color Wheel, Figure 19–8)*
1. Complementary colors	Red and green, the colors directly opposite each other.
2. Split complementary colors—actually a triad, two colors adjacent to the direct complement of the third color	Green-blue and green-yellow, the two colors adjacent to green, the direct complement of red.
3. Triads—three colors equidistant from each other	Red, yellow, and blue.

COLOR AND LIGHTING

As mentioned earlier in this chapter, color has a significant influence upon the lighting of an office. Light colors increase the utilization of light; dark colors decrease the lighting intensity. This is because light colors reflect the light rays, whereas dark colors absorb the light rays. For these reasons, any normally dark area will lighten up when lighter colors are used for the ceiling, walls, and floors.

Natural lighting varies slightly in color. Light predominantly from one particular direction usually has a characteristic tinge; to compensate for this condition, the use of complementary colors is usually recommended. This is illustrated below:

When Predominant Natural Light Source Is—	*Light Is Slightly Colored by—*	*Recommend Use of—*
Northern light	Bluish tinge	Warm color
Eastern light	Neutral	Neutral color
Southern light	Yellowish tinge	Cool color
Western light	Reddish tinge	Cool color

Furthermore, the use of color influences the apparent proportions of an area. This is due to the reflecting and the contracting light effect brought about by the different colors. Dark colors seem to advance an area, light colors to retreat it. Hence, the dimensional effect of a long narrow room can tend to be equalized by the use of a dark color on the end walls and a lighter shade of the same color, or of a harmonizing hue, on the other walls. Similarly, the proportions of a square area can be made to appear elongated.

MUSIC CONDITIONING

Music serves as an environmental work aid because it uses the physiological and psychological power of sound in musical form to produce an improved behavior pattern. "Music while you work" programs are designed to improve working conditions, relieve mental and visual fatigue, reduce nervous tension, and make the employees feel better.

Results of numerous tests, involving thousands of office employees, in offices where music conditioning is present point conclusively to extremely favorable benefits being obtained by both the employers and the employees. To illustrate, increased productivity of from 6 per cent to 21 per cent, depending on the type of work, improved employee morale, and a decrease in absenteeism and nonessential employee conversations are among the important employers' advantages reported.[3] The effect of music upon key-punch productivity in a large public utility office is shown in Figure 19–9.

In a survey of over 35,000 employees questioned, 90 per cent stated they liked music while they worked; an equal number credited music with making their work more enjoyable; and nearly 85 per cent said it helped to break the monotony of their work.[4] The types of office work showing the maximum benefits include filing, mail-room, typing, reception, key-punching, and verifying.

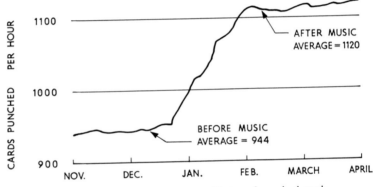

FIG. 19–9. Effect of music on production of punched cards.

The music is functionally controlled, which means that it is specifically arranged, orchestrated, and recorded to accomplish a specific goal. Distracting and attention-getting music, such as heavy brass effects and solos, is excluded. The music is stimulating and designed to create a favorable and pleasing mood. Neither directly nor consciously does the employee listen to the music, just as he does not minutely examine colorful wall designs that help create a pleasant working environment.

Programs are tailored to fit the music to the specific office work as well as to the temperament of the employees. That is to say, programs utilize different types of music and take into account the "standard energy curve" of employees. For example, maximum low ebbs of energy usually occur at 10:30 A.M. and 3:30 P.M. Around these times, music of maximum stimulus is applied. In contrast, music during the first part of the morning consists of a bright opener followed by moderately bright

---

[3] "Will Work Music Really Cut Your Labor Costs?" *Business Management* (Greenwich, Conn.: Management Publishing Group), July, 1959, p. 41.

[4] *An Answer to Worker Tension* (a booklet published by the Muzak Corporation, New York, 1960).

music, such as several waltzes. Light classics and slower swing tunes are usually predominant in programs for office employees. A definite schedule is followed—the music is played for specific intervals only, because best results are usually obtained from this type of pattern.

The music is either "piped" or transmitted from a central sending studio to the subscribing office, or an entirely self-contained unit for providing the music is installed in the office. The expense is nominal, especially in view of the results achieved. The cost approximates $1.00 per day for a small office and 10 cents per month per employee for a large office. The self-contained unit can be obtained on either a purchase or a rental basis. The inexpensive addition of a microphone to the subscriber's equipment automatically converts the installation to a public-address system. Thus, managerial messages can be conveyed to all or part of the premises.

AIR CONDITIONING

Air conditioning regulates atmospheric conditions by controlling the four basic elements of temperature, circulation, moisture content, and cleanliness. It is possible to control only three, or two, or, in fact, just one of these elements; but such control is more correctly referred to as partial rather than complete air conditioning. In addition to aiding human health and comfort, air conditioning offers economic advantages. Higher productivity and decreases in cleaning and decorating costs are prominent. Reports of productivity gains due to air conditioning are quite common. In one study, office employee efficiency showed a 20 per cent gain after air conditioning was installed.[5]

Air conditioning can be supplied from a central unit or from an individual unit. Varying sizes and capacities are available. Individual units for a small group of offices or for part of a floor area have grown in popularity. Some are designed for a single room and are portable. The cost of air conditioning has been greatly reduced. A well-engineered individual unit is now available for as low as several hundred dollars.

TEMPERATURE AND VENTILATION

The temperature in many offices is too high. This leads to drowsiness and tends to retard the execution of office work. Regulators should be installed on the heating apparatus so that excessive temperatures are not reached. It is well to become "thermometer-conscious" and to keep the office temperature within reasonable limits. The recommended office temperature is about 70 degrees F.[6]

---

[5] Norris Wells, "Is Investment in Air Conditioning Sure to Pay Off?" *American Business* (Chicago: Dartnell Publications, Inc.), April, 1954, p. 31.

[6] If air conditioning is used, the recommended temperature range is from 68 to 82 degrees Fahrenheit, depending upon the outside temperature. Too great a differential between outside and air-conditioned areas is undesirable.

Ventilation or the movement of air is also important. Lack of proper ventilation can make a person feel sleepy and unduly tired. At 70 degrees Fahrenheit, an adult human body at rest gives off heat at the rate of about 5 b.t.u. sensible heat per minute, an amount about equal to the heat given off by a 100-watt incandescent light bulb.[7] This heat must be carried off by the surrounding air; otherwise, the body becomes unduly heated, resulting in discomfort and lack of energy. The normal ventilation requirement is about 2,000 cubic feet of air per person per hour. Drafts should be avoided. Usually, the best practice is to have the air circulating from a number of outlets so that it is distributed evenly over the entire area. For nonair-conditioned areas, fans and window ventilators will help considerably in providing more adequate ventilation. Electric fans can be used. Window ventilators permit incoming fresh air without direct drafts blowing on any one person. Disagreeable odors can be eliminated by the use of specially designed electrical units and of deodorant air-cleaning products which are available in packaged bottle form. Furthermore, the practice of opening windows and airing the office for short, stated periods during midmorning, noon, and midafternoon will do much toward expelling stale air and freshening up the office.

HUMIDITY

The amount of moisture in the air definitely affects the comfort and efficiency of a human being. At the same temperature, moist air feels hot, and dry air feels cool. Excessive dampness may cause physical discomfort of a respiratory nature and induce a heavy, languid feeling. Likewise, excessive dryness or very low humidity frequently induces a feeling of parchedness and nervous irritability.

The term "relative humidity" is used to describe the intensity of moisture saturation in the air. A recommended relative humidity for an office is from 40 to 60 per cent. For example, when the relative humidity is 20 per cent, the office air is too dry; when the humidity is 70 per cent, the air is too moist.

SOUND CONDITIONING

A noisy office is seldom an efficient office. Noise is unpleasant, distracting, and costly. It makes for difficulty in concentrating, in using the telephone, and in turning out accurate office work. According to physicians, noise causes transient changes in blood and brain pressure, a quickening pulse rate, and indigestion. So-called "getting used to noise" is misleading. One may temporarily be unaware of its effects; but over a period of time, one becomes excessively fatigued and irritable as a result of noise.

---

[7] Herkimer, Herbert and Herkimer, Harold, *Air Conditioning* (New York: Chemical Publishing Co., Inc., 1947), p. 257.

TECHNICAL ASPECTS OF NOISE AND SOUND

Noise can be briefly described as discordant or unwanted sound. Noise has no definite pitch and quality; whereas in a musical tone, these properties are fairly well defined. Sound can be defined technically as "vibrational energy." The oscillation of these waves of energy, or sound waves, traveling through the air stimulates the auditory nerves; and this, in turn, results in a perception of the sensation and a consciousness of sound.

The characteristics of sound depend chiefly upon its (1) pitch—the frequency of the vibrations, (2) intensity—the energy of the vibrations, (3) quality—the mode or type of vibration, (4) reverberation—the sustaining qualities after the sound has stopped at its source, and (5) the

VALUE OF NOISE LEVELS EXPRESSED IN DECIBELS

Threshold of hearing	0
Noise in average home	32
Quiet office	37
Quiet radio in home	40
Noise in city (residential district)	45
Restaurant clatter	50
Noisy office	57
Stenographic room (large office)	70
Noisy factory	85
Boiler factory	97

Source: Americana Corporation, "Encyclopedia Americana,"
Vol. I (New York, 1955), p. 107.

FIG. 19–10.

expectancy and acceptance of the individual. From the practical viewpoint, loudness is probably of greatest concern. Loudness is primarily determined by both intensity and pitch, with emphasis on intensity. Actually, the phenomenon of increasing loudness follows a rather complex physical law. For this reason, and in order to have a relative measurement of the range of intensities which are handled in noise control, a unit of measurement called a "decibel" is used.

A decibel is approximately the smallest change in sound which it is possible for the human ear to detect. The decibel scale shows the relative values from the lowest to the highest human audible sound intensity. For convenience, the scale is measured logarithmically. The lowest value is zero, the beginning of human audibility, to approximately 110, which represents the sound of thunder. Figure 19–10 shows a table of sound identification and the corresponding decibel ratings.

MEANS OF CONTROLLING NOISE AND MANAGERIAL ADVANTAGES THEREFROM

In addition to the human comfort benefits, probably the greatest advantage derived from office noise control is increased productivity and, even more important, increased accuracy. In one study of noise control conducted in a large insurance office, the over-all production increased 8.8 per cent, typists' errors decreased 29 per cent, and machine operators' errors decreased 52 per cent.[8]

The means for controlling noise include the following:

1. *Reduce and, if possible, eliminate the source of noise.* Felt pads placed under typewriters and adding machines, and rubber cushions under various types of office equipment, will help considerably in noise reduction. Soundproofing cabinets which fit over the machine like a hood, with a front opening for the operator, can also be used. Adequate maintenance and proper lubrication of file drawers, doors, desks, and chairs contribute further to noise reduction. Appeals to employees can be made, stressing consideration for others and the importance of eliminating unnecessary conversations.

2. *Locate office in a quiet space.* The top floors of a building are usually less noisy, since they are further removed from street traffic. Relocation within the building, so that the office is not directly exposed or adjacent to objectionable noise sources, is another possibility. Finally, moving to a quiet area should be considered. Less congested areas are usually less noisy than highly congested areas.

3. *Segregate noise sources from the rest of the office.* A great deal can be accomplished by placing all noisy equipment in one place. A separate room to house the noisy office operations works out very well. If this is not feasible, concentrating the chief noise sources in one area is usually better than having them scattered all over the office.

4. *Use sound-absorbing materials for office floors, ceilings, and walls.* Sound travels in waves and is reflected from glazed or non-porous surfaces in the same way that light is reflected. Under these conditions, sound continues to travel in all directions and bounces back and forth until its energy is absorbed; then the sound dies out of its own accord. This condition usually makes for a noisy office.

When acoustic treatment or sound-absorbing material is used, the sound dies out faster. The same identical sounds exist as before, but they are not permitted to reflect repeatedly until dissipated naturally. Carpet eliminates virtually all floor noise such as that from walking or from pushing a chair across the floor, and it serves as an effective sound blotter absorbing most air-borne noises. Office noise is definitely reduced by means of carpeting. Also, drapes and curtains made of soft fabrics help to absorb sound.

Ceilings and walls can be covered with acoustic material which is available in many forms. One common and popular type is a fibrous,

---

[8] Celotex Corp., *Twenty-Five Answers to Questions on Sound Conditioning with Acousti Celotex* (rev. ed.; Chicago, February, 1954), p. 8.

mineral tile, about 12 × 12 inches in size and perforated. The tile is available in thicknesses ranging from ½ inch to 1¼ inch, and can be attached either by a special cement or by means of nails or screws. Another common variety is a mastic type of acoustic material which is spread on the surface and dries, leaving a porous surface. In some instances, a loose, fibrous material is used, along with a separate hard facing material that has numerous perforations.

QUESTIONS

1. Discuss the meaning and importance of brightness in supplying adequate office lighting.
2. Of what importance is the following statement to an office manager? "The effective light for seeing is the reflected light, not the light from the source."
3. Discuss the subject of "Sources of Light" for the office of today.
4. Of the five major factors of physical working conditions in an office, which one do you believe is most important? Justify your answer.
5. Are the major factors of physical working conditions discussed in this chapter interrelated? Explain.
6. What are some important considerations in the "seeing system" of an office?
7. At an office management meeting, Mr. Alexander Messinger, an office manager, tells you that his general office is quite noisy. What suggestions can you give Mr. Messinger to combat the office noise?
8. Discuss the psychological effect of color upon office employees.
9. An office manager heard many favorable comments concerning the adoption of "music while you work" in various offices. Believing this might be desirable in his own office, he arranged, through the office supervisors, to ask his entire office force if they would like to work to music. The response was overwhelmingly in favor of having music. Accordingly, the office manager purchased a wide selection of "long-play" records and two record-playing machines—one machine for each of the two main office areas. What benefits or difficulties do you feel might result from the office manager's action? Explain your answer.
10. Outline the important considerations to be taken into account in the arrangement of lighting fixtures.
11. What is the meaning of each of the following terms?
    a) Monochromatic colors in an office.
    b) Decibel.
    c) Color wheel.
    d) Relative humidity.
12. In your opinion, can the use of music conditioning be considered a sound investment by an office manager? Justify your answer.

CASE PROBLEMS

Case 19–1.   Consolidated Truck Terminal, Inc.

The general offices of Consolidated Truck Terminal, Inc., occupy the top floor of a three-story building which is about sixty years old and located in the older industrial section of a large midwestern city. The total area is approximately 100 feet wide by 250 feet long. The building faces north, and windows make up almost the entire walls on the west, south, and east sides, or on a 250-, a 100-, and a 250-foot side.

Natural lighting is usually sufficient for the two rows of desks by the windows on the west and east sides of the office. However, occupants of the inside four rows of desks must use artificial lighting at all times. Indirect filament-bulb lighting is used and, in the opinion of many of the office employees, does not give enough light for eye comfort. Even the outer rows of desks do not have ideal lighting conditions, as the direct sunlight comes in through the windows on the east and west sides.

The desks and chairs in the office are as old as the building itself. The desks for sorters, bookkeepers, calculating clerks, typists, other clerical help, and supervisors are all of the same type—double pedestal, made of wood. It is not uncommon for the employees to pick up slivers of wood in their legs or arms while working at these desks. The chairs are also old and wooden. They are swivel type, without armrests. The chairs have rollers; and as an employee works at his desk, the chair tends to roll away, that is, unless the wooden caster wheels are flat on one side. Many of the female employees have complained of getting snagged hosiery from either the chairs or the desks.

For ventilation, the windows are opened from the top and bottom with a board resting on the sill at an angle to deflect the direct breeze upward. This is usually all right for the occupants of the outer two rows of desks; but the four inner rows get all the breeze, which is fairly strong with a normal wind. Hot-water radiators are located along the walls at the base of the windows. In the winter, the men employees complain that the office is too warm and open the windows; then, the women complain that the office is too cold. Since the office is on the top floor, the heat from the roof in the summer is terrific; the office is not aired out at night.

The general manager agrees that the physical working conditions in the office are bad, but states that the corporation does not have the money "to fix up the whole office." However, repeated employee complaints about the working conditions led him to the decision to air-condition the office. In his opinion, this was the worst condition that should be corrected. As an alternative, he reasoned he could gradually fix up the office section by section, but concluded that this might give rise to even greater problems than he now has. Accordingly, the general office was air-conditioned.

The first day of the air-conditioning operation was a hot day in August. Many of the employees praised the new installation as a real contribution and some progress in providing a decent place in which to work. Quite a few employees, mainly female, complained about the office being too cold and of drafts from the air ducts. They said they could not stand the blasts of cold air.

Problems:

1. Evaluate the actions taken by the general manager.

2. Would you have made the same decision as the general manager? Justify your answer.

3. How would you handle the present complaints about the air conditioning?

Case 19–2.   The Gidney Company

Charles M. Kingman, assistant treasurer of the Gidney Company, is visiting the regional branch office of the company in Buffalo, New York. During his visit, he observed the physical working conditions of the general office area. In his opinion, a satisfactory amount of light is present in one corner of the area. This corner has window openings to the outside permitting daylight to enter. He estimated the lighting in the remaining area to average about 20 foot-candles at the most.

The current lighting fixtures are a filament-bulb, direct-lighting type. The luminaires are suspended from the ceiling by means of chains. Mr. Kingman estimates the floor-to-ceiling height as about 13 feet 6 inches, and the height of the luminaire from the floor as approximately 11 feet. The luminaires, spaced 8 feet center to center, are arranged in rows running the length of the office. There are about 8 feet between each of several rows of luminaires. Each luminaire is equipped with a 100-watt bulb.

Supplementary lighting in the form of desk lamps is used by some supervisors. Upon inquiry, Mr. Kingman found that the lamps were brought in by the employees and do not belong to the company.

The desks have a highly polished dark mahogany finish. The walls of the office area are painted a medium brown color up to a height of 4 feet from the floor; from this level to the ceiling, the walls are a medium gray, with the ceiling a grayish white color. The floor is dark green vinyl asbestos tile. Mr. Kingman was informed that it was installed about three years ago.

Problems:

1. What is the problem in this case?
2. Outline what you recommend to solve the problem.
3. Should Mr. Kingman take any specific action? Why?
4. Explain how you would gain the Gidney Company managers' agreement to act upon your recommendation as stated in question No. 2, above.

Chapter 20

OFFICE LOCATION AND BUILDING

The rung of a ladder was never meant to rest upon, but only to hold a man's foot long enough to enable him to put the other somewhat higher.

—Thomas Huxley

ONE MORE area subjected to office planning remains to be discussed. This area is office location and building. The various papers, people, equipment, machines, layout, and physical working conditions must be united within suitable housing. This means that the location for the office and the choice of building must be decided.

LOCATING THE OFFICE

Most offices are located in one of the following places: (1) in the factory building, (2) in a separate building adjacent to or near the factory building, or (3) in an office building far removed from any factory building. In the first two cases, the office location depends upon the factory location, which is usually determined with reference to factory needs only. However, in the third case, the office location can be determined in line with the particular needs of the individual office. For any of these three cases, the office space within the prescribed or selected building must also be determined. True, a choice of space within a given building is not always available, but study can be conducted to confirm the suitability of a given space or to select a space within selected building.

Normally, a number of factors should be considered, including (1) the characteristics of the building, (2) the building facilities, (3) the proximity of the office building to business factors, (4) the cost involved, (5) stability of tenants, (6) adaptability of space, (7) natural lighting and ventilation provided, and (8) freedom from dirt and noise. It should be noted that in the case of a new office building constructed specifically for a certain office, some of these factors may not apply. But the following information is useful for office planning purposes; the extent of its helpfulness depends upon the individual circumstances.

CHARACTERISTICS OF THE BUILDING

Under this heading are included the general appearance of the building, its size, reputation, age, available services, and technical factors. In considering these things, decisions are made whether the building is modern or old, whether the building name is in good repute, whether the name and address are easy to pronounce and remember, and whether the building is well advertised. The building services, including the elevator service, janitor service, and night protection, should also be considered.

An important technical factor is the allowable floor live load. At least 75 pounds per square foot are needed for office operations. A value of 100 pounds is desirable for complete versatility of layout. Also, the floor-to-ceiling heights must be taken into account. A minimum of 8 feet is usually recommended; however, for large open areas, 10–12 feet may be appropriate. Low ceilings create a feeling of congestion and make the office difficult to ventilate; high ceilings make lighting, noise-reducing, and heating efforts difficult. Furthermore, columnar spacing must be considered, for it affects office layout, especially the location of main partitions that are joined to columns. A spacing of 20 × 20 feet or more is acceptable; spans less than 18 feet are normally unsatisfactory for efficient office space. The need for moving partitions, adding offices, and accommodating new pieces of office equipment is best met by maintaining flexibility in the office layout. This flexibility is provided in most of the new office buildings which feature a constant dimension of approximately 5 feet, center to center of window sections, or alternating windows and piers.

THE BUILDING FACILITIES

The meaning of building facilities is sometimes not clearly understood. Normally, the term includes any device or feature incorporated in or attached to the building which assists in using the space with convenience and efficiency. In brief, a building facility must be fastened to the building, or installation is required to finish the building. Building facilities include a long list of items, among which are entranceways, elevators, stairways, electrical and telephone facilities and outlets, wiring arrangements, heating and ventilating ducts, air conditioning, hallways, columnar spacing, janitor closets, water accessibility, noise control features, means of fire protection, and other fixed facilities. To highlight the importance of building facilities, a brief discussion follows of telephone outlets, wiring needs, and cellular steel floors.

WORK SHEET FOR TELEPHONE SYSTEM

EXCH. _____

CENT. OFC. AND TEL. NO. _____

ATTACH TO ORDER _____

DESIGNATION →	A	B	C	D	E	COMMON EQUIPMENT This Col. for Plant
ROOM NO. →	PX 1234	PXEX 1234	PXEX 1234	PX 1235	PXEX 1235	
	PH LL BL	PH LL BL	PH LL BL	PH LL BL	L. STA	
PX 1234	PH LL BL	PH LL BL	PH LL BL	PH LL BL		
			C Z	C B		

~CODES~

L — LINE STATION OR CONTROLLED LINE STA.	H R — HEAD RECEIVER
B — BELL	L — LINE LAMP
C — CUT-OFF	B — BUSY LAMP
P — PICK-UP	PUSH BUTTON — BUZZER
P H — PICK UP AND HOLD	S — Z
E — EXCLUSION	

In case bell, buzzer or key is not included in station set, add "X" to the code.

FEATURES

PART OF SET	H P S C	E B Z	CX BX ZX	H P S C	E B Z	CX BX ZX	H P S C	E B Z	CX BX ZX	H P S C	E B Z	CX BX ZX	H P S C	E B Z	CX BX ZX
	HX PX SX			HX PX SX			HX PX SX			HX PX SX			HX PX SX		
NOT PART OF SET															

EQUIPMENT

TYPE SET ● HCK DL / ILL / HCK DL / HC DL

OTHER EQUIPMENT

SUBSCRIBER'S NAME / OTHER INFO. _____

SEE: _____

● Such as: Handset, Combined Hand

TELEPHONE REQUIREMENTS

SHEET	LOCATION	LINES	EXTENSIONS	HC	HCK			100 A				KEY				S	Z	INTER COM	LLBL
					2	4	6	3	6	9	12								
	12th floor	25	54		2	18	10					24				12	8	4	12
	13th floor	40	65		4	25	12					12	12			14	10	3	18

INSTRUMENTS / FEATURES

FIG. 20–1. Telephone work sheets used in space planning.

Courtesy: Illinois Bell Telephone Co., Chicago

Telephone Outlets. Modern office space planning should include an adequate number of properly located telephone outlets. This requirement for telephone service should be developed by space planners, equipment people, or telephone company personnel. Knowledge of the building facilities, and of the functional needs of the persons using the office, supplies the basic information. Figure 20–1 shows portions of work sheets to assist in determining telephone requirements and locations. Without this planning, it may subsequently be found that telephones have to be changed, outlets are incorrectly located, and unsightly conduits must be attached to the floors and ceilings.

Wiring Needs. Adequate wiring facilities are one of the big considerations in building facilities today. Separate runways are used for (1) low voltage, including telephone and communication systems, and (2) high voltage for normal electrical current as well as that of higher voltages. For electrical current, many office buildings are wired for about 2 watts per square foot of floor area; but with the increase in the amount of light and the power necessary to operate electric office units, this figure is no longer adequate. The current recommendation is about 6 watts per square foot. Wiring capacity is limited by the cross-sectional area of the conduit, and to increase wiring capacity requires either larger conduits or new-type conductors. The former is expensive, since most conduits are buried in concrete. One alternative is to attach a new, larger conduit on the surface. This is costly, but not so costly as making a new trough and recessing the conduit in concrete.

Recent developments have made possible a new type of wire with very thin but effective insulation. Its use permits greater copper capacity in the conduit; hence, in many instances, old wiring can be replaced with this new type and the present conduits employed. Usually, this is an economical practice.

As stated in Chapter 4, an electronic processing system requires disturbance-free electrical power; regulated temperature, dust, and humidity conditions; and adequate floor construction to support the various machines. To insure precise leveling of the units, a new floor in the computer area is frequently constructed over the old floor, with sufficient space in between the two, in some cases 6 inches, to permit adequate wiring channels.

Cellular Steel Floors. The modern need for quantities of electrical wires has given rise to the use of cellular steel floors. At the top left portion of Figure 20–2 is shown a series of galvanized steel cells spaced close together, providing continuous in-floor passageways throughout the entire floor area. Various cross-sectional areas and spacings of the cells are available. These steel cells serve as a subfloor over which the concrete is poured. However, before pouring concrete, steel header ducts are

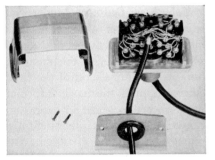

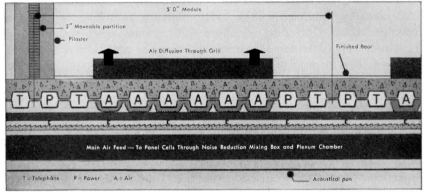

Courtesy: Inland Steel Co., Chicago

FIG. 20–2.   Top left: Close-up of cellular floor construction. Top right: Components of telephone outlet fitting. Bottom: Suggested arrangement for use of cellular floor for telephone, power, and air needs.

fastened directly on top of the steel cellular flooring and at right angles to the cells. Header ducts provide passageways from the main distribution points to the cells. Connections between header ducts and cells are made at access units, which are spaced as required. The illustration shows the removable top of the access unit featuring a simplified three-screw leveling design permitting exact adjustment to the finished floor level. Outlet fittings connect the cell to the desired point of use. In other words, the main feeder lines in the header ducts are connected to the desired distribution lines in the cells, from whence the proper distribution line is connected to an outlet. In the illustration, two outlet fittings are shown. Easily installed anywhere along the cell length, they are available in many designs to meet various functional requirements. For example, in the top right illustration of Figure 20–2 are shown the components of a compact aluminum outlet fitting for telephone service; it features three connecting blocks with a capacity of 15 pairs of telephone wires or 30 separate wires. Additional flexibility is made available by cellular steel floors in that, via conduit underneath the cells, additional wire connections between designated points can be utilized.

However, cellular steel floors provide raceways for purposes other than electrification. The dry, unobstructed underfloor ducts can be used for heating and air conditioning, as well as other uses. A gain in usable floor and window areas is among the outstanding advantages of the cellular steel floor design. The bottom illustration of Figure 20–2 suggests a combination of air, electrical, and telephone cells.

PROXIMITY OF OFFICE BUILDING TO BUSINESS FACTORS

When an office building location is to be selected, the following factors should be given careful consideration because office efficiency is greatly influenced by them.

Customers and Others in Same Business. The proximity of the building to those who are in almost daily contact with the office is a very important consideration. In the first place, closeness to customers is generally considered advantageous. This is especially true when personal interviews and associations are frequent. However, in those cases where most activities can be handled by telephone or by correspondence, the importance of proximity to customers is greatly diminished.

Second, closeness to others in the same line is usually considered sound business practice. This closeness of association encourages discussions of common problems among occupants, helps simplify the problems of the building manager, and adds to the convenience of customers and clients dealing with occupants of the building. There is, for example, a tendency for offices of financial houses, law firms, real estate firms, insurance agencies, and public utilities to locate in buildings in the financial district. On the other hand, offices of physicians, dentists, and advertising agencies are frequently found in the shopping districts. Also, in many cities, specialized buildings to accommodate particular types of business offices are available; for instance, motion-picture offices may be located in the Film Exchange Building, grain offices in the Grain Exchange Building, and physicians' offices in the Medical Building. It is interesting to observe, however, that with the exception of medical buildings, these specialized buildings become, in time, occupied by a good proportion of general tenants.

Transportation Facilities. In the selection of an office location, it is imperative to determine that the location is served by adequate transportation facilities. Convenient and low-cost means of getting to and from the building must be available not only to employees but also to outside representatives, visitors, and delivery and messenger men. Out-of-the-way places, necessitating transferring and long waits for busses, trains, or taxicabs, are a distinct disadvantage. As a result of incon-

venient transportation facilities, the enterprise might suffer unneces-
sarily—frequent association with others in the same business would be
limited, and the personnel problem of recruiting and maintaining employees would be greatly increased.

Shopping Centers, Restaurants, and Hotels. Convenience to shopping
centers might well contribute to the growth of the business. For example,
domestic financing enterprises have found it helpful to locate in or near
the shopping areas; medical doctors likewise find that shopping areas are
good locations. The availability of restaurants is another consideration.
Employees like to have a selection of handy eating places for noon
lunch, or for evening meals when overtime work is necessary. A lack of
eating places might necessitate the providing of a company cafeteria,
dining room, or place where employees can eat their lunches. Also, near-
ness to hotels is, in many cases, a distinct advantage in the location of
an office. In cases where many out-of-town representatives call at the
office, the advantage of close proximity to hotels is apparent.

Mail Facilities. The handling of incoming and outgoing mail is of
great importance in any office. Good mail facilities should always be
secured and given prime consideration in the selection of an office location. Frequent pickups and deliveries, with convenient accessibility to a
post office, can contribute very materially to operating efficiency.

THE COST INVOLVED

The cost of office space is of cardinal importance; however, it should
never be considered the sole basis for selection of the office location or
space, but it should always be considered along with the other location
factors discussed. The universal unit for expressing the cost of office
space is dollars per square foot of floor area per year. To illustrate, assume an office measures 30 × 40 feet and the rental is $5.00 per square
foot. The cost per year is:

$$30 \times 40 \times \$5.00 = \$6,000$$

or, on a monthly basis:

$$\frac{\$6,000}{12} = \$500.$$

The annual cost per square foot varies with many factors, such as the
size of the city and general business conditions; but in order to gain
some idea of the range in rates, a high of around $7.00 to a low of
around $0.25 per square foot can be used. The top figure represents
space in the better locations and buildings of the larger cities, while
the latter may be converted factory space in a relatively poor location.
The following data indicate further some of the spread in rates:

Type of Enterprise	Rate per Square Foot per Year
Financial houses	$6.50
Advertising agencies	6.00
Real estate	4.00
Law firms	4.00
Physicians and dentists	4.00
Insurance agencies	3.50
Public utilities	3.00

The square foot cost usually includes many services, such as air conditioning, running water, wall maintenance, and elevator service. In many respects, the price is subject to negotiation as to what is included.[1]

STABILITY OF THE TENANTS

It is generally considered advantageous to locate an office in a building where the tenants are stable. Frequent moves by tenants in and out, and alterations, are undesirable from the viewpoint of solid, substantial enterprises. Various studies seem to indicate that real estate companies, law firms, and financial houses are among the most stable. Their office needs remain fairly constant, and they seem disposed to remain in one location for relatively long periods. In some cases, their tenure in the same location extends for 25 years and longer. In contrast, manufacturers' agents and advertising agencies tend to move more frequently. However, many of these remain in the same location for 10 or 15 years; and while this is relatively less, it still reflects a strong element of stability.

ADAPTABILITY OF THE SPACE

The space chosen should permit suitable arrangement for the various office divisions; it should also be of adequate size and shape to permit the best arrangement of office equipment and machines. For the most part, rectangular shapes are best; and where requirements permit, occupancy of an entire floor is usually preferred. Individual circumstances alter cases; but normally, it is more economical to travel 10 feet vertically, i.e., between floors, than 150 feet horizontally, i.e., on the same floor. As already discussed in this chapter, the space should be adaptable from the viewpoint of building facilities such as heating and ventilating ducts, adequate soil pipe, water, and electrical wiring.

The difference between "gross space" and "usable space" should be noted. Usually, one pays for gross space, in some instances called "rental area," which is the area measured between the inside surfaces of the outer boundaries. It includes areas for columns, projections, pilasters, and window arrangements necessary to the building. The usable space is the effective area which can be used for the office. Frequently, 10 per

---

[1] See also page 394 for discussion of "Provisions of Lease."

cent of the gross space cannot be used; and in some buildings, the column locations further add to the uneconomical use of space, rendering the space efficiency as low as 65 per cent. The heavy black portion in the top illustration of Figure 20–3 shows space with low usability. This can easily be an area 5 feet by 1 foot, or 5 square feet. Some of this can be utilized by ingenious arrangements of files or odd pieces, but much will be unusable. Modern buildings omit columnar obstructions on the inner face of outside building walls, and the columns are spaced to per-

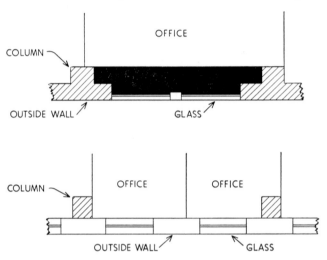

FIG. 20–3.   *Top:* The columnar spacing and inside wall offsets make economical use of space difficult. The solid black area has low usability. *Bottom:* Modern building columnar and window arrangement emphasizes maximum usable space and facilitates subdivision of space.

mit effective subdivision of the space. This is shown by the bottom portion of Figure 20–3.

As stated earlier in this chapter, the space selected should permit future alteration and office expansion. Attention to future requirements means more than just securing space greater than that needed for current requirements. Consideration must be given to where and how future changes will alter present space provisions. Usually, future considerations are taken care of either by leasing entire floors and subleasing what is not now required or by securing options on adjoining areas. Some office executives feel it is desirable to provide space arrangements to accommodate at least five years of future expectations.

NATURAL LIGHTING AND VENTILATING PROVIDED

As discussed in the previous chapter, lighting is very important in an office. The availability of daylight and the building facilities for providing artificial light should receive prime consideration. Any area that provides much daylight is normally favorable. Exposures facing the north are generally preferred, as northern light is of a steady and soft type. Eastern exposures are next in preference, followed in order by southern and western exposures. Normally, the outside wall areas should utilize a maximum of glass area and be not less than one fifth of the floor area. Windows extending almost to the ceiling permit a maximum amount of natural light to reach the inner areas of the floor space.

However, in addition to daylight, artificial light is usually required. For this purpose, adequate fixtures, electrical outlets, and lighting provisions must either be available or be provided. Agreement on the amount of artificial light to be utilized and the cost of installing and maintaining the necessary fixtures is a further important consideration.

It is imperative that an office be well ventilated. Careful observation should be made of the prospective space area to determine if adequate ventilation is possible. Spaces with few windows, a small number of openings to air ducts, low ceilings, and window openings on inside courts normally do not provide sufficient ventilation. However, with air conditioning, many of these shortcomings can be overcome.

FREEDOM FROM DIRT AND NOISE

Certain elements are extremely disturbing to office workers and should be avoided whenever possible. Dirt, smoke, and soot are objectionable, and the possibility of their presence in an office location and area should be taken into account. Street noises are bothersome and interfere with efforts of mental concentration. In addition, the surrounding tenants' types of businesses, with special reference to the amount of traffic and the operations performed, might also be important from the viewpoint of noise.

LOCATION AND SPACE SELECTION CHART

In most cases, it is difficult to evaluate all the above factors and give the proper weight to each in order to determine the best location and space selection. To overcome these obstacles, a location and space selection chart like that shown in Figure 20–4 can be used. The selection factors are listed on the left, and beneath each factor are statements designed to help identify the intended meaning of the factor. Opposite each factor is a series of numbers indicating the range of points or values which have been assigned to that factor.

The factors and weights shown in the illustration are suggestive only. In an actual case, the factors selected and the weights given each one are determined by the evaluator. However, to make comparisons among different possible locations valid, the same chart is used for evaluating the several sites under consideration.

In the chart shown, the values or points assigned to each factor are not equal. The maximum for factor 1 is 24 points; the maximum for factor 2 is 60 points; etc. This simply means that, based on the evalu-

	Excellent	Good	Fair	Poor
1. Characteristics of the building: Does the building have a favorable appearance, good name and address that are easy to pronounce and remember, and adequate floor load and ceiling height?	24	18	12	6
2. Building facilities: Are entranceways, wiring arrangements, outlets, ducts, fire protection, and other *fixed* facilities adequate?	60	45	30	15
3. The proximity of office building to business factors: Is the building near to customers; to transportation facilities; to shopping centers, restaurants, and hotels; and to mail facilities?	44	33	22	11
4. The cost involved: Is the rate reasonable and in keeping with competitive prices?	40	30	20	10
5. Stability of tenants: Do tenants of the building tend to stay put (are moving and transferring the exception)?	20	15	10	5
6. Adaptability of space: Is the space adaptable to the needs of the office? Is there room for expansion?	60	45	30	15
7. Natural lighting and ventilating provided: Is the exposure on the north, east, south, or west? Does it have large glass areas? Do windows face the street or open lots? Are ceilings high?	28	21	14	7
8. Freedom from dirt and noise: Is the general area free from dirt and noise? Is the area itself clean and quiet?	24	18	12	6
Maximum total..................	300	225	150	75

FIG. 20–4. Chart used to determine location and space selection.

ator's judgment and experience, the relative value of the factors is of different weight or importance.

ILLUSTRATING THE USE OF CHART

Suppose five possible office spaces are being considered. To evaluate the various spaces, the chart is used. Assume the total selection points for each location are as follows:

Space	*Total Points*
Location No. 1	156
Location No. 2	243
Location No. 3	178
Location No. 4	145
Location No. 5	206

Based on these data, the decision would be to select location No. 2, with a total of 243 points.

BUILDING CODE REQUIREMENTS

It should be noted that construction and remodeling work is subject to building code requirements, which specify the design and the type of construction that is permitted. For example, use of certain materials may be forbidden for certain uses, or stated design principles must be followed for certain structural parts. Requiring all buildings to have at least two entranceways, one on each of two sides of a building, may be included in a building code, the purpose being to reduce the fire hazard. Code requirements are enacted and enforced usually by local government.

Before launching a space-planning project, it is well to consult the building code requirements. Frequently, some flexibility is provided in the code, certain alternatives and choices being designated. Portions of some building codes have remained the same for a number of years, while others have been modified from time to time. Keeping informed and up to date on the requirements can prove very helpful.

OWN OR RENT

In most discussions regarding the selection of office space, the question usually arises: "Is it better to own or to rent?" This question involves basic policy and can actually be answered only by the top managers. Certain considerations should be made, however, and these are as follows.

The advantages to an enterprise of owning its own office building can be listed:

1. The building can be tailor-made for, or remodeled within technical limits to meet, the particular needs of the enterprise. However, needs change; sometimes, the building becomes obsolete or at least not as convenient as first planned.

2. There is an element of prestige for an enterprise in owning its own office building. The name of the enterprise can be used for the building, and the publicity value can be quite high.

3. There is a possibility of income from renting out a portion of the building. This procedure allows also for flexibility in future expansion.

4. Permanency of location is obtained. This might lend stability to the enterprise and, in addition, permit continuity of a desired name and street address.

5. A relatively safe investment is afforded. An office building represents an equity in which the capital invested is fairly secure.

In contrast, the main advantages of renting an office building are:

1. Freedom of top managers from care and worry in connection with ownership. The problems of building maintenance and repairs are avoided.

2. Finances of the enterprise are more flexible. Large amounts of capital are not tied up in one relatively long-time investment. The renter is free to invest any surplus in the most productive channels.

3. Changes in office location can usually be made more freely. The enterprise is not wedded to one location.

4. A satisfactory arrangement is provided for the small enterprise whose office requirements are not elaborate.

The "sale and lease back" arrangement is being heard of more and more frequently. This describes a transaction in which an investor buys a building from a seller and in the same transaction gives the seller a long-term lease on the building. The seller continues to occupy the building, pays rent, and is free of the responsibility of building upkeep and operation. For the seller, the deciding issue to enter into a "sale and lease back" arrangement is his financial position, especially that of taxes and his desire for a sound "brick and mortar" investment.

PROVISIONS OF LEASE

When space is rented, the legal right of a tenant to occupy a given office space is usually consummated by means of a lease. Actually, *a lease is a form of contract by which one party conveys real estate to another party for a period of time at a specified compensation.*

A lease is in effect for a stated period of time. Office leases usually run for one, three, five, ten, or twenty years, and in some instances longer. Payments are usually made monthly, with the first payment due at the time the lease is executed; this first payment customarily applies as rent for the first month or stated period. Sometimes, an advance of three months' rent is made at the beginning of the lease period, and this is held by the lessor as evidence of good faith and intentions on the part of the lessee.

It is well to remember that a lease is a legal document; and in dealing with matters pertaining to leases, the services of a competent lawyer are advisable. It is well, however, that the office manager has a general knowledge of a lease, especially of its more common provisions.

A lease may contain many different agreements or clauses. The aggregate depends upon the type and value of the real estate involved and also upon the number of subjects upon which the lessor and the lessee believe a definite written agreement is advisable. A lease can be specially written, or it can be a standard form. Normally, the lessor provides janitor service, heat, running water, elevator service, window shades, and fire-protection apparatus. On the other hand, the lessee usually provides floor coverings, partitions, Venetian blinds, awnings, ventilators and fans, and intercommunication telephones. In addition, the lessor usually has the right to change the name and street address of the building; designate all sources for sign painting, ice, towel service, and the like; have passkeys to the premises; and enter the premises at all reasonable hours for inspection, repairs, and alterations.

QUESTIONS

1. Discuss the subject of building facilities as applied to office location and building.
2. Various office spaces may be classified as undesirable because of certain factors involved. Discuss briefly some points that may determine that a space is not acceptable.
3. Discuss the meaning, purpose, and application of cellular steel floors in office buildings.
4. Of the various major factors given consideration in locating an office, which two factors do you believe are most important? Justify your viewpoint.
5. In your own words, explain the illustration of Figure 20–3.
6. Explain how a location and space selection chart can assist in locating an office.
7. As an office manager, would you favor the "sale and lease back" arrangement in connection with acquiring suitable office space? Why?
8. Define each of the following:
   a) Rental area.
   b) Gross space of an office area.
   c) Building facility.
   d) Allowable floor live load.
9. Evaluate the statement: "Closeness to others in the same line of business is usually considered unsound business practice."
10. What is a lease, and what advantages does it provide for the lessee? For the lessor?
11. Read the "Offices for Rent" classified advertisements in your local newspaper, and determine the cost for various types of office space. Do your data seem to be in line with the average space cost figures given in this chapter? Discuss.
12. Select two office buildings in the community in which you now live, and make a survey to determine their suitability with respect to (a) the characteristics of the building, (b) the cost involved, (c) the adaptability of the space, and (d) freedom from dirt and noise for each of the following prospective tenants:
    a) A sales representative requiring desk space and a room for small samples.
    b) An insurance office requiring a total of about 1,800 square feet, including a reception room, a room about 15 × 25 feet for salesmen, and general office space.

c) A medical doctor who needs a reception room, an examining room, and, if possible, a small room to one side for his records and library.

Write your results in a suitable form, using a sentence outline type of presentation.

CASE PROBLEMS

Case 20–1. Nikko-Sanwon Chemical Company

This company, an integrated manufacturer of vinyl plastics, produces and sells three major categories of such plastics, including (1) vinyl chloride polymer resins, (2) "PUC" compounds, and (3) calendared vinyl sheeting and polyethylene film. These products are used in a variety of applications such as insulation for wire, flooring, toy components, luggage, and bookbinding.

The sales office of the company is located in the Merchandise Mart, near the loop in Chicago. In this office, 12 salesmen and 26 clerical personnel are employed. The office is convenient for buyers, and is a prestige location where a representative can bring customers and impress them favorably. In addition, "the Mart" is very accessible for employees, who can live in any part of the greater Chicago area and reach the office without trouble.

One of four manufacturing plants of the company is located in the southwest area of the city, some nine miles from the loop area. Adjacent to this plant is a large warehouse which was constructed two years ago. There is ample space available in the warehouse to house the sales offices, now in the Merchandise Mart. In the opinion of Mr. Tashio Umeda, president of the company, the sales office should be removed to the warehouse. This would reduce overhead and consolidate Chicago operations in one location. However, through Mr. Leonard Griffin, the vice president of sales, Mr. Umeda discovers that many of the salesmen and office personnel do not favor such a move. Some of them have stated that they will quit if the move takes place.

Mr. Umeda strongly feels that the move would be best for the company over the long-range viewpoint. However, he wishes to retain all his present employees if this is possible, and suggests that the company (1) reduce the working hours to 7½ hours daily from the present eight hours, but keep the pay the same; (2) establish a free service to assist employees to find satisfactory housing quarters in the southwest area of the greater Chicago area; and (3) organize car pools, with the company compensating the employees whose cars are used.

Problems:

1. What additional information do you feel appropriate for Mr. Umeda to consider before reaching a decision on whether to move the sales office?

2. Outline the program of action that you recommend Mr. Umeda take. Substantiate your recommendations.

Case 20–2. The Boulevard Bank

The Boulevard Bank is located in a fast-growing suburb east of the city of Los Angeles. In 1946, this bank erected a new, modern two-story building with ample space and modern equipment to take care of the needs of its customers. The building faces 75 feet on the main street of town and is 150 feet in depth. It does not have a complete second floor but a balcony only, extending all around and designed for small commercial offices. The basement is used for the bank's safety deposit vaults, storage space, washrooms, and building maintenance equipment.

Today, the bank has outgrown its present building facilities. More space is definitely needed if the bank's growth is to continue. The bank's managers are conservative and efficient. The bank is financially very strong. To date, the managers have not arrived at a decision aimed to solve the problem of expansion.

In an effort to gather some basic facts, the president of the bank has obtained the following information:

1. Additional office space believed needed is 5,600 square feet.

2. No ground is available for purchase or lease on either side of the bank's present building.

3. An additional floor to the bank's present building cannot be made due to the design of the building.

4. Present bank building is owned by the bank and is free of debt.

5. Available office spaces in buildings within 200 yards of the bank building include (*a*) 6,000 square feet at $2.00 per square foot on a ten-year lease basis and (*b*) 10,200 square feet at $1.85 per square foot on a five-year lease basis.

6. Size of balcony space in the present bank building is 4,000 square feet.

7. Estimated cost of remodeling the balcony for the bank's use is $8,500.

8. To demolish the present bank building and erect a new three-story bank building, the cost is estimated at $750,000.

9. Annual rentals from occupants of balcony offices are $10,820.

Problems:

1. Discuss the arguments for, as well as those against, the erecting of a new building by the bank.

2. Are you of the opinion that the bank should seek a new location? Why?

3. What decision do you suggest the bank managers take?

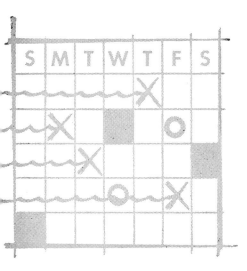

Part 5

CONTROLLING IN OFFICE MANAGEMENT

Controlling, a fundamental function of office manage-ment, consists of determining what is being accom-plished, evaluating it, and, if necessary, applying corrective measures. Basically, controlling is performed to see to it that what is planned is being accomplished.

Controlling is extensive; there is no single type of man-agerial control that is all-inclusive. Some types have to do with the accuracy to be achieved, while others con-cern the practices to follow, the amount of work to accomplish, or the dollars to expend. Seven chapters comprise Part V of this book, and they cover completely the essentials of managerial controlling as applied to office work.

Chapter 21

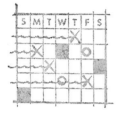

OFFICE STANDARDS; CONTROLLING FORMS AND SUPPLIES

What the superior man seeks is in himself, but what the small man seeks is in others.

—Confucius

CONTROLLING is performed by the office manager to insure that the provisions of his planning will take place. It can be viewed as the familiar management follow-up either to confirm operations taking place as desired, that is, according to plans, or to reveal deviations that necessitate corrective action so that the office goals will be achieved. In some instances, the planning may be quite meager, perhaps a statement of the amount of work desired, with practically no plans worked out as to when and how the work should be performed. Nevertheless, controlling can be applied, but it is fundamental that the most effective controlling can be applied to only complete and well-thought-out plans.

CONTROLLING AND STANDARDS

Controlling is an activity and consists of determining what is being accomplished, evaluating it, and, if necessary, applying corrective measures. The first two of these steps answer what is being done and how well it is being done. For these purposes, measurement in terms of definite units is preferred.

Standards are basic to these accomplishment and evaluation tasks of controlling. *A standard is something established by either custom or authority in order to gauge such things as quality, performance, and service of any factor used in management.* A standard is a reference line of management; or it may be thought of as a basis of reckoning, i.e., a basis of comparison. Most standards represent the best current knowledge of an item or practice formulated and accepted to meet the needs of present conditions.

IMPORTANCE OF STANDARDS

Standards serve as an accepted basis against which an actual action or object may be judged, thus providing a sound comparison between similar types. In this manner, the work of controlling is facilitated. However, standards are also important to the other fundamental functions of management, including planning, organizing, and actuating. For example, in planning, standards are the essential media for determining what components are required for establishing the sequence of successive operations. In other words, standards provide the common language for carrying out managerial work in areas such as expressing what is to be done, discussing, allocating, and instructing.

EXTENT OF STANDARDS

Standards apply to all factors of an enterprise. For example, there exist, in management, standards for each of the six M's—i.e., Men, Materials, Machines, Methods, Money, and Markets. This means that modern managers have established recognized bases of reference for each of the six factors. For example, concepts such as "standard" material and "standard" machine are common in the office, but less commonly identified standards are "standard" man and "standard" money. The concept of a standard man is frequently used in personnel work when considering what qualifications a man must possess to fill a particular job, while standards in money or the financial part of an enterprise are very well illustrated by expressions of standard costs.

In many offices, the basic types of standards, along with the type of area covered by each, are shown by the following:

Basic Standard	Area
Work:	Measurements of the quantity and the quality of accomplishment
Tools:	Desk, file, machine
Conditions:	Amount of space, equipment layout, lighting, floor covering
Process:	Filing methods, mail distribution, handling of accounts receivable, duplicating process

Under tools, for example, a standard for a machine might designate the specific type, capacity, speed, and possibly the name of the manufacturer. Furthermore, this designated machine would probably be expected to be used for certain work. In this case, the machine standard serves for purposes of controlling.

MEANS OF EXPRESSING STANDARDS

Various means of expressing standards can be used, including the following:

1. *Written specifications.* Simply a detailed statement of the requirements that must be followed or that must be met by the factor under consideration.

Factor	Written Specification	Model	Accepted Rule or Regulation	Unwritten Customary Procedure	Verbal Communication
Men	X	...	X*	X	X
Materials	X	X	...	X	X
Machines	X	X	...	...	...
Methods	X	...	...	X	X
Money	X	...	X	X	...

* Particularly in the case of government and public institutions.

FIG. 21–1. The means most commonly used to express standards according to the factors of management.

2. *Model.* A typical sample, a miniature representation, or an exact representation of a specimen of the factor considered standard.

3. *Accepted rule or regulation.* An established course or guide prescribed by a person in authority.

4. *Unwritten customary procedure.* The habitual usage or generally recognized practice as shown by past experience.

5. *Verbal communication.* The conveyance of thoughts and opinions concerning the standard by means of spoken words.

Convenience has tended to associate or group certain of these means with certain factors employed by managers. For example, a standard method is usually expressed by one of three means—a written specification, an unwritten customary procedure, or a verbal communication. In contrast, a standard material might be expressed by any of these means plus a model. Figure 21–1 shows the means most commonly used to express standards according to factors. To illustrate, for machines, the standard is usually expressed by a written specification or by a model. Figure 21–2 shows a methods standard expressed by means of a written specification. In this case, the method is precisely stated; it tells exactly what to do and minimizes the possibility of misunderstanding.

INTERDEPENDENCE OF STANDARDS WITHIN AN ENTERPRISE

Standards are changed not only because improvements are made but also because, within an enterprise, standards are interdependent. For a given task in an office, assume standards have been set up for the material, machine, and method. These three standards are interdependent and may be called "associated standards." The employee, in order to accomplish the task, must use the standard material in the standard machine and follow the standard method. Figure 21–3, in the sec-

Every error which is made in posting a passbook or ledger card must be corrected by an adjusting entry on the savings machine, as described in the following paragraphs. No erasures are permitted.

If the wrong old balance is posted in the machine, the correction should be made as follows:

1. If the old balance is picked up incorrectly and detected immediately, the Clear and Sub-Total lever is merely brought to the "Clear Balance" position and the balance cleared.

2. If the error is found after posting the old balance and the deposit or withdrawal, but before extending the new balance, the incorrect old balance is to be set up and the Overdraft key depressed (with the book and card out of the machine), and the correct old balance is to be set up on the Old Balance key. The book and card are then to be inserted and the correct new balance extended.

3. If the error is not detected before the new balance is posted, the correct old balance is to be picked on the Old Balance key (with the book and card out of the machine). If the entry was a deposit, the amount is to be recorded under the Overdraft key. The card and book are then to be inserted and set to the line immediately below that on which the incorrect balance appears and the correct new balance extended. The word "Balance" is to be written beside it and an ink line drawn through the incorrect balance.

4. If the error is not detected until the cards are proved at the end of the day, the procedure in (3) above is to be followed, except that the card only can be corrected. A Caution signal should be placed on the card so that the book will be corrected when next presented. The customer should be advised of the error and asked to present his passbook for verification as soon as possible.

Source: First National Bank of Boston, "Manual for Savings Tellers" (Boston, 1943), pp. M1 and M2

FIG. 21–2. A methods standard in the form of a written specification.

Factor	Present Standards	Standards after Changes	Reasons for Changes in Standards
Material....	12# white bond paper, size $8\frac{1}{2}'' \times 11''$	16# white bond paper, size $17'' \times 22''$	New sheet size requested by top management members. Larger sheets necessitate heavier paper.
Machine....	$11\frac{1}{4}''$-roll typewriter	$19\frac{1}{4}''$-roll typewriter	Larger roll needed to accommodate new paper size.
Method.....	Insert paper in machine, make five copies, leave $\frac{1}{2}''$ spacing between vertical columns.	Insert paper in machine, make four copies, leave $2''$ spacing between vertical columns.	Number of copies reduced from five to four because of heavier paper used. Increased spacing improves appearance of sheet.

FIG. 21–3. Illustrating the interdependence of associated standards. The standard for material was changed upon request of top management members. This change in the standard for material necessitated a change in the standard for machine and also in the standard for method.

ond column, illustrates the present standards for the material, machine, and method. It can be seen that the employee is to use 12-pound, 8½ × 11-inch paper in a 11¼-inch-roll typewriter, and that he is to make five copies, using ½-inch spacing between vertical columns.

Now, suppose that a change is made in the standard of the material from 12-pound, 8½ × 11-inch paper to 16-pound, 17 × 22-inch paper. In order to handle this new weight and size of paper, it is necessary to change the machine standard from a 11¼-inch to a 19¼-inch-roll typewriter and to change the method standard from making five copies to four copies and from allowing ½-inch spacing to a 2-inch spacing between vertical columns. These changes in standards and the reasons for making them are shown in concise form in Figure 21–3.

In general, a manager should review all standards when any one standard is revised. This is especially important for associated standards, but it also applies for standards of the same group. To repeat, *standards are not independent; they are interdependent.*

It will frequently be found that when only the one standard is changed, the associated standards remain entirely compatible with the revised standard. But a manager does not know this until he reviews and studies all the associated standards after each revision. In similar vein, a change in any one of the standards of a *similar group* necessitates a review of all standards in that group. For example, *all methods standards* should be reviewed whenever a change is made in any one methods standard, because in this way possible sources of improvement and the bettering of all methods standards can be discovered and adopted.

STANDARDS AND PERFECTION

The establishment of a standard does not mean that perfection has been reached. For example, a material standard for paper designated by an office *does not* imply that paper meeting all those particular specifications is the best paper obtainable; it may actually be paper of an inferior quality. What the standard actually means is that paper of these specifications is the type desired by the manager and is satisfactory for the specific purpose in mind, taking into account such things as the type of printing press, the price range, and the desired finished product. Material standards specifying a low grade of material are not uncommon, for they simply reflect a manager's belief that for the process and use to which the material is going to be subjected, the low grade of material is satisfactory.

Experience shows that after a standard has been set, it is common to try to improve the standard and to move it toward perfection. This is as it should be, for progress in management is dependent in large measure upon improvements in standards. In addition, the setting of a standard seems to place a level below which future standards will not be set;

that is, once a standard is set, changes that are not in the direction of improvement are discouraged.

AMERICAN STANDARDS ASSOCIATION, INC.

Since 1947, the American Standards Association, Inc., with assistance by the National Office Management Association, has directed its efforts to the establishing of office standards which it is hoped will prove useful to many managers. The American Standards Association does not set standards; it provides the machinery whereby every group concerned in any project has a right to participate in the setting of the standards. The program includes the establishment of office standards for each of the following major groups: office equipment and furniture, paper for office use, office supplies, business machines, personnel, physical and physiological factors, and office forms, records, and procedures. Figure 21–4 shows an office standard for basic sheet sizes and standard stock sizes for bond papers and index Bristols. By its use, a reference level for managerial controlling is provided.

ADVANTAGES OF STANDARDS

The advantages of the use of standards in management are tremendous and include the following:

1. *Aid managing.* The performance of the management process is expedited by the use of standards. Identification and measurement of quality, performance, and capacity of the factors used by a manager constitute the supports upon which the managerial functions can be predicated.

2. *Provide a common basis for understanding.* Standards provide a common terminology, or a common language, between the employee and supervisor or between the buyer and seller. Through the use of standards, it is possible to determine exactly what is being discussed or investigated.

3. *Aid in securing co-ordination.* Standards serve as focal points around which revolve most problems of management. The synchronization of the various factors used by a manager depend, in the final analysis, upon the synchronization or interplay of the various standards which are brought together.

4. *Reduce waste.* Standards help to determine definite requirements. Losses resulting from obsolete equipment, inefficient methods, and excess materials are kept at a minimum when good standards are employed and strictly enforced.

5. *Promote better utilization of employees.* Standards help to achieve the goal of utilizing personnel within carefully defined and known limits. Executives are encouraged to do executive work—not rou-

Division 2
Paper
NOMA
N2.1 - 1955
•
ASA
Reg. U. S. Pat. Off.
X2.2.1 - 1955
*UDC 676.3.001.3:389.172
•

NOMA
OFFICE STANDARD

Basic Sheet Sizes and Standard Stock Sizes
for Bond Papers and Index Bristols
(An American Standard)

1. Scope

1.1 The scope and purpose of this standard is to list the basic sheet sizes and standard stock sizes of bond papers and index bristols in order to encourage the use of normally available sizes.

2. Definitions

2.1 For purposes of this standard, the terms listed below are defined as follows.

2.1.1 Basic Sheet Size, as defined in the Dictionary of Paper* is a certain sheet size recognized by buyers and sellers as the one upon which its basic weight is figured Usually, it is also the one which prints, folds, and trims most effectively.

2.1.2 Standard Stock Sheet Sizes are the sizes of paper normally stocked by most paper merchants and most paper mills and from which the sizes commonly used in the office are cut with a minimum of waste.

2.1.3 Bond Paper⁵ is a grade of writing or printing paper originally used where strength, durability, and permanence are essential requirements, as in government bonds and legal documents. Its use has extended into other fields, such as business letterheads and forms, where strength and permanence, though important properties, are not so essential; this accounts for the wide range of quality in this type of paper. These qualities are obtained through the use of rag pulp, bleached chemical wood pulps, and mixtures of these fibers in the manufacturing process. Although bond paper is a typical writing paper, almost all of it is subjected to some form of printing before use. Therefore, it must have good printing qualities which, however, are not as important as writing and erasing qualities, clean-

liness, formation, finish, color and freedom from fuzz. It is usually made in basis weights from 13 to 24 pounds (17 in. x 22 in. per 500 sheets).

2.1.4 Index Bristols* are bristols used principally for index records, business and commercial cards. They are a group of cardboards made on the Fourdrinier or cylinder machine of homogeneous stock (such as rag, sulphite, or bleached sulphate pulp) or by pasting together two or more plies of the same kind of paper, and finished and sized for pen and ink work. The usual basis weights are 180, 220, 280, 340, and 440 pounds (25.5 in. x 30.5 in. per 1000 sheets).

*The Dictionary of Paper, published under the auspices and direction of the American Paper and Pulp Association, 122 East 42nd Street, New York, N. Y. (Copyright Second Edition 1951.)

3. Standard Stock Sheet Sizes†

(All Dimensions in Inches)

Bond Papers (Rag Content or Chemical Wood Pulp)	Index Bristols (Rag Content or Chemical Wood Pulp)
17 x 22‡	20½ x 24¾
17 x 28	22½ x 28½
19 x 24	22½ x 35
22 x 34	25½ x 30½‡
24 x 38	
28 x 34	
34 x 44	

† The Standard Stock Sheet Sizes listed in this standard, except for the 22½ x 35 size Index Bristol, are identical with those listed in Simplified Practice Recommendation R22-40 for Paper of the U. S. Department of Commerce.

‡ Basic Size.

NOTE: When the direction of the grain is important, it should be specified.

• **Approved as American Standard by the American Standards Association, Inc.—Aug. 16, 1955**
• **Sponsor: National Office Management Association.** *Universal Decimal Classification

NATIONAL OFFICE MANAGEMENT ASSOCIATION
WILLOW GROVE, PA.

Courtesy: American Standards Association, Inc., New York; and National Office Management Association, Willow Grove, Pa.

FIG. 21–4. A written office standard.

tine work. Likewise, supervisors are expected to carry out the job of supervising—not that of an operative employee with only the title of supervisor.

6. *Encourage simplicity.* Standards tend to eliminate unusual and complicated practices. The very nature of standards and their interre-

latedness tend to encourage the use of simple descriptions and easily understood terms. Also, wide usage encourages understanding of the standard.

7. *Act as stimuli to research.*   Standards help to localize areas which improvements might be made. They serve to help state the problem and to assist the researcher in concentrating on a problem of relatively limited scope.

8. *Provide effective connecting links between the findings of research and the application of research results.*   Standards serve as the contact points for the application of research findings. New discoveries and improvements are introduced via the standards; and in this manner, the beneficial contributions of research are utilized with a minimum of time and effort.

9. *Provide interchangeability of part and machine.*   Each component may be so specified and accurately determined by the use of standards that it is entirely feasible to use any one of a group of similar components. By means of standards, it is possible to insure that all units of part X will be identical within the limits set up by the standards.

10. *Make mass production possible.*   Standards permit the handling of each component separately; thus, specialization may be practiced and the gains thereof realized. Difficult and complex jobs requiring long and strenuous training periods are reduced by the use of standards to relatively simple tasks, yet at no sacrifice in the total amount of work accomplished.

OFFICE STANDARDIZATION

The wide adoption of a limited number of standards in a particular area can lead to standardization. For example, when a company adopts certain stated standards regarding the type and size of desks it will use, the practice is known as standardization. A degree of uniformity is implied in all standardization. In many instances, standardization deals with an industry, not with just one enterprise. Both the needs and the benefits of standardization are in proportion to the complexity of managing the particular enterprise or industry.

Typically, a number of considerations must be included in standardizing an office item. For desks, the considerations might include size, appearance, utility, comfort, interchangeability, construction, maintenance, depreciation, and initial cost. How much weight to give to each of these factors is primarily a question of judgment, although weights in proportion to the relative costs of the factors might be developed. Standardization can be applied to any number of office areas such as chairs, files, machines, lighting, forms, procedures, employment qualifications, and training programs.

ECONOMIC AND SOCIAL ASPECTS OF OFFICE STANDARDIZATION

From an *economic* viewpoint, there is little doubt that office standardization is beneficial. Such economic factors as simplified control, greater quantities of work achieved, advancement of office production techniques, and assistance in managerial decision making are among the virtues generally pointed out.

However, from the *social* viewpoint, there has been much discussion regarding the real benefits of standardization. Proponents claim the level of both the skilled and the semiskilled employee has been raised; a measurement of performance is provided; the uniformity among similar jobs has made the employee's services more in demand; and the employee can develop proficiency in a definite, prescribed area of endeavor. In contrast, those opposed to office standardization claim the employee is deprived of his dignity as an employee—valuable skill and enthusiasm for his job are lost; the range within which the employee may exercise his skill is narrowed; the employee is without the over-all picture, of which his efforts are a small part; and the dull and drab work life, with work interest and outlook impeded, can made the employee an undesirable citizen in his community.

THE CHALLENGE OF OFFICE FORMS

An area in which controlling is very important is that of office forms. These are basic to much office work. The accomplishment, efficiency, and economy of the office are greatly affected by the office forms utilized. Adequate controlling of office forms is mandatory for good office management.

In nearly all enterprises, forms have a tendency to continue indefinitely regardless of need. The root of much office inefficiency stems from this situation. In many instances, an outmoded form is extended deep traditional and almost reverent consideration. To question its value or suggest the possibility of its elimination amounts to heresy.

There is also a tendency, almost an obsession in some cases, to start new forms regardless of whether the information desired is now contained in existent forms or can be secured by a slight modification in these forms. The viewpoint can be described as narrowed to the particular needs for a particular problem of a particular person. Individualism is emphasized to the exclusion of practically all other considerations.

Study after study shows that the great majority of executives believe there are operations in their respective enterprises where greater efficiency could result if proper control over office forms were exercised. Ample opportunity exists for improving the information-handling tasks through the medium of forms. In addition, research shows another highly significant fact: that the processing and using of forms represent not only much the greater cost of forms, but also the greater opportunities for improvement. True, the size and weight of paper, cost of printing, and kindred considerations are worthy of the manager's attention; but it is not these *physical* considerations that represent the lion's share of expenditures. It is the *functional* considerations of office forms, identified by answers to questions such as how much time is spent by whom in using what forms, and how effectively the forms assist in getting the information recorded, transmitted, and processed. Various estimates show that for each dollar spent for office forms, somewhere between $15 to $25 is spent to process these forms. Taking the average of $20, this means that a five-copy form costing $60 per thousand involves a processing cost of $1,200. A 10 per cent reduction in these processing costs, a reasonable possibility, is equivalent to twice the total physical costs of the form.

CONTROLLING OF OFFICE FORMS

The initial step in the controlling of office forms is to find out what is being done. For this purpose, current information on the various forms now being used, what respective purposes they serve, and specific data on their contents and identification are required. To these ends, the following steps are recommended.

1. Announce to all employees and explain the existence of the forms control unit, its function, and its authority. Be specific as to who is the head of it. In many cases, the head may be the office manager. Other members of the unit should include key personnel who are qualified and can give support to the office forms control efforts from different departments of the enterprise.

2. Freeze all forms activity at its *status quo*. Announce that any additions or changes must be taken up and cleared through the forms control unit.

3. Obtain at least two copies of every office form used in the enterprise. File one copy in a centralized forms control file. Use the other for purposes of analysis, as described below.

4. File each form in the centralized file according to function. This will bring together every form that is similar in nature regardless of its design, its name, or where it is used. Office forms are employed to assist in any of the following functions: report, request record, instruct, follow up, authorize, cancel, order, apply, acknowledge, estimate, route, schedule, and claim. Segregating the forms by their major function assists analysis.

5. Secure a listing of all the office procedures used in the enterprise.

6. Mark all forms in the centralized file according to the procedure in which they are used.

EVALUATION OF PRESENT FORMS

The second step is to determine how well the present office forms are serving the enterprise. For this goal, several different but related activities can be undertaken. Questionnaires sent to those using the forms frequently prove effective. It is helpful for the person in charge of forms control to meet separately with each department head and discuss improvements. These meetings can be followed by group meetings for all department heads in order to decide what improvements can be made in forms that affect more than one department.

In evaluating the present office forms, it is not uncommon to analyze the existent forms to determine if any can be (1) eliminated, (2) combined with others, or (3) improved. The emphasis is upon functional considerations. The form's adequacy to meet the work requirements consistent with efficient office management is of foremost importance. Results achieved are sometimes amazing. In the case of one prominent Chicago company, the total number of office forms was reduced from 1,182 to 368.

Figures 21–5 and 21–6 show how forms can be combined to improve office efficiency. Originally, four separate forms—shipping label, invoice, shipping memorandum, and packing slip—were typed separately. Subsequently, the four forms were combined and now require only one typing. In Figure 21–6, a copy has been raised to show the shipping label in the upper left corner, the receiving memorandum in the upper right, and the packing slip below. These are separated by tearing apart at the perforations.

In addition, physical considerations are taken into account—the size of the forms, correctness for filing, cut without waste, and easy folding for enclosure in an envelope. Also, the weight of paper for the original and each carbon, the use of different colors of paper, and their essentiality in the particular form are carefully reviewed. Specifications are checked— the type of ink, punches, and perforations are investigated. The ordering quantities and rates of consumption are compared.

These efforts culminate in establishing standards for forms believed to be best suited to meet the company's requirements. Such forms are desirable because they give stability, uniformity, and continuity to the controlling efforts over office forms. This does not mean that the work of forms control becomes static. Quite the contrary; it is dynamic. As the needs of the company change, the forms used will also change. The person in charge of forms control work must recognize this fact.

Standardized forms expedite training, help insure measurable results of accomplishment, and promote the maintenance of satisfactory outputs. In the majority of cases, it is desirable to standardize the size of paper, paper stock, and printing style. Forms of an odd size should be avoided because they involve difficulties in office handling as well as paper waste

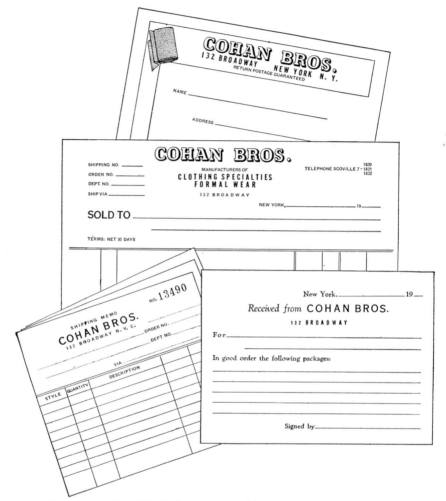

Courtesy: American Sales Book Co., Inc., subsidiary of Moore Corp., Ltd., Niagara, N.Y.

FIG. 21–5. Forms used by a clothing manufacturer. *Top to bottom:* Shipping label, invoice, shipping memorandum, and packing slip.

in manufacturing. Standardizing paper stock and printing style simplifies ordering, eliminates chances for error, and insures uniformity of records—an important consideration when forms are retained over a period of years.

REMEDIAL ACTION

The third step in controlling office forms is remedial action by the forms control unit to bring about the establishment and use of office forms deemed by them to be proper and effective. Specifically, this group should have the authority to purchase forms and to review, pass

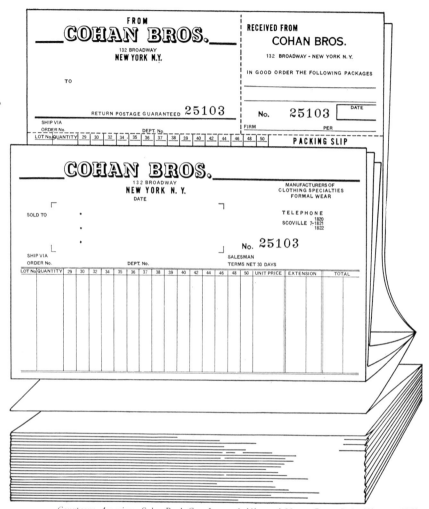

Courtesy: American Sales Book Co., Inc., subsidiary of Moore Corp., Ltd., Niagara, N.Y.

FIG. 21–6.   A combination of the four forms shown in Figure 21–5. Now, the same amount of work is accomplished in one typing operation instead of in four.

on, or reject any and all forms in the enterprise. Competent help should be assigned to the forms control organizational unit, and it should be given sufficient status so that others will take it seriously. The members must work well with those of the other organizational units. Suggestions by others should be encouraged and their co-operation won.

OBJECTIVES OF CONTROLLING FORMS

Many existent inefficiencies of an office can be eliminated, and the usefulness of office forms improved, by adequate controlling of office forms. Specifically, by means of forms control, a manager seeks (1) to use and retain only those forms which are necessary, (2) to insure that the needed forms give the greatest assistance at the least cost, (3) to produce the required forms by the most appropriate process, (4) to distribute forms to those having justifiable reasons for receiving them, (5) to study proposed or revised forms for essentiality, and (6) to review periodically all forms in use in order to keep them in line with current needs of the enterprise.

CONTROLLING OFFICE SUPPLIES

Important, but sometimes neglected, is the activity of office supplies. Office employees need proper supplies if maximum productivity is to be attained. The lack of a typewriter ribbon, an order pad, envelopes, or letterheads might cause serious delay in getting out important office work. In addition, supplies represent an investment of capital. An office of one hundred employees might easily have $10,000 worth of stationery and office supplies on hand; and unless these are properly looked after, deterioration and waste might take place.

Unless reasonable controls are exercised over office supplies, it is certain that there will be extravagance, needed items out of stock, excessive prices paid for certain items, and obsolete material in the stock room. Simple but effective control measures can be taken to alleviate inefficient stock-room conditions. For one thing, marginal stock items, such as infrequently used and slow-moving items, should be eliminated. Most office stock rooms are burdened with such supplies, which interfere with the smooth operation of the stock room. Also, it should be determined if less costly items could be substituted for certain present supplies. Usually, an arrangement providing for pretesting different products, or at least a willingness to try them out, is in order. Standardization of some items can assist controlling efforts and reduce costs. Likewise, periodic campaigns are helpful to reduce waste of supplies by employees. Informal surveys and studies of supplies used will show whether waste apparently is getting out of hand. Many measures may be taken, but the most effective long-range remedy is to appeal to the employees to cease wasteful practices and help curtail needless expense for supplies.

POINTS FOR SUPPLIES CONTROL

To provide acceptable service and to eliminate needless expenditures for office supplies, the following steps appear essential:

1. Locate the stock room in a convenient space that is not desirable for clerical work. Be sure it is clean and dry. Enclose the area, and keep it under lock and key. Provide adjustable shelving, arranged for easy accessibility to supplies and most effective use of space.

2. Arrange the stock according to some orderly plan. Index all items

by number or code, and have a handy reference available to locate any item quickly; arrange forms by their numbers. Place heavy items on the lower shelves and light items on the upper shelves.

3. Establish realistic maximum and minimum quantities for each item, as well as the ordering point. These can be based on judgment guided by past experience. The analysis of the requirements for each item will help attain a balanced inventory of supplies. As a normal practice, it is usually best to buy small quantities at frequent intervals. For each item, the amount purchased should be in line with the rate of consumption, the time required to receive a replenishment from the supplier, the quantity considered minimal for the functioning of effective management, and the savings in cost, if any, which are achieved through larger-quantity purchases of the item. Some companies find it desirable to carry a one-, two-, or three-months' supply of the principal items. When delivery is made, a reorder with specific date of delivery is immediately issued in order to maintain an adequate and balanced amount of stock. Some companies put bulk items on contract purchase, ordering a six-months' total with deliveries released on a monthly basis. Substantial savings are claimed from this practice, especially for stationery items.

4. Limit the quantity of supplies issued at any one time to about a two-weeks' supply. Large quantities of supplies encourage waste; too-small quantities involve excessive requisitions and trips to the stock room. Also, in many cases, it has been found that the practice of packaging supplies in small units helps to economize their use. Furthermore, all issuance of supplies might be confined to one day out of the week or to certain dates during the month. This tends to promote planning the need for office supplies and to concentrate the work of control over supplies. In the event that supplies are needed in the interim, a special requisition and approval from the office manager can be required. This practice tends to discourage requests for supplies at irregular times.

5. Place one person in charge of the stock room, and delegate complete authority and responsibility to him.

6. Issue supplies only upon authorized written requisitions, which should be made out, in most cases, by the department head or by the supervisor of the unit receiving the supplies. File these requisitions in case they are needed for future reference. Maintain a journal or record by departments of what is issued, when, and to whom. Make a periodic inspection of this record to ascertain if consumption of supplies appears to be normal in the light of past requirements and volume of work handled.

7. Inform supervisors, by means of monthly statements, of the costs of office supplies issued to their respective units. This will help to keep the supervisor conscious of the importance of office supplies; and the supervisor, in turn, will reflect this attitude to the individual employees.

8. Exercise periodic follow-up to help insure that the supplies are needed and meet requirements. An effective practice is to select at random a requisition for supplies and investigate it thoroughly. Find out how the item is used, who uses it, whether it is the best for the specific use, and whether the price paid for it is reasonable and in line competitively. Answers to these questions either will confirm that a satisfactory job of acquiring supplies is being done or will uncover areas which require remedial action.

QUESTIONS

1. Discuss the extent and importance of standards in the field of office management.
2. Do standards imply perfection? Explain your reply.
3. What part does the American Standards Association play in the work of establishing office standards?
4. In your opinion, what are the three most important advantages of standards in office management? Point out and discuss your major reasons for selecting these three advantages.
5. Can controlling take place without the use of a standard? Elaborate on your answer.
6. Do you favor office standardization? Cite reasons to support your viewpoint.
7. Why is it important to review all standards when one standard is revised? Illustrate your answer by an example taken from your experience or by an incident with which you are familiar.
8. In efforts to improve existent office forms used in an office, should emphasis be given to functional or to physical considerations? Substantiate your answer.
9. Write out a standard with which you are familiar, and explain how it probably helps in the management of the factor concerned. It is suggested that you select any common factor in office work which you have performed or observed in school, at work, or at home.
10. Is the controlling of office supplies of major importance to an office manager? Why?
11. As an office manager, what actions would you take to provide adequate management over office supplies?
12. Discuss briefly the six steps essential to finding out what is being done as the initial work in connection with controlling office forms.

CASE PROBLEMS

Case 21–1.   Benton-Donohue Company

For the past several months, Mr. Richard E. Schubert, the office manager, has been giving serious consideration to the establishing of standards for posture chairs which his company purchases. Mr. Schubert believes that standards are necessary for three chair classifications—executive, supervisory, and clerical. For each of these groups, a particular model, design, upholstery, and color would be determined and used throughout the entire office.

To substantiate his viewpoint, Mr. Schubert points out that the use of such standards would greatly improve the appearance of the office and save much time in purchasing. Also, chair purchases could be made at better prices for the company. But probably of even greater importance would be the elimination of comparison of chairs by employees of the same general organizational level. For example, one supervisor would not compare his chair to that of another supervisor and feel that he had a better or an inferior chair by comparison. Chair equality would be attained.

The controller suggests that the employees of each office division should be permitted to select the chairs they want. In other words, chair standards should extend within an office division only. Any other standards arrangement would conflict with personnel interests and possibly with the type of work performed. Furthermore, he believes that the company should give its chair business to several suppliers. Competition should be encouraged; otherwise, the company might find itself at the mercy of one supplier.

The president of the company does not see anything wrong with employees of the same organizational level using different chairs, and he asks two questions of the office manager: (1) "How are you going to determine the standards for chairs in our office?" and (2) "What are the tangible savings from adopting the use of chair standards?" As the president sees it, the answer to question No. 1 is so involved that the company should not undertake the project. In addition, many employees would question the results and their use regardless of what would be determined. In answer to the second question, it appears that additional expenditures, not savings, would be incurred. Not one, but groups of chairs would probably have to be purchased if chair standards were adopted. Also, the possibility of taking advantage of lower prices on the chair market would be minimized, and further improvements in chair design and manufacture would be discouraged.

Problems:

1. Do you agree with the viewpoint of the controller? Discuss. Of the president? Discuss.

2. What action do you recommend that the office manager take? Why?

Case 21–2.   Arnold Electronics Corporation

Among the many areas in which efforts to reduce costs were being directed, that of office supplies was of special interest to Miss Lena Walker, assistant office manager of the Arnold Electronics Corporation. The total number of office employees was 135, and the type and quantity of office supplies consumed seemed excessive to Miss Walker. She therefore concentrated her efforts to find out why certain items were used and the amounts that were used.

Her investigations led to these facts: The supplies were stored in a large locker which did not have ample space or shelves. Many employees used company envelopes and stationery for private correspondence and for scratch paper. A rather large percentage of the supplies had to be discarded from time to time because they became dusty and soiled in the locker. There seemed to be no standard sizes of stationery. Whenever anyone wanted any supplies, he simply went to the locker and "helped himself." No records were kept of when a new order for supplies should be placed; and at times, the supply of certain items was depleted. Anyone who noticed that the supply of a given item was getting low was empowered to inform the office manager who, in turn, wrote a request to the purchasing department. The locker was kept locked part of the time; the key was in the custody of the secretary to the office manager—anyone in the office had access to the key, since it was kept in the secretary's top desk drawer and almost every employee knew this.

Problems:

1. Are you of the opinion that Miss Lena Walker has adequate information to facilitate a decision regarding the controlling of office supplies?

2. What recommendations do you believe Miss Walker should make? Why?

3. What program for implementing your recommendations do you suggest? Discuss.

Chapter 22

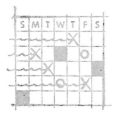

CONTROLLING QUALITY AND OFFICE WORK FLUCTUATION

The man who graduates today and stops learning tomorrow is uneducated the day after.
—NEWTON D. BAKER

ONE OF the important areas for which controlling is applied in an office is quality of work. Poor quality impedes the essential services of an office. A poorly typed letter, an incorrectly executed office form, an error in extending the cost data, or a misspelled name on a customers' list diminishes the effectiveness of information handling. Some of the work must be done over, some can be "fixed up" by additional expenditure of time and energy, and some is used "as is"—with errors or misstatements undetected, and promising the possibility of subsequent waste.

RESULTS OF POOR OFFICE QUALITY

Generally speaking, lack of adequate control over quality can result in three types of losses. Paper work errors can cause a wrong decision to be made. Failure to process an inquiry properly might result in the loss of the prospective sale from a very important customer. Also, poor quality can result in loss of good will. A customer's payment improperly posted, or an incorrect billing, are examples. Furthermore, loss in time and money is incurred in detecting and correcting office errors. Frequently, this loss is unnoticed; nevertheless, it is present.

OFFICE QUALITY CONTROL APPROACHES

Faced with the necessity of maintaining a satisfactory level of quality, the office manager can select one of several alternatives. The approach to be used depends upon individual considerations. Usually, the particular type of office work, the personnel, the cost of maintaining quality, and the possible effect of an error in the work are given high priority. First, a practice of checking every segment of all work can be followed. This constitutes 100 per cent inspection—i.e., each letter or each column of figures is gone over to verify the correctness of the work. Second, a policy of either spot or sample checking can be followed. In the case of spot checking, every third or perhaps fifth document or segment of work is checked. For sample checking, a group which is representative of the total is determined statistically and is subsequently checked to determine the quality level of the total work being performed. Third, the office work can be inspected by means of statistical quality control. This approach is based on statistical methods and the laws of probability. It will be discussed in elementary terms in the next several pages of this chapter.

STATISTICAL QUALITY CONTROL

Natural phenomena and their relationships are statistical in character. Repeated productive operations of the same thing will provide a distribution of values. This can be evidenced either by measurement on each of a quantity of similar items or by repeated measurements of the same thing on the same item. This follows because of the inherent characteristics of the measuring method.

The distribution of values can be shown graphically by means of a curve, with the values represented on the horizontal scale and the frequency of the values on the vertical scale. For our purposes here, it can be stated that when the phenomena are natural, sufficiently large, and of random selection, most of the values will cluster in the center around a representative average value, while other values in the group will tend to

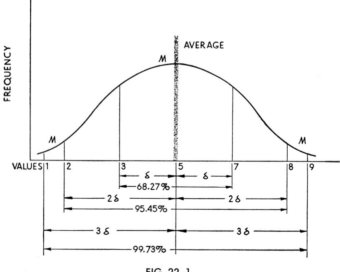

FIG. 22-1.

taper off to the left and to the right of this average. The result is what the statistician calls a normal, or bell-shaped, curve, as shown by the curve *MMM* in Figure 22–1. To illustrate, if the errors of inventory recorders are counted, it will be found that most commit, let us say, five errors, while a few commit three, and still fewer commit one error. Likewise, to the right (or greater than five errors), there will be some with seven errors, and a few with nine errors.

Based on statistical mathematics and the laws of probability, the statistician can determine the normal dispersion or spread of these data. Commonly, a value known as a standard deviation is calculated. Within a standard deviation to the left and to the right of the average are contained 68.27 per cent of the values of the series. Within two standard deviations to the left and to the right are 95.45 per cent, and within three standard deviations, 99.73 per cent of the values. These concepts are shown in Figure 22–1.

CHANCE AND ASSIGNABLE CAUSES

These statistical relationships are utilized in developing effective means to control the quality of work. For a series of data, it is known statistically what variations from the average can be expected on account of the inherent characteristics of the phenomena. Variation within a definable area is inevitable and is the result of chance. However, variation outside the definable area can be discovered and subsequently corrected. In other words, statistical quality control reveals when a variation is due to other than chance, i.e., when an assignable cause is present. But it does not tell what the cause is. Investigation and analysis are required to find and remove the assignable cause.

CONTROL CHART

A graphical device known as a control chart is constructed and used for plotting data and showing variations from the acceptable goal or standard. The values of the limits placed on the chart are determined statistically. In this work, the statistical concepts of the normal curve, the average or normal quality value, and the limits of variations that are due to chance are determined.

Figure 22–2 illustrates a control chart. This can be thought of as developed from a normal, or bell-shaped, curve placed on its side, so that the area in which variations due to chance occur is represented by a horizontal band. In the illustration, this band is from 3.0 to 7.0 errors. The average or normal expectancy due to the inherent nature of the work is 5.0 errors; however, the quality of the work will vary from 3.0 to 7.0 errors because of chance. It is inevitable and is not assignable to a cause. When the quality measurement goes outside this pattern of variations—

for example, as indicated by points 1 and 2—the cause is not chance but an assignable influence which should be discovered and eliminated. It might, for example, be a defective tabulating key mechanism on the typewriter, paper slipping in the machine, or a space bar that is not working properly.

In a control chart, the frequency of plotting the data depends upon the quality and value of the product controlled. Usually, the values are obtained from a sample of the work—that is, a representative number of

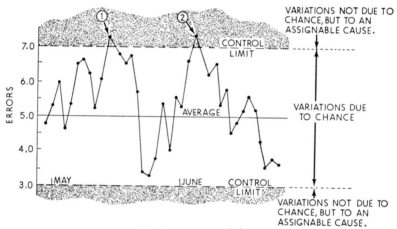

FIG. 22–2. A control chart.

the total are selected and checked. This may be once every fifteen minutes, or perhaps once a day. The value of these selected units is representative statistically of the total being processed.

A different control chart is usually established for each control station. This is done because the work being quality-controlled at one station may differ considerably from that at another station.

It should be noted that statistical quality control stresses preventive rather than remedial action. When more than 7.0 errors are found in a batch of work, indicated by point 1 in Figure 22–2, the work is stopped, and the reason for this assignable amount of errors discovered and corrected before the work is permitted to continue. A large quantity of work is not processed; and subsequently, much of it found defective. Statistical quality control emphasizes a "look-see" while the work is being done, not a "look-see" after the work is completed. Also, the trend of the readings is usually indicative. For example, the increasing readings climaxing to point 2 in Figure 22–2 point to the occurrence of such a reading as 2 outside the control limits. Many feel that trends leading to readings near the control limits can be used as signals to look for an assignable cause without waiting for the actual reading to exceed the control limits.

PROGRAM TO FOLLOW UNDER STATISTICAL QUALITY CONTROL

To initiate statistical quality control, it is first necessary to find out the current quality level of the operation. A fact-finding survey of from two to four weeks is recommended, the exact time depending upon the variety and complexity of the work being done. A description of the error, its probable cause, and an estimate of the time required to correct it provide additional helpful information.

The quality levels and the control limits should then be determined. It is usually best to concentrate on the key areas or locations. This tends to give control over the entire work of the office. Some errors can be eliminated entirely by the use of such techniques as process improvement, machine operation, and simplified office forms. When the error can be eliminated—i.e., all the factors causing it, the need to control such errors is likewise eliminated.

The next step is to establish the sampling plans so that economical and statistically sound representations of the total values will be used. This resolves itself into a problem of statistics, but a practical understanding of the included problem is necessary.

Installation of the program is usually a simple task, but close supervision and expert assistance, if needed, should be supplied. Like all new programs, that of statistical quality control gives rise to questions and to situations demanding on-the-job decisions.

The program should be reviewed periodically to check on results and make minor adjustments deemed advisable. Of course, if the nature of the work changes, the quality control efforts should be reviewed to determine if any modifications are needed.

CONTROLLING OFFICE WORK FLUCTUATION

Another important area involving office controlling is office work fluctuation. In most offices, the volume of work is likely to be quite large during some periods and, conversely, quite small during other periods. This fluctuation appears to be in the general nature of office work, and it complicates controlling efforts. Hence, various means to minimize the fluctuations have been devised.

A study of the demands upon an office over a comparatively long period of time will usually reveal a rhythmic pattern in office activities. For example, it may be found that peak loads are generally experienced on the first day of each week, every Friday, or the last few days of each month.

In such cases as these, controlling can be directed to help take care of the peak periods, since these are known in advance and an adequate means for handling them can be determined. In other cases, however, the demands upon an office are continually changing; and where this condition exists, the work of controlling is extremely difficult. Special control efforts may be required to meet the situation.

PROBLEMS INCURRED

Perhaps the most important problem incurred by the fluctuation of office work is that of getting the work finished when it is needed. Adequate control can assist tremendously in this respect. Also, work fluctuation creates a "feast or famine" situation in the factors utilized in performing the work. For any given period, how many people to hire, what machines to employ, and which methods to adopt are typical questions. On the one hand, the reduction of idle machine and personnel time are paramount; while on the other hand, lack of sufficient capacity in machine or manpower is of foremost consideration. Another disturbing problem is the designating and the handling of rush or special work. In most instances, this designation means little in determining work priority, because the terms are applied to practically all the work. Furthermore, the supplying of accurate information concerning the status of certain work in the office is complicated by work fluctuation. Information about such things as the progress of a particular job, the number of units completed, and the probable finishing time is not readily supplied when the work volume is characterized by steep peaks and deep troughs.

CONSIDERATIONS IN CONTROL EFFORTS OVER WORK FLUCTUATION

Certain fundamentals must be taken into account in controlling office work fluctuation. Among the more important requirements are the following:

1. *The controlling should help in getting the work accomplished.* Controlling is a part of the management process performed to accomplish specific work. The controlling efforts should be selected and utilized on the basis of achieving the goal, not perpetuating a control mechanism or program as such.

2. *All control efforts should be carefully co-ordinated, so that both unity and a minimum of wasteful overlapping efforts are achieved.* Controlling of work fluctuation cannot be left to the individual employee. When this is done, sporadic, unbalanced, and somewhat haphazard results are common. Generally, the best practice is to have the controlling under the direction of one individual or a division designated to handle this function.

3. *All management members must realize that the controlling efforts are intended to help them.* The controlling should be constructive in its ultimate effect; as a result, management members should be able to give more attention to such duties as getting the work out, handling grievances, making decisions, improving methods, and reducing costs.

4. *Complete data on personnel, machines, procedures, and cost must be known.* Intelligent controlling can take place only when adequate knowledge and information about the things being controlled are available and supplied. As stated in Chapter 21, these data may be in the form of standards.

5. *The office work should be expressed in readily measurable units.* Some expression for describing accurately the quantity of work is necessary. Control efforts are usually most effective when applied to a specific amount of work which is known and understood by all affected by it.[1]

6. *Knowledge of time standards for all major operations within the office should be available.* The reasonable time expectancies for completion of work are basic tools to control work fluctuation. Knowing when, how much, and for how long the controlling efforts are applied are decisions which should be guided by the utilization of office time standards.[2]

7. *The sequence of operations on each type of work should be established and utilized.* In many instances, the office procedure will supply this information, but details covering a specific job or a portion of the entire work are sometimes also necessary. This is especially true in the case of congested or "bottleneck" areas.

8. *Accurate and fast means of communication between the one doing the controlling and the employee doing the actual physical office work must be provided.* In the smaller office, or where the supervisor initiates his own means of control, no particular difficulty is encountered with this requirement. However, when centralized controlling is used, fast intercommunication service is necessary between the line operators and the controlling unit.

MEANS OF CONTROLLING OFFICE WORK FLUCTUATION

The question now arises: "What specifically can the office manager do in order to meet the problems inherent in the fluctuation of the office work volume?" The answer lies in employing one or several means at his disposal. The choice depends upon his preference and the circumstances of the particular office. Eight possibilities are discussed in the following pages.

1. *Employment of part-time help.* This possible solution is self-evident and will not be treated in any detail here. In certain cases, the use of part-time help is entirely satisfactory; but experience seems to indicate, in general, that part-time help may not be as reliable, efficient, and co-operative as regular employees. Also, the cost of recruiting, hiring,

---

[1] Measuring and timing office work is the subject of Chapter 25.
[2] *Ibid.*

and training part-time employees might be excessive. Flexibility of the work force, however, is gained by the use of part-time people.

2. *Overtime work.* Although commonly resorted to, this solution to the problem of work fluctuation is not entirely satisfactory. For occasional overloads, it may represent the simplest solution. However, when the amount of work during regular hours is light and frequent peak loads are common, the working of overtime is open to serious question as the best way of handling the problem. For one thing, overtime increases unit labor cost considerably. Consider a common case in which an employee works eight hours overtime. These eight hours are paid for at the rate of time and one half. In effect, these overtime hours increase the unit labor cost by 8.33 per cent, calculated by dividing 52, the hours paid for, by 48, the hours worked, or 1.0833, an increase of 8.33 per cent.

There is also the question of employee fatigue. Over an extended period, there is reasonable question whether the rate of output during the overtime hours will be the same as that during the regular work hours. The rate of production during overtime tends to fall below the normal production rate. Most office managers will concur in the statement that an office employee working an extra two or three hours after a normal eight-hour working day will not produce an extra two eighths or three eighths of a normal day's work. The amount will be less—in some instances, considerably less.

Furthermore, legal restrictions must be taken into account. Federal and state laws regulate the type of work and the hours which an employee can work in certain occupations. Where female employees are involved, the regulatory statutes may be of special importance.

3. *Forming mobile units.* In some offices, it is possible to form "flying squadron" units which are moved from area to area to help handle excessive work loads. Generally speaking, the office must be fairly large to utilize this method. However, the same idea is used informally in most small offices by shifting the employees around when and as the work requires.

The mobile unit arrangement necessitates employees with comprehensive training in a number of different types of office work. Hiring and maintaining such employees present some difficulties, but can be managed satisfactorily.

4. *Calling service bureaus to do the work.* Office overloads or work which is of a special nature can be handled by outside enterprises which specialize in this type of work. Most of these so-called "service bureaus" are independently owned business firms, but some are units of office machine manufacturers. Service bureaus are located in all major cities throughout the United States; several are nationwide in scope. Some are specialists operating, for example, computer or punched-card installations only; but many offer complete services in typing, calculating, tabu-

lating, filing, transcribing, duplicating, and direct mailing. Service bureaus offer vast experience and competent, specialized personnel to handle complex jobs. The service is fast. For example, one service bureau completed, for a client, inventory calculations involving 3,500 hours of work within three working days. In view of the service provided, the cost of service bureaus is usually reasonable.

It should be observed that these outside service bureaus are useful to the office manager for more than meeting peak loads or emergency problems. They are also helpful when purchase of particular office machines cannot be justified by the office because of its size or the amount or character of the work. Also, a service bureau can be engaged to serve as a laboratory to test the value of a new means of handling office work before the necessary equipment is purchased.

5. *Stress centralization in organization.* One of the strongest justifications for centralization in office organizing is the more effective handling of peak loads.[3] When the excess work is (1) mainly basic activities such as typing, computing, copying, sorting, and filing, and (2) concentrated in different departments at different times, the centralized organizational approach has real merit.

6. *Use of cycling.* Cycling is an arrangement whereby papers are processed throughout a period according to an orderly plan rather than as a group, for example, at the beginning or end of each period. In other words, by means of cycling, the work is spread out evenly throughout the period. The practice of cycling has been used in connection with the mailing of statements and is commonly referred to as cycle billing. The same practice, however, can be applied to other types of office work.

Cycling has been used for a long time by public utility companies in sending out their bills for service. Meters are read, for example, in a certain section of the city, bills mailed, and payments specified by a certain date. Several days later, other meters in another section of the city are read, bills mailed, and payments requested by a date which is a few days after that of the previous group.

Many department stores operate on a cycle-billing basis under which each account is posted once a month, but statements are mailed for a different section of accounts on different days throughout the month. The accounts can be divided into twenty or fewer groups, depending upon such things as the volume of postings, the number of accounts, and the number of trays required to house the accounts.

Figure 22–3 shows a chart which gives the divisions for twenty cycles. Going from the outer to the inner circle of this chart, the data represented are, respectively, the accounts, the cycle numbers and closing dates, and the cycle mailing dates. For example, to the right of and

---

[3] See Chapter 28.

slightly above the center of the chart, accounts "Cle to Coon" have cycle number 6.01. The 6 of this number indicates that the closing date is the sixth of the month. The cycle mailing date is 10, i.e., the tenth of the month, which allows four days after closing accounts to prepare the statements for mailing to customers.

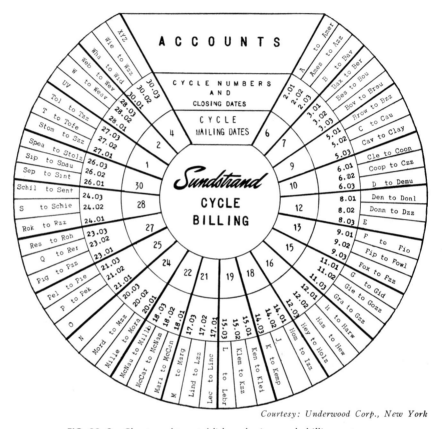

Courtesy: Underwood Corp., New York

FIG. 22–3. Chart used to establish cycles in a cycle-billing system.

7. *Maintain work backlog.* This means utilizes a reservoir of work, so to speak, in order to level out the peaks and valleys of the office work flow. When certain work can be postponed or moved up, this approach works out quite satisfactorily. The attempt is to make each day an average day.

An alternate approach is to mix urgent with nonurgent office work. Certain tasks of the office, such as bringing records up to date, replenishing supplies, and putting headings on certain papers, can usually be performed during slack periods. When work having high priority is received, it is processed immediately, the nonurgent work being laid aside for the time being.

8. *Orderly work flow through routing, scheduling, and dispatching.* This approach consists of establishing specific channels by which the office work is to be accomplished, placing time values on each successive step so arranged, receiving information on progress of work, and issuing authorization for work to proceed from step to step. It emphasizes the controlling of the work quantity and the use of time in work performance. Each of the major components of this approach—routing, scheduling, and dispatching—will be discussed.

ROUTING

Routing is the determining of the route or channel through which the work travels and the sequence of operations required for the completion of the work. For most offices, routing is determined by the procedure used. In some instances, the choice of a particular machine or of a certain area may be fixed by the routing process, but this is the exception rather than the rule with most office work. Commonly, a route sheet, showing the sequence of operations, is prepared. In addition, for each operation, the allocated time and the department in which the work is to be performed are indicated.

A practice sometimes followed is to place the office work in a heavy Manila envelope with the route sheet attached on the outside. A copy of the sheet is retained by the person or department doing the central control work. In some instances, the form of the route sheet is printed on the envelope to prevent possible loss of the route sheet in the office.

SCHEDULING

Scheduling is the assigning of time values to the work sequence—the determination of when each operation starts and when it should be completed. The extent to which office work can be scheduled depends upon the individual circumstances; but usually, a great deal can be scheduled, including billing, key punching, tabulating, transcribing, check writing, order writing, and inventory taking.

The common practice in scheduling is to work backwards from the time specified for completion. An allowance is made for each operation required by the work; and in this manner, a starting time is determined. For example, if the time set for completion of a job is 4:00 P.M., Thursday, June 12, and the work requires 18 hours' time, this means that the work should start 18 hours before that time and date, or 2:00 P.M., Tuesday, June 10.[4]

The Folder System. In certain instances, a simple and quite effective informal method of scheduling office work can be used advantageously.

---

[4] This is based on working hours from 8:00 to 12:00 noon and from 1:00 to 5:00 P.M., five days a week.

This is known as the folder system. Under this plan, a given number of units of work are placed in a folder. These are distributed by the supervisor, who notes to whom the work is given, the starting time, and the machine or workplace used. Upon return of the completed work, the time is noted, and the process is repeated. The supervisor is the key person under this plan. He has knowledge of the work on hand, the amount completed, the amount in process, and when it should be finished.

Use of Visible Index Cards. The data necessitated by more formal and complete scheduling, usually for fairly large quantities of work, can be handled on cards. When cards are used, a visible index type, providing signals for control purposes, works out very well.[5] A separate card is made out for each machine, desk, or workplace. The signals featured by this type of equipment are moved to specific positions along the margin of the card to designate specific scheduled times. Scanning the cards quickly reveals what equipment is available for work and what jobs are currently being worked on.

Use of Charts. Another effective means of recording scheduling data is by the use of charts. One of the original types, called the Gantt chart, was devised by Henry L. Gantt. The basic principle used is that work planned and work accomplished are shown on the same chart in relation to each other and also in their relation to time. The items are listed in a column, with corresponding capacities or data on maximum scheduling loads shown in an adjacent column. Other columns are used for time units, such as hours, days, weeks, or months.

Figure 22–4 shows a Gantt chart representing the scheduling of work for Department 13, in which six posting machines are used. In this figure, a main time column represents one week, as shown by the date filled in at the right and top of each time column. To illustrate, the column headed "Dec. 3" means the week ending December 3. In this case, there are five divisions under each main time column; the divisions represent

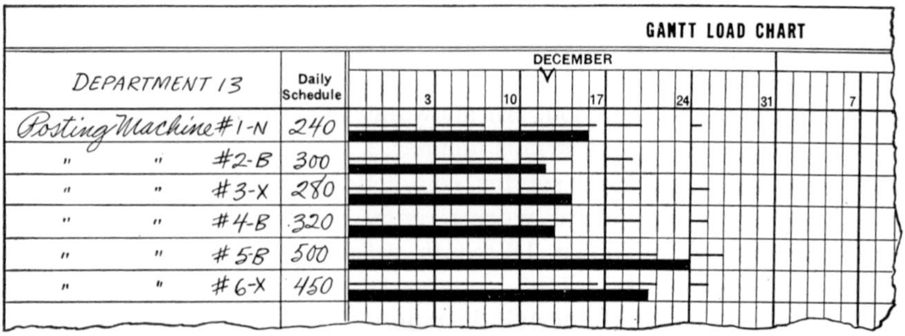

FIG. 22–4. Gantt load chart, showing graphically the degree of utilization of machines, idle time, and time available for scheduling.

[5] See Chapter 12 for discussion on visible equipment for filing.

the five working days in the week. The data for each machine are shown in the identified horizontal sections of the chart, i.e., machine No. 1–N by the top horizontal section, machine No. 2–B by the second horizontal section, etc. For each machine, the work, scheduled by weeks, is indicated by the light line and the total cumulative work scheduled by

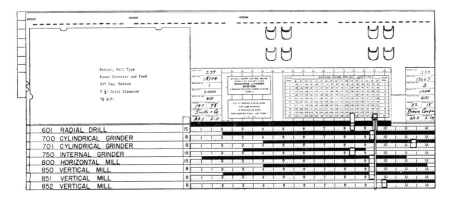

601	RADIAL DRILL		
700	CYLINDRICAL GRINDER		
701	CYLINDRICAL GRINDER		
750	INTERNAL GRINDER		
800	HORIZONTAL MILL		
850	VERTICAL MILL		
851	VERTICAL MILL		
852	VERTICAL MILL		

Courtesy: Remington Rand, Inc., New York

FIG. 22–5. *Top:* Close-up of scheduling chart. *Bottom:* Installation in office of a large manufacturer.

the heavy line. Thus, for posting machine No. 4–B, work time scheduled for the week ended December 17 is three days, which represents 960 postings (3 × 320); and the total amount of time scheduled for this machine for the six weeks' work in twelve days. The **V** mark on the top of the chart shows that the chart represents the status as of that date, which, in the illustration, is December 14. This type of Gantt chart is termed a load chart, since it graphically represents the load assigned to each machine and likewise reveals the idle or available time. Successive additions can be made on the chart by extending the proper lines; a redrawing is not necessary.

The "combination visible card–Gantt chart" is another type of scheduling chart, which is increasing in use and combines the principles of the visible card and the Gantt chart. This newer chart has the general appearance of a large, visible card file with the overlapping card pockets hanging vertically. See Figure 22–5 on page 431.

The scheduled items, such as operations, machines, or work stations, are shown in the extreme left column of the chart; time is indicated along the horizontal axis. A separate pocket is used for each scheduled item. At

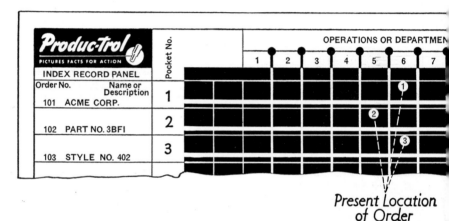

FIG. 22–6. A close-up view of the peg-string board.

the extreme left of each pocket is placed a card which gives frequently used information about the scheduled item, with the identifying data appearing in the visible margin. The remaining portion to the right in each pocket is used to show graphically the scheduled operations and times allotted for the particular item. To do this, two types of cards are used: time insert cards and operation cards.

Operation cards are printed card forms used to indicate data concerning the operation and the time scheduled for the operation on the time scale. The information about the operation is written on the card. The scheduled time information is shown in the bottom margin of the card. Time insert cards are printed strips of paper which are placed in the visible margin to show the time scale along the horizontal axis. The strips are folded lengthwise, with the turned-up stub showing the printed scale.

When the operation card is tucked in the visible margin and behind the insert card, only the colored strip of the operation card is visible; and the length of this strip indicates the amount of time required to do the work. The exact placement of the card is determined by the scale of the insert card in the visible margin. Since a colored strip indicates scheduled time, it follows that white space indicates free or unscheduled time.

DISPATCHING

Dispatching is putting into action and adequately following up the routing and scheduling plans; it is a signaling to go ahead and a check to see that action is taking place when and where it is wanted.

Dispatching in the office is usually quite simple. It is frequently done informally by the supervisor; however, when the volume and different

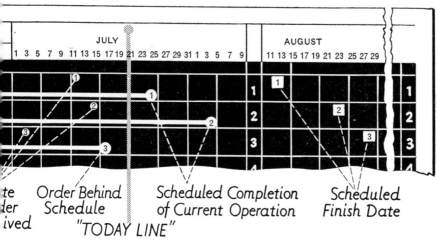

te   Order Behind   Scheduled Completion   Scheduled
ler   Schedule   of Current Operation   Finish Date
ived   "TODAY LINE"

Courtesy: Wassell Organization, Westport, Conn.

kinds of office work warrant it, employees doing only dispatching work can probably be employed advantageously. Quite often, it is desirable to use a central control board which graphically visualizes the dispatching of the many different jobs which are started, moved through the office, and completed.

Types of Dispatching Control Boards. There are many types of control boards, including the three-hook, peg-string, grooved-strip, and spring-clip types. The discussion here will be confined to the peg-string and the grooved-strip boards, since they are probably most adaptable to office work.

Figure 22–6 shows the usual pattern of a peg-string board, which has the controlled items on the left side and such things as time, operations, and departments in separate sections across the top. The board has a series of small holes into which pegs are inserted. For each item in the left column, there are two horizontal rows of holes. The top row is used to indicate the scheduled operations, the bottom for the actual progress. Thus, comparison between the two is easily made.

To show the scheduled operations, a peg with a string attached is inserted in the proper hole corresponding to the operation and time value. The string, which extends from the left of the board to the peg, is always taut, thus giving the impression of a horizontal line. Pegs inserted in the bottom row of holes show the actual progress. To expedite quick reference, an assortment of different pegs, having contrasting colors, shapes, and markings on the top, is employed.

A quick glance at the board shows the times for dispatching, what work is behind schedule, and what work is ahead of schedule. A vertical cord representing a specific time and date, frequently a "today line," is used to assist in visualizing these conditions. Each day, for example, the cord is moved to the right a distance equal to one day on the time scale. All data are kept up to date on the board by moving the pegs to the proper positions representing the current condition.

Referring again to Figure 22–6, the first line, pocket No. 1, covers order No. 101. The large round peg shows that this order is in department No. 6. To the right and under July, the small round peg indicates that the order was received July 11. The peg with the string attached to it is shown under July 25, which is the scheduled completion date of the current operation. The "today line" is at July 21. Hence, this order is to be completed in four days. In contrast, order No. 103, in the third pocket, was scheduled for completion on July 16 and is five days behind schedule. This order is in department No. 6, which should be consulted to determine what can be done to get the order moving. The square pegs to the extreme right of the board indicate the scheduled dates for finishing the orders. Order No. 101, for example, is to be completed August 12.

In contrast, the grooved-strip board has horizontal cardholder strips for insertion of tickets representing work lots. The extreme left column is used for work-lot numbers, and the remaining columns are headed by department names. Cards are made out for each work lot. As the work progresses, the cards are moved on the board to correspond with the correct department location of the work. In some instances, the time is shown horizontally. When this is done, separate tickets can be made for each operation on each work lot, as well as for the scheduled starting and finishing times indicated on each card. In this manner, the helpfulness of the board is increased by showing the scheduling function.

QUESTIONS

1. What different approaches can an office manager follow with regard to quality control? Discuss.
2. Does statistical quality control stress remedial or preventive action? Use Figure 22–2 in explaining your answer.
3. An office manager receives daily reports on the results of statistical quality control work in key locations of the office. Aside from quality informa-

tion, in what ways can the office manager use these reports to improve the accomplishment of the office work? Discuss.

4. Many feel that office work must be 100 per cent accurate and free from mistakes. In the light of statistical quality control, is this belief reasonable? Should an office manager expect this degree of quality? Discuss.

5. As an office manager, would you favor working your employees overtime to meet work requirements? Justify your stand.

6. Discuss three fundamentals to be taken into account in considering the control of office work fluctuation.

7. Identify each of the following:
   a) Unassignable cause in statistical quality control.
   b) Cycle billing.
   c) Mobile units to take care of work fluctuation.
   d) "Folder system" of office work scheduling.

8. Relate the meaning of Figure 22–6 in your own words.

9. Talk with an office manager and inquire if work fluctuation is a problem in his office. If so, evaluate the practice followed to minimize it. If not, how do you account for its absence? Make a brief report of what you discover.

10. For each of the following, indicate what means probably would be used to handle the peak office work load caused by:
    a) Finishing a payroll by Friday morning of each week.
    b) Issuing statements to customers the first of each month by a large department store.
    c) Completing an inventory over a week end for a large manufacturing company.
    d) Issuing licenses to car owners of a state during the first two months of the year.

11. An office manager believes that scheduling all the work in his office would cost more than the advantages to be gained from such scheduling efforts. He feels, however, that scheduling certain operations only would be possible from the standpoint of cost. In your opinion, would the scheduling of certain operations only probably prove satisfactory? Why, or why not?

12. Point out the relationship, if any, in each of the following pairs:
    a) Scheduling and office machines.
    b) Routing and office layout.
    c) Standards and office work fluctuation.
    d) Quality control and dispatching.

CASE PROBLEMS

Case 22–1. Dallas Dandy Petroleum Products, Inc.

Distribution of "Dallas Dandy" petroleum products is made by sales to independent dealers and by direct sales to certain customers by the corporation's bulk plants and commission agents. These bulk stations number about two hundred and are widely dispersed geographically. Products sold directly by bulk plants are recorded by means of customer delivery tickets which are listed on a sales report by an office employee at the bulk station. On any given sales report, there might be listed 15 to 500 tickets. The bulk plant reports from one to five times a week, depending upon its volume of business.

Because of customer billings, sales reports, and tax reports, a particular month's business must be processed for all bulk plants within the first three days of the following month. Hence, all bulk plants must have their sales reports in the office by the second working day of the following month. This creates a large volume of work at the first of each month and a limited period within which to complete its processing. The department that initially receives the work is not sufficiently staffed for this heavy, short-term load, nor are the succeeding departments to which the work is passed.

Initially, it was hoped that in some way the problem would solve itself, and the office manager did very little toward its solution. After a while, he exerted pressure upon the supervisors in an attempt to get more work from the clerks. This helped to a certain point; but with the same story every month and an increasing volume of work, it was evident that something more would have to be done.

Giving the problem much study, the office manager decided to establish a group of "special clerks." These were chosen from various departments and were selected because of their experience and flexibility. Their regular assignments were normally work of little priority value; they could be done at any time during the month. When the month-end volume of work arrived, these special clerks, as many as were needed, were added to the first department which received the work. As the work moved along to subsequent departments, so did the special clerks. When the rush period was over, they returned to their regular assignments.

The arrangement devised by the office manager worked satisfactorily for several months; then, complaints grew from customers regarding errors in papers sent them. For the month just ended, 378 complaints were received. Normally, about 50–60 complaints had been received each month, none of them too serious. Since there were about 20,000 active customer accounts, the office manager had accepted 50–60 as probably a normal state of affairs. But when the complaints jumped to 378, he became very concerned. He discussed the problem with the various supervisors, who assured him they would make special efforts to insure better-quality work. The following month, the mistakes reported by customers reached 443. The office manager was certain that corrective action must be taken at once. How many papers erred in favor of the customer, about which the company heard nothing, also worried him. He was certain his superior would find out about the situation and demand a solution to the problem. He reasoned that he had better have the right answer and a plan in operation before he was "called on the carpet."

Problems:

1. What are some of the major alternatives open to the office manager?
2. Do you believe the present "special clerks" arrangement can be made to operate satisfactorily? Substantiate your answer.
3. What program of action do you recommend for the office manager? Why?

Case 22–2.   Steadman Company

For the past few weeks, the volume of office work has increased about 18 per cent. Unfinished work is piling up, and the office manager does not know if a temporary peak or a permanent new office work level is being attained. Data on the present office force are:

Type of Work	Three Accountants	Six Typists	Seven Clerks	Receptionist and Switchboard Operator
Accounting..........	100	....	....	....
Typing..............	....	190	22	5
Filing...............	12	19	196	....
Miscellaneous........	8	31	62	35
Hours per week.......	120	240	280	40
Average hourly pay rate.	$2.35	$1.80	$1.40	$1.50

The sales manager suggests that the office staff work overtime in order to complete the work. He realizes that time and one half will be paid for overtime hours; but in his opinion, this is the best answer.

The office manager personally dislikes the idea of overtime. He wants to go home to his family at the regular quitting time. Also, he will not receive overtime pay himself, because of his payroll classification. He favors hiring extra help.

The president of the company suggests that a service bureau be used to handle the overload. A friend of the president has told him that a service bureau, the Keystone Office Services, does excellent work and gives fast service. If the work is taken to its office, the bureau charges for accounting work $4.00 per hour and for typing and general clerical work $2.75 an hour; or it will send help to the client's office, for which the charge is $4.50 and $3.50, respectively, an hour per employee supplied by Keystone.

Problems:

1. What important factors should be considered in arriving at a decision? Discuss.

2. What action should the office manager take? Justify your answer.

Chapter 23

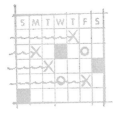

QUANTITY CONTROL—
OFFICE PROCEDURES

No man really becomes a fool until he stops asking questions.

—CHARLES P. STEINMETZ

QUANTITY control, as applied to office procedures, deals with the amount of papers processed or the amount of work done on any one paper. Quantity control is a vital part of all the effort of managerial controlling in an office. If office work is to be done efficiently, the essential information must be handled in the best manner possible. Work which is actually not required or poorly performed should be identified and the condition remedied as a result of quantity control practices in the office.

OFFICE WASTE ELIMINATION

Evaluating the office work being done quite frequently leads to the strong conviction that the work can be done in a simpler and better manner. The controlling activity of comparing what is being done with what should or can be done is centered around processing and is usually expressed in terms of objective accomplishment. If the predetermined goal is gained, the office procedure is considered satisfactory. This goal achievement criterion tends to emphasize elimination of nonproductive or wasteful elements of a procedure, that is, those parts not contributing directly to the desired end results. Examples include delays at desks, waiting for instructions, and long moves from work station to work station.

In other words, the elimination of waste is paramount. Waste exists (1) in doing unnecessary office work and (2) in doing necessary office work inefficiently. Each of these groups offers a tremendous challenge to everyone interested or employed in office work.

The evaluating of office procedures, seeking to improve their effectiveness, and eliminating waste, leads logically to the subject of work simplification, which is extremely important. Dynamic quantity control of office procedures leads to work simplification; but the two terms are not synonymous, as will be shown in the immediately following pages.

OFFICE WORK SIMPLIFICATION

Getting rid of unnecessary office work and doing only what is necessary and doing it efficiently are commonly accorded unanimity of approval. Everybody is for this plan of action, but relatively few do anything about it. Actually, its conception and implementation is more of a philosophy, an attitude, a type of thinking, and a belief about office work accomplishment. Some have termed it "office work simplification," and formally define it as common sense organized to eliminate waste of material, equipment, time, energy, and space in the performance of office work.

Office work simplification can be applied to a procedure, method, form, arrangement, machine, equipment, or layout. In this book, it is first discussed in relation to an entire office procedure. The application of work simplification to an individual's job is treated in the following chapter. It is believed that this is the correct order—i.e., first simplify the procedure, and then simplify the elements making up the procedure. To reverse this order would mean that individual jobs would be improved before determining whether they are necessary.

Work simplification deals with such things as determining the proper work sequence and the various steps making up that sequence, the least-effort manner of performing each required office task, the arrangement of the work station, the type of machines used, the skill required to do the work, the make-up and size of the form, who sees the form and what he does with it, and how long it remains at each desk. The possibilities for securing work simplification are limited only by the ability, imagination, and aggressiveness of the person doing the simplification work. There is no secret formula.

Many office procedures have been subjected to quantity-controlling efforts over and over again, and improvements have resulted from each study. The best way, in keeping with the right quantity control, is a theoretical concept. Excess in office work will usually be found as work requirement change, new machines are developed, new materials become available, and informed office personnel aggressively seek improvements.

TOP MANAGEMENT SUPPORT

A work simplification program should have the approval and support of the top managers for full benefits to be derived. They must be convinced that work simplification is the means to pursue to get rid of waste. Support from the top not only gives prestige and status to the program, but it also serves to inform all members of the enterprise that work simplification is in keeping with the mode of operation the top managers want to exist.

PRINCIPLES OF OFFICE WORK SIMPLIFICATION

Over a period, many lists of principles or guides of office work simplification have been compiled. Some are quite lengthy; but for our purposes here, six principles will be discussed.

1. *Promote "participation with know-how" by every office employee by means of training in and encouragement of the use of work simplification.* Enthusiastic employees with initiative and imagination in formulating the means and in co-operating in efforts to eliminate waste are of fundamental importance. A will to want an improved procedure to work satisfactorily and an understanding of the reasons for developing procedural improvement to eliminate waste are cardinal considerations in any work simplification program. For the most part, these are not won by having an expert simplify the work and then telling the employees how the work should be done. In contrast, these considerations are won by encouraging employee participation in the work simplification efforts; for in this way, employee interest, self-expression, acceptance, and co-operation are motivated and utilized.

But participation alone is insufficient. Nothing is more frustrating to the employee than to be asked to take part in an activity about which he knows little or nothing. This means the know-how must be supplied. Short, effective training programs are in order. Information and examples must be made available to the office employee. Thus, the "participation with know-how" is supplied.

The best improvements in the manner of office work performance may produce discouraging results because of employee attitudes and reactions. This has been summarized in four words, "employee resistance to change," but such a phrase appears incomplete and actually misleading.

Most office employees dislike being "pushed around," being criticized, and not being informed of developments of changes which affect them. Factors such as these cause the employee to desire the *status quo* and to view with disdain a new means of work performance suggested by outsiders. In addition, fear of the unknown effect of improvements contributes to the employee's nonco-operative attitude. At the bottom of this is the employee's natural suspicion of what might happen to him as a result of the change. Typical of these fears are the questions: Will my job be eliminated? Will lower prestige and loss of esteem by fellow employees result? Will my favorite desk location be lost? Is a loss in pay involved? These fears must be eliminated in order to gain the full benefits of procedural improvements.

What is the best way to do this? The answer is primarily employee "participation with know-how" in the work simplification program. A person will usually accept what he himself proposes. Give the employee the technique and the means for improving office work; the resultant improvement will usually have acceptance and the strong will to make it work satisfactorily. Even though the improvement does not represent the zenith of what probably can be done, it is well to remember that an average improvement with employee acceptance and enthusiasm will commonly outproduce a superior improvement with employee passive resistance.

In addition, frank information pointing out the need for improvements to keep the enterprise competitive or to give greater security to the employee should be provided. It is not necessary that an office employee lose his job as a result of work simplification. A policy of retraining and transferring to other jobs can be followed. In many cases, the normal labor turnover will take care of the number of employees needed; those leaving the company are not replaced. But these facts should be explained in simple language to the employees, so that they know what is going on and where they fit into the picture. Also, the ideas of acquiring a real sense of accomplishment and of getting things done the simple way are strong appeals to many office employees. If a manager cannot win the employees' enthusiastic co-operation for the cause of eliminating office waste, it is almost a certainty that no really significant gains from quantity control are going to be made. And under such a condition, the total potential of office employee productivity will never be reached.

2. *Make the series of activities productive and simple.* As a group, the series of work activities that are adopted should represent the best possible combination for achieving the finished work, taking into account the facilities and conditions under which the work must be accomplished. Simply stated, justify each activity for its essentiality, and eliminate all the unnecessary ones. As far as possible, those contributing directly to the goal, or so-called "productive" elements of a procedure, should be maximized; and conversely, the nonproductive elements should be reduced to an absolute minimum. Normally, this provides for the greatest productivity. However, in most procedures, there are usually nonproductive elements that cannot be eliminated entirely; some are required to maximize the productive elements.

The more effective activities or series of activities are usually simple in their make-up. Involved ways of performing work should be avoided because they invariably include waste, especially of time and of quality. The specific goals for performing most office work are relatively simple, and the process can be simple. But there is some tendency to get imbued with details or excessively concerned with the frills. These must be guarded against and eliminated for improved work efficiency.

3. *Combine work activities wherever possible to avoid recopying.* Unless carefully controlled, it is common to find needless copying of data over and over again as a built-in practice of an office procedure that is followed. As a matter of fact, it is so prevalent that it has won acceptance in some offices as the accepted manner of getting information processed. There is nothing uncommon, for example, in having the salesman write an order, his branch office recopy it, the factory recopy certain portions of the order, the billing department recopy on an invoice, and accounts receivable recopy on the proper ledger card.

Most of these writing activities can be combined into a single operation. Various form combinations, such as a purchase order and receiving sets, packing list and bill-of-lading sets, or any group of papers combined in such a way as to permit a single writing, may be used advantageously. Or the source data can be put into a form that permits subsequent reproduction either in total or in part as the procedure requires. This normally necessitates the utilization of certain machines.

4. *Reduce distances traveled to the shortest amounts feasible.* Movement of papers or of people are costly and wasteful, since the great majority of such activities do not represent purposive effort. Therefore, movements should be closely scrutinized; if not essential, they should be eliminated. For office procedures, distances must be traveled, but these should be reduced to a minimum.

It is usually better to move the paper than the person. Sometimes, the machine can be brought to the work; or mechanical handling devices, such as conveyors, pneumatic tubes, and gravity feeds to deliver or to take away the papers, can be used. When messengers are employed, perhaps more items per trip are in order. Different arrangements of the office layout might also offer worth-while improvements.

5. *Arrange activities to provide a smooth flow from one clerical step to another or a rhythmic pattern for an employee at a workplace.* Excessive amounts or spurts of unduly heavy work loads tend to discourage the office employee. As a result, the feeling of never "getting on top of the work" or having a sense of accomplishment plagues the employee. In contrast, the situation of carefully throttling the work in order to keep busy is equally annoying. A steady, constant flow of work which is adequate and reasonable is especially significant in determining the most satisfactory office procedure.

Provide for a steady, constant flow of the work whenever possible. Once the paper work starts "through the mill," it should continue to progress until the completion of the procedure. Delays and hesitations should not be permitted. Much time and energy are dissipated by tolerating the jumping-around from one batch of work to another, then returning to the initial batch. It takes time to adjust mentally to the different batches of work, not to mention the lost time in stopping one and starting another, and in interrupting the smooth work flow.

For the individual employee, a rhythmic pattern of work actions should be encouraged by the arrangement of the work. Getting a swing or emphasis upon certain parts of the work helps to lessen fatigue and monotony. Motions along curved, not straight, lines should be used.

6. *Provide employees with pleasant physical surroundings and comfortable, correct workplaces.* Almost every day, additional evidence is found demonstrating that pleasant physical working conditions add materially to employees' satisfaction and productivity. Waste is decreased. Adequate light, for example, is an important factor in keeping errors in office work at a minimum.

An employee should be comfortable. This means that his chair, desk, table, or machine should be of such dimensions that the work can be accomplished with ease, that is, without excessive physical exertion or strain. When possible, it is usually desirable to have the employee sit part of the time and stand part of the time. Some change is apparently necessary for maximum comfort.

NOMINAL HEAD OF PROGRAM

It is usually advisable to have one person in the office serve as nominal head of the work simplification program and be responsible for coordinating the various efforts, stimulating interest in the program, and acting in the capacity of a clearinghouse for the various projects. Specifically, the day-to-day activities of this head include conducting all or some of the training sessions, counseling trainees and graduates of the training, publicizing the work simplification program, making periodic reports to top managers on the progress of the program, and budgeting the program's expenses.

A satisfactory arrangement is to have the person in charge report to a committee made up of the office manager and several department heads. By this means, proposed changes can be talked over, and an exchange of ideas is provided for. This medium also serves as a basis for keeping the department heads informed about procedural improvements, as well as for reminding them of the importance of effective procedures in office work. It may be desirable to have a member of top management on the committee, so that vested interests on the lower levels will not be perpetuated.

If the volume of work warrants, a work simplification organizational unit staffed with full-time employees can be formed. Regardless of the organizational arrangement, the principle of "participation with know-how" should be followed. Outside consultants can be used to bring in specialized knowledge and broad, fresh, objective viewpoints. They are especially effective in training employees in the techniques of work simplification.

THE FIVE-STEP PATTERN

An effective approach used in work simplification of office procedures consists of five steps, including the following:

1. Select the office procedure to be evaluated and improved.
2. Get all the facts about this procedure.
3. Analyze and evaluate these facts by means of pertinent questions.
4. Devise the improvement.
5. Apply the improved procedure for accomplishing the office work.

Experience has shown this pattern to be an excellent basis for exercising quantity control over office procedures work. Discussion of each step follows.

SELECT THE OFFICE PROCEDURE TO BE EVALUATED AND IMPROVED

Generally speaking, this is a trouble-giving situation, i.e., the number of work activities is too large, the time taken to do the work is excessive, costs are unduly high, or the end result seems unjustifiable. It may be a procedure that limits other office work or one in which labor requirements appear completely out of proportion.

Whatever the procedure selected, it must be defined. This clarifies the objective and avoids the mistake of attempting to simplify office work without first gaining a clear concept of the work objective. Defining the procedure assists in its simplification because all efforts can be concentrated and directed toward this goal. Questions to help in formulating the definition include: What is the end result of this work? Is it essential? Is this end result achieved now in part or in total by another procedure? How is the information from this office procedure used? Who takes action as a result of this work completion?

GET ALL THE FACTS ABOUT THIS PROCEDURE

The next step is to find out how the work is currently being handled. Details of the present procedure are obtained from available record sources, i.e., job descriptions, charts, lists, outlines, and sample forms. Supplemental information can be obtained from talks with members of management. This is followed by an inspection of the actual procedure in action, so that the type of work and the equipment used can be observed.

All the facts are needed to perform a competent analysis. For example, it is insufficient to note: "Purchasing department copy filed." Additional information is required: Is this the best place to file the copy? How many copies are filed per day or month? Is this a full-time job for one employee? Are any copies not filed? Why? Are they filed alphabetically?

To aid in getting all the facts and to gain a clear comprehension of them, graphic representations or charts have been developed. Charts show the complete action in concise form; they bring out the salient

OBJECTIVE	CHART TO USE	CHART ILLUSTRATION
TO IDENTIFY AND ANALYZE THE VARIOUS DETAILED STEPS OF THE WORK PROCESS	PROCESS CHART IDENTIFIES THE VARIOUS STEPS AND DIFFERENTIATES PRODUCTIVE FROM NONPRODUCTIVE ELEMENTS	
TO IMPROVE THE ARRANGE-MENT OF PHYSICAL FACILITIES	MOVEMENT DIAGRAM INDICATES MOVEMENT OF A PERSON OR A PAPER IN CONNECTION WITH PERFORMING WORK	
TO DETERMINE WHAT TYPES OF JOBS ARE PERFORMED AND WHO DOES THEM	WORK-DISTRIBUTION CHART— BASICALLY A SPREAD SHEET OF SUMMARIZED DATA	
TO ANALYZE THE DISTRIBUTION AND USE OF COPIES OF A MULTI-COPY OFFICE FORM	PROCEDURE FLOW CHART SHOWS NUMBER OF COPIES, WHO PREPARES, AND WHERE THEY ARE USED	

FIG. 23–1. Various types of charts used in evaluating and improving office procedures in quantity-controlling efforts.

points vital in the analysis. There are many different types of charts that can be used; the major ones used for office procedures are shown in Figure 23–1. For each chart, the objective, suggested usage, and illustration are given. Observe that each of these charts has a particular purpose and value, and it is neither necessary nor practical to use every type of chart in a particular study. Frequently, more than one chart is used, and the right combination of several charts usually reveals information and clues for work simplification. There will be more discussion about charts later in this chapter.

ANALYZE AND EVALUATE THESE FACTS BY MEANS OF PERTINENT QUESTIONS

Using the factual information about the entire procedure as a guide, the next step is to analyze and evaluate these facts. This phase might be described as one of challenging or of questioning each detail of the work. For this purpose, questions pertaining to Why, What, Where, When, Who, and How are extremely helpful. The facts obtained in step No. 2 show what is done, where, when, by whom, and how. To this, the big Why must be added. In other words, the questioning now is: What is being done and Why? Where should it be done and Why? When should it be done and Why? Who should do it and Why? How should it be done and Why? The use of these questions has been referred to as a questioning attitude or an open mind. The answers help to relate essentials, reveal unncessary work, and provide clues for improving the procedure.

Every activity of the procedure is subjected to this questioning, and the answers are evaluated in terms of the office work simplification principles discussed above. For example, the answers to the double question: "Where should it be done and why?" should comply with the principle: "Reduce distances traveled to the shortest amounts feasible."

Additional questions of a more specific nature can also be asked. The exact content will depend upon the individual case and to a very great extent upon the initiative and imagination of the questioner. Examples of specific questions include the following:[1]

1. Purpose of operation:
   a) What is the intended use of the form?
   b) Is the form used as intended?
   c) What purpose is served by the report?
   d) Could the information given on the form or the report be obtained from another source?
   e) Do numbers, ratios, or variations best answer and serve the needs of the procedure?
   f) Is the cost of preparing the form or report justified by the results it accomplishes?

---

[1] Adapted from H. B. Maynard and G. J. Stegemerten, *Guide to Methods Improvement* (New York: McGraw-Hill Book Co., Inc., 1944), pp. 25, 28, 31, 35, 39, 40, 45, and 46.

2. Design:
   a) Is the design of the form such that no portion is unused?
   b) Is the size of the form best suited to its use?
   c) Would a change in color of the form facilitate its use?
   d) Is the information by which the form will be filed located in the most convenient place from a filing standpoint?
   e) Can a special type of form, such as Activisible, Kardex, or Keysort, be used to advantage?
   f) Can large forms be designed so that, when folded, they will fit in standard files?

3. Process analysis:
   a) Is the operation duplicated at any point in the procedure?
   b) Should the form be filed permanently or temporarily, or be destroyed?
   c) Can two or more records be produced at one writing by combining forms?
   d) Can the copying of information be eliminated by using original records?
   e) Is information compiled in the manner best suited for subsequent sorting, filing, or use?
   f) Should permanent records be made on 35-mm. film to conserve filing space?

4. Inspection:
   a) Is the form or work legible?
   b) Is the form or report easy to interpret?
   c) How is work checked for errors?
   d) Is it important that all parts of the work be letter-perfect?
   e) Would the use of mechanical devices improve the accuracy of the work to a desirable extent?

5. Material:
   a) Is the paper stock used for the form the best for its purpose?
   b) Is the size of the form most economical from a material standpoint?
   c) How can waste of forms and office supplies be reduced?
   d) Are office materials analyzed for suitability and ordered in most economical quantities?

6. Material handling:
   a) Can the flow of a form through the procedure be expedited by improved office layout?
   b) Can the amount of time the form is delayed while awaiting action be reduced?
   c) Is messenger service adequate?
   d) Can pneumatic tubes or other forms-conveying systems be used to advantage?

    e) Should special arrangements be made for keeping forms clean during handling in the shop?

DEVISE THE IMPROVEMENT

    Improvement is obtained by seeking to eliminate, combine, change, or simplify the steps of the procedure. Answers to the question "What is being done and Why?" may point out activities that are unnecessary and can be eliminated. If so, eliminate them, for this is the zenith of work simplification. Questions of Where and Why, When and Why, and Who and Why will suggest combining or changing procedural elements as to place, time, and person, respectively. An improved procedure will result. The question "How and Why?" emphasizes simplifying the activity.

    Devising the improvement is assisted by conforming with work sim-

Key Questions	Major Principles*	Resultant Action	
What and Why?	1. Promote "participation with know-how." 2. Make activities productive and simple.	Eliminate	
Where and Why? When and Why? Who and Why?	1. Promote "participation with know-how." 3. Combine work activities—avoid recopying. 4. Reduce distances traveled. 5. Provide a smooth flow from one step to another.	Combine or change	the Place the Time the Person
How and Why?	1. Promote "participation with know-how." 2. Make activities productive and simple. 6. Provide pleasant employee surroundings.	Simplify	

    * Refer to pages 440–43.

    FIG. 23–2. Key questions, major principles, and resultant actions used in devising the improvement of an office procedure.

plification principles. For example, the answer to the question "Where and Why?"—suggesting a change in the place the task is done—is guided by consideration for principle No. 4: "Reduce distances traveled to the shortest amounts feasible," as discussed on page 442. Figure 23–2 is helpful in devising an office procedural improvement because it shows the relationships between the key questions asked, the major principles of work simplification utilized, and the resultant actions.

    The sequence of the questioning and subsequent improvement action is logical and practical. If the activity can be eliminated, there is no need to study it further for possible combination or change. Likewise, the "Who and Why" question precedes the "How and Why" question because the former might lead to improved labor utilization, and this should be determined before the manner of doing the work is improved.

APPLY THE IMPROVED PROCEDURE FOR ACCOMPLISHING THE OFFICE WORK

This last step includes obtaining approval for the installation of the improved procedure, installing it, checking to see if the estimated decrease in waste is being realized, and following up periodically to see that the gains are maintained. A common practice is to have a form filled out comparing pertinent information of the present with that of the proposed procedure. Savings expected in terms of man-hours, equipment, material, and dollars are the type of information included. Such information is essential for obtaining approval for the installation of the new procedure.

Acceptance of the improved way is sometimes predicated upon the results of a test installation. In this way, weaknesses can be spotted and corrected, and the assured savings can be validated. As already pointed out, acceptance of the improved procedure is facilitated by practicing "participation with know-how." To complement this, everyone concerned should be advised as to the proposal and what is being attempted. Full credit should be given to all who helped in the improvement.

The simplified procedure should be reviewed at reasonable intervals, possibly every three months, in order to make certain that it is being followed. The value of the improved procedure is minimized if it is only partly followed. It is important to know how the procedure is working out and if its action is effective.

CHARTS IN PROCEDURES WORK

As pointed out under step No. 2 above, "Get all the facts about this procedure," various types of charts are commonly used to show these facts and to help in the subsequent analysis and improvement. The balance of this chapter pertains to the more common and helpful of these charts. Included are (1) the process chart, (2) the movement diagram, (3) the work distribution chart, and (4) the procedure flow chart.

Before discussing these charts, it is well to point out their purposes. These include: (1) to assist in securing, organizing, and visualizing the facts, (2) to aid in analyzing and evaluating these facts, (3) to help formulate an improved procedure, and (4) to assist in convincing others of the value of the improved procedure. Unless the chart serves one or more of these purposes, it should not be drawn.

PROCESS CHART

A process chart shows in detail the successive steps in a process; it is probably one of the most helpful tools in work simplification. The steps are indicated by brief statements and symbols arranged vertically in chronological order, with the first step at the top of the sheet. There are four commonly used symbols: (1) a large circle, ◯, for an operation such as writing, posting, sorting, and filing; it is used whenever anything is being changed or created or added to; (2) a small circle, ○, for transportation such as movement of paper from place to place or the walking of an individual; (3) an inverted triangle, ▽, for storage or delay, such as an office form remaining in place awaiting further action; and (4) a square, ▢, for inspection which includes checking or verifying, but not changing the paper. To illustrate, signing a letter constitutes an operation and would be represented by a large circle. Sending the letter to another office unit is transportation and is shown by a small circle. Filing the letter is represented by a storage triangle. Checking the letter for errors constitutes inspection and is represented by a square.

OPERATION – ORIGIN OF RECORD

OPERATION – ADDING TO RECORD

TRAVEL OR MOVE

DELAY – AVOIDABLE

FILE

COPY DISCARDED OR DESTROYED

INSPECTION

FIG. 23–3. Symbols for process charts preferred by some analysts.

Some recommend the use of symbols modified from those given above. One such set is shown by Figure 23–3. It can be observed that the "operation" has been refined into two types: (1) those that represent origin of the record and (2) those adding information to the record. Likewise, an arrow, symbolic of travel, and a large *D*, standing for avoidable delay, are utilized. A separate symbol for "copy discarded" is also used. Many analysts have found that color is helpful in charting work. For example, the "do" operations, constituting direct processing work and adding value to the product, are distinguished by the use of a special color. In contrast, for the "do" operations used but not adding value, no special color is used. Included in such "do" operations are those for "make ready" and "put away," or those done for preparatory or cleaning-up purposes.

The intended purpose of the process chart and the symbols is to give a clear picture of the office procedure and assist in analyzing and improving it. Any reasonable set of symbols can be used; the best is the set that assists the analyst most in his determination to eliminate paper work waste. In addition, it is customary to include on a process chart the time required, the distance covered if movement is involved, and a summary by type of action.

A process chart can be drawn for an entire procedure covering many departments, or it may be confined to a part of a procedure. The details will vary accordingly, but a process chart always shows the basic types of actions throughout the area covered.

Figure 23–4 illustrates a process chart. It shows the process of stopping an incorrect charge credit in a large department store. It is drawn for the credit form papers. This work is brought about by the following situation.

An article of merchandise is purchased by a customer, Mrs. John T. Smith, with a charge account. The merchandise is returned, but the clerk incorrectly writes Mrs. John F. Smith on the credit memorandum. Later, the customer telephones and informs the adjusting department of the store that the name is not Mrs. John F. Smith, but Mrs. John T. Smith. Meanwhile, the credit memorandum is in process in either the sales auditing department or the accounts receivable department, both located several floors away from the adjusting department. Hence, a "stop notice" is prepared and a duplicate copy sent to sales auditing or accounts receivable, telling them not to bill the credit memorandum made out to John F. Smith. This stop notice, along with the credit memorandum to John F. Smith, is returned to the adjuster who handled the telephone call.

The placing of the credit memorandum and stop notice on the desk constitutes step No. 1 of the chart illustrated in Figure 23–4. Therefore, on line No. 1, this action is briefly described in the column to the left. This action is an operation, in that something happens to the papers; hence, it is represented by a large-circle symbol and is indicated on the chart by filling in the large circle under "operation" on line No. 1. Appropriate notes are made in the column to the right.

Next, the forms are picked up. Hence, on line No. 2, this action is expressed and represented by a large circle. In a similar manner, the entire process is described and charted. The totals of each action and of the distances traveled are then determined and recorded in the summary table at the top of the sheet. In this illustration, the figures are:

Operations..........................17
Transportations.....................7
Storage.............................5
Distance traveled...................92 feet

A study of the chart shows that this procedure can be simplified. To do this, the work simplification principles and the questioning attitude, as already discussed, were applied. For example, when step No. 3— placing paper in drawer—is subjected to the question "What is done and

PAGE..........

MARSHALL FIELD & COMPANY

FLOW PROCESS CHART

JOB Stopping an incorrect Charge Credit

SUBJECT CHARTED Credit form

CHARTED BY Ethel Marable

DATE November 19—

DEPT. Customer's Service SEC. Adjusting

SUMMARY			
METHOD	PRES.	PROPD.	SAVG.
NO. OF OPERATIONS	17		
NO. OF TRANSPORTATIONS	7		
NO. OF STORAGES	5		
NO. OF INSPECTIONS			
MAN HOURS OR MINUTES			
DISTANCE TRAVELED	92 ft.		

	DETAILS (PRESENT ~~PROPOSED~~) METHOD	OPER. / TRANS. / STORAGE / INSPECT.	DIST. IN FEET	TIME IN MINUTES	WHY? WHAT? WHERE? WHEN? WHO? HOW?	NOTES
1	Placed on desk	Oper.				Credit and duplicate Stop attached—sent from Sales Auditing or accounts receivable
2	Picked up	Oper.				
3	Placed in drawer	Trans.	2			
4	Waits	Storage				Time indefinite—may have other work of priority nature
5	Taken out of drawer	Trans.	2			
6	Placed on desk	Oper.				
7	Waits	Storage				Makes out request for Claim which acts as out-of-file notice
8	Attached to request	Oper.				
9	Carried to central files	Trans.	15			
10	Placed in basket	Oper.				
11	Waits	Storage				For central file Clerk
12	Picked up	Oper.				
13	Carried to file cabinet	Trans.	25			
14	Waits	Storage				Looking for claim under correct name
15	Attached to claim	Oper.				
16	Carried to out basket	Trans.	25			
17	Placed in basket	Oper.				
18	Waits	Storage				for pick up
19	Picked up	Oper.				
20	Carried to desk	Trans.	15			
21	Placed on desk	Oper.				
22	Stop taken from claim	Oper.				Original stop now placed on claim
23	Credit voided	Oper.				write "Void", Claim number and initials
24	Picked up	Oper.				
25	Placed in house envelope	Oper.				
26	Picked up	Oper.				
27	Carried to house mailbox	Trans.	8			
28	Placed in house mailbox	Oper.				
29	Waits for pickup	Oper.				

24-01-01 Form 187

Courtesy: Marshall Field & Co., Chicago

FIG. 23–4. A fill-in type of process chart covering the work of stopping an incorrect charge credit.

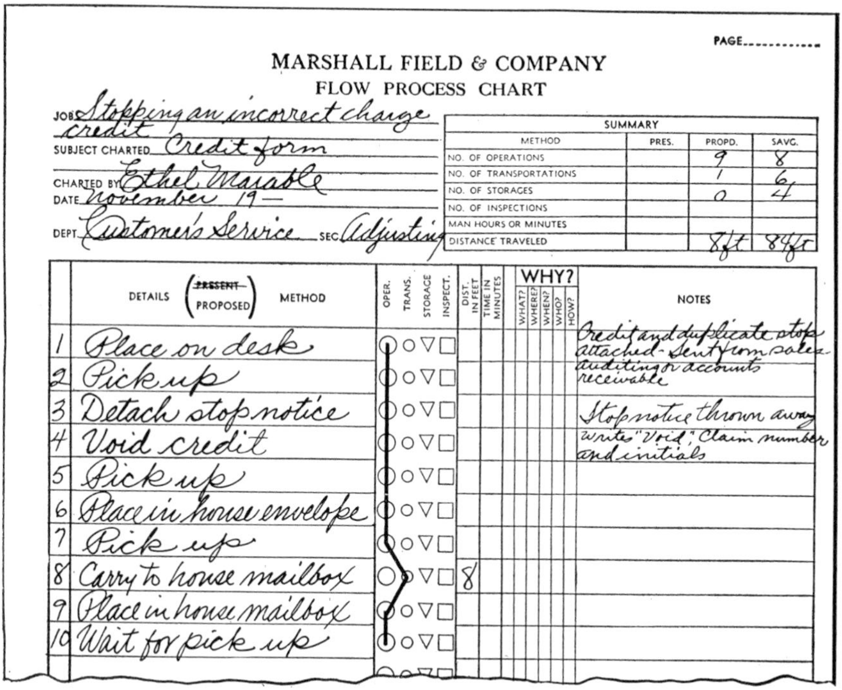

PAGE..........

MARSHALL FIELD & COMPANY
FLOW PROCESS CHART

JOB Stopping an incorrect charge credit
SUBJECT CHARTED Credit form
CHARTED BY Ethel Marable
DATE November 19—
DEPT. Customer's Service SEC. Adjusting

SUMMARY			
METHOD	PRES.	PROPD.	SAVG.
NO. OF OPERATIONS		9	8
NO. OF TRANSPORTATIONS		1	6
NO. OF STORAGES		0	4
NO. OF INSPECTIONS			
MAN HOURS OR MINUTES			
DISTANCE TRAVELED		8 ft	84 ft

	DETAILS (~~PRESENT~~ / PROPOSED) METHOD	OPER. / TRANS. / STORAGE / INSPECT.	DIST. IN FEET	TIME IN MINUTES	WHY? WHAT? WHERE? WHEN? WHO? HOW?	NOTES
1	Place on desk	OPER.				Credit and duplicate stop attached - Sent from sales auditing or accounts receivable
2	Pick up	OPER.				
3	Detach stop notice	OPER.				Stop notice thrown away
4	Void credit	OPER.				Writes "Void", Claim number and initials
5	Pick up	OPER.				
6	Place in house envelope	OPER.				
7	Pick up	OPER.				
8	Carry to house mailbox	TRANS.	8			
9	Place in house mailbox	OPER.				
10	Wait for pick up	OPER.				

Courtesy: Marshall Field & Co., Chicago

FIG. 23–5. An improved procedure over that shown in Fig. 23–4.

Why?" it is found to be unproductive and hence can be eliminated. In similiar manner, every operation, transportation, storage, and inspection not proved necessary is eliminated; and actions found necessary are combined wherever feasible, or changed to provide better accomplishment of the work. Finally, each necessary step is simplified as much as possible.

Figure 23–5 shows an improved procedure over the one shown in Figure 23–4. In the light of what has been written, it is suggested that a careful comparison of these two charts be made in order to gain an insight as to how a procedure can be improved. Under the new procedure, credits are voided with a claim number on them and sent to sales auditing or accounts receivable. The stop notice can be discarded, since its duplicate is already on the claim. The elimination of requests to pull claims out of the central file accounts for getting rid of steps No. 7 through No. 21 of the original procedure. Also, steps No. 3 through No. 6 have been eliminated; they were simply delaying actions brought about by the make-up of the original procedure. The improved procedure requires eight less operations, six less transportations, four less storages, and less than 10 per cent of the former distance traveled.

MOVEMENT DIAGRAM

A movement diagram portrays motion through space. It is drawn on a scaled layout of the office floor plan so that the movement can be measured and viewed in proper relationship with the physical factors. These charts are helpful in spotting backtracking, visualizing the physical motion involved, and locating congestion and bottlenecks.

Movement diagrams are of two types: those showing paper movement and those showing employee movement. The entire chart should be of one type or the other. Attempting to follow first one and then the other on the same chart leads to confusion. As the name implies, paper movement charts depict the successive lines of travel for a paper form, i.e.,

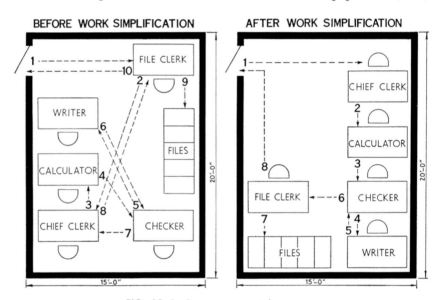

FIG. 23–6. Paper movement diagrams.

from desk to desk or from department to department. Figure 23–6 illustrates paper movement diagrams, showing the movements before and after work simplification.

In many instances, however, the paper is not moved by simply handing it to the person at the adjacent desk or by messenger service; it is carried by the person last working on it to the next successive station. This is part of the procedure. It is therefore apparent that an analysis of employee movement is equally as important as an analysis of paper movement. Charts showing employee movement are especially helpful where the work is nonrepetitive and where the employees operate over a large area. The employee movement chart is similar in appearance to the paper movement chart.

OFFICE FUNCTIONS	TOTAL MAN HOURS	LOIS MILLER Unit Supervisor	MAN HOURS	BETTY HEIDT Stenographer	MAN HOURS	RUTH TORFF Order Clerk	MAN HOURS	EDITH WRIGHT File Clerk	MAN HOURS	SYLVIA GAZEL Telephone Switchboard Operator	MAN HOURS
Correspondence	54	Read and route Dictation	9 10	Takes dictation Transcribes	10 20	Types labels and materials for files	5				
Computing	32	Figures prices	3	Figures prices	2	Figures prices	15	Figures prices	12		
Filing	21					Files correspondence Finds letters in file	2 5	Files correspondence Finds letters in file Classifies correspondence	4 6 4		
Handling mail	26	Opens mail Time stamps mail	2 5	Stamps mail	2	Opens mail	5	Stamps mail	4	Opens mail Stamps mail	3 5
Miscellaneous	67	Answers questions Answers telephone inquiries Supervises	8 2 1	Cleans typewriter Gets supplies Arranges advertising stuffing material	1 2 3	Answers telephone inquiries	2	Errands for postage stamps and supplies Maintains tickler file for follow-ups	8 2 8	Operates switchboard	32
	200		40		40		40		40		40

FIG. 23-7. Work distribution chart.

WORK DISTRIBUTION CHART

Proper distribution of work, facts on who is doing what, and the full utilization of labor skills on tasks for which they are best suited are fundamental to good management. In order to know what types of jobs are done and who performs them, a work distribution chart can be used. This is basically a spread sheet which shows, for a given time period—usually a week—the type of work and the time spent on each job by each employee in the office unit under review. The basic information can be obtained from the supervisor or the employees. Probably more objective data are obtained by observing each employee and recording information on his activities. However, this approach is relatively expensive.

Figure 23-7 shows a work distribution chart. A vertical column is used for each employee, along with one to indicate the time spent on each activity. The functions performed are listed in the first column on the left. This chart gives a graphic, over-all picture of the work done

---

1. Is the work distributed properly—one employee does not have too much, another too little to do?
2. What is each employee's contribution?
3. Are efforts being expended on relatively unimportant work?
4. What activities take the most time? Should they?
5. Does there appear to be excessive shifting from task to task?
6. Is job specialization being followed?
7. Are skills and abilities being utilized fully?
8. Is a fairly steady work flow being maintained?

FIG. 23-8. Questions to ask in utilizing the data provided by a work distribution chart.

and the relative amounts of time put on each job. It shows, for example, whether major activities are given the most time or, in contrast, how much time is being spent on relatively unimportant functions. It reveals whether special skills are being wasted, whether too many employees are performing the same function, and whether an employee is doing too many unrelated tasks. Pertinent questions to ask in connection with work distribution charts are listed in Figure 23–8 on page 455.

PROCEDURE FLOW CHART

This type of chart is very effective where multiple-copy forms are used. It depicts graphically the distribution and subsequent steps for each form from physical inception to permanent storage or destruction. Generally, this type of chart is not difficult to construct.

Figure 23–9 shows a procedure flow chart of work performed for handling uniform express receipt-collect shipments. Four separate writings are required for each package. These include separate typings for each of two labels, a packing slip and duplicate, and the copies of the uniform express receipt-collect. As indicated in the chart, the labels are put on the package. One copy of the packing slip is sent to the billing department for filing, the other copy placed in the package. Other operations can be determined from the chart.

A procedure to accomplish the same objective, but with much waste eliminated, is shown in Figure 23–10. As illustrated, a seven-part form is written at one time from the sales order. The writing is checked, and then the copies are sent to the shipping department, where they are distributed and used as indicated on the chart. The total number of operations has been reduced from 30 to 17, a saving of nearly 45 per cent. Waste elimination has been achieved by giving special attention to making activities productive, combining operations, eliminating others, and increasing the accuracy.

ADDITIONAL QUESTIONS FOR CONTROLLING PROCEDURES

In addition to what has already been stated, certain questions can be asked periodically to determine if changes seem in order for existent office procedures. The following eight questions make up an effective check list.

1. Is any part of any office procedure now in use being justified simply because "that's the way it's always been done"?

2. Are codes for such things as office forms, procedures, and work flows being used effectively? Can the codes be shortened or simplified?

3. Are any procedures being performed in an awkward, inefficient manner due to lack of equipment or machines?

4. Are batches of work of the proper amount and frequency to permit easy handling and balancing?

5. Are related tasks combined to the maximum extent?

6. Are employees doing the type of tasks for which they have special aptitude, training, and experience?

7. Are all instructions simple and clear?

8. Are cleanup tasks performed effectively and in time to avoid confusion created by things lying around?

PERT AND CRITICAL PATH

Quite a few companies have adopted a novel approach to help keep tab on complex projects involving a number of procedures. In defense work it is called PERT (Program Evaluation and Review Technique); in other fields it is known as the Critical Path approach. In either case, the purpose is to highlight the key jobs or work in a multistage industrial operation and to indicate possible solutions if trouble appears. The office is involved in that these efforts require additional or revised information on short notice or new information as necessitated by changes in plans and schedules.

In most cases, PERT or Critical Path takes the form of special charts indicating the sequence and progress of many interdependent steps required for completion of the project. Commonly, separate charts are constructed for each major division of the total project, then these charts are combined to reveal the composite necessary operations for the total project. From this composite chart, the time for the longest sequence of operations is now computed to determine the estimated project completion time. This longest sequence is the "critical path" because a delay in any job along this path would necessarily delay completion of the entire project. In contrast, delay in any other jobs of the project not included in the critical path could, within limits, be delayed without retarding the whole project. Usually some 85 per cent of the individual jobs are found in this category. In other words, 15 per cent of the jobs are critical in content and sequence to the completion of the entire project within a stated period.

QUESTIONS

1. What are the four major purposes of charts as used in work simplification for office procedures?

2. Comment on this statement: "Obtaining the best possible office procedure is the job of the office manager, not the office employee or the office employees. To improve procedures, it is the office manager's responsibility to determine what changes are to be made, when, and how. This being accomplished, the office manager informs the employee or employees of the procedure to be followed."

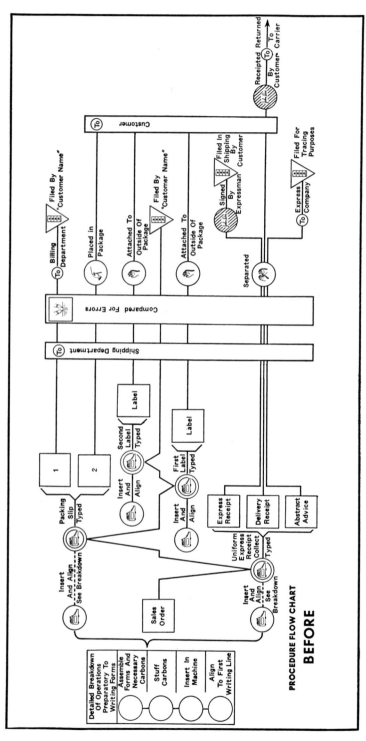

PROCEDURE FLOW CHART

BEFORE

FIG. 23–9. A procedure flow chart before work simplification.

Courtesy: Standard Register Co., Dayton

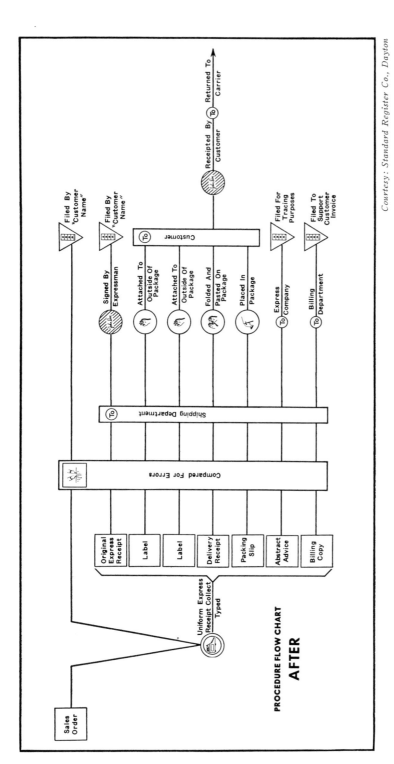

FIG. 23–10. The improved procedure over that shown in Figure 23–9, after work simplification.

Courtesy: Standard Register Co., Dayton

3. List the six principles of office work simplification, and briefly discuss the one you feel is most important.

4. Identify each of the following by a simple statement:
   a) "Make ready" operation.
   b) Questioning attitude.
   c) Office work simplification.
   d) Quantity control of office procedures.

5. Should office work simplification be applied first to a procedure and then to methods, or vice versa? Why? Are there any outstanding exceptions to your answer? Explain.

6. In your opinion, do office employees resist change to procedural improvements? Discuss.

7. Explain Figure 23–2 in your own words.

8. Can all the elements of a procedure be productive? Explain.

9. Is there a uniform code for symbols used in process charting? Should there be? Why?

10. Do you agree with the following statement? "Whenever a change is made in an office procedure, certain employees will complain, others will not care, and still others will enthusiastically welcome it. It is usually impossible to please all employees all the time. The most expeditious course is to make all the changes for improvement in a procedure at one time and thus gain the benefits as quickly as possible."

11. What are some considerations to be taken into account to determine what office procedure should be evaluated and improved?

12. Is it practical to simplify office procedures without the use of charts? Why?

CASE PROBLEMS

Case 23–1.   Tostomero Music Publishers

In an effort to reduce waste and cut costs, Mr. Benito Grassi, the president, decided to institute a paper work simplification program in this company. An expert in work simplification was hired for a period of six months. It was believed that within this time the program could be well established, and further use of the expert's services would be unnecessary. During the first day at work, the expert observed the entire office and finally selected the job of opening mail and sorting the contents as the first job for analysis and simplification. The job was improved considerably, and the new method was demonstrated by the expert to the supervisor of the mail department, who agreed that the new method was a big improvement. Together, they went to one of the four employees performing this work and showed her the new method. She was requested to perform the job in the new manner. Within the next day or so, all four employees on this work had been instructed in the new method and were using it.

For the following two weeks, production records kept by the supervisor of the mail department showed that the productivity of the four employees increased approximately 30 per cent. It was found that the mail work for the day was nearly finished by midafternoon. Three of the girls were sent to the shipping department, where they were given work of verifying the sheet music gathered for an order against the items called for on that order.

The expert, quite pleased with the achievements to date, reviewed other jobs for analysis. He wrote a short note to Mr. Grassi informing him of the success of the program. The following day, he received a telephone request from the mail department supervisor to come to that department at once. The expert complied, and the supervisor related that the four girls had come to him in a group asking for more money. He told them the plan was to give them an increase but they had beat him to it. Beginning a week from next Monday, their pay would be raised from $60 to $70 a week. The supervisor inquired of the expert if this was correct. The expert assured him that was the amount the company had agreed upon.

"Did the girls react favorably to the pay increase?" asked the expert.

"They seemed to be satisfied. They didn't say much of anything."

Over the next six weeks, the production of the four girls decreased until it was practically the same as it had been before the simplified method was installed. The decline was fairly uniform for each of the four employees. The expert checked the operators several times and observed that the employees were still using the new method. He spoke to them individually, but none had any complaints, nor did any have an explanation for the current level of production.

Problems:

1. Discuss the important ramifications of this problem.
2. Evaluate the work of the expert. Explain.
3. What action do you now recommend for the company? Why?

Case 23–2.   A. P. Judson, Inc.

The procedure followed for handling order-invoice papers is as follows:

1. The customer's order, received by telephone, mail, or telegraph, is checked for accuracy, completeness, and pricing by the order department.

2. The order is then forwarded to the credit department, which checks the credit of the customer; if satisfactory, the order is returned to the order department. If the credit is not satisfactory, the order is held, and a letter is written to the customer.

3. Upon return to the order department, the order is given to an order typist, who prepares and proofs the order master for use on the duplicating machine.

4. The master is sent to the duplicating unit, which runs off the following copies, subsequently sent to the following respective parties:

a) Customer's acknowledgment copy, to customer
b) Alphabetical copy, to order department's open-order file
c) Salesman's copy, to salesman
d) Production order copy 1, to production department
e) Production order copy 2, to production department
f) Shipping order, to shipping department
g) Packing slip, to shipping department
h) Bill of lading, copy 1, to shipping department
i) Bill of lading, copy 2, to shipping department
j) Bill of lading, copy 3, to shipping department
k) Bill of lading, copy 4, to shipping department

5. Production department copy 1 accompanies the finished goods ordered and is sent to the shipping department.

6. Production department copy 2 is retained by that department for its records.

7. Upon receipt of production department copy 1 by the shipping department, this department forwards the shipping order copy and bills of lading 1 and 3 to the billing department.

8. Bill of lading 2 is given to the carrier.

9. Bill of lading 4 is retained by the shipping department for its records.

10. The packing slip is enclosed with the goods.

11. The billing department runs off the following copies, which are used as indicated:

a) The original invoice is retained by the billing department.

b) The duplicate invoice is mailed to the customer, along with bill of lading 1.

c) Bill of lading 3 is filed in the billing department.

d) The salesman's copy is given to the salesman.

e) The invoice-posting copy is sent to the accounts receivable department.

Problems:

1. Draw a procedure flow chart of the above procedure.

2. In your opinion, does this appear to be an efficient paper-handling procedure? Discuss.

Chapter 24

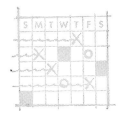

QUANTITY CONTROL—
OFFICE METHODS

Seven national crimes: (1) I don't know, (2) I don't think, (3) I don't care, (4) I'm too busy, (5) I "leave well enough alone," (6) I have no time to find out, and (7) I'm not interested.
—William J. H. Boetcker

QUANTITY control does not stop with procedures; it also includes methods. In other words, we first make sure that the procedure is bringing about the desired results in the best possible way. Then, we seek to make sure that each element making up the procedure is being done in the best possible way to meet the procedural requirements.

Improvements in office methods are obtained by following the same fundamental approach already discussed in the preceding chapter under "Office Procedures." In general, the same principles and techniques of work simplification apply to office methods as to office procedures. Facts are obtained, charts are used to visualize the work, every detail of the task is questioned to uncover clues for improvement, employee participation is encouraged, and greater productivity and accuracy are sought. The goal is to eliminate waste.

OFFICE METHOD STUDY

The fundamental basis of all physical work is the execution of motions. Task performance usually involves physical movements on the part of the employee. For example, movements by the left hand and arm or by the right fingers and wrist are typical movements for many office tasks.

Evaluation and improvement efforts concentrated on a method, or the manner of work performance of an employee performing a given type of work, is commonly referred to as "motion study." In fact, historically, the initial attention toward improvement in the manner of performing work was directed to individual tasks. Frank B. and Lillian M. Gilbreth, pioneers in this area of management, define motion study as follows: "Motion study consists of dividing work into the most fundamental elements possible; studying these elements separately and in relation to one another; and from these studied elements, when timed, building methods of least waste."[1] In other words, it is the careful analysis of an employee's motions with the view of finding the best way of doing the task, i.e., eliminating waste of all kinds.

One of the prime ways of eliminating waste is to eliminate unnecessary motions. Those movements which do not contribute to the fulfillment of the task are discarded. Only the essential motions are retained, and these are arranged to accomplish the work with a minimum of time, effort, and fatigue. This results in greater output per employee and in a reduction of fatigue and waste. The gains possible from motion study are tremendous, for, as the Gilbreths wrote:

> The greatest waste in the world comes from needless, ill-directed, and ineffective motions. These motions are unnecessary and preventable. Their existence in the past was excusable, because there was no knowledge of how to dispense with them. That excuse no longer obtains. The methods and devices of waste elimination are known and are being constantly used. But the knowledge of how to make these great world-wide economies is being disseminated at an astonishingly slow pace.[2]

Motion study is not speed-up. Motion study does not imply speeding up the movements of the employee; rather, it implies an increase in the rate of work production. There is a significant difference between these two concepts, and this difference should be clearly understood. Speeding up the employee means to hurry *all* the steps, *both the necessary and the unnecessary ones.* In contrast, increasing the rate of production through motion study means *performing only the necessary steps in a normal manner.*

APPROACH TO EVALUATING AND IMPROVING OFFICE METHODS

Since the approach followed for evaluating and improving an office method is similar to that for evaluating and improving an office procedure, discussed in detail in Chapter 23, the material of this chapter is concentrated on pointing out considerations and information especially helpful for office methods. The basic five-step pattern of work simplification will be followed, but the discussion under each will be material not yet presented in this book. This five-step pattern, for purposes of this chapter, includes the following:

---

[1] Frank B. and Lillian M. Gilbreth, *Applied Motion Study* (New York: Macmillan Co., 1919), p. 43.

[2] *Ibid.*, p. 57.

1. Select the office method to be evaluated and improved.
2. Get all the facts about this method.
3. Analyze and evaluate these facts by means of pertinent questions.
4. Devise the improvement.
5. Apply the improved method for accomplishing the office work.

SELECT THE OFFICE METHOD TO BE EVALUATED AND IMPROVED

In selecting the method to be improved, it is best to start with repetitive tasks. They lend themselves most readily to analysis, since they occur in volume and over a period of time, making a detailed study possible. Furthermore, they offer large savings possibilities. The savings on each task performance might be small, but doing the task over and over again results in cumulative savings of a sizable amount.

In the experience of one company, the annual savings amount to $340 per office task improved. This may appear relatively small; but on the average, over 150 such improvements are developed each year, making a yearly savings of over $50,000—a truly worth-while goal.

Selecting repetitive tasks for simplification does not mean that special tasks do not warrant study. *Any task can be improved with sufficient study.* In many instances, worth-while savings on regular tasks have been made from analysis of special tasks. Actually, the job selected and the extent and thoroughness of the analysis depend upon a number of things, such as the continuity of the work, the amount of processing required, the total cost or number of people engaged in the work, the value connected with the paper handled, and the interest of the operative employee, supervisor, or analyst.

GETTING ALL THE FACTS

As in the case of procedural improvement, it is necessary to have all the facts about the work to make a proper and meaningful analysis. This information is obtained from a number of sources. Of particular interest here is the use of charts, among which the more common include the left- and right-hand chart, the production study chart, and the operator-machine chart. (See Figure 24–1.) All of these pertain to the individual employee performing a specific task. They differ in content and make-up, but not in purpose, from the charts used for procedural analysis. A detailed discussion of these charts, along with examples, is included at the end of this chapter.

THERBLIGS

To assist in getting the facts, the Gilbreths developed the idea that all motions are made up of elements called "therbligs" (coined from the

OBJECTIVE	CHART TO USE	CHART ILLUSTRATION
TO ANALYZE THE HAND MOTIONS OF THE OPERATOR	LEFT AND RIGHT HAND CHART SHOWS THE DETAILED MOTIONS OF EACH HAND IN PERFORMING THE WORK	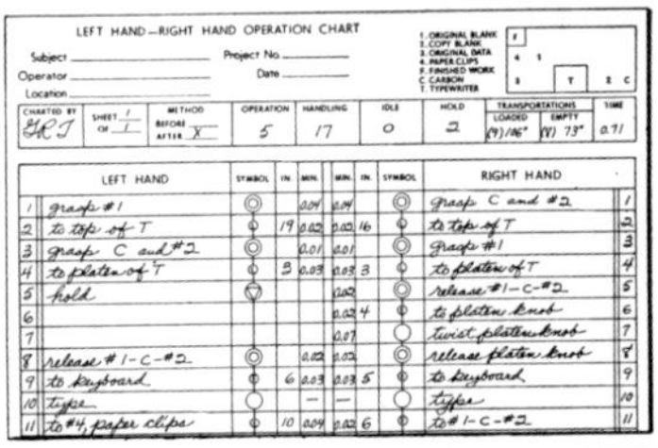
TO STUDY HOW AN EMPLOYEE SPENDS HIS TIME	PRODUCTION STUDY CHART SHOWS AN EMPLOYEE'S TIME BY ACTIVITIES	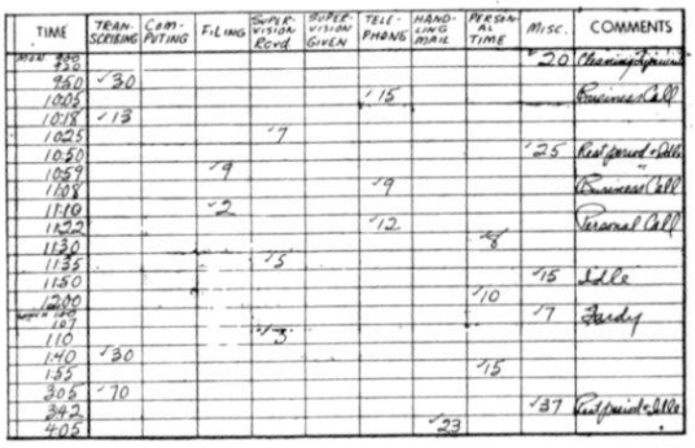
TO SHOW THE WORK RELATIONSHIPS BETWEEN OPERATOR AND MACHINE	OPERATOR-MACHINE CHART SHOWS CORRELATION BETWEEN OPERATOR AND MACHINE IN PERFORMING THE WORK.	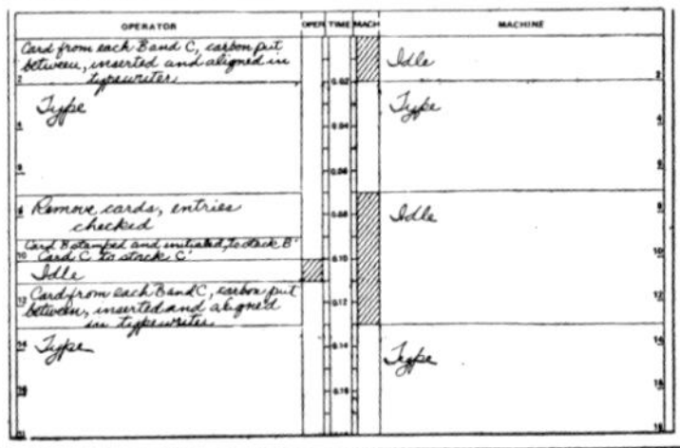

FIG. 24–1. Various types of charts used in simplifying office methods.

spelling of the name Gilbreth backwards, except for the *th*).[3] Most manual work consists of a relatively few basic motions repeated again and again. Gilbreth designated 17 therbligs; other motion analysts have arrived at a slightly different number. Figure 24–2 shows 16 commonly used fundamental motions as classified by Professor Ralph M. Barnes.

The use of therbligs is helpful in detailed studies and refinements. However, motion analysts frequently do not use the therbligs as such, but they do employ them as fundamental to their thinking. For example, it is generally recognized that economy in motion is realized when both the right and the left hands start their therbligs at the same time. The motion economist will strive to attain this condition, but he might not make a therblig analysis.

---

[3] There is a difference of opinion as to the correct definition of a therblig. Some writers call it an elementary motion, while others feel that it is fundamental but of a compounded, not an elemental, nature and concerns work accomplishment.

Name of Fundamental Motion	Symbol	Description
Select	St	Select refers to the choice of one object from among several.
Grasp	G	Grasp refers to taking hold of an object.
Transport loaded	TL	Transport loaded refers to moving an object from one place to another.
Position	P	Position consists of turning or locating an object in such a way that it will be properly oriented to fit into the location for which it is intended.
Assemble	A	Assemble consists of placing one object into or on another object with which it becomes an integral part.
Use	U	Use always consists of manipulating a tool, device, or piece of apparatus for the purpose for which it was intended.
Disassemble	DA	Disassemble consists of separating one object from another object of which it is an integral part.
Inspect	I	Inspect consists of testing a piece to determine whether or not it complies with standard size, shape, color, or other qualities previously determined.
Pre-position	PP	Pre-position refers to positioning an object in a pre-determined place in such a way that it may be grasped in the position in which it is to be held when it is needed.
Release load	RL	Release load refers to that part of the cycle during which the hand is letting go of the object grasped, allowing it to slip out of the hand.
Transport empty	TE	Transport empty consists of moving the empty hand in reaching for an object.
Rest for over-coming fatigue	R	Rest for overcoming fatigue is a fatigue or delay allowance provided to permit the worker to recover from the fatigue incurred by his work.
Unavoidable delay	UD	Unavoidable delay refers to a delay beyond the control of the operator.
Avoidable delay	AD	Avoidable delay refers to any delay of the operator for which he is responsible and over which he has control.
Plan	Pn	Plan refers to a mental reaction which precedes the physical movement, that is, deciding how to proceed with the work.
Hold	H	Hold denotes the retention of the object after it has been grasped, no movement of the object taking place.

Source: Ralph M. Barnes, "Work Methods Manual" (New York: John Wiley & Sons, Inc., 1944), p. 68

FIG. 24-2. Names, symbols, and descriptions of commonly used fundamental motions. The motion "select" is sometimes segregated into three separate motions: "search," "find," and "select."

ANALYSIS AND EVALUATION OF FACTS—THE QUESTIONING APPROACH

The questioning approach is advantageous in seeking simplification of office methods. It is actually more an attitude than technical knowledge. It can be developed by anyone who approaches the job with an open mind and who believes that the manner of doing the work can be improved. Each detail of the work manner is questioned for its essentiality, possible change, combination with other motions, or simplification. The questions "What and Why?" "Where and Why?" and so forth, are utilized, as in the previous chapter.

Additional questions of a method-improving nature and with purposeful intent should be developed and used. They should lead to betterment, not just a conglomeration of queries. Generally speaking, good questions are required in order to get good answers. The following list includes a number of selected questions which are worded to provide practicality and to furnish answers that are useful in bringing out possibilities for improvement.[4]

1. Questions regarding setup or workplace layout:
   a) Is the recipient of the form provided with a proper place to keep it?
   b) Are pens, pencils, erasers, and forms properly prepositioned?
   c) Are desk tops and drawers kept in an orderly condition so that time spent looking for lost articles is reduced to a minimum?
   d) Is a desk necessary, or could the work be done as well on a flat-top table?
   e) Should a specially designed table be provided to facilitate the use of office machines?

2. Questions regarding tools and equipment:
   a) Can gathering or sorting aids be used?
   b) Should a machine replace hand methods?
   c) Are office machines properly maintained by qualified maintenance men?
   d) Can any foot-operated devices, such as a foot-operated stapler, be used?
   e) Is the type of typewriter suitable for the use to which it is put?

3. Questions regarding working conditions:
   a) Are unnecessary noises and disturbances eliminated?
   b) Is privacy assured for telephone conversations of a confidential nature?
   c) What precautions are taken to prevent the spread of colds and other infectious diseases throughout the office?
   d) Are suitable facilities provided for personal belongings?
   e) Could certain clerical operations, such as payroll work, be handled to better advantage on a three-shift basis?

DEVELOPING THE IMPROVED METHOD

This can be viewed as consisting basically of two closely interrelated functions: (1) improving the employee's motions and (2) providing a

---

[4] Adapted from H. B. Maynard and G. J. Stegemerten, *Guide to Methods Improvement* (New York: McGraw-Hill Book Co., Inc., 1944), pp. 51, 56, 60–61.

suitable workplace area. In the former, the step-by-step examination to eliminate, combine, change, or simplify the motions is followed. To assist in these efforts, the principles of work simplification, included in Chapter 23, are applied, along with questions such as "What and Why?" and "Where and Why?" as previously illustrated in Figure 23–2. Certain helpful hints that have widespread application in office methods are given in Figure 24–3.

HELPFUL HINTS
TO
SIMPLIFY YOUR JOB

1. Have source document and end result in same format, if possible.
2. Use precomputed tables or graphic indicators.
3. Avoid writing the same information twice.
4. When a pencil is satisfactory, use it in preference to making insertions into a typewriter.
5. Use a file copy in preference to making entry in register.
6. Make only the number of copies that are needed and used.

FIG. 24–3. Points to remember in simplifying an office method.

In addition, certain basic guides generally helpful in improving office methods should be utilized. These include the following:

1. Do the work by machine, not manually, if possible. Develop the best motion for the operator with the machine being utilized.

2. Use both hands for doing work, avoiding the use of either hand as a holding device. Both hands should begin and complete their motions at the same time, moving simultaneously in opposite and symmetrical directions.

3. Analyze and eliminate, if possible, all hesitations and searches in the method to be followed.

4. Employ a minimum of motions to complete the task. Use hand motions only or, if necessary, hands and eye motions only. Arm, leg, and body motions should be infrequently required.

5. Count therbligs required by the method; the minimum number usually identifies the best method.

6. Build an agreeable sequence of motions, so that a desirable rhythm is followed in performing the task.

7. Include continuous, curved motions in preference to motions having sharp changes in direction, because the former are both less demanding and less tiring.

8. Strive to have high-priced office help do high-priced office work only. Minimize, for example, the private secretary doing strictly typist work.

9. Provide good office physical environmental factors. (See Chapter 19.)

10. Have all operations located conveniently so that the operator does not have to reach.

11. Preposition papers, cards, and working tools so that they are handy and ready for use as required.

12. Arrange the workplace so that the operator can stand or sit, as he wishes.

PROVISION OF SUITABLE WORKPLACE AREA

The last four guides listed above relate to the provision of a suitable workplace area. This subject warrants some discussion because of its importance. The best motion cycle and the maximum elimination of waste are not possible unless the proper workplace area is provided.

In considering the workplace area, there are usually many possibilities for improvement. Among the most helpful are the following:

1. *Place only what is needed for the task on the desk or table top.* Do not clutter up the work area with such things as paper clips, pads, miscellaneous folders, magazines, and books which are not required in performing the task. Supplies and tools not needed should not be in the employee's way. When they are allowed to remain, inefficient motions as well as unsightly work areas are evident.

2. *Keep the employee's supplies and tools not needed for the particular task in desk drawers or in cabinets.* Supplies and tools should be stored neatly and systematically; the arrangement used depends upon the individual circumstances. Materials placed in cabinets should be indexed according to some simple plan that facilitates finding.

3. *Utilize the normal and the maximum working areas.* The *normal* working area for the right hand on a desk top, for example, is the area determined by swinging the extended right hand and forearm only across the desk. The pivoting is at the elbow, with the upper arm being relaxed at the side of the body. The arm tends to swing out a little at the outer end of the arc. In a similar manner, the normal working area for the left hand is determined. These two normal areas overlap in front of the employee, and this overlapping area represents the location in which work requiring both hands can be performed most readily.

The *maximum* working areas are the areas determined by swinging the extended hand and entire arm, pivoting at the shoulder. Figure 24–4 shows graphically the normal and maximum working areas with dimensions for an average employee.

Paper being worked on should be located within the arcs of the normal working areas common to both hands. Supplies should also be conveniently located, i.e., within the normal and never outside the maxi-

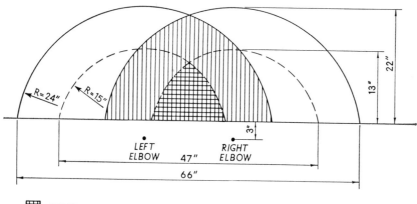

DENOTES NORMAL WORKING AREA COMMON TO BOTH HANDS

DENOTES MAXIMUM WORKING AREA COMMON TO BOTH HANDS

FIG. 24–4. Illustration of normal and of maximum working areas.

mum working areas. It should be noted that the periphery of this area is arc-shaped and not rectangular. The arrangement of the supplies and tools should also follow a pattern determined by motion principles.

4. *Provide a comfortable and effective arrangement.* For minimum fatigue, the chair should support the employee slightly above the small of the back and should permit him to sit erect with his weight supported by the bone structure of the body. It is desirable that the height of the seat and of the back, and the relative position of the back to the seat, be adjusted in order to meet individual needs. Correct chair height is achieved when the weight at the knees is supported by the feet and when no pressure exists between the upper leg and the front edge of the seat. The back support should be such that the occupant can sit back in the chair. These suggestions were made in Chapter 16 and attention is again directed to Figure 16–3.

The height of the workplace should be such that comfortable support is given the underside of the forearm at a point slightly below the elbows. In cases where the hands are self-supported and a desk or table is used, the workplace should be of such height that the hands work at a level slightly higher than that of the elbows.

In typing, for example, the forearms should be parallel to the slope of the keyboard, with the wrists slightly lower than the knuckles. The typist should sit in a position that will cause her upper arms to slope slightly forward. Sitting erect in the chair directly in front of the machine with feet flat on the floor makes it possible to type comfortably and easily.

Materials and devices normally required in the execution of the work should be provided and conveniently arranged. This includes such things as supplying devices to hold papers while typing; locating frequently used supplies such as paper clips, stapler, and rubber stamps on a rotor where easy access is possible; and putting reference materials, including books, catalogues, and lists, on convenient racks within easy reach or vision of the operator.

The arrangement of unitizing can also be followed. Under this plan, each operating unit is considered a separate entity and is supplied individually with all the tools and supplies necessary for its work. The required papers, books, supplies, and the like are located on a wall rack or in a floor cabinet near the operator's desk. For the most part, this arrangement brings best results when a large portion of the office consists of widely dispersed and fairly independent units, although it is not limited to this particular type of setup.

APPLICATION OF THE IMPROVED METHOD

After an improved method has been worked out, it is a relatively simple matter to apply it, provided the employee has participated in the simplification work and has an understanding of and confidence in the management members of the enterprise, as discussed in the preceding chapter. There is no adequate substitute for gaining and maintaining wholesome understanding between the management and nonmanagement members. The purpose of methods evaluation and improvement should be clearly set forth, and the reasons for their importance in the enterprise made crystal-clear to every employee. Along this line, it is frequently helpful to show examples of what has been accomplished with methods improvements in other offices, and to indicate that it is one of the media through which the combination of high wages and short hours has come about.

Everyone must realize the importance of motions in performing office work and see possibilities for improvement. This includes all department heads, division heads, supervisors, and operative employees. To achieve this goal, training can be provided; meetings with department heads and supervisors are common. They can be conducted separately for each group or combined into one group, depending upon the individual circumstances. In certain instances, supervisors may not partake freely in the discussions if management heads are also present. When this condition exists, separate groups can be formed, but management heads should never be excluded from the program; otherwise, they may lose touch with the progress and fail to see the supervisors' viewpoint.

THE LEFT- AND RIGHT-HAND CHART

An important tool of methods improvement is the left- and right-hand chart, which shows the actions and motions of each hand. In this case, six symbols are generally used, including:

1. Large circle ○ Means operation—such as something created, changed, or added to.

2. Large double circles ◎ Means handling—such as select and pickup.

3. Double triangles, points down ▽ Means idle.

4. Large circle with triangle inside, point down ⊽ Means hold.

5. Small circle with letter *L* inside Ⓛ Means transportation loaded.

6. Small circle with letter *E* inside Ⓔ Means transportation empty.

Here again, there is no universal agreement on the type and number of symbols to be used in this charting work. The important concepts, however, are to make certain that all the facts about the method are collected and to visualize the method being used. The symbols are merely to assist in these endeavors.

Some believe it is best to observe the actions of both hands and to indicate these data on the chart as the work progresses. Others prefer to prepare the chart by following the actions on the right hand only, the actions of the left hand only, and then combining the two charts in order to show the relationships existing according to time of execution. Attention must be given to details. A few seconds saved on an action or the elimination of a short movement, perhaps 3 or 4 inches, may seem small; but when the task is repeated over and over again, the cumulative savings in fatigue and time become highly significant.

An Original Method Described. Figure 24–5 illustrates a left- and right-hand operation chart for typing, in duplicate, original sales data sent in by field representatives. The workplace layout is sketched at the top of the chart. A number or code system can be used to identify the various materials and equipment used. Also, provisions for the inclusion of other pertinent data are made at the top of the sheet. Of special interest is the summary information, which shows the total actions by type, along with the distance the hands travel and the time taken to perform the task.

In this case, the task begins with the operator reaching with the right hand to the pile of copy blanks positioned to the right and forward of

LEFT HAND—RIGHT HAND OPERATION CHART

Subject_____　Project No._____

Operator_____　Date_____

Location_____

```
1 = ORIGINAL BLANK
2 = COPY BLANK
3 = ORIGINAL DATA
4 = PAPER CLIPS
F = FINISHED WORK
C = CARBON
T = TYPEWRITER
```

F		1
	4	2
3	T	C

CHARTED BY	SHEET 1 OF 1	METHOD BEFORE X AFTER____	OPERATION	HANDLING	IDLE	HOLD	TRANSPORTATION		TIME
IRJ			6	23	4	3	LOADED (10) 131"	EMPTY (12) 136"	1.25 (X)

(X) NO TYPING

	LEFT HAND	SYMBOL	IN.	MIN.	MIN.	IN.	SYMBOL	RIGHT HAND	
1	idle	▽			0.05	20	Ⓔ	to #2	1
2					0.02		◎	grasp #2	2
3					0.05	16	Ⓛ	to top of T	3
4					0.01		◎	release #2	4
5					0.04	9	Ⓔ	to C, carbon paper	5
6					0.02		◎	grasp C	6
7					0.04	13	Ⓛ	to top of T	7
8					0.01		◎	release C	8
9					0.06	25	Ⓔ	to #1	9
10					0.02		◎	grasp #1	10
11					0.06	25	Ⓛ	to top of T	11
12					0.02		◎	release #1	12
13	grasp #1-C-#2	◎		0.01	0.01		◎	grasp #1-C-#2	13
14	to platen of T	Ⓛ	3	0.03	0.03	3	Ⓛ	to platen of T	14
15	hold	▽			0.02		◎	release #1-C-#2	15
16					0.02	4	Ⓔ	to platen knob	16
17					0.07		◯	twist platen knob	17
18	release #1-C-#2	◎		0.02	0.02		◎	release platen knob	18
19	to keyboard	Ⓔ	6	0.03	0.03	5	Ⓔ	to keyboard	19
20	type	◯	—	—	—	—	◯	type	20
21	to #1-C-#2	Ⓔ	6	0.03	0.03	5	Ⓔ	to T platen knob	21
22	grasp #1-C-#2	◎		0.02	0.02		◎	grasp platen knob	22
23	remove #1-C-#2	◯		0.05	0.05		◯	twist platen knob	23
24	to top of T	Ⓛ	3	0.03	0.02		◎	release platen knob	24
25	hold	▽			0.03	3	Ⓔ	to top of T	25
26					0.03		◎	grasp C	26
27					0.05	13	Ⓛ	to "C" on desk	27
28	release #1-C-#2	◎			0.02		◎	release C	28
29	to paper clips, #4	Ⓔ	15	0.06	0.05	13	Ⓔ	to top of T	29
30	grasp paper clip	◎		0.02			▽	idle	30
31	to #3, original data	Ⓛ	10	0.04					31
32	grasp #3, original data	◎		0.03					32
33	to top of T	Ⓛ	20	0.05					33
34	release original data card on #1-#2	◎		0.02	0.02		◎	grasp #1-#2	34
35	attach clip	◯		0.04			▽	hold #1-#2	35
36	to "F" on desk	Ⓛ	25	0.06			◎	release	36
37	release	◎		0.02			▽	idle	37
38	to T	Ⓔ	25	0.06			▽		38

FIG. 24–5.

LEFT HAND—RIGHT HAND OPERATION CHART

Subject _____ Project No. _____
Operator _____ Date _____
Location _____

1. ORIGINAL BLANK
2. COPY BLANK
3. ORIGINAL DATA
4. PAPER CLIPS
F. FINISHED WORK
C. CARBON
T. TYPEWRITER

CHARTED BY	SHEET 1 OF 1	METHOD BEFORE___ AFTER X	OPERATION 5	HANDLING 17	IDLE 0	HOLD 2	TRANSPORTATIONS LOADED (9)106" EMPTY (8)73"	TIME 0.71

#	LEFT HAND	SYMBOL	IN.	MIN.	MIN.	IN.	SYMBOL	RIGHT HAND	#
1	grasp #1	◎		0.04	0.04		◎	grasp C and #2	1
2	to top of T		19	0.02	0.02	16		to top of T	2
3	grasp C and #2	◎		0.01	0.01		◎	grasp #1	3
4	to platen of T		3	0.03	0.03	3		to platen of T	4
5	hold	▽			0.02		◎	release #1-C-#2	5
6					0.02	4		to platen knob	6
7					0.07		○	twist platen knob	7
8	release #1-C-#2	◎		0.02	0.02		◎	release platen knob	8
9	to keyboard		6	0.03	0.03	5		to keyboard	9
10	type	○	—	—			○	type	10
11	to #4, paper clips		10	0.04	0.02	6		to #1-C-#2	11
12	grasp paper clip	◎		0.02	0.01		◎	grasp #1-C-#2	12
13	to #3, original data		8	0.03	0.02		○	pull #1-C-#2 from T	13
14	grasp #3, original data	◎		0.03	0.02	2		to top of T	14
15	to top of T		18	0.04	0.01		◎	release #1-C-#2	15
16	release on top #1-C-#2	◎		0.02	0.03		◎	grasp C	16
17	grasp #3 and #1-C-#2	◎		0.04	0.05	12		to "2" on desk	17
18	hold	▽		0.02	0.02		◎	release	18
19					0.03	16		to left hand	19
20					0.02		◎	grasp clips	20
21					0.04		○	attach to #3, #1-#2	21
22	to "F" on desk		25	0.06	0.02		◎	release	22
23	to #1 on desk		10	0.04	0.03	16		to "2" on desk	23

FIG. 24–6.

the typewriter. This action is "transportation empty," since the hand is empty, and is indicated on line No. 1 by a small circle with an E inside under the symbol column for the right hand. The description "to No. 2" is written in the description column on the right. In making this transportation, the hand travels 20 inches; and this is recorded in the distance column, right hand, on line No. 1. While this is going on, the left hand is idle, so a double triangle is inserted under the symbol column of the left hand and the word "idle" written in the description column on the left.

Next, the right hand grasps a copy blank. This is a handling action and is shown by large double circles on line No. 2 under the right hand.

"Grasp No. 2" is written on the same line in the description column. During this particular operation, the left hand was idle. Since this is the same as the previous entry for the left hand, no new symbol is necessary on the chart.

In a similar manner, each step of the operation is observed and noted on the form. It is important that all details be included and that extreme care be exercised to insure accuracy in this work.

Improving an Original Method. A study of Figure 24–5 shows that the method can be improved. In this figure, it should be observed that the right hand moves first to No. 2, the copy blank pile. The analyst will question the necessity and purpose of this action. He will ask questions such as "Is this necessary?" "What is its purpose?" and others which will help to achieve improvement. Also, he will observe that the right hand successively makes six transportations—three empty and three loaded—all to the same general area. Are these necessary? Can they be eliminated, combined, or simplified? Can they be made productive? Further, it will be observed that in the beginning, the right hand is occupied, while the left hand is idle. As already pointed out, motion economy results from both hands moving simultaneously in opposite directions. Therefore, arrangements should be made to have both hands moving at the same time, and in opposite directions if possible. By following this minute and careful consideration of each action, the analyst is able to simplify the work, make it easier to do, and eliminate waste.

Figure 24–6 on page 475 shows improvements for accomplishing the same work. The new work layout is sketched at the top of the sheet. Idle time has been eliminated, and simultaneous hand motions have been made a part of the method. The two transportations—empty and loaded —to the copy blanks and the two transportations to the carbon paper have been combined. A comparison study between the two charts will reveal other work simplification accomplishments. The tabular comparison shows:

	Present Method		Proposed Method	
Operations..................	6		5	
Handling....................	23		17	
Idle.......................	4		0	
Hold.......................	3		2	
Transportation loaded.......	10	(131 inches)	9	(106 inches)
Transportation empty.........	12	(136 inches)	8	(73 inches)
Time......................	1.25 minutes		0.71 minutes	

Worth-while savings have been accomplished.

PRODUCTION STUDY CHART

The production study chart shows how an employee spends his working time and the major functions performed. Either the employee can record his activities, or the supervisor or an analyst can obtain the data by means of observation. In any event, the employee should be informed of the study and its purpose, and told why and how the recordings are made. For meaningful results, the job content should be fairly consistent from day to day, and the observed employee should neither hasten nor retard his normal efforts. The data should be collected for several consecutive days, preferably a week, in order to arrive at what would seem to be a normal pattern. Such information assists in controlling quantity through office methods because it reveals what types of work are being done by what employee and for how long.

Recording the Data. There are several ways in which the information of a production study chart can be recorded. One method consists of using graph paper with sections representing time units throughout the working day. These sections are filled in with colored pencil according to a color-identification key for the various functions performed. Another method consists of simply marking down in tabular form the various types of work done and the time each job is started and finished.

Figure 24–7 illustrates an effective form for a production study chart for office work. The usual identification data—employee name, date and the like—are shown at the top. A series of vertical columns are used for the various functions, with the extreme left column utilized for time and the extreme right for comments. Since the study begins at 9:00 A.M. Monday, the insertion "Mon. 9.00" is written on the first line under the Time column. The employee is observed cleaning her typewriter, so a check mark (✔) is made on the first line under Miscellaneous and "cleaning typewriter" is written under Comments. She finishes this task at 9:20 A.M. and begins transcribing. Hence, "9.20" is written on the first line under Time, and a check mark is made under Transcribing on line 2. She stops transcribing at 10:05 A.M. to telephone. Hence, on line 3, a check mark is made under Telephone, and the entry "10.05" is made in the Time column. In a similar manner, entries are made throughout the entire day.

Performing Calculations. The calculations for figuring the elapsed time per function can be made as the study progresses or at the completion of all observations. In the illustration, the ordinary 60-minute watch has been used. For the first line, the elapsed time between 9.00 and 9.20 is 20 minutes, which is recorded in the same square as the check mark under Miscellaneous. For the second line, the elapsed time is 9.50 minus 9.20, or 30 minutes. The itemized totals are shown at the bottom of the form along with the percentage figures. For example, the total time spent on transcribing is 143 minutes. This constitutes 34.1 per cent of the total day's working time, calculated by dividing the transcribing time, 143 minutes, by the total day's working time, 420 minutes.

These types of data are important in work simplification effort. They

PRODUCTION STUDY CHART

Sheet _1_ of _5_ Sheets

Date __3/2/__

Study By __ERH__

Computations By __ERH__

Employee's Name __Nancy Taussig__

Division or Unit __Transcription – 32__

Job Title __Transcriber__

TIME	TRAN-SCRIBING	COM-PUTING	FILING	SUPER-VISION Rcvd.	SUPER-VISION GIVEN	TELE-PHONE	HAND-LING MAIL	PERSON-AL TIME	MISC.	COMMENTS
MON. 9:00									20	Cleaning typewriter
9:50	30									
10:05						15				Business Call
10:18	13									
10:25				7						
10:50									25	Rest period + Idle
10:59			9							
11:08						9				Business Call
11:10			2							
11:22						12				Personal Call
11:30								8		
11:35			5							
11:50									15	Idle
12:00								10		
LUNCH 1:00 / 1:07									7	Tardy
1:10				3						
1:40	30									
1:55								15		
3:05	70									
3:42									37	Rest period + Idle
4:05							23			
4:15								10		
4:25						10				Business Call
4:45			20							
4:58									13	Idle
5:00									2	Cleaning up Desk
TOTALS	143	—	31	15	—	46	23	43	119	420
PER CENT	34.1	—	7.4	3.6	—	11.0	5.4	10.1	28.4	100.0%

FIG. 24–7. Chart showing how an employee spends her working time. Data are secured by observing the employee.

tell what the status of the jobs is at present and give, per employee, a picture of the over-all work pattern which might form the basis for remedial supervision, equalization of the work load, and further analysis to improve efficiency. They can also be used to supply basic information for the construction of a work distribution chart.[5]

For example, a production study chart may reveal that a typist, with a typing speed of 50 words per minute, spends only 50 per cent of her time typing. The remaining 50 per cent is spent on other activities, most of which are nonessential, including positioning papers in typewriter,

---

[5] See Chapter 23 for discussion of work distribution chart.

checking work, removing papers from typewriter, separating copies, cleaning typewriter, answering telephone, filing papers, and getting information from the supervisor. In this case, the effective typing production is at a rate of only 25 (50 per cent of 50) words per minute. In too many offices, the sole emphasis is upon the speed of the operator. True, this is important; but when the methods analysis reveals only 50 per cent of the employee's particular skill being utilized, it is a challenge to the manager to eliminate such waste. The production study chart reveals such situations and assists in correcting them.

OPERATOR-MACHINE ACTIVITY CHART

As the name implies, this chart shows the relation between the operator and the machine. Its use is somewhat limited in office methods, owing to the general nature of most office activities. It is chiefly employed to determine idle machine time and the number of machines which one operator can reasonably handle, thus in effect controlling the quantity.

Figure 24–8 shows an operator-machine activity chart. Pertinent data and a sketch of the workplace layout are included at the top. Time is represented by vertical distance on the scale shown in the center column of the sheet. For example, two scale units represent two minutes, four scale units four minutes, etc. The activities of the operator are listed in the left column, those of the machine on the right.

The vertical height of each spacing in these respective columns is determined by the time devoted to the particular activity. For example, in the illustration, the first action by the operator was to "take a card from each *B* and *C*, put a carbon between, insert and align in typewriter." This required two tenths (0.2) of a minute, so a horizontal line was drawn two units down from the beginning horizontal line. During this time, the typewriter was idle; hence, a horizontal line was drawn across the right column under Machine, two units from the same beginning line, and "idle" written in the space so formed.

Next, the operator typed. This action continued five tenths (0.5) of a minute, so a horizontal line was drawn across the Operator column five units below the last horizontal line, or in this case opposite the 7 mark on the time scale. The space so formed was marked "type." Since the typewriter action stopped at the same time, a horizontal line was also drawn across the Machine column opposite 7 on the time scale, and the space above was marked "type." In a similar manner, the entire chart was constructed.

This method can be improved very easily. The use of multicopy stub sets with interleaved carbon offers one possibility. This would reduce the labor time per unit and increase the operating time of the machine—both contributing to greater efficiency. However, a more significant improvement would be the use of continuous-strip office forms with carbon

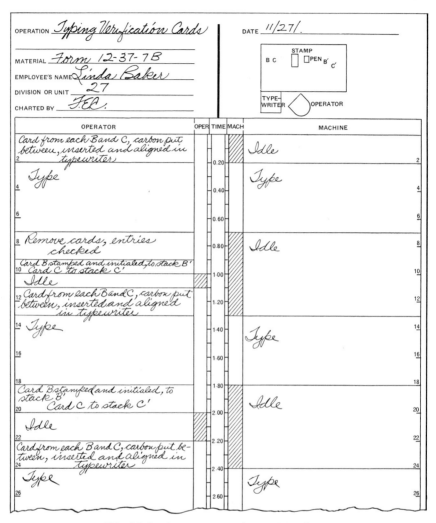

FIG. 24–8. An operator-machine activity chart.

interleaved, thus permitting the operator to type continuously until a quantity of work is finished. The checking and separating of the forms could subsequently be handled on this quantity. This method would provide a smooth and rhythmic flow of work, permit specialization upon the immediate task, and eliminate unnecessary reaching, as well as excessive finger and arm motions. Elimination of much waste would be achieved.

QUESTIONS

1. In your opinion, are the greatest improvements more likely from quantity control of office procedures or of office methods? Justify your viewpoint.

2. For each of the following pairs, carefully point out the difference between the two identities:
   a) Production study chart and motion study.
   b) Normal working area and maximum working area.
   c) Therblig and the "What and Why" question.
   d) A "handling" and a "transportation loaded."

3. Discuss eight guides in achieving motion economy, using illustrations to demonstrate your answers.

4. How is it possible for motion study to bring about greater work accomplishment without speeding up the employee? Explain.

5. Comment fully on the following: "For a given quantity of work, it is entirely possible for methods improvements to reduce employee fatigue in performing that quantity. But methods improvements usually result in increasing the amount of work performed; and as a result, the employee spends the same amount of energy or more than before the improvement. Hence, the employee is quite likely to be just as fatigued under the improved method as before the improvement."

6. List the therbligs performed for each of the following:
   a) An executive receiving a letter and signing it.
   b) A shipping clerk answering the telephone.
   c) A stenographer folding a letter, inserting it in an envelope, sealing it, and placing it in the outgoing mail basket on her desk.
   d) A typist inserting a card in a typewriter, preparatory to typing.

7. From question No. 6, above, select one of the activities listed and chart it, using a left- and right-hand chart. Point out the motions depicted on the chart which in your opinion can be eliminated, changed, combined, or simplified in performing this work.

8. Does motion study take into account individual differences among employees? Explain.

9. Discuss Figure 24–7 in your own words.

10. As an office manager, would you agree to the suggestion that the employees fill out the data on their own respective production study charts and turn these data in to you for analysis and interpretation? What would be the advantages under such an arrangement? The disadvantages?

11. Discuss the subject of "Application of the Improved Method" in the field of office management.

12. Analyze your motions in typing a letter, or taking notes from a reference book, or sorting and then filing cards in a file. What do you conclude from your study? Discuss.

CASE PROBLEMS
Case 24–1.   Owens Direct Mail Sales, Inc.

For purposes of sales analysis and taxes, customer orders are sorted by state. A seventh copy of the invoice prepared by the company is used. The volume fluctuates from week to week, but an average weekly volume is fifteen thousand orders. To do the sorting job, a rack, laid out in a straight line with eight sections horizontally and five sections vertically, is being used. The rack, which is 10 feet long and 4 feet high, sits on a long table. The forty-way sort is used because several of the states are grouped.

The operator, a tall girl, holds a batch of orders in her left hand, reads the state on the order at the top of the batch, picks the order up with her right hand, and inserts it into the bin of the rack for the particular state. The operator walks back and forth to cover the distance of the rack. She is expected to accomplish a rate of twenty orders sorted a minute, and succeeds in doing so.

Because of the volume, all the orders cannot be sorted by the operator using the rack. The overflow is sorted by another girl, who spreads the work out in little piles over several tabletops. Although the second girl works all day at this job of sorting orders, she does not accomplish as much as the girl working with the rack. From this, the office manager concludes that the rack idea is better than sorting on the tabletops. He is about to order another rack for use by the second girl; but before doing this, he has requested you to study the work method and see if any improvements for this order sorting can be developed.

Problems:

1. What are some tentative methods you feel should be investigated to find a possible improvement?

2. What is your recommendation to the office manager?

Case 24–2. Mildred Clevenger

With her approval and knowledge, typist Mildred Clevenger was observed during a workday by analyst Herman Wright for the purpose of making a production study chart. The data recorded included the following: Miss Clevenger read the newspaper till 9:00 A.M., the official starting time. Promptly at 9:00 A.M, she checked her typewriter and arranged work on her desk; at 9:12, conversed with a messenger boy; at 9:21, answered a business telephone call; at 9:29, typed; at 10:05, talked with supervisor; at 10:20, idle; at 10:30, rest period; at 10:45, typed; at 11:13, made a personal telephone call; at 11:42, typed; at 12:00, lunch; at 1:00, typed; at 1:55, idle; at 2:12, answered a business telephone call; at 2:24, idle; at 2:35, typed; at 3:00, rest period; at 3:15, typed; at 3:25, made a personal telephone call; at 3:55, typed; at 4:17, took typed material to advertising department; at 4:35, typed; at 4:41, answered a business telephone call; at 4:55, put work away and covered typewriter; and at 5:00, official quitting time, left her desk.

Problems:

1. Draw the production study chart.

2. Calculate the itemized totals of the activities of Mildred Clevenger.

3. What interpretations do you make from these data? Discuss.

4. What action do you recommend as a result of the factual data assembled? Why?

Chapter 25

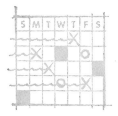

DETERMINING AND APPLYING OFFICE TIME STANDARDS

Make use of the passing Now, for in another moment it will become forever a worthless, unuseable thing.

—J. A. WORSHAM

UP TO THIS point in our discussion of controlling, we have covered controlling of office forms and supplies, quality control, and quantity control. Another important area of controlling is that of time use. Succinctly stated, this area deals with work accomplishment *within specific time limits.* It is very well to get the office work completed, but how long should it take to do it in keeping with fair, reasonable, and adequate time controls?

OFFICE WORK MEASUREMENT

Before we can apply time standards, it is necessary to know the amount of work to which the time controls are being applied. To state that the work should be completed within 5.5 minutes implies a given quantity of work completed within this period. This means that measurement of office work is required.

To measure means to determine quantity. For time control, we measure work, we measure time, and relate the two together. To illustrate, it is common to speak of so many orders processed within a given time. The number of orders becomes meaningful when tied with the quantity of time.

Measurement of work concerns accomplishment or productivity. It has to do with results; it does not deal with the amount of energy expended, although in many cases this may be in direct proportion to the work output. Measurement provides data showing the amount of work done, and this information is helpful in determining whether the office is being managed efficiently, and the amount of work achieved by each employee.

Work measurement can be considered a tool in that it helps to know what is going on; but in and of itself, work measurement does not change anything or exercise any control. But it does help the manager (1) to distribute work loads fairly, (2) to define job success in tangible units, (3) to analyze employee performance, and (4) to highlight where remedial help is needed.

Much of the work in an office can be measured fairly accurately and inexpensively. The extent in any given case will depend upon the particular type of office tasks performed; but usually, from two thirds to three fourths of all work in an office can be measured. It is true that difficulty in measurement is encountered, for example, when the office work is nonrepetitive and irregular, or when it is primarily mental rather than manual. These are impediments; but with study and analysis, the ultimate objectives of measuring the office work can be achieved and surprisingly useful and reliable results obtained. It is erroneous to accept the belief that work measurement cannot be set for office work.

MEASURING UNIT

To measure requires a recognizable unit. There are many different units that can be used, the selection depending mainly upon the type of office work. For example, typewritten work can be measured by typing area or sheets, and purchase orders by the number written. Sometimes, the quantity can be determined very easily by means of counting devices on machines; and frequently, the relationship of the weight of paper to the amount of work can be employed. Other examples of work-measuring units in the office are the number of invoices written, the amount of postage (dollar value) used on outgoing mail, the weight of incoming mail handled, the reams of paper used in duplicating work, the number of pay checks prepared, the inches of card stacks filed, and the number of credit investigations made.

The unit used should be easy to identify, count, and understand. For each related application, it should possess uniformity of scope and definition. Generally speaking, the unit preferred is that which comes into existence as the result of an essential, clear-cut office operation. This characteristic aids identifying and counting.

In some instances, the selection of a satisfactory unit is extremely difficult; while in other cases, there are several available and acceptable units. In the latter case, for example, typewritten work can be measured in units of (1) pages, (2) standard-length lines, (3) key strokes, (4) square inches of typed material, or (5) cylinders or disks from which material is transcribed. The choice is guided by the individual characteristics of the work under consideration. No one unit is best under all conditions. For example, the number of pages is satisfactory provided the pages are approximately uniform in the amount of typed material and in difficulty.

Accurate measurement is desirable and should be sought; but in the case of office work, this can be carried to uneconomical extremes. Too precise or too detailed measurements can result in bulky and sometimes cumbersome data which are ineffective in practical application.

MODIFIED WORK MEASUREMENT UNITS

Because, in many cases, office work contains a number of variables and the job of an office employee may consist of several related but independent tasks, the use of a modified unit to measure office work is sometimes used. In other words, a purchase order may constitute the basic work measurement unit. But not all purchase orders of a company are identical. Some require five lines of typing, others eight lines; and for exceptional orders, the filling-out of special forms is necessary.

To combat these hurdles, modified work measurement units can be employed. One common example of this is to use a "block of orders" instead of a single order as the basic measurement unit. A quantity of 200 orders may make up a block of orders. The content of the individual order may vary considerably, but the content of 200 orders will normally be quite like that of another 200 orders. Thus, a work measurement unit possessing reasonable comparability is provided.

Also, the work measurement can be considered over a period of time, i.e., for 10 or 15 days. During such a period, the average make-up of the modified unit will be fairly constant, that is, comparing one 15-day period with another 15-day period.

Another approach is to employ what can be termed "the core operation." Under this modified work measurement unit, the office work of an entire procedure, or any part of it, is expressed by a single unit, considered the core or the most important operation and the one around which most of the other work of the procedure, or the totality being measured, depends. To illustrate, the incoming order might be considered the core. All processing in connection with this order, such as credit investigation, correspondence, billing, and the like, is tied up with the handling of the incoming order. These activities increase as the incoming orders increase, and vice versa. By measuring the core, it is feasible to get a reasonably accurate measurement of the entire procedural work. Core operations employed include number of policies handled, applications processed, orders received, items on order, units shipped, sheets duplicated, bills sent out, requisitions made, or checks written.

TIMING OFFICE WORK

Common practice associates time measurement, or the aspect of duration, with the work measurement. Time is an all-important factor. To punch a given number of cards or to file a definite quantity of orders is an accomplishment, but the important question is: Within what time limits can this be done? How long should it take? How much time should elapse from the start to the finish? Time is the element which is basic and common to all work. It is a vital basis of effective controlling.

For any given case, it is customary to identify the measurement of work and also that of time as "time study." Formally defined, *time study is the determination of a satisfactory work output and of the time required to complete a given number of work units regularly.* The unit may be an entire task or any part thereof. Time is usually expressed in minutes per piece or one hundred pieces, or at a rate of so many pieces per hour.

The values from time study are called "time standards" and are used by managers as bases of reference for controlling. More specifically, time standards help the manager of office work, in that:

1. *A basis for work distribution is provided.* Time standards give the office manager the means for determining the volume of work and the number of employees required to get the work out. They afford the establishment of a "fair day's work," and they make it possible to plan the office operations.

2. *The office work can be scheduled.* Knowledge of the time to be allocated to different tasks expedites the arrangement of the order of work according to a predetermined timetable. By this means, full utilization of all production factors can be more nearly attained. Available times of machines or of employees for emergency or special rush jobs can be readily determined, as well as information on the starting and completing dates for the various tasks, all of which helps the office to provide excellent service to the remaining parts of the enterprise.

3. *Effectiveness of department, division, or individual can be determined.* An indication of what the working force should accomplish is provided. The question is not "Is the employee always busy?" but "What does the employee accomplish?" The actual productivity compared with standard productivity is known. It is therefore possible to distinguish the efficient from the inefficient employee or group. Remedial action to improve the work of the inefficient personnel can be taken.

4. *Control over costs can be exercised.* Time standards make it possible to compare standard against actual costs. Some control can thus be used effectively, since information as to where costs are out of line is supplied.

5. *Morale and labor relations are improved.* With time studies, the employee knows what is expected of him, and this makes office work more interesting. Having an objective—an end in view—lends encouragement so that office work does not seem like an endless mass of detail. Generally, the employee will be happier and do better work when he

knows what and how much he is supposed to do, and upon what basis his efforts will be judged. Time standards remove favoritism; they provide factual information and treat all employees alike. In addition, by means of standards, basic data can be obtained which are extremely helpful in considering employee promotions and in formulating training programs.

MEANS FOR DETERMINING OFFICE TIME STANDARDS

Standard time for office work can be determined in six different ways: (1) by subjective judgment, (2) by past performance records, (3) by work sampling, (4) by standard time data, (5) by stop-watch study, and (6) by standard data from time study.

Before discussing each means, it should be noted that regardless of the means followed, several key initial considerations should be observed.

1. Identify and carefully note what is the beginning and the end of the task for which the time standard is being established. It is usually helpful to have the end of the task cycle followed immediately by a repetition of the task cycle. When the selected task cycle requires the exclusion of work or time between the cycles, difficulties may be encountered in identifying adequately the time standard calculated.

2. Tell the office employees that time standards are being determined. Usually, this is by far the best course, but it may have lesser importance when the means of subjective judgment or past performance are used. Time standards affect employees, and they will want to know about the standards. Enlightened managers take the initiative and share information concerning the purpose, means, and personnel doing the work of establishing standards. Furthermore, managers should answer all questions directly about the time standards program because it is realized that the ultimate success of the program depends greatly upon the employees' co-operation.

3. Select the means of determining standards that appears best considering the particular circumstances involved. As will be pointed out in the following discussion, the various means of establishing standards vary in their respective costs of determination, application to group or individual accomplishment of work, and relative accuracy. To highlight this information, Figure 25–1 has been included. For example, work sampling is of medium cost, is satisfactory for group or individual work, can be used when the work fluctuates either as to volume or as to type, and gives results of relatively medium preciseness. In contrast, comparable data for the stop-watch study means differ from those of the work sampling means as indicated by the Figure. These data are relative and serve as a guide only. Individual considerations determine which means to utilize in a specific case.

MEANS	COST OF DETERMINING	GROUP OR INDIVIDUAL WORK	SATISFACTORY FOR WORK VARIATION BY:		RELATIVE PRECISENESS
			Volume	Type of Work	
Subjective judgment.........	Low	G or I	Yes	Yes	Low
Past performance records.....	Medium	G or I	Yes	Yes	Medium
Work sampling..............	Medium	G or I	Yes	Yes	Medium
Standard time data..........	High	I	No	No	High
Stop-watch study............	High	I	No	No	High
Standard data from time study.	High	I	No	No	High

FIG. 25–1. Various means of determining office time standards compared by pertinent factors normally taken into account in selecting the means employed.

SUBJECTIVE JUDGMENT

Time standards set through subjective judgment are sometimes referred to as rule-of-thumb standards. They are based only on the experience and guess of the management member. It is strongly recommended that the manager refrain from the use of such time standards. Even when an accurate guess in establishing the standard has been made, it is extremely difficult to explain and justify the estimate. Frequently, disagreement over the guess arises and may cause problems.

PAST PERFORMANCE RECORDS

Under this plan, a count is made of work done on a particular class, unit, or item of office work. It is a recording of what is happening. To illustrate, assuming billings written as the unit, the records will show accomplishments day by day or week by week as follows: the number of units on hand at the beginning of the period, the number received during the period, the number completed, and the number at the end of the period. These are basic data; and after a short lapse of time, it is possible, with some adjustment, to arrive at the actual performance time standard derived by dividing the number of total man-hours worked by the number of orders processed. With sufficient data, trends, variations, maximum work loads, and the like can be evolved and subsequently utilized in time-controlling the work.

Data can be gathered either by the supervisor recording the amounts of work completed along with the corresponding times taken for each of his employees, or by having each employee record his work completed and the time taken to do it. Simple forms can be used, and co-operation of the employee is essential. To secure this, it is well to explain carefully and in some detail the purpose, operation, and need of the plan.

Standards arrived at from this approach have management value.[1] In

---

[1] For example, they are usable in federal offices where watch time study is prohibited by clauses in appropriation bills.

many respects, they are particularly helpful for groups of office employees doing fairly similar work. It should be observed, however, that standards obtained from past performance records are really *records of "what is,"* rather than *"what should be."*

WORK SAMPLING

Work sampling is a means employing random observations whereby the ratio of delays and of elements of work to the total process time is determined. It is based on the law of probability. If a comparatively large number of observations are taken at random intervals, the ratio between the observed frequency of a particular activity to the total number of observations taken will approximate the correct percentage of that activity. The technique consists of intermittent but frequent spot checking of the activity of one or more office employees and the recording of the activity at the moment it is observed. From this work sample, the time spent on each type of operation in relation to the total time available is determined.

Work-sampling data can be secured by means of observations by the supervisor. This method can be carried to any desired degree of detail, is economical, and measures cyclic effect, a very important concept in most office work. Care must be taken to avoid purposeful behavior on the part of the employee being observed. For example, when the observer enters the work area, the employee may not continue to work at his normal pattern, but strive to appear busier and begin moving papers, straightening up his desk, and engaging in similar activities. Such actions decrease the accuracy of the data. One means to combat purposeful behavior is to have a stationary observer throughout the study. With an observer ever present, the employee does not know when to exercise purposeful behavior. However, the stationary observer eliminates cost advantages of work sampling and reverts to the all-day study with its relatively high costs. Probably the best ways to eliminate purposeful behavior are (1) to use and train the supervisor as the observer and (2) to explain thoroughly the need and manner of performing the study in order to win the employee's complete co-operation.

From work-sampling data, it is possible to determine effective utilization of time, causes and extent of interference with effective accomplishment, flow of work through an office, and the amount of time devoted to various activities by an employee. For example, use of work sampling can provide the proportion of time a stenographer spends in typing, taking dictation, answering the telephone, and filing—information as shown graphically by a production study chart, discussed in Chapter 24. The office manager of a large insurance company found, by means of work sampling, that a low utilization of personnel and machines existed in the company's data-processing center. Using these facts as a springboard, the manager, within eight months, by means of control programs, increased machine utilization 17 per cent, released twelve rental machines, and won enthusiastic support of supervisors and employees for work sampling as a technique for making jobs less complicated and more productive. There are many who believe work sampling is one of the most practical and economical means for appraising the time required to perform office work.

STANDARD TIME DATA

The data for this method of determining time standards are based upon fundamental motions or muscular movements for which basic time standards have been developed. The time values vary with the nature of the motion and the conditions under which it is made. For example, movement of an arm 4 inches is given a certain time value, turning the wrist has another value, etc. Most standard time data are expressed as tables of values. To utilize this material, the standard time data man analyzes each manual operation into the basic motions which are necessary in performing the task. The time for each required basic motion is taken from the table of values and added to determine the time standard for the entire task.

OPERATION NAME: Obtain and put an original sheet of paper into typewriter DEPT. Sales Analysis SHEET 1 OF 2

NO.	ELEMENTAL DESCRIPTION	MOTION ANALYSIS	ELEM. TIME	CUMULATIVE TIME		ELEM. TIME	MOTION ANALYSIS	ELEMENTAL DESCRIPTION	NO.
	LEFT HAND							**RIGHT HAND**	
1					.0080	.0080	A20 D	R to sheet	1
2					.0080	-	Ct Gr	1st Gr	2
3					.0103	.0023	F1P	Separate	3
4		Wait	.0119	0119	.0119	.0016	F1	Gr	4
5	R to sheet	A20D	.0080	0199	.0199	.0080	A20D	M sheet to typewriter	5
6	Gr sheet	1/2 F1	.0008	0207	.0207	.0008	Hold		6
7	Approach typewriter roller	A1SD	.0034	0241	.0241	.0034	A1SD	Approach typewriter roller	7
8	A1 (OTS-TD .074")	1-1/2A1SD	.0051	0292	.0249	.0008	1/2 F1	R1 sheet	8
9	GD 5"	1-1/2A1SD 30%.0015		0307	.0303	.0054	A8D	R to roller knob	9
10	IND	A1SD	.0034	0341	.0311	.0008	1/2 F1	Gr roller knob	10
11	INS	A1D	.0026	0367	.0367	.0056	Wait		11
12	R1 paper	1/2 F1	.0008	0375	.0398	.0031	FS180°	Turn roller knob	12
13	R to carriage release	A80	.0054	0429	.0406	.0008	1/2 F1	R1 roller knob	13
14	Gr carriage release	1/2 F1	.0008	0437	.0437	.0031	FS180°	R to roller knob	14
15					.0445	.0008	1/2 F1	Gr roller knob	15
16					.0601	.0156	.0078x2	Repeat elements Nos.12-15	16
17		Wait	.0192	0629	.0629	.0028	FS45°SD	Turn to final line	17
18	Depress carriage release	F1	.0016	0645	.0645	.0016	Hold		18
19	Push carriage to 1st position	VA4SD	.0048	0693	.0693	.0048	VA4SD	Pull carriage to 1st position	19
20	A1 (OTS-TD .100")	1-1/4A1SD	.0043	0736	.0736	.0043	1-1/4A1SD	A1 (OTS-TD .100")	20

TOTAL SELECT TIME: _____ X _____ CONVERSION = _____ HPC   STANDARD PRODUCTION PER HOUR (100 + HPC) _____ EHO

REMARKS:

Courtesy: Work-Factor Co., Inc., Haddonsfield, N.J.

FIG. 25–2. Data from a standard time study.

Figure 25–2 shows the standard time values for the elemental motions required to obtain and put an original sheet of paper into a typewriter. On line 4, for example, right hand, the elemental time of 0.0016 of a minute is the time allotted for a motion, *F1*, meaning fingers open 1 inch; and the elemental description is *GR*, standing for grasp. Similarly, on line 5, the standard time value of 0.0080 of a minute is given *A20D*, arm extended 20 inches to *M*, or move, sheet to typewriter.

Standard time data are predetermined time values for definite basic motions. By their use, time standards can be set before the work is actually performed. Knowing or determining the basic motions required, the standard time for each element is determined, and all are added to obtain the total standard time value for a particular task. No stop watch is needed.

STOP-WATCH STUDY

This means of determining time standards emphasizes a relatively precise measurement of a particular task or an individual segment of office work. The time standard developed from this source applies to specific work done under specific conditions, such as workplace, method, and material. It is not a universal time standard. The work selected for study should be repetitive and of sufficient volume to warrant careful analysis. The proper workplace should be resolved and the work motions economized. There is no point in establishing carefully set time values for work that is performed ineffectively and that is soon to be improved. The variable job elements which are affected by changing conditions should be under control. It should be noted that stop-watch study is also helpful in determining waste, many studies in fact being made for this purpose. The stop watch should be one which reads directly in one hundredths (0.01) of a minute. Keeping all values in minutes and hundredths of minutes simplifies calculations. The watch should also provide means for snapping back the hands to zero after each reading if the "snap-back" method is desired.

The employee selected for observation should be an above-average type, not because he accomplishes more work, but because he will probably have the best motions and rhythm in his work. This does not mean that the time standards to be determined will require an above-average worker. Discussion of this point is given several paragraphs below. Complete co-operation of the employee must be secured. This means, among other things, explaining what is being done, and why, plus answering any questions the employee may have. When ready, take a position a little to one side of and behind the employee. To become familiar with the task, watch the completion of it several times.

The job is divided into components or small motions that can be observed and timed. An illustration of such components for the work of posting material requisition notices on card files is shown by Figure 25–3. The eight components heading up a like number of columns are hand-printed across the top of the form.

Next, the time observations are recorded. The starting time is written in the space provided (upper left of Figure 25–3). Make certain the stop-watch hands are set at zero. Start the stop watch at the beginning

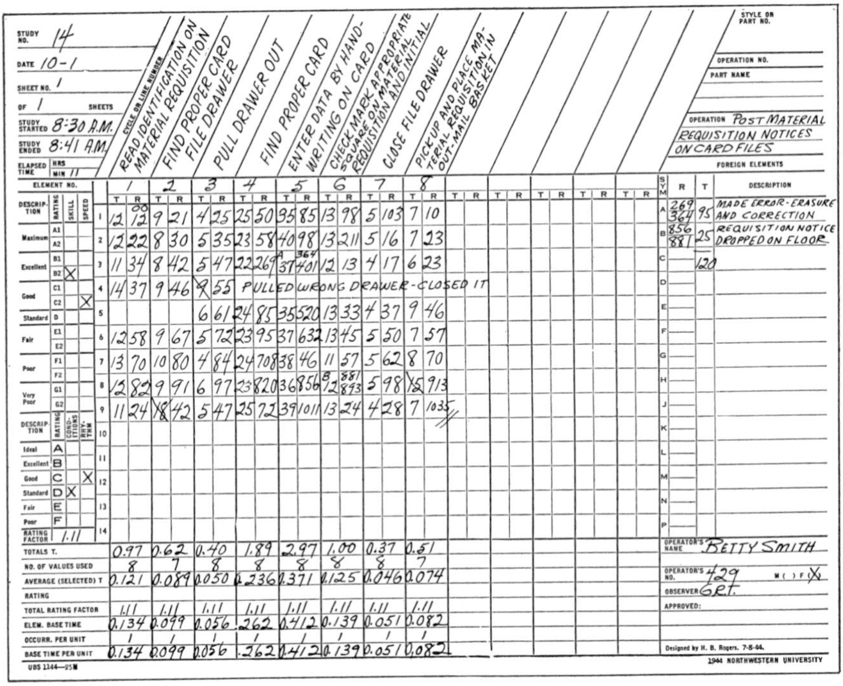

STUDY NO. 14
DATE 10-1
SHEET NO. 1
OF 1 SHEETS
STUDY STARTED 8:30 A.M.
STUDY ENDED 8:41 A.M.
ELAPSED TIME HRS MIN 11

STYLE OR PART NO.
OPERATION NO.
PART NAME
OPERATION POST MATERIAL REQUISITION NOTICES ON CARD FILES

Elements: 1 READ IDENTIFICATION ON MATERIAL REQUISITION; 2 FIND PROPER CARD FILE DRAWER; 3 PULL DRAWER OUT; 4 FIND PROPER CARD; 5 ENTER DATA BY HAND-WRITING ON CARD; 6 CHECK MARK APPROPRIATE SQUARE ON MATERIAL REQUISITION AND INITIAL; 7 CLOSE FILE DRAWER; 8 PICK UP AND PLACE MATERIAL REQUISITION IN OUT-MAIL BASKET

CYCLE OR LINE NUMBER	1 T	1 R	2 T	2 R	3 T	3 R	4 T	4 R	5 T	5 R	6 T	6 R	7 T	7 R	8 T	8 R
1	12	00 12	9	21	4	25	25	50	35	85	13	98	5	103	7	10
2	12	22	8	30	5	35	23	58	40	98	13	211	5	16	7	23
3	11	34	8	42	5	47	22	269	A 37	364 401	12	13	4	17	6	23
4	14	37	9	46	9	55	PULLED WRONG DRAWER-CLOSED IT									
5					6	61	24	85	35	520	13	33	4	37	9	46
6	12	58	9	67	5	72	23	95	37	632	13	45	5	50	7	57
7	13	70	10	80	4	84	24	708	38	46	11	57	5	62	8	70
8	12	82	9	91	6	97	23	820	36	856	B 12	881 893	5	98	15	913
9	11	24	18	42	5	47	25	72	39	1011	13	24	4	28	7	1035
10																
11																
12																
13																
14																

	1	2	3	4	5	6	7	8
TOTALS T.	0.97	0.62	0.40	1.89	2.97	1.00	0.37	0.51
NO. OF VALUES USED	8	7	8	8	8	8	8	7
AVERAGE (SELECTED) T	0.121	0.089	0.050	0.236	0.371	0.125	0.046	0.074
RATING								
TOTAL RATING FACTOR	1.11	1.11	1.11	1.11	1.11	1.11	1.11	1.11
ELEM. BASE TIME	0.134	0.099	0.056	.262	0.412	0.139	0.051	0.082
OCCURR. PER UNIT	1	1	1	1	1	1	1	1
BASE TIME PER UNIT	0.134	0.099	0.056	.262	0.412	0.139	0.051	0.082

DESCRIPTION	RATING	SKILL	SPEED
Maximum	A1		
	A2		
Excellent	B1		
	B2	X	
Good	C1		
	C2		X
Standard	D		
Fair	E1		
	E2		
Poor	F1		
	F2		
Very Poor	G1		
	G2		

DESCRIPTION	RATING	CONDITIONS	RHYTHM
Ideal	A		
Excellent	B		
Good	C		X
Standard	D	X	
Fair	E		
Poor	F		

RATING FACTOR 1.11

FOREIGN ELEMENTS

SYM	R	T	DESCRIPTION
A	269 364	95	MADE ERROR-ERASURE AND CORRECTION
B	856 881	25	REQUISITION NOTICE DROPPED ON FLOOR
C		120	
D			
E			
F			
G			
H			
J			
K			
L			
M			
N			
P			

OPERATOR'S NAME BETTY SMITH
OPERATOR'S NO. 429 M ( ) F (X)
OBSERVER G.R.T.
APPROVED:

UBS 1144—25M
Designed by H. B. Rogers. 7-8-44.
1944 NORTHWESTERN UNIVERSITY

FIG. 25–3. Time-study data sheet for an office task.

of the first element; and at the completion of this element, note and record the watch reading on the first line in the first column under the letter *R*, which stands for Reading. At the completion of the second element, note the watch reading and record it on the first line of the second column under the letter *R*. In similar manner, read and record the watch readings for each of the elements.

In Figure 25–3, the reading at the completion of element 1 is 12; at the end of element 2, 21; at the end of element 3, 25; at the end of element 4, 50; and so on. In this illustration, the "continuous reading" method is being followed, not the "snap-back" method.

At the end of the last element, let the watch continue to run; and in like manner, repeat the task-cycle-recording readings on the second line. Continue this procedure until a sufficient number of cycles have been timed to indicate some commonness in the elapsed time per element. Usually, about eight or ten cycles should be recorded, but some analysts claim readings should be taken for at least 15–20 minutes. It is also possible to determine mathematically how many cycles represent a reliable sample so that a true representation of the work is obtained.

Variations from the proper sequence are recorded as "repeats" on the immediate line below, or, in the case of interruptions, by footnoting and explaining in the space located on the extreme right of the form. To illustrate, referring to Figure 25–3 again, on the third line under element 5, an interruption occurred and is footnoted by the letter *A*. At the right of the form, a description is given that the employee made an error, erased, and corrected. This "foreign element" took place between watch readings of 269 and 364, or a total of 95, which is actually $^{95}/_{100}$ of a minute. Another interruption is shown by footnote *B* on the eighth line under element 6.

We want the time standard not for the above-average employee ob-

SKILL			EFFORT		
+0.15	A1	Superskill	+0.13	A1	Killing
+0.13	A2		+0.12	A2	
+0.11	B1	Excellent	+0.10	B1	Excellent
+0.08	B2		+0.08	B2	
+0.06	C1	Good	+0.05	C1	Good
+0.03	C2		+0.02	C2	
0.00	D	Average	0.00	D	Average
−0.05	E1	Fair	−0.04	E1	Fair
−0.10	E2		−0.08	E2	
−0.16	F1	Poor	−0.12	F1	Poor
−0.22	F2		−0.17	F2	
CONDITIONS			CONSISTENCY		
+0.06	A	Ideal	+0.04	A	Perfect
+0.04	B	Excellent	+0.03	B	Excellent
+0.02	C	Good	+0.01	C	Good
0.00	D	Average	0.00	D	Average
−0.03	E	Fair	−0.02	E	Fair
−0.07	F	Poor	−0.04	F	Poor

Courtesy: Stewart M. Lowry, Harold B. Maynard, and G. J. Stegemerten, "Time and Motion Study" (New York: McGraw-Hill Book Co., Inc., 1940), p. 233

FIG. 25–4. Performance-rating chart.

served, but for the average or normal employee. The adjustment to normal is known as "leveling"; to do this, observations of the observed employee's skill, effort, working conditions, and consistency are made during the study. Recordings for these factors are written on the left side of the form in Figure 25–3. As a guide, a leveling chart, such as that shown in Figure 25–4 (page 493), is usually used. The algebraic values of the ratings are obtained from this chart; and in the case illustrated, the following will apply:

Attribute	Rating	Algebraic Value
Skill..............................	B2	+0.08
Effort or speed....................	C2	+0.02
Conditions........................	D	0.00
Consistency or rhythm.............	C	+0.01
Total.........................	...	+0.11

This total added algebraically to unity gives 1.11, which is the leveling or rating factor and is indicated on the form near the bottom of the left-hand column in Figure 25–3.

The time elapsed for each element is calculated by subtracting the preceding from the immediately following cumulative reading and recording under the appropriate column headed T, which stands for Time. To illustrate, in Figure 25–3, on the first line, the value 9 under T in element 2 is obtained by subtracting 12 from 21; the value 4 under element 3 is obtained by subtracting 21 from 25. Other values of time elapsed for each element are obtained in like manner.

Now, the time standard can be calculated by:

1. *Finding the representative, observed, elemental time.* To do this, study the time taken by elements shown by each vertical column under T, strike out the abnormal times, and find the average—usually the arithmetic average of the remaining times. In the illustration given in Figure 25–3, the abnormal time of 18 for element 2 on line 9 has been discarded. The average of the selected T values is 0.089, as shown near the bottom of the column. This was calculated by dividing 0.62 by 7.

2. *Apply the leveling factor.* To do this, multiply the average T value by the leveling factor. In the case illustrated, this is 0.089 times 1.11, which gives 0.099, the elemental base time. Since the T value occurs once per unit, the base time per unit is the same, namely, 0.099, which is written on the bottom line of the column.

3. *Add allowances for personal needs, fatigue, unavoidable delays, and the like.* This can be expressed either as a lump percentage or as separate percentages for each allowance. This is shown in Figure 25–5. The sum of the base time per unit is 1.235. An allowance of 20 per cent

TIME STUDY OBSERVATION SHEET

| STUDY NO. 14 | DATE 10-1 | DEPT. OR LOCATION 13 | DWG. NO. — | DWG. SUB OR ISSUE — | PART OR STYLE NO. — | OP. NO. — |

OPERATION: Post Material Requisition Notices on File Cards

Base time per unit — element base times:

Element No.	Base Time
1	0.134
2	0.099
3	0.056
4	0.262
5	0.412
6	0.139
7	0.051
8	0.082

(A) 1.235	TOTAL BASE T.	
(B) 1.20	ALLOWANCE FACTOR	
(C)	ALLOWANCE TIME	
(D) 1.482	STANDARD TIME	DESK HEIGHT: 29¾"
(E) 1.482	TOTAL STD TIME/UNIT	General overhead illumination
(F) 100%	% OF CYCLE	LIGHTING: 40 CANDLE POWER ON DESK TOP
(G) 40.5	STD. UNITS PER HOUR	
(H)	$ HRLY BASE RATE	REQUISITION: FORM B 761
(J)	STRAIGHT PIECE RATE	
(K)	$ HRLY PREM. RATE	FILE CARD: FORM R 97
(L)	TASK: UNITS PER HOUR	
(M)	PREM. PIECE RATE	
(N)	PREM. PIECE RATE	

NET OVERALL TIME, PER UNIT OR CYCLE:

$$\frac{1035 - 120}{8} = \frac{915}{8} = 1.14$$

CONDITIONS: SIT/100 % STAND ___ % TEMP 70 DEGREES

SKETCH: PART, TOOLS, OR WORK AREA — 42", 54", 4 Cabinets @ 12 slides in each, Vertical Section, Requisitions

REMARKS: Vertical files of drawers contain visible index cards

FIG. 25–5. Reverse side of time-study data sheet shown in Fig. 25–3.

as a lump sum has been added, and the new value is 1.482. This is, of course, in minutes. Expressed as units per hour, the value is 40.5. Figure 25–5 also illustrates other pertinent data which are included on the time-study sheet. Information regarding the conditions, the material used, and a sketch of the workplace area is usually included for identification and future reference.

STANDARD DATA FROM TIME STUDY

This is the last means for establishing time standards discussed in this book. Like standard time data discussed above, this source, or standard data from time study, utilizes predetermined values which are selected and added in order to synthesize the entire operation for which the time standard is desired.

From the data of many actual time studies, it is possible to determine the basic allowable times for elements which are common to many tasks.[2] To do this, relationships between time and some meaningful variable, such as distance, size, or weight, are determined. For example, con-

---

[2] "Elemental motions," as used here, means the smallest motions that can be observed and read for time. It does not mean elementary motions or therbligs, which are discussed in the preceding chapter. Therbligs usually are of too short a duration to be measured by a stop watch.

sider the element "pulling file drawer out." From many actual time studies, the time values for this element are obtained. Some of these values will be for pulling file drawers out a distance of 6 inches, others 10 inches, still others 14 inches, etc. By mathematical analysis of these data, the relationship between time and distance traveled for the element "pulling file drawer out" can be determined. From this relationship, the amount of time for this element can be predetermined, based on the distance the drawer travels. In similar manner, relationships can be determined for the size of the drawer and the weight of the material in it. The relationships so developed can be expressed as tables of values, as equations, or as graphs.

EXAMPLES OF OFFICE TIME STANDARDS

The following office time standards have value in connection with various types of office work. They are included here to be helpful in a comparative way only. They were determined for specific conditions prevailing in a particular office and should be used as guides, not goals.

Units per Hour

1. Typing:

Type name and account number on card............................. 180
Type labels from typewritten copy..................................... 135
Type ledger cards.. 105
Type report, double space on $8\frac{1}{2} \times 11$-inch paper, one original and one carbon copy.. 10
Type address on envelope... 85

2. Calculating and checking:

Compute products of 3-digit number by 3-digit number, using machine..... 500
Add 20 numbers in a column (each number is 3 digits) by machine........ 2
Compare columns of figures on tape or report, with columns of figures in like order (number of digits per figure compared equals 5)..................4,800
Count items on a tape, or lines on a sheet............................9,400

3. Accounting:

Pull from source, post account to ledger sheet by machine, and replace sheet... 130
Make entries in ledger (manual)....................................... 40

4. Filing and sorting:

Sort correspondence papers for filing................................. 480
File correspondence papers in alphabetical file....................... 180
Sort 5×3-inch cards alphabetically........................... 300
Locate and pull addressing plates from alphabetical file.............. 420

5. Miscellaneous:

Hand-fold $8\frac{1}{2} \times 11$-inch sheet with one fold..........1,200
Seal ordinary envelope (manual)....................................... 450
Assemble three sheets of paper, $8\frac{1}{2} \times 11$ inches, and insert in large 9×12-inch envelope.. 575

QUESTIONS

1. Give an example of a modified work measurement unit in connection with office work, and explain how it is used.

2. Why is it necessary to measure office work? Why not just time the work and determine the time standard from these data? Discuss.

3. Indicate what measuring unit you would recommend, and your reasons why, for each of the following:
   a) Duplicating a monthly report.
   b) Verifying the accuracy of bank checks written.
   c) Answering correspondence dealing with sales.
   d) Receiving office visitors.

4. Explain Figure 25–1 in your own words.

5. Discuss the application of standard time data to the managerial controlling of office work.

6. Why should a stop-watch time study be made only after the proper workplace has been provided and the motions economized? Are there any exceptions?

7. Explain the following: "Past performance records are actually 'what is,' rather than 'what should be.' "

8. Name and discuss four major advantages in having time standards. Are these advantages to managers exclusively, to nonmanagement members exclusively, or to both managers and nonmanagement members? Explain.

9. For what type of office work and under what conditions would you recommend time standards established by past performance records? Discuss.

10. Carefully distinguish between the concepts in each of the following pairs:
    a) Work sampling and "snap-back" watch readings.
    b) Time study and stop-watch study.
    c) Purposeful behavior by employee and definition of task.
    d) Leveling factor and allowance for personal needs.

11. Do you agree with the statement: "Stop-watch study for determining time standards is a scientific process"? Explain your answer.

12. Comment on the following: "The adjustment of observed data to give proper consideration for what is an average employee appears vital in a stop-watch time study. In contrast, the concept of an average employee is ignored when the means of work sampling is followed. This is inconsistent and demonstrates that neither means provides accurate time standards."

CASE PROBLEMS

Case 25–1.   Ideal Insurance Company

The time data on page 498 are for tabulating daily receipts. For this work, an allowance of 12 per cent is given for personal needs and delays. Office hours are from 8:00–11:30 A.M. and 12:30–4:30 P.M., with a fifteen-minute "break" in midmorning and again in midafternoon.

The operator is seated at a desk. Envelopes containing customers' payments have been slit across the top by machine, and these envelopes are placed in front of the operator about an arm's length away. The first work element is reaching for and tearing open the sides of an envelope by means of the index fingers, thus permitting quick access to the contents. The succeeding elements are indicated on the time-study sheet. On the desk to the upper right of the operator is a basket for checks; to the right center, the daily receipts sheet; to the lower left, a basket for bills. On an average, two

								STYLE OR PART NO.
STUDY NO. 62-331								
DATE April 27							OPERATION NO.	
SHEET NO. 1							PART NAME	
OF 1 SHEETS								
STUDY STARTED 9:20 A.M.							OPERATION Tabulating	
STUDY ENDED 9:28 A.M.							Daily Receipts	
ELAPSED TIME HRS / MIN 8							FOREIGN ELEMENTS	

Column headings (diagonal):
1. Reach for envelope
2. Remove contents, move bill to left and check / tear sides open
3. Compare check with bill for accuracy / to right
4. If O.K. enters times and amount of check on Daily Receipts Sheet
5. Stamps bill and places check in basket to lower left
6. Puts check in basket upper right

ELEMENT NO.	1 T	1 R	2 T	2 R	3 T	3 R	4 T	4 R	5 T	5 R	6 T	6 R
Maximum A1 (1)	.04	.04		.10		.20		.42		.50		.54
A2 (2)		.57		.65		.77	1.02			.11		.16
Excellent B1 (3)		.21		.28		.40		.58		.67		.74
Good C1 X (4)	2.71			.77		.87	3.07			.19		.25
Standard D X (5)		.30		.38		.46		.65		.75		.80
Fair E1 (6)		.84		.92	4.03		5.55			.62		.67
Poor F1 (7)		.71		.78		.92	6.13			.22		.26
Very Poor G1 (8)		.31		.38		.50		.70		.79		.85
(9)		.92	7.01			.10		.29		.36		.41
(10)		.47		.53		.64		.87		.96	8.01	

FOREIGN ELEMENTS:

	R	T	DESCRIPTION
A	1.74 2.65	.91	Top not slit-Opened entire envelope
B	4.03 5.39	.36	Error in spelling Erased & corrected

	1	2	3	4	5	6
OCCURR. PER UNIT	1	1	1	1	1	1

Bottom rows: TOTALS T. / NO. OF VALUES USED / AVERAGE (SELECTED) T / RATING / TOTAL RATING FACTOR / ELEM. BASE TIME / OCCURR. PER UNIT / BASE TIME PER UNIT

OPERATOR'S NAME Nancy Reilly
OPERATOR'S NO. 22   M ( ) F (X)
OBSERVER L.D.T.
APPROVED E.M.

U86 1144—25M   Designed by H. B. Rogers. 7-8-44, Revised 7-26-47
1944 NORTHWESTERN UNIVERSITY

out of a hundred envelopes contain payments that are incorrect for the amount of the bill. When such receipts are discovered during element No. 3, the contents are placed in a basket located on the desk to the upper left of the operator.

Problems:

1. Compute the time standard for the indicated work in receipts posted per hour.

2. How many receipt postings would you expect during a regular working day? Explain.

3. How many incorrect payments would you expect an operator to have during a regular working day? Show all calculations.

Case 25–2. Snyder Cold Storage, Inc.

Four employees process orders which are received from dealers throughout a six-state area. The work consists of (1) picking up a bundle of orders from an incoming order tray, (2) reading orders and sorting them into several categories by quantity of order, (3) checking prices by referring to a catalogue, (4) entering the order manually on a three-part carbon form, (5) separating the three copies of the form, (6) folding and inserting copy No. 1 into a window envelope—this is the dealer's acknowledgement, (7) filing copy No. 2 into a tub file, and (8) placing copy No. 3 into a tray to be sent to the stockroom.

Mr. Jason Phillips, the office manager, has compiled the data shown in the accompanying table. This information was obtained by reviewing records maintained by the office on work output. He is confident that the data reveal the true situation for the four employees processing orders.

Month	Days Worked	Hours per Day	Number of Clerks	Hours Absent	Total Hours Worked	Number of Orders Processed	Actual Performance Standard
January...	22	8	4	15.5	688.5	3,682	.187
February..	19	8	4	16.0	592.0	2,574	.230
March.....	21	8	4	35.0	637.0	3,959	.161
April......	21	8	4	7.5	664.5	3,046	.218
May......	21	8	4	8.0	664.0	2,415	.275
June......	22	8	4	5.0	699.0	2,470	.283
July.......	22	8	3	2.0	526.0	1,898	.277
August....	22	8	4	7.0	697.0	2,247	.310
September.	21	8	3	3.5	500.5	1,498	.334
October...	22	8	4	30.5	673.5	3,617	.186
November.	20	8	4	20.0	620.0	3,690	.168
December..	19	8	4	24.0	584.0	3,720	.157
					7,546.0	34,816	

Average $= \dfrac{7,546}{34,816} = .216$ hours per order processed

The company anticipates a 14 per cent increase in orders for the forthcoming year. Mr. Phillips reasons that a 14 per cent increase could require an additional 0.56 of a girl. His casual observation of the four employees during the past two weeks shows that they are busy and appear to be working at a normal pace. The processing of orders has never given any trouble to the office manager.

Problems:

1. Evaluate the actual performance standards calculated by Mr. Phillips.
2. What decision should Mr. Phillips reach? Justify your viewpoint.
3. Relate how you believe Mr. Phillips should implement the decision of question No. 2, above.

Chapter 26

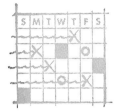

OFFICE COST CONTROLLING AND BUDGETING

Ask thy purse what thou shouldst spend.

—Scottish Proverb

ANOTHER IMPORTANT area of controlling in office management is cost. It is implied in every office accomplishment not only that the work is completed satisfactorily, but that it is completed within a certain cost. In fact, managerial success in many cases lies in understanding the nature of true costs. Answers to what things cost, how these costs are figured, and the meaning of the final results in terms of cost are fundamental to the work of the effective office manager. In addition, questions of cost must be answered if the enterprise is to continue. Cost knowledge is essential to survival, at least from a long-range point of view.

COST DEFINED

For purposes of this book, cost can be defined as *the dollar amount expended for the ownership, use, or service of every component making up and employed in the execution of the work.* Cost is a matter of money outlay for manual or mental work accomplished, planned, or in process of being achieved.

IMPORTANCE OF COST

Cost is basic to nearly all business activities; some consider it the common controlling medium, since other types, such as those for quality and quantity, can be expressed in terms of cost. But cost data should be employed prudently; other media and techniques of controlling should be used when they are believed to be superior under the particular circumstances. Cost is not an objective in itself, but a guide to help manage, especially in the activity of controlling, the various activities in order that the aims of the enterprise will be realized. It is simply a means, but an important one, used by a manager.

The making of a managerial decision is usually influenced very much by the consideration of cost information. Questions as to whether to install a new procedure, to purchase a new office machine, to perform a new service, or to revise a form design are decided with the aid of cost information. Sometimes, the question is answered almost entirely on the basis of cost. In addition, cost also helps justify a managerial action. Recommendations for a change usually include the cost before and the cost (estimated) after the change is effected. Likewise, if an alteration has been made, the wisdom of this move is frequently confirmed by a "before and after" cost picture. Figure 26–1 illustrates one type of form that can be used.

COST SAVINGS ESTIMATE

DEPARTMENT NO. ___78___

DATE __9/7/__

DESCRIPTION __Adopt work layout and method described by M-240__

NOTE: ALL COSTS FOR ONE YEAR

COSTS	PRESENT	PROPOSED	SAVINGS
LABOR	$2875	$2130	+$745
MATERIAL	925	800	+ 125
MACHINE TIME	750	1035	- 285
OTHER (WRITE IN)			
TOTAL	$4550	$3965	$585

ACTION ___Recommended and approved on Oct. 3, 1958 by executive___

___committee, R. C. McGinnis, Chairman.___

APPROVED AND PUT INTO EFFECT BY ___CRM.___

FIG. 26–1. A cost savings estimate.

It is by means of cost that an office manager keeps informed of basic bench marks of the office operations. Many of the items in the reports dealing with accomplishments and in the ordinary financial statements are expressed in cost. The number of employees; supplies used; inventory on hand, in process, or finished; charge for floor space occupied; charge for office machines usage; and the like are expressed in dollar values, estimated from cost information.

Cost serves as an effective medium for co-ordinating managerial activities. For example, it is helpful in determining the program of action that will achieve the required results, yet maintain the proper balance. The selection and extent of managerial efforts, their timing, and direction can be executed in an orderly manner. Actions predicated on guesses or on hit-and-miss bases are minimized.[1]

Another reason for the importance of cost is its use to supply clues to places where waste can be reduced or eliminated. While curbing waste is a desired result of all controlling, it is especially so in the case of cost. The very nature of cost information focuses attention on what was paid out and what was received. This leads to waste reduction. To illustrate, a study of duplicating costs might uncover uneconomical runs and the use of improper paper for the specific purpose. In addition, cost information reveals fluctuations in cost which can be followed up by investigations to determine the reasons and subsequently apply remedial measures.

The effective use of cost information leads logically to the maintaining of satisfactory cost levels and, beyond this, to the lowering of these cost levels. Progressive reductions in cost appear to be a normal state of affairs in a progressive economy. The eternal challenge is to achieve better office work at less cost.

APPROACHES TO COST REDUCTION

To gain significant office cost reduction, three approaches appear essential: (1) Concentrate on the items offering greatest cost reduction opportunities, (2) develop a cost-consciousness among all employees, and (3) establish an effective cost control program. This three-pronged attack, when efficiently applied, is practically certain to reduce costs.

ITEMS OFFERING GREATEST COST REDUCTION OPPORTUNITIES

Certain items normally offer greater cost reduction possibilities than others. Those representing the big items, the ones on which the most money is now being spent, and those of a cumulative and repetitive nature, usually offer the best opportunities for lowering costs. Some research and probing may be required to find this type of information for a particular office.

In most offices, however, the major expense is wages and salaries— employees are the key cost. A breakdown of total office expenses under typical conditions is usually of a pattern similar to the following:

Item	Percentage of Total Costs
Office wages and salaries	70%
Supplies, postage, telephone	15
Purchase and maintenance of office equipment and machines, rent, light, and heat	15
Total Costs	100%

---

[1] The budget, discussed later in this chapter, is also helpful in utilizing cost data for effective managerial purposes.

In other words, nearly three out of every four office dollar costs are for people. To increase efficiency, this suggests the use of less employees, or the more efficient use of those presently employed. Stressing people as the core of office cost reduction, Fred E. Shelton, Jr., suggests careful examination of four areas: (1) office supervision, (2) habit patterns, (3) servile attitudes, and (4) methods of administration.[2]

COST-CONSCIOUSNESS AMONG EMPLOYEES

Cutting cost is not a job restricted to managers. It is a job in which every employee can and should participate. Interest in costs is fundamental because it is a means contributing to employee security. To reduce costs is a way of keeping an enterprise fit so it can continue to operate successfully and meet its responsibilities.

Cost information can be used to develop a cost-consciousness among employees. A feeling of the importance of cost and its use throughout

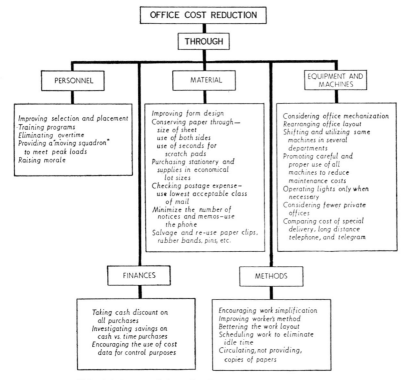

FIG. 26–2. Possibilities for the reduction of office costs.

[2] Fred E. Shelton, Jr., "Wanted: Cost Reduction," *Office Executive* (Willow Grove, Pa.: National Office Management Association), June, 1956, pp. 9–11. This is an excellent article. Mr. Shelton is office manager of the Standard Register Company, Dayton, Ohio.

the entire enterprise must be achieved for cost to have greatest value. Every member on the payroll, from the top executive to the lowest employee, should be made aware of and encouraged to think in terms of cost. When the employees are cost-minded, a basic and broad beginning toward improving operations has been accomplished. Thinking in terms of cost is necessary for greatest efficiency.

To accomplish this aim, suggestions pointing out possibilities for lowering office expenses are helpful. Figure 26–2 on page 503 shows this in graphic form and brings out the fact that cost permeates all office activities. Every employee has the opportunity to be cost-minded and to reduce costs. In addition, accurate cost information should be disseminated to all supervisors and employees who are charged with those costs and for which they are responsible. By this means, cost is given important and meaningful status. Employees are quick to recognize this and will seek to use cost as a guide in their everyday tasks.

ESTABLISH EFFECTIVE COST CONTROL PROGRAM

As pointed out throughout this book, controlling consists basically of determining what is being done, evaluating it, and taking corrective action if necessary. The same holds true for cost control. An effective cost control program consists of these five steps: (1) Assemble facts on cost, (2) know what cost is satisfactory, (3) compare actual cost with the cost deemed satisfactory, (4) take remedial action if necessary, and (5) provide adequate and proper follow-up.

ASSEMBLE FACTS ON COST

The initial step in cost control is to get together the facts on cost, classify as to type, and arrange so that handy reference and quick comparisons can be made. Sources of cost information include ledgers, cost journals, payroll records, purchases, and records of service charges. To expedite this work, it is usually advisable to concentrate the efforts in several selected areas.

In assembling the factual cost information, it is well to take into account these considerations:

1. *The data should be accurate, timely, and identified.* In the modern office, frequent changes may be made in the effort to improve operations. These changes are sometimes of a major sort and necessitate a new collection of cost data in order to reflect an accurate measurement of current expenditures. Even in the case of minor adjustments, the resultant effect may be sufficiently large to invalidate a considerable portion of previous cost information. Cost data should be closely affiliated and apply to the current situation; otherwise, their value is questionable.

There are so many different kinds of cost that the term "cost" in and of itself is practically meaningless. The variety of costs is almost endless, the different kinds depending upon the degree and type of work covered. To facilitate understanding, information concerning "cost of what to whom" is needed.

Several common identification arrangements will be given. The first, based on the factors or elements of material, labor, and overhead, includes the following:

Element	*Segregation and Meaning*
Material cost:	Direct material cost—expenditures for materials which are or become a part of the product (office forms and letterheads).
	Indirect material cost—expenditures for materials which are not a part of the product but are necessary in the carrying-out of the work (typewriter ribbons, erasers).
Labor cost:	Direct labor cost—expenditures for labor attributable to and having a bearing upon the product or service (billing-machine operator, typist).
	Indirect labor cost—expenditures for labor not attributable to or in an unbroken connection with the product or service (methods man, janitor).
Overhead cost:	Expenditures which do not belong exclusively to any part of the material or labor (rent, light, heat, managerial expense, telephone).

The second arrangement utilizing a functional basis consists of total costs made up of:

I. Production costs, under which are:
   A. Production overhead costs
   B. Office cost consisting of:
     1. Office overhead cost
     2. Prime office costs
       a) Direct office material cost
       b) Direct office labor cost
II. Sales costs, under which are:
   A. Sales overhead cost
   B. Promotion, travel, and advertising cost
   C. Salesmen's compensation cost
     1. Wage payment cost
     2. Commission and bonus cost

This outline is for illustrative purposes only and is not complete.

2. *The data should apply to well-defined components.* Usually, in studying cost data, the most important figures are not the totals but the individual cost figures, covering each component of those which collectively make up the total cost. Sufficient details must be included in all

cost information to maximize its managerial value. No single factor tells the whole cost story.

In addition, the "cost per unit" should be used. The unit cost is the important concept. Comparison of a $300 actual cost with a $200 expected cost is not valid. If the work accomplished is 150 units and the expected output was 100 units, the true values become:

$$\text{Actual} = \frac{\$300}{150 \text{ units}} = \$2.00 \text{ per unit,}$$

$$\text{Expected} = \frac{\$200}{100 \text{ units}} = \$2.00 \text{ per unit,}$$

which demonstrates that the actual unit cost did not exceed but is equal to the expected cost.

3. *The identification and presentation form must be simple and complete.* The operation covered should be clearly specified, so that the data are identified with the correct kind of cost. Such things as date, location of operation, operation number, and other pertinent information should be included. The arrangement can be in properly headed, simple tabular columns. However, in special cases, it might be advisable to have the data in coded form in order to preserve their confidential nature. Either cards or letter-size paper can be used, depending upon custom and individual requirements.

KNOW WHAT COST IS SATISFACTORY

This can be determined in a number of ways. The amount may be arrived at from past experience, giving due consideration to general economic changes and conditions. A general evaluation of what is received for a given expenditure may also be used. However, probably most satisfactory are standard costs; if available, they should be employed.

Standard cost is a computed predetermined cost which represents the amount of expenditure for direct material, direct labor, and overhead considered normal for the performance of the work. Theoretically, when the work is done by a standard employee with standard material and under standard conditions, the total dollar expenditure should be the standard cost. In some cases, the standard cost, having been established some time ago, must be adjusted to reflect current conditions. These adjustments are called variances and are applied to the cost standard to determine the cost currently considered acceptable. Variances may be either positive, i.e., added to the standard, or negative, i.e., subtracted from the standard.

The use of standard costs gives rise to several outstanding advantages. These include the following: Basic references are provided to orientate managerial efforts; strict accountability for deviations from the established standard cost can be placed on those responsible for the deviations; and cost analysis is simplified. In contrast, standard cost usage has its shortcomings. For example, the units of expression are dollars and hence are subject to fluctuating value; personnel must be especially trained for standard cost work so that proper interpretation and use of the standard data are made; and in cases of special work, standard cost data cannot be used unless serious adjustments are made. While all these objections are valid, they are not particularly serious. Dollar values tend to remain *relatively* the same even though they do fluctuate in absolute value. It is probably true that some guide to acceptability, although it be found wanting in many respects, is better than none at all. Also, most efforts to guide the performance of work must, of practical necessity, be tempered with judgment.

COMPARE ACTUAL COST WITH COST DEEMED SATISFACTORY

This shows whether expenditures are greater, the same as, or less than an acceptable level. It indicates the performance efficiency expressed in dollars. If the expenditure is less than the amount considered satisfactory, an investigation is made to determine if the work performed was of acceptable quality and quantity and if the satisfactory cost level is proper. On the other hand, where the actual cost exceeds the established satisfactory level, an investigation might be made to check the satisfactory level or, more likely, to analyze the actual cost to see in what way it can be brought into line.

The comparison work is expedited by cost reports giving detailed information on expenditures and compiled at the end of each day, week, or month. For maximum assistance, the report should show the plus or minus deviations from the standard for each item and, what is very important, should include sufficient data to establish trends. In many instances, the comparison of actual with standard cost is included under budgetary control, which is discussed later in this chapter.

TAKE REMEDIAL ACTION IF NECESSARY

For the most part, this includes efforts to reduce expenditures in those cases where actual costs are exceeding the satisfactory cost level. In many cases, the data apply to what has already happened, so that the remedial action is for some future date. However, it is vital to evaluate costs and to seek the reasons for present values. To illustrate, investigation of an increasing trend in office personnel costs may reveal poor selection techniques and high turnover. The remedial action might include a testing program, retraining of interviewers, and specific employee training efforts.

Although costs are detailed in terms of specific office functions, it is necessary to retain the over-all viewpoint in deciding the remedial action.

A reduction in one expense might increase another, making a total net gain in expenses. For example, centralized office costs may be reduced, but the work has been shifted to branch offices where the costs increase. Other illustrations are reducing the amount of light, resulting in an increase of time required to do the work; and eliminating interoffice telephone service, with the resultant increase in time spent by employees in delivering messages personally.

Another consideration is to utilize all time and space savings effected. There is no gain in doing work in less time or less space unless the savings are transferred to other work. For example, a job may be improved to the point where what formerly was an eight-hour task becomes a six-hour task, thereby saving two hours. But actually, there is no saving unless these two hours are used to perform other work. Likewise, an office machine may save the time of one person out of three; but unless the third person is transferred and put to other work, the net result costwise is not a saving but only a machine added.

PROVIDE ADEQUATE AND PROPER FOLLOW-UP

To make cost control effective, it is necessary (1) to check up and see that the remedial steps are followed and (2) to know, as a consequence of these revisions, what the new results will be. The first point is achieved through personal means—observation and working with supervisors. For the latter point, some simple type of reporting can be instituted. For these reports to have greatest value, they should be made on a weekly and, in some instances, on a daily basis. It is important to know immediately if costs are getting back into line. Receiving reports at relatively long intervals of time might mean needless continuation of costly practices or receipt of information when it is too late to do anything about it.

Cost control is a job that never ends. It varies in intensity with the particular needs of the enterprise, the skill of the personnel assigned to and interested in it, and the beliefs of the top management members. It takes time and is laborious work, but it is well worth the effort. Best results are usually obtained from continuous, not sporadic, efforts.

OFFICE BUDGETS

Among the important responsibilities of an office manager is the maintenance of a proper balance among all office activities and the achievement of objectives within certain predetermined limits. To help accomplish these goals and exercise the necessary controlling, the office manager can use a budget.

BUDGET AND BUDGETARY CONTROL

When a manager speaks of using a budget, he actually has two concepts in mind: the budget and budgetary control. Each of these can be defined formally in the following manner: *A budget is a device consisting of an orderly arrangement of statistical data determined by computed guesses and covering all phases of the enterprise for a definite future period of time.* On the other hand, *budgetary control is the process of using the budget by comparing actual results with the computed guesses in order to correct either the estimates or the causes of the differences.*

The budget and budgetary control are interrelated and must always be considered jointly. A budget without budgetary control is useless from the managerial viewpoint; and budgetary control without a budget is meaningless.

KINDS OF BUDGETS

It is possible to draw up a budget for almost any department or division of an enterprise. Frequently, separate budgets are made for sales, production, purchasing, finance, labor, and general expense. These are then combined into one budget, which is sometimes termed the "master budget" or simply the "budget."

A budget can be expressed in dollars, physical units, or any other term which is useful and convenient to use. The dollar is probably the most frequently used. Quite often, where physical units are employed, the dollar values are also shown. When this practice is followed, it should be noted that not only units but also unit cost, i.e., price, must be forecast, and this can prove quite difficult.

It is sometimes desirable to show in a budget not only the allowances at a certain level of activity but also the allowances at various other levels. Such a budget is referred to as a *step budget*, and its value lies in predetermining and thinking through the action to be taken should variations from the estimated goal arise. Actually, the work of preparing a step budget is not as difficult as it may at first appear. Deviations are estimated from the allowances for the established goal. Some items will vary directly with the volume; others will tend to rise or fall with the operating level, but not in direct proportion to it; others will remain the same regardless of the operating level.

ALL BUDGETS CONCERN THE OFFICE MANAGER

The office manager should use all the budgets employed in an enterprise to find out the plan or projected trends in operations which will affect the amount of office work. Included in the various budgets of an enterprise are those for sales expense, production, purchasing, and general expense, as will be mentioned in the following pages. From these various budgets, knowledge of changes such as an increase in advertising literature to be mailed, a change in the number of bills payable, the development of new sales markets, a new policy regarding billing practices, and a reduction in the number of purchasing orders can be ascertained and this information utilized to have the office provide its necessary functions.

Ordinarily, the office manager is active in the preparation of (1) the cash budget and (2) the office expense budget. In the case of the cash budget, the extent of office activities affects the cash requirements of the enterprise. The purchase and trade-in of office machines and equipment, the expansion or contraction of any office function in order to keep it in balance with changes elsewhere in the enterprise, or simply action to cut down office expenditures are illustrations of the office's influence on the cash budget.

The office expense budget is the individual budget covering office activities and is one in which the office manager is vitally interested. Typical items include supervision, clerical payroll, stationery, supplies, postage, telephone and telegraph service, reception and messenger service, purchase and maintenance of office machines and equipment, rent, and light. As already indicated, comparisons are made with the estimated amounts.

Figure 26–3 shows a portion of an office expense budget. In this case, entries of actual expenditures have been made for the months of January

OFFICE EXPENSE BUDGET FOR THE YEAR 196–

ITEM	JANUARY		FEBRUARY		MARCH	
	Estimate	Actual	Estimate	Actual	Estimate	Actual
1. Stationery and envelopes...	$ 75	.....	.....	$ 83	$ 50	
2. Supplies...............	50	$ 68	$ 35	21	35	
3. Postage...............	35	35	35	35	35	
4. Telephone and telegraph....	185	173	185	186	185	
5. Reception and messenger service...............	450	440	450	440	500	
6. Magazine and book subscription.............	18	18	.....	.....	.....	
7. Maintenance of machines and equipment*........	40	53	40	62	40	
8. Purchase of machines and equipment*...........	440	291	.....	165	200	
9. Rent...................	80	80	80	80	80	
10. Light.................	22	21	20	21	20	
11. Traveling expenses*.......	80	135	80	40	80	
12. Employees' welfare.......	50	60	50	47	50	
13. Clerical payroll*..........	3,750	3,870	3,750	3,920	4,000	
14. Supervision payroll*.......	1,140	1,140	1,140	1,170	1,300	
15. Miscellaneous (list)........	25	.....	25	.....	25	
Install new electric outlet.	.....	3	.....	.....	.....	
Fix door at north exit....	.....	.....	.....	18	.....	
Total.............	$6,440	$6,387	$5,890	$6,288	$6,600	

* These items must be justified by details on supplementary sheets.

FIG. 26–3. An office expense budget. Supplementary sheets are used to show the details of certain items which are selected on the basis of judgment and experience.

and February. Expenses for February are nearly $400 in excess of the estimate. A study of the itemized data for this month shows that clerical payroll, machine and equipment purchases, and supervision payroll are the items chiefly responsible for the increase. Further investigation of these expenses should be made.

PREPARATION OF THE BUDGET

An interesting graphic representation of the sequence of budget preparation is shown in Figure 26–4. The total estimated income is deter-

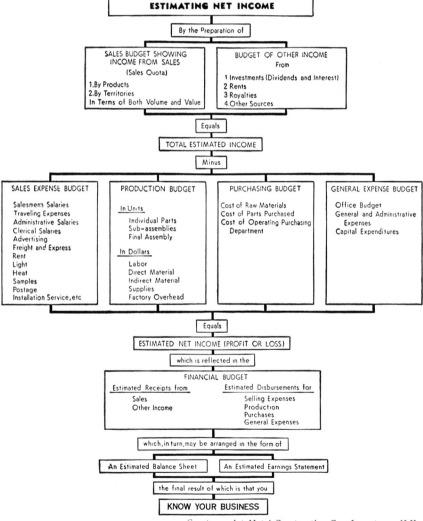

Courtesy: Art Metal Construction Co., Jamestown, N.Y.

FIG. 26–4. A normal sequence of budget preparation. The chart shows the co-ordination of the various individual budgets and the type of information found in each one.

mined from expected sales and other sources of income. From this total estimated income are subtracted the expenses of sales, production, purchasing, and general expenses. This gives the estimated net income or loss, which can be reflected in the financial budget, an estimated balance sheet, and an estimated earnings statement. The chart shows some of the details included under each individual budget.

Usually, the sales budget is developed first, since in many cases all other activities are predicated on what the sales expectancy picture is. Using the predicted sales as a basis, the plan for production, purchasing, and the like can be drawn up.

However, in some cases, this approach is reversed. The beginning is made by estimating the approximate income needed to provide a fair return on capital invested in the enterprise; then, one works back to determine the sales required, the production, and so on. There are variations of these two approaches, as well as other methods.

Most procedures for budget making consist of a series of steps somewhat like the following:

1. A conference of top management members is held to discuss trends and general outlook, and to formulate broad policies regarding activities throughout the coming year.

2. The basis for the entire program, including sales and net income, or some other entity, is first drawn up by the executive in charge of the particular activity. It is then submitted for discussion and approval to the remaining top management members.

3. Each department head then prepares a budget for his own separate activity, guided by the data in the basic budget.

4. These budgets covering separate departments are submitted to the officer in charge of the budget. Generally, this is the controller or the budget officer.

5. A conference between the designated officer and each department head is then held for the purpose of thoroughly discussing and, when necessary, revising the respective individual department budget. Sometimes, a budget committee is used, in which case the budget officer transmits the estimates to the committee along with his recommendations.

6. After a tentative agreement on each individual budget has been reached, the master budget meeting is called. At this time, each individual budget is submitted and discussed. If necessary, adjustments are made, and final approval is obtained. This approval is generally contingent upon a final O.K. by the general manager or the president.

7. When finally determined, the budget is written up in its approved form, and copies are sent to all persons charged with carrying out a major portion of the plan. In like manner, copies covering specific parts

of the master budget are distributed to lesser executives who are responsible for the execution of a particular portion of the plan.

THE BUDGET PERIOD

The data of a budget apply to a definite period of time. The length of this period varies, however, because of several important considerations, one of which is the ability to make reasonable forecasts covering conditions affecting the work. All comparisons are made with the forecast data. It therefore follows that for valid comparison, the budget should cover only a reasonable future period, usually one year or less.

Another consideration is the normal cycle for completion of the work. The period selected should be long enough to include seasonal or any characteristic variations so that the "up and down" changes are covered. In other words, the budget cycle should cover the sales and production cycles.

The length of the fiscal period should also be taken into account. Many budgets are concerned with income and expenditure and are expressed in dollar units. In these cases, the budget period should coincide with or fit into the time pattern already existing for other financial controls.

Also, the intended use of the budget influences the budget period selected. For example, if the budget is to serve as a quarterly check, the time period should include a three-month period. If the purpose is a semiannual check, a six-month period will be used.

The most common period covered is one year, with breakdowns for quarterly and monthly periods. The year usually coincides with the calendar year, although if operations are on a fiscal basis, the fiscal year is used. Customarily, the forecasts are subjected to revision and addition, either monthly or quarterly, as new conditions become known.

REVISION OF BUDGET

Generally, the forecast will be made during November and December for the following year. Then, the revising and adjusting can follow any of a number of plans, but the following three are the most frequently used.

1. *Periodic budgeting.* This plan provides for major revisions three times a year—in March, June, and September—for the remaining months of the year. For example, in March, a reforecast for the period April through December is made. If needed, revisions can be made at other times of the year as well.

2. *Progressive budgeting.* This arrangement furnishes definite times for major revisions throughout the year, such revisions covering

definite periods following the revision date. For example, assume that revision times are bimonthly or at the end of February, April, June, August, October, and December, and that the period covered is six months. At the end of February, revisions would be made for the following six-month period, March through August; at the end of April, revisions are made for the period May through October; and so on. Revisions made at times other than the definite dates usually apply to the current budget only.

3. *Moving budgeting.* Under this plan, a forecast for 12 months is maintained by adding a month as each month is completed. To illustrate, at the completion of October, 1963, a forecast for October, 1964, is added; therefore, the 12-month forecast would cover November, 1963, through October, 1964. Revisions in the forecasts covering the intervening months are made when necessary.

USE AND EVALUATION OF BUDGETS

To a great extent, the budget's practical use and effectiveness are predicated on the interest and enthusiasm of the executives and supervisors. If they have had a part in its formulation and want to make it operative, the use of the budget will normally be successful. Periodic statements and comparisons should be issued so that all management personnel are informed and their interest maintained. Enforcement of the budget is achieved by making individuals responsible for carrying out the prescribed operations. In the final analysis, there is no substitute for this fixing of responsibility. Sometimes, certain conditions need to be corrected to attain the goal set up by the budget. But when fixed responsibility is placed with the individual, these conditions will be either corrected or promptly reported to the manager for remedial action.

Budgets provide important advantages to an office manager. Of major significance is that assistance is supplied in achieving a desired balance among the various office activities. The over-all viewpoint is encouraged. The use of a budget also helps to reveal weaknesses in the office organizational structure. Those units in which expenditures are excessively high can be signaled out for managerial attention. Furthermore, emphasis on planning, and especially on orderly controlling, is assisted by the budget's formulation and use. In addition, the decision making of a management member is expedited and is facilitated by the factual information and records of accomplishment shown by the budget.

On the other hand, it should be noted that a budget is a managerial tool—a means of assistance to a manager, not management itself. Budgets are not automatic in their operation. Care in their compilation and wise, meaningful interpretation of the data are required. In addition, the use of budgets requires time. Current ills are not cured overnight by budgets. The discovery, correction, or elimination of undesirable conditions cannot be hurried. Finally, budgets are limited by the accuracy of the forecasts. Reviews about every month or three months should be scheduled so that new developments or changes of conditions are reflected in the budget.

QUESTIONS

1. Would you say that costs are important in the making of most major decisions by an office manager? Why?
2. Name the major approaches to office cost reduction, and discuss briefly the one you feel is most important.
3. What are the outstanding advantages is using standard costs for office controlling purposes?
4. State concisely the meaning and give an example of each of the following:
   a) Unit cost.
   b) Indirect material cost.
   c) Cost-consciousness by employees.
   d) Cost control.
5. Cite the major reasons for cost being important in office management.
6. Which of the following can serve as objectives of an office manager?
   a) Costs.
   b) Reduction of costs.
   c) Budgets.
   d) Standard cost.
   Explain your answers.
7. In your opinion, can an office be managed effectively without a budget? Defend your answer.
8. Discuss the importance of employees as the key to reducing office costs.
9. Miss A believes that if an item is in the budget, it is sufficient justification for spending that amount in order to utilize funds advantageously and keep them in balance. In contrast, Miss B claims that, whenever possible, savings on every budget item should be made in order to keep costs at a minimum. With whom do you agree? Give your reasons.
10. Do you agree with the statement: "All budgets concern the office manager"? Explain your answer.
11. Discuss the subject "Preparation of the Budget" in the typical enterprise.
12. As an office manager, what basic arrangement for revising the budget would you follow? Why?

CASE PROBLEMS

Case 26–1.   Office Automation Institute

This institute is contemplating offering a ten-day seminar on the use of computers for various office work. Such a seminar will be the first of its kind offered by the institute. Three- and five-day seminars in programming and in systems analysis have been offered in the past; and for these courses, an average paid enrollment of around forty was registered.

For the contemplated ten-day seminar, it is estimated that 1,500 announcements will be mailed at a cost of 10 cents each for the mailing and

$250 for preparing and printing the announcements. In addition, each registrant will receive seminar materials estimated to cost the institute $27.35 per enrollee. Meetings will be held at the conveniently located Hotel Davis, which charges $25 a day for a conference room having a capacity of ninety-two. The group will be served lunch each conference day in a special catering room of the hotel, for which a charge of $2.50 per person, including tips, is made. Also, hot beverages will be supplied at midmorning and again at midafternoon in the rear of the conference room. For this service, a charge of 75 cents per day per enrollee will be made. A total of eight instructors will be used to cover the various subjects; but only two different instructors for any one day will be scheduled, each handling the group for half a day. Compensation for an instructor for half a day is $75.00 plus his lunch regardless of whether he instructs in the morning or in the afternoon. Special equipment, including a slide and a motion-picture projector, will be needed for three days; it is estimated that this will cost $25.00 per day.

As a policy, the institute requires a margin of approximately 30 per cent of the total income from a seminar. That is, if the total income is $1,000, the institute strives to keep expenses at no more than $700. Registrations from mailings for other seminars have ranged from 1.9 per cent to 5.1 per cent of the total number of mailings sent out. However, the managers of the institute are at a loss to know whether these response ranges are valid for a seminar such as they are now planning.

Problems:

1. Discuss the major problem facing the institute.
2. Calculate the approximate registration fee that the institute should charge for the office automation seminar.
3. What plan of action do you feel the institute should follow? Why?

Case 26–2.   Apex Finance Company

In the collection department of this company are four bookkeepers, paid $375 each a month, and one credit clerk, who receives $285 a month. They are expected to handle 20,000 accounts per year. It is not anticipated that the requirements of the company will exceed this amount for some years to come. This standard is believed equitable; but for the past several months, the rate of output has been around 1,500 per month. To meet the required standard rate of 20,000 accounts per year, the bookkeepers are working overtime. In addition to labor costs, there are also the following annual costs in connection with the handling of the accounts: postage, $312.00; office forms, $211.75; miscellaneous supplies, $125.00; and overhead expenses allocated to this department, $522.00.

The office manager, Mr. Jeffrey Morgan, wants to reduce costs of getting this work accomplished. Accordingly, he called the representatives of several office machine manufacturers and found that a machine to do the bookkeeping work would cost the company $2,650 a year, including depreciation, maintenance costs, interest on capital invested, etc. This figure is based on a ten-year period. An operator to run the machine will cost $5,200 a year. The operator would perform all credit work in connection with accounts handled. By use of the machine, a production of 16,000 accounts per year is estimated. However, two employees in addition to the machine operator would be required. Each of these two employees would be paid $300 per month.

Furthermore, mechanization would necessitate new forms costing $475 a year. The cost of other supplies would remain the same. Mr. Morgan was informed by the treasurer of the company that the same overhead costs would continue to be charged the department whether or not a change in the manner of doing the work was made. At some future date, an adjustment might be made; but for the present, the same overhead cost should be included.

Mr. Morgan also spoke with a representative from the Voss Office Services and received a quotation of $123.70 per hundred accounts to do the work. This quotation includes pickup and delivery of the work that would be done in the offices of the service bureau company.

Problems:

1. Evaluate the viewpoint and action of the office manager.

2. Compute the cost of performing the work under the present plan and under each of the suggested plans.

3. What is your recommendation to this company? Why?

Chapter 27

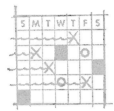

OFFICE MANUALS

The possibility of succeeding even occasionally in getting students to want to develop fully their intellectual powers is more wonderful to me than the possibility of launching any number of sputniks.

—JULIAN HARRIS

USE OF OFFICE manuals assists in obtaining the desired control of the employees' efforts in an enterprise. Information dealing with an employee's duties and responsibilities, the regulations under which he shall work, and the policies and practices of the enterprise for which he is working can be given in a simple, direct, uniform, and authoritative manner by means of manuals. *An office manual is a written record of information and instructions which concern and can be used to guide the employee's efforts in an enterprise.* Actually, it is a guidebook—a source for data believed essential for the highest performance of the job.

WHY USE MANUALS?

Essentially, an office manual is a device to help in the orientation of employees. It can help to make instructions definite, to state policies and procedures, to fix responsibility, to provide quick settlements of misunderstandings, and to show how the employee can contribute to the achievement of company objectives as well as to his relationship with other employees. Manuals relieve management members of having to repeat similar information, explanations, or instructions. Uniformity, accessibility, and deliberation are among the advantages of a manual. In many enterprises, manuals are considered a "must."

In contrast, there are some managers who do not advocate the use of manuals for any of a number of reasons. Among the more common adverse criticisms are that manuals "cost too much," "are too much work," "stifle initiative," or "won't work in our case." In some cases, these objections are no doubt justifiable; but for most enterprises, the use of manuals appears to be beneficial.

Figure 27–1 lists the basic requirements for success of office manuals.

1. Center authority and responsibility for the manual program.
2. Write to the level of the employee who will use the manual.
3. Maintain a distribution list—distribute only those manuals that are needed in each case.
4. Use color to emphasize identity of binder or printing matter.
5. Keep manual simple in arrangement of material and in language used.
6. Adopt adequate indexing and cross referencing.
7. Use numerous visual aids—charts and illustrations.
8. Keep manuals up to date.
9. Highlight changes and revisions.
10. Audit the material periodically.

FIG. 27–1. Basic requirements for success of office manuals.

More will be included about these requirements throughout the pages of this chapter.

TYPES OF OFFICE MANUALS

Different offices have need for different manuals. The type is determined by answering the question: "What is the purpose to be served?" In some instances, a single purpose only is served; while in others, several purposes are to be fulfilled. The number and the kind of purposes are determined by the individual circumstances.

Manuals can be written to cover a variety of subjects, including policies, organizational structure of the enterprise, employment, indoctrination, job instruction, standard work practices, history of the enterprise, and specialized or departmental practices such as in the accounting, engineering, purchasing, or sales department. However, for convenience, the major types of manuals, along with their respective purposes, can be set forth as follows:

Type of Manual	*Purpose*
Manual of policies	To state the policies of the enterprise or office.
Manual of operations, or standard practices manual, or job instruction manual	To inform employees of established methods, procedures, and standards.
Manual of office rules and regulations, or handbook on employment	To give concise information on benefits, operating rules, and employment regulations.
Historical Manual	To provide historical information about the enterprise.
Multiple-purpose manual	To supply selected items from any area or subject deemed desirable and helpful in the work performance.

MANUAL OF POLICIES

As set forth in Chapter 14, a policy is a basic guide to action. It prescribes the over-all boundaries within which activities are to take place and hence reveals broad managerial intentions or forecasts broad courses of managerial action likely to take place under certain conditions. To illustrate, promoting employees solely on the basis of merit is a policy. It states the guide for promoting, but it does not tell who will be promoted. Likewise, the payment of salaries above the prevailing amounts in the community for similar work, consistent with the economic well-being of the enterprise, is another example of a policy. Knowing the policies of an enterprise provides the main framework around which all actions are based. Policies furnish the background for an understanding of why things are done as they are.

A manual of policies puts into writing the policies of an enterprise. It has been said that a policy does not really exist unless it is in writing. To decide each case on its individual merits and to convey this decision verbally is not in keeping with modern management thinking. Proponents of a manual of policies cite these advantages: (1) Written policies require managers to think through their courses of action and to predetermine what actions will be taken under various circumstances; (2) a general program of action for many matters is provided, and only the unusual or exceptional matter requires the attention of the top managers; (3) a framework is provided within which the manager can operate freely; and (4) written policies help to insure equitable treatment to all employees.

On the other hand, there are those who object to having a manual of policies. Among the important points they mention are the following: (1) Policies are extremely difficult to write accurately and completely— the interpretation of words and phrases sometimes leads to serious misunderstandings; (2) written policies make it difficult to keep policies flexible, as is frequently required by changing conditions; and (3) knowledge of policies should be confined to those persons charged with their execution—the top executive, department heads, or supervisors, as the case might be.

MANUAL OF OPERATIONS

A manual can serve as a convenient source for information on how the work is to be done. The authorized steps can be listed; and supplementary information, in the form of diagrams, sketches, and charts, can be included in order to clarify the data. The standards and guides to be followed are usually included.

The contents of this type of manual can be pointed toward any one or all of the following:

1. *Individual tasks and jobs.* Illustrative is the manual which explains how to operate and use an adding machine. The importance of keeping accurate records can be emphasized and information included describing the parts and operations of an adding machine, practice lessons, and an explanation of the practices of the company. A glossary of terms is sometimes included to clarify the work.

2. *Departmental practices.* Manuals of this type contain a statement of the duties of the department. Its divisions are defined, the supervisors listed, and their responsibilities indicated, along with outlines and procedures for operating. The work of departments, such as sales, purchasing, accounting, and research, is often set up and described in departmental manuals.

3. *General practices in a special field.* This type of manual is becoming more popular, for it furnishes valuable general information which is usable in special lines of work. Its adoption is mainly in large offices, although in certain instances the small office can benefit from manuals of this type.

MANUAL OF OFFICE RULES AND REGULATIONS

Manuals are an excellent medium in which to explain employee benefit plans, including such things as group insurance, hospitalization, and savings facilities. Questions regarding the use of the company library, cafeteria, and recreation club can also be answered. In addition, the prescribed guides for conduct are included and cover such items as sick allowances, the use of rest periods, conduct regarding smoking, solicitation for money in the office, the sale of tickets, hours of employment, holidays, vacations, office etiquette, rest periods, telephone usage, and recreational provisions. As already stated, a manual of this type is identified either as a manual of office rules and regulations or as a handbook on employment. However, for psychological reasons, the manual may be given a title like "You and the XYZ Company" or "Getting Along at XYZ." Such a manual helps to orientate and to inform the employee by giving him specific answers to all the elements of his work surroundings, thus promoting understanding and harmonious relationships. Figure 27–2 shows a sample of the type of information included in this kind of manual.

HISTORICAL MANUAL

Many employers feel that it is important to give employees information regarding the history of the company—its beginning, growth, accomplishments, present management, and current status. This gives the employee an insight into the tradition and thinking behind the enterprise with which he is associated. It probably makes for better understanding, increases morale, and helps the employee to feel that he "belongs"—

GENERAL OFFICE ROUTINES

DESKS—Keep your desk clean. It's a workbench, not a catchall. Never allow a lot of old-fashioned relics to accumulate on it. File everything away in its natural place, and dispose of obsolete matter. (The job of filing is an important one and is not to be neglected or allowed to pile up.)

Avoid having decorations on the desk that might tip and spill, such as flower containers, ink bottles, sponge cups, etc. Keep such things in safer places.

Clear all desks and tables before leaving the building. Any papers or letters of a confidential nature must be put away, never left on the desk top. All lights are to be turned off, fans and ventilators disconnected, and blinds raised. Typewriters should be covered when not being used.

DUSTING—Each office is to be thoroughly dusted each morning—during the day too if necessary. No one need resent dusting—it's part of the job.

Pens should be filled, pencils sharpened and water bottles filled first thing in the morning. See to it that ash trays are kept clean throughout the day. If blotters are used, make sure soiled ones are replaced.

Typewriters should be dusted morning and night, type cleaner applied weekly.

SUPPLIES—If you are responsible for handling supplies for the office, check them regularly and make sure that you are not running low. Keep a list at your desk of supplies that will soon need to be requisitioned (use form 527 for ordering). All requisitions must be authorized by the department head.

HOURS—Arrange hours if possible so the office will not be unattended at any time. If it is impossible for someone to be present during lunch hour, do not leave without making arrangements with someone else to take any important calls.

CALLERS—It is much better to have an understanding with your superior regarding his wishes in the matter of announcing callers, the persons he wishes to see and those he does not, rather than to guess at the proper procedure in each instance.

Keep an accurate, up to date list or notebook of telephone numbers and addresses, business as well as personal. Such a list should be readily accessible. Add to it regularly so it will be of value both to you and your superior.

Source: Butler Brothers, "Secretaries' and Stenographers' Handbook" (Chicago, 1946). p. 20 Reproduced here by special permission.

FIG. 27–2. Page of a manual used by a large national distributor of general merchandise.

that he is a part of the company. Giving an employee a picture of the whole helps him to fit himself into the total picture. Manuals, of course, are excellent means for conveying this type of information to employees. The story of the enterprise usually can be told on several pages; and quite frequently, it can be a part of a message written by a major officer. Historical information is commonly included as the introductory portion to a manual of office rules and regulations.

MULTIPLE-PURPOSE MANUAL

This type of manual represents a combination of any two or all of the types discussed above. The company's needs, the size of the enterprise, and the philosophy of the top managers usually determine the make-up. The outline of a multiple-purpose manual might include the following:

1. Title.
2. Foreword.
3. Table of Contents.
4. Company History.
5. General Policies of Company.
6. Organization.
7. Company Departments—Functions, Authorities, and Responsibilities.
8. Office Regulations.
9. Office Supplies and Maintenance.
10. Personnel Points—Hiring, Promoting, Terminating, Sick Leave, Employee Benefits, and Social Activities.
11. Miscellaneous.
12. Index.

SOURCES FOR MANUAL MATERIAL

Probably one of the best sources of material for a manual is manuals used by other enterprises. Looking over what has been included in manuals of another company suggests what topics might be covered. However, the manual should be personalized to meet the particular needs of an enterprise.

Additional data can be secured from a number of other sources. Such data might include (1) minutes of board of directors' meetings, (2) reports of executive conferences, (3) speeches and published articles of executives, (4) bulletins and company circulars, (5) agreements with employees and contracts with unions, (6) grievance records, (7) company magazines or similar publications, and (8) interviews with executives, especially the personnel manager, training director, and supervisors.

Experience shows that, with time, it will be desirable to eliminate certain material and to add other material. The additional material might be secured from the above sources or, because of the unique nature of the information, may be secured from a special source. For example, instructions in the correct use of a new office machine would probably be secured from the manufacturer or seller.

PREPARATION OF MANUALS

Some orderly process must be followed in the preparation of manuals if they are to be inclusive and to be completed within a reasonable period of time. The process followed depends a great deal upon the individual in charge of this work. In general, however, it will be helpful to follow a procedure along these lines:

1. *Announce to all members of the enterprise that a manual is to be prepared.* Solicit their suggestions and ideas as to what should be included. Appointing a committee of employees often encourages their participation in the preparation of the manual. As a result, better understanding and greater acceptance and use are usually gained. Special attention should be directed to supervisors, for they are usually rich sources of excellent material.

2. *Draw up a list of all the subjects to be covered by the manual.* The purpose of the manual, the cost, and managerial judgment will determine, for the most part, what items are included. Proper subheadings should be made under each main topic, and the list should be arranged according to the contemplated main divisions or sections of the manual. A big timesaver in this respect is to use a separate card for each topic and file behind guides. By this means, material can be classified quickly and the list or outline changed with a minimum of effort.

A logical arrangement of the material is most commonly used, but this sequence is not necessarily the most effective in all cases. Consideration should be given to placing the vital information or that which is most interesting in the beginning, using the last portion of the list for data of less importance.

3. *Write the information under each subject.* Check the source data to help insure accuracy in all writing. Source material can be numbered and indexed, and this means of identification tied in with the writing by means of marginal notes. Keep the prospective reader in mind—write so he will want to read the manual and understand what it is intended to mean. A simple, friendly, and sincere style is best. Short words and sentences should be employed. Include charts, diagrams, and examples of proper forms, letters, and reports in order to gain greater clarity. These illustrations should be in an inexpensive, rough form until it is decided, as described below, whether they will be included in the final manual. All material should be presented in the "normal flow of work" sequence. The amount of detail depends upon the importance of the subject.

4. *Prepare a limited number of copies for key executives, supervisors, employee or union representatives, and several key employees.* Have them read the manual and submit criticisms and suggestions. Quite often, better ways of expression are found in this way. Sometimes, subjects can be combined, major items previously overlooked can be added, minor points strengthened, and the entire manual improved.

5. *Revise the manual and give it to top management members for approval.* Corrections and suggestions from the previous step are in-

corporated. It is well to include a separate statement to the effect that the entire contents are in agreement with the philosophy of top management members and are acceptable to the employees.

6. *Send the approved manuscript to the printer or the party doing the actual mechanical production work.* The manual can be published by any of several different methods, including mimeographing, letterpress, or offset printing.[1] The quantity, appearance, and cost will probably determine the process used. Details regarding size, paper, and type of binding must also be decided. Generally, it is well to seek competent advice in these matters.

The size 6¼ × 4½ inches is excellent for a booklet intended for carrying in the pocket. If the manual is to be used as a reference book on a desk, an 11 × 8½-inch size is very satisfactory. Other popular sizes include 9⅛ × 6 inches, 8½ × 5½ inches, and 5⅛ × 3¾ inches. Pages of these sizes can be cut, with minimum waste, from sheet sizes usually carried by the printer.[2]

The number and size of the pages in the booklet generally determine the weight of paper used. When the number of pages does not exceed

---

PAGE SIZE—

If printed, the 6 × 9-inch page size is effective. This is the typical book size.

If typed, the 8½ × 11-inch page size will be preferred by most employees.

ARRANGEMENT OF MATERIAL—

Place sections most frequently used at front of manual.

Related sections should be placed close together and interrelated by cross references.

Set sections apart by stiff divider page of different-colored paper.

Either tab sections for ready reference, or use a divider of page size to facilitate a margin index.

REMEMBER TO—

Make the cover attractive by using a clear, brief title and well-selected art work.

Include a table of contents and an index so that the reader can quickly find that for which he is looking.

FIG. 27–3. Helpful suggestions for preparation of manuals.

---

[1] See Chapter 9 for discussion of duplicating processes.

[2] In the case of loose-leaf and many bound manuals, it is customary to give the dimension of the binding side first. Thus, an 11 × 8-inch size means the binding is on an 11-inch side. The dimensions used in this discussion follow this practice. In contrast, and at times somewhat confusingly, in specifying dimensions of index cards, the horizontal dimension is named first, followed by the vertical dimension. For example, an 8 × 5 card means 8 inches horizontally and 5 inches vertically.

about twenty-four, a thick paper can be used; but where a greater number of pages is involved, a thinner stock is used, to eliminate unnecessary bulk. For page sizes under about 8½ × 5½ inches, a paper of about 60 pounds is used. When the size is greater, paper of about 70 pounds is employed.

It is advisable to set off the reading material by headings. These can be made to stand out on the page by the use of white space around them, or color may be employed. Color increases the cost; but in many cases, the effect brought about by such things as a colored border, headline, or illustration justifies the additional expense. For additional suggestions see Figure 27–3 on page 525.

The type of binding may be either side or saddle wire stitching, screw post, prong fasteners, ring binder, and wire or plastic edge binding. The choice will depend primarily upon usage, amount of material, appearance, and cost.[3]

DISTRIBUTION OF MANUALS

It is paramount that the distribution of the manuals provide a copy to everyone concerned with and in need of the information the manual contains. The extent of distribution depends upon the size of the enterprise; in most cases, one copy of the manual should be available for ready reference in at least each department or division. In cases where manuals pertain to specific jobs, copies should be readily available to every employee on such jobs.

To increase the readership of the manual, it is sometimes given to the employee only during an interview. His attention is directed to specific pages, and he is encouraged to read the entire booklet. In some cases, depending upon the type of manual, it is mailed to the employee's home with an accompanying letter. Forewarning that the manual is to be used as the subject for a forthcoming meeting or group discussion is a very effective means of encouraging readership. In addition, sometimes the employee is requested to sign and to return an enclosed card in the manual as evidence of reading the complete booklet; and in other instances, questions are asked on the card to measure the employee's understanding of the manual contents.

MANUAL MAINTENANCE

The problem of keeping the manual up to date is ever present. In most enterprises, changes are taking place constantly, owing to new work being added or improvements in current work being made. Revisions of and additions to manuals are constantly in process. New pages must replace the old and be distributed to all holders of the manuals.

---

[3] See Chapter 9, pages 167–68, for detailed discussion of this subject.

These changes may be covered either by single sheets or by entire supplements. Frequently, amendments are written on colored paper to attract attention to the change. Also, notations made in red ink in the manual will point out those parts which have been changed, omitted, or amended. When many changes cause the manual to be difficult to read and use, it should be rewritten.

All revisions should be cleared through a central control unit so that proper authorization and conformity in results are obtained. If this is not done, needless confusion and misunderstanding will result. The revised sheets should follow the established form of the manual. New material will probably be added every three to six months, together with certain modifications in the old material. Limited research shows that nearly 90 per cent of all managers prefer a three-ring binder, which facilitates the insertion of revised sheets.

QUESTIONS

1. List and briefly comment on six basic requirements for success of office manuals.
2. What are the general subject areas that usually make up the contents of a manual of operations?
3. Are you of the opinion that for most offices a manual is beneficial? Substantiate your answer.
4. Distinguish carefully between the elements in each of the following pairs:
    a) Manuals and standards.
    b) Historical manual and manual of office rules and regulations.
    c) An 11 × 8½-inch manual and an 8½ × 11-inch manual.
    d) Managerial controlling and manuals.
5. If the office manager of a medium-sized office was limited to one type of manual, what type would you recommend? Why?
6. It has been suggested that a manual be written that would be adaptable for use by all offices. Spaces for individualized "fill-ins" would be provided. Do you believe such a manual is feasible? Explain.
7. Do you feel that office manuals reduce the need for training of office employees? Explain.
8. Enumerate and discuss briefly the major steps in the preparation of a manual.
9. Name and evaluate the important sources of material for manuals.
10. What kinds of information should be in an office manual?
11. Discuss the subject of manual maintenance.
12. Is an office manual of greater importance in a large or in a small office? Justify your answer.

CASE PROBLEMS

Case 27–1. Sovereign Products Company

During a conversation with a business friend at the Meadowdale Country Club, Mr. Gregory E. Brady became very interested in office manuals and their use in the management of an office. His country club friends told him a public relations firm, Richards and Associates, had gotten together a very attractive and informative office manual for them. Mr. Brady is vice president of finance for Sovereign Products Company. Several days later, he called his office manager, Mr. Rodney Custer, to his office, and the following conversation took place.

BRADY: I've asked you to come in, Rod, to discuss the use of an office manual in our office. What do you think of our having a manual?

CUSTER: Well, Mr. Brady, you will recall—or no, I guess that was before you came here, that—well, we had an office manual some eight years ago. But its usage declined; and during the past year or so, I guess you could say we have no manual at all.

BRADY: That was my understanding—we do not have an office manual. How come we got away from having a manual? Why don't we use it, Rod?

CUSTER: I don't know, sir. It doesn't seem to be missed.

BRADY: Others use one. Maybe we are missing out on something. I think we should have one. Seems to me in an office our size, with 72 employees, we. . . .

CUSTER (*interrupting*): It's 82, sir.

BRADY: Are we up to 82? The more we could use a manual, I would judge. It would help reduce office costs and lighten the burden on our office supervisors. Don't you think so?

CUSTER: Well, it could, I suppose.

BRADY: Yes. Custer, I'd like you to see what you can do toward bringing out a new, up-to-date manual for our office.

CUSTER: Yes, sir. I am very busy right now, sir, and I really don't have anybody who can write well enough to do this.

BRADY: Well, see what you can do, and let me know.

Mr. Brady held the matter in abeyance for four weeks. He then called a representative of Richards and Associates to his office and discussed the possibility of this firm writing a manual for the Sovereign Products Company's office. He gave the representative a copy of the old manual used by the office at one time, and offered several suggestions about what the contents of a new manual should include. Immediately after this conversation, he telephoned Mr. Custer, told him what he (Brady) had done, and requested that Mr. Custer submit any ideas about the new manual and its contents to him.

Five weeks passed, and there was no word from Mr. Custer. Richards and Associated were called in again by Mr. Brady, who authorized them to proceed and make up a sample or dummy copy of a proposed new office manual. A month later, the sample was submitted and approved by Mr. Brady and also by Mr. Custer, whom Mr. Brady asked "to look it over." Subsequently, the manual was printed and distributed to key personnel.

Now, six months later, Mr. Brady has information based on sources he considers thoroughly reliable that the office manual is not being used.

Problems:

1. Is there a problem faced by the company? Substantiate your answer.

2. Discuss the actions taken by Mr. Brady, emphasizing what you consider the good and the bad points.

3. What do you recommend Mr. Brady do now? Why?

Case 27–2.   Meredith-Piedmont Wood Furniture Company

Eighty-five persons are employed in the office, consisting of the following organizational units: office services, correspondence, order billing, accounting, purchasing, filing, and records retention. The office manager believes that having an office manual would help in informing office employees about their work and in achieving a well-co-ordinated office force. He requests authorization to proceed with actions to write, print, and distribute such a manual.

In contrast, the president of the corporation takes the viewpoint that (1) an office manual would represent an additional expenditure for which little return would be realized; (2) it would tend to "freeze" activities as they now are, i.e., retard progress; and (3) he questions whether it would be used, since the corporation has never had a manual.

Problems:

1. Write the preface to the proposed manual, and prepare the table of contents.

2. Evaluate the president's viewpoint.

3. What action should the office manager take? Why?

Part 6

ORGANIZING IN
OFFICE MANAGEMENT

Organizing is the next fundamental function of office management to be discussed. This includes apportioning the office work to be done as determined by planning, assigning the distributed work to specific members of the work group, and establishing the proper work relationships among them. Effective organizing is essential in managing an office. The five chapters that follow deal with office organizing.

Chapter 28

ORGANIZATION OF
THE OFFICE

No man is so great as mankind.

—THEODORE PARKER

ORGANIZING becomes a necessity when two or more people work together. Decisions must be made regarding who does what work, who reports to whom, and who decides what types of issues. Organizing deals with these basic questions.

IMPORTANCE OF ORGANIZING

Organizing makes possible the effective operation of a group. It is the basis for teamwork. Members of the group can serve as a single unit directing all their various efforts toward a common goal. Each member can contribute his maximum and his specialty toward the major objective. A management member can be effective only when he knows specifically what work he is to manage, who is to assist him, to whom he reports, and what members are in his work group. In addition, the management member should know in general terms what work is to be done by other management members and how their work affects or might affect his managerial efforts. Likewise, a nonmanagement member must know how he and his work fit into the total picture; to whom he reports; what he is to do; when he is to do it; and who, if anyone, helps him.

Of significant importance is the fact that organizing enables a manager to enlarge his scope of operation or effectiveness. Organizing makes it possible for a manager to accomplish much more than he could as an individual. It provides the means for using effectively the work of other people, and it sets the groundwork for the development of people. In fact, failure to organize properly limits any manager's ability to manage. Many problems of management stem in part from poor organizing. According to various estimates, some one half of all management problems originate from organizational defects. The study of organizing is therefore of great importance.

OBJECTIVE AND PURPOSE OF ORGANIZING

Organizing, like the other fundamental functions of management, is influenced and guided by the objective being sought. Organizing is, or should be, performed to achieve a definite objective, and this goal determines the organizational type and structural make-up needed.

To evaluate competently an office organization requires relating it to the particular objective for which the organization is designed. The question "For what objective is the group organized?" is a cardinal consideration in organizational efforts. The paper work required in one enterprise may differ from that in another enterprise. The centers for paper work processing are not identical in all organizations. Top managers' ideas of what paper work should be performed by what departments differ among enterprises. Some companies are local, others national, and still others international in scope. Also, some have only one line of related products, while others have multiple lines of products. These considerations help shape the objective and, in turn, are utilized to mold the organization.

PURPOSE OF ORGANIZING

From what has already been stated, it follows that organizing is done for many reasons: It is to assist in the manager's job of achieving the objective in the best manner by means of a group consisting of an informed and satisfied work force. It is to help blend together the group's efforts and facilities into a concerted unit directed toward achieving a stated goal efficiently. It avoids needless duplication of effort. It gets individuals to work effectively as members of a team, not separately as single individuals. It avoids confusion and misunderstanding as to who is to do what work. It prevents "buck passing," an excessive number of managers and nonmanagers, and misinformed members of the group.

MEANING OF ORGANIZING

Organizing is the allocating of the total work to be done among the work group, establishing the relative authority and responsibility of each individual who is placed in charge of each work component, and supplying the proper work environment. In organizing, a manager is concerned with (1) work—how to distribute it, (2) people—who is going to do what work, (3) relationships—what is the relative authority and responsibility among the "organization units" formed by the work distribution and the respective people doing it, and (4) work environment—what tools and workplaces will best contribute toward maximum work accomplishments. From the managerial viewpoint, organizing results in the determination of an "organization structure." This can be thought of as the over-all framework joining the functions of an enterprise and establishing definite relationships among the personnel who perform the respective functions.

Organizing is a dynamic, not a static, process. As a result, changes take place in an organization structure; this is the common occurrence rather than the exception. Changes in organization structure take place for many reasons, such as changes in the objectives of the enterprise, changes in personnel, and changes in the conditions outside the enterprise. The student of management must fully realize that organization structure is a living, present, dynamic entity—it is not a static concept. The effective manager normally changes his organization structure from time to time in order best to meet the current requirements of the enterprise. This subject of organizational dynamics is so important that an entire chapter in this book, Chapter 31, is devoted to it.

RELATION OF OFFICE TO ORGANIZATION OF ENTERPRISE

Since office work and its management are performed to supply a needed service to other major activities of an enterprise, it is advisable first to consider office organization in relation to the organization of the entire enterprise of which the office is an important part. It is common to think that in the typical organization, the major activities to be performed are production, sales, and finance. Each must be done satisfactorily if the enterprise is to survive. The creating of a utility for others is basic for most enterprises. This, in turn, necessitates selling efforts, so that the product or service is made available to buyers. The producing and selling efforts necessitate financing activities, in that ample capital must be obtained and maintained.

In addition to these three major activities, there are frequently personnel and the office, which are included to assist the main functions. Many feel that both personnel and the office are major activities, and that each should be accorded organization position and status on a par with production, sales, and finance. Sound arguments can be advanced to justify this viewpoint. In the case of the office, for example, the trend toward more and more automation, the use of computers, and the general recognition of the vital contributions of the office give increasing weight to this viewpoint. In keeping with this approach, and as pointed out in Chapter 1, many prefer the term "administrative management" to "office management," the belief being that the former more accurately describes the content and importance of processing paper work and the contributions of such efforts to an enterprise.

Any attempt to justify one major activity as the most important in an enterprise is purely academic. Actually, all the major activities are needed. For example, production requires sales, financing gives rise to paper work, personnel assists production, and paper work expedites sales efforts. Our interest here is organization in the management of the office; and the vital concept for our purpose is to remember that office work is done to help fulfill other major functions—it is not performed apart from them. Production activities such as cutting, sewing, machining, assembling, painting, drying, and packing are assisted by the work of the office. Likewise, typical sales activities such as merchandising, analysis of markets, and selling efforts are helped by the office. And the same is true of finance and personnel, for many records and papers are needed in each.

ORGANIZATIONAL CONTENT AND PLACEMENT OF THE OFFICE

The questions can now be asked: "What activities should be included in the office?" and "Where should the office organizational unit be placed in the organization of the entire enterprise?" The answers must be known so that organizational relationships can be identified both within the office itself and between the office and major organizational units of the enterprise. These relationships can be termed (1) intradepartmental—among the activities making up the office, and (2) interdepartmental—among the office and other major organizational units of the enterprise. The interdepartmental viewpoint is especially helpful because it emphasizes the facilitating and service aspects of office work.

Actually, to designate an organizational unit as "the office" can be confusing, for it is likely neither to be in one location nor to include all office activities. To reiterate, office work is not an activity in and of itself; it is a part of and employed in almost every function. Office work contributes information needed in performing the major functions of production, sales, finance, personnel, and other functions such as engineering, research, and purchasing, which are necessary in a particular organizational structure.

Logically, from the organizing point of view, the required office work should be located where it can be performed at lowest cost and with highest service to those using it. This is determined by giving consideration to a number of factors, of which the following are important:

1. *Type and nature of the enterprise.* The content and the placement of the office function are affected greatly by the dominance of the production, sales, finance, or personnel activities. If the enterprise is primarily one for production—a large manufacturer, for example, selling its entire output to several large buyers—the office unit probably will be of relatively small importance. However, in a predominantly financial enterprise, the work will be of relatively great importance. To illustrate, in a bank or insurance company, office work is usually of much greater importance than it is in a manufacturing company. Likewise, in a govern-

mental enterprise, the office unit normally occupies a position relatively high in the organizational structure.

2. *Importance attached to office work.* If top managers of an enterprise recognize the work of the office as of relatively high significance, the tendency will probably be to bring it together into one organizational unit and place this unit high in the organizational structure. But if office work is considered minor, although necessary, it probably will be performed by the department needing it and co-ordinated as completely as possible with the primary activities of the respective department.

3. *Extent of centralization of office functions.* Since office work occurs throughout the entire enterprise, from the president's office to the lowest-paid clerk, it is possible to have it performed in dispersed locations, under the jurisdiction of the unit in which it arises. When this practice is followed, the office function is dispersed and either combined with, or made subordinate to, other organizational units. In its fullest application, this dispersion extends to the smallest and lowest organizational unit of the enterprise. In contrast, a directly opposite arrangement might be used. In this case, the office work is fully concentrated and is placed in the hands of a single executive who is completely responsible for all office activities in the organization.

These two conditions, however, are extreme. From a practical viewpoint, seldom is either used. An intermediate or modified arrangement between these two extremes is commonly followed:

1. Office work is located and performed by major departments, and each department head is fully responsible for the office activities in his own department.

2. Office work is distributed among all departments, but one person is placed in charge of this office work in order to achieve reasonable co-ordination.

3. Certain office work is centralized in one unit and placed under one manager. The remaining office work is performed in the unit in which it arises and is supervised by the regular department head of that unit. This arrangement is quite popular. It is interpreted in different arrangements, and the more common of these are discussed in the following paragraphs.

THE OFFICE SERVICES ORGANIZATIONAL ARRANGEMENT

As pointed out and discussed in Part III, so-called "office services," including writing and correspondence work, calculating and checking, filing, record retention, handling the mail, and communicative work, are frequently included in the office organizational unit and placed under the "office services manager" or in some cases the "office manager." However, all these services are not always centralized, the notable exception being writing and correspondence work, and calculating and checking. Furthermore, even when all these services are referred to as being centralized, they are only partially so—some of certain services being performed in various units throughout the entire organization structure.

The adoption of an "office services" unit arrangement means that the manager in charge of office work has a dual managerial task. First, he should manage the services unit; and second, since office work is being performed in various other units in which it arises, he should counsel with the executives of these various units and help them accomplish their office work in the best manner. This second task is of paramount

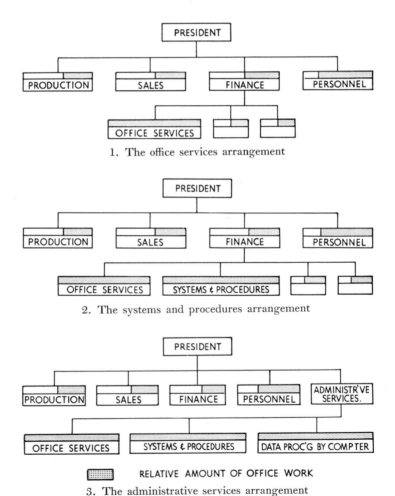

1. The office services arrangement

2. The systems and procedures arrangement

RELATIVE AMOUNT OF OFFICE WORK

3. The administrative services arrangement

FIG. 28–1. Arrangements of centralizing certain office work with reference to the entire enterprise.

importance and in many respects establishes the true status of the office manager in any organization structure. Actually, it is identifying what office work is and demonstrating to other managers in the organization structure how best to accomplish this type of work. It can also be considered as providing the office work viewpoint to all managers of the enterprise. All use office work; hence, help in how to use it effectively constitutes a real service. Figure 28–1, top illustration, shows graphically the arrangement of the office services arrangement.

THE SYSTEMS AND PROCEDURES ORGANIZATIONAL ARRANGEMENT

As the recognition and need for better management of office work have increased, organizational units to achieve special desired efficiencies have been established by many companies. The exact format, content, location, and authority of this organizational unit varies considerably from company to company. For our purposes here, it is identified as the "systems and procedures department"; but other common titles are systems department, procedures department, methods department, or business services department. Probably none of these titles identify completely and clearly the work performed. Any or all of the following activities may be included in the systems and procedures organizational unit: (1) office procedures and methods—to determine the proper office operations, their best sequence, and the manner of performance to get the office work accomplished efficiently; (2) office equipment and machine analysis—to advise what type of equipment or machine should be used for a specific type of office work under the prescribed conditions; (3) office layout and working conditions—to recommend the most effective arrangement of office facilities and the physical surroundings to supply; (4) office standards—to relate useful levels of performance or frames of reference in order to evaluate achievement; and (5) office work simplification—to point out ways to eliminate waste of all kinds and get the office work out more effectively. The systems and procedures arrangement is illustrated by the center illustration of Figure 28–1.

THE ADMINISTRATIVE SERVICES ORGANIZATIONAL ARRANGEMENT

Primarily because the electronic computer has gained favor for the processing of office information and, in addition, more attention is directed to the management of office work, the concept of an "administrative services" organizational unit on a par with other major units of an enterprise has developed and is gaining favor. This arrangement places most of the office work under a single administrator. The bottom illustration of Figure 28–1 shows the administrative services arrangement. For illustrative purposes only, the units under administrative services are shown as office services, systems and procedures, and data processing by computer. Modern electronic machines make it feasible to handle a large part of the paper work of an enterprise in one organizational unit. However, even under the administrative services arrangement, some office work is performed in other major units, simply because it is easier, more convenient, and of greater service to perform some of the office work in these other units.

CENTRALIZATION IS A KEY ISSUE

An essential issue in office organization is the degree of centralization which is adopted. As already indicated, the degree of centralization of "office services" varies among different enterprises; by no means do all or even a majority of enterprises have a department akin to the systems and procedures department, and relatively few have an administrative services department. Equipment analysis, for example, may be handled by the executive handling the particular function for which the equipment will be used; likewise, the executive of the operating department may have charge of standards applying to paper work in his unit. Data processing by the computer may be an activity subordinate to the vice president of finance or the controller. The particular organizational pattern followed depends upon many factors, such as the personal preference of top management members, the capability of the manager of office work, the size and general nature of the enterprise, the quantity of office work, and the repetitiveness of the office work. Judgment, background, and experience play very large roles. However, because a key issue is the degree of centralization adopted, further comment on this subject is warranted.

CENTRALIZATION OF OFFICE ACTIVITIES

"Centralization of office activities" means the physical concentration of such activities into a single group, and the management over them vested in one person. For example, in centralized filing, all filing work for an entire office is done by a filing section and managed by a filing chief. Centralization is concentration.

Actually, the concept of centralization can be considered from the viewpoint of (1) physical location or (2) management. This, in turn, permits four possibilities, namely, (1) physical location centralized and management centralized, (2) physical location not centralized and management centralized, (3) physical location not centralized and management not centralized, and (4) physical location centralized and management not centralized. Illustrations of these four possibilities, along with comments for each, are shown in Figure 28–2.

ADVANTAGES OF CENTRALIZATION

Since the question of centralization is important and is frequently confronted in office organizing, the advantages and disadvantages of

POSSIBILITY 1

PHYSICAL LOCATION : CENTRALIZED
MANAGEMENT :   CENTRALIZED

POSSIBILITY 2

PHYSICAL LOCATION: NOT CENTRALIZED
MANAGEMENT :   CENTRALIZED

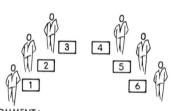

COMMENT: COMMON CONCEPT
OF CENTRALIZATION

COMMENT : COMMON BUT SOMETIMES
NOT FULLY COMPREHENDED
AS A TYPE OF CENTRALIZATION

POSSIBILITY 3

PHYSICAL LOCATION: NOT CENTRALIZED
MANAGEMENT :   NOT CENTRALIZED

POSSIBILITY 4

PHYSICAL LOCATION: CENTRALIZED
MANAGEMENT: NOT CENTRALIZED

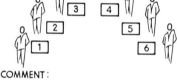

COMMENT :

SERIES OF INDIVIDUAL UNITS.
ACTUALLY NO CENTRALIZATION
CONCEPT EXISTS

COMMENT :

RELATIVELY RARE CONCEPT OF
CENTRALIZATION - LITTLE USED

FIG. 28–2. The four possibilities of centralization.

centralization will be enumerated. Among the important advantages are the following:

1. Flexibility is given the organizational structure. Work peak loads can be readily handled, office machinery utilized fully, and the effects of labor shortages reduced to a minimum.

2. Equitable wage schedules are fostered. The measurement of office output is encouraged, and comparisons of wages for similar work are possible.

3. Training of office employees is expedited. New employees can be added to centralized groups without seriously affecting the operations of the group. The retraining of old employees for new jobs is also well adapted to a centralized type of organization.

4. Methods of office operation can be applied uniformly and quickly. Standards and procedures common to all divisions can be established, and improvements can be installed with a minimum of effort.

5. Cost of performing office work is decreased. Supervisory costs are lowered, the costs of investment and maintenance of machines are lowered, and the amount of floor space is frequently reduced.

6. Labor specialization is practiced. Employees become highly efficient and are continuously employed on work necessitating their highest individual skill and ability.

DISADVANTAGES OF CENTRALIZATION

These are the most important reasons why the centralized type of arrangement may be undesirable:

1. Much office work is confidential and should be handled by the unit in which this confidential trust is placed.

2. The work is performed by those who may not be familiar with the detailed requirements. Minor changes and corrections cannot be made on the spot.

3. Effective planning and controlling are difficult to exercise since the executives most familiar with the use and purpose of the paper work are not near at hand.

4. Work is done without regard for urgency or importance to the individual office unit. Delays may take place. The efficiency of each unit may be hampered.

5. Costs may increase due to nonproductive transporting and handling time required.

6. Employees of a "generalist" nature are not developed. Some versatile persons with over-all viewpoints are essential in all enterprises.

TREND TOWARD CENTRALIZATION OF OFFICE WORK

As seen from the above lists, centralization of office work has its advantages and also its disadvantages. However, the current trend appears to be toward centralization. Terms like "central accounting," "service center," and "central office of services" are being used in office organization. Rounding up and consolidating fragmental clerical functions, using office automation, and taking measures to stop the spiraling of overhead costs are among the major reasons for this trend.

Several illustrations will be of interest. A prominent insurance company centralized correspondence work with the result that efficiency, measured in terms of quantity of work performed, increased nearly 25 per cent. Also, clerical work formerly done in its more than 230 agencies is now done faster and at a lower cost in 42 large clerical units. A large oil company centralized its credit card accounting and shifted much office work from the sales department to a centralized office services department. The result was an 18 per cent payroll reduction. A suggested procedure to follow in considering the feasibility of centralization of the office is discussed in Chapter 31.[1]

THE OFFICE ACTIVITIES

For instructional purposes, it is helpful to enumerate the various office activities that can exist in an enterprise in order to afford a panorama of office work. As indicated above, the location and arrangement of office activities assume a variety of patterns and relations. The following is not intended to represent any particular office or serve as a specific recommendation.

The many and various office activities, segregated by six major divisions, include:

1. Electronic data processing (deals with activities of computer utilization).
   1.1 Operation of electronic units.
   1.2 Program determination.
   1.3 Storage of media—punched cards, punched tape, magnetic tape, and so forth.
   1.4 Filing of computer operational data.
2. Office services (includes activities commonly thought of in reference to office work).
   2.1 Correspondence and office reports.
       2.11 Stenographic and typing work.
       2.12 Billing.
       2.13 Duplicating work.
   2.2 Computing.
       2.21 Cost data.
       2.22 Statistical data.
   2.3 Facilitating services.
       2.31 Mail and messenger services.
       2.32 Reception service.
       2.33 Telephone and telegraph.
       2.34 Storage and issuance of supplies.
   2.4 Filing.
   2.5 Records retention.
3. Office planning (encompasses activities dealing with what office work will be performed, when, where, and how).
   3.1 Determination of objectives, policies, procedures, and methods.
       3.11 Routines and flow of office work.
       3.12 Design and use of office forms.
   3.2 Use of office machines and equipment.

[1] See pages 603–5.

3.3 Research.
4. Physical facilities of the office (consists of activities pertaining to the securing, using, and maintaining of physical factors needed for performing office work).
  4.1 Location and arrangements.
    4.11 Office layouts.
    4.12 Office lighting.
    4.13 Ventilation and noise abatement.
  4.2 Purchasing.
    4.21 Office machines.
    4.22 Office furniture and equipment.
      4.221 Desks, chairs, and filing cabinets.
    4.23 Office supplies.
      4.231 Office forms and paper.
      4.232 Pencils, clips, and miscellany.
5. Office controlling (consists of activities of work measurement and comparison to see that office work is performed as planned).
  5.1 Operational analysis.
    5.11 Office standards.
      5.111 Office forms.
      5.112 Office machines, furniture, and equipment.
      5.113 Office procedures and methods.
    5.12 Office work simplification.
    5.13 Office work measurement.
    5.14 Office manuals.
  5.2 Work and cost control.
    5.21 Routing and scheduling.
    5.22 Peak work load handling.
    5.23 Cost analysis.
      5.231 Office budgets.
      5.232 Forecasts.
6. Office personnel (includes employee motivation and his relationships with fellow employees, with his job, and with the public of the enterprise).
  6.1 Office employment.
    6.11 Recruitment, selection, and placement.
      6.111 Interviews, tests, and references.
    6.12 Transfers, promotions, and terminations.
  6.2 Salary administration.
    6.21 Job description and evaluation.
    6.22 Job performance rating.
  6.3 Office training.
  6.4 Welfare.
    6.41 Grievances.
    6.42 Suggestion system.

6.43 Office safety.
    6.431 First-aid treatment.
    6.432 Accident prevention work.
6.44 Office employee benefits.
    6.441 Pension and sick benefits.
    6.442 Restaurant and recreation.

QUESTIONS

1. Justify the statement that organizing is important in management.
2. Do you agree with this statement? "Organizing is the work of setting up a hierachy of managers and determining who supervises whom and what unit does what thing or things." Explain your answer.
3. If specialization helps in getting work accomplished, should not all office work in an enterprise be performed in a centralized location and under the management of one head? Justify your answer.
4. What are the major purposes of organizing?
5. Elaborate on the statement: "No organizational unit should be designated as 'the office.' Such a statement is both incorrect and confusing."
6. What relationship, if any, exists between managerial objectives and organizing? Discuss the significance of your answer in the study of management.
7. Discuss Figure 28–1 in your own words, pointing out what you consider the chief points of interest from the viewpoint of organizing.
8. Discuss the meaning of the term "centralization" as used in managerial organizing.
9. Justify your answer to each of the following:
    a) Does centralization give flexibility to an organization structure?
    b) Do organizing and organization structure have essentially the same meaning?
    c) Does the concept of centralization in organization always mean from the viewpoint of management?
    d) Is co-ordination the main purpose of organizing?
10. What are some major difficulties you would anticipate in placing one person over all department heads in order to co-ordinate their heretofore separate office management efforts?
11. Briefly discuss what in your opinion are the four most important advantages of centralization. Of decentralization.
12. Comment on this statement: "In any organization structure, some functions must be on a decentralized basis—otherwise, an organization structure would not exist. Hence, the disadvantages of decentralization are present to some degree in all organization structures."

CASE PROBLEMS

Case 28–1. Mohawk Telephone Company

Among the employees of the Mohawk Telephone Company is a group of service representatives whose activities embrace answering complaints and general questions of customers, and making adjustments. Much of this work is completed over the telephone, but a great deal of customer contacts must be handled through the mail. The entire group is divided into three districts, which are further subdivided into approximately three units each. Each unit handles a number of exchanges in proportion to the volume of work involved.

The requirements of this group for typing service consist of dictation from managers of each district and local managers of each unit. This work normally should be in the mail the same day it is dictated. In addition, the service representatives themselves have occasion to submit letters for typing, but the great majority of their letters are of a form or standardized type and do not require individual dictation. Other work of the typing department for the group, accounting for nearly three fourths of its total work, consists of filling in various office forms and envelope addressing, neither of which require same-day attention.

The eleven typists and one supervisor are consolidated into one group located on the third floor of the building. Current practice to handle priority work of the managers, all of whom are located on the second floor of the building, is for the manager to telephone the typing supervisor and request a typist. The supervisor then sends a typist to the manager. There, she takes the dictation and then returns to the typing department, where the material is typed. Work prepared by a service representative is sent by messenger to the typing department. It is picked up once an hour, carried to the central distribution point, and then routed to the typing department. All finished typed work, whether for manager or representative, is returned as soon as it is completed through the messenger service. If there are any corrections to be made, the material is returned by messenger service. This means a delay is encountered. In some instances, work of a priority nature is delayed as much as two days.

Complaints have been made by the managers, and the office manager admits that some delays have been excessive. He suspects that the accuracy and general efficiency of the typing group have also probably declined, but he has no proof of this.

Problems:

1. Do you feel this is mainly a problem in managerial organizing? Defend your answer.

2. If you were one of the managers of a district included in the group, what recommendations would you make?

3. What action do you suggest the office manager take? Why?

Case 28–2.   Wrightwood Manufacturing Company

Eugene Beesley, aged 36 years, an industrial engineer, came to the Wrightwood Manufacturing Company about two years ago. He was assigned to the industrial engineering department of the manufacturing division. His work record showed him to be a highly competent and qualified man, and the company felt very fortunate in acquiring his services. During the first few months with the company, he handled several projects admirably well; and when the office requested an engineer to assist in some office work measurement, Beesley was given the assignment. Soon he became extremely interested in office work and the possibilities it offered for improvement. To his way of thinking, "the papermill" offered tremendous opportunities. He worked diligently and established many standards.

Nearly a year ago, the office manager quit to move south on account of his wife's health. Beesley's dynamic qualities and eagerness, together with his competency, suggested to the company's vice president of general services that he was the man for the office manager's job. Discussing the proposition with several of his colleagues and finding no opposition, the vice president offered the office manager's job to Beesley, who accepted.

He was elated at the prospect. Within his first two months on the new job, he submitted a new co-ordinated plan for office operations which would save the company a considerable sum. His office supervisors believed the plan excellent and supported him. Beesley held many conferences with several top executives, including the vice president of general services, the vice president of sales, and the vice president of finance. He also talked with various groups in each of several units. Beesley believed he should talk to these various personnel of the company because many of his proposed changes in paper work would affect them.

After six months of trying to make headway with the office improvement program, Mr. Beesley began to feel that he was not getting anywhere. His superior, the vice president of general services, kept giving him special work to do, which work Beesley classified as strictly "busy" work and of no real importance. One job was an investigation of the reception service; another, of the trend in the number of items included on a typical order received by the company. Also, at the suggestion of the president of the company, Beesley visited several large offices using computers and also spent several days each with two different computer manufacturers. Reporting back to the president on the results of these visits, Beesley's impression was that the president had little interest in the visits and would rather not hear about them.

Another three months passed, and things continued about the same. Beesley kept busy on special assignments which he believed were whims of the company's top executives. He felt that he was achieving nothing that could not be accomplished by reports from company people in the various units affected. He arranged an interview with his superior and challenged the situation. He received a vague response. Thinking over the situation for several days, Beesley decided to quit and tendered his resignation.

Problems:

1. Should the company accept Beesley's resignation? Why?
2. What do you thing the real problem is in this case? Explain.
3. What action should be taken, and by whom? Discuss.

Chapter 29

OFFICE ORGANIZING— WORK DIVISION AND PEOPLE

Success story: You'll usually find that the man who was kicked upstairs prepared for it in more ways than by bending over.

—N. D. Stoyenoff

THE ORGANIZATIONAL location and content of the office was emphasized in the last chapter. The importance of centralization in office organizing was set forth, and the necessity for dividing the total office work was implied. By this division, clusters of somewhat similar work are formed, providing nuclei of organizational units. This approach along work lines is helpful in gaining a clear insight to the initial task of organizing. It is sometimes referred to as thinking along functional lines or specific activities. More needs to be said about the use of functions in dividing the work for organizational purposes.

THE MEANING AND IMPORTANCE OF FUNCTIONS

A function is the normal or characteristic operation of an activity or performance. It may also be thought of as the proper action of anything. Filing, for example, is a function in that it is an activity which always has characteristic identities, and these indentities are usually considered the proper action of filing. In management, it is common to speak of "functions," such as the function of producing, the function of selling, and the function of financing. The function of producing means the normal or characteristic action of producing goods or services; likewise, the function of selling means the normal or characteristic action of selling goods or services.

In turn, any function covering a broad scope of action can be broken up into component functions covering actions of a relatively limited scope. To illustrate, the broad function of producing can be divided into component functions, such as the function of designing, the function of plant layout, the function of inspection, the function of production control, and the function of purchasing.

THE FUNCTIONAL APPROACH IN ORGANIZING

Although functional analysis is important and is the initial step in most organizing, it must be remembered that it is only one part of organizing. The work must be *performed by people*, relationships established among the organizational units, and proper work environment supplied. It is advisable to think first of functions, then of individuals performing these functions. This approach is effective because (1) a manager must co-ordinate functions, i.e., what is done, not who is doing it; (2) functions are usually permanent, the interests and abilities of personnel tending to change with time; and (3) personnel emphasis often results in unusual combinations of duties that are difficult to manage and for which the securing of replacements is arduous.

It is important to note that the same function may be performed by two or more people. Likewise, the same person may perform two or more functions. The former case may be illustrated by a group of clerks all doing the same work, for example, checking billings in a department. The latter case is illustrated by the receptionist who greets and directs visitors, opens and sorts the mail, and types letters.

Grouping common activities or functions to form an organizational unit is the common approach. However, other means for departmentation are used: (1) by process, (2) by customer, (3) by product, and (4) by territory. An organizer can use any means he desires; and commonly, several means are employed in the same organization structure. What best helps to achieve the objective should be used. In a bank, for example, for the top levels, functions may be used; whereas the loan department may be divided by customer—loans to manufacturers of plastics, chemicals, and paper; loans to manufacturers of food processors and package machines; or by product—commercial loans or personal loans. Office work division by territory is common for offices designed to serve sales organizations. The territory divisions constitute the main segments of the sales organizational structure, and the offices serving such organizations are likewise segregated and located throughout the country.

INDIVIDUAL JOB CONTENT

From the organizing viewpoint, individual job content is the contribution to the objective made by the individual performing the particular job. The activities assigned or the individual job content can be viewed as what the employee is required to perform because of the organizational position and relationship occupied in the organization structure.

Effective organizing requires that each employee have a definite task that he understands and can perform. When these requirements are met and the necessary physical facilities and adequate supervision are provided, the individual is in a work situation where ideal accomplishments can be reached.

The division of work to be done must be carried out to the individual job level. That is, the department functions must be divided ultimately into jobs for each individual. Unless this is done, the managerial work of organizing is incomplete, and the group of people connected with the enterprise cannot perform as a whole or contribute with a unity of action.

JOB SPECIALIZATION

Specialization is a demonstrated successful fact. Its benefits are tremendous. Complex work can be segregated into relatively simple components, each accomplished effectively by employees specializing in that single or similar group of operations. Training is simplified and reduced, yet skill in a limited area can be greatly increased. Specialization has been stimulated by the trend toward mechanization, which usually necessitates large volumes of similar work, thus creating specialized and concentrated work areas for the attendant operators.

JOB SPECIALIZATION—HOW FAR?

All organizing requires some specialization. Most managers agree that no one person can do everything equally well. The need for allocating total work and capitalizing upon what a person can perform best have resulted in job specialization. The question is not whether to have job specialization but to what extent job specialization should be carried. In organizing, the office manager must decide this question as exemplified by determining the work make-up of each organizational unit and what is done by each member of that unit.

Too many and too varied tasks for one employee are generally avoided. On the other hand, a job of very limited scope is not used, presumably to minimize the problem of monotony and lack of employee interest in his work.

In some enterprises, where the organizing has utilized job specialization to a great degree, provisions such as job rotation, "music while you work," rest periods, and keeping the employee informed of all major enterprise operations have been adopted to maintain high morale and to make the organizational structure effective. For the most part, the degree of specialization has not been questioned. However, in some companies, an attempt to broaden the job scope has been advanced. This is commonly referred to as *job enlargement*. The results of these efforts have been surprising. In several interesting examples, job enlargement brought about reduced office costs, improved quality of work, better teamwork, and lower absenteeism. These results, which must be interpreted carefully, indicate that there are both economic and social limits to social specialization. What degree and form of job specialization to follow presumably depend upon the type of office work and the individual doing it. However, more specific information is needed to derive definite recommendations; at the same time, it appears that reconsideration of prevalent ideas concerning job specialization is in order.

WORK DIVISION ARRANGEMENTS

Generally speaking, work divisions for the top level of an organizational structure are made on the basis of functions. Divisions for the intermediate levels usually are either by type of product, by customer, or by territory. Common at the lower office organizational levels are work divisions by any of these three arrangements: (1) serial, (2) parallel, and (3) unit assembly. Work division by product, customer, or territory is self-explanatory; but further discussion of the serial, parallel, and unit assembly is warranted.

In the serial arrangement, the work division is extended to a series of small tasks, each task being performed by a specialist in that particular type of work. Moving progressively from task to task, the work advances until completed. The serial arrangement is the same basic plan as the familiar factory assembly line, commonly found in production plants. In some quarters, the term "production line basis" is used to describe the serial arrangement in the office. "Consecutive handling" adequately describes this arrangement.

The parallel arrangement permits a series of needed and separate tasks to be performed by one individual or a work team. The employee or employees, as the case might be, do not specialize in performing one task but gain proficiency in accomplishing several tasks. Frequently, the tasks are related, but this is not necessary. To implement the parallel arrangement, the total work is divided into two or more major parts, and each part is assigned to an employee or group of employees. The basis for dividing the work into parts can be any of many factors, for example, by letter of the alphabet, number, territory, type of merchandise, or major subject. From the individual's viewpoint, the scope of the work is relatively large under the parallel arrangement. The term "concurrent handling" can be used to identify this arrangement.

The unit assembly arrangement provides for different employees to perform different work steps upon the same work items at the same time. It can be termed "simultaneous handling." Each step is done by a specialist in his particular type of work. Co-ordination of the various tasks is a prime requirement under this arrangement, for the separate tasks usually do not require identical times to perform. The unit assembly arrangement can be thought of as a cross-blending between the serial and the parallel arrangement.

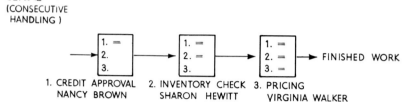

SERIAL
(CONSECUTIVE
HANDLING)

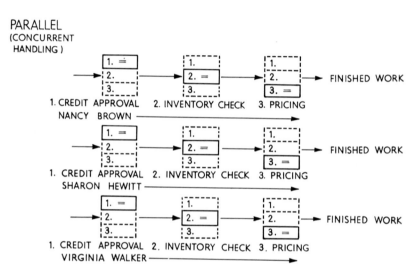

PARALLEL
(CONCURRENT
HANDLING)

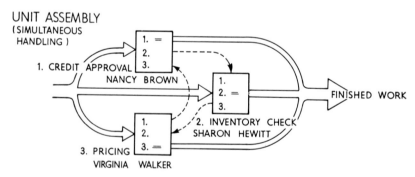

UNIT ASSEMBLY
(SIMULTANEOUS
HANDLING)

FIG. 29–1. Illustrating the serial, parallel, and unit assembly arrangements of work division.

Figure 29–1 shows these three basic arrangements in graphic form. The work considered pertains to the handling of customers' orders and consists of three separate operations, including (1) credit approval, (2) inventory check, and (3) pricing. Assume a work force of three employees, Nancy Brown, Sharon Hewitt, and Virginia Walker. The serial arrangement is shown at the top of the figure. For simplicity, each separate operation has been considered a separate task, and one employee has been assigned to each task. In contrast, the parallel arrangement is shown at the center of Figure 29–1. In this illustration, the total customer order-handling work has been divided into three parts that parallel each other. Each part consists of all three separate tasks of the work, that is, credit approval, inventory check, and pricing. As illustrated, employee Nancy Brown performs all three tasks or operations, and so do each of the other two employees, Sharon Hewitt and Virginia Walker. The bottom illustration of Figure 29–1 shows the unit assembly arrangement. Here, specialization is practiced by each employee, but the work sequence is not identical for each item. Nancy Brown performs credit approval; while at the same time, Sharon Hewitt performs inventory check, and Virginia Walker does pricing.

WHAT ARRANGEMENT TO USE

Like many other practices, the question of whether to use the serial, parallel, or unit assembly arrangement cannot be fully answered by a "Yes" or "No." Normally, for any given office, the tendency is toward the prevalence of one, but seldom will it be used exclusively. Individual circumstances govern, with consideration given to cost, employees' interest in their jobs, quality of work, preferences of managers and employees, and the over-all objectives.

More specifically, the serial arrangement of work division requires a sufficient work quantity of a particular type to keep an employee fully occupied in its performance. Quantity and specialization are close "buddies." Also, mechanization tends toward a serial arrangement. Most office machines handle a large volume of work, and their cost usually requires a high percentage of utilization throughout the workday. In some instances, the job content is so complex and the tasks so heterogeneous that some breakdown in the work is necessary to acquire and maintain employees for the work. When this is the case, the serial arrangement is usually followed. In addition, some office work, if performed by one employee, would incur a sizable loss of time in shifting from one operator to another. For example, a job consisting of typing, then calculating, followed by checking and resumption of typing, may show low efficiency. Selecting the serial plan frequently follows when the skill needed is of a special type, due to scarcity or the amount of training that can economically be provided. It is usually not feasible to dilute the efforts of the employee possessing a needed skill in a specialty. An expert in operating punched-card equipment should not type and file letters as a part of her regular job duties. Another condition normally suggesting the adoption of the serial arrangement is when great uniformity in handling certain portions of the office work is required. The signing of checks and bank drafts can be cited as an illustration.

In contrast, the parallel arrangement is usually followed when better work performance appears to be associated with a complete understanding and handling of the particular subject matter. An overcharge in a billing to a complaining customer might best be handled in its entirety by one employee. Furthermore, when the "start to finish" period for the work performance must be reduced, the parallel arrangement may be superior. Under this pattern, delay in work processing, or loss in time by papers traveling from operation to operation, is avoided. Less handling and idle time generally result when the papers are processed by employees working under a parallel arrangement. In some cases, by keeping the division of work too small, an employee is deprived of helpful overall checks in the work. When this situation exists, the parallel arrangement automatically provides the solution. It should also be observed that with parallel groups performing similar cycles of work, it is possible to hold contests, compare work accomplishments of each group, and inject other competitive devices in managing the work. Such measures help stimulate high productivity. In addition, the parallel arrangement helps to eliminate duplication of efforts such as reading and checking if such is present when high specialization is followed. Under the parallel pattern, one employee familiarizes herself with the contents of the paper by a single reading and a single checking. Finally, the parallel arrangement is suggested where the circumstances indicate that greater interest and enthusiasm by employees probably will be gained from having a greater variety of work in the job make-up.

The unit assembly arrangement permits work to start at an operation other than the first in the sequence of tasks. This makes it possible to start processing the work simultaneously at different operational stages. In other words, the performance of work operation No. 3 need not wait until No. 1 and No. 2 are completed. In certain situations, this is a definite advantage. Furthermore, flexibility in machine utilization and in work scheduling are provided. Usually, completed work is obtained more rapidly under the unit assembly arrangement; for this reason, it is employed for special rush and emergency work. Specialization is practiced to a great degree under this arrangement; but as stated above, sometimes the co-ordination of the individual work processing poses a difficult problem.

JOB ANALYSIS

Job analysis is a formal means of determining the job content. It can be defined as follows: *Job analysis is the process of critically examining the components of a job, both separately and in relation to the whole, in order to determine all the operations and duties.* In short, job analysis deals with facts about jobs and what is required for competent performance. Typical of data included are the forms and materials handled, the equipment and machines used, the methods utilized, the frequency of the operations, the amounts and kinds of skill required, and the degree of concentration needed. Such information is extremely useful in management because (1) the scope of the job becomes definite, (2) the identity becomes fixed, and (3) definite association between job title and content is established.

Job analysis is customarily and quite correctly thought of as an activity logically a part of personnel activities because it is basic in the performance of many personnel department functions. For example, job analysis is the basis for determining the relative worth, compensation-wise, of jobs; it facilitates hiring and placing, can be used for formulating training needs, and serves to identify promotions and transfers. These are truly personnel in character or a part of the management, and are discussed in Part VII of this book. However, inasmuch as job analysis does identify and establish the job and its content, it is included in this discussion dealing with organizing. As already pointed out, really effective and complete organizing work requires specific work divisions at the individual level. Job analysis helps supply this requirement.

OBTAINING JOB ANALYSIS DATA

In the case of new work or a new organizational unit, the manager doing the organizing must decide the characteristics of the newly craeated job or jobs, including their content and relation with other jobs in the enterprise. He may not formalize this work to the extent or in the detail that is common in the usual job analysis efforts. Nevertheless, information of the job analysis sort is helpful in organizing, and the indicting statement can be made that many difficulties in organizing begin with the manager's failure to make greater use of job analysis information.

In a going office, there are three different methods of securing job analysis data: (1) interviews and observations, (2) conferences, and (3) questionnaires. Whatever the method, it is advisable to secure, within practical limits, as much information as possible about every job. It is usually better to have too much than too little data. To foresee all the uses to which the data may eventually be put is not always possible. Experience shows it is best to provide for expansion of the job analysis program.

When the interview and observation method is used, the analyst goes to the employee, asks questions about the job, and observes what the content of the job is. While this method is satisfactory for office jobs, it is probably most popular for factory jobs.

In the second method, the employee is called into conference and verbally describes his job to the analyst, who records the information. This method usually requires more time than the others, takes the employee from his job, and may interfere with the work routine.

In the third method, a questionnaire is sent to the employee, who fills in the information. This method is used in cases where the employees can intelligently handle clerical details and are more or less accustomed to paper work. It is commonly used for most office work. The federal government has employed this procedure successfully for nearly fifty years. However, it is frequently advisable to supplement the questionnaires with short observations and interviews, especially on the more important jobs, for this brief contact usually gives the analyst a better idea of the job content.

JOB ANALYSIS REPORT

The data of job analysis commonly are recorded on a prepared paper form, sometimes referred to as a job analysis report. The form serves as a reminder to answer definite questions and thereby secure all the needed facts, so that no part of the job is overlooked. In addition, it provides a means of recording the data in a standardized manner, thus making it easier to handle and interpret the information. Figure 29–2 shows a portion of a job analysis form.

JOB ANALYSIS

Present title of job _____ Department _____

1. What is the general purpose of this job?
2. What duties are performed in the *usual* course of the work? (Tell from where work is received, what is done with it, and where it is sent.)
3. What duties are performed only at stated intervals? (Group answers by daily, weekly, monthly, etc.)
4. In what organizational unit is this job presently located?
5. Does the job entail supervising other employees? (Explain.)
6. If there are any special courses in school essential in order to perform the duties of this job satisfactorily, name them.
7. What past experience is *necessary* for a new employee to have in order to perform the duties of this job?
8. What are the *most* difficult parts of this job?
9. What are the *least* difficult parts of this job?
10. About what proportions of this job require sitting, _____%; standing, _____%; moving about, _____%?
11. What machines or other equipment are operated?
    Regularly:
    Occasionally:

FIG. 29–2. Portion of questionnaire used for job analysis.

JOB DESCRIPTION

The information on the job analysis form actually describes the job. However, when this information is written in a more descriptive style, the term "job description" is frequently used.

The general make-up of job descriptions varies among different enterprises. In most cases, however, a summary of the job, the work performed, and the qualifications are generally considered essential. See Figure 29–3.

Job descriptions are useful in the work of organizing. The duties and the lines of authority, if any, are clearly set forth. In addition, job descriptions help bring about better understanding within an enterprise because the qualifications required of the successful employee on a particu-

---

JOB DESCRIPTION

DATE_____

JOB TITLE___JUNIOR ACCOUNTANT_____GRADE_VI____CODE_____

SUMMARY: Under general direction of Comptroller and immediate supervision of Accountant, performs general accounting duties and prepares special reports as assigned.

WORK PERFORMED: Maintains records of cash receipts and/or disbursements, posts related subsidiary records. Posts various journal entries and adjustments, maintains record of Supply Department receipts and prepares minor financial statements.

Handles correspondence, verifies tabulations and reconciles bank statement. Assists in distributing work to temporary help, prepares monthly reports and special statements. Performs related work, such as figuring per capita and expense ratios. Operates office machines as required.

May supervise work of accounting clerks, typists for temporary periods, etc. and performs similar duties as assigned.

QUALIFICATIONS: Normally requires three to five years' training and experience, including two years' general accounting training plus three years' company accounting experience as an Accounting Clerk.

Courtesy: J. D. Moore Organization, Park Ridge, Ill.

FIG. 29–3. A job description written in an effective form.

lar job are pointed out. Furthermore, job descriptions help in selecting persons best fitted for the requirements of the job, in acquainting the new employee with the job to which he is being assigned, and in crystallizing scattered information into a clear job picture.

Current practice tends to use the terms "job description," "job statement," and "job title" to identify progressively contracting descriptions of the job. A job statement is used to furnish a quick picture of the job. To illustrate, in Figure 29–4, the job content of "programming man-

---

Programming Manager: Reports to director of computing center. Supervises administrative assistant programming. Is responsible for planning and organizing all programming activities for the computer; maintaining essential records of the programming department; directing, motivating, and evaluating personnel; and participating in the planning of electronic data processing.

FIG. 29–4.   Job statement of programming manager.

ager" is condensed to a single paragraph. A job title is simply a common name for a job. Job titles are commonly inadequate and do not identify the job satisfactorily. For example, the common job title of "secretary" is used for jobs of different make-up, as illustrated by the

---

Secretary: Takes dictation, using shorthand, and transcribes the dictated material into a neat typed format; makes appointments for executive and reminds him of them; answers and makes telephone calls; handles personal and important mail; writes routine correspondence on own initiative; maintains executive's files.

Secretary: Takes dictation, using either shorthand or a machine; transcribes dictation from either shorthand notes or a machine; interviews people coming into the office, directing to other employees those who do not warrant seeing the executive; answers and makes telephone calls.

FIG. 29–5.   Job titles may be identical, but the respective job statements may differ.

two job statements in Figure 29–5. This situation is further illustrated by the following interesting remarks:

Another thing we have found in office jobs is that there is no consistent terminology. What is a clerk? I wish somebody would tell me. In one plant he is the chief accountant and in the next plant he is sorting tabulating cards. They both have the same title. We go into engineering departments—what is a draftsman? One is a detail draftsman and one is a layout draftsman, but they are classified the same. Why? Certainly more is required from the standpoint of skill and experience of a designing draftsman, or a layout draftsman, than of a detailer. Classifications of bookkeepers indicate amazing differences. Anybody running a calculating machine is a bookkeeper, whether he knows anything about accountancy or not. Those who are just following instructions are bookkeepers.[1]

The point is this: *The title plus the job content are necessary for accurate identification.* This is important in organizing where work division and organizational unit creation must be decided.

IMPORTANCE OF PEOPLE IN ORGANIZING

As stated in the beginning of this chapter, organizing can logically start with work division, and the divisions created serve as focal areas for organizational units. In turn, the work within each organizational unit must be accomplished, directly or indirectly, by people. Up to this point, attention has been directed to the work aspect of organizing; but equally important, and in the opinion of many of greater importance, is the "people aspect" of organizing. In fact, it would be difficult to overemphasize the importance of people in organizing.

Successful organizing helps provide the means for getting effective results through people's efforts. It provides for the adequate development and placement of people. While both the division and the assignment of work are important, they are not the end objective in organizing. The main goal is to make it possible for a group of people, called employees, to work co-operatively and efficiently as a unit. The total work is segregated by functions so that each individual of the work group can perform a portion of the total work in the best possible manner. The expression "Organization is people" is trite; nevertheless, it stresses the importance of people in the work of organizing. It brings out the basic idea that people constitute the center about which revolve the organizational concepts of the work to be done, the authority, and the work environment.

In the final analysis, the organization structure is a tool—it provides the grouping of specific activities and of people for the purpose of applying management. Work is accomplished by people or machines operated by people. Organizing does not accomplish any work objective; it must be implemented with people. Hence, one of the biggest jobs of a manager is to form or maintain an organization structure which permits the proper placement and the development of employees. Some claim that almost any organization structure will prove satisfactory as long as the right people are operating it. Others lay great stress on the proper division of work and relationships. No doubt, both are important. However, the point here is that people are vital in organizing; they can make or break any organization structure.

It follows, therefore, that a sound organization structure is necessary

---

[1] C. J. Uhlir, "Job Evaluation—A Tool of Management," *Annual Conference Proceedings, National Office Management Association, 1944* (Philadelphia), p. 19.

for effective employee performance. This is true because organizing deals with and sets forth such basic issues as what is to be done and by whom, and who decides what. This view of organizing has been compared to that of writing the story for a motion-picture film. It sets the stage and predetermines what is to take place. How well it takes place, i.e., the quality of the motion picture, depends in great measure upon the actors—the personnel element.

Organizing affects and is affected by the human side of group activities. The sought-for co-ordination among different activities is more correctly stated as the co-ordination among *the employees* performing the different activities. After all, the work is divided so that it can be accomplished by the group. How effectively the various members of the group work together as a unified team toward achieving the objective is the paramount consideration.

PERSONNEL UTILIZED IN AN ORGANIZATION

Some managers prefer to build their organizational structure around the available men and women taking into account their special talents and ambitions. Secondary consideration is given to the function. Grouping the people, then assigning the activities, is the order of this approach. While excellent results have been reported from this approach, it involves serious handicaps. For example, organizational units encompassing unique combinations of functions may be present, and portions of the organization may take on identities that are difficult to define and manage. Furthermore, replacement of personnel who perform strange combinations of activities is made more difficult.

Personnel has a decidedly marked effect upon the structure of an organization. When, for example, the ratio of skilled to unskilled employees is high, the pattern of the organizational structure might be far different from that for one where the ratio is low. The reason for this, in part, is the relative importance of supervision and the placement of different functions at different levels in the two structures.

MANAGER'S ATTITUDE AND ORGANIZING

Organizing reflects a manager's attitude and thinking. That is to say, there is a personal managerial influence in organizing. It reveals the understanding of a manager for the essentiality of the human element and the determination of how this element is to be regarded. Just allocating the work, assigning employees to neatly conceived endeavors, and granting carefully defined authority to selected persons are insufficient. The people assigned to certain tasks and the creation of certain working relation among themselves must be handled with care, for they are of great significance in the success of the organizing work. There is genuine skill in having logical work divisions tie in respectively with an adequate consideration for who is to do each respective component of work.

An office manager implements regard for the human element in his organizing work by recognizing and appreciating the value, as well as the limitations, of his employees. This is not a one-shot proposition but a continuing, ever-searching effort to keep up to date on how the employees available to him can best be brought together to work toward a common goal. The supervisor in charge of the mail room, for example, reflects from the human-element viewpoint the office manager's thinking, organizationwise, of the supervisor's value, including his strong and weak points for his particular supervisory job. The job content, a result of work division, is presumably what the office manager thinks it ought to be; likewise, the authority granted is what the office manager thinks it ought to be—all or at least a big portion of it is with reference to the office manager's human-element evaluation of the supervisor. In this sense, it is sometimes said that an organization structure reflects the shadow of its manager. However, it appears more appropriate to state that an organization structure *reflects the light or understanding* of its manager.

ORGANIZATIONAL INTEGRITY AND PEOPLE

The office manager who experiences greatest success in organizing practices integrity in assigning his personnel to organizational units. Above all, he is a realist and accepts people available to him for what they really are. He recognizes that most organizational structures, and particularly the area of which he is a part, are the result of many decisions which took into account various considerations, some of which were controversial and contained imponderables. He also realizes that organizing is a "give and take" proposition between what is to be done and who is assigned to do it. Essentially, it has a compromise characteristic. The chief criterion, however, is to get the work accomplished adequately and maintain a continuity of satisfactory work achievement.

Good organizing is assisted by viewing people in the light of what they can do well. Concentration on men's strengths pays organizational dividends. A manager holding firm convictions about an employee's abilities to perform the work competently tends to instill confidence in the employee and develops his will to do successful work. At the same time, the manager must grasp the limitations of his people. Not all men can do all things, and for a manager to assume otherwise in his organizational work can lead to disaster. Yet, by proper managerial motivation, leadership, and lifting a man's vision to higher planes, the common man can be stimulated to achieve uncommon things.

CHALLENGE OF ORGANIZATION AND PEOPLE TO MANAGERS

A major challenge of organization and people is to integrate fully the work being done by the people of the various units into a co-operative and co-ordinated whole. This sounds fairly simple, but acquiring it in actual practice is a different story. People are not entirely unpredictable, yet they certainly cannot be considered the same as machines. Based on available knowledge, the intricacies of the human mind are far more difficult to understand than the chemical reaction of several compounds. Consider, for example, an individual working as a member of a group. He is an individual but, at the same time, is group-affected. If removed from the group and analyzed, the investigative results would have to be greatly qualified because he is not the same person he was when integrated into his organizational unit.

Another and perhaps eternal challenge is to develop a favorable organizational climate or atmosphere in which people are stimulated and permitted to grow so that they can perform a greater quantity and better quality of work and assume greater responsibility. The organizational structure must supply the needed background. Favorable surroundings conducive to the development of a way of life, operating under the arrangement devised by organizing, must be provided. The competency of an employee may be curbed due to improper organizational relationships, or his full contribution may never be realized if he is placed in the wrong organizational unit or is not supplied the proper work environment. In the best of organizing work, there is spirit, an attitude of mind, a belief in people and what they can accomplish. A solid organization structure is not built on form or body alone.

Finally, in the work of organizing, there is the challenge of utilizing all available resources, especially people, to their utmost. The tendency is to create new authorities, new units, and to go out and get "new faces." Adequate regard should be paid the tried and true. It is not always wise to discard the traditional for something new, mainly because it is new. Good organizing requires concentration on fundamentals. From a practical viewpoint, a manager must use in the best possible manner what is available to him. At the same time, changes and newness cannot and should not be avoided, for progress demands and is a part of something different.

QUESTIONS

1. What are the significant differences between the concepts in each of the following pairs?
    a) Job statement and office function.
    b) "Organization is people" and work divisions.
    c) Parallel work division arrangement and job analysis.
    d) Job enlargement and job specialization.

2. Explain the meaning and importance of individual job content in managerial organizing.

3. Relate the more common bases of departmentation at the various levels of the organization of an enterprise.

4. Of what value are job descriptions in managerial organizing? Elaborate on your answer.

5. Explain Figure 29–5, highlighting the main concepts that this illustration shows.

6. Discuss the means for obtaining office job analysis data. Which means do you prefer? Why?

7. You have been asked to give a short talk on the subject, "The Effect of an Office Manager's Attitude upon His Organizing Work." Outline the main topics of your proposed speech.

8. Do you agree with the following? "Organization structure is a tool; in and of itself it does not accomplish any work objective." Explain your answer.

9. Under what general conditions would you recommend the serial arrangement of work division? Justify your answer.

10. As you see it, is the condition of expanding or of decreasing activities of an office the more challenging to an office manager in his organizing work? Give reasons for your answer.

11. Do you believe it possible to overemphasize the importance of people in office organizing? Elaborate on your answer.

12. Relate why organizing is a challenge to the alert manager.

CASE PROBLEMS

Case 29–1. King-Mullin Corporation

Manufacturers of devices to control, confine, and utilize the flow of liquids under pressure, this corporation has grown tremendously during the past five years. Its fluid system components are being used in the aircraft field, missiles, lift trucks, hydraulic accumulators, air control valves, and similar applications. Currently, there are a total of 20 persons in the headquarters or Los Angeles office, including the general manager, who is the chief executive of the corporation and runs the business for the small number of owners. In addition, there are two salesmen who are on the road most of the time, nine engineers in a research and development unit reporting to the production manager, and 156 persons in manufacturing. The 20 people in the office and the work done by each are as follows:

1. *Assistant to the purchasing agent.* Types the letters of this department and handles the files of this unit. Reports to the purchasing agent and personnel director.

2. *Assistant sales manager.* Handles advertising; works with the advertising agency; plans catalogues and brochures, displays, and sales portfolios; corresponds with distributors and customers. Reports to sales manager.

3. *Billing clerk.* Types the invoices, maintains her own files of the customers billed. Reports to the controller.

4. *Bookkeeper.* Keeps the books, types bills, and also does some filing work. Reports to the controller.

5. *Controller.* Directs the work of the accounting department; makes up various financial reports, cost analysis, and office employees' payroll; and hires new employees for the office. Immediate superior is the general manager.

6. *Correspondent.* Dictates letters on machine and sometimes to a file clerk or typist, makes up shipping schedules and cost estimates. Reports directly to the sales manager.

7. *Cost accountant.* Makes up factory payroll, assists the controller with cost analysis work and other reports, and does some typing and filing. Reports to the controller.

8. *File clerk and typist.* Alternates between filing and typing, takes shorthand, and is responsible for office supplies. Is under the direct supervision of the sales manager.

9. *General manager.* Actually the president of the corporation, he coordinates the entire operations of the corporation, makes major decisions, and interprets broad policies.

10. *Order clerk.* Enters incoming orders, and is secretary to and reports directly to the sales manager.

11. *Purchasing agent and personnel director.* Handles all purchasing and is personnel director for factory workers only. Immediate superior is the general manager.

12. *Sales manager.* Handles contacts with customers, either personal or by mail; travels about 50 per cent of the time; and manages the work of the sales department. Reports to the general manager.

13. *Salesman.* Calls on prospects and customers, secures orders, takes care of customer inquiries by telephone. The sales manager is the immediate superior of all salesmen.

14. *Secretary to the general manager.* Performs secretarial work for the general manager, which work requires about 35 per cent of her time; during the remainder of her time, she helps the other departments. Reports directly to the general manager.

15. *Switchboard operator.* Operates the telephone switchboard and does some typing. Reports to the general manager.

At the present time, in the Los Angeles office, there are two correspondents, two file clerks, and four salesmen. For each of the other classifications, there is one employee.

Within the next four months, a small computer will be delivered and installed at the company. This addition is mainly the result of the efforts of the general manager, who is confident that it will prove very valuable for problems in the company's research and development work, analyzing sales, and improving office work. For this latter application, he has received little or no encouragement from the controller, who, to date, has shown little interest in the forthcoming computer or its application to the regular paper work of the corporation and prefers not to disturb the present means of processing papers.

Problems:

1. Draw an organization chart of the office.

2. Evaluate the present office organization, pointing out what may be its strong and weak points.

3. Where do you suggest the forthcoming computer unit be placed from the standpoint of organization? Why?

Case 29–2. The Rozell Bank and Trust Company

An important division of this company is the machine accounting division, which prepares reports for all other divisions in the company. At the present time, this division is organized as follows: Reporting to an assistant manager are three supervisors, one each for the control section, the machine room section, and the punch section. The assistant manager is a good technician for planning office work for machines. He is an excellent designer of required paper forms for machine operations and is highly respected. He appears to get along best with people interested in operating office machines. He is a poor writer, and many do not understand about what he is writing in his memorandums to the people in his unit or to those in other units of the company.

The control section supervisor, a liberal arts college graduate, is ambitious, thinks in broad concepts, and feels that the work of both the machine room and the punch sections should be subordinated to him, since their work is for control purposes, the function his unit performs. In the control section are (1) the cash unit, headed by a group leader with six employees reporting to him; and (2) 12 employees working on reports and statements, and reporting directly to the control section supervisor.

Reporting to the machine room section supervisor are two group leaders. The first directs 15 machine operators, the second supervises seven file clerks. The general concensus is that the machine room supervisor is a specialist in office machine operations. He has been in this type of work for eight years. He is a detailist, very precise, and ignores verbal orders. He wants and requests that all orders and suggestions affecting him be put in writing. Most who know him agree that he has a very keen mind.

The supervisor of the punch section has 10 key-punch operators reporting to him. He is a happy-go-lucky, hard-working man whose chief interest is to keep a steady job so that he can maintain a reasonable standard of living for his wife and three children.

Each time a report is late in delivery or wrong in content, the two supervisors of the control and machine sections blame each other. There is almost constant dispute between them and little, if any, co-operation. A sizable amount of overtime work is put in by both sections to complete reports now and then needed.

Problems:

1. What is the problem in this case?
2. What do you feel should be done? Why?

Chapter 30

AUTHORITY AND ORGANIZATIONAL RELATIONSHIPS

I think luck is the sense to recognize an opportunity and the ability to take advantage of it. Every man has bad breaks, but everyone also has opportunities. The man who can smile at his breaks and grab his chances gets on.

—SAMUEL GOLDWYN

ORGANIZATIONAL units are formed as a result of (1) dividing the total work to be done and (2) assigning people to these work divisions. For an organization structure to exist, however, these organizational units must be related or formally tied together, so that they make up a unified or concerted group, and so that the various people assigned to various tasks can operate effectively in unity. Discussion of this relationship leads to the subject of authority.

AUTHORITY DEFINED

Authority is the right to act or to exact action by others, within a prescribed area. With the concept of authority is associated the power to make decisions and to see that they are carried out. The compliance concept is a vital part of the meaning of authority. However, this compliance need not be and, as a matter of fact in office management, is seldom confined to coercion or force; more commonly, it is gained by means of persuasion and requests.

Authority as a part of and emitting from organizing has definite limitations. In managerial practice, authority must be used in conformity with the efforts to achieve the accepted goals of the organizational unit as a part of the enterprise. Authority, acting through organization relationships, helps to achieve these goals. Authority is not used by an office manager as his whims or wishes might suggest. Also, the use of authority is influenced by the people with whom it is being employed. The exacting of certain actions by others must be within their capacity to perform. To illustrate, trying to enforce a decision impelling an inexperienced file clerk to operate a modern bookkeeping machine would be a ridiculous misuse of authority. Furthermore, the beliefs and habits of the individual over whom authority is being exercised should be taken into account. When the individual is convinced that the action requested is proper and in order, he will respond readily. In contrast, when this condition does not exist, the effectiveness of the authority used may be limited; and in some instances, the content of the authority may be altered.

Authority is dynamic. Its make-up changes according to the specific conditions and requirements of the group or the individual. Authority is a tool, not the end result, of an office manager; it exists and is used to accomplish specific work goals.

AUTHORITY AND THE ORGANIZATION STRUCTURE

Within any one enterprise, authority connects the various organizational units, establishes relationships, and gives meaning to an organization structure. Vertical authority relationships are those between different organization levels and concern the superior-subordinate association. Horizontal authority relationships deal with organizational units within an organizational level and concern the manager-to-manager association within the same organization level.

The establishing of authority within an organization structure is usually conditioned by several factors. The relative position in the structure normally indicates the degree of authority from the formal viewpoint. But the amount of decision-making power and ultimate enforcement may be modified by the popularity or acceptance of the one in authority by the person being influenced by that authority. Managerial competence to gain enthusiastic co-operation, to acquire respect, and to inspire may be lacking despite the formal authority established by position in the organization structure.

Furthermore, a person may have little or no formal authority established by reason of position in the structure. Yet, that person might actually possess extensive authority due to his integrity, knowledge, and skill. In punched-card accounting, for example, others might seek suggestions from a certain individual and do what he recommends. Although the person may not be formally in charge, he actually possesses significant authority. Situations of this type may be of a temporal nature or may exist for long, continuous periods.

In many office organizational units, situations of an unusual or emergency nature arise from time to time. They may not be provided for in the regular organizational arrangement. In such circumstances, the person assuming the authority has derived it from what is called the "authority of the situation." This usually is temporary and exists until the person normally in charge assumes authority over the unusual event.

DELEGATION OF AUTHORITY

By means of delegation, an executive spreads his area of managerial influence and makes an organization structure meaningful. Without delegation, an executive restricts his managerial actions to those that he himself can perform. In fact, organizing does not become fully effective until delegation of authority is practiced.

Figure 30–1 illustrates the importance of delegation of authority in an organization. In the top illustration, office executive A has three assistants, 1, 2, and 3. In turn, assistant 1 has chiefs 11 and 12 reporting to

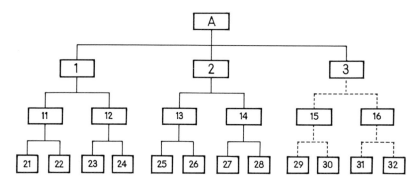

FIG. 30–1. Failure to delegate authority by office executive 3 tends to paralyze the organization established under him.

him; likewise, chief 11 has subordinates 21 and 22; and chief 12, subordinates 23 and 24. The employees reporting to executives 2 and 3 are shown by the illustration. President A delegates proper authority to his executives 1, 2, and 3. The former two, 1 and 2, delegate authority to their subordinates; and in turn, these subordinates delegate authority to their subordinates. In contrast, executive 3 is trying to do all the managerial work of his organizational unit himself. He does not delegate authority to either 15 or 16, who likewise do not delegate to 29, 30, 31, or 32. This failure to delegate authority actually paralyzes this portion of the organizational structure under executive 3. To a great extent, the employees reporting to executive 3 may just as well not be management members of the organization.

Delegation of authority is the act of granting or conferring authority by one executive or organizational unit to another. Delegation is usually thought of as moving from a higher to a lower level. It is important to note, however, that delegation can be from a lower to a higher level and from one level to another on the same plane, as found in the organization of some governmental and religious groups. Hence, delegation can be downward, upward, or outward.

In delegation, the delegator always retains his over-all authority for the delegated duties. He does not surrender or permanently release his authority. He does grant the right for others to act officially within the specific areas. Only the authority needed to carry out successfully the assigned functions is or should be delegated. This makes for the tapering concept of authority and simply means that in most organization structures the authority becomes successively smaller or tapered as successively lower horizontal levels of the structure are considered.

From the practical viewpoint, delegation of authority is either specially granted or inherently implied in the job. In the former case, it is given to an individual in order that he may act to perform the management which is essential in achieving the objective. In the latter case, the authority is inherently tied up with the job, so that whoever holds the job or performs the delegation function in the organization structure automatically possesses the authority which goes with that position. In any enterprise, therefore, authority is contingent upon such things as the delegation of those already in authority, the traditional structure of the organization, and the character and mental characteristics of the individual.

PROBLEM OF DELEGATION

One of the big problems in organizing is to get executives to delegate authority. Ideally, the proper delegation should exist at each delegator-to-delegatee level throughout the entire structure, and the delegation should extend as close to the level or point of action as possible. This makes for effective organizational action and encourages initiative by employees at each organization level. But in practice, some managers are reluctant to delegate. They fear that if authority is delegated, the right decision may not be made, and the work will not be handled correctly. Their belief is that they must keep in close touch with activities and decide most issues. In some instances, they may not fully realize the amount of authority needed by a subordinate to get the work done properly. In other instances, the executive states that he has delegated authority but at the same time criticizes his subordinates when they make and enforce decisions without his advice.

Delegation of authority is not easily acquired. The natural tendency is to do work yourself if you are the one charged with doing it. And if the work is important, there is all the more reason for doing it yourself to make certain that it is done right. These habits develop quite commonly because most persons acquire managerial status after doing nonmanagerial work. The latter type emphasizes doing the work yourself and doing it well; the reward can be promotion to managerial work. But success in managerial work requires getting work achieved by and through others. Failure to realize this fact plus difficulty in making the needed change in thinking, i.e., acquiring the managerial viewpoint, not the direct operative viewpoint, contribute to the lack of delegation by a manager.

It is common for the amount and extent of delegation of authority to be arrived at informally by trial and error. The subordinate makes a decision or tries out a certain practice; and if no reprimand results, he assumes the management work performed is within his province. In many cases, the status of delegation of authority is the result of an infiltration process over a long period of time. Slowly but surely, authority for certain matters has been turned over to the delegatee. Commonly, verbal statements establish the amount of delegation of authority; and in a relatively few instances, the superior gives specific delegation of authority in writing.

DEVELOPING DELEGATION OF AUTHORITY

The first requirement for developing delegation of authority is to realize the need for it. A manager must recognize that as long as he is limited to doing what he can accomplish himself, he will always be short of time and limited in his achievements. The alternative is to acquire aides, train them, and permit them to do the job, even if their manner of doing it differs from how the manager might have done it. Competent aides are mandatory for group efforts to reach greatest heights. A manager's need is to multiply himself. It is nonsense to try to lead the band and play all the instruments, too.

Furthermore, for delegation to work effectively, certain criteria can assist materially. Important is the establishment of definite goals and clear policies, for these give guidance to the subordinate and keep him from going too far astray in the fulfillment of the tasks. Work which is routine and which is covered by definite policies should offer little delegation difficulty. Clear and timely communication, complete instructions and orders, and definite job identifications are also helpful. And the use of broad controls expedites delegation, for they can supply the desired checks to determine whether the work is being accomplished satisfactorily.

Lastly, belief in delegation is necessary. An office manager must want to make delegation successful; he must strive to help it succeed. Among other things, he will not interpret delegation as distributing the work to others, sitting back, and observing if they make good or not. Rather, he will select the delegatee carefully and offer counsel readily to him, being careful not to give him answers, but to help him find the answers himself. The office manager must be willing to see his subordinates make mistakes and charge the cost to management training and the strengthening of his organization. Effective delegating does not just happen. From the very beginning, it takes much effort, time, and persistence to develop the art of authority delegation and to keep it alive.

SPAN OF AUTHORITY

In writing of relationships among organizational units and the subject of authority, the question arises: How many immediate subordinates can a manager manage effectively? The number is commonly referred to as "span of control" or "span of management." For our purposes here, it is believed the term "span of authority" is appropriate and helpful.

In a given case, there is probably an optimum number of employees who should be immediately subordinate to an executive in order that most satisfactory managerial results are obtained. The number should be large enough to utilize the executive's full time and ability, yet not so large that his efforts are diluted over too wide a span. The proper span of authority depends upon many considerations.

The organizational level at which the managerial work is performed appears to be important. At the higher levels, few might report to their immediate superior; while at the lower or operative levels, many might report to one superior. Also, the type of work is important. To illustrate, a supervisor of draftsmen might adequately direct the work of fifteen draftsmen, depending upon the particular type of drafting work performed. Generally speaking, a relatively broad span of authority can be used. In addition, adequate consideration must be given to whether all the immediate subunits are of equal size and importance, whether they must be given equal attention by the supervisor, and whether the caliber of personnel requires a large or a small amount of supervision. Where the make-up of the work is fairly stable and little communication between units is required, a broad span of authority usually proves satisfactory. Furthermore, the geographical distance between activities affects the span utilized.

Some managers prefer a span numbering from four to eight. Originally, this quantity came from the military, where rapid change in plans and operations may be necessary because of enemy action. However, in business organization, the span should be determined by keeping in mind the considerations mentioned above. The number used may well be four to eight, but it need not necessarily be this amount. The span of authority appears to be increasing in many business enterprises. In some instances, successful operations are reported with spans of 10 to 12 persons at the top levels and with 20 to 25 persons at the lower levels. In the final analysis, the number of subordinates reporting to a manager should be limited to what he can effectively manage.

It is appropriate to point out that span of authority deals with the number of persons reporting to a manager, not the number of persons having access to a manager. The two can be greatly different. Also, span of authority is confined to *formal* authority relationships. Actually, in most enterprises, there are usually many informal authority relationships. These result from the existence of social interests and relationships among employees, and are frequently different from the economic formal relationships established.

ORGANIZATIONAL RELATIONSHIPS AND SPAN OF AUTHORITY

It is interesting to note how the number of relationships increases as the number of persons supervised increases. First, consider a manager, M, with two supervisors, A and B. In this case, there are six relationships: M with A, M with B, and A with B, plus the reverse of each, assuming the initiative is taken by the second-named party; i.e., the additional three are A with M, B with M, and B with A. Now, assume that M increases his power to delegate, that is, he increases the number of supervisors from two to three, or an increase of 50 per cent. What happens to the number of relationships with which M may now be concerned? They increase from six to 18, or an increase of 200 per cent. The third supervisor, C, makes for these additional 12 relationships: M with C, B with C, A with C, M with AB, M with BC, and M with AC, plus the reverse of these six relationships. This is summarized in Figure 30–2.

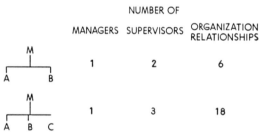

FIG. 30–2. Data showing the rapid increase in organizational relationships as the number of persons increases.

It can be concluded that wide spans of authority make for a high number of organizational relationships, while short spans make for a low number of relationships. Not all the relationships are of equal importance, but they should be taken into account when determining the span of authority.

RESPONSIBILITY

When a subordinate is delegated authority to perform specific work, an obligation to perform the work is created. The acceptance of this obligation is known as responsibility. Sometimes, the responsibility takes the form of a list of duties. These can be assigned; but as stated above, compulsion or persuasion to perform them arises from authority, which is the medium through which a manager operates.

Responsibility is the obligation for the carrying-out of a duty and what one is answerable for in the execution of an assigned task. That is, responsibility can be viewed as having two parts: (1) the obligation to secure results and (2) the accountability to a superior—the delegator of authority.

Since an authority delegator retains in the ultimate all his authority, he likewise retains in the ultimate all his responsibility. He cannot elude a failure of a subordinate by saying it was the fault of the subordinate. The superior retains the ultimate responsibility and is accountable for what is or is not achieved by his organizational unit.

1. Do you make a continuing review of excess office processing capacity?
2. What five office work areas require most of your time? Should they?
3. Have you investigated to find out if your instructions are understood?
4. Are you keeping up with the latest developments in office machines that might be used in your organizational unit?
5. Are written procedures brought up to date?
6. Do you receive any useless reports or documents?
7. Do you take an individual interest in each of your subordinates?

FIG. 30–3. Questions to develop management responsibility.

However, the delegator of authority usually does not spell out every detail of how the job is to be performed. He confers the right to make and enforce decisions to the delegatee in connection with that delegatee accomplishing the work. This means that the delegatee has a certain leeway in getting the work done; and in turn, this provides some flexibility in the specific manner of work performance and the responsibilities assumed by him. Efforts to develop management responsibility in delegatees take many different forms, but an effective practice is to provide the delegatee with a list of questions to stimulate his enthusiastic acceptance of responsibility and improve the exercise of his granted authority. Figure 30–3 illustrates the type of questions that can be asked.

LINE AUTHORITY AND STAFF AUTHORITY

There are two major types of authority: (1) line and (2) staff. An executive can have either or both. An executive having line authority, called a "line executive," normally exercises direct command over the work of all members in his unit; but there are certain exceptions, as discussed below. Characteristically, the authority relationship is of a superior-subordinate type, forming "a line" from the top to the bottom of the structure. It is the authority used to accomplish directly the major goals of an enterprise.

Staff authority can be divided into several classifications, including

(1) advisory staff, (2) functional staff, (3) service staff, and (4) control staff. Although all of these are commonly termed "staff authority," they are dissimilar in important respects, and the common identification of staff is unfortunate. An executive with staff authority is a staff executive. A clear understanding of the various types of staff authority helps clarify vital relationships in organizing. Hence, a brief description of each type will now be given.

ADVISORY STAFF AUTHORITY

The word "staff," according to Webster, means "a pole carried in the hand for support." Therefore, staff authority pertains to assistance or support, and this concept was the initial identification and use given staff authority. Much of this assistance and support takes the form of being

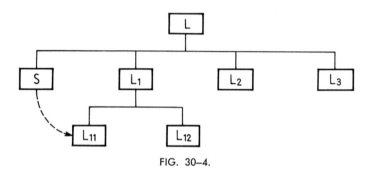

FIG. 30–4.

advisory and is appropriately called advisory staff authority. Specifically, a manager with advisory staff authority normally counsels or advises, in his specialty, the manager having line authority. Advisory staff is a manager-to-manager relationship and can exist within any organizational level.

In Figure 30–4, line manager L has four subordinates, S, L_1, L_2, and L_3. The latter three are line executives, while S is an advisory staff executive. His job essentially is to counsel and advise L in his (S's) specialty so that L can do a better job. The counsel and advice of S can be accepted in whole or part and utilized by L in managing the organizational group; or L can reject the advice of S, since L is in direct command of the unit. In some companies, the practice of "compulsory staff service" is followed. This requires a line executive to listen to his staff executives, but the final decision and enforcement rests with the line executive. When the managers are competent, this practice aids them in their respective tasks. Also, in some enterprises, the "completed staff work" doctrine is followed. This emphasizes the presentation of complete solutions by the advisory staff to the line executives. Piecemeal recommendations are avoided; and stress is placed on supplying assistance, not placing the line man in a predicament with questions regarding what he wants investigated or what data should be included in a report. Of course, the line man and the staff man should talk things over, but in a constructive way, with each making contributions.

FUNCTIONAL STAFF AUTHORITY

In office management, the use of functional staff authority is especially common. It concerns specific functions only and is delegated from one manager to another manager who is not related to the former by formally established authority channels. It can be conferred by a line to a staff manager, or vice versa. To illustrate, in Figure 30–4, line manager L may delegate to his subordinate staff executive, S, the authority for S to issue orders concerning a specific work activity directly to L_{11}, who is a line manager. In this case, the authority possessed by S is functional staff. Actually, L is delegating a qualified amount of line authority for a specific activity to S. The delegated authority is limited to a particular activity and applies only to the authority relationship in this activity between S and L_{11}. Good management practices would include L's informing L_{11} and L_{12} that this functional staff authority exists. Functional staff authority expedites efficiency and is convenient. Its use, however, must necessarily be limited; otherwise, established authority relationships are neutralized. Some specialized activities of the office from time to time require a competent office executive to explain and enforce office procedures to nonoffice personnel in order to insure proper handling and good administration. Such situations are solved by the use of functional authority.

SERVICE STAFF AUTHORITY

When speaking of office organizing, the term "service unit" commonly arises. Its justification is primarily economy and improved work performed or service offered by the unit. Purchasing, general office services (mail, telephone, and reception service), and legal counsel are examples of service organizational units. Generally, the head of such a unit possesses service staff authority which actually includes some line authority, as persons are expected to request the service organization to perform for them a service included in the service unit's make-up and, furthermore, to be bound by the decisions made by the service unit in its specialty. To illustrate, the manager of billing may not purchase supplies and equipment. This is done for him by the purchasing unit, and the billing manager abides by the decisions and actions of the purchasing unit.

Service staff authority applies both within and outside of the service unit as it pertains to this specialized service work. In addition, some service organizational units utilize functional authority when delegated, that is, they have jurisdiction over specific work performed by others not normally or formally under the authority of the service unit. In some instances, the service unit's authority is limited to the strictly advisory. The unit recommends and counsels in work regarding its specialty, but the decision as to what to do and its enforcement are not within the province of the service unit.

CONTROL STAFF AUTHORITY

In many organizations, there are units that perform essential work for achieving the major goals of the enterprise; yet, their work is of a specialty nature and is not supplied on a strictly advisory basis. The contribution is indirect in so far as the chief objectives are concerned; but when necessary enforcement of decisions is present, considerable line authority over the particular function in the enterprise may be present. For example, these conditions frequently exist for a financing and auditing or an industrial engineering organizational unit. Financing and auditing are normally required for successful management. Requests by such a unit to line managers to supply certain financial information, to use financial standards supplied, and to abide by prescribed auditing practices are not on a "take it or leave it" basis by the line managers. The requests are essential for required managerial control and can be enforced by the financial and auditing unit. Such a unit has control staff authority. In a very real sense, it includes aspects of ultimate line authority. Enforcement is usually voluntary because the line managers realize that the specialty offered is important and that, if necessary, compliance to requests can and will be forthcoming.

ORGANIZATION CHARTS

An organization chart is a graphic representation of an organization structure. It can be thought of as a picture of the organization structure; it shows the organizational relationships and the existing lines of authority.

The drawing of an organization chart is simplified by using the outline approach. First, list the main functions; next, place those functions which are subordinate to the main functions under the proper main function in the outline list; then, place under each subordinate function the minor functions which properly belong under the respective subordinate function. In this way, a list is developed which shows the main functions, the subordinates under each main function, and the minor functions under each subordinate. This outline form is then transformed into the graphic form which makes up the organization chart.

The chart may also be prepared by starting with the person of highest authority in the organization structure and working down by determining who reports to this top person and what activities each person handles. This procedure provides the information for the first level of management below the chief executive and may be followed for each consecutive layer. From the information so gathered, the organization chart can be constructed.

ADVANTAGES OF AN ORGANIZATION CHART

An organization chart insures neither good organization nor good management; it simply helps in visualizing the organization structure and, for this reason, assists in obtaining a better organizational structure. An organization chart compels the organizer to put down in black and white what the structural relationships are. This crystalizes his thinking and clarifies fuzzy, but important, details which might otherwise be overlooked. Specifically, the main advantages of an organization chart can be listed as follows: (1) a clear, over-all concept of the organization is obtained; (2) the main lines of authority and responsibility are brought out in full relief; (3) promotional possibilities are provided; and (4) the assignment of titles is simplified.

THE LINE ORGANIZATION

The line, or scalar, type of organization, which was used extensively in our early industrial development, is one of the oldest organization forms. It uses line authority exclusively. This type of organization is still quite popular and is frequently employed by proprietors of small business and for other enterprises where the number of employees is small.

The line organization is characterized by direct lines of authority from the top executive to the various assistants, and direct from them to the employees at the operative level. Each member is fully responsible for the carrying-out or the actual performance of the job to be done. Throughout the entire structure, each member is in complete charge of all activities within his particular organization segment. Authority and responsibility are greatest at the top, and reduce or taper as successively lower levels of management are considered.

The line type of organization is illustrated in Figure 30–5. Line authority exists between the president at the top to the employees at the bottom. The line authority may be thought of as a scalar type, in that it reduces by scales or steps. To illustrate, the connection is from the president to the vice president of production, to the superintendent of steel products, to the foreman of the foundry section, and to the workers of this section. The vice president of production is in complete charge of production, including the work of the superintendent of steel products and the superintendent of wood products; the superintendent of steel products is, in turn, in complete charge of that particular segment of the organization and specifically over the foremen of the foundry, machine, and assembly sections.

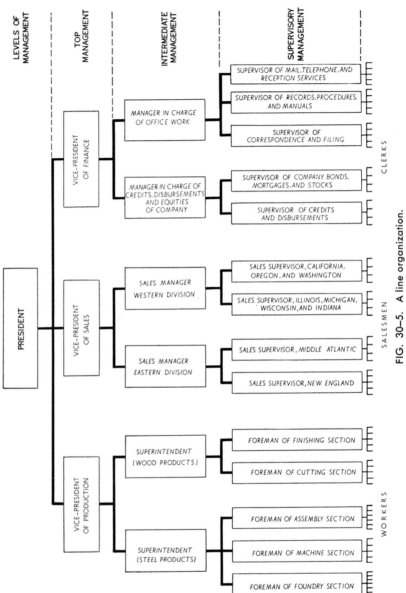

FIG. 30–5. A line organization.

Advantages. The advantages of the line organization include the following: Authority and responsibility are definitely fixed, and the person who has that authority and responsibility is known to all; the structure is very simple and hence readily understood by all personnel; discipline is easily maintained, since each worker and each boss knows what is expected of him and in which areas he is to operate; decisions can be quickly reached; the oneness of the boss who is in complete charge makes for a minimum of delay in decision reaching; and lastly, the line organization offers splendid training opportunities for the development of executive talent. The line officer is charged with getting things executed; he must be a doer; he must get the work accomplished.

Disadvantages. The line organization also has its disadvantages. Perhaps the most outstanding one is that, relatively, specialization of work is not practiced. Particularly is this true at the intermediate and supervisory management levels. Another disadvantage is the difficulty of securing co-ordination. Each lord is master of his own house or his unit of the organization, and the co-ordination between any two line units of the same organizational level is obtained solely by the strong leadership of the man at the top in charge of the several line units. The tendency is for the head of each unit to develop a rather independent unit and to think only of his own unit's activities, without due regard for other necessary functions of the enterprise. In fact, some writers believe that the line organization probably places too much emphasis on the managers. Another disadvantage is the difficulty of forming organizational units; this is particularly true in cases where the unit is not suggested by the procedure or process. Frequently, insufficient opportunity is afforded to modify and to change existing units from the viewpoint of the total organization structure.

THE LINE AND STAFF ORGANIZATION

When staff authority relationships are added to a line organization, the resultant organization is called a line and staff organization. Since this is the type most extensively used, a clear understanding of its authority relationships is essential. In the line and staff organization, line executives have line authority to carry out the activities, but their efforts are qualified by staff executives who have authority to carry out their particular work. Both line and staff executives are considered essential, and all are believed needed to accomplish the work most effectively. That all the managers are essential and needed means that they comprise a winning team of managers with varying degrees and types of authority. In the team effort, all are required. None should be thought of as inferior; for if in fact they are, then either they should be replaced or their area of operation should be eliminated.

The chart of a line and staff organization is shown in Figure 30–6.

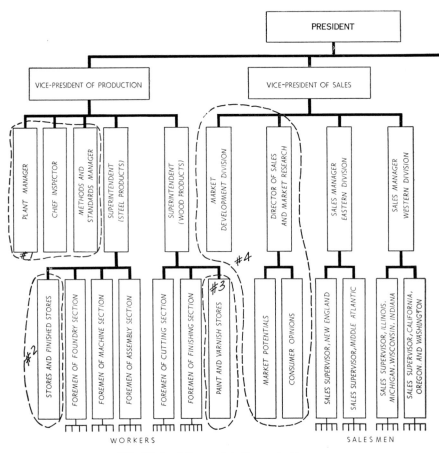

FIG. 30–6. A line and staff organization.

The line part of this organization, basically the same as that shown in Figure 30–5, is represented by the diagram *outside* the areas of the dotted circles, and the areas *inside* the six circles represent staff organizational functions. On the left, under production, for example, the jobs of plant manager, chief inspector, and methods and standards manager constitute staff activities. Likewise, under the vice president in charge of sales, the jobs of market development and sales and market research constitute staff functions. The entire portion of the chart to the right, under personnel, is circled, since personnel is a staff function to the entire organization. Areas enclosed by circles 2 and 3 represent staff functions at lower levels of management. Staff functions can exist at all levels. Note in particular that even though a function is staff, the organization for carrying out that function may be of a line organization type. To illustrate, under the vice president of sales, the directorship of the sales and market research division is a staff activity to the organization

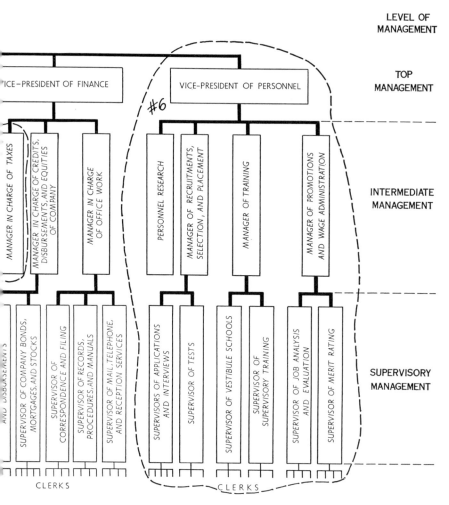

structure as a whole; but the sales and market research division itself is organized as a line organization, with the work of market potentials and consumer opinions under it.

Advantages. The advantages of the line and staff organization include the following: First, the lines of authority are fairly well fixed, good discipline can be attained, decisions can be reached after desirable deliberation, and the principle of specialization can be utilized to the extent of practical limits. Second, co-ordination can be improved because the line officers are supplied with factual data concerning activities both within and outside their own units. Third, flexibility is provided for the organization structure to expand or contract, as conditions warrant. New activities can be added and old ones discarded without seriously affecting the organization structure. Fourth, proper balance among all the activities, line as well as staff, can be maintained. Fifth, more opportunities are afforded to match the desires, capacities, and interests of personnel with the job, since a greater variety of jobs involving different duties, responsibilities, training, and background is required.

Disadvantages. The disadvantages of the line and staff organization center around the relationships existing between the line and staff officers. In the first place, the line officer may tend to ignore the advisory staff officer's counsel, so that the expert information provided is never used. Second, the staff officer may tend to ignore the ideas of the line officer simply because specialization and expertness are supposed to be under the jursidiction of the staff officer. Third, the staff officer may overstep his prescribed staff authority and even attempt to take over line authority which is out of his realm of activity. Fourth, a considerable number of staff officers are not good salesmen, and many staff contributions are not fully used partly because other executives are not convinced of the merits of the staff's work. Fifth, line orders, staff advice, and staff orders may be confused by members of the organization structure, with the result that the *what, when, where*, and *how* of activities are not clearly known to either the managers or the nonmanagement members.

USE OF COMMITTEES

Committees constitute an important part of most organization structures. They can exist at any organizational level, be of short or of long life, and deal with various subjects. Many are delegated line authority, that is, they not only discuss and decide issues but also secure compliance of others with the decision. Such a committee is sometimes called a "plural executive." However, probably most committees have advisory staff authority. Their purpose is to discuss and recommend. In some cases, they simply receive information, classify it, and make it available for others to use.

The committee may be viewed as an important modification or addition to the main type of organization. Just as staff modifies the line to form a line and staff organization, so the committee may also be added to form a line, staff, and committee organization, which is probably the best type of organization yet devised. In this case, the committee element adds an excellent medium to the organizational structure for discussion and educational group meetings. Also, the committee acting in an advisory capacity serves as an excellent addition.

A committee offers several outstanding advantages. First, it permits organization members to take an active part; thus, better co-operation is obtained. Second, it helps to secure co-ordination. Men and women from different departments have the chance to see the organization's needs as a whole; they have a chance to discuss these problems with their fellow supervisors and employees. Third, the committee is an excellent source of collective advice, ideas, and opinions for top managers. Fourth, the committee offers an excellent medium for educational and training purposes.

In contrast, a disadvantage of the use of a committee is that it divides responsibility. There is no single individual fully responsible. Second, the committee is weak in carrying out activities. It lacks decisive action and follow-up. Third, most of a committee's decisions are the result of compromise—a "straddle the fence" variety. Usually, the majority rules; and this might tend to bring prejudice, secret agreements, and bargaining, rather than facts only, into the committee's decisions. Fourth, committee meetings usually require a great deal of the members' time. There appears to be little doubt that a sizable amount of this time is wasted and might better be spent by members on their individual tasks.

QUESTIONS

1. Discuss several ways in which the delegation of authority by an office manager can be developed.
2. For what reasons does an office manager use an organization chart?
3. Explain the meaning of Figure 30–1 in your own words.
4. Point out the difference between the terms in each of the following pairs:
   a) Span of authority and responsibility.
   b) Service staff authority and a line organization.
   c) Organization chart and horizontal authority relationship.
   d) Compulsory staff advice and plural executive.
5. Mr. A is a line executive of Department X. Also in this department is Mr. B, an advisory staff executive reporting to Mr. A. Clearly state the organizational relationship between Mr. A and Mr. B.
6. Is it possible for an enterprise to have a member without (*a*) authority, (*b*) responsibility, or (*c*) authority and responsibility? Explain.
7. Of what importance is span of authority in office organizing? Discuss fully.
8. How can management responsibility be developed in delegatees? Use an example to illustrate your answer.
9. Enumerate and briefly discuss the advantages in a manager using a line and staff organization.
10. The organization chart of the Stevens-Elwood Company shows that Tom Clements, an office employee with twenty-eight years of service in the mail department, has no formal authority; yet, on many occasions, questions requiring decisions are addressed to Tom, and the employees of the mail department follow his suggestions. How do you account for this state of affairs?
11. Relate the advantages and disadvantages in the use of committees in office organization structures.
12. Discuss the meaning and use of control staff authority.

CASE PROBLEMS

Case 30–1.   The Webb Compny

Ernst Simpson, assistant treasurer of the Webb Company, is in charge of the accounting department, employing 18 persons, and the office services department, employing 11 persons. He has a manager for each department and permits the accounting manager to direct his department, but is constantly telling the manager of office services what to do and what decisions to follow. Whenever one of the office service employees has a question, the manager refers the employee to the assistant treasurer. Either the manager does not want to handle the matter, or he has been requested to refer employees to the assistant treasurer.

The assistant treasurer has enough work from his superior to keep him occupied, but he does not seem to find time to handle all of it. Certain matters are poorly done; and others are delayed not for days, but for weeks. Ernst Simpson has been urged to hire more people; but as yet, he has not done so. Apparently, he prefers to struggle along with the same number of employees.

It appears that the employees of accounting and of office services like Ernst Simpson. There has been no grievance by the employees, and the departments appear to be work groups of satisfied persons. On the other hand, no work standards exist within the two departments, so there is no scientific yardstick for determining how efficient a job is being done. If a person is sick or on vacation in office services, the manager fills in on the vacant job, as no one else is acquainted with the work. The storeroom for old filed material is really a mess. There are ample storage cabinets, but it is a time-consuming job to find anything. Microfilming equipment was purchased eight years ago, but has not been used very much lately. The storeroom is kept locked, the key being held by the manager of office services. Anyone in the office having need of an old record can get the key from the manager without any trouble and look for the record he needs.

You have been given the above information by the treasurer of the company, who requests that you try to improve the operations under the assistant treasurer.

Problems:

1. What is the problem here?
2. What actions would you take? Discuss fully.

Case 30–2.   Paul Lawrence Chadwick

Paul Lawrence Chadwick is the head of a staff unit, the office procedures improvement unit; he reports to the office manager. In turn, the office manager reports to the president of the company. Chadwick works hard, has a multitude of ideas, and at times becomes discouraged because of the delay and inactivity on many suggestions for improvement made by his organization unit.

What he believed to be an excellent suggestion, from the viewpoint of both less effort required to do the work and lower cost, was submitted to the office manager in a report some six weeks ago. Since that time, Chadwick has asked the office manager several times what he thinks about the suggestion and receives the answer: "We are looking into it." Chadwick feels, however, that the office manager is just "stalling."

A few days after the last time Chadwick spoke to the office manager, the latter suffered an injury in an automobile accident. It was announced that he would be unable to come to work for at least four weeks; while he was absent, his duties would be taken over by the assistant office manager. Chadwick has little respect for the assistant office manager's abilities. Likewise, the assistant office manager feels that Chadwick is too precise and spends company money on a lot of impractical ideas. The two do not get along too well.

Chadwick believed the suggestion embodied in the last report to the office manager to be so important that, in the company's best interests, delay in its adoption should not be tolerated. Based on past experience, he was convinced the assistant office manager, now in charge, would take no action on it. Accordingly, he explained the new procedure to the supervisor whose department, direct mail, is affected and to a small number of line employees in that department. The new procedure was installed. For the next several weeks, careful records of time expenditures were made by Chadwick, and these were compared with expenditures under the previous procedure. Savings of $23 a day, or approximately $6,000 a year, were indicated through the use of the new procedure. Chadwick wrote the report concerning the installation and the results obtained, and submitted it to the president of the company, with a copy of the report being sent to the "office of the office manager."

Two days later, the office manager returned to his job; and during the course of "welcome back" conversations, the president referred to the report and asked a few questions about it, which the office manager could not answer, explaining he was not familiar with it. Returning to his office, the office manager called in his assistant and inquired about the new process being used in the direct-mail department. The assistant knew nothing about it. The office manager's secretary, overhearing the conversation, located the copy of Chadwick's report to the president and gave it to the office manager.

Problems:

1. What action do you feel is proper for the office manager to take? Why?
2. Do you approve of Mr. Chadwick's action? Justify your answer.
3. What general impression do you gain concerning the organization of this company?

Chapter 31

THE LIVING OFFICE ORGANIZATION

That person is most cultivated who is able to put himself in the place of the greatest number of persons.

—JANE ADDAMS

IN CHAPTER 28, it is stated that "organizing is a dynamic, not a static process." This statement merits elaboration. The effect of change upon organizing and the viewing of organizing as a vibrant, living entity are the chief considerations of this chapter. Organizing should never be looked upon as a routine task of assigning people to divisions of work, granting them authority, and putting organizing on the shelf, assuming that it need not be used again until a problem in organizing arises.

Using organizing effectively requires adequate consideration of current and future needs of the enterprise and shaping the organization to supply these needs best. The astute manager knows that organization is vital in management and can be extremely helpful in his managerial efforts, especially if the organizing is updated and the best possible work groupings, personnel, and relationships are employed in keeping with current demands.

PROBLEM OF OBTAINING GOOD ORGANIZATION STRUCTURE

Too often, an enterprise expands or contracts without any real plan of organization structure. New functions and new personnel are added, and the enterprise just grows; or in contrast, existing functions are combined, peculiar relationships established, and management personnel placed on jobs requiring but a small portion of their capacities.

From the viewpoint of efficient management, the absence of any real plan of organizing usually leads to undesirable conditions, including the following:

1. The functions become disproportionate in their relationship to each other when judged by the relative importance of each function to the objectives of the enterprise.

2. Important functions are neglected, or they are subordinated to other functions; either condition makes it difficult to carry out the requisite activities.

3. New functions of a planning nature which might greatly strengthen the organization are ignored.

4. Capable men are confined to mediocre jobs.

5. Authority relationships become blurred; differences arise over who is supposed to decide what.

6. The necessary co-ordination among the major functions is decreased, since the personnel for each major function tend to stress their individual activity exclusively.

PHILOSOPHY OF TOP MANAGEMENT MEMBERS

When it is all said and done, the organization used, be it the result of recognizing the dynamics of organizing or failure to do so, is influenced greatly by the philosophy of the top management members. Their attitude and thoughts tend to mold the organizational structure used. They cast the die and decide, sometimes arbitrarily, what the form of organization will be and when changes in it will be made. Organizational structure, therefore, reflects top managers' thinking; and over a period of time, the organizational structure mirrors the instrumentality through which top managers wish to operate.

To some degree, top managers can be influenced by their subordinates regarding what changes in the existent structure should be made. But in most cases, suggestions initiated by the subordinates are conditioned by them in order to insure approval by the top managers. The location, timing, and extent of any organizational modification is regulated ultimately by the top managers. So their thinking controls whether the dynamics of organizing are recognized. Especially is this true in the organization of the office primarily because of the relation of the office to the entire organization of the enterprise.

ATTENTION TO CONTINUITY

The development and modification of an organizational structure should be restudied at frequent intervals for possible improvements. In some companies, this task is assigned to one individual within the organization. He works closely with the various management members, discussing possible organizational improvements with the managers who would be affected by such changes, and encouraging them to offer their ideas and participate in developing needed organizational improvements. Having an individual to head up the activity of possible organizational changes helps insure that attention will be given this important work. In some large companies, several leading steel manufacturers, for example, a special organizational unit exists for the purpose of studying and recommending organizational changes and improvements.

The continuity of demand for the products or services of an enterprise is also important. This consideration can be viewed from the standpoint of the flow of work and also from that of the type of work. A steady flow of work resulting from a fairly constant demand usually results in a relatively stable organization structure. Modifications in the structure are likely to be minor and infrequent. The line as well as the staff functions are usually well defined and known. On the other hand, when demand for the products or services is irregular, the predominant idea is usually to meet current requirements; and generally, the organization is of a line type, with relatively few staff functions. It tends to be a "nothing or all" existence.

Under the consideration of type of work, assume that office A handles the same work day in and day out and that office B handles a certain type of work X for a part of a month, work Y for another part of a month, and work Z for still another part of a month. The structural organization of office A will probably differ from that of office B, and the personnel must be attuned to changes periodically as a normal state of affairs. Office A probably will emphasize staff elements. Office B, on the other hand, will tend toward a line type of organization in which most workers can perform several activities with equal skill.

Organizational continuity is also affected by the time element. A structure set up temporarily to accomplish an emergency task might be far different from one set up to exist over a long period of time. Organization structures having little continuity are usually very simple. An office group to handle registrations for a one-day convention might well be organized quite differently than a group organized to handle tax registrations. Or consider the example of a crowd of people organized to put out a fire in the neighborhood. They probably will be organized far differently from the firemen of the local fire department. The crowd of people will probably form a line type of organization, with every member doing something physical to put out the fire. It is unlikely that there would be any staff members. Also, speed of action would be paramount, and this consideration emphasizes a line rather than any other type of organization. At the conclusion of the fire extermination, the group would be dissolved. In contrast, the local fire department probably utilizes a trained staff of experts in the business of fire fighting. Through time, the fire department has developed an efficient, highly coordinated organizational structure. And it is permanent—it is not dismantled after each fire-fighting experience.

NEED FOR ORGANIZATIONAL BALANCE

Normal changes within an organization take place in different areas and to different degrees. This results from current popular interest, research, or personal managerial intent. To illustrate, the records retention unit spurts in size due to a strong swing in managerial thinking to its importance; or systems and procedures develops into a central activity of those concerned with paper work processing, and organizational units within which this type of work is performed are expanded and given greater authority.

The result of these localized changes may tend to make the entire organization unbalanced. In some instances, the strengthened unit needed just that to place it in proper balance with the other organizational units. But frequently, the strengthening does not stop at the point of balance; it continues until a state of unbalance among the units is again present.

Organizing effort should attempt to keep the various units in balance, but the meaning of balance is subject to a great many interpretations. Good organizing will maintain the relative importance of the various functions, and this is an important consideration of organizing. Too frequently, managers continue to improve what is already relatively effective. Bettering the weak areas would be more helpful from the viewpoint of the entire organization. An important part of the problem is not to place all strong managers of the enterprise in one or a few organizational units. Success begets success. Commonly, the strong manager tends to attract trainees with the greatest managerial potential, and the more proficient manager tends to develop good managers under him.

In analyzing an office organization, it may be found that correspondence or billing is grossly overemphasized relative to its importance in view of all the other office activities. Further observation frequently reveals that the past experience and work of the office manager was in the area now seemingly too large or being given too much emphasis. Why is this? Because, as stated in the beginning of this chapter, any organization tends to reflect the thinking and experience of its manager. A man most interested and experienced in correspondence work will tend to have this unit organized and managed well. If he knows very little about office personnel research, this activity may be somewhat neglected and not developed to its required relative importance.

Organizing, to be effective, must represent a balance among the various activities in relation to their real worth and contribution. An office is not all procedures, all filing, or all anything else. It is a proper balance and blending among the many activities believed essential. The effective organizer thinks in these terms and realizes that for superior long-term gains, the office organization must represent a balanced picture of all the office functions.

PROCESS AND MACHINES USED

One of the important influences bringing about changes in an organization is the process and machines used. As pointed out in Chapter 29, the process quite often determines the main components of the organization structure. In the handling of a purchase order, for example, receiving, costing, billing, and mailing may contribute the main components. However, research and concentrated efforts for improvement may evolve a different process for the handling of purchase orders. Information in a different form or time sequence may be adopted to reduce costs. It is also possible that some electronic development or duplicating improvement might revolutionize the old process into one that is different and brand new. This, in turn, would mean organizational changes.

Closely allied with process changes are the machines used. Mechanization may use the identical process, but it may perform the work in such a manner and at such speed that changes in the organizational pattern are necessary. Certainly, when the office work is being accomplished largely by manual means and is changed to one of mechanical processing, organizational modifications are in order. Mechanization may eliminate functions, including hand labor, and in their place cause to be instituted other functions, necessitating different people, at least in the sense of the displaced people being retrained for the new work, and new relationships within the organization being established.

PERSONNEL AND ORGANIZATION DYNAMICS

Since organization is basically a means to get people to work together effectively as a group, it follows that many organizational modifications result from changes in the personnel aspect. These personnel changes come about in three different ways: (1) The manager believes a different organizational arrangement will prove advantageous; (2) the manager recognizes that some personnel have changed and desires to utilize better their possible contributions; or (3) the manager is confronted with the problem of labor turnover—some employees leave, and replacements must be found for them, or the employee requirements of the office change.

Certain types of people tend to work together effectively as a group, while others never seem to reach the level of expected co-operation. The reasons are many; but presumably most important are differences in personalities, capacities, and relationships among the group's members. Various predetermined personnel measurements and devices can be employed to place employees better, but trial-and-error, probationary, or temporary placement approaches are widely used. Nothing, it seems, completely takes the place of actually trying it out and observing what is achieved from this trial. This shuffling of personnel makes for organizational changes and is done in the interests not only of employee social satisfaction, but also for production efficiency.

Most managers recognize the fundamental truth that with time, their employees change. They acquire new knowledge, new skills, new interests, and new attitudes. This is inevitable; in fact, it is promoted by managers in management development programs and many efforts of motivation. But it is perhaps more important that people change because it is a natural evolutionary process which takes place as a person increases in age, participates in more experiences, and reflects on life and its meaning. An office job satisfactory to a young woman of 20 probably will not satisfy her when she reaches 26. She will seek a change, and the alert manager will recognize this and do something about it. Later, at age 35, it could well be that no job in industry will satisfy her, as her interests and desires are now centered on work in connection with her own family. The point here is that no person remains static. Some change more rapidly than others, but change they do. Managers, in their organizing work, should take these personnel changes into account; and this means the organization structure will be dynamic.

Sooner or later, all offices have the problem of employee replacement due to the normal state of affairs of some employees leaving the office or the employee requirements of the office changing as the office work either expands or contracts. A basic need of every office is to supply and to maintain a satisfactory working force. To do this, likely candidates must be located and those best qualified selected and hired. This brings up the important subject areas of recruiting and selecting office employees. These are vital activities in maintaining the living organization, and the next several pages will be devoted to a discussion of them.

RECRUITING

The recruitment of employees is a permanent activity. Increased emphasis is placed upon this work during peak business periods, but the problem of securing the right employees confronts most offices most of the time. There are always separations because of marriage, illness, voluntary leaves, terminations, and death.

Recruiting involves four major aspects: (1) the determining of future needs, (2) the evaluating of the recruiting process for different types of office jobs, (3) the establishing of contacts helpful for referrals of candidates, and (4) the preparing and distributing of appropriate material used to promote recruiting efforts. Knowing the quantity and quality of candidates to seek and when to seek them constitutes the first requirement of effective recuriting. People of the skill, attitude, and interest that the office requires should set the background for recruiting efforts. Following this, attention should be directed to the sources utilized and the contacts established. Many office managers have found that appropirate recruiting literature is definitely helpful in aiding recruiting efforts.

Limited data reveal that the number of applicants hired to the number rejected is in the ratio of 1 to 7, and that about $150 is spent for each office employee hired. These data suggest that recruiting can be improved. What can be done? Probably foremost is the use of more accurate and complete job specifications. When the job requirements are vague, the likelihood of finding a satisfactory candidate is considerably lessened. No available source can supply its maximum recruiting assistance when the information supplied is insufficient and not clearly stated. Another improvement possibility is the avoidance of delay in hiring the likely candidate. In too many cases, a qualified candidate is lost because of a lack of promptness in dealing with the applicant from the time of application to the time the decision to hire or not to hire is rendered. A third area is developing the reputation of the particular office as being a good place to work. The office possessing this valuable public good will commonly has a satisfactory group from which outstanding candidates can be selected.

SOURCES OF OFFICE HELP

Generally speaking, a variety of labor sources is desirable and needed to meet recruitment goals. The "best" source usually must be qualified regarding the type of office job, the geographical location, the prominence of the company, and the skill with which the recruiter uses a particular source. The proper personnel viewpoint is to work with a number of different sources of office help. Better people usually can be selected if there is a group from which to choose.

Among the more common sources are:

1. *Persons recommended by present employees.* This is usually a very good source, but caution must be exercised to avoid favoritism. Some companies post notices on bulletin boards encouraging employees to recommend friends who might be seeking employment.

2. *Former employees.* This group constitutes an excellent source. However, careful screening and selection techniques are required to avoid a "come and go" atmosphere. Frequently, satisfactory part-time employees can be obtained from this source.

3. *New employees.* The person just hired usually knows somebody else who is looking for a job. Satisfactory results are usually obtained if candidates are put through the regular selection channels.

4. *Employment agencies.* It is well to utilize this source. Some are public, others are private. The former charge no fee; the latter do, and the charge commonly is made to the employer. Agencies have broad contacts and experience; they try to supply likely candidates for vacancies.

5. *Schools—including vocational advisory boards.* This is one of the better and larger sources of office employees. Some companies keep in close touch with high schools, business colleges, and universities, and send representatives to talk with students about to graduate. Many

schools have placement offices and will co-operate fully with prospective employers. It is well to develop schools as a source of office help. The candidates usually have formal training but limited business experience.

6. *Institutions for the rehabilitation of handicapped persons.* Frequently, very capable people can be secured from this source.

7. *Voluntary applicants.* It is a good practice always to see people who come in looking for a job. Frequently, this source offers excellent personnel, but it cannot be relied upon as the sole source of help.

8. *Advertising.* Newspaper, radio, and television advertising are effective media for securing a number of candidates. Good coverage is usually obtained; but all respondents will not be fully qualified, and the normal weeding-out process must be used.

SELECTION OF OFFICE HELP

Choice of a candidate is normally based on a comparison between (1) what the job requires for successful execution and (2) what the applicant has to offer. For the most part, the better the balance between these two factors, the better the selection work, and the more likely is the attainment of a satisfactory working force. Under job requirements are such attributes as the amount of formal education, knowledge, experience, and physical considerations. Under what the applicant offers are his fund of knowledge, experience, intelligence, physical attributes, and personality. This matching effort, however, must not be thought of as an exacting operation. On the contrary, it is quite flexible. Job requirements should be used as a guide. Frequently, a satisfactory person does not have the *exact* qualifications desired; but with time and experience, he may well prove satisfactory on the job.

The use of vocational requirements facilitates the selection. For example, the suggested minimum vocational requirements for the job of beginning stenographer might be established at ability to type at a rate of 55 words per minute on straight copy material for a 10-minute period, with five errors or less; to perform shorthand writing at 100 words per minute; to transcribe notes of unfamiliar material at the rate of 35 words per minute for a 10-minute period, and to produce work of mailable quality; to transcribe from a machine, at the rate of one cylinder per hour, cylinders of approximately 10–12 letters, each letter consisting of two to three paragraphs. Progress is being made by various associations in getting office managers to request employees who meet definite vocational standards and in getting schools to train students toward these standards.

TOOLS OF PERSONNEL SELECTION

There are a number of selection tools that assist in deciding which candidate should be placed in what job of an office organization structure.

Discussion here includes the tools of (1) application form, (2) interview, (3) references, (4) physical examination, and (5) tests.

1. *Application form.*   *The application form is a written record providing a means of securing and maintaining the more obvious personnel information, such as identification, education, work history, and activities of the applicant.* It is particularly helpful for selection purposes. Sufficient information should be obtained, but superfluous information should be avoided. All questions asked should serve a definite purpose in evaluating the candidate's possible value to the office.

For the higher-level jobs, it is often quite helpful to ask several questions designed to gain some insight into the candidate's general attitude toward life and his ability to write and to organize material. To illustrate, questions such as the following might be asked: "In narrative form, give us a résumé of your major accomplishments, hopes, and ambition." "Will you tell us about your special qualifications not covered elsewhere in this application?" "What unusual business situations have you encountered, and what did you do about them?"

2. *Interviews.*   One of the basic tools in the selection process is the interview. It provides the opportunity for meeting the applicant and observing his verbal ability, appearance, general personality, and attitude, as well as the chance to "get together and talk it over." The face-to-face meeting with the applicant offers possibilities of information afforded by no other means.

The objectives of the employment interview are to exchange information and to make a favorable impression upon the applicant. Unless these conditions are accomplished, the interview is not wholly satisfactory. The exchange of information is essential to intelligent selection. Winning a favorable impression reflects the interviewer's ability to gain public goodwill by securing a favorable attitude of the applicant toward the office, whether he is hired or not.

To assist interviewing, it is a good practice for the interviewer to have a list of items he wishes to cover. The accuracy and quality standards on previous jobs held by the candidate, the supervisory practices liked, and the grades received in school are illustrative of areas to cover that will make for effective interviewing. Second, rating charts can be used. By this means, a written record of the relative intensities of the important factors is made by the interviewer. A third interviewing aid is oral trade questions. An idea of the candidate's competency is obtained through the use of these questions, which are concerned with names of office machines, office operations, general knowledge of office jobs, and the like. Fourth, an interviewer's guide, designed to help secure essential information, can be used. The interviewer asks the questions on the guide and records the answers given by the applicant as favorable or unfavorable.

Fifth, interviewing practices shown by experience to be effective should be followed. These include:

a) Putting the applicant and yourself at ease.

b) Explaining clearly what the job is—the duties, responsibilities, chances for promotion, working conditions, and so forth. If possible, read or let the candidate read the job description.

c) Using language appropriate to the educational and experience background of the applicant—language that does not reveal your own attitude.

d) Encouraging the applicant to talk by asking questions that begin with *why*, *when*, and *how*. Avoid questions that can be answered by a "Yes" or "No."

e) Interrputing the applicant only when what is being said is irrelevant. Start speaking after the applicant has paused for at least ten seconds.

f) Letting the applicant ask questions.

g) Granting sufficient time for the interview, but not prolonging it to the point of boredom or useless repetition.

h) Keeping your interviews fresh. Periodically change the questions and the sequence in which they are asked.

3. *References.* Managers usually like to obtain information on the applicant from previous employers and responsible persons currently acquainted with him. Reference checking is a helpful means in appraising not only the candidate's co-operation and dependability but also the candidate's probable skill, interests, and abilities. On the other hand, there are many who believe references are frequently unreliable. Members of this school claim inaccurate evaluations are provided; either excessive praise or excessive criticism is supplied.

The value of references depends upon the knowledge and character of the person supplying the reference information. Qualifications include being fully familiar with the demands of the job, knowing the candidate extremely well, supplying information with absolute honesty, and exercising sound evaluating judgment. These qualifications appear to be filled best by professional people and by former employers.

In a great majority of cases, agreement on these points exists:

a) References from former employers are more reliable than those supplied by personal friends of the candidate. Former employers can verify dates of employment, salaries, type and quality of work performed, and attendance record.

b) Telephone reference inquiries produce better results than mail. By telephone, a depth of detail can be acquired, and people given as references are usually more willing to speak frankly than to put the same comments in writing.

c) Reference information should be obtained *before* a full interview. Data can be checked, and selected areas for discussion or further probing can be chosen for the interview.

4. *Physical examination.* The main purpose of the physical examination is to determine the type of work the applicant is physically best suited to perform. It is a selection device and should not be used for seeking out hidden ailments in the applicant.

Results of the physical examination should show one of several situations: (*a*) that the candidate is physically able to do certain types of work; (*b*) that he is fit for limited service only in specific jobs; (*c*) that with certain adjustments and treatments, he will be suited for jobs of a particular sort; or (*d*) that he is physically unfit, and proper corrective action cannot be taken. Physical examinations help to raise the standard of physical fitness, to increase work output, to lower accident rates, to decrease turnover, and to lessen the amount of absenteeism caused by sickness.

5. *Tests. Tests are measurements of personnel aspects secured by scientific methods of observing and recording in certain standard situations.* The measurements are normally qualitative and seek to determine the degree or intensity of the attribute being measured. The qualities or personal characteristics measured are believed to be definitely related to success in performing the work. Tests determine what a candidate can do, but not what he will do. The test score is actually a probability grade. It is not a mark of certainty but an indication of the probability of the candidate's success or failure as determined by his possession of the attributes measured and the importance of these attributes in the work accomplishment.

Several terms in connection with tests should be familiar to the office manager. These include:

a) Validity of test. This refers to the relationship between the test score and accepted or known facts about the attribute measured by the test. To illustrate, the most desirable employees among the present employees should make a high score; the average employees, a lower score; and the least desirable employees, the lowest score.

b) Reliability of test. This deals with the consistency of the test in yielding similar results when given on different occasions. In other words, the same approximate results should always be obtained with the same group and the same test.

c) Standardization of test. When a test has been found, through a process of experimentation, to have both validity and reliability, it is commonly referred to as a standardized test.

d) Norms of test. A series of numbers indicating performance scores of large numbers of persons who have taken the test are called "norms." They serve as guides for comparison of scores.

Testing is a specialized field, and best results are usually obtained when the work is performed by qualified testing experts. Trained personnel, either on a part- or full-time basis, can be engaged.

TYPES OF TESTS

There are on the market today a great number of tests designed to measure the many different attributes considered significant in personnel work. A complete list of these tests is beyond the scope of this book.[1] Some tests are designed to measure the acquired skill and knowledge of the applicant, while others examine his potentialities. For greatest proficiency, most office work necessitates certain skill and personality attributes plus an ability to perform several or all of the following: typing, stenography, arithmetic computations, spelling, correct grammar, and reading comprehension.

The National Business Entrance Tests, sponsored jointly by the National Office Management Association and the United Business Education Association, offer a battery of tests covering machine calculation, stenography, typing, bookkeeping, filing, and business fundamentals. Those who pass these tests are given a card or certificate of proficiency which is evidence of having successfully passed certain standardized clerical tests.

A twelve-hour examination program is utilized for Certified Professional Secretary candidates. The examination, prepared annually, consists of personal adjustments and human relations, economics and business organization, business law, secretarial accounting, stenography, and secretarial procedures. Successful candidates are given a CPS identifying card and are permitted to wear a CPS pin.[2]

Among the many types of single-trait tests, the following are probably of greatest importance in office management: (1) the intelligence test, (2) the clerical test, (3) the personality test, and (4) the interest test. Figure 31–1 shows a comparison of these four types of tests, revealing for each one the contribution, general content, basic implication, names, and main purpose.

CHANGES IN ORGANIZATIONAL RELATIONSHIPS

As mentioned earlier in this chapter, the living office organization is not only brought about by changes in work division and in people of the

---

[1] For an informative work giving voluminous help in locating, identifying, and evaluating tests and books on testing, see Oscar Krisen Buros (ed.), *The Fifth Mental Measurements Yearbook* (Highland Park, N.J.: Gryphon Press, 1959). Also recommended is Herbert Moore, "Experience and Employment Tests," *Studies in Personnel Policy, No. 32* (New York: National Industrial Conference Board, 1941).

[2] For further information on the National Business Entrance Tests, write the National Office Management Association, Willow Grove, Pennsylvania; for information on the Certified Professional Secretary tests, write National Secretaries Association, 222 West Eleventh Street, Kansas City, Missouri.

Name	Contribution	General Content of Test	Basic Implications	Examples of Standard Tests	Main Purpose of Test
Intelligence and Mental Alertness Tests	Indicates one's adequacy in a number of types of work.	Problems on information and of judgment and reasoning. Questions dealing with contrast or comparison. Memory tasks.	What a person has absorbed is a fair indication of what he will or can absorb. Differences in background are not taken into consideration. Little indication of how the indicated ability may be applied.	Army Alpha (Original and Several Revisions) Benge Test of General Knowledge The Henmon-Nelson Test of Mental Ability The O'Rourke General Classification Test Otis Self-Administering Test of Mental Ability The Pressey Senior Classification and Verification Psychological Corporation Scott Company Mental Alertness Test	To make preliminary selection. To gain an insight to the applicant's ability to understand and to manage ideas.
Trade and Clerical Tests	Helps to show the degree of achievement possessed by a candidate for this specific type of work.	Questions appraising vocabulary level. Ability to notice details. Problems in simple calculations and arithmetic reasoning. Competency in performing clerical work.	Candidate having achievement of certain level and above will probably execute the job requirements most effectively.	Benge's Clerical Test Blackstone Stenographic Proficiency Tests Minnesota Vocational Test for Clerical Workers National Business Entrance Tests O'Rourke's Clerical Aptitude Test Psychological Corporation Shellow's Intelligence Test for Stenographers Thurstone Examination in Clerical Work, Form A	To determine applicant's knowledge of a specific trade or profession. To select candidates having at least a certain minimum of relative ability to perform work in a particular field.
Personality Tests	Indicates the presence or absence of traits, or group of traits.	Single item questions which are answered with "Yes" or "No." Single words suggested—applicant names words which he associates with this single word.	Applicant will answer questions honestly. The make-up of the personality is related to the situational demands of a job.	Beckman Revision of Allport A-S Test California Test of Personality Heidbreder's Personal Traits Rating Scale, Form 2 Humm-Wadsworth Temperament Scale Laird's Personal Inventory C-2	To appraise those qualities which are pivotal in a situation and probably will determine the degree of future success of candidate on the job.
Interest Tests	Aims to determine the extent of the candidate's genuine interest in a particular type of work.	Questions to indicate the correct use or identity of machines and devices.	One's latent or developed interest in a certain type of work is closely related to the energy, persistence, and contribution which he gives to that work.	Brainard-Steward Specific Interest Inventory Strong's Vocational Interest Blank, Form A Thurstone Vocational Interest Schedule	To determine the degree of interest which a candidate has for different types of work.

FIG. 31-1. Comparison of various tests on significant factors.

organization, but also by changes in organizational relationships. These latter changes can be quite simple in the case of a small organization. Frequently, many functions are grouped together under one heading, and the total number of headings is usually small. Under such circumstances, there is no need for an elaborate organizational structure. Quite often, the line type of organization is used by a small enterprise. In contrast, when the divisions of functions are numerous, the organization structure may become quite complex, and the relationships are of a relatively high number. The relative importance and the relationship of the various activities necessitate a different pattern from that of a small organization structure of few segments. As an organization expands, the problem of an increasing number of authority relationships is encountered. Organization dynamics bring about this problem.

In addition, when a relatively large number of specialized functions are performed, the organizational structure tends to stress the staff characteristics. Likewise, when specialized functions are scattered throughout the enterprise, it is quite likely that the staff elements will be numerous, with emphasis on the staff components. This makes for organizational relationship changes. Also, if the functions are quite distant and apart, the committee type probably will be extensively used in order to help to co-ordinate the widely separated activities. Here again, organization relationships are affected.

There is an old saying that "authority clusters around the person willing to accept it." The employee of managerial competence, ambition, and desire for authority tends to acquire additional wanted authority. Hence, over a period, authority tends to be increased by such individuals; and as a result, organization relationships change, at first in practice, and ultimately are formally established in keeping with conditions as they have developed.

REORGANIZATION IS COMMON

In the great majority of situations, it is reorganization of an existent organization rather than organization of a new structure that confronts the manager. He must figure out ways to shift certain functions and people from one unit to another unit, to eliminate an entire organizational unit, or to initiate a new one involving new people and new authority relationships. All the changes must be accomplished with minimum friction; in fact, enthusiasm for the new organizational arrangement must be won. The task is frequently made more difficult in that most organizations grow without regard to adequate planning and design.

Work of reorganizing should follow a definite plan. The following five-step program is effective:

1. *Make an inventory of the present organization.* It is absolutely essential to know the precise identity of the organization structure from

which the reorganizing is to be made. Assumptions and guesses in this respect lead to unnecessary trouble and work. The correct name of each organizational unit, the exact work performed, the employees performing what work in each unit, and the line and staff authority relationships existing among all the units should be carefully ascertained and set down in writing.

2. *Write a description for each job.* Although it requires much time and detailed effort, preparing a written description of each job is usually extremely helpful. In no other way will the reorganizer fully realize the exact content of the various work segments and how they are related. Preparing written descriptions also greatly assists in securing clues as to what work might better be placed other than where it is in the present organization.

3. *Analyze current organization, and evaluate proposed changes.* This step is guided mainly by the objectives of the entire organization and the part that each component is expected to contribute to the goal accomplishment. Knowledge of the people available to perform the various tasks is also essential. This can be gained by researching the personnel records and talking with the supervisors or with the employees themselves. Some means of recording information in a logical order should be followed. Data common to all employees should be obtained so that reasonable comparisons can be made.

From all this information, the proposed organization is gradually evolved. Several different ideas, encompassing different work divisions, people, and relationships, are tentatively drawn up. Subsequently, each arrangement is evaluated, noting what appear to be its strong and its weak points, the probable hurdles involved in putting it into force, the effect upon the personnel to be changed, the possibility of acquiring needed new personnel, the training which will be required, and similar considerations. Tentative arrangements should be discussed with various management members and affected personnel to gain their appraisals and exchange reactions regarding the advantages and disadvantages to be incurred and the consensus regarding what should be done. Based on the results of this over-all investigation, the decision is made as to the make-up of the reorganization to be used.

4. *Determine the phases or steps to be taken from the present to the proposed organization.* It may be deemed wise to institute the reorganization at once. In situations where an extremely inefficient or costly organizational structure exists, it may be best to implement the change without delay. However, in many cases, the gradual shifting from the present to the ultimate organization takes place in several phases or steps. Normally, this makes for greater acceptance by the employees, who will go along with a small change but will balk if the modification is too large or believed radical from their viewpoint. Indi-

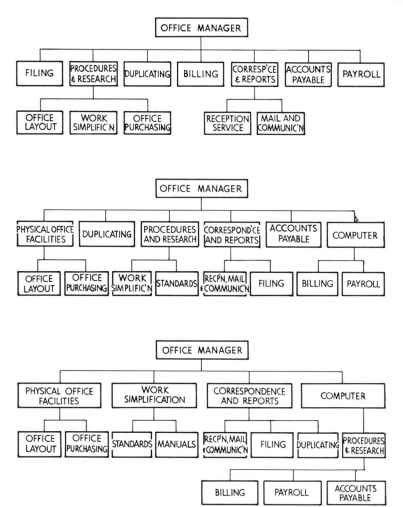

FIG. 31–2. Phase charts are commonly used in reorganizing. The present organization is illustrated by the top chart. The first phase of changes to be made is shown by the middle chart. Subsequently, the organization of the middle chart is changed to that shown by the bottom phase chart.

vidual situations may govern the timing of the change. For example, the retirement or resignation of a key executive may signal the most opportune time to adopt change. However, regardless of the reason, in each instance the plan of what is to be done and by whom should be worked out in advance. To reorganize without adequate predetermination and study usually leads to poor results.

Figure 31–2 illustrates the phases of reorganization that might be followed by a company whose present office organization is like that shown by the top diagram. Note that seven managerial chiefs report to the office manager. It is desired to reduce the number of chiefs reporting directly to the office manager, to install and use a computer, and to consolidate relative functions in order to get a more tightly knit and effective organization structure.

The first phase in this reorganization is shown by the middle illustration of Figure 31–2. Procedures and research has been given the subfunctions of work simplification and the newly created standards section. Under the new unit of physical office facilities is placed office layout and office purchasing. The correspondence and reports unit now includes filing along with reception, mail, and communicative services consolidated into one subunit. The computer unit is added and initially will process data in connection with billing and payroll. Accounts payable remains a separate unit, as does duplicating; the head of each reports directly to the office manager.

The second and final phase consists of transferring the procedures and research unit to the computer section, where it will serve in a staff authority relationship. Work simplification with standards, and a manuals unit under it, report directly to the office manager. Duplicating is transferred and becomes a subunit under correspondence and reports, while accounts payable is placed under the computer organizational unit.

5. *Take necessary reorganization action.* The last step is to put the reorganization into action. Once it is decided what changes to make and a time schedule established, definite action should be taken. To hesitate or display indecisiveness can hamper the entire reorganization. A positive viewpoint, fairness, and pointing out the "reasons why" generally assist in getting good results.

It is important to give the reorganization time to prove itself. Time is required for people to adjust to new assignments, become familiar with new authority relationships, and utilize new formal channels of communication. All managers should be thoroughly indoctrinated in the reorganization, be able to answer questions concerning it, publicize its advantages, and counsel any employee in need of such help. Successful reorganization plans always include these important follow-up features.

Specific attention should be called to the fact that the above list does not include copying the organization of another enterprise in a similar business. Organizing is highly personalized and should be tailor-made for the specific objectives, type of work, and people of a given enterprise. Needs and circumstances vary. Basic guides are available for the construction of an effective organization and should be used in keeping with the basic requirements. The work is similar to the architect designing a building. The best architect does not copy an existing building. He employs basic guides of building and engineering, and creates a structure that meets the specific and personal needs of his client.

CENTRALIZATION AND OFFICE REORGANIZATION

In Chapter 28, it was pointed out that there is currently a trend toward centralization in office work. Adopting such a change necessitates major reorganization in the case of many enterprises. The change should not be made simply because another company is doing so or because several competitors are following such a program. The soundest

CLERICAL FUNCTIONS INVENTORY					
COMPANY:		INFORMATION BY:		DATE:	
WORK GROUP	LOCATION AND DEPARTMENT	NUMBER OF EMPLOYEES		MAJOR WORK PERFORMED	OFFICE MACHINES AND EQUIPMENT USED
		SUPERVISORY	NON-SUPERV'Y		

FIG. 31–3. Recording form to simplify inventory of clerical functions.

approach is to make an objective study within the given enterprise. For this purpose, a four-step program can be followed:

1. Determine the major centers of office work activity.
2. Ascertain the productive efficiency of these centers.
3. Establish the optimum number of major office work centers.
4. Decide on the location of the major office work centers.

Step No. 1 is essentially an inventory showing, by centers, the name, location, number of employees, major work performed, quantities of work, and equipment utilized. From these data, it is possible to identify the areas offering the greatest potential for improvement. The use of a simple form such as that shown in Figure 31–3 is helpful in this recording work.

With the knowledge gained from step No. 1, the key areas of major significance can be selected and subjected to step No. 2, which consists of finding out if any relationship exists between the volume of work processed by a group and the work output per person in that group. In general, a high volume of available work per person is related to high individual productivity. This results partly from the fact that there must be a sufficient work volume to keep an employee busy throughout the work period.

Data such as those in Figure 31–4 show that for a given enterprise, the greater the number of billings processed, the higher the employee productivity or billings processed per employee. Each dot in the figure represents a district office of the company. In the case of two district offices, the number of billings processed is about 420, and the corresponding productivity per employee is 73 and 77, respectively. When the volume of work is higher, at 700 or 750, as in other district offices, the productivity jumps to 97. This suggests gains to be derived by centralizing all billing work; but before this conclusion can be reached, the analyst should conduct similar investigations for other clerical work performed in the district offices, such as credit and collections, and ac-

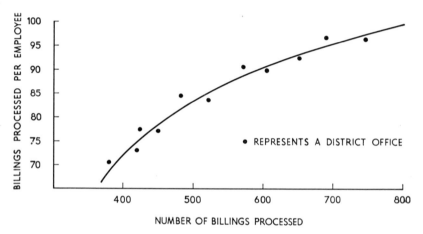

FIG. 31–4. Relationship between average productivity per employee performing billing processing and number of billings processed for each of eleven district offices.

counts receivable, to determine if a similar pattern emerges. From this range of information, the feasibility of consolidation can be demonstrated.

Step No. 3 answers the question: To what degree should the centralization be pursued? Do you collapse office work done in eleven district sales offices to six or three regional office service centers, or some number in between? In some cases, the optimum size can be determined for the data utilized in step No. 2 by noting the volume point at which definite plateauing takes place, that is, employee productivity remains constant regardless of the work volume. Using this optimum work volume as a base, the number of district offices can be determined. But this mathematical answer usually must be qualified by nonmeasurable factors. To illustrate, the answer usually must take into account the influence of considerations such as the potential for using office mechanization, the need of communication between the organizational units, the cost of conversion, employee training required, and the vulnerability and risk involved should the centralized units become incapacitated due to equipment breakdown, strikes, or disaster.

Along with the optimum number of centers is the question of where the consolidated units should be located. This constitutes step No. 4. This task is essentially one to be decided within criteria established by the top managers, the present organization structure, the personnel involved, the availability and cost of labor, and the likely direction of the company's future growth and paper work requirements.

BENEFITS OF GOOD ORGANIZATION

A good organization is well worth the effort required to design, evaluate, and modify it as changing conditions demand. There are numerous benefits derived from good organization, among which it can be stated that good organization:

1. *Enables a manager to multiply himself.* One man can accomplish a limited amount of work; but by means of organizing, he can spread his influence and achieve much more work. A man through good organizing attains greater work accomplishments than is humanly possible working alone.

2. *Prevents needless duplication of work.* The entire work to be done is analyzed and divided with the resultant necessary work components determined. No more and no less work than that made up by these components need be done.

3. *Encourages labor specialization to be practiced.* The dividing of the work, necessary for organizing, is compatible with the use of labor specialization. Special skills and work efficiencies are harnessed by good organization.

4. *Provides a basis for evaluating performance and capabilities of employees.* Good organization helps define specific work to be done, outlines in what areas decisions are to be made, and indicates who is accountable for what work.

5. *Reveals logical personnel advancement possibilities.* The sequence of promotion, which jobs are related, and the relative importance of each are stressed by good organization.

6. *Assists salary and wage administration.* The relative importance and difficulties of different jobs revealed by organization can assist in developing an equitable salary and wage administration. In some cases, jobs of the same organizational level have similar wage ranges.

7. *Expedites formal communication.* Definite channels of relationships among all organizational units are established by organization.

and these channels serve as official means for communication among the organizational members.

8. *Resolves differences among managers concerning identity and coverage of their respective managerial authority.* Organization spells out the relative authority for each management member. The areas in which decisions and their enforcement are authorized are clearly established; they are not left to chance.

9. *Minimizes by-passing established authority relationships.* Who is to report to whom is clearly established in good organization, and every manager knows who is to help him accomplish a definite task.

10. *Increases co-operation and co-ordination of the group's efforts.* Good organization places emphasis upon co-operation with others; and the formal division of work, together with specified authority relationships, fosters co-ordination.

11. *Places activities into manageable units.* The work of each unit can be planned effectively, expanded or contracted as required, and adequately controlled. In addition, the group can be of a size and composition which permit high morale, commonness of purpose, and effective leadership.

12. *Permits an orderly approach to reorganizing.* A known structure exists within which employees can work together effectively. Mistakes in this structure can be brought to light quickly; they need not be perpetuated. Necessary changes can be planned, considering all important aspects of the change; correction by expediency is unnecessary.

QUESTIONS

1. Give two examples to show that organizational continuity is affected by the time element.
2. Comment fully on this statement: "The old adage of keeping an organization in balance is so much academic nonsense. Activities are never in balance; some are always more important than others. Hence, it is perfectly natural and nothing to worry about to have organizations that are not in balance. It is a natural state of affairs."
3. In what ways do you believe the recruiting of office employees can be improved? Are you of the opinion that these improvement means are practical and can be accomplished? Explain.
4. What are some of the undesirable conditions that result from a lack of any real planning for organizational change?
5. Carefully identify each of the following:
    a) Certified Professional Secretary.
    b) Vocational requirements.
    c) "Validity of test."
    d) The living office organization.
6. Are the tools of personnel selection helpful when a company with four different jobs to be filled as a result of organization dynamics has only one applicant? Explain.

7. You are in need of a file clerk, a junior accountant, and a messenger boy. How would you recruit candidates for these office jobs?

8. Are organizational changes brought about by changes in the process and machines used? Elaborate on your answer.

9. A friend of a present employee has been interviewed, tested, and her references checked. She is recommended to the supervisor of Department K–5, who hires her. At the end of a four-week period, it appears she cannot perform the work satisfactorily. Is the personnel selection, supervision, company, or employee at fault? Explain your answer.

10. Stage an interview with an applicant for the job of correspondent. Bring out the important factors that make an interview successful. Summarize your techniques.

11. Explain the meaning of Figure 31–2 in your own words.

12. What are the four major steps to follow in determining by objective study whether to centralize certain office work? Discuss briefly one of these steps.

CASE PROBLEMS

Case 31–1. Express Cartage Company

Some twenty years ago, this company started with one truck and one driver, who is now president of a thriving cartage business. Initially, Mr. Tom Flanagan, nicknamed "Gabby" by all his close friends, had his wife, Angela, prepare all the paper work in connection with the business. As the business grew, he hired Phideas Plummer, then aged 43 years, as a bookkeeper, and soon, there were a junior bookkeeper reporting to Phideas and a sales manager with two salesmen reporting to Mr. Flanagan. A little later, August Wagner served as an assistant to Mr. Flanagan in the operations department, which had grown to six trucks and drivers.

About five years ago, it became apparent that something would have to be done about Phideas Plummer, who, although quite proficient at keeping books, was indeed a poor manager. At this time, Phideas had the title "office manager," with two bookkeepers and a file clerk reporting to him. He seemed to have become very irritable, was curt with the employees, and seldom was able to supply Mr. Flanagan with information requested. Since he had been with the company for fifteen years and knew the business, there was reluctance to let him go. Accordingly, one of the bookkeepers, Mrs. Myrtle Ashenbrenner, aged 48 years, was made the office manager and given two girls, one who would take care of billings and the other to do the filing. Mr. Plummer continued to handle bookkeeping, including accounts receivable, and had one helper.

About six months ago, further changes appeared imperative. Phideas Plummer was getting more cantankerous and just did not seem to know the meaning of co-operation with the other employees. However, his three people, an accounts receivable accountant and two general accountants, voiced no difficulty with him. Myrtle Ashenbrenner, now with the company eleven years, failed to show any aggressiveness in managing the office. She seemed content to run only her unit, consisting of herself, handling credit matters, a billing clerk, and a filing clerk. It was quite obvious that she and Phideas Plummer did not get along, even though there was no evidence of discord between them. The company now had a very competent sales manager, Peter Ferreti, who had a secretary, a file clerk, and three salesmen reporting to him. "Gabby" Flanagan was very well pleased with the work of Mr. Feretti; and in talking over the problem of having a better office manager, they agreed that Miss Eileen Fogarty, currently private secretary to Mr. Flanagan, should be given this job. Miss Fogarty is a very reliable employee; all of her six years with the company have been as Mr. Flanagan's private secretary. Her present age is 29 years. When offered the new job, Miss Fogarty was not too enthusiastic, but stated if it was what Mr. Flanagan wanted, she would accept it.

At that time, the office unit consisted of a telephone switchboard operator, two stenographers who also did filing work, a watchman, and a purchasing clerk who bought items up to $300; over this amount, the purchasing was done by Mr. Flanagan. The operations unit, still headed by August Wagner, had a file clerk and sixteen drivers and trucks.

Mr. Flanagan is today still dissatisfied with the operation of the office. He does not know what to do about it and has asked you for assistance.

Problems:

1. What are your reactions to the changes made in the organization of this company?

2. Draw a chart of the current organization.

3. In your opinion, what are the major problems requiring managerial attention?

4. What recommendations would you give Mr. Flanagan? Substantiate your suggestions.

Case 31-2.   Sharpe Products Company, Inc.

Mr. Brown is the office manager of the Sharpe Products Company, Inc. Over a period of the last seven years, the office force has expanded from 10 to 91 people. The production and the sales activities have expanded tremendously, but the expansion percentagewise of the office force has been greatest. There is not, however—and never has been in the company's history—a formal organization of the office employees.

The president of the company requested that Mr. Brown investigate and study the organization of the office force and improve it, in order that the company could operate more effectively. Accordingly, Mr. Brown held several meetings with his key people and discussed the general problem and challenge. It was decided to distribute questionnaires requesting each employee to supply information including a list of his duties and the name of the person he considered his boss.

The results showed that about 65 per cent of the employees listed Mr. Brown as their boss—the one to whom they brought work for approval and from whom they received instructions. Some 15 per cent listed as their boss four of the oldest employees, those from whom they had learned their particular job when they first started with the company. Many of the returned questionnaires listed quite a few duties that were identical. This would seem to indicate needless duplication, but Mr. Brown interpreted this to mean the use of the same term by different employees to designate different duties.

A list of the total office force includes:

Position	*Number*
Office manager	1
Assistant office manager	1
Chief accountant	1
Credit manager	1
Credit clerks	3
Accountants	20
Order clerks	10
Billing clerks	10
Inventory clerk	1
Typists	21
File clerks	5
Calculating machine operators	4
Duplicating machine operators	2
Receptionist	1
Switchboard operators	2
Mail department	3
Messenger service	2
Stock room clerk	1
Janitors	2
Total	91

Problems:

1. Evaluate the approach taken by Mr. Brown and the possible usage of the organizational information obtained.

2. Based on the data given in this case, what major organizational units do you recommend be established? Justify your answer.

3. For each of these major units (in answer to No. 2, above), enumerate what activities or people you would include.

4. What other activities might logically be added to each of your major organizational units? Do you recommend that they be added? Why?

Chapter 32

HELPFUL PRINCIPLES OF OFFICE ORGANIZING

A strong leader knows that if he develops his associates he will be even stronger.

—JAMES F. LINCOLN

EFFECTIVE ORGANIZING is a challenge to every manager. It cannot be achieved by any mechanistic discipline or technological process. The best approach appears to include knowledge of basic organizing truths plus skill in their application, taking into complete account the individual considerations. Improving organizing practices and maintaining sound organizing concepts are continuous tasks and commonly must be sought amid ever-changing economic and social atmospheres. Fortunately, in these efforts, valuable aid, based on experience and reasoning, is available in the form of principles of organizing.

THE IDEAL ORGANIZATION STRUCTURE

Theoretically, an ideal organization structure can be set up for each enterprise. Such a structure would include all the desirable characteristics of an organization structure, determined by philosophizing as to what the functional relationships and the personnel performing them should be in order to approach perfection.

In actual practice, the ideal organization structure is seldom, if ever, obtained; and there are several reasons why this is true. In the first place, the personal influence of top executives upon the structure of the organization is exceedingly important. Men differ in their beliefs, and not all top executives view an organization structure with identical opinions and convictions. Also, the enterprise may lack the funds required to set up the ideal structure. Certain functions, recognized as important, are not a part of the organization structure simply because top managers cannot see their way clear to finance these activities. In addition, there is a tendency to stay with the old and established form of organization structure rather than to change to a new and untried form. Enterprises tend to build up customary practices, and these traditions tend to maintain an organizational *status quo*. Finally, the ideal organization structure may never be attained because of agreements, bargains, and favors which exist among members of the enterprise. Contracts with certain individuals to perform certain functions, and understandings among members of an immediate family or relationship, may be cited as examples.

ORGANIZATION PRINCIPLES

Although the ideal organization structure can probably never be attained, it is entirely possible to improve most structures. Over a period of time, definite organization principles have been developed. These principles are general truths and should be viewed as common guides to action. They are universal and apply with equal validity to an organization structure set up for the accomplishment of office work or to one set up to achieve any other major objective. Their specific application to office organizing can be particularly helpful to the progressive office manager.

It is well to think in terms of principles instead of isolated instances. This makes for trust and confidence; at the same time, skill in applying knowledge is enhanced. Success in the specific application of any organization principle depends upon the individual circumstances. In certain instances, these principles are merely some of the factors which should be taken into account, along with other factors considered important in the individual case.

CONSIDERATION OF THE OBJECTIVE OF THE ENTERPRISE

The very first principle to be considered is the objective of the enterprise. Answers to the question "What is the aim of the enterprise?" or "What is the enterprise trying to accomplish?" are fundamental considerations in any organizing effort. The objective permeates all activities within an enterprise, and influences their number and the extent to which they are carried out.

It is extremely difficult to judge the effectiveness of an organization structure without an adequate knowledge of the objective of the enterprise. What would be considered efficient for one objective might well be considered very inefficient for another objective. For example, the objective of cleaning the streets in a small town after a heavy snowstorm might require an organization structure which is entirely different from the structure needed when the objective is to distribute samples of products in ten cities throughout the United States. Or consider the organizational differences between two offices, one for a large insurance company using a computer, the other for a small manufacturer of necessity using basically manual office methods. Because the objectives are

different, the type, number of functions, and personnel of the one structure would be entirely different from those of the other.

UTILIZATION OF FUNCTIONS AS ESSENTIAL COMPONENTS

The essential functions of the enterprise should constitute the main
elements of the organization structure. The true relationship of the
functions gives the true organizational setup. The nature of the enterprise determines the main functions; and these, in turn, determine the
essential components upon which the organization structure should be
built.

Furthermore, the functional approach provides continuity. Functions
remain and can grow almost indefinitely; they are not limited in span
of time or in ability, as are individuals. Also, the functional approach
promotes the objective viewpoint in organizational structures and minimizes the subjective influences of the individual.

The grouping-together of similar functions helps to form strong major
groups; the tendency to split activities is minimized. Not only does grouping of like functions with like functions afford great strength to an
organizational structure, but it also provides great flexibility; functions
may be modified, new functions added, and old functions eliminated
easily and simply without disturbing the essential structure of the organization.

In addition, the utilization of functions as the essential organization
components helps to define clearly the various functions and to prevent
uneconomical overlapping and duplicating. Working directly with
functions helps to concentrate attention on them, and clear concepts of
activities tend to be developed.

ESTABLISH REASONABLE ORGANIZATIONAL UNITS

The functional approach assists in dividing the total work along a
logical basis. To form practical organizational units, the various work
divisions must be assembled into effective units from the standpoint
of organizing. In establishing these organizational units, consideration
must be given to many physical factors such as the size of the unit, the
quantity and scope of work, the way it is done, the need for verifying
the work of one unit by another, the extent of continuous flow, and the
permanent nature of the work. The advantages of specialization should
be sought, but job interest of the employee must also be won. In addition, and possibly of greater importance, is consideration for the management member who will take charge of this unit. What are his special
attributes, his shortcomings, ambitions, accomplishments, and training?
If no manager is available, what qualifications will be sought; and is
there a reasonable possibility that such a manager can be hired? Furthermore, adequate thought must be given to evaluating the proposed nonmanagement members of the unit, the capacity and skills required, per-

sonnel associations to be integrated, and the wishes of the contemplated prevailing management member.

In addition, the reasonableness of the organizational unit is affected by the influence of the span of authority. If organizational units of relatively small work scopes are established, there normally is a tendency to use wider spans of authority than if the reverse—units with large work scopes—is adopted. The span should always take into account the preference and managerial ability of the supervisory executive.

DEFINITION OF EACH JOB

To define each job of an organizational structure makes for better organizing. The activities to be performed should be prescribed in complete yet simple language. The duties and the responsibilities should be noted as well as the authority relationship between the job being defined to that of other jobs in the structure. Such work helps the organizer to utilize constructive and creative thought in his efforts and to see more clearly the division of work and the relative organizational position of the person assigned each component work segment.

Organization charts and job descriptions are helpful media in this work, but special attention should be given organization manuals. The format can follow any one of many different patterns; but specific information regarding the title, the organizational unit, responsibility, and authority are usually included. Getting this information down in black and white helps to clarify overlapping operations, eliminate duplications, and assign duties to specific areas. However, when the material for an organization manual is collected and written by each manager in charge of each respective unit, interest is stimulated in better organizing work, and general understanding among executives throughout the structure is gained. Organization manuals are also helpful in training the executive incumbent as well as his successor, and they provide official answers to organization questions for the given enterprise.

CONSIDERATION OF THE HUMAN ELEMENT

The motivating power behind any organizational structure is the personnel of that structure. For a function to be performed, a responsibility to be assumed, and an authority to be exercised, the presence of human beings is required. Therefore, adequate consideration for the human element of any organizational structure is of prime importance.

Psychologically, the fact of individual differences is well established. People differ in their desires, in their capacities, and in their interests.[1]

---

[1] This idea is taken from the excellent discussion of capacities, interests, and opportunities of personnel as developed in *Personnel Management*, by W. D. Scott, R. C. Clothier, and W. R. Spriegel (6th ed.; New York: McGraw-Hill Book Co., Inc., 1961), chap. ii, pp. 12–23.

What one person seeks, another abhors. The capacity of one might be unusual for creative work, while that of another is such that he can think of a new idea only after extended and considerable effort. Likewise, the chief interests of one person might be along the line of mathematical details, while those of another are in broad generalities.

The various functions to be performed also differ so that in any organizational structure, there are many functions to be performed by many different types of persons. This condition is not paradoxical, as might first be expected. Rather, it is extremely fortunate, for it makes it possible to match a person of certain desires, capacities, and interests with the particular function which requires those particular characteristics.

Placing the right person in the right job provides an enormous motivating power within the organizational structure. It makes for over-all harmony within the organization and helps determine whether the person fits into the aims and purposes of the organization and methods of operation. Secondly, it provides for high efficiency among the organization members. A person does his best when he is engaged in a function which satisfies fully his individual desires, capacities, and interests. Thirdly, there is the advantage of a better social order. The employee feels that he is doing the things which he believes are worth while and that he is contributing to society according to his individual ability. In addition, he is engaged in work which places him in an environment which gives him social satisfaction.

In some cases, the entire organizational structure is built around the available personnel, giving minor consideration to the functions. A big advantage in this approach is that all the unique characteristics of all the available personnel are utilized to the very utmost. Good results can be obtained. However, the big disadvantage in such a practice is that the necessary replacements are extremely difficult to make, because it is frequently almost impossible to find a person with the exact characteristics of the person being replaced.

PROVISION OF EFFECTIVE LEADERSHIP

Leadership is always outstanding in the success of any enterprise. The structural relationships of an organization may be very poor; yet, wonders may be accomplished through effective leadership. On the other hand, the relationships may be excellent; yet, little can be achieved if its leadership is poor.

Leadership implies the ability to show others the way to attainment of wanted goals. Managers have excellent opportunities to do this by means of their organizing efforts. For example, the manager can, through his organizing, assist the subordinate in concentrating his efforts on work which not only is in keeping with the enterprise's demands, but also supplies satisfaction and status to the subordinate. Also, by placing subordinates on jobs that challenge the best of their abilities and lending needed encouragement and help to them by means of leadership and example, the strength of the organization is increased, and the manager can accomplish more with less effort and time.

Organizational units can serve as focal points around which employee enthusiasm and accomplishments revolve, provided adequate leadership is utilized, along with effective organization. Leadership can provide the real spirit of an organized group and stimulate the group to peak performance far above what they actually thought could be attained.

UNITY OF COMMAND ATTAINMENT

One of the main purposes of organizing is to secure unity of effort by the group. The different segments of the organization should be put together into a neat mosaic that permits and encourages the total as well as each part to contribute its maximum toward the work to be done.

No one should report to more than one superior, and there should be one superior for every organization member. An attempt to operate under any other set of conditions results in conflicting orders, confusion by the employee, and dissatisfaction by the manager. In addition, the manager faces the problem of proper allocation of his time, giving loyalty to divided interests, and spreading his efforts too thinly.

Violation of the "unity of command" principle is sometimes found in a filing organizational unit where the file clerks receive orders from several superiors and no head of filing exists. Under such conditions, the filing work is usually poorly managed. Papers are misfiled and lost, several of the file clerks do the majority of the work, and the lazy or inefficient ones are given an "out."

DETERMINATION OF CLEARLY DEFINED CHANNELS OF AUTHORITY AND RESPONSIBILITY

In every structure, there is some personnel directive which is manifested through the instructions, orders, and procedures that are transmitted through organization channels. This personnel directive is one of the most important means of obtaining effective group effort, and it can operate efficiently only when clearly defined channels of authority and responsibility are provided within the organizational structure.

Each member of an enterprise not only must know what to do, but must know that his work is looked over to determine if it is being done correctly. Definite channels eliminate the so-called "horizontal gaps" in organization structures, i.e., areas at any given organizational level which are not covered by a channel of authority and responsibility. When horizontal gaps exist, the functions and activities of the personnel in such areas are not adequately synchronized with those of the other parts of the structure, and inefficient overlapping of personnel control activities is usually present.

ESTABLISHMENT OF DEFINITE AUTHORITY AND RESPONSIBILITY

Not only must the channels through which authority and responsibility flow be clearly defined, but also the authority and responsibility themselves must be definite and known to all concerned. Defining the authority assists in gaining the needed co-ordination among the various component efforts, and it enables vertical co-ordination between superior and subordinates throughout the entire organization to be effective.

Defining authority does not mean spelling out every detail of what a manager can and cannot do. It prescribes in what broad areas the manager shall make decisions; and by means of objective identifications, policies, and communication, the manager directs his efforts to specific work. Thus, the manager's initiative, creativity, and enthusiasm are stimulated, not thwarted, by the careful defining of his authority. This makes for effective management.

Responsibility implies an individual trust, a dependence upon an individual to perform an assigned task promptly and efficiently. When one is vested with responsibility, it is up to him and to him alone to see that the job is carried out satisfactorily. Defining responsibility tends to develop the individual and to increase his reliability. When an individual knows exactly the task and the activity for which he is being held fully responsible, he tends to overcome common obstacles and to perform his tasks promptly and thoroughly. Human beings like to measure up to the requirements made of them. In addition, defining responsibility aids in getting work accomplished. When responsibilities are defined, it is known who is responsible for each particular activity; and with this knowledge available, the proper person for a specific function can be seen quickly and directly, without waste of time.

Responsibility should be fixed at a level as low in the organization structure as is consistent with the capability of the personnel at that level to assume responsibility. The lower the level, the greater the benefit to the total organization personnel. Furthermore, benefits of developing future managers of the enterprise, increasing the individual's feeling of worth, and minimizing disciplinary problems can be cited.[2]

ESTABLISHMENT OF CLIMATE FOR DELEGATION OF AUTHORITY

Delegation of authority by a manager is vital because it makes organization meaningful. Failure to delegate means failure to reap the

---

[2] For a thorough discussion of responsibility in organization, see R. C. Davis, *Industrial Organization and Management* (3d ed.; New York: Harper & Bros., 1957), pp. 56–63.

benefits of organizing. Many managers are reluctant to delegate; and frequently, delegation is practiced to a limited degree only. To request a manager to delegate seldom brings about the desired practice. Other steps must be taken.

Establishing a work climate that is free from frustration and fear is probably a cardinal guide to follow in encouraging delegation. Managers must be made to feel that turning over carefully selected assignments to their subordinates is the proper thing to do and that their superiors approve of such action, even when the subordinate does not perform the assignment in the same manner that the manager would and the results are short of the expected accomplishment. The deficiency is charged to the development of managerial skill.

The climate should be one of managers believing in their subordinates, recognizing their competence or lack of it, and willing to take a calculated risk to gain ultimately a better work force. The underlying theme followed is that a manager grows greatest when he builds subordinates the most.

PROVISION FOR COEQUALITY OF AUTHORITY AND RESPONSIBILITY

Another important principle of organizing is that the authority of any manager should be coequal with his responsibility and, vice versa, his responsibility coequal with his authority. The association between authority and responsibility is intimate and arises from accomplishing the same work. As pointed out in Chapter 30, making decisions and enforcing them regarding specific work (authority) also entails the obligation to perform this work (responsibility) by accepting and using the delegated authority.

Authority and responsibility are therefore akin to an object and its image in a mirror. If one exists, the other exists also in a coequal status. Authority commensurate with responsibility is needed before responsibility becomes meaningful; and likewise, responsibility without commensurate authority has dubious managerial value. Effective managers keep this principle of organizing in mind and see to it that for any executive, coequality of authority and responsibility is present.

HOLD THE ORGANIZATIONAL LEVELS TO A MINIMUM

In the interests of having an organization that is closely knit, adaptable to necessary changes, and high in productivity, it is normally advisable to hold the organizational levels to a minimum. What the precise number of levels should be depends mainly on the size of the enterprise and the type of work performed. For most business enterprises, seldom should there be more than five levels beneath the chief executive. To have more encourages "run-arounds."

The number of organizational levels is closely associated with the span of authority followed. Wide spans usually make for few levels, whereas narrow spans normally necessitate a larger number of levels. In the former case, the organizational structure is referred to as a "flat organization"; in the latter, as a "tall organization." Co-ordination vertically is relatively easily obtained in the flat organization; and in contrast, it is more difficult in the tall organization because of the depth created by the organizational levels. On the other hand, and because of the same reasons, co-ordination horizontally is relatively easy within the tall organization, but relatively difficult within the flat organization.

Communication is more effective and direct when few levels of organization are used. This follows because organizational levels tend to distort and to serve as insulators to communication. When communication must penetrate many levels of organization, both the content and the speed of the communication may be altered with each succeeding level pierced. The difficulties exist in communication not only from the top down, but also from the bottom up.

ATTENTION TO CO-ORDINATION OF THE ACTIVITIES

Co-ordinating implies the smooth working-together of the various activities which make up the total effort expended in achieving the prescribed work. Co-ordination can be thought of as aiming toward a perfect meshing or a harmonious adjustment. By means of co-ordination, a manager obtains a smooth synchronization of all necessary activities, each performed at the desired place and time. An illustration of a situation in which co-ordination is paramount is that of a symphony orchestra, where various musical sounds of many instruments, consisting of different tone qualities, pitches, timbres, and quantities, are all coordinated or blended together in such a manner that the end result is smooth, melodious music.

Organizing is intended to provide a vital means for co-ordinating the activities of a group. This integration of efforts, in the opinion of many, is the ultimate deciding factor in organizing. Without order and arrangement, there are quite likely to be disjointed efforts and a hodgepodge of mental and physical toil incompatible with the objectives of the enterprise.

Each member of a group should know not only his own immediate goal but also the common goal of his fellow workers, so that recognition can be made of a common interest and the obligation of mutual service. To reach the peak of co-ordination, each member must accept the basic purpose of the enterprise, understand why this achievement is essential, know his part in these efforts, and be informed of the progress as it is achieved. This implies a self-imposed type of discipline by each member upon himself in order to win status as a true "mutual server."

PROVIDE FLEXIBILITY IN ORGANIZATION

In all organizing work, it is fundamental to remember that no organization remains the same for long. Recognition of this dynamic quality should be taken into account in all organizing, and this necessitates providing flexibility in the organization. Within a given period, products and services are added, others are discontinued, while many others are modified. Likewise, processes change, with resultant change in make-up and relationships of organizational units.

It is in personnel that the most prominent changes will take place. As pointed out in Chapter 31, in the normal course of events, some people will leave the enterprise, and others will join it. Some will request transfers; others, because of new skills or experience acquired, will seek better jobs both within and outside the enterprise. Also, changes in process, mentioned above, contribute to the need for personnel changes. The astute manager realizes that these changes are inevitable and provides some flexibility in his organization to cope with them. Organizations change, some increase, some decrease. None remain completely constant.

APPLICATION OF SIMPLICITY

Simplicity has been defined as "that delightful perfection between too much and too little," and the best all-around organization structures are those which encompass simplicity in their make-up. A complex structure is almost certain to make difficulties for a manager. Likewise, an organization structure that excludes necessary functions is a serious handicap to the success of the enterprise. A good organization structure includes only the necessary functions, no more and no less, and establishes the relationship among the necessary functions in the simplest possible manner.

The known rules of nature are comparatively simple; the natural way to perform a task, to relate one's work to that of another, or to accomplish a common goal, is to do it the simple way; it is against normal business instincts to do anything in a complex and involved manner. The true concept of a particular function—what is to be done, when, and how—is best understood by people when they are informed in simple language and in a direct manner.

Efforts to make an organization structure seem profound by adding unnecessary functions, giving old functions new names, and developing complex relationships between the functions make for confusion. Efficient managers work with things that are simple; they understand them better; and they know that simplicity brings the best results.

It is appropriate to quote from a statement attributed to Sir Henry Deterding of the Shell Oil Company, who said:

There is a master key to success with which no man can fail. Its name is simplicity, simplicity I mean in the sense of reducing to the simplest possible terms every problem that besets us. Almost every man can succeed if only he will simplify everything in his life. That has been my working theory for forty years. As a very young man I stumbled upon this fundamental truth that everything that is complicated is wrong. Simplicity rules everything worth while. Whenever I have met a problem which after taking thought I could not reduce to simplicity, I have left it alone.

If more managers would follow this suggestion, our managerial efforts would certainly improve.

QUESTIONS

1. What is an organization principle, and how can an office manager use it?
2. Discuss the meaning of the following statement: "To assist in gaining the benefits of effective organizing, a manager should establish a climate of delegation of authority."
3. Are you of the opinion that organizing is performed primarily to achieve needed co-ordination of various necessary activities? Why?
4. Is there such a thing as an "ideal" organization? Why?
5. A great deal of importance is attached to the objective in evaluating an organization structure. Why is this?
6. Discuss the organizational principle "Establish reasonable organizational units."
7. Relate an example illustrating the attainment of the unity of command in an organization, and comment briefly on its desirability.
8. When a manager delegates authority to make his organizing effective, is he not increasing the organizational levels which should be held to a minimum? How do you resolve these seeming differences in organization principles?
9. What basic guide or guides in organizing have been violated in each of the following?
   a) Failing to recognize and include certain functions in the organization structure.
   b) Assigning the responsibility for a single function to three people.
   c) Organizing an office exactly like that of another highly successful office.
   d) Excessive "buck passing" when emergency work fails to be completed on time.
10. As business operations become more complex and the paper work arising from them becomes more voluminous, do you feel it practical to feature simplicity in an office organization structure? Explain.
11. What is the meaning of each of the following managerial terms or concepts?
    a) "Flat organization."
    b) Leadership.
    c) "Horizontal gaps" in an organization structure.
    d) Organizational flexibility.
12. Why is the establishment of definite and fixed responsibility important in organizing?

CASE PROBLEMS

Case 32–1.   The Ryan and Harrison Company

A total of 52 employees are classified as office workers in this company. The office manager is in charge of one telephone operator, two mail clerks, four timekeepers, two billing clerks, two duplicating machine operators, and a receptionist. The controller is in charge of 10 accounting clerks, three bookkeepers, a purchasing agent, and three purchasing clerks. The sales manager has a regular force including 10 stenographers and three file clerks. The remaining office workers are dispersed throughout the company and report to the chiefs of their immediate and respective units.

The office manager believes his unit should include the correspondence work, but the president of the company has done nothing about the suggestion. He is not sure that the office manager could handle the work properly, and he does not want to interfere with getting sales correspondence out promptly nor to offend the sales manager. The controller is a very forceful and conscientious man who keeps in close touch with every operation performed in his unit. He insists that all decisions concerning work of his unit be cleared through him. He justifies this practice as an effective means of keeping costs in line. His work load is very heavy, but he has repeatedly turned down the suggestion to appoint an assistant, explaining it would increase office costs too much. It is common for the controller to work until 7:00 o'clock several evenings a week and to come down to the office for a part of Saturday morning. Some of his associates chide him by telling him: "You can win a promotion in an easier way" or "You should work steady during regular working hours." The controller resents these comments, but says nothing in reply. The sales manager, being a very busy man, has only limited time to supervise the stenographers; so he has the secretary to the president, an elderly woman, take charge of the stenographers and file clerks.

There is very much independence between units with little co-operation between them. The stenographers usually will not type any letters unless they pertain to sales. Occasionally, the controller comes into the office manager's department and directs people what to do. The purchasing agent does not co-operate with the office manager, giving as the reason that the office manager has no authority over purchasing. The general atmosphere around the office spells independence. Some of the clerks feel that they are being "picked on" because more work is piled on them, while others just sit around and look busy.

Problems:

1. In your opinion, what are some plausible reasons leading to the present condition of this company's office, that is, what might lead to the formation and existence of this office?

2. From the viewpoint of organizing, evaluate the present office of this company.

3. What action do you feel should be taken to improve the company's office organization?

Case 32–2.   George C. Nance Company

The George C. Nance Company manufactures fractional horsepower electric motors and employs a total of 360 people, of whom 47 are office employees. The active head of the business is George C. Nance, now 63 years old and sole proprietor.

Mr. Nance is not satisfied with the performance of the office of the company. He feels that the present office manager, Mr. Jerome Cleary, aged 37 and with the company for 11 years, lacks decisiveness, shuns responsibility, and neglects some of the six units in his office organizaiton structure by devoting most of his time and interest to several favorite ones.

To correct this situation, Mr. Nance at first thought it best to terminate the employment of Mr. Cleary, but after some consideration believes this would probably be too drastic, even if accomplished on an amiable and mutually agreeable basis. He feels the best solution is to place Mr. Cleary in charge of one office unit along with similar heads of the other office units and have all reporting to him (Mr. Nance).

The personnel manager believes Mr. Nance's suggestion will result in confusion and might cause ill feeling toward the company. He reasons that if Mr. Cleary is demoted, the effect of such a move might be very detrimental to the present office morale, which he judges to be less than average. Also, he questions whether Mr. Cleary will accept the lower-level job.

The sales manager disagrees with Mr. Nance, saying that it would be better to select the most promising man in the office and promote him to the office manager's job. Mr. Cleary's position could be determined later, or possibly his employment terminated as soon as possible.

Mr. Nance countered that in his opinion, there is no qualified candidate for the office manager's job among the present office employees. The vacancy of the office manager's job might stimulate some present employees to prepare themselves for this opening, but Mr. Nance believes that eventually a man from the outside will have to be hired.

Problems:

1. In line with Mr. Nance's suggestion, do you feel that having the heads of the various office units reporting directly to Mr. Nance would probably prove successful? Explain.

2. What significance do you give to the statement by Mr. Nance that there is no qualified candidate for the office manager's job among the present office employees?

3. What action do you feel Mr. Nance should take? Why?

4. Assuming Mr. Nance's suggestion is followed, should Mr. Cleary (a) accept the demotion, try to improve himself, and profit by the experience; or (b) quit the company? Elaborate on your answer.

Part 7

ACTUATING IN OFFICE MANAGEMENT

This last part deals with the fundamental managerial function of actuating. To many, this is of foremost importance in the performance of management. When employees are inspired and are called upon to use their highest attainable skills and capacities in work they are genuinely interested in doing, the task of management is considerably lightened.

Actuating includes the creating and the continuing of the desire by each employee to achieve work goals willingly and enthusiastically. It can be thought of as the ability to get others to do the work you want done because they want to do it.

The following six chapters are devoted to office managerial actuating.

Chapter 33

MOTIVATING OFFICE PERSONNEL

Lack of something to feel important about is almost the greatest tragedy a man may have.

—Dr. Arthur E. Morgan

WITH ALL the developments in office automation, techniques, and new mathematical means for solving managerial problems, it is easy to lose sight of the fact that in the ultimate, management must be accomplished by and through people. In the final analysis, it is people who make or break the management of any office. Experts in management recognize this. They state that a vital activity of management is the motivating of employees. To build men and women is management's greatest role. Materials, equipment, and machines can all be readily replaced; they can even be insured against loss. But capable and loyal human beings cannot be replaced, nor can their loss be adequately insured. Efforts to develop and maintain competent and cooperative human beings must be made and this means that human motives must be understood and actions taken according to that understanding.

BASIC VIEWPOINTS TOWARD LABOR

The Industrial Revolution brought about centralized production activities, transformed skilled workmen who were their own employers into employees of others, separated many employees from the buyers of their products, and widened the gap between the employer and the employee. As a result, the status of the employee and his relationship with his employer underwent significant changes.

At one time, the employee was considered in the same light as a commodity—something to be bought on the open market, and of a fairly uniform quality. Later, the so-called "machinery conception" of labor became prominent; the employee was considered a producing unit and his value measured in terms of the goods produced. After years of struggle and unhappiness, a new concept of employer-employee relationships gradually evolved. It was that an employee is a human being and that his welfare is important; hence, the employer should encourage and supply various welfare services deemed desirable. A paternal attitude toward the employee developed. This represented an improvement over the employee's previous status, but it was not the answer to satisfactory employer-employee relations. Many employees were suspicious of these welfare efforts and resented being the children of a paternalistic policy. Since the period of around 1915–20, the concept that an employee is a human entity and must be treated as such has gained headway. This means that consideration for an employee's psychological make-up and recognition and utilization of his desires, attitudes, interests, and motives are as important as attention to his physical efforts, perhaps even more so.

As thinking along this human-entity line progressed, the basis for a great many current practices developed, including the idea that individuals vary in their personal aptitudes and interests, that different jobs require different abilities, that the emotional make-up of the employee is important, and that the prevailing spirit or feeling of the work force affects its productivity. A "mutuality of interests" between employer and employee is being recognized. This means that both have an interest in the well-being of the enterprise and that the relationship between employer and employee should be a harmonious working-together toward their common objectives, which are compatible over the long-run period of time.

MOTIVATING EMPLOYEES

The question can be asked: "How do you motivate employees?" A logical approach is to find out the wants of the employees and either satisfy these wants in managerial activities or supply reasonable explanations why they cannot be fulfilled. Many studies have been conducted to discover the important wants of employees. The survival or biological needs, sometimes referred to as economic, include the desire for adequate food, clothing, and shelter. What constitutes adequacy in these areas will differ among people, and likewise the degree of motivations to acquire satisfaction of these needs will vary. However, in normal economic times, these survival needs are met; and when they are taken care of, much of the employee's concern is then turned to the satisfaction of emotional and social needs. For example, he wants to know that what he is doing is worth while and has merit, that he is accepted and approved by his fellow men. For most employees, their daily work is expected, at least in part, to supply these needs by providing an opportunity to demonstrate their talent, acquire prestige, and gain recognition.

Studies along this line reveal listings of the psychological and social wants of employees. The wants vary somewhat depending upon the study, but most include the following: job security, opportunity for expression, chance to develop and grow, information about changes that will affect them, equitable pay, personal help when requested, recognition for accomplishments, treatment as human beings, and effective supervision.

Knowing these wants, the next step is to set operations in action in order to satisfy them. Here is where the real skill of motivating enters. Employees' wants are not identical for each group or for each member of a group. Furthermore, the wants do not remain constant; they vary from day to day. And the reaction to the same stimuli may differ widely among employees.

Most people want to do their share—and more. It is the task of the manager to provide a working climate in which this basic desire of an employee is completely fulfilled. From time to time, a person is encountered who wants to "get by" without doing any work, dislikes most fellow employees, has little ethics in his dealings with others, and is against most proposals by people with whom he is associated. Such a person is sick emotionally and mentally. Study shows that in many instances, this is not the way he would like to be; but he got this way owing to his past experiences, his beliefs, or the conditions to which he was exposed. Quite frequently, it is found that this type of person actually wants help. Proper understanding and motivating can straighten him out, but it may take much time and patience.

MOTIVATION BASIS

Our knowledge of motivating is being added to every day; and although a great deal is known about it today, there still remain many unknowns. Agreement is usually voiced with the statement that every employee has a motivation response and this response can be utilized by managers creating opportunities, removing obstacles, providing guidance, and encouraging growth. However, the triggering of the response, or the taking of actions, rests with the employee. In other words, the emphasis is upon self-direction by the employee. Hence, successful motivation usually results when a manager provides the proper climate and permits the employee to act in order to satisfy his own needs.

Figure 33–1 lists some basic concepts to remember in dealing with people. These concepts can be utilized in motivating employees, the application depending upon the particular circumstances in the individual case.

COMMUNICATION

High on the list of what to do to gain effective motivation is communication. Employees want to know what is going on and especially to be informed about achievements, problems, or changes that affect them.

1. People like to help others. Ask for their opinions.
2. People like to be encouraged. Help them see the successful accomplishment of their aims and ambitions.
3. People like good listeners. Let people talk about their accomplishments and disappointments.
4. People like a word of praise whenever merited.
5. People like a choice, if possible. Let a person decide for himself; help him reach conclusions, but do not make decisions for him.
6. People like to avoid embarrassment and being "boxed in a corner." Give a person an "out" and a chance to save face.

FIG. 33–1. In dealing with people, remember these concepts.

The normal tendency is to underrate the importance of communication. An aggressive and sincere communicative effort will do wonders toward achieving a co-operative, confident, and enthusiastic working force. An informed employee is usually a good employee. Employees like to be told firsthand about new policies and why they are being adopted, and they feel that they have a right to know about changes to be made in existing conditions.

Most difficulties of communication can be classified under the headings of either telling too little or assuming complete understanding of communication. Both of these habits tend to detract from our communication effectiveness. Managers should take the initiative and supply full information to employees. Dependence upon "word of mouth," or believing that "everybody knows that—it's common information," leads to incomplete and frequently incorrect information. The employee is eager to know any news in which he is involved. He wants to be informed, not coddled. Any information that will help him do a better job ranks high in his preference.

Tell an employee something you want him to understand, and the chances are twelve to one he will not fully understand you. Why is this? Because many believe if they write or tell a person certain news, they have fulfilled their job of communicating. But to communicate effectively requires definite skills and knowledge. Included among these criteria are the following:

1. *Communication is two-way.* One tells, informs, or requests; the other listens, asks, or interprets. Without listenership, the communication just does not exist. As Thoreau put it: "It takes two to speak the truth—one to speak, the other to hear it." Listening is an art and requires effort. For best results, involve the listener as soon as possible. Asking leading questions such as the following are effective: "How do you feel about . . . ?" "Well, what do you think—will it work?" "Now, what other information can I give you?"

2. *Think before you write or talk.* Some people are so intent on communicating that they start to write or talk before evaluating the situation and organizing their thoughts. As a result, they confuse the reader or listener. Before communicating, it is a good idea to decide: (1) Why do you want to say anything? (2) What do you want to say? (3) What is the objective in saying this? and (4) What do you know about the receiver or listener?

3. *Use effective words—focus words and mutually known words.* Focus words help to spot the key points in a communication. The listener or reader is assisted by phrases such as: "Our goal is to. . . ." or "To summarize, ..." These expressions aid in drawing inferences and value judgments. The use of mutually known words is essential. To describe the wage structure as "lucrative" reduces real communication if the receiver does not know the meaning of the word.

4. *Practice empathy.* Communication is assisted by the sender placing himself in the position of the receiver and judging the message from the receiver's point of view. This guide helps win acceptance by the receiver and emphasizes his interests, goals, and fears by giving the receiver what he wants to hear or read.

5. *Create a follow-up.* The recipient should be given the feeling that he can return with questions or ask clarification on any part he fails to understand. Offering assistance and closing with expressions such as: "Call me if any questions arise," or "Let's get together again next Monday noon and . . . ," are usually effective in this respect.

COMMUNICATION MEDIA

Normally, the formal lines of communication should be employed. These are the same connecting links as "lines of authority," discussed in Chapter 30. Organization shows relationships, and these relationships are made meaningful by exercise of both authority and communication. In fact, authority to put decisions into action necessitates communication. The traditional office grapevine is effective as a dispenser of information. It can never be completely eliminated, people and communication being what they are. The wise manager recognizes this and uses the grapevine as an auxiliary, but is exceedingly careful that accurate, complete, and timely messages are conveyed through the normal channels so that half-truths and incomplete information are not spread by the grapevine.

Many media are available. The selection depends chiefly upon the type of information and the type of employees to be reached. Figure 33–2 suggests the features and the organizational level for six selected media.

SUGGESTION SYSTEMS

A suggestion system is a means by which employees can submit their ideas to a manager and, if these ideas are adopted, receive an award,

Medium	Features	Organizational Level for Which Effective
Conversation	Man-to-man, forthright personal relationship	All organizational levels
Letters	Excellent for statistical data and where permanent record is desired	Top managerial and supervisory levels
Pamphlets and booklets	Suitable for large volume of material	All organizational levels
House organs	Adequate coverage satisfactory for reminders and announcements	All organizational levels
Motion pictures, radio, and television	Dramatize presentation; helpful in training, relating company history, and special achievements	All organizational levels
Speeches	Impressive for special events and celebrations	Top managerial and supervisory levels

FIG. 33–2. Media available for communication purposes.

usually consisting of an amount of cash. Generally, the suggestions concern ways to save time, to reduce waste, to improve quality, or to simplify practices and procedures. A suggestion system can be a strong employee motivator because the employees are given the opportunity to say something, to feel that the company is "their company," to think of constructive ideas, and to contribute to the progress and betterment of the enterprise.

In addition, the economic gains can be quite large. Financial gains are made by the company as well as by the successful suggester. But these gains should not be stressed to the exclusion of the others mentioned. A suggestion system is far more than a mechanism for the buying of useful ideas.

Each and every suggestion should be answered promptly with reasons for decisions reached. Replies can be by individual letters or personal interviews; it is not a good practice to post lists on the bulletin board. Replies to turndowns, i.e., those suggestions receiving no award, must contain the reasons why such action is taken. This practice is recommended because it (1) lets the employee know that his suggestion was evaluated; (2) reveals whether the judging committee understood his idea; (3) helps him to become better informed, inasmuch as he is told why his idea was not worthy of an award; and (4) prompts him to continue to try and stimulates further thinking. The amount of the reward must be worth while and must offer some inducement to the employee. Many companies have found that $5.00 is a minimum figure to use and that maximum awards based on 10 per cent of the savings for the first year are satisfactory.

Suggestion systems have a tendency to become dormant; for this reason, they must be continually promoted. Showmanship, publicity stunts, and promotions can be used to keep the program alive. Devices which have proved successful include the following: attractive suggestion forms; appealing and well-located suggestion boxes bearing the sign "Have you deposited your suggestion here today?"; attention-getting posters; reminders in payroll envelopes; and notices in company papers.

The suggester's identity is unknown to the investigator in some systems. This anonymity is obtained by means of a numbering and coupon arrangement on the suggestion form. The suggester retains a numbered coupon which corresponds to the number of the suggestion. Under this arrangement, impartiality on the part of the investigators is promoted. In contrast, other systems require the suggester's signature, a practice which affords close contact with the suggester.

Suggestion stimulators can be directed to all employees in order to encourage their participation in the suggestion systems. Letters and announcements can be used; or more direct and definite means may be utilized, such as the manager asking: "What can you suggest to save time in the filing department?" Employees then start thinking of ways to improve that department. This practice appears to bring usable results, but it involves a serious disadvantage. A suggestion system is supposed to enable the employee to take advantage of the things he already knows but which have not as yet been used to full advantage; directing his attention to new fields, therefore, might mean a loss of excellent ideas stemming from employee on-the-job knowledge.

MERIT RATING

The typical employee wants the answer to the question: "How am I doing?" If highly successful, he would like to know it; if mediocre or even unsuccessful, he would like to know it, and why. Furthermore, it is motivating to him to know that his employer has an interest in him, is willing to give praise when deserved and to point out his shortcomings when existent, so that he can improve himself and satisfy his superior.

Merit rating, also commonly termed performance rating, should not be compared to the inspecting of a product on an assembly line. It is not an X ray of the employee. It is a two-way understanding between the employee and his supervisor involving the setting of objectives for the employee to develop himself and the means for achieving these objectives. Merit rating can be viewed as an inventory of the most valuable asset of the enterprise—its employees. Such efforts are essential to effective management; they constitute an important tool of managerial actuating and provide information helpful in many ways. Among the important uses of merit rating are:

1. To assist in developing the supervisor's critical evaluation of the employee's worth.

2. To provide a record of the progress of new employees or those in training.

3. To indicate areas where training is needed.

4. To let the employee know what management members think of his performance.

5. To uncover employees of unusual abilities along specific lines.

6. To guide personnel work in promoting, demoting, or transferring an employee.

7. To justify increases in wages within the established job range.

MERIT-RATING PLANS

Merit rating is accomplished by rating the employee on a number of predetermined factors. These factors are considered to be directly associated with, as well as indicative of, the employee's performance on the job. Many different forms of employee ratings have been devised. In each case, however, the factors selected are considered to be applicable to the employee, not to the job.

There are four basic types of merit-rating plans: (1) employee comparison, (2) man-to-man basis, (3) check lists, and (4) charts. The first is an elementary form of ranking in which a comparison of the relative performance of employees is determined. Normally, the employees under a given supervisor or in one department are ranked, from the most satisfactory at the top of the list to the least satisfactory at the bottom of the list. The ranking can be by separate traits or on an over-all basis.

In the man-to-man type, the employee is rated by comparing him to another employee believed to exemplify the highest rating of the particular factor being considered. Sometimes, a rating scale, established by the highest, middle, and lowest exemplary employees, respectively, is used. Thus, on the quality of dependability, for example, employee A is compared with each of the three employees included in the rating scale and is then given a rating it is believed he deserves. The man-to-man basis is not widely used in offices because it is rather complex and time-consuming. Difficulty is encountered in selecting the employees to use in the rating scale, and wide variations in the characteristics of those selected appear common.

Check lists consist of a series of statements or questions dealing with the employee's performance. Frequently, the statements have different values or weights which are unknown to the respondent. Questions which can be answered either "Yes" or "No," or by "It applies to this employee" or "It does not apply to this employee," are used. The following illustrates a portion of a check list:

Item	*Scale Value**
1. He works at a slow but steady pace	5
2. He is usually ahead of his work schedule	3
3. He gets along with fellow employees	8
4. He makes few mistakes in his work	10
5. He asks for considerable time off	7
6. He usually thinks of the company first	4

* Not included in form supplied to rater.

Charts are probably the most common type of merit rating used in an office. This is because they are easy to use, readily understood, and accepted by both the raters and the ratees. The chart type consists of a list of selected traits, each accompanied by a scale indicating different degrees of the trait. The rater indicates on each scale the extent to which the employee displays that respective trait in his work. For guidance to the rater, short descriptions for various degrees are usually provided. Figure 33–3 shows a performance-rating chart.

MERIT-RATING FACTORS

The factors used in merit rating should be carefully selected, although they will vary somewhat with the individual requirements of the office. Only those factors that are necessary to give adequate data about the employee in his particular job should be included. Usually, six to eight factors are sufficient, as the use of too many factors might lead to carelessness in rating, and too few might distort the ratings. Information which is available elsewhere, such as attendance, punctuality, and length-of-service data, should not be included in the merit-rating form.

ADMINISTRATION OF MERIT RATING

Merit ratings are formally made about twice a year. The supervisor normally is charged with the responsibility of rating employees. Sometimes, assistance is given by his superior or by a member of the personnel department; and in some instances, several superiors who are in intimate contact with the employee rate him, in order that more than one judgment of his performance will be available. In most cases, the supervisor knows or should know most about the performance of the employee in his division or unit. Actually, no competent supervisor depends upon a rating form or waits for a given time of the year to appraise his employee. It is a continuous job. Formal and periodic merit rating helps codify results and insures that some orderly appraisal is taking place.

An interview between the employee and the management representative affords an opportunity for a forthright discussion on the employee's performance. Each factor of the merit rating can be discussed in a constructive and factual manner. Recognition of the employee as an indi-

BLUE CROSS - BLUE SHIELD PLANS
CHICAGO

PERFORMANCE RATING

NAME:_____   DATE of RATING:_____

DEPARTMENT:_____   JOB CLASSIFICATION:_____

JOB KNOWLEDGE	How Well Does This Employee Understand The Requirements Of Job To Which Assigned:				
	Thoroughly understands all aspects of job.	More than adequate knowledge of job.	Has sufficient knowledge to do job.	Insufficient knowledge of some phases.	Continually needs instruction.
QUALITY OF WORK	How Accurate, Neat And Complete Is The Work:				
	Consistently neat, accurate and thorough.	Careful worker seldom needs correction.	Work is acceptable.	Occasionally Careless —needs checking.	Inaccurate and careless.
CO-OPERATION	Does This Employee Work Harmoniously And Effectively With Co-Workers And Supervision:				
	Exceptionally willing and successful as a team worker.	Usually tactful and offers to assist others.	Gets along well enough, no problem.	Cooperation must be solicited, seldom volunteers.	Tends to be a troublemaker.
RESPON-SIBILITY	How Does This Employee Accept All The Responsibilities Of The Job:				
	Accepts all responsibilities fully and meets Emergencies.	Conscientiously tries to fulfill job responsibilities.	Accepts but does not seek responsibility.	Does some assigned tasks reluctantly	Indifferent—avoids responsibilities.
INITIA-TIVE	How Well Does This Employee Begin An Assignment Without Direction And Recognize The Best Way Of Doing It:				
	Self starter: makes practical suggestions	Proceeds on assigned work voluntarily and readily accepts suggestions.	Does regular work without prompting.	Relies on others: needs help getting started	Must usually be told exactly what to do.
QUANTITY OF WORK	How Much Satisfactory Work Is Consistently Turned Out By This Employee:				
	Maintains unusually high out-put.	Usually does more than expected.	Does sufficient amount of work.	Inclined to be slow	Inadequate turn-out of work.
DEPEND-ABILITY	How Faithful Is This Employee In Reporting To Work And Staying On The Job:				
	Places company interests ahead of personal conveniences	Punctual and does not waste company time.	Generally on the job as needed.	Some abuses — occasionally needs to be admonished.	Chronic abuses of working schedules.

COMMENTS:_____

_____

_____

Rated By:_____   Discussed With Employee: By_____

Is any action being taken to help this employee improve his performance? ☐ No ☐ Yes—Specify_____

_____

_____ Dept. Manager_____

RB—9-7-59   (See Reverse Side For Instructions in Rating)

Courtesy: Blue Cross–Blue Shield Plans, Chicago

FIG. 33–3. An effective performance-rating chart.

vidual can be increased and employee good will enhanced. The interview can be highly objective, because preplanning and concentration upon specific topics are feasible.

Employee self-appraisal is another helpful technique. When office employees are fully informed in advance of the purpose, operation, and application of merit rating, they make remarkably accurate self-appraisals. There is some tendency, however, for the better employees to underrate themselves, and the problem employees may overrate themselves. Employee self-appraisal helps to give the *how* and *why* of merit rating to the employee. He knows what is expected of him and uncovers areas in which improvements can be made. Self-analysis encourages self-development. Self-appraisals can be recorded on special forms provided for this purpose. They supplement the regular ratings determined by management-designated raters.

Since judgment and subjective factors are so important in merit rating, it is advisable to supply a training program for raters in order to help secure intelligent and well-considered ratings. Training helps to implement the plan properly and constructively. The rater must understand the purpose of the form and what method to follow. Competent rating work is a key area of satisfactory merit rating. Also, it is important to provide retraining periodically, so that new developments in employee-rating work and future plans can be brought to the attention of the raters. A retraining program also aids in reviewing the principles of good rating with each rater before each rating period.

Review by a management panel is highly successful in many companies. Funneling all ratings within an enterprise through one body makes for better control and greater uniformity of ratings. Employees who are qualified for promotions, transfers, training, and salary increases are readily identified. Likewise, those requiring remedial action are identified, and proper measures can be taken.

PRACTICES TO FOLLOW IN MERIT RATING

Many practices could be listed to help insure accurate and useful merit ratings, but the following probably represent the major considerations to be given attention:

1. Top management backing for merit rating is essential to its success.

2. Merit rating should serve to motivate employees, to inventory personnel, and to improve the working force.

3. The rating form should include only those traits that cannot be measured objectively by standard personnel records.

4. Only those traits of greatest importance to an employee's progress should be utilized; usually, eight to ten traits are adequate.

5. To expedite comparisons and the rating work, rate all employees on one trait, then all on the second trait, and so forth.

6. Normally, and in keeping with statistical probability, of the ratings for many on a single trait, a few will be low, a few will be high, and the greatest number, perhaps 60 per cent, will be average.

7. Each trait should be a single one, not compound; should be defined objectively, not subjectively; and should be in terms of work performed on the job.

8. Ratings should be based on observations of definite and concrete actions.

9. Ratings of an employee should be discussed with him in private by the rater.

10. Periodic training and retraining of raters are essential for success of a merit-rating program.

LEADERSHIP

People prefer to be with a successful leader. Being a part of victorious accomplishments, following a man who has demonstrated an ability to get things done, and having firsthand experience in observing successful management in action are in and of themselves highly motivating to an employee. Members of a group receive strong stimuli from effective leadership; and in turn, a strong leader acquires his position, in part, because of his ability to motivate members of his group.

What is leadership? It has been defined in a number of different ways; but for our purposes here, we can consider that leadership implies a threefold meaning:

1. *Skill to direct—to show the way.* A leader possesses the ability to guide people—to point out the proper means for attainment. This leadership characteristic usually means that the leader is out in front leading, not in back pushing. While not directly applicable, the principle can be illustrated by considering a piece of ordinary wrapping twine. When the front end of the twine is directed and guided along desired paths, the rest of the piece of twine will follow. In contrast, when the twine is pushed, it follows no predetermined path and flounders in an aimless direction.

2. *Ability to win co-operation and loyalty.* A leader is able to get people to act jointly and to work toward a common goal. All efforts of the group are knit together and concentrated into one large force toward the attainment of the objective. This unity of operation is accomplished by strong and enthusiastic feelings, so that each member has a deep sense of obligation to the leader.

3. *Courage to carry on until the assigned task is accomplished.* A leader is dauntless and ever confident that the task to be done will be completely accomplished. He has implicit faith in the success of his ac-

tions, and gives a feeling of confidence and positiveness to all associated with him.

People like to be led by a dynamic leader. They like to be led by a person who clearly envisages the goal, who knows how to achieve that goal, and who goes out after it. Effective leadership is an important entity at all levels of management in an organizational structure. It is not confined to top levels alone but is equally important for managerial personnel at lower levels, i.e., for supervisors and group leaders.

EFFECTIVE PERSONNEL MANAGEMENT

The task of motivating employees is the duty of every management member. However, in most managerial discussions, this task is usually considered under personnel management, since this area is concerned primarily with people. The following definition is simple and useful: *Personnel management includes those activities dealing with the procuring and the maintaining of a satisfactory and a satisfied working force.*

Specifically, the goal of personnel management is to assist in this major objective, i.e., to obtain people capable of doing the work, to motivate them favorably, to develop their abilities, and to help them find satisfaction in and be satisfied with their jobs. Personnel management efforts are directed not toward the achievement of one big happy family of employees as such, but toward the achievement of this happy and contented group as an essential in accomplishing the task to be performed. Or, stated in a different way, such efforts are directed toward making an employee's work life happier by making his work more meaningful to him and hence attaining stated objectives more effectively.

The number and the intensity of activities performed to accomplish effective personnel management vary with such things as the size of the office, the general type of office work, the organizational pattern, and the philosophy of the top managers. In a small office of 10 employees, the work of personnel management is probably handled on an informal, highly personal basis by the owner. In contrast, in a large office of 1,000 employees, the activities are probably functionalized and definite programs set up and executed in order to provide for each employee's development and for desirable relationships.

PROMOTIONS, ABSENTEEISM, AND TARDINESS

Promotions afford satisfaction to the average individual in his desire to develop, to advance, and to improve his status. Most companies have the policy of promoting from among their present employees whenever possible. This requires keeping a sharp eye open for the discovery of promotable personnel—those people who demonstrate a desire to advance by qualifying for a better and more responsible job. Quite a few managers, however, feel that some of the vacancies for better jobs should be filled by candidates from outside the enterprise. By this means, it is contended, new ideas, new attitudes, and different methods of operation are brought in which tend to foster an active, healthy condition.

The initiative for promotion work belongs with the manager. Without prodding, the manager should see that worthy people are promoted. The knowledge of whom to advance is gained through records covering each employee's merit, competence, and length of service. Actually, promotion implies two-way action. It calls for action by the managers—to open up avenues along which employees can advance; and it calls for action by employees—to qualify themselves for advancement.

The failure of an employee to report on the job when scheduled to work is one of the difficult personnel problems with which the average office manager must cope. Absenteeism disrupts the smooth flow of work; either the work stops completely, or extra work is forced upon another employee.

There is no single cure for absenteeism, for it is an individual problem and the correction must individually suit the particular case. Records revealing who is absent, how long, how often, and why are helpful.

Among the various motivating means used to reduce absenteeism are pointing out to employees the importance of being on the job, talking with each absentee upon return and thoroughly discussing the cause and explanation offered, checking to see if the right person is on the right job, maintaining a continued health program, allowing a definite number of days off per year, requiring absentees to make up time, and showing some outward thanks and appreciation to those employees who are always on the job.

Bad timekeeping on the part of employees indicates a disrespect for others and a lack of dependability. Tardiness is contagious. When one or two continue to come into the office late, the idea gets in the minds of other employees that such behavior has managerial approval. Being early is as much a habit as being late. The hour at which work starts has little influence on the problem. The tendency to procrastinate must be corrected and the importance of keeping time obligations stressed.

An effective motivating means consists of creating a strong employee interest in promptness. Supervisors should set good examples and always be on time themselves. They should also keep reminding the employees about the importance of being on time. In many instances, the employee simply fails to allow himself sufficient time to get ready for work. Dependence upon hairline transportation connections and failure to allow extra time for travel under bad weather conditions are common causes. The means of correction here are self-evident.

In many offices, a tardy employee is required to report first to the office manager or to the timekeeper, where an explanation is given verbally for the tardiness and a form filled out indicating the reason why.

The idea of going through a "lot of red tape" helps discourage tardiness. The imposition of a penalty, such as making up time lost or doing the least desirable work, proves effective. However, before using such a plan, it should meet the approval of the employees, who should agree to "go along with it." One company uses a unique plan which brings surprisingly good results. An employee's name is selected at random from the payroll list; and promptly at starting time, the employee is called on the telephone. If he answers, indicating presence and promptness on the job, he receives a reward of $20.

EMPLOYEE ECONOMIC SECURITY

Aside from the freedom of choice of work and the opportunities to improve oneself, there are now available various beneficial insurance arrangements whereby the employee is provided some economic security in case of sickness or old age. Also, at the time of his death some assistance is given to his dependents. These arrangements have been brought about through the efforts of companies and employees and the influence of state and federal laws, among which are unemployment insurance regulations, workmen's compensation laws, social security regulations, and fair labor standards regulations. The form, purpose, and content of these various plans vary considerably, and require some special training and experience for complete understanding.

The discussion here will be confined to three arrangements, including:

1. *Hospitalization plans.* These plans are a form of insurance which pays nearly all hospital expenses resulting from all nonoccupational illnesses or accidents suffered by the employee. Premiums are usually paid by the employee, although in some instances the company contributes toward the plan. Under a typical plan, costs might be $7.00 per month for an unmarried employee for semiprivate accommodations. The amount of cost varies with such factors as the number of employees in the plan, their sex and age, and the benefits provided.

2. *Pension plans.* These are orderly processes whereby regular payments are made to one retired from service. Data show that many employees reach retirement age without sufficient means of support. To meet this condition, pension plans have been set up by quite a few companies. These plans make it possible not only to give needed relief and to grant rewards for long service, but also to retire older employees, thus permitting the employment of younger persons as replacements. This helps keep the work force alive and vibrant, and the existence of a retirement pension plan makes for high morale and attracts better employees.

The cost of a pension plan can be paid by either the company or the employees, or both. The amount of retirement pay generally provided is about 50 per cent of the average rate for the five-year period preceding retirement. The trend is toward a reduction in the waiting period for eligibility and the elimination of high age requirements of participants for pensions. Programs under which the employee contributes are also becoming more common. The plan should be based on a sound actuarial basis. It is usually advisable to employ the services of specialists in this field.

3. *Group insurance plans.* Protection for individual employees as members of a group is provided by group insurance plans. Usually, employees are eligible only after a stipulated period of service and in an amount relative to their earnings. The company or the employees may pay the full cost of the plan, or the cost may be assumed jointly. Employees are usually able to secure protection at a cost below that of individually purchased insurance of the same protection. The exact nature of the policy varies with different plans; the basis of all is straight life insurance coverage, but this frequently is supplemented with other benefits.

EMPLOYEES' RECREATIONAL ACTIVITIES

Recreational activities have motivating influence, but they also help provide a balance between work and play. A well-rounded program of recreational activities is an important part of personnel activities because it improves employer-employee relations, increases efficiency, and makes for healthy, satisfied employees.

Such activities may include the following: archery, baseball, softball, basketball, tennis, horseback riding, golf, bowling, horseshoe pitching, swimming, hiking, band, glee club, photography club, and amateur shows.

The participation of management members in recreational activities should consist of a readiness to furnish advice, to offer suggestions, and to lend assistance *upon request.* Managers should not attempt to force inclusion of certain activities or to run the program. Any semblance of paternalism should be avoided.

In guiding the development of the program, the following approach is usually helpful:

1. Measure the adequacy of the activity to find out the total number of employees who can participate.

2. Examine each existing activity to see if it is attracting a capacity number of employees.

3. Investigate public and private recreational facilities to determine how and when they can be used.

4. Find out what is included in programs of other companies.

5. Publicize the existence of the activities so that all employees who can and want to participate may do so.

SUGGESTIONS FOR EFFECTIVE MOTIVATING

Certain general guides which, in many offices, have proved successful in motivating employees will now be given. To some extent, these are a review of what has already been stated; but in the following form, they can prove helpful and convenient.

1. *Believe in yourself and in other people.* Effective motivating starts with a genuine belief both in yourself as a management member and in the people under your direction. A manager must sincerely believe that he can motivate and must want to motivate his employees. Belief in employees means thinking and promoting the idea that they can plan better, exercise authority better, and do their work better, and giving them the opportunity to do so.

2. *Set a good example.* The management member should demonstrate by his actions the kind of effort he would like his employees to exert. Performance on the part of the leader, his attitude, and his work habits tend to set a pattern which employees copy. Important in this consideration is to keep busy—everyone, including the supervisor, should have enough meaningful work to do. Failure to provide ample work results sooner or later in employee dissatisfaction and a lack of justification for the money spent in their employment.

3. *Place employees in proper jobs.* Employees normally will give their best efforts in work they like and feel competent to perform. They need to have assignments they are capable of performing. Finding the field of endeavor best suited for each individual employee's capacity and interest, as well as following up to insure that each member is on the best job for which he is currently adapted, will assist in stimulating the employee's best efforts.

4. *Stress participation.* Rare indeed is the person motivated to unusual achievement without some participation in the planning, discussion, and decision making of the activity in which he is going to take a part. Actually, this is a basis for practicing delegation of authority.[1] An employee wants to say something about conditions that affect him. Employees want to be asked their opinions about factors involving their work. They appreciate an audience. By such means, the employee gains the feeling that his employer has an interest in, and cares about, those working for him. Likewise, the desire "to get ahead"—to advance, to win status and prestige—tends to be satisfied when participation is stressed. In some companies, weekly meetings among members of a department are held in order to bring the employees into the task of operating the department by seeking their counsel.

---

[1] See Chapter 30.

5. *Keep employees informed.*   It is a natural human tendency to want to know what is going on, why this or that operation is important, and what changes are being considered—in short, to be kept informed. This adds to an employee's sense of belonging and of being an integral part of the organizational structure. Employees want to feel they are valued members of the team. Communicating effectively with people is essential in motivating them.

6. *Give adequate, incentive and reward.*   This can and does take many different forms including the amount of wages, the granting of special privileges, the conferring of titles, and the instilling of competition between departments or among employees. To illustrate, the amount of compensation, as well as a proper differential between jobs, is important. Employees want comparable pay for comparable jobs, and salaries that are "in line" with those of other enterprises in the area. They may be less interested in the amount of their own pay than in the relationship of their pay to that of other employees. Individual recognition, awarding of honors, and seniority can be cited as common means of granting special privileges, but these rewards are conferred within the limits of well-publicized policies. Employees can be greatly motivated when the reward offered has significant value to them.

7. *Recognize achievements of employees.*   Most employees want to feel useful; they want their efforts to be appreciated. In short, they want recognition. Credit where credit is due and a sincere expression of satisfaction from the employer for a job well done are effective motivating means. The practice of holding periodic talks in private with each employee is also highly recommended. In this way, the employee is individualized, he is afforded recognition, he can voice his feelings about aspects of his job, and a better employer-employee understanding can be established.

8. *Develop group spirit.*   Motivation is assisted by making employees feel they are a part of the group and are needed on the team. In this respect, various employee recreational activities can be used to good advantage. The group spirit among an interested and participating number of employees is also fostered by giving them certain facts and an objective, then letting them, as a team, come up with a recommended course of action. In one company, the employees are given a profit and loss statement based on the work they performed and are requested to tie this in with the major objectives of the company.

9. *Give information about the job itself.*   To be motivated effectively, each employee must believe his work is wholesome and important. The relationship of his assignment to the entire office and to the aims of the company should be clearly brought out. It is helpful to point out why the particular equipment and machines are supplied so that an attitude

of pride in performing work well and in being a part of the enterprise is developed.

10. *Provide an opportunity for job security.* Almost every employee is concerned about having steady work—not being laid off or losing his job. Security is the main reason for demanding restrictions on the type of work that an employee can perform. Also, adequate financial support for old age or to take care of illness or accidents is an important security want of the employee. Providing this wanted security can have a stimulating effect upon the employee. However, it is necessary to keep him aware of it and to point out that work accomplishments effectively attained are the best means of achieving and maintaining job security.

11. *Employ fear judiciously.* Fear is a negative force; but when properly used, it can serve as a very strong motivator. The apprehension of not wanting certain happenings to take place can cause a person to exert unusually strong efforts in the direction away from the unwanted event.

12. *Exercise strong leadership.* All normal persons are motivated by competent leaders. The typical employee wants a leader who knows what he is doing, can speak authoritatively, never makes promises he cannot keep, builds confidence, and takes prompt disciplinary action whenever necessary.

RESEARCH IN ACTUATING OFFICE EMPLOYEES

Why is the successful actuating of office employees one of the most helpful of all managerial skills? The answer, in part, is because typically the office employee calls upon only a fraction of his full potentiality in performing his job. Managers commonly do not tap the ultimate of what an employee is capable of doing. The main reason is because available motivating tools and their application are inadequate. Much more needs to be known about motivating and how to apply it.

It is hoped that research will supply the answer. Research is a lucrative source of new techniques, new methods, and new information. It seeks to appraise by objective means. It strives to answer such questions as "How well is the job now being done?" "Can it be improved?" and "What will happen if certain changes are made?"

Good research starts with basic factual knowledge about each employee—facts that can be used to increase the employee's satisfaction and to help assure a maximum of work output. In addition, personnel records are necessary in dealing with many outside agencies, particularly those of the state and federal governments.

Success in maintaining helpful personnel records depends chiefly upon the content and number of records used, the accuracy of the recorded data, and the analysis and interpretation of the facts. Available standardized forms will be found helpful, but these should be evaluated in terms of what is essential for the particular program. Among the common personnel records are the following: personnel history of the employee; employee's application form; physical examination findings; results of selection tests; identification record; data on training; merit ratings; seniority ratings; safety record; first-aid record; record of attendance, warnings, and demerits; salary and earnings; and termination.

In addition, a personnel record folder on each employee is very helpful. This folder consists of a collection of all personnel records pertaining to the employee; it gives the complete story on that employee and makes this information available for instant reference. Normally, it contains the records listed above; but in some cases, either more or less records may be retained.

QUESTIONS

1. How important do you feel the actuating of office employees really is? Elaborate on your answer.
2. What is meant by each of the following?
   a) Focus words in communication.
   b) "Machinery concept" of labor.
   c) Employees' recreational activities.
   d) Check lists for merit rating.
3. Contrast the "paternalistic" viewpoint toward employees with that of the "mutuality of interests" viewpoint. In your opinion, which has the greater motivating potential? Why?
4. Six months ago, company XYZ established a suggestion system, which unfortunately has proved to be very ineffective. You are asked to investigate the system and make recommendations for improvements. Describe your approach to a procedure in this assignment.
5. Referring to Figure 33–1, select one concept that in your experience was used very successfully. Relate this experience, emphasizing its importance in dealing with people.
6. Draft a merit-rating chart that to you seems satisfactory for a "general clerk—computer section." Justify your recommended chart.
7. Relate an experience in which you, as an individual or as a member of a group, were motivated in accomplishing a task. Indicate the means of motivation and how successful you believe it was. Do you feel other means of motivation would have been more successful? Why?
8. Name eight merit-rating practices that normally should be kept in mind for most satisfactory results from the viewpoint of both employee and employer.
9. Discuss the need for research in the efforts of office managerial actuating.
10. Are hospitalization, group insurance, and pension plans effective motivating means for employees? Give reasons for your answer.
11. Of the twelve means of motivating employees given in this chapter, which five, in your opinion, are probably the most effective for most cases? Why?
12. Discuss leadership as a motivating force in management.

CASE PROBLEMS

Case 33–1.   Polly Miller

Miss Miller is middle-aged and has been employed by the Des Plaines Company for sixteen years. She is single, and her progress in the company has been somewhat less than average. For some years, she has been receiving the maximum wage for her classification. Her rating is that of an average employee. Miss Miller has a comfortable apartment in the city and lives alone. She is plain-looking and dresses conservatively. She is inclined to be a retiring type socially and primarily associates with the older group of employees, who are in the minority. She is not an outstanding employee; and her supervisor, Marie Duncan, considers Polly Miller something of a problem.

One day, Miss Miller came to Marie Duncan's office and said she would like to talk with her. Miss Duncan asked her to be seated. Without any other approach, Miss Miller said: "The only pay increases I have had in ten years are where the top rate has been raised. Everyone else gets those increases. I think I should get an increase once in a while that isn't due to the top being raised."

MARIE DUNCAN: Well, we can't pay you more than the ceiling rate.

POLLY MILLER: I've got a good attendance record, it seems to me, when I see all the people coming and going as employees of this place. I've stayed right here and have been loyal. But you don't seem to want to recognize that.

MARIE: You're asking for a raise just because you come to work every day? Other employees have good attendance records, too, you know. You are expected to be on the job. That's part of the reason why you are still here. We take into account everything about your work performance and arrive at a pretty good decision as to your worth to the company.

POLLY: That merit rating is just a lot of opinions. I do little extra things around here, and nobody says anything. When a pet employee raises her little finger, she is praised to high heaven. For your information, I happen to know, but I am not going to tell you how I found out, but I happen to know all right, that another girl in one department doesn't do as much as I do, but just 'cause she goes around "yes-ing" everybody she gets credit and praise all the time, and she got a raise. I'm as good as she is.

MARIE: Yes?

POLLY: Yes. It's the truth, and I know it, and so do you. This place needs some changes. A decent person like myself, a good loyal employee, shouldn't have to complain, . . . and . . .

MARIE: You believe that?

POLLY: Of course I believe that; otherwise, I would not tell it to you. I'm honest. Ask any of the girls in my group, and they'll tell you so.

Problems:

1. What is the problem here, as you see it?
2. Evaluate Polly Miller, based on the limited information provided.
3. As Marie Duncan, what would you do? Why?

Case 33–2.   Greenleaf Chemical Company

Miss Allison was hired by the Greenleaf Chemical Company of Kingsport, Louisiana, directly upon her graduation from high school and was placed in the payroll office as a typist. She was intelligent, quick, cheerful, energetic, and had a pleasing personality; however, she looked delicate and was somewhat lacking in self-confidence. The paymaster had asked for a girl who was good at figures, who could type with reasonable speed and accuracy, and who could take shorthand. Miss Allison more than met these qualifications.

There were twenty girls in the paymaster's office, and Miss Allison readily made friends with all of them. She not only adapted herself quickly to the job but also enjoyed the work. She was usually the first to arrive in the morning and was frequently spoken to for her failure to quit work at noon or at night. She became an asset to the department head; and within a year, she had demonstrated to the employment manager that she was in line for promotion. Consequently, when the employment manager received a requisition for a secretary to one of the sales executives, Miss Allison immediately came to his mind. He went to the paymaster and suggested Miss Allison's release for transfer. The paymaster was reluctant to let Miss Allison leave his department because of her efficiency. He at first suggested that he pay her more money; but this was not feasible, since she was now receiving the top rate for her present job classification.

The employment manager called Miss Allison into the office and suggested the change to her. She asked for a few days in which to think it over. After three days, there was no answer from her. She seemed to be very upset and unable to do her work, and apparently was unable to reach a decision.

Problems:

1. In your opinion, what are the relative responsibilities of the paymaster and the employment manager in respect to the promotion of Miss Allison? Explain.

2. Evaluate the attitude and action of the paymaster.

3. How do you explain the behavior of Miss Allison after the change was suggested to her? Discuss.

4. What action do you recommend the employment manager take? Why?

Chapter 34

OFFICE SUPERVISION

A leader has two characteristics. First, he is going somewhere. Second, he is able to persuade other people to go with him.

—W. H. Cowley

A KEY figure in the managerial work of actuating is the supervisor. Almost every plan, policy, and decision originated at the top of the organization structure must filter down through the supervisory level. Because of his strategic location both to influence and to implement the many actuating techniques, the supervisor is extremely influential in motivating employees, in training them, in promoting safety, and in building teams which carry out specific duties.

Actually, many of the problems of management are reduced to relatively simple tasks if the supervisors are able to get complete and enthusiastic co-operation from all employees. The accomplishment of satisfactory office production and the establishment of a favorable work climate depend in large measure upon the quality of office supervision. The supervisor is charged with seeing that the work in his unit is performed within a reasonable time and at a reasonable cost. Many of the problems and hurdles interfering with getting the office work accomplished involve questions of supervision.

THE SUPERVISOR'S STATUS

The supervisor represents the focal point about which the top managers' wishes are distributed and the operative employees' desires are concentrated. He is the point of contact between management members and nonmanagement members. To many employees, the supervisor represents management.

Usually, a supervisor is thought of as being below the executive level. The supervisor's work is similar to that of the executive; but the scope of the work, the matters on which decisions must be made, and the general over-all executive work are not as broad in the case of the supervisor as in the case of the executive. For convenience, a "supervisor" can be defined as *a management member working at an organizational level where*

647

personal oversight of tasks assigned to small groups is assumed in order to assure satisfactory performance.

DUTIES OF THE SUPERVISOR

The supervisor's job is to direct the activities within his group in keeping with top management policies and directives, and to develop the employees under him. Fundamentally, this resolves into the ability to get work performed properly by others. This is the heart of supervisory success. A person who insists upon doing everything himself never makes a satisfactory supervisor. Many failures in supervision are in getting things done through people. It is not always the employee's fault, although this is the common explanation.

The precise duties of a supervisor differ from one job to another; but in general, there are certain universal duties carried out by a supervisor. Probably foremost is that dealing with subordinates. The supervisor is expected to utilize his employees' capacities and interests effectively. He assigns employees definite work, points out certain goals, and gets them to want to perform accurately and do a satisfactory volume of work. Various means can be used by the supervisor, depending mainly upon the type of employee, the work situation, and the kind of office work.

Most supervisors are called upon to review and evaluate the work performance of their employees, to answer questions concerning the methods in action to accomplish the work, and to instruct and give direction and orders in achieving the work. These duties can be grouped and identified as performing technical matters. The complexity of these technical elements varies considerably among supervisory jobs. Normally, supervisors of unskilled or highly routine work require the least technical competence, while those in charge of highly skilled or professional work require the most.

The supervisor's manner of dealing with subordinates and in performing the technical considerations of his job give rise to the supervisor's duty of utilizing effective human relations. Strictly speaking, this is not in addition to but rather an integral part of dealing with subordinates and performing technical matters. The practice of human relations is not performed in isolation by the supervisor but is integrated with his choice of whom to assign the work, what motivating forces are to be used, and how best to explain technical situations about the work. The supervisor's duty is to create employee interest in the objectives of his office unit, practice friendliness and fairness, give clear instructions, keep the employee informed of new developments, and express genuine interest in the employee's welfare.

In addition, many supervisors devote a sizable portion of their time to improving work methods and training employees. The extent of these activities will depend upon the individual situation. Where highly developed staff units in these areas exist, the need may be relatively small; but even in such cases, at least a modicum of method improving and training are a part of the supervisor's job.

THE WORK OF THE SUPERVISOR

It is possible to classify the work of the supervisor in a variety of ways. Since the supervisor is a management member, the following outline appears logical and helpful.

Under planning, the supervisor has such activities as:

1. Participating in the formulation of establishing objectives for his unit.
2. Understanding and knowing the work to be done.
3. Knowing and interpreting company policies to the employee.
4. Keeping up with new developments.

Controlling encompasses the following work by the supervisor:

1. Following stated practices and procedures.
2. Evaluating work output in terms of cost.
3. Checking accuracy and quantity of work.
4. Minimizing peak work loads.

Organizing efforts by the supervisor include:

1. Delegating work to others.
2. Allocating the work among members of the unit.
3. Placing similar work in the same unit.
4. Establishing proper authority relationships among members of a unit.

The supervisor's managerial actuating efforts deal with:

1. Informing employees of changes.
2. Disciplining employees.
3. Developing understudies.
4. Securing teamwork and harmony among employees.
5. Increasing the value of employees.

NEEDS OF THE SUPERVISOR

To perform his work effectively, the supervisor must have certain knowledge and must be able to do skillfully certain activities. Knowledge requirements of the supervisor vary from one office to another, but the ability to perform certain activities skillfully is fairly constant regardless of the office and its type of work.

The basic knowledge needs are:[1]

---

[1] The five points have been adapted from U.S. Civil Service Commission, "Supervision Improvement Program," *A Program for Supervisors in the Federal Service* (Washington, D.C., August, 1944), p. 2.

1. *Knowledge of the work.*   Knowledge of materials, office forms, equipment, routines, and the manner in which results are used are included in this need. Much of this knowledge might be acquired while one is serving in a nonsupervisory capacity. The supervisor should know enough about the detail work that is done to provide the necessary leadership to those performing the tasks and to plan and control their work so that orderly and reasonable rates of accomplishment are realized.

2. *Knowledge of responsibilities.*   This includes comprehension of the company's policies, rules, and regulations; of the extent of the supervisor's authority and responsibility; and of matters on which he can make final decisions. An acquaintance with basic information about organization, management, collective bargaining, communication, budgeting, and any area of direct or indirect concern in the particular supervisory job appears to be a minimum requirement.

Basic needs concerning what the supervisor must be able to do are:

1. *Skill in instructing.*   Whether a supervisor gives specific instructions on a particular task or makes assignments in fairly broad terms, it is necessary that he pass along his knowledge to others. This, in turn, calls for skill in instructing and is a prime means for making supervision more effective. Generally, an employee is more satisfied, has greater interest, and will be more industrious when informed clearly what work is wanted and how it is to be performed. This means that the supervisor should have skill in instructing, so that a well-trained work force is available.

2. *Skill in improving methods.*   Better utilization of materials, machines, and manpower is the constant aim of progressive managers. Some methods of performing work are inherited, others are hastily thrown together, while still others are copied from similar operations. All can be improved. Skill in analyzing, supplemented by ingenuity, usually results in improved ways of performing work.

3. *Skill in working with people.*   This sometimes suffers as a result of the pressure and volume of day-to-day work. Working with and getting along with people are vital to the supervisor. This emphasizes the important areas of understanding the behavior and attitudes of individual employees and of recognizing basic human motivations.

RELATIONSHIPS WITH OTHERS IN ORGANIZATION

The destiny of a supervisor is controlled largely by other people. Almost everything he achieves comes as a result of their approval. Good relationships with others in the organization are therefore paramount for the supervisor. For convenience of discussion, these relationships can be viewed as those dealing with organization members (1) above the supervisor and (2) below the supervisor.

The supervisor carries out the directives of his superiors; he is expected to implement a specific portion of a plan at the operative level. To do this, the supervisor receives instructions and specialized assistance from various staff members, attends indoctrination meetings, and communicates with his superiors. In these relationships, the astute supervisor discovers that certain practices assist him appreciably.

First, and above all else, the supervisor must believe in the essentiality of the work he is performing. For the office supervisor, this means that he must be convinced that the office is a vital part of the enterprise and that his efforts to help manage the office work are fundamental to the success of the enterprise. He should reveal this belief by viewing enthusiastically his opportunity to contribute to the success of the office.

Appeals to top and middle managers should focus upon those areas in which they have greatest interest. Normally, these include improved service, lower costs of operation, and increased net income. The office supervisor who shows how his unit will help achieve these goals will capture the attention and support of his superiors. Actually, with some concentrated thinking, it is not difficult to do this, but some showmanship should be used in presenting the idea. For example, for a project lowering the costs of operation, the mere statement, "The savings to be realized are $12,000," is not nearly as effective as "The savings to be realized are greater than the net income realized from increasing our sales $125,000." Both statements mean the same thing, but the second one is far more effective to top-level managers.

It should also be recognized that there is a certain amount of human resistance to almost anything new. Many people favor a *status quo* policy —a sort of "do not disturb things, let them be as they are" attitude. Especially is this true if there are no complaints and things are running quite smoothly. The feeling is: "Why take a chance? Let well enough alone." Being human, some members of top or middle management have this complacent attitude. The possibility of this condition's existing in any particular case should be realized and taken into account by the office supervisor.

Finally, the supervisor should conduct himself so that he gains recognition as a member of management. Too frequently, such recognition is lip service only. Office supervisors are considered management members by decree alone. Nothing tangible is done to make supervisors a part of management or to make them feel that they are. A recognition of certain factors by top management members is necessary. These include written statements outlining the supervisor's authority and responsibility, adequate compensation, and direct two-way flow of management information. These activities, along with other important ones and the tools for achieving them, are shown in graphic form in Figure 34–1.

With reference to the second category of relationships—those with organization members below the supervisor—a number of considerations can be stated. Much of the success of a supervisor depends upon his abil-

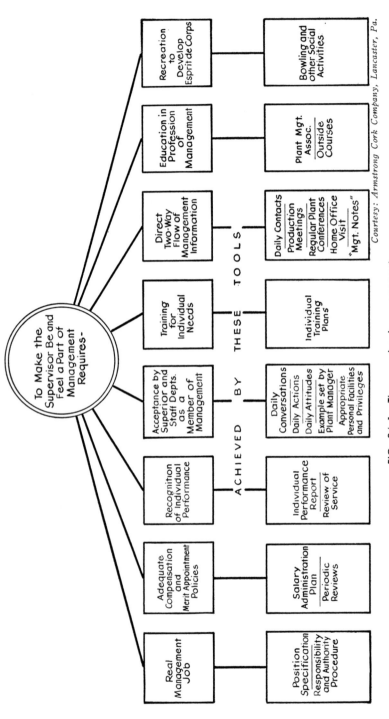

FIG. 34-1. The supervisor in management.

Courtesy: Armstrong Cork Company, Lancaster, Pa.

ity to develop and maintain good relationships with his work group because, as a manager, he accomplishes the work by means of this group's efforts.

Of prime importance in relationships with members of his group, a supervisor should:

1. *Judge members of his group by their good qualities.* Work is achieved by positive attitudes, not by stressing lack of abilities and skills.

2. *Make every personal contact helpful and constructive.* Take the viewpoint that you are trying to assist every member of your group achieve the ultimate of his potential.

3. *Get your group members to participate in your plans.* Modify plans to strengthen them and to uncover and eliminate objections; and adopt the plan that will achieve the predetermined goal most effectively and serve the interests and desires of the group to a maximum.

4. *Eliminate opposition of interests among your group.* Find out common motives and areas of identical purpose. These should be emphasized in supervisory work. Strive toward group unity and effective teamwork.

5. *Give instructions clearly.* Be certain the basic idea is identified and transferred to the recipient of the instruction. Do not take anything for granted. Provide sufficient details.

Figure 34–2 shows a daily check list to rate a supervisor in his relationships with his work group.

	Yes	*No*
1. Do I impress people as knowing my job?	_____	_____
2. Do I plan my work so that each member of my group is fully occupied?	_____	_____
3. Do I follow the rules that I require of my members?	_____	_____
4. Do I have time to talk over with my members problems that are bothering them?	_____	_____
5. Do I have control of myself before I discipline any member of my group?	_____	_____
6. Do I maintain recognized quality standards?	_____	_____
7. Do I insist that each member meet reasonable work outputs?	_____	_____
8. Do I see that each member keeps his working place in an orderly condition?	_____	_____
9. Do I make certain that satisfactory working conditions are maintained?	_____	_____
10. Do I treat each member of my group as I would like to be treated?	_____	_____

FIG. 34–2. Daily check list for supervisor's self-appraisal.

THE SUPERVISOR AND PLANNING

Effective supervision requires thorough planning. The successful supervisor has found that planning enables him to gain his goal with a minimum of effort. Planning helps the supervisor to maintain the proper balance in his work; major objectives are given the major portion of his time and effort. Also, planning makes for orderliness in supervision; actions are thought through. Likewise, areas of nonaction are predetermined. The supervisor knows what he is going to do and when he is going to do it.

Failure of the supervisor to plan his work results in inefficiencies and makes the job of supervision more difficult. Frequently, the lack of planning results in a failure to meet expectancies or to anticipate and to prevent supervisory problems before they occur. Other indications of lack of planning are tardiness in getting work accomplished, excessive costs, not enough time to finish the work, low morale, lack of direction to the group, waste of material, loss of employees' time, and an absence of over-all co-ordinated effort.

Adequate planning will help disclose to the supervisor the proper time for the presentation of an idea or program to his superiors or to his subordinates. Logically, this is when they are in a receptive mood or are puzzled with a problem for which the idea or program is a solution. Timing, however, is very important; and in many cases, it is wise to draw up an entire plan, *file it away*, and let it stay filed away until the most opportune time arrives.

When this time arrives, the best technique is to submit the plan, request approval or acceptance, and give reasons why it should be followed. This approach gives the initiative to the supervisor, and the advantage commonly lies with the one having the initiative. An army with unrivaled offensive power is usually the victor; a basketball team with a terrific offense is extremely difficult to defeat. Games are usually not won by the team which cannot score.

THE SUPERVISOR AND CONTROLLING

Controlling of the supervisor's efforts is needed to assure that a proper balance is maintained among the various facets of the supervisory work. An equitable appraisal of all the integrated parts must be made and compared with established levels of satisfactory performance.

Data on important factors such as cost, quantity of work achieved, quality of work, number of grievances, number tardy, number absent, and labor turnover rates are illustrative. Trends in these data are significant. Also, changes in some factors may help predict future changes in others—frequently before either the difficulty or the favorable accomplishment is revealed by standard operating reports.

Adequate controlling can also give an awareness to a supervisor of the need for effective utilization of his time. Mastery of fundamental supervisory knowledge and skills is insufficient; wise use of time on the job is also required. Some office supervisors complain about lack of time to do all that is expected of them; but the president of each of the respective companies has no more time, yet accomplishes much more. Why is this? In part, because of better time utilization.

Successful supervisors concentrate on essentials—the really important tasks. They perform key tasks only and do not let themselves get involved in endless details. Unnecessary work is quickly identified as such and abolished.

The common office slogan "Do it now" can be overdone, but it has virtue in that it seeks to eliminate the practice of delay. For most supervisors, the completion of a task once it is started makes for efficient time utilization. Tasks not quite finished are the vexation of many supervisors. Staying with a job until it is finished and not giving in to interruptions are key habits to be followed.

The budgeting of one's time is also a timesaver. The time-minded supervisor decides what tasks he has to perform, estimates the time for each, and schedules these time periods through his workday. This approach helps utilize time more effectively and establishes goals that are achieved during the day, thus providing a sense of satisfaction.

The last suggestion is to acquire speed in reading and become more selective in what is read. Few adults receive reading training beyond the elementary school level. Many people read at this pace, which is a serious detriment to their efficiency in time utilization. Data based on accelerated reading courses indicate an average increase of about 75 per cent in the reading efficiency of their members. When such increases can be achieved, the supervisor can utilize his time more effectively.

THE SUPERVISOR AND ORGANIZING

In a relatively small enterprise, the manager, who in many cases is also the owner, maintains close supervisory relations with each employee. He is in a position to exert a real influence on the employee's development to meet job requirements, and to keep him informed about changes and progress of the business. But with growth of the company and the resultant spreading of the gap between top management and nonmanagement members, it is generally agreed that supervisors must narrow the gap and conduct many of the needed managerial relations with employees.

The size and complexity of the enterprise, as well as the viewpoint toward employees, tend to modify the supervisor's organizational status and his authority. Unfortunately, in many offices, it is not clear what the office supervisor is expected to do. The former concept of the supervisor "running his unit," with complete authority to hire, fire, change work sequence, make improvements, and handle operations in any way believed satisfactory, has changed considerably in many offices. This lack of a clear-cut understanding is due to the very nature of the job—the fact that the work of supervision is so varied, the scope so large, and the activities involved so numerous. However, the transition can be said to have been brought about by the use of staff members to assist and to render advice to the supervisor in carrying out his work. In some cases, it is believed that the work of office supervising has become so complex that expert help to the supervisor is an absolute necessity. In contrast, others are of the opinion that staff helpers usurp authority and take over activities which constitute the fundamental duties of the supervisor. For example, in many offices, the supervisor does not interview and select new employees, but he does have a voice in the final hiring.

SELECTION OF OFFICE SUPERVISORS

Effective supervision can be said to start with the methods used for supervisory selection. From what has already been discussed, it follows that a supervisor's qualifications are different from those of an operative employee. The employee having the longest service, the highest production volume, or the longest no-tardiness and no-absenteeism record is not necessarily the best selection for a supervisory job. Much of the work the supervisor is called upon to perform differs from that of the operative employee.

The first step in the selection of office supervision is to determine the background and characteristics needed for the supervisory jobs. Such information can be used to set the minimum employment qualifications and standards. Preparation of such information should take into account the realities of the specific condition.

The actual task of selection is assisted by the use of any one or all of the following: (1) appraisals of the candidates, (2) written tests, (3) interviews, and (4) evaluation of experience and training. The first, or appraisal of candidates, can take many different forms, including inquiry of the candidate's present superior, talking with those acquainted with the candidate's work performance, and discussing with friends the candidate's activities in clubs and other groups outside the office.

Written tests are increasing in usage, but they probably do not yet qualify as a common means for office supervisory selection. Tests are designed to measure work, personality, and technical factors. They provide a means to screen initially a large number of candidates, and they stress objective evidence instead of someone's opinion and judgment. However, considerable criticism has been leveled against tests in which it is pointed out that they concentrate on selected areas rather than the "entire man," that some candidates are practically certain not to reveal their true ability by written word, and that the candidates answer test questions for a prescribed situation in one way, yet for the same situation perform in a different way under actual working conditions.

As pointed out in Chapter 31, interviewing is perhaps the most common means of selection, and this statement includes supervisory selection. The face-to-face meeting, the opportunity to clarify ambiguous written statements, and the flexibility to shape the interview to the individual case make for the wide use and popularity of the interview method.

Finally, the evaluation of experience and training provides a practical element to the selection method followed. A detailed investigation of the candidate's work history is sometimes undertaken. Thus, elements which might be overlooked in the other selection approaches are brought into the program. Knowledge of the enterprise and technical competence are illustrative of these elements.

THE SUPERVISOR AND ACTUATING

As already pointed out, the ability of a supervisor to apply actuating efforts to his employees is a vital portion of his job. At this point, attention is directed to actuating work applied to supervisors by their superiors. For example, top managers are interested in having a comprehensive training program for office supervisors for many reasons, including improvements in both the quantity and the quality of work, better understanding of company policies, effective development of employees, improvement in employee-employer relations, and reductions in labor turnover and operating costs.

Strictly speaking, any educational activity designed to prepare the candidate for supervisory work or to improve the supervisor in carrying out his duties successfully can be termed "supervisory training." The field is quite broad and deals with many, yet related, subjects. Supervisory training is not confined to learning to perform a set of movements more efficiently but includes the development of attitudes, control of emotions, and the broadening of one's views.

To keep the supervisor fully informed constitutes one of the biggest problems in securing effective supervision. Conditions are constantly changing; new developments are taking place; and in most cases, the supervisor finds himself confronted with new personnel, new attitudes, and new problems.

Among the many means of supervisory training are included:

1. *Company supervisory schools* in which organized classes in problems of supervision are studied.

2. *Individual study* of the various available materials on the theory and practice of supervisory work.

3. *Conferences and seminars* that afford discussions with supervisors of other departments, group training, and an opportunity to talk over problems of mutual interest.

4. *Dramatized meetings* in which supervisors act out their problems, this acting-out to be followed by discussions and comments to bring out possible improvements in the handling of problems.

5. *Observation of and talks with employees* to gain a better insight into their jobs and their attitudes.

6. *Interviews with top management members* to gain advice and suggestions regarding what supervisory action might be taken under various circumstances.

7. *Involvement in an actual situation*, handling the work of supervision with a "learn by doing" technique. Usually, some background data are desirable before using this means of obtaining information.

TRAINING WITHIN INDUSTRY FOUNDATION

Excellent work in supervisory training is being accomplished by the members of the Training Within Industry Foundation, a nonprofit organization which advocates gaining maximum results from employed people through better supervision. Years of intensive research and many office tryouts with groups of supervisors have helped develop highly successful training programs for supervisors. Among the more important for normal office use are:

1. *Job instruction.* The *JI* course consists of five two-hour sessions and is intended to give skill in instructing. It is especially helpful where there is work involving long break-in periods, numerous errors, or difficulty in getting the office work out on time. To illustrate the content, the course consists of four main parts: (*a*) preparing the employee, (*b*) presenting the operation, (*c*) trying out the performance, and (*d*) following up on performance.

2. *Job relations.* Known as the *JR* course, this also consists of five two-hour sessions. It helps provide skill in leadership and is recommended where there are too many misunderstandings among employees and complaints are numerous in the human relations area.

3. *Job methods.* This *JM* program likewise is five two-hour sessions. It gives skill in improving methods through practice sessions and on-the-job coaching. This program is effective in finding better methods of accomplishing office work.

4. *Job economics training.* Known as the *JET* course, this requires five 1½-hour sessions and presents the basic principles upon which the American economy operates.

5. *Discussion leading.* This *DL* course of four three-hour sessions is designed to give skill in getting participation in meetings and in discussing thoroughly matters of common interest.

6. *Program development.* The *PD* course is intended for the instruction of one person in a company who has responsibility for designing and conducting training programs in his company or some unit thereof. The normal time required for this course is five days, dispersed among two or three weeks, to permit specific application of program material to the trainee's company.

SECURING EFFECTIVE SUPERVISION

Much material is available concerning how to be an efficient supervisor. Some of it is quite idealistic and contains many platitudes. The subject is broad, but the following ten points are included in order to indicate, in general, the type of activity which is recommended.

1. *Treat all workers alike—show no favoritism.* The successful supervisor operates objectively; his personal likes and dislikes are not permitted to influence his work.

2. *Practice consultative supervision.* This practice includes talking things over with the employees and giving them an opportunity to suggest the best way to accomplish a task. Such a procedure makes for a co-operative work force and recognizes the fact that no one has a monopoly on good ideas.

3. *Enforce all rules and regulations promptly.* Usually, nothing is gained by delaying action in cases where violations are involved. In fact, delay might be interpreted as a lack of decisiveness and an inability to cope with the situation.

4. *Keep your instructions simple, and repeat them frequently to the new employee.* Good supervision requires mutual understanding between the supervisor and the employee. In addition, a patient, helpful attitude must be assumed, particularly in working with the employee who is not yet fully familiar with all the job requirements.

5. *Insist upon and stress the need for each employee to give a full day's work for a full day's pay.* Satisfactory work outputs are the chief responsibility of every supervisor.

6. *Watch waste—material loss and time loss.* One of the chief foes of efficiency is waste. Guarding against this enemy will add significantly to the work output.

7. *Keep fully informed on company policies and their interpretation.* The supervisor is constantly called upon to interpret company policies to the employees. Knowing the policies and keeping informed of any changes and additions is a supervisory "must."

8. *Secure employees' opinions regarding supervision.* Through some means, such as attitude surveys, spot interviews, casual conversations, and discussion groups, find out what is bothering the employees and what "gripes" are developing. Adequate and correct information at the right time and place may avoid much needless trouble.

9. *Develop capable assistants.* Good management requires that qualified replacements be available to maintain the supervisory force at a satisfactory number and caliber. Failure to develop an understudy jeopardizes the supervisor's chances for promotion.

10. *Let top management members know what you are doing and why.* Because supervision is vital to the enterprise, top management members should know what supervisory action is taking place. Effective supervision requires complete backing by these members, and one of the best ways to retain this endorsement is to tell them what is going on, along with the various reasons why.

QUESTIONS

1. Discuss the duties of an office supervisor in what might be considered a typical office.
2. Identify each of the following:
   a) Supervisor.
   b) *JI* course for supervisory training.
   c) "Employees favoring the *status quo.*"
   d) Consultative supervision.
3. Justify your viewpoint toward this quotation: "With more and more specialists and expert staff people being used in the modern office organizational structure, the importance and status of the office supervisor has decreased. He is not as important as formerly. In many cases, he decides virtually nothing, his superiors telling him what to do."
4. What are the basic skills an office supervisor needs? Discuss briefly the one you feel is most important.
5. Mention some activities an office supervisor performs in the area of organizing; of controlling.
6. Does the fact that to many employees the supervisor represents management make the supervisor a manager? Why?
7. Discuss some personal attributes that appear to be closely related with supervisory success.
8. Draw up a program for the recruitment and selection of office supervisors for a large office. Assume candidates will be recruited from both within and outside the enterprise.
9. "The advantage usually lies on the side taking the initiative." Explain this statement, citing examples from your own experience.
10. As an office manager, what practical recommendations would you make to assure more efficient supervisory services? Explain.
11. Discuss the relationships between the supervisor and those above him in the organization.

12. An office supervisor tells you he is refraining from developing an understudy because he feels that success in such an undertaking will mean the loss of his (the supervisor's) job. As office manager, how would you cope with this situation? Explain.

CASE PROBLEMS
Case 34–1. Peerless Products, Inc.

In the accounting department are fourteen employees who—Edgar Crawford, the supervisor, believes—make a very effective team. One employee, Bernard Oakton, aged 30 years, married, with three children, started a tax service company last year. He assisted a number of people to prepare their income tax returns and made several hundred dollars extra. As a result of this work, he secured the part-time job of keeping the books for two small businesses. By working several evenings and week ends, he was able to do this work. Although it was confining, he did not mind, as he could use the extra money; and he thought that with some luck, the business might develop into an independent accounting firm of his own.

Oakton has never said anything about this outside work to Edgar Crawford, who nevertheless knows about it through friends and the grapevine. There is no company policy pertaining to such matters, and Crawford has said nothing to Oakton about the outside work. But he has observed that Oakton looks tired, even the first thing in the morning, and for the past six weeks has been absent quite often from his regular job. About two weeks ago, he heard that Oakton had hired a part-time helper to assist him on these outside assignments.

Last week, Oakton was absent for a day and a half. When he reported for work at noon, Edgar Crawford requested that he come to his office and fired him.

BERNARD OAKTON: This is the rawest deal I ever heard of. I wasn't here because my wife is ill. I wanted to explain this to Marcey (*the telephone switchboard operator*); but while holding the line, I was cut off.

EDGAR CRAWFORD: You know something? I do not believe you.

OAKTON: Well, now I. . . .

CRAWFORD: You're trying to misrepresent your absence, which is another reason why you deserve to be fired. And if you were cut off on the switchboard, why didn't you call back to offer your explanation? You know as well as I do that company rules require notification from anyone who is not going to report for work on a regular workday.

OAKTON: Sure, I know that. But the phone call has nothing to do with it. You're sore because of my outside business.

CRAWFORD: I did not say that.

OAKTON: It's what you're thinking, all right. I know. But let me ask you this, Mr. Crawford. You've known about my outside work and never said anything. So what gave you the right to get tough about it all of a sudden and terminate my employment?

Problems:

1. What do you believe Bernard Oakton should do now? Why?
2. What should Edgar Crawford do? Why?
3. Could the circumstances that led to this problem have been eliminated? Explain, showing how and why.

Case 34–2.   Strayer Manufacturing Company

Herman Ellinger, supervisor of the accounting department, has turned in his resignation, with regret, in order to become a member of a public accounting firm in which he is promised an ownership interest. His assistant, Arvid Juhl, aged 61, has been offered the supervisor's job; but he has rejected it, explaining that he does not wish to take on this responsibility at his age and honestly feels it should be given to someone else. Several attempts to persuade Juhl to change his mind and accept the promotion have failed.

The accounting department consists of 16 employees exclusive of the supervisor and the assistant. Of these 16 employees, 10 are women. The oldest, from the viewpoint of company service, is Mary Ann Gebhardt, aged 52, who has been with the company 28 years. She is well thought of, an excellent worker, accurate, and dependable. The second oldest from the employment standpoint is Hazel Sims, having been a company employee for 24 years. She is 49, quiet, reserved, has little to say, works steadily, and accomplishes much work.

Henry Crawford, aged 37, has 17 years of company service, the longest of any male employee in the accounting department. He completed two years of college before joining the company; for the past seven years, he has been attending evening university classes and expects to receive his degree, with a major in accounting, a year from next June. He is ambitious and is for one Henry Crawford, first and last. Close associates say he is rather blunt in his conversations and expects things to be done immediately. Crawford does not get along too well with Arvid Juhl. From the viewpoint of age, John Donner is the oldest, being 44. He joined the company in 1948 and is a satisfactory accounting department employee; but in the opinion of Mr. Ellinger, he should not be appointed the new supervisor.

The president of the company has stated informally that perhaps a new man should be brought in from the outside. However, the president indicates he is not fully familiar with the situation and has no definite opinion or suggested decision concerning it.

Problems:

1. What is the major problem in this case? The minor problems?

2. Discuss your recommended action to resolve the company's major problem, as you see it.

3. What person or persons (title or titles) should probably carry out your recommended action? Explain.

Chapter 35

DEVELOPING OFFICE EMPLOYEES

I don't feel the least hostile to young people or bothered about them. I don't understand them, but when I was young, people didn't understand me. It's a perfectly natural process.

—E. M. FORSTER

ANOTHER VITAL area of managerial actuating is formal employee training, which can be defined as *a planned development of people*. It is an enlargement of work habits which are useful in solving office production problems. It assists people to acquire skill through the use of what they have learned.

Employee training is an everyday activity in most enterprises. Employees acquire their training either by means of planned and well-administered programs or by a hit-or-miss method which includes learning by mistakes, by trial and error, and by absorption. Since training goes on continually, progressive managers have set up definite training programs so that proper direction and control can be given to make the employees more useful to the enterprise.

VALUE OF TRAINING

One who really manages makes use of training to help him manage. Planning, controlling, organizing, and actuating are each helped by training. For example, creating effective plans, building a satisfactory organization structure, delegating authority, stimulating employees, and seeing that objectives are achieved via the planned avenues are all assisted by good training.

A well-trained group of office employees will usually show a greater increase in, and a higher quality of, work output than will an untrained group. Employees do a more intelligent job and make fewer mistakes when they possess the know-how, have an understanding of their jobs and of the interdependence of one job and another, and know the *why* of the company's policies and procedures. Furthermore, morale can be boosted *after* the employee knows what to do.

In addition, the responsibility of supervision is lessened. Training does not eliminate the need for good supervision, but it reduces the requirement for detailed and constant supervision. A well-trained office employee is self-reliant in his work, because he knows what to do and how to do it. Under such conditions, close supervision is ordinarily not mandatory.

Also, the best available methods of performing the work can be standardized and made available to all employees. High levels of performance become the rule rather than the exception. The advantages of past knowledge and experience can be retained.

These values, however, are not obtained without a price. Certain difficulties and possible losses are incurred and should be recognized in any training program. First of all, regular office work is likely to be interrupted or delayed by time spent in training. The output of the trainee might be temporarily reduced. Also, training might foster dependence upon others for solutions to challenges which the employee should think through for himself. Self-reliance and capacity for new ideas might be stifled. Furthermore, competent training leaders are difficult to obtain. When mediocre instruction is utilized, not only may the results of the training be below what is expected, but they may prove harmful.

OBJECTIVES OF SUPERVISORY TRAINING

From what is known, although admittedly probably incomplete, it appears that three basic skills are common to most successful supervisors. Included are technical proficiency, facility in visualization, and ability in human relations. Under technical skill are included such things as effective application of one's knowledge of specific techniques in record keeping, office practices, office layout, and the like. Essentially, technical skill deals with tangible operations and is the most common type of skill possessed.

Skill in visualization means the capacity to picture mentally the managerial operations, to envision their relations, to exercise creativeness, and to evolve means for accomplishing definite goals. It involves intangibles, it includes perception of the management process, and it implies possession of an all-inclusive conceptual viewpoint and understanding about all the elements through which the major tasks will be accomplished. It is especially important for the office supervisor.

Skill in human relations is essential to supervisory ability and growth. Much of the discussion in this section of the book deals with this topic; but for emphasis, it can be repeated that skill in human relations deals with manager-nonmanager relationships, the general attitude toward people, the evaluating of human motivations, and the winning of loyalty, support, and willing co-operation.

OBJECTIVES OF EMPLOYEE TRAINING

Comparing respective job requirements to the qualifications of the employee performing the jobs will reveal certain areas in which employee training might prove helpful. Future plans of the office, anticipated increases in personnel, and changes in methods are direct and basic sources for determining the objectives of a training program.

Each employee should have complete knowledge of what constitutes his job and what its relationship is to other jobs in the organization. All too frequently, this is left to chance or to the belief that with time the employee will pick up the required knowledge. A manager should use a well-planned training program to get job-content information to each employee. Improved relations are a certainty when the employee understands completely what his job is, the relationship of his work to other work in the department, and, in time, that of his department to the entire organization structure.

Each employee should have knowledge of the best methods of doing his job. It is not sufficient for managers alone to know the best methods; a manager must see to it that the employees know, for only then is maximum efficiency in work output possible.

Up-to-date knowledge of operating policies and procedures is another important and common objective in office training. Information on personnel practices should be made known to all. Likewise, the general scope of desired public relations and the quality of paper work required are among the types of information which should be a part of every employee's knowledge.

Each employee should have ample opportunity for recognition and advancement when ability is demonstrated. Employees want to acquire proficiency in order that they may be more valuable to the enterprise. This may take the form of improved status, public recognition, promotion, or increased earnings. These must be available if the results of training are to be fully satisfactory. It is a mistake for an enterprise to develop an employee for a better job or to improve or add to his knowledge and skill without subsequently offering him a job on which he can use the newly acquired ability, either in the present or at some near future date, within or outside the enterprise.

FUNDAMENTALS OF TRAINING

Most employees are acquiring knowledge and skill most of the time. This appears to be a natural process, but the acquisition need not necessarily be applicable to the employee's job. The sources can be personal performance, behavior of other employees, hearing, observing, and imitating. These means are commonly referred to as "experience." It places a strong emphasis on what is practical and is conditioned extensively by experiment and accident. As such, it is not an efficient means.

Intentional efforts to teach someone can be far more effective, provided the efforts are properly managed. Beginning with what the trainee now knows and can perform, it is possible to determine what the trainee must know and be able to do in order to perform successfully particular work assignments. The differential between what is now known and what is needed constitutes the gap which training seeks to fill. This gap is reduced gradually, because learning is a gradual process. An employee learns bit by bit, not all at once. Knowing the gap to be filled and considering the gradual doses which can be absorbed by the trainee and in what sequence, the formal training operation can be set in motion.

---

1. A person learns best what he likes best.
2. A person learns by doing; watching or listening is insufficient.
3. A person remembers longer if he understands the *why* of the knowledge.
4. A person tries harder for rewards than he does because of punishments.
5. A person learns fastest when the teaching makes it easier for the learner to learn.

FIG. 35–1. Some key points in learning.

Usually, tie-ins or association of new concepts with knowledge or skills already possessed by the trainee proves effective in training work.

There are, however, basic considerations in the activity of acquiring knowledge and skill. Of prime importance is the trainee's personal interest in wanting to learn. Economic or social gains may motivate him, but a stimulus must be present. Necessarily, people start from where they are in any training effort, and they are most likely to want to learn when they see what is taught is helpful to them. In addition, the trainee must be in a receptive mood, emotionally settled, and free from worries, personal troubles, and anxieties. Lastly, it must be recognized that the trainee must learn for himself; he must subject himself to the learning process. The instructor's role is primarily one of guidance and stimulation.

Figure 35–1 lists some key points in learning. Keeping these simple truths in mind will assist anyone who is helping others to develop.

TYPES OF TRAINING

Training can be classified in many ways. One useful classification is training for present jobs and training for future jobs. Another is training for any or all of the following: job knowledge, job skills, and attitudes. Still another is training for basic information, for personal development, and for specific production in definite work application. A useful list showing the range and types of training may be outlined as follows:

Pre-employment Training. This deals with the type and amount of instruction needed by inexperienced employees prior to their entering the office. This training is generally provided by educational institutions outside the enterprise, such as high schools, universities, business colleges, night schools, and correspondence courses. Pre-employment training is generally broader and more fundamental than the other types of training. Likewise, it often is of a theoretical nature, in contrast to the practical aspect of the other types; it seeks to provide an intellectual background and to develop the art of thinking and reasoning.

Induction Training. The objective of induction training is to provide the new employee with the information necessary for a complete knowledge and understanding of practices and procedures of the enterprise. Included in this aspect of training are welcoming the new employee to the company, explaining the office rules and regulations, acquainting him with employees' benefits, informing him of the company's policies and operations, and telling him what is expected of him as an employee. The new office employee's impression of the company is frequently formed during the first several hours at the new job. Introductions should be made to the new employee's department head, fellow employees, and those supervisors with whom he will be associated. If it is possible, an introduction to one of the officers is also helpful, as this gives the new employee a feeling of worth and helps him to visualize the extent of the company. Experience shows it is a good idea to give the employee some job which he can do without too much instruction and then leave him by himself. This gives the new employee a chance to digest some of the new surroundings. Follow this up with contacts about every hour or so throughout the rest of the day. Encourage the new employee to ask questions.

On-the-Job Training. This type of training aims to give the employee the necessary skill required for a specific job. It seeks to fill the gap between the ability the worker can supply and the ability the job requires. The job can be either that of the present or some future assignment. In some cases, the job is of a higher grade than the employee's present one; in other words, the employee is being prepared for promotion. The make-up of on-the-job training takes many different forms, including lectures in specific subjects, practice on new machines, job rotation—including all jobs of a certain group, special assignments of a temporary nature, understudying a junior executive, special courses, reading assignments, and special workshops by professional associations. On-the-job training stresses just that—on the job—but some of the training may be acquired, in part, outside the enterprise. The entire program, however, should be carefully co-ordinated.

Supervisory Training. One of the most important types of training in any enterprise is supervisory training. Training of supervisors is vital because of their essentiality in management. Special courses in supervisory training have been designed, and many of these are generally considered effective. Discussion of supervisory training is included in the chapter on office supervision (Chapter 34).

TYPES OF TRAINING GIVEN TO VARIOUS CLASSIFICATIONS OF
EMPLOYEES

Classification of Employee	Type of Training	Training Required
New	Induction	To give information relative to the job and to the policies and practices of the company.
	On-the-job	Specific training in the important details of the employee's job. To help the employee acquire the necessary knowledge and skill.
Seasoned	On-the-job	To instruct in changes in procedures, routines, policies, and new equipment. Also, to prepare for jobs of higher grade (promotion).
Transferred	Induction	To give information relative to new duties and work environment.
	On-the-job	Specific training in the important details of the new job. To help the employee acquire the necessary knowledge and skill.
Supervisor	Supervisory	To give information relative to the theory and practical application of supervisory techniques.

FIG. 35–2.

Figure 35–2 indicates the type of training which is given to employees of different classifications or circumstances. For example, the new employee is given induction training and on-the-job training. The former provides information relative to his new job and to the policies and practices of the company; the latter includes specific training to help him acquire necessary skill.

MAKE-UP OF TRAINING PROGRAM

In addition to ample consideration for the objectives sought and the types of training available, the make-up of any training program should include sufficient thought to (1) the trainees, (2) the instructor, (3) the training period, (4) the training material, and (5) the training methods.

Trainees. Proper selection of trainees is of major importance if permanent, gainful results are to be obtained. A trainee should be trained for the kind of job he likes and is fitted to perform. In this respect, training is closely related to the selection of personnel. Evidence is quite conclusive that careful screening of candidates for training raises the effectiveness of the training work.

In the case of supervisory training, it is best to include all supervisors and those considered for promotion to such posts. Excluding some employees on the basis that they do not need the training or that they are already doing their work satisfactorily is a poor policy. Even outstanding supervisors profit from well-managed training programs, and their presence assists in many ways the less competent supervisors in attendance.

Instructor. A key figure in a good training program is the instructor. A capable teacher contributes immeasurably to the success of a training program. Qualified instructors may be obtained from inside or outside the company; however, many office employees are not good teachers. The efficient employee does not necessarily have the ability to teach. Instructors need many qualifications besides knowing how to do the work. A good teacher has the skill to instruct and is tolerant, understanding, and patient. Also important is an appreciation for the value of the training work in relation to the enterprise and an understanding of what the employee goes through in order to acquire the skill and knowledge which the program is designed to achieve.

Training Period. The length of the training period depends upon the skill to be acquired, the trainee's learning capacity, and the training media used. For example, a simple indoctrination program for clerks may require an hour a day over a period of a week, while a course in accounting machines may be given two hours a week for fifteen weeks. The use of effective visual material usually helps to reduce the training time. Some training directors claim that effective visualization reduces the teaching time by upwards of 35 per cent.

To maintain interest and to secure maximum accomplishment, no single session should last longer than two hours. One hour is even better. The best practice is to pay employees for training time if the course relates in any way to their work. Many states have laws or rulings affecting training time; and in addition, certain federal laws are applicable. Controversial issues are likely to appear if the employee does any productive work during the training time, if the training is outside regular working hours, or if the training work is intended to train the employee for a new or additional skill.[1]

Training Material. A text or some written material is usually desirable as a basis for instruction, review, and reference. For most subjects, a satisfactory book can be selected; but in instances where the

---

[1] Federal and prevailing state laws should be checked to help determine whether trainee or company time should be used.

course content is of a special nature, it may be well to prepare material for this specific use. A complete outline of the entire course should be made with the main topics included under each meeting or session. When a text is used, the parts to be covered must be clearly indicated; and assignments which require some preparatory time should be made for every meeting. This helps to keep the program on schedule, points the meeting toward definite subjects, and usually assists in the progress and satisfaction of the trainee.

Training Methods. There exists today many different schools of thought about the method of training. However, the objective should be foremost in determining the form of training to provide. Fundamentally, all instruction should (1) proceed from the known to the unknown, (2) go from the simple to the complex, and (3) follow the order of "prepare, present, and apply."

Training methods can be classified into ten major groups: lectures, demonstrations, conferences, problem solving, role playing, job rotation, understudy method, coaching and counseling, guided experience, and actual practice. Choice of training method depends upon many factors, including the objectives of the training, the number of trainees, the preferences of the instructor, the type of material to be covered, the cost, the time allotted, and the wishes of the trainees.

The lecture is an effective means of initially explaining the material to the trainees. It should be carefully prepared, reinforced by the use of charts, sketches, and models, and presented by a qualified speaker. Demonstrations provide forceful presentation of how the job is done. This means stresses learning by eye, rather than by ear, and is especially helpful for jobs where physical skills are vital. The conference method permits trainees to express themselves orally and to exchange thoughts, and enables the instructor to judge the trainee's understanding of the subject material. The conference method is especially popular in supervisory training. Trainees are encouraged to express themselves freely. A group of about twenty participants is the ideal size for best results from the conference method.

Problem solving is effective when the problems are well selected and bring out considerations pertinent to the work at hand. In short, solving the problems should meet specific development needs, such as an ability to analyze and relate given facts, to determine the problem to be solved, to read and to substantiate the recommended actions to be taken. Unless a developmental need is met, this method of training may be inadequate, time-consuming, and ineffective. Role playing narrows the gap between talking about what should be done and actually doing it. For training purposes, the playing-out of a typical problem situation can be quite effective. It is especially helpful in situations involving employee relations. The method permits the trainees to participate, to gain an insight into their own behavior, and to look at the problem from many different viewpoints.

Job rotation, sometimes referred to as the "merry-go-round" basis, rotates trainees among different organizational units, thus providing the trainees with over-all knowledge of the company's operations and the work done by each unit, and the opportunity to participate in the affairs of the various units. This method assists the individual to think in terms of universal managerial principles rather than the immediate activities at hand. By means of the understudy method, the trainee works as an assistant or helper to his teacher, thus acquiring familiarity with the work and practices of his teacher, who normally is an employee at the same or higher organizational level as the trainee. Experience with dynamic events and acquaintance with the atmosphere and position in which the trainee will eventually perform are acquired. On major issues, the trainee may be required to submit complete data affecting the issue along with his recommendations for action. In this way, thinking is stimulated, and the accepting of responsibility is encouraged. Both job rotation and the understudy method are commonly used in supervisory training.

Coaching and counseling are normally work-centered and fact-centered individual efforts aimed to convey useful work information and to improve skill. Coaching emphasizes "setting up the plays," but permitting the employee to carry them out as best he can. Motivation and practical instruction are essential. The instructor must have the respect of the trainee, understand how he feels, and possess an ability to use analogies and demonstrations. Counseling stresses assisting an employee to recognize his strengths and weaknesses in fulfilling the requirements of his job. The counselor spends most of his time listening. His role is to help the trainee help himself, to become independent in his own right, and to build confidence in himself. The amount of direction and assistance given depends upon the individual being counseled. Both coaching and counseling emphasize a person-to-person individualized relationship. Essentially, it is an informal rather than a formal method of training.

The guided experience method utilizes evaluation of the trainee to reveal his weaknesses; then, the causes of these weaknesses are decided, and experience to remedy them is planned. Extreme care is taken to select the proper work assignments so that the trainee's shortcomings are ultimately removed. The assignments vary and include such things as writing reports, serving on committees, solving specific problems, performing research work, and working on normal day-to-day tasks. Like coaching and counseling, the guided experience method can be considered a highly personalized, informal type of training.

The last training method to be discussed is actual practice, which stresses the performance of the office work. "Learning by doing" might be said to describe this method, which is believed by many to be the most important of all training methods. Each employee learns how to apply what he knows to the problem that confronts him at the particular time.

COST OF TRAINING

Training costs money. Many analyses of its cost are unrealistic, in that comparisons are made between the expenditures of "no training" —actually a misleading term—and those of a formal training program. The fact is that training costs are tangible and intangible. Erroneously, the latter group is commonly ignored in the cost of training.

Under tangible training costs are training materials, nonproductive time of trainee, and nonproductive time of employee instructor, or fee charged, if an outsider. Under the intangible classification are such things as a longer time for the trainee to attain a reasonable level of production, loss of employees seeking better job opportunities, time of experienced employees asked to "show me how to do this" by the trainee, loss due to work spoilage and errors, practicing of poor work methods, and improper work viewpoints and attitudes being permitted to develop and spread.

Training is a necessity in modern management, and reasonable expenditures for it should be made. The amount depends upon the needs and the aims of the office. However, whatever the costs, they should be kept under control. Management members should have some idea of what is being accomplished for the expenditures being made. This brings up the question of training effectiveness.

EFFECTIVENESS OF TRAINING

From the managerial viewpoint, it is an excellent idea to measure the effectiveness of training efforts. The evaluation, however, must be in terms of a particular training problem. This problem may be expressed in the form of questions, such as:

1. Has the training increased production?
2. Has there been a decrease in the number of errors?
3. Has the number of accidents decreased?
4. Has there been a reduction in labor turnover?
5. Has there been a reduction in absenteeism, requests for transfers, and number of grievances?
6. Has the amount of material spoilage been reduced?

It is usually best to measure effectiveness by departments or by some homogeneous group, for the problems of measurement become quite complex when the entire office is considered. It is advisable to make comparisons between office groups as units. A good procedure is to use as a control one group which is characterized by little or no formal training, by training of a particular type, or by a different method of training. Special care should be exercised to see that the groups compared are reasonably similar with respect to such factors as age, sex, and time of week, month, or year.

Evaluating the results of training is not, however, a simple matter. Many companies make little effort to evaluate training results as such, or they are satisfied with general over-all indications of the training's worth. It is difficult to differentiate what factors contribute to increased production and employee development. Many of the products of training are intangible and are extremely difficult to measure. However, many personnel practices tend to measure indirectly, at least in part, the results of training, including such practices as communication and employee merit rating.

Training can be overdone to the point that the efforts and costs in its behalf exceed the highest estimates of benefits within a reasonable period. Training should be carefully managed; it should not be engaged in simply because "it is the thing to do." It is a continuous, not an "off and on," activity. It can start on a small scale and subsequently increase as the benefits become known and the needs and progress of the enterprise dictate. As a guide, these points should be kept in mind: (1) Office training is desirable and necessary, and is performed regardless of whether a formal program is carried on or not; (2) office training must be tailor-made to fit the specific need of the enterprise; (3) the questions of *what* training should be conducted, and *when, where,* and *how,* require answering; (4) office training should be based on the needs of the office as shown by job analysis, prevalence of errors, low work output, employees' attitudes, and supervisory effectiveness; (5) office training should be preceded by careful selection of trainees; and (6) the training of office supervisors is vital.

QUESTIONS

1. In your opinion, is training a vital actuating force in management? Justify your viewpoint.
2. Can the gap between the beginner and the average employee be filled by proper training? The gap between the average and the expert employee? Explain your answers.
3. Carefully identify each of the following:
    a) Guided experience method of training.
    b) Training period.
    c) Induction training.
    d) Intangible costs of training.
4. What interpretation do you give to the following statement? "One who really manages makes use of training to help him manage."

5. Point out and briefly discuss the significant differences between the objectives of supervisory training and those of employee training.

6. Using Figure 35–1 as a guide, relate a learning experience that bears out the validity of several key points listed.

7. Do you agree with the following statement? "In the office, it is advisable that the new employee be let alone during the first day on the job. This permits adjustments to new surroundings in a manner that is not only acceptable to but also normal for the new employee."

8. Give an example illustrating an occasion when you would recommend the use of role playing in office training. The use of lectures. The use of actual practice.

9. Do you believe an employee-training program is a good investment? Why?

10. A new employee has just completed a two-week indoctrination training program given by a bank. The training director of the bank has rated the new employee as unsatisfactory, basing his opinion on the training results. Should the new employee be placed on the job, asked to repeat the training, or dropped from the payroll? Explain your answer.

11. As an office manager, would you try to evaluate the effectiveness of office training programs? Why?

12. Evaluate and justify the use of the understudy method for office training purposes.

CASE PROBLEMS

Case 35–1.   Schmidt Company

"Here's your desk. You can get yourself squared away, and I'll be back as soon as I can," stated supervisor Ruth Frey to new employee Harriet Walters. The desk was similar to a seeming multitude of other desks, all inhabited by employees working on their jobs. All, that is, except those wondering who the new employee was, how she got the job, and what kind of person she was. After standing a few minutes, Harriet Walters sat down at her desk, pulled each of the six desk drawers open in sequence, and scanned the miscellaneous papers thereby revealed. She came across an old newspaper and out of curiosity placed it on the top of the desk and began reading a news item. After reading for perhaps ten minutes, Harriet suddenly sensed that someone was standing at her side. Looking up, she saw a well-dressed, middle-aged man, Mr. Joseph McMurry.

McMurry: Reading of newspapers during office working hours is not permitted, Miss . . . a . . . er. . . .

Harriet: Walters. Harriet Walters is my name.

McMurry: Yes. Yes, thank you, Miss Walters. So may I suggest that you put the newspaper away and be on with your work?

With this statement, Mr. McMurry walked away. Harriet thought she had better tell Mrs. Frey about the incident, so she walked over to Mrs. Frey's office and told her. Mrs. Frey listened, smiled, and then stated: "Don't worry about it. Here, take this manual back to your desk and scan the material. Some of it is outdated, but you'll find it informative and interesting. I'll be over just as soon as I can."

Harriet returned to her desk and read the manual for over an hour. Then,

Mrs. Frey brought a batch of papers and requested that Harriet check the addition of a column of figures on each paper. Any errors were to be indicated by writing in the correct figure in red pencil. This work continued until a bell rang, and Harriet noticed everyone leaving his desk. Glancing at her wristwatch, she noted it was 12:00 noon. Assuming it was lunchtime, she grabbed her purse, walked to the lobby, and started to leave by the main entrance. Stopped there by a watchman who requested her "pass" to leave, Harriet returned to the office, but found no one around whom she could ask about the needed pass. After Harriet had spent several minutes wondering what to do, she saw a girl from the factory processing office walk by; after a formal greeting, and learning of Harriet's plight, she asked Harriet to join her for lunch in the company cafeteria.

Shortly after the start of the afternoon session, Ruth Frey approached Harriet at her desk, told her she (Ruth Frey) was free now, and proceeded to explain how to perform a fairly simple job of arranging cards alphabetically. In addition, Mrs. Frey brought several more batches of paper on which lists of figures were to be added and checked. After spending some fifteen minutes with Harriet, Mrs. Frey left. She returned twice during the afternoon and found Harriet busy and doing the work correctly.

Problems:

1. Is there a problem here?
2. What suggestions do you feel are in order to Harriet Walters? To Ruth Frey? Discuss.

Case 35–2. Serbur Textiles, Inc.

As an industry, textiles have been suffering from overproduction and soft prices. Sales volume is down. Business activity has been declining for Serbur Textiles, Inc. Currently, its sales are 30 per cent less than they were two years ago; and Mr. Benjamin Geiss, the treasurer, believes adjustments in the company's personnel must be made in order to keep the company solvent and competitive. Accordingly, he has suggested, among other reductions, that four members of the office training unit be laid off indefinitely. This would leave the director of the unit and an assistant remaining. Mr. Geiss points out that the office force as a whole has been reduced nearly 20 per cent during the past eighteen months; and with this smaller work force, plus the fact that relatively few new employees are being hired—only in cases of absolute necessity—a reduction in training personnel is a logical place to trim costs.

Objections to Mr. Geiss's plans are voiced by the office manager, Mr. Julius Lieberman, who explains that office training is vital and that competent instructors skilled in office training work are difficult to replace. The instructors would certainly find employment elsewhere; thus, a great permanent loss to the company would be suffered. Mr. Lieberman suggests trimming costs elsewhere—areas where the situation is not so critical.

Mr. Geiss counters with the statement that the pruning of any organization structure is difficult—every function and every employee seems essential. He cannot see where office training is going to be needed for months to come. He also questions the contribution that this training unit has made. As best he can make out, the company's cost for processing various paper work has been about the same for the past four years, except where new office machines were installed. He requests Mr. Lieberman to send him a report indicating what office personnel should be reduced and specific data to show that the office training unit should remain as is.

Problems:

1. What do you think about the viewpoint of Mr. Geiss? Discuss.

2. Point out the major contents of the report that Mr. Lieberman is to prepare.

3. What action do you feel the company should take? Why?

Case 35–3. Gulf Grocery Wholesale Company

Total management personnel from the supervisory level up is 87 men and women, of whom 45 are operative supervisors. Main office organization units include credit and collections, order writing, billing, accounting, purchasing, personnel, stock, correspondence, mail handling, advertising, filing, research, company library, and watchman services. The company's executive committee wishes to initiate a formal supervisory development program. Business is expected to increase on an average of 10 per cent per year for the next decade. The company operates in six states and sells grocery items to over 1,400 retail grocery outlets.

Problems:

1. Outline the general features of your recommended program, noting the probable schedule of events.

2. Do you feel a program such as that requested by the executive committee is the best way to develop office supervisors for the company? Why?

Chapter 36

OFFICE SALARY ADMINISTRATION

If you would have a happy healthy harmonious life you must train your thoughts.

—LOWELL FILLMORE

THE MONETARY reward for performing definite work is a fundamental consideration in managerial actuating. A number of avenues can be followed in salary determination, but the core of most approaches is (1) job evaluation which determines the relative worth of the job, (2) consideration of how well the incumbent is doing his particular job, (3) regard for the amount paid for "fringe benefits," and (4) social and economic influences such as career influence and supply of and demand for jobs, and for employees of specific skills.

But it is not the granting of an equitable yet finite number of dollars that provides the total motivation of employees from salaries. There are also influences of a number of related actuating considerations, many of which have already been discussed in previous chapters. These include the salaries of executives which employees read about, the calibre of supervision provided, the way they feel about their fellow employees, the gossip they hear from other employees, and the profit reports they read in newspapers.

JOB EVALUATION

The concept of the job and its relative worth are considered in job evaluating, which can be formally defined as follows: *Job evaluation is the determination of the relative value of each individual job in an enterprise and is arrived at by means of a systematic procedure using jobs or selected job factors for comparison or measurement.* There are four main methods of carrying out job evaluation work, including ranking, classification, factor comparison, and point.

Ranking Method. The jobs within an enterprise can be arranged according to their relative difficulty. A ranking of the jobs is thus obtained; and in this manner, the relative importance of each one is established. The job at the top of the list has the highest value, and the job at the bottom of the list has the lowest value. The usual procedure is (1) to rank the jobs in an individual department and (2) to combine all departmental rankings into one composite ranking.

Figure 36–1 illustrates the results which might be obtained from this method. For example, the job of "accounting clerk I" was con-

ARRAY OF JOBS ACCORDING TO RANKING METHOD

Rank No.	Name of Job	Earnings per Week*
1	Accounting clerk I	$105
2	Purchasing clerk	101
3	Traffic clerk I	97
4	Cashier	93
5	Accounting clerk II	89
6	Traffic clerk II	85
7	Cost clerk	81
8	Tabulating-machine operator	77
9	General bookkeeper	73
10	Correspondent	69
11	Stenographer	65
12	Switchboard operator	61
13	Typist I	57
14	File clerk	53
15	Typist II	49
16	Office boy	45

* In uniform variation from top to bottom.

FIG. 36–1.

sidered of greater value than the job of "purchasing clerk," while the job of "office boy" was ranked lowest in the office. If the weekly salary of the top job is set at $105 and that of the lowest job at $45, then the rank order of the intermediate jobs, assuming a straight-line or uniform variation, is shown in the last column in the illustration.

Classification Method. Under this method, a predetermined number of job classes or groups are established, and the jobs are assigned to these classifications. For example, the job classes, from highest to lowest, might include:

Class A.　Executive
　　Office manager
　　Office departmental supervisor
Class B.　Skilled
　　Purchasing clerk
　　Traffic clerk
　　Cashier
Class C.　Limited skilled
　　Tabulating-machine operator
　　Stenographer
　　Switchboard operator

Class D. Unskilled
   File clerk
   Office boy

In this method, the jobs within each grade frequently must be graded further to show more adequately the existing relationships. To do this, the ranking method, previously described, can be employed.

Factor Comparison Method. Jobs can also be evaluated according to predetermined factors which have been established as a measure of ranking. Customarily, a key-job comparison scale is established and used for this purpose. Job factors are listed across the top and the dollars per week or salary-rating schedule in the left column. The scale provides the means for applying *salary rates* to job relatives as needed.

Assume four job factors: education, experience, responsibility, and working conditions. On each of these factors, each key job is ranked. Generally, eight to ten jobs are considered key jobs, selected on the basis of the jobs requiring widely different amounts of the job factors being utilized. To illustrate, for the "accounting clerk I" job, the rating values given for each of the job factors might be:

Education	$ 32.00
Experience	24.00
Responsibility	40.00
Working conditions	9.00
Total	$105.00

In other words, from the key-job comparison scale, it is possible to determine what portion of the present salary of a job is being paid for each factor.

This scale is the measuring device for evaluating all other jobs in the company. Other jobs are fitted into this scale, with the key-job evaluations being used as guides. To illustrate, consider the job of "tabulating-machine operator." The evaluator would first read the job analysis sheet for this job. Then, concentrating his attention on the factor of education, he judges where under the education column the job of tabulating-machine operator seems to fit. He might decide that this job requires a little more education than a certain key job but less than another key job. Hence, he would evaluate "tabulating-machine operator" between the two considered key jobs. In similar manner, the job is evaluated according to the other job factors, and the other jobs in the company are evaluated in a similar manner.

Point Method. In this method, job factors are selected, and each is assigned a maximum number of points or credits. For example:

Education	300 points
Experience	250 points
Responsibility	250 points
Working conditions	200 points
Total	1,000 points

The selection of job factors is qualified by the following: that each job factor (1) exists in all the jobs to be evaluated, (2) varies in amount in the different jobs to be evaluated, and (3) is mutually exclusive of other job factors. The maximum point value assigned to each factor is de-

4. Responsibility for Loss

Level	LEVEL DEFINITION	Points
A	Nature of work involves negligible opportunity for loss. Normal or reasonable care required and all work is verified or proved by repeating entire operation.	3
B	Nature of work is such that more than normal or reasonable care is required to prevent loss. However, work is checked by proving against totals or some standard rather than by repetition of operation.	15
C	Nature of work involves moderate but constant opportunity for error, limited only by daily or subsequent spot check or examination. Great care should be exercised to prevent loss. Potential serious loss from errors in transcription or computation.	27
D	Good judgment must be exercised regularly to prevent loss. Work is of such nature that complete and correct performance is hard to control, reliance being placed on the individual. Work subject to general supervision and occasional review.	38
E	Work of such a nature that commitments are made which may involve the entire bank. Work is frequently released without any check being made or is checked only by individual doing the work. A high degree of financial responsibility is involved.	50

Courtesy: J. D. Moore Organization, Park Ridge, Ill.

FIG. 36–2. Illustrating the different levels of "responsibility for loss" and the number of points assigned to each level.

termined by its relative importance. This is governed primarily by the judgment and experience of the analyst. Normally, from eight to fourteen factors are used. Those most common include skill, experience, education, responsibilities, working conditions, effort, and supervisory requirements.

Each selected job factor is defined in clear and simple language. The degree or intensity of each selected factor is broken down, and points are assigned for each level of the factor. Figure 36–2 shows these data for the factor "responsibility for loss," which has been given five levels, *A* through *E*, ranging in value from a low of 3 to a maximum of 50 points. Figure 36–3 illustrates eleven job factors selected for use in the evaluation of clerical and supervisory jobs. In this case, the data showing the level and the points of rating, along with pertinent comments for the job of "junior accountant," are indicated for each factor. Note that under factor No. 4, "responsibility for loss," the rating level of *B* is valued at 15 points, which was arrived at by referring to the guide shown by Figure 36–2.

PRICING THE JOB

The ultimate aim of job evaluation is to determine the job price or rate of pay. Jobs of high evaluation should command high rates of pay; in general, the higher the evaluation, the higher the pay. The immediate problem is to determine what the rate of pay should be when the evaluation is a known amount. The job prices to be established must be consistent (1) externally (rates within the enterprise are in line with the rates paid outside the enterprise) and (2) internally (rates within the enterprise are directly associated within the evaluations).

External Consistency. This is accomplished by securing the current wage rates in the area from private companies specializing in this type of work or from local governmental offices. Sometimes, however, a thorough labor market survey must be made. It is also well to remember that accurate job descriptions are necessary for meaningful labor market surveys.

Internal Consistency. This can be determined by comparing the job evaluations with the rates paid. In some cases, this can be done by a simple comparison of columnar data. Very often, however, a graphic representation helps to visualize this comparison, especially when the point system of evaluation has been used. Commonly employed is a chart or scatter diagram in which existent wage rates are plotted on the vertical axis and evaluations on the horizontal axis. A curve showing consistent relationships between rates and evaluations can then be drawn on the chart. The deviations of actual rates from this curve can readily be spotted, and jobs overpaid or underpaid with respect to their evaluation can be quickly observed.

Figure 36–4 is a scatter diagram showing the relationship between wage rates and evaluations. The plotted points are indicated by the small circles. Curve *AA* has been drawn in and represents what is considered to be a consistent relationship between rates and evaluations. Curves *BB* and *CC* have been drawn in for reasons discussed in the paragraphs that follow.

Code .... Salary Grade .... VI ....

Job Title .... JUNIOR ACCOUNTANT ....

CLERICAL AND SUPERVISORY EVALUATION

	NO.	FACTOR	RATING LEVEL	RATING PTS.	JOB REQUIREMENT
SKILL	1	Essential Knowledge	D	84	Requires a knowledge of advanced accounting methods and procedures and a working knowledge of company financial policies.
	2	Experience and Training	G	73	Normally requires 3 to 5 years' training and experience, including 2 years' accounting training plus 3 years' company experience as an Accounting Clerk.
	3	Analytical Requirements	C	27	Requires analysis of figures and data which vary in content but follow general patterns of application
RESPONSIBILITY	4	Responsibility For Loss	B	15	Requires more than normal care to prevent loss due to miscalculations. However, work is usually checked against totals.
	5	Confidential Information	B	6	Involves preparation and use of limited confidential matters in the Accounting Department.
	6	Contacts Public and Internal	B	28	Involves routine contacts with persons where detailed subject matter must be presented satisfactorily.
	7	Individual Initiative	B	12	Involves initiative in planning details of own work.
EFFORT	8	Mental Effort	C	15	Requires moderate mental effort to solve problems of accounting.
	9	Physical Effort	A	6	Involves light physical effort with intermittent standing and sitting at comfortable intervals.
	10	Work Conditions	A	0	Working conditions are excellent.
	11	Supervisory Requirements	FX	18	Involves immediate leadership over Accounting Clerks and Typists.
		BASE POINTS		400	
		TOTAL POINTS		684	

FIG. 36–3. Job factors, ratings, and comments for the job of "junior accountant."

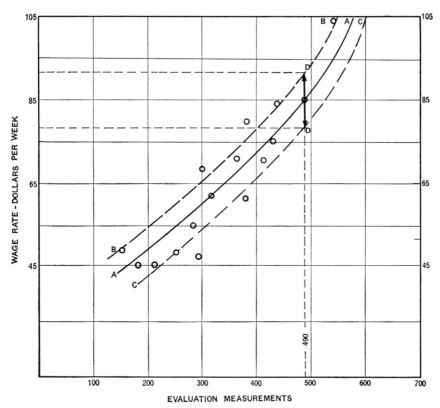

FIG. 36–4. Scatter diagram showing relationship between wage rates and evaluation measurements.

JOB PRICE RANGE

From a practical viewpoint, the office manager is interested in more than a job price for each job. What he really wants is (1) *a price range for each job*, not a single price for each job; and (2) *a price range to cover a group of jobs*, not just one job. A price range provides flexibility and makes for a better salary plan. Furthermore, when a group of jobs are within one price range, the entire task of wage determination is simplified.

Referring again to Figure 36–4, a wage range has been indicated by the two curves *BB* and *CC* drawn on the chart.[1] The job of "traffic clerk I," for example, evaluated at 490 points, has a range from $77 to $93 per week, indicated by ordinate *DD* on the chart.

To provide a group of jobs within one price range, it is customary to

---

[1] Frequently, a constant percentage change from the center line is used to establish the outside range lines. For example, for $50 median, the range is $45–$55; for $90 median, the range is $81–$99.

group jobs into classes so that all jobs in the same class have the same price range. In other words, jobs of the same worth are put into the same class. The number of job classes depends primarily upon the total number of jobs, and the spread between the highest and the lowest job. Usually, a total of six to ten job classes is sufficient in most offices.

As already discussed, the classification method of job evaluation automatically puts the jobs into various classes. On the other hand, when any of the other methods of job evaluation are used, the alignment of jobs is arbitrarily divided into different numbers and levels or classes.

ADVANTAGES DERIVED FROM JOB EVALUATION

A solid foundation for an equitable salary administration is supplied by job evaluation because it (1) shows the relative value of jobs within a company, (2) assists in the evaluating of new jobs, (3) helps obtain a satisfactory wage level for all jobs within the company, (4) helps to eliminate salary inequalities by putting jobs having similar requirements in the same salary range, and (5) affords factual data for the settling of salary disputes. It should be pointed out, however, that the work of determining job content, grades, and price ranges should be kept up to date by regular, periodic checkups. The content of many jobs changes in the normal course of events; and this, in turn, frequently changes the relative values of the jobs. Likewise, changes in the general wage levels appear to be the usual rather than the exceptional happenings.

HOW WELL THE INCUMBENT IS DOING HIS JOB

Up to this point, job evaluation has been discussed. This determines the relative worth of the job. Next in salary administration, it must be determined how well the incumbent is doing his job. For this purpose, several different approaches can be followed. Commonly, merit rating or seniority is used.[2] Some offices use special bonus arrangements or financial incentive plans. These two arrangements warrant further discussion.

BONUS ARRANGEMENTS

These forms are payment of bonuses on special occasions, such as Christmas, a birthday, or an anniversary commemorating continuous employment. Frequently, these payments amount to sizable sums— perhaps an extra month's pay or, in some cases, as much as 20 per cent of a year's salary. They are usually given to share the results of profitable operations, to recognize outstanding service, to continue a traditional custom, or to improve employee morale.

---

[2] Merit rating is discussed in Chapter 33.

FINANCIAL INCENTIVE PLANS

These plans are wage payment methods of paying the employee to some extent for the amount of work accomplished instead of strictly on the basis of time spent at work. Generally speaking, financial incentive plans are not common in offices, but their use is growing. The more common incentive office operations include transcribing, order processing, and billing.

There are two fundamental concepts in practically all incentive plans: (1) a base or standard amount of work output and (2) the amount of wage payment which will be given for production below standard, at standard, or above standard. The first concept, the base amount of work output, can be determined by past performance records, by time studies, or by guess. Customarily, this standard amount of work is expressed as 100 per cent. The amount of work which is established as standard is extremely important, for it is commonly, but not always, the point at which the incentive pay begins. The second concept, or pattern of the amount of wage payment, varies with the incentive plan. Some plans guarantee base rates up to standard; others do not. Some divide the excess above standard equally between employee and employer, while others share the overflow according to various percentages.

The same general type of plan can be used for a group instead of a single employee. This arrangement can be used when the nature of the work is such that segregation of work by individual employees is very difficult or costly. The group incentive pay is figured first, then divided among the members according to either the individual base wage rates, the number of hours worked by each member, the individual gross base pay, or on some other agreed basis.

MAJOR GUIDES FOR INCENTIVE PLANS

Incentive wage plans should be tailor-made to suit the particular office and to achieve the particular objectives desired from the plan. The following guides are helpful:

1. Incentive plans should have the backing of the top managers.
2. The best incentive plan is usually the simple plan. It should be thoroughly understood by all concerned.
3. There should be a close relationship between reward (incentive pay) and results (contribution).
4. An incentive based on the individual employee is generally better than one based on a group.
5. The work output should increase as well as the amount of salaries.
6. The base or standard production amounts should be carefully determined—preferably by measured time studies.

7. The number of temporary standards should be held to a minimum. When standards are temporary, this fact should be known to all concerned.

8. The incentive wage should be neither guaranteed nor limited. In most instances, the base wage should be guaranteed.

9. The standards should be reviewed for possible revision whenever any change is made in the material, machine, or method used.

10. If indirect production employees, such as messenger boys, receptionists, and telephone operators, are included in the plan, they should be affiliated on some measurable basis, such as the maintenance of an acceptable ratio between the total indirect man-hours to the total direct man-hours, or the total indirect man-hours to total work output. This tends to keep the indirect man-hours under control.

FRINGE BENEFITS

Important in most modern salary administration plans are fringe benefits, which include such items as vacation with pay, group insurance, hospitalization plans, and sick leave. Various estimates point to an average of about 18–20 per cent of total base payroll costs constituting expense for fringe benefits. The trend in the amount of fringe benefits has been steadily upward during the last decade.

Many office employees give considerable weight to the fringe benefits included in a job. The dollar "take home" pay is adjusted in view of the fringe benefits received; and it is common to find an office employee preferring to work for a particular concern where the dollar salaries are average or even low, but the numerous fringe benefits provided make for an attractive total remuneration.

SOCIAL AND ECONOMIC INFLUENCES

There are a number of factors that could be discussed under this heading; but for our purposes here, discussion will be limited to career influence and the supply of and demand for jobs, and for employees of specific skills. Career influence is made up of what an employee is looking forward to when he accepts a job and the influence of this ambition on his work. The pay for a job may be too low, in terms of what the job requires; but because of career influence, the employee willingly forgoes the higher and appropriate pay in order to get ultimately to a job he wants. The case of a young law graduate in a law office illustrates this point. On the other hand, the career influence may cause a job to be rated too highly by the employee, based on the actual job requirements. The job might be of the dead-end type and offer no usable training or advancement beyond a well-known level. In this case, sufficient salary must be paid to secure and hold the proper type of employee.

For the most part, salary rates are affected by the condition of supply and demand. These economic factors are dynamic; they change with time and exert a "push and pull" effect on salary rates. As a matter of practical consideration, recognition must be given to significant changes in the supply and demand for employees of specific skills. *Temporarily,* minor adjustments might have to be made in order to alleviate serious labor shortage difficulties. For example, current conditions may make it necessary to start a new employee at a figure higher than the usual starting wage but still within the range of the job. Or in unusual cases, the rate may be outside the job range; but such a condition usually does not last and might be viewed as an emergency case. If it does persist, however, it is well to revalue the job and change the classification, thus giving reality to the salary administration plan.

This does not mean that the wage ranges established primarily through job evaluation should be ignored whenever the labor market is either generally tight or loose. It does mean some deviation for some jobs—generally very few—which have become out of line because of the effect of current economic forces. As a matter of fact, the job-evaluating factors, such as education, experience, and responsibility, are themselves functions of time and of the economic forces of supply and demand. It is therefore reasonable to expect some minor adjustments in salary rates as a result of the influence of supply and demand for employees of specific occupations.

QUESTIONS

1. Would you say that job evaluation is scientific in its determination of the value of a job? Why?
2. Describe the factor comparison method of job evaluation in your own words.
3. Define each of the following:
   a) Career influence upon salary administration.
   b) Job evaluation.
   c) Financial incentive plan.
   d) Job factors in job evaluation.
4. In what ways are job evaluation data helpful in settling controversial salary problems confronting an office manager?
5. Which method of job evaluation do you consider the simplest? The most accurate? The easiest for employees to understand? Substantiate your answers.
6. For an office employing 750 employees, can the wage rates be externally, but not internally, consistent? Internally, but not externally, consistent? Elaborate upon your answers.
7. As an office manager, would you favor a financial incentive plan as a part of your salary administration program? Justify your viewpoint.
8. Discuss the subject of "Job Price Range" as used in job evaluation work.
9. Discuss the effect that supply of and demand for office jobs, and for applicants for office jobs, have upon office salary rates.

10. In your opinion, are bonus payments to employees effective actuating efforts? Why?
11. What steps do you feel might be taken to make an office employee more aware of the fringe benefits he is receiving?
12. What basic employees' desires does a financial incentive provide? Are these of major or minor importance in office management?

CASE PROBLEMS
Case 36–1.   Sawyer-Chesky, Inc.

The office manager, Ron Seydell, is of the opinion that fringe benefits for the office employees have become excessive. Some years ago, the company started the practice of giving all office employees coffee and doughnuts free of charge during the morning and afternoon "breaks." Mr. Seydell favors cutting this out. Also, a parking space was leased by the company several years ago, and office employees were permitted to park free on this lot. With the increase in business and office employees, the lot has become inadequate. There is a second parking lot available; but rather than keep adding to company costs, Mr. Seydell feels that the whole idea of the company supplying free parking space should be abandoned.

In talking over the situation with his associates and the personnel director, Mr. Seydell has met opposition to his proposal. The personnel director, in particular, feels very strongly that the employees will resent, even though they may not openly say so, any action by the company to take away the parking service and convenience. True, this costs the company an average of about 36.7 cents per week per employee, points out the personnel director, but he contends that it is money well spent. The free coffee and doughnuts involve 16.2 cents per day per employee.

The office manager agrees that the grumbling should be held at a minimum when the company stops picking up the "tab" for these extras. He contends that office costs must be reduced. Something has to be done about these fringes, which are excessive, in his opinion. What started as little extras and niceties are getting out of hand. The parking question will get the company involved more and more as time goes on. And in his opinion, the advantages, if any, of the company supplying free coffee and doughnuts are quite intangible; and to think of this as being a favor to the employees is simply ridiculous. To quote Seydell's own words: "The company is paying the employees a good wage. Let them buy their coffee and doughnuts if they want them. It's not the company's responsibility."

Problems:
1. What do you think of Mr. Seydell's recommendations? Why?
2. Can you see any merit in the company retaining these benefits? Discuss.
3. What plan of action do you feel the company should take? Why?

Case 36–2.   Lawrence P. Strong Corporation

President Strong of this corporation believed that certain salaries of his office personnel were out of line. Accordingly, he brought in an outside group of management consultants to make a job evaluation of the office jobs. After these jobs were evaluated and classified, the data revealed the facts shown in the accompanying table.

MONTHLY SALARIES	JOB CLASS								
	9	8	7	6	5	4	3	2	1
Accountant.................	475	...	...	...	...	...	...	...	...
Auditor....................	550	...	...	...	...	...	...	...	...
Calculatng machine operator..	...	...	...	...	275	...	...	...	...
Draftsman..................	...	...	500	...	...	...	...	...	...
Expediter..................	...	500	...	...	...	...	...	...	...
File clerk A................	...	...	...	...	240	...	...	...	...
File clerk B................	...	...	...	...	...	200	...	...	...
Junior accountant...........	...	...	400	...	...	...	...	...	...
Junior stenographer A........	...	...	...	...	...	230	...	...	...
Junior stenographer B........	...	...	...	...	...	...	230	...	...
Messenger..................	...	...	...	...	...	...	...	...	175
Price clerk.................	...	...	...	325	...	...	...	...	...
Rate clerk.................	...	...	...	325	...	...	...	...	...
Receptionist................	...	...	...	...	...	...	190	...	...
Senior stenographer..........	...	...	...	...	300	...	...	...	...
Senior stock clerk...........	...	...	...	...	...	...	...	...	170
Statistical typist............	...	...	...	...	...	275	...	...	...
Systems analyst.............	...	450	...	...	...	...	...	...	...
Telephone operator..........	...	...	...	...	...	...	225	...	...
Typist A...................	...	...	...	...	...	...	220	...	...
Typist B...................	...	...	...	...	...	...	...	200	...
Voucher register clerk........	...	...	...	...	...	...	...	195	...
Established minimum........	530	440	370	310	270	230	200	170	150
Established maximum........	620	530	440	370	310	270	230	200	170

Problems:

1. What are some possible reasons for the various salaries being out of line with the established range?

2. How should salaries falling above or below the established salary range be handled?

3. In your opinion, do any of the salary ranges and respective classifications appear out of line? If so, which ones? If not, how do you explain that they are in line?

4. Graph the data, using "wages in dollars" vertically and the nine "job classifications" horizontally.

5. Using this chart or graph, what further considerations can you draw from these data?

Chapter 37

OFFICE TRADE UNIONISM

Some people will never learn anything for this reason, because they understand everything too soon.
—ALEXANDER POPE

TRADE UNIONS among office employees have existed for a number of years. Among the oldest are the editorial employees of some newspapers, organized around 1890; the National Association of Letter Carriers, created in 1892; and the Brotherhood of Railway and Steamship Clerks, organized in 1899. These early unions were loosely organized, judged in terms of present-day standards; but they were unions, and their members were clerical employees.

During the following several decades, other office unions came into being, among which are the following: the National Federation of Post Office Clerks (organized in 1906), the American Federation of Teachers (1916), the National Federation of Federal Employees (1917), and the American Federation of Governmental Employees (1932). Since about the middle thirties, there has been increased interest in the unionization of office employees. Stimulus was brought about as a result of various labor laws enacted. Today, there are several hundred strong office employees' unions within the boundaries of the United States. Estimates vary as to their total membership, but it is probably about 6–7 per cent of the total number of office employees. This may appear minor, but it is a composite figure of all office employees; and in certain enterprises, the extent of office unionization assumes a prominent position.

WHY OFFICE EMPLOYEES JOIN OR DO NOT JOIN UNIONS

The growth in office unionization has been relatively slow compared to that of factory employees. Various surveys reveal that office employees do not join a union for these major reasons:

1. *Possible loss of social status and prestige.* Identification of office employees is with "those in the know." The typical office employee works in street clothes; he is around, sees, and sometimes meets the executives of the company. He believes his work is of a high type, is dignified, and has prestige. Frequently, it is looked up to.

2. *Receiving certain benefits of unionism without being members.* In many instances, the benefits negotiated by unions of nonoffice employees are passed along to the office employees of that enterprise. This practice has been termed "a free ride" for the office employees. The practice may be questioned, but it does exist.

3. *Satisfactory working conditions.* Most office employees feel that they work in an area which is cleaner than that in which many other employees work. Also, they may consider the work safer and not as physically tiring.

4. *The basic characteristics of most office employees.* They are conservative and inclined to stay with the old rather than to try out the new. In addition, about two thirds of the office employees are women, many of whom are interested in working in offices for only a limited period of time.

In contrast, what is the answer to "Why do office employees join unions"? Among the various reasons, these appear most prominent:

1. *Discontent with present earnings.* Especially is this true when comparisons with wages of factory employees are "near at hand" and the differential between the two are great. Included among the greatest contributors to this discontent are slower rates of wage increases for office compared to factory employees, shrinking advantage in fringe benefits enjoyed by office employees, and wage raises for lower-class office jobs without comparable wage adjustments in middle and top office job classes.

2. *Lack of security.* The wide changes taking place in the office, especially growing automation, add to the office employee's fear of losing his job.

3. *Supervisors who are not well trained or informed.* The employees want better work guidance, communication, and participation in matters that affect them.

4. *Lack of a feeling of justice.* Formalized procedures to permit handling of grievances of office employees or to represent them adequately to management representatives are not provided. The employees believe there is no adequate means for them to get their "gripes" to top managers' attention.

OPERATION IN THE UNIONIZED OFFICE

When a union exists in an office, managers are required to bargain with the authorized representatives concerning "wages and other conditions of employment." In other words, a process which might be called "collective co-operation" is used, whereby employers and representatives of employees arrive at agreements covering compensation and the conditions under which employees will work. This usually means that policies concerning matters such as wages, discharge, discipline, and transfer must be discussed with the union representatives and incorporated into a mutually agreed-upon labor contract. Subsequently, decisions utilizing these policies are made by management members but are frequently subject to question by and explanation to the union, via an established grievance procedure. The net effect is to challenge the decision-making process of management members, regardless of the level of management. The union wants to be consulted and to present its views in matters affecting its members during the decision-making process so that the decision reached will be in keeping with its views. To reiterate, the ultimate decision is made by a management member; but from the practical viewpoint, the decision must be acceptable to the employees in order to be entirely effective.

CHARACTERISTICS OF CONTRACTS

The majority of current office-union contracts are tailor-made to suit the special conditions of the individual offices. There is, however, some similarity of contracts, since most of them cover the same subject topics. Most contracts contain clauses covering such matters as recognition of the union, union status, union security, salaries, hours of work, seniority, employment procedures, transfers and dismissals, grievance procedures, penalties, maternity leaves, and severance pay. A discussion of several of these subjects follows.

Union Recognition Clause. A "recognition of the union" clause points out that the union named in the contract is fully recognized by the employer; frequently, it also states what jobs and what employees are covered by the contract. Sometimes, a statement is included to the effect that the union will not accept into membership those employees in the excluded groups.

Status of Union. Union status concerns the relationship of members of the union with the company. In general, there are three kinds of union status:

1. *Union shop.* Nonunion members may be hired; but after a certain period, they must, as a requirement of employment, become union members.

2. *"Mainteneance of membership"* shop. All employees are not required to join the union, but all present union members must retain membership during the time the contract is in force.

3. *Exclusive bargaining shop.* The union is recognized as the exclusive bargaining agent for all employees, but no employee is compelled to join it or to remain a member.[1]

---

[1] The Labor Management Relations Act of 1947 outlawed in interstate commerce (1) the closed shop—in which the employer agrees to hire only union members, and all employees must continue their good standing in the union during their terms of employment, and (2) the preferential shop—in which preference in hiring and in layoff is given union members.

Wage Rates. Clauses on wage rates frequently include the recognition of job classifications and wage rates for each class. Minimum rates only might be stated. Uniform adjustments, either in amount or in percentage, may be provided; and the effective date of such adjustments may be included.

The following is a typical contractual statement pertaining to wages.

SECTION 2. The wage schedules as set forth in this schedule, attached hereto as Exhibit B and made a part hereof, shall apply and be in effect as of July 1, 1962, and shall remain in effect for the life of this agreement.

SECTION 3. Overtime compensation and deductible time lost shall be computed by dividing the monthly salary by one hundred seventy-three and one third (173⅓) to arrive at an hourly rate to be used for such computations.

Layoffs and Seniority. While most unions favor the governing of layoffs and rehires on seniority, they will grant a statement to the effect that seniority shall govern when the employee involved has the ability to do the work under question. Questions arising in connection with seniority are sometimes clarified by the practice of preclassifying employees either by occupation or by departments or divisions. In this way, employees making up a fairly comparable group are associated together.

To illustrate:

SECTION 3. A reduction in working forces resulting in demotions and layoffs will normally be on a departmental seniority basis except for stenographers and filing clerks, who will be on a company-wide basis.

Penalty Clauses. Penalty provisions provide punishment for members who violate parts of the contract. Penalties might be in the form of reductions in pay, temporary or permanent layoffs, or less severe disciplinary measures, depending upon the nature of the violation.

CONTRACT LIMITATIONS

It is not feasible to write a collective bargaining contract which covers every possible source of difference between the employer and the employee. A brief contract stating the points in simple terms usually is sufficient. Attempts to cover all contingencies in great detail will result in complicating the contract and in making it extremely difficult to interpret. Arguments about language technicalities lead to disputes which usually cause trouble.

There must be a spirit of co-operativeness on the part of both interested parties; they must want the contract to work. When both parties have this attitude, even the skimpy and legally poorly written contract can help to expedite harmonious relations. Without this attitude, the success of a well-written contract can be seriously curtailed.

In many respects, questions involving the legal rights are peripheral quizzes—they do not penetrate to the real core of management-union co-operation. Managerial actions and techniques conducive to production and mutual co-operation are paramount considerations, as well as the union's appreciation of the inherent characteristics and conditions under which the office must operate. Recognition must be given to the development of the various elements and changes affecting the general background in which the contract is made. These include technologic, economic, and social modifications that today's enlightened managers and nonmanagers recognize and accept.

LABOR MANAGEMENT RELATIONS ACT OF 1947

A long list of labor laws make up our current legal background upon which current management-union co-operation is administered. But for our purpose, the provisions of the Labor Management Relations Act of 1947, commonly referred to as the Taft-Hartley Act, and the Landrum-Griffin Act of 1959, can be considered as making up the current labor legislation. The Landrum-Griffin Act of 1959, among other things, permitted employees to file with the government complaints about the acts of their union leaders. Most of the complaints to date have dealt with questions pertaining to voting by union members in union affairs, and the misuse of the dues by union officers.

The Labor Management Relations Act of 1947 is the important legislation that sets forth the major provisions of management-labor co-operation. By this law, a National Labor Relations Board was established with the power to hear testimony, render decisions, and decide the appropriate unit for purposes of collective bargaining. The board serves mainly in a judiciary capacity. A general counsel and his staff prosecute the cases brought before the board. Among the other important provisions of this law are unfair labor practices, strike controls, and checks on unions.

Unfair Labor Practices. The Taft-Hartley Act forbids unfair labor practices by the employer and also by unions or their agents. The employer list includes (1) interfering with or restraining employees from forming or joining a labor union, (2) dominating or influencing a labor organization, (3) discriminating in the hiring or in the conditions of employment of any employee because he is a member of a union, (4) terminating employment or discriminating against any employee for any charge made or testimony given under this law, and (5) refusing to bargain collectively with representatives of his employees.

Practices which constitute unfair labor practices by unions or their agents include (1) coercing or restraining employees in connection with their joining a union, (2) charging "excessive or discriminatory" union initiation fees (the meaning of "excessive or discriminatory" is determined by the labor board in cases where there is an authorized union shop contract), (3) refusing to bargain collectively with the employer, (4) participating in jurisdictional strikes, and (5) practicing "feather-bedding," i.e., making the employer pay for services not performed.

Charges of unfair labor practices on the part of either employer or union are investigated, complaints issued, and prosecution carried on before the National Labor Relations Board by the general counsel, who has exclusive authority to prosecute unfair labor practices. He is appointed by the President of the United States and has general supervision over all attorneys employed by the board, except trial examiners and legal assistants to board members.

Basing its decision on the preponderance of evidence and testimony, the board decides whether any defendant named in the complaint is guilty of an unfair labor practice. If he is not guilty, the findings are stated, and an order is issued dismissing the complaint. If he is guilty, the board states its findings and causes a cease and desist order, prohibiting the continuation of the unfair practice, to be served on the guilty party. For enforcement of its orders, the board has the power to petition the Circuit Court of Appeals with jurisdiction where the unfair labor practice occurred.

Strike Controls. The Taft-Hartley Act provides that 60 days' notice must be given the other party before the normal termination of a labor contract. The Federal Mediation and Conciliation Service must be notified at least 30 days after the 60-day notice if no agreement is reached. This provision is, of course, intended to help settle the differences of opinion. Lockouts and strikes are prohibited during the notice period. There is no compulsory arbitration or court injunction right against a legitimate noncritical strike, i.e., one not threatening "national health and safety" or affecting an entire industry.

In contrast, threatening lockouts or strikes affecting "national health and safety" or an entire industry may be delayed 80 days by the President in this manner: A board of inquiry may be appointed to determine the facts involved in the dispute. A report stating these facts, along with each party's statement of its position, is filed with the Federal Mediation and Conciliation Service, and the contents are made known to the public. In addition, the President at this time may, through the Attorney General, seek a court injunction against the lockout or strike. If the injunction is issued, there follows a period of 60 days in which to bring about a settlement. If this is not reached, the National Labor Relations Board holds, within the ensuing 15 days, a company-by-company election on each employer's last offer of settlement and certifies same within five days to the Attorney General, who then moves to dissolve the injunction. Then, the President submits a comprehensive report of the proceedings to Congress, along with any recommendation which he deems fitting and proper for appropriate action.

Checks on Unions. In order that a union may take advantage of the National Labor Relations Board under this act, that is, seek a board election or file an unfair labor practice charge with the board, the union must previously file (1) pertinent union information and (2) noncommunist affidavits by each officer of the union.

The pertinent union information is filed annually with the Secretary of Labor. The report must include name, title, compensation, and allowances for each of the union's three principal officers and for any other officer or agent of the union if the aggregate compensation and allowances of any one of these persons exceeded $5,000 for the preceding year. The report must also include the manner of election or appointment of these officers or agents; the amount of initiation fees and regular dues; a statement showing the procedure followed for such things as qualifications for union membership, levying of assessments, authorization for bargaining demands, for strikes, for disbursement of union funds, and for the basis for expulsion of members; and a report showing receipts and expenditures for the fiscal year and total assets and liabilities at the end of the fiscal year. All union members have a right to a copy of their union's financial report.

The affidavits by union officers can be filed either contemporaneously with a union action privileged by the act or within the preceding twelve-month period. The affidavit is a sworn written statement signifying that the union officer is not a member or affiliate of the Communist Party and does not believe in, belong to, or support any organization believing in or teaching the overthrow of the United States government by force or by illegal or unconstitutional methods.

Other Major Provisions of the Act. Additional important provisions of the act include the following:

1. Union shop agreements must be in accordance with the prevailing state law and are void in states that forbid them.

2. An employee or a group of employees can petition that the union's authorization to enter into a union shop contract be withdrawn; such a petition must contain the signatures of 30 per cent of the employees represented by the union. However, only one election on union security can be held each year.

3. In instances of authorized union shop contracts, the failure of a member to pay union dues and initiation fee is the only cause for loss of good standing with the union for which an employer can be forced to discharge an employee.

4. Union dues checkoff is allowed only with the employee's written consent.

5. If the majority of professional workers desire a union, they can be represented, if they wish, by a union other than that representing the production workers.

6. The individual employee can present grievances directly to his supervisor, provided the union representative is informed and given an opportunity to be present. Settlement of the grievance can be made if such settlement is not contrary to any terms of the existing union contract.

7. The employer can refuse to bargain with a union of foremen or supervisors. They can have their union, but the employer need not bargain with them if he does not choose to do so.

8. Unions as well as employers can sue and be sued for violations of contract under this act. Judgments against unions must be collected from them, not from the individual employees.[2]

HANDLING OF CONTROVERSIES

Ideally, the manager and the union representative should solve their differences by means of interpreting the labor contract, bargaining, or mutual agreement. In practice, however, this does not always take place. Hence, to handle controversies, several methods are available, including the following:

By mediation. Both parties agree to use a third party, or mediator, in order to compromise or reach an agreement. He may relay one party's opinion to the other or act as a chairman in getting the parties together to relate their beliefs and opinions. In addition, the mediator may define the basis of the dispute and show the legal meaning of the agreement, thus indirectly demonstrating how settlement might be reached.

By conciliation. Each party may ask for a conciliator who serves as an intermediate and seeks to settle the dispute. In contrast to that of the mediator, the work of the conciliator is aggressive; he may be said to take the offensive. The conciliator may induce one party to accept certain requests of the other or may give advice as to the manner of settling the dispute. To bring about agreement, conciliators depend upon such things as their ability, prestige, and knowledge of all facts in the case. They have no legal power to compel acceptance of any terms.

By arbitration. The parties may use voluntary arbitration to settle their differences. To do this, both parties agree to submit the case to a neutral, impartial third party or umpire. It is usually agreed that the arbitrator's findings will be accepted as final.[3]

In actual practice, the terms "mediation" and "conciliation" are used synonymously. As previously stated, the Taft-Hartley Act provides that a thirty-day notice of a change in or termination of a labor contract must be filed with the Federal Mediation and Conciliation Service. This

---

[2] An excellent source on this subject is Selwyn Torff, *Collective Bargaining: Negotiations and Agreements* (New York: McGraw-Hill Book Co., Inc., 1953).

[3] K. Braun, *The Settlement of Industrial Disputes* (Philadelphia: Blakiston Co., 1944), p. 29.

"Arbitration," as discussed here, applies to reaching a contract agreement and is not the common type of arbitration which deals with the interpretation and application of existing contracts to specific disputes.

makes it possible for the service to get the differences settled before an open break has occurred.

THE CHALLENGE OF BARGAINING

Fundamentally, the aims of management members and of unions are reconcilable. It may at first appear that the differences in goals between the two are very great. But when the aims of each are analyzed, they appear compatible and able to exist in harmony. Figure 37–1 shows diagrammatically the position of collective bargaining in relation to the major goals of managers and of unions.

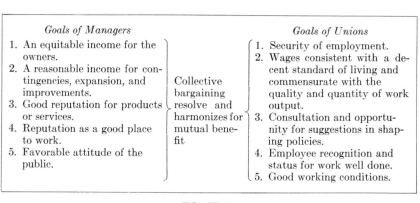

Goals of Managers
1. An equitable income for the owners.
2. A reasonable income for contingencies, expansion, and improvements.
3. Good reputation for products or services.
4. Reputation as a good place to work.
5. Favorable attitude of the public.

Collective bargaining resolve and harmonizes for mutual benefit

Goals of Unions
1. Security of employment.
2. Wages consistent with a decent standard of living and commensurate with the quality and quantity of work output.
3. Consultation and opportunity for suggestions in shaping policies.
4. Employee recognition and status for work well done.
5. Good working conditions.

FIG. 37–1.

To bring about greater improvement, harmony, and mutual benefit in management-union co-operation, the major areas requiring satisfactory solution deal with (1) more intense utilization of competent manpower in working and thinking about labor relations, (2) the rights of management, (3) recognition of all interested parties, (4) the scope and viewpoint of labor relations, and (5) the basis for conducting collective bargaining.

More Intense Utilization of Competent Manpower. This area is probably of greatest importance. The more intense application of the best minds toward finding ways and means to assist management-union co-operation appears fundamental to its continued progress. Time has brought improvement, but more remains to be done. Progress in the following areas would be highly beneficial: bettering the communication with and motivation of employees, smoothing out the business cycle, improving management techniques, training more efficient employees, and broadening the educational background of managers and of labor leaders.

Rights of Management. This is a vital area. Management members desire freedom to meet their responsibilities and resent any restrictions in carrying out functions which they believe essential for performing their job. Traditionally, managers want no restrictions on their right to hire, fire, discipline, and maintain order and efficiency. On the other hand, unions feel that one of their main functions concerns the welfare of their members. They are interested in all matters which involve the employee; conditions of employment, they reason, are of vital concern to them.

Experience shows that the planning and the executing done by managers determine to a significant degree what action the union takes. By and large, unions are opportunistic and operate on a basis of practical consequences. It is possible to include in the contract the principal managerial rights and specify these as managerial functions; but acceptance by the union is a debatable question and depends upon individual circumstances and precedents, and the character of the rights. There are some who feel that a policy of specifying managerial functions has a limiting effect, since unions might claim participation in matters not specifically stated. However, this might be handled by an additional statement to the effect that all existing functions now carried out by members of management shall remain functions of members of management.

Recognition of All Interested Parties. It is well to note that there are actually *three, not two,* interested parties in a labor contract: (1) the employees, represented by the union; (2) the owners, represented by managerial personnel; and (3) the consumers, or general public. The negotiators are usually only the managers and the union representatives, but their agreements should be consistent with the public interest. Disagreements resulting in strikes or shutdowns obviously affect public interest. Likewise, agreements which are contrary to the public interest can be very damaging; although more subtle, they can probably have a greater effect upon certain members of society than upon the initial disputants.

Scope and Viewpoint of Labor Relations. Generally speaking, the manager's viewpoint of labor relations is of limited scope in comparison with that of unions. Many managers think of management-union cooperation as limited to their particular shop or office, the whole subject being concerned with their employees. In contrast, many unions are typically interested in all employees throughout an entire industry or occupation. They want to maintain their organizational strength and to secure protection from other unions. This explains, for example, the demands for uniformity of wages among similar employees, for the union shop, and for the "maintenance of membership" clauses.

Basis for Conducting Collective Bargaining. Most managers would like to operate on the familiar business basis. The process is orderly, and contracts represent agreements satisfactory to both, which in case of violation means redresses enforceable by court action. However, evidence seems to indicate that in some instances, unions are not certain that the traditional business code is the best medium. They are driven by a passion for improvement of the employees' lot and, in many respects, believe collective bargaining and the attainment of satisfactory management-union co-operation are more in the nature of a social and political procedure than a business procedure. That is, they feel the relationship of employees to employer is basically different from that of the typical business process.

SUGGESTIONS FOR IMPROVEMENT

There is probably no single course of action that can or should be recommended, but certain approaches seem to be in order. Although somewhat idealistic in their make-up, the following suggestions appear essential and form the basis for realistic progress.

Management members should take the offensive and acquire an enlightened view of their role in collective bargaining. They should find out the real reasons behind the union demands. Management must be active, not passive. It should supply intelligent leadership and play an important part in pioneering in and seeking for improved methods and relationships.

Managers and unions should both strive further to recognize fully the problems of each other. Neither party should ask for concessions which, if granted, jeopardize the existence of the other. Both should seek for something workable, since any other approach leads to strife.

In addition, closer association should be developed among managers, employees, and the unions. Managers should know the employees, employees should know the managers, and both should know the union. They should know each other as fellow human beings working together. A spirit of co-operation and understanding must prevail; for all three are bound together, and they must strive for mutual, not separate, survival.

Both managers and unions should be capable and willing to accept complete responsibilities. Agreements made in good faith should be carried out, and any subsequent adjustments found desirable should be made in accordance with the mutually agreed-upon procedure.

Also, it must be realized that time is required to bring about changes in things. This is especially true with matters pertaining to management-union co-operation. Both parties must allow time for ideas to be absorbed. Improvements do not just happen overnight; they evolve; they take time.

QUESTIONS

1. Of the various reasons given in this chapter for office employees not joining unions, which one do you believe is probably most important? Why?
2. In your opinion, do trade unions help, hinder, or have no effect upon the actuating efforts of a manager? Elaborate on your answer.

3. Do you feel that the extent of office unionization will increase, decrease, or remain about the same? Why?

4. On what basis do you believe office layoffs and rehires should be handled? Justify your viewpoint.

5. In a unionized office, should an office employee take his work problems to his supervisor, the union steward, or a member of the personnel department? Justify your answer.

6. In company RST, the office employees are nonunion, and the factory employees are members of a union. Recently, as a result of collective bargaining, a 4 per cent increase in wages was given factory employees. At the same time, a like increase was given office employees.

   a) Do you feel the office employees are justified in accepting this increase?

   b) How can the managers of the company justify the increase to office employees?

   c) Should the office employees join the union?

   Give reasons for your answers.

7. In your opinion, does an office employee suffer possible loss of social status by joining an office union? Why? Is this primarily an individual or a group consideration? Elaborate on your answer.

8. Is the work of the office manager changed by the existence of a union in the office? Explain.

9. Relate briefly the meaning of each of the following:

   a) Union shop.

   b) Mediation.

   c) Landrum-Griffin Act of 1959.

   d) Closed shop.

10. Discuss the subject "Contract Limitations" as it applies to a management-labor written collective bargaining contract.

11. What interpretation and significance do you attach to the following statement? "Unions offer an effective vehicle to nonmanagement members for reaching managers about grievances and personal needs."

12. What are some important union unfair labor practices forbidden by the present federal labor law?

CASE PROBLEMS

Case 37–1. Eberhart Machine Company

The supervisor of the duplicating department asked two duplicating machine operators to clean up their desks and tidy up several cabinets of paper located in the department. The operators refused, claiming such work was neither in their job classification nor in their job description. The discussion went on for thirty-five minutes, with no work of any kind being done. Finally, the supervisor stated: "Either the two of you do the work as I direct and file a grievance about it later if you like, or you go home." The operators went home. They stated: "Our union will back us up. We don't have to do cleanup work."

The following morning, when they reported for work, the personnel manager came to their places of work and told them each had been given a five-day suspension for refusing instructions of their supervisor. One of the operators replied: "We didn't disobey our supervisor. She gave us a choice either to do the work or to go home. We chose to go home. She did not warn us we were subject to disciplinary action if we went home. Ask her; she is standing right over there."

Said the personnel director: "The supervisor didn't have to warn you. Employees are supposed to work as directed and not go home. There is nothing in the job description that says you're not supposed to do reasonable cleanup work, and the request made of you was certainly reasonable. You chose to ignore supervisory direction and to risk discipline."

"We'll take this up with our steward and higher-ups if need be," replied one of the operators. "You can't do this to us."

Problems:

1. What action should be taken now by the personnel director? By the supervisor?

2. What decision do you believe should be reached? Why?

Case 37–2.   The Chandler Manufacturing Company

Hilda Zimmerman worked twenty-two months as a file clerk before being laid off. Her rate of pay was $1.50 an hour. She was soon recalled and given the job of general clerk at a pay rate of $1.30 an hour. About a week later, during a lunch recess, Hilda met a friend, Ethel Kessler, who had been working as a clerk in the production planning department of the company. Hilda had introduced Ethel to the employment manager about a year ago and helped her get the job. During the conversation, Hilda learned that Ethel had been laid off but was recalled two days ago and was now working as a clerk in records retention at $1.40 per hour, with a promise of 10 cents increase after six months if her work was satisfactory.

Hilda reported the circumstance as a grievance to her union steward, who took the case to the assistant personnel manager who handled such matters. The steward contended that Hilda should be given the records-retention job instead of Ethel because of Hilda's seniority and her desire and capacity to do the work.

The assistant personnel manager denied the requests, stating the situation was investigated thoroughly before action was taken. The records of Hilda Zimmerman showed she was rated "fair" in co-operation with others and "poor" in dependability. An interview with the filing supervisor revealed that Hilda seemed to waste time and do a lot of complaining about the work assigned to her; when informed of her unsatisfactory rating, she said she would try to do better, but no improvement was accomplished.

Problems:

1. What action should the steward take? Why?

2. What action should the company take? Why?

3. Other than pay, what factors do you feel might be important in this case? Explain.

Chapter 38

OFFICE SAFETY

*To profit from good advice requires more wisdom than
to give it.*

—CHURTON COLLINS

PROVIDING a safe place in which to work and promoting safe work habits are conducive to favorable motivation of employees. Losses caused by accidents are costly not only from the humanitarian but also from the economic viewpoint. Office accidents represent an inexcusable waste of experienced employees. Even slight injuries received in an office can result in loss of working time and the disrupting of normal working conditions. Managerial attention must be paid to safety in the office.

ACCIDENT OCCURRENCE

Accidents can and do happen to office employees; they enjoy no automatic exemption. These accidents come about in a number of ways. For example, typewriters, calculators, and other office machines frequently need cleaning. Some cleaning fluids are inflammable, and cases are on record where the fumes from the cleaning fluid were ignited by a spark from the electric motor of the machine, resulting in a flash fire which caused severe burns to office employees. Severe falls and injuries have resulted from slipping on highly polished floors and running on stairways by women in high-heeled shoes. Reclining too far back in a chair can result in the occupant's being thrown with considerable force; and serious, sometimes permanent, injuries have been suffered by office employees in this way. Illustrations of practices that frequently result in accidents are shown in Figure 38–1.

A CAUSE FOR EVERY ACCIDENT

There is a cause for every accident that happens. It is some defect of action or lack of action which must be corrected in order to prevent a recurrence of the accident. Falling down a stairway is not a cause; it is a result—an accident. The causes may be loose papers on the stair

Courtesy: "GM Folks," General Motors Corp., Detroit

FIG. 38–1. Accidents are caused by carelessness. The practices illustrated commonly result in accidents. These pictures were especially posed for accident prevention promotional work.

treads, inadequate lighting on the stairway, or the employee's failure to watch where he is stepping. These conditions must be rectified in order to achieve better safety results.[1]

Some writers have classified the causes of accidents under three headings: mechanical, physiological, and psychological. These terms are self-explanatory. Under mechanical causes, for example, are classified such things as improper lighting, unguarded machines, and technical defects in equipment. Physiological causes include bad eyesight and age of employees; psychological causes cover such things as the employee's tendency to take unnecessary chances, horseplay, and temporary emotional and mental disturbances. These causes are interrelated and must be attacked jointly in most practical activities designed to reduce accidents.

MANAGERIAL COURSE OF ACTION

Experience and records show that accidents can be reduced; in fact, many can be prevented entirely. The best course of action for preventing accidents depends upon the circumstances in each particular case. Some advocate the so-called "triple E" program, which consists of engineering, education, and enforcement. That is, the first step is to

---

[1] For an excellent discussion of this subject, see Rollin H. Simonds and John V. Grimaldi, *Safety Management* (Homewood, Ill.: Richard D. Irwin, Inc., 1956), chap. iv.

engineer all equipment and machines with safety guards, cutoff switches, and other devices to make them as safe as is technically possible. Next, education to all employees is provided, to instill work habits and practices for winning high safety achievements. Last, enforcement insures that safety regulations are carried out.

This means that the initiative rests with the manager, but he must win the co-operation of the employee to make office safety really effective. Aggressive managerial action is required. Merely supplying a safe working place is insufficient. The manager must also see to it that safety measures are recognized and enforced; but what is more important, he must accomplish this with enthusiastic approval and encouragement by the nonmanagement members. For this worthy goal, competent management is needed. Pertinent suggestions as to what actions to take are included on the following pages.

PLANNING EFFECTIVE SAFETY ACTIONS

Before hazards causing accidents can be eliminated, they must be identified. Available safety information reveals that the main types of office accidents have to do with slipping, tripping, handling materials, being hit by falling objects, and striking against objects. Among the more common hazards which result in office accidents are:

Defective electric cords lying across aisles, and loose connections
Paper clips and thumbtacks on the floor
Loose linoleum or carpeting
Slippery floors
Open desk drawer or file drawer
Tilting backward too far in office chair
Sharp burrs on edges of metal office equipment
Sharp pointed pencils placed in upright position in handkerchief coat pocket
Broken glass desk top
Exposed moving parts of office machines
Splinters and loose veneer on wood desks and chairs
Bottles, papers, or books stacked on top of filing cabinets
Protruding pencil sharpeners and power and telephone outlets
Reading while walking
Running in aisle, on stairways, or through doorways

Especially helpful in locating and knowing what hazards to eliminate in a given office is a check list. An illustration of such a form is shown in Figure 38–2. In addition, an analysis of the accident reports can help in locating areas that need attention.

With factual data as a background, steps can be taken to incorporate each of the following safety actions into the program.

Education of Employees to Possible Dangers. Each employee should be made thoroughly aware of all the possible dangers of his job. All the details that make for safety should be carefully explained. These efforts

OFFICE SAFETY INSPECTION DATA

Carefully inspect the office, and for each question, check whether a hazard exists. If "Yes," briefly note the important details.

QUESTION	DOES HAZARD EXIST?		COMMENTS (GIVE LOCATION AND DETAILS.)
	Yes	No	
1. Are aisles obstructed?............................			
2. Do pencil sharpeners project over desk or table?..			
3. Are file drawers kept closed when not in use?......................................			
4. Are machines properly guarded?....................			
5. Are glass desk tops broken?.......................			
6. Are there any sharp metal projections on any equipment?................................			
7. Is electrical wiring concealed?.....................			
8. Are office accessories insecurely placed?............			
9. Are papers and waste properly disposed of?........			
10. Are facilities for smokers adequate?...............			
11. Are materials stacked on desks or cabinets?...			
12. Are extension cords used extensively?..............			
13. Are floors too highly polished?....................			
14. Is carpeting loose or worn?.......................			

FIG. 38–2. Portion of a form designed to assist in determining safety hazards.

can be planned and made a regular part of the job process and the training work. In this manner, the correct and usual way of doing the job, which is also the safe way, becomes habitual. Safety is built right into the job—it is a part of the job. Simple visual aids to help in this work are shown in Figure 38–3.

Provision of Safe Work Areas. Safety planning should include all necessary provisions for safe working places and equipment for employees. Office floors should be covered with nonslippery material; adequate lighting should be provided; desks and chairs should be free of sharp edges.

Promotion of First-Aid Service. Adequate first-aid service should be included in the safety planning. Insistence upon first-aid treatment for minor injuries means little if adequate facilities are not available. When these facilities are provided, managers show that they wish all injured employees to receive treatment promptly. Furthermore, such provisions reflect adequate safety planning by the managers.

Availability of Safety Clothing. The use of special clothing and protective equipment designed to protect employees from injuries is another area to be included in safety planning. Finger guards should be furnished to employees doing work where the chances of suffering paper cuts are quite high. Likewise, plastic aprons should be available to em-

Courtesy: National Safety Council, Inc., Chicago

FIG. 38–3. Visual aids to help educate the office employee to possible dangers on the job.

ployees working around large quantities of ink, gluepots, and cleaning solutions.

Inclusion of Good Housekeeping Practices. Good housekeeping in the office is essential for good safety work. The habit of orderliness and cleanliness should be included in safety planning, and adequate provisions made for its promotion and follow-up. Stairways should be kept clear of all loose objects; aisles should be marked for traffic lanes; an adequate number of wastepaper baskets should be furnished; and regular clean-up service should be provided. A clean, orderly office sets a good example for the employee and helps to keep the office personnel safety-minded.

OFFICE SAFETY WORK AND CONTROLLING

Effective accident prevention work requires that adequate records be kept of all accidents. It is important to know what accidents happened, where, and when. Adequate records will also show the type of injuries and the conditions which caused them. By studying such data, a manager is able to take intelligent corrective action and knows where to stress safety efforts.

Content of Safety Records. Safety records should include such things as the date of the accident, the employee's name, the department, the injury suffered, a concise description of the accident, and a report of the action taken to prevent a recurrence. Other information might be

added, depending upon the experience and the use which it is desired
to make of these data.

Safety Indexes. There are also two widely used and accepted indexes
in safety statistics: (1) the frequency rate and (2) the severity rate.
These names are self-explanatory: The frequency rate measures the occurrence of accidents, and the severity rate measures the seriousness
of accidents. The indexes are used to show the relative values and trends
within any group and the comparisons among different groups.

1. *Frequency rate.* The frequency rate can be defined as the number
of disabling injuries suffered per million man-hours worked. The formula is:

$$\text{Frequency rate} = \frac{\text{Number of disabling injuries} \times 1,000,000}{\text{Total number of man-hours worked}}$$

Disabling injuries are frequently referred to as "lost-time accidents
arising out of and in the course of employment." The National Safety
Council classifies the following types of injuries as disabling injuries:

a) Death.

b) Permanent total disability. Any injury or combination of injuries
suffered in one accident which permanently and totally incapacitates an
employee from following any gainful occupation. Loss of both eyes or
of both hands is an example.

c) Permanent partial disability. Any injury suffered in one accident
which results in the loss of any member or part of a member of the
body but which does not result in death or permanent total disability.

d) Temporary total disability. Any injury suffered in one accident
which results in no permanent injury but which prevents the injured
person from returning to a regularly established job within twenty-
four hours after the start of the shift during which he was injured.

The total number of man-hours is best obtained from payroll records or timecards. If these are unavailable, the number can be estimated by multiplying the average number of employees by the average
number of hours worked during the period considered.

2. *Severity rate.* The severity rate is the number of days charged as
a result of injuries per million man-hours worked. The formula is:

$$\text{Severity rate} = \frac{\text{Time charged (in days)} \times 1,000,000}{\text{Total number of man-hours worked}}$$

Days charged are sometimes called "days of disability." However,
the time charged away from the job does not accurately measure the
severity of the accident. Therefore, tables have been set up indicating
an arbitrary number of days which should be used for various types of
accidents. For example, an accident resulting in death or in permanent
total disability is charged at the rate of 6,000 days for each case. This

is approximately twenty years. A permanent partial disability resulting in the loss of a hand is charged at 3,000 days.

Available safety data show that the office frequency rates and severity rates are among the lowest of any industry classification. This is shown in Figure 38–4. It is encouraging to note that with the exception of very few, the rates are declining for every industry—safety is progressing.

THREE-YEAR FREQUENCY AND SEVERITY RATES OF SELECTED INDUSTRIES

INDUSTRY	FREQUENCY RATES					SEVERITY RATES				
	1954–56	1955–57	1956–58	1957–59	1958–60	1954–56	1955–57	1956–58	1957–59	1958–60
Offices........	1.40	1.37	1.41	1.48	1.39	115	112	115	117	104
Automobile......	2.76	2.64	2.55	2.41	2.34	296	303	310	274	258
Chemical........	3.73	3.57	3.52	3.56	3.54	535	526	530	533	528
Construction....	18.77	19.38	19.03	18.35	17.97	2352	2440	2412	2386	2350
Lumbering......	27.09	23.47	24.81	23.90	23.82	3163	2790	2605	2471	2375
Printing and publishing........	6.45	6.32	6.41	6.48	6.66	165	266	311	308	369
Steel..........	3.87	3.83	3.75	3.52	3.29	888	866	814	801	794
Tobacco........	3.50	3.87	3.95	3.70	3.65	137	121	180	164	207

Compiled from National Safety Council, Inc., "Accident Facts" (Chicago, 1955–61)

FIG. 38–4. Comparison of safety statistics.

ACCIDENT COSTS

Costs are another means of controlling safety, inasmuch as the amount of expenditure has some relationship to the efforts directed to this area. Budgets of these costs are desirable, and actions to get the most benefits for a given expenditure should be encouraged.

It is a well-known fact that accidents are expensive. The loss might be in money, skill, time, human suffering, work output, or interruption in the flow of work. The hidden or incidental costs of accidents are much greater than the measurable direct costs. Such things as the cost of hiring and training new employees, the interference with production, and the loss of good will are sizable expenses not generally thought of in connection with the costs of accidents. The ratio of hidden to direct costs of accidents may be as high as 4 to 1, which means that total accident costs are far greater than most people realize.

ORGANIZING AND THE SAFETY WORK

It is important that there be a recognized head of office safety work. This person should be given complete responsibility for the direction and guidance of all office safety efforts. The person in charge might be the office manager himself, or the office manager might appoint a subordinate to the job. Generally, the safety director need not spend all of his time on safety, but it is advisable for him to devote a certain amount of time regularly to the program.

Importance of Supervisors. Department heads are the key personnel in accident prevention work. In many respects, the success of the entire safety program depends upon the supervisors. The entire program is promoted by the co-operation of the department heads, and they can do more than anyone else toward keeping the employees safety-minded. Furthermore, supervisors can correct unsafe conditions, they can see that safety rules are followed, that first aid is provided in case of accident, and that proper reports are filled out.

Safety Committees. Because participation promotes acceptance for safety efforts, safety committees with rotating memberships are recommended. A five-member committee, with membership rotating bimonthly, usually works out very well. The system of replacements should be such that not more than two new members are added at any one time, thus insuring that the remaining three members are familiar with the work of the committee.

The work of this group is advisory. It fulfills a staff function to the safety head and submits suggestions for the reduction of accidents within the office. Frequently, the safety committee may also:

1. Make regular inspections of the office.
2. Supervise the maintenance and use of first-aid equipment.
3. Make fire-prevention inspections.
4. Sponsor accident-prevention contests.
5. Help prepare safety rules.
6. Review safety suggestions made by the employees.
7. Supervise the display of safety materials on the bulletin boards.
8. Accumulate and transmit safety training material to the other employees.[2]

ACTUATING ALL EMPLOYEES BY PROMOTING SAFETY CONSCIOUSNESS

The mental attitude of the employee toward safety is exceedingly important in accident prevention work. There is a great deal of truth in the saying: "The best safety device in all the world is located an inch or two above the eyebrows." The employee who "thinks safety" and who has developed a safety consciousness "from the ears up" has gone a long way toward preventing accidents.

All efforts designed to keep safety on the employee's mind and to keep accident prevention a live subject in the office will help substantially in the safety program. Although it may seem strange, it is a common occurrence for people to be careless. Safety-mindedness requires alert-mindedness. Safety work is a continuous process, requiring constant reminders to the employee to work safely, to avoid taking chances, and to keep safety foremost in his thoughts. The task is not an easy one,

---

[2] National Safety Council, Inc., *Industrial Safety Guide* (Chicago, 1960), p. 5.

but persistence and steadfastness of purpose will achieve good results.

It is a truism that for the most part, people attach the same degree of importance to activities as do their leaders. If the managers believe and are actively engaged in accident prevention work, then this same spirit will be picked up by the employees. The safety example set by managers is important in attaining a good safety record.

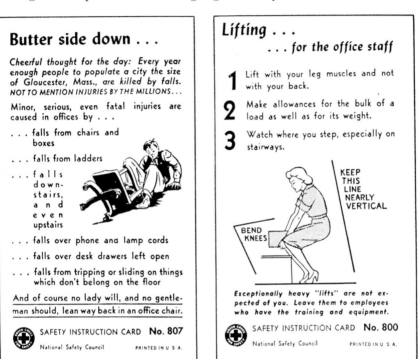

Courtesy: *National Safety Council, Inc., Chicago*

FIG. 38–5. Safety instruction cards.

Explain Safety Rules. Safety rules should be explained, and the reasons for their rigid enforcement given to the employees. The entire safety program can be seriously handicapped if there is any letdown in either the education or the enforcement of safety rules. Quite often, having the rules in writing is helpful and can be fulfilled by issuing mimeographed, typewritten, or printed forms.

Inform Office Employees of Safety Fundamentals. This can take various forms, including articles in company papers, talks at meetings, informal suggestions to employees, movies, and safety instruction cards. This latter medium provides the employee with pertinent suggestions about safety and serves as a series of timely reminders, helping to keep safety on the minds of the employees. Figure 38–5 shows several examples of safety instruction cards.

Employ Bulletin Boards. Pictures, posters, and cartoon sketches can also be used to arouse the employee's interest in safety. It is usually best to have this material specific in nature, telling the employee what to do under particular conditions. Giving the employee general safety cautions and slogans is probably of limited value. Also, it is usually well to supplement this type of safety promotion with intensive individual follow-up. The bulletin boards used should be located in areas that are

Courtesy: *National Safety Council, Inc., Chicago*

FIG. 38–6. An effective safety poster.

frequently seen, accessible, and in full view. A poster with exceptionally lively layout is shown in Figure 38–6.

Promote Safety Contests. This approach stresses the competitive spirit and usually relies upon the employee's desire to excel. An award in the form of a plaque, banner, special pin, or money may be given the individual, group, or department having the best safety record for a given period. A reversal of this technique can also be used, and it is generally effective. In this case, a booby prize is given the unit having the poorest safety record, with the requirement that this "award" be displayed prominently. This approach appeals to the employee's pride and to his desire to escape any designation which makes him look ridiculous. Like all promotional plans, safety contests must be publicized and made acceptable to the employees.

QUESTIONS

1. Is it true that office employees must be educated to the possible dangers of their work and surroundings? Elaborate on your answer.
2. Do you agree with the following statement? "Office safety is readily accepted by the employee mainly because it is for his own benefit. Rigid enforcement of safety regulations smacks of the dictator approach. An employee is a human being and does not have to be pushed into being a safe employee."
3. Support the belief that there should be a safety program for office employees.
4. Assume you have just been appointed safety head in an office employing 150 people. What steps would you take to initiate an effective safety program?
5. Select one of the two illustrations shown in Figure 38–1. Assume you are an office supervisor and observe the condition shown by your selected illustration. What action would you take? Be specific.
6. Discuss the subject of accident costs in an office.
7. Are committees effective in promoting safety among office employees? Substantiate your answer.
8. Do you agree with the following? "Anyone who has worked in office safety programs realizes that certain accidents happen no matter what precautions are taken. Accidents are in the nature of things where people are working. To think otherwise is to ignore plain facts." Why?
9. With reference to office safety, explain in your own words what is meant by a frequency rate of 8.0? A severity rate of 160.0? If the severity rate is divided by the frequency rate, such as 160.0 divided by 8.0, giving a value of 20.0, what is the meaning of the value 20.0? Discuss.
10. Discuss the meaning of Figure 38–4 in your own words.
11. Comment on the statement: "Safety instructions should be integrated with office training, regardless of the particular job and the trainee."
12. Explain the meaning of the statement: "The best safety device is located an inch or two above the employee's eyebrows."

CASE PROBLEM

Case 38–1. Western Marbury Company

Several months ago, the office manager announced that smoking by the office employees at the workplaces during working hours would be permitted by the company. This decision came about when it was found that a great deal of working time was lost by crowding into the rest rooms "for smokes" during working hours. The employees had asked that the ban on smoking in the office be lifted and had been quite aggressive in securing the present concession of smoking being permitted at the desks.

Ten days ago, a fire started in the purchasing division of the company's office. Two employees suffered minor burns in extinguishing the flame, and some damage was done to a desk and to carpeting. An investigation revealed that the cause was carelessness on the part of an employee, who had placed a lighted cigarette on the edge of his desk. The lighted cigarette had fallen into a wastebasket filled with papers, and the fire had started.

The following day, the office manager issued a memorandum to every office employee, requesting full co-operation in helping to keep the office a safe place in which to work. The employees were urged to be especially careful about smoking in the office, and it was explained that a serious fire could mean a loss of jobs and valuable property. In addition, an attractively illustrated poster was put on the office bulletin board, suggesting: "Be careful. Watch where you place your lighted matches and cigarettes. Help avoid a serious fire which might result in physical injury to you and the loss of your job." At the same time, the office manager personally spoke with all the office supervisors, requesting that they stress office safety to their respective employees and especially caution them about the handling of lighted matches and cigarettes.

Yesterday, a repetition of the fire incident occurred in the office; however, this time, the fire was in the cost accounting division. The fire got a fairly good start and damaged one corner of the office. The damage is estimated at about $1,800. The cause is not known. The supervisor of the cost accounting division feels it might be similar to that of the previous fire, but he has no proof of this. Close questioning of the three employees who work in the area where the fire started does not reveal any careless use of matches or cigarettes.

Problems:

1. What are your reactions to the handling of the situation by the office manager after the first fire? Explain.

2. Should the office manager continue to allow smoking in the office? Discuss.

3. What action do you recommend that the office manager now take? Why?

INDEX

Index

717

This book has been set on the Linotype in 10 point Monticello, leaded 2 points, and 9 point Monticello, leaded 1 point. Part and chapter numbers and titles are in Lydian Bold. The size of the type page is 27 by 46 picas.